CRIMINOLOGY, CIVILISATION
AND THE NEW WORLD ORDER

Frontispiece: Survivors lie outside among the dead at the newly liberated Ebensee concentration camp, Ebensee, Austria, May 1945. (Credit: USHMM, courtesy of Benjamin Ferencz)

The most ultimately righteous of all wars is a war with savages, though it is apt to be also the most terrible and inhuman. The rude, fierce settler who drives the savage from the land lays all civilised mankind under a debt to him. American and Indian, Boer and Zulu, Cossack and Tartar, New Zealander and Maori, in each case the victor, horrible though many of his deeds are, has laid deep the foundations for the future greatness of a mighty people … it is of incalculable importance that America, Australia and Siberia should pass out of the hands of their red, black and yellow aboriginal owners, and become the heritage of the dominant world races. (Theodore Roosevelt, two term Republican President of the US and winner of the Nobel Peace Prize for negotiating the cease fire in the 1905 Russio-Japanese war, in *The Winning of the West*, Vol. 4, 1890.)

> The settlement of the North American continent was … a consequence not of any higher claim in a democratic or international sense, but rather of a consciousness of what is right that had its sole roots in the conviction of the superiority and thus of the right of the white race. (Adolf Hitler, cited in Mills 1997: 106)

Blood was to be shed. This act – this work – was never to be undone. A landmark in history, it was cast in 'monumental' proportions … This was no episode. It was a deed.

In the middle of the end, a final cognition was felt. The perpetrator was gazing upon a forbidden vista. Under the murky huts of Auschwitz, Germans stood alone as they lined up their victims, herding them into gas chambers. These guards were living through something ultimate. Experience *Erlebnis* was reaching its outer limits. The act had become knowledge, and that knowledge was unique, for the sensation of a first discovery is not repeatable. (Raul Hilberg in speculating on the nature of the Holocaust 1965: 36)

CRIMINOLOGY, CIVILISATION AND THE NEW WORLD ORDER

Wayne Morrison
School of Law
Queen Mary College,
University of London

Director
The External Undergraduate Laws Programmes
University of London

Routledge·Cavendish
Taylor & Francis Group
a GlassHouse book

First published 2006
by Routledge · Cavendish
2 Park Square, Milton Park, Abingdon, Oxon, OX14 4RN

Simultaneously published in the USA and Canada
by Routledge · Cavendish
270 Madison Ave, New York, NY 10016

A Glasshouse book
Routledge · Cavendish is an imprint of the Taylor & Francis Group, an informa business

© 2006 Wayne Morrison

Typeset in New Baskerville by Newgen Imaging Systems, Chennai, India
Printed and bound in Great Britain

British Library Cataloguing in Publication Data
Morrison, Wayne
Criminology, civilisation and the new world order.
(Criminology)
1. Criminology
I. Title
364

Library of Congress Cataloging in Publication Data
A catalog record for this book has been requested

ISBN10: 1-904-38588-5 (cased)
ISBN10: 1-904-38512-5 (pbk)
ISBN 13: 978-1-904-38588-2 (cased)
ISBN 13: 978-1-904-38512-7 (pbk)

In memory of Eryl Hall-Williams and Kerry Flood

Contents |

Acknowledgements

This book was written while I have been Director of the External Law Programmes of the University of London. That position has contributed to developing a global perspective reflected in this text although I would not have been able to complete scholarly work in the face of its administrative and pedagogical demands except for the exemplary administrative support provided by Ms Martina Moore, my heart felt appreciation. Much of the travel and other assistance was linked in with this duties and made possible as part of my Director's Budget and small research support from School of Law Queen Mary, University of London. Thanks are due to the able stewardship of Mr John McConnell of the finances of the external system of the University and other support he offered.

Thanks to the staff of the Holocaust Memorial Museum, Washington (USHMM); the Anti-Slavery Society, London; the Royal Anthropological Institute, London (RAI); Mary Evans Picture Library, London (MEPL); Royal Africa Museum Tervuren, Brussels, Belgium; The British Museum and the British Library; the Horniman Museum, London; the Liberation War Museum, Dhaka, Bangladesh; Alexander Turnbull Library, Wellington, New Zealand; Tasmanian Museum and Art Gallery, Hobart and the Art Gallery of South Australia, Adelaide, Australia; for assistance and permission to reproduce images as indicated in the text.

During visits in Dhaka I have had the privilege of staying in the household of Mr Nur-e-Alam Siddique, one of the student leaders of the language and liberation struggle and subsequent politician and businessman. In these troubled times for relations between the supposed blocks of the West and Islam, Nur-e-Alam is living proof that charm, intelligence, personal courage and integrity, holding to a global perspective and the ability to be successful at business while recognizing social ties to workers and family, are in no way incompatible with devotion to the Muslim faith. The chapter that appears herein can not attempt to do justice to the struggles he and others were and are engaged in nor to the beguiling and complex, wonderfully contradictory, attractive yet repelling social arena that is contemporary Bangladesh. But at a time where that space is being labeled as fertile ground for terrorist threats (some of which is very real) it is an attempt to indicate the interdependencies of our world and my plea for the necessity for allowing justice to be something other than the possession of supposed 'civilised space'.

Beverley Brown, Chris Cunneen, David Fraser, John Pratt and Howard Senter have at various times read early drafts of at least part of the text and their comments and encouragement have been valuable as have the positions taken in their published work. Some of the ideas structuring this work were first published in a chapter co-written with Keith Hayward appearing in *Law After Ground Zero* (Glasshouse 2002), aspects of Chapter Eight were presented at the First International Conference on Cultural Criminology, London 2003, jointly organized my Keith Hayward and myself, and published in the special edition of *Theoretical Criminology* that came out of that conference.

During this study I came across the work of the travel writer, Sven Lindqvist, and the common transversing of some ground may be evidence of degree to which one encounters the 'facts' of genocide in traveling – if, that is, one is prepared to see. If a reader is surprised at contention that the holocaust is in part Europe turning its colonial impulses upon itself, the work currently been produced by writer such as A. Dirk Moses and Jurgen Zimmerer may soon make that part of the accepted canon.

This text is jointed dedicated to the memory of Eryl Hall Williams and Kerry Flood. Eryl Hall Williams was not only my Phd supervisor but instrumental in my staying in London to work. He is greatly missed for his humanity and encouragement. My regret concerning his own scholarly production is that during World War II he was a conscientious objector who served instead in social and medical support teams and was one of the first to enter Belsen concentration camp where he played an important role establishing conditions that saved the lives of many of the inmates they found. That he never put that experience, one of the defining moments of his personal existence, into his scholarly work was in large part thanks to the positivism that so structured a view of disciplinary boundaries that rendered that experience 'personal', not suitable as a resource for doing proper criminology. I hope he would appreciate my attempt herein to produce a very different criminology. With Kerry Flood I shared not only university and rugby but the experiences of confronting the quiet demons of the everyday civilized space of urban New Zealand. That those demons may be said to have scored a victory with his death robbed me not only of a friend with whom to engage with on my trips to New Zealand but that place of a fine and humane lawyer who was concerned to offer his best for his fellows.

Finally this work would not have been possible without the personal support and companionship of Michele, in respect of which special thanks is an understatement.

Introduction

I would think because of what has happened, we won't have to use U.S. forces around the world. I think when we say something is objectively correct ... people are going to listen. (US President George H. Bush, 1 March 1991 at a Presidential Press Conference at the end of 1st Gulf War)

When western cultural theorists were growing more laid back, the collapse of the twin towers was a sign that the grand narratives might be over in San Diego but not in Saudi Arabia. ... Osama bin Laden had evidently not been reading Francis Fukuyama. (British cultural theorist Terry Eagleton, quoted THES 2003)

The exception is that which cannot be subsumed; it defies general codification, but it simultaneously reveals a specifically juridical formal element: the decision in absolute purity ... There is no rule that is applicable to chaos. Order must be established for juridical order to make sense ... A regular situation must be created and sovereign is he who definitely decided if this situation is actually effective. (Carl Schmitt [1922]1985: 19–20)

For a limited period the United States has the power to write the terms for international society, in hopes that when the country's imperial hour has passed, new international institutions and stable regional powers will have begun to flourish, creating a kind of civil society for the world. (Kaplan 2003: 83)

America's destiny is to police the world. (Title of article by Max Boot, *Financial Times*, 18 February 2003)

The argument and composition of this book

Subject matter. The relationship between a modern discipline's presentation of truth and modernity, globally conceived. A relationship conceived through a reworking of the history and composition of criminology – the discourse of crime and its ordering – in the light of two circumstances: September 11, 2001, and the prevalence of genocide in modernity.

Argument. We live in the political and scholarly grip of the territorial state, yet we inhabit a global modernity: a modernity that was created in large part by imperial projects now officially discarded. In the West our concern is with living the 'good life' within 'civilized space', blind to the interconnection that render that space in a dependent relation to its external. The result is an intellectual incoherence and existential imbalance that is no longer sustainable, even if we are not yet able to think ourselves out of our situation.

Project: descriptive and normative. It is descriptive in its analysis of criminological history and its current substantive marginality; it is normative in its related argument that the absence of a global criminology is not only indicative of the nature of global governance but also evidence of failures both intellectual and social.

Prescriptive statement. Justice must transcend the territorial limits it has operated within modernity.

Disciplinary focus and organisation of the material. The argument for a global criminology works through an analysis of the excluded. Criminology is excluded from the discourses of post-September 11, and genocide is excluded from the discourse of criminology. Criminology has confined itself to a supporting role for civilised space, a territorial imagination that excludes from view the uncivilised, the other, utilizing strategies that are imperially effective but domestically clean. These exclusions provide the point of reference by which the constituting powers of the subject – criminology – may be gauged and may concomitantly reflect the constitution of our world order. The text traces this through analysis of the statistical, anthropological and everyday assumptions of criminology's history and our civilised everyday civilised spaces which exclude global conceptions as they are constituted by them; the argument rejects, however, current analyses that describe September 11, 2001 and the responses to it as exceptions that either destroy or reveal the absence of a global legal order. Instead September 11 confirms the nature of the world order of modernity; it can rather be read as a return of repressed features that display constituting powers and offer temptations for their enhancement.

Reflexive implication for security. Only a global awareness, which locates imagery of what is lost, of what is not present, can hope to counter the positivism that finds September 11, 2001 so astonishing and avoid the temptations of a new world order to criminalises politics in the shadow of a new militarist imperium.

Immediate background for writing

For those in my position – a well-educated, white, 'Western' professional – the last decade of the twentieth century was meant to be a time of celebration: with the collapse of the Berlin Wall and the Soviet Union, the cold war – perhaps the last clear division of the globe into spheres of neocolonial influence – was over. The Japanese American social commentator and ex-US State Department official, Francis Fukuyama (1989, 1992), announced the end of the social and political battles of modernity. Modern history, we were assured, culminated in the 'unabashed victory of economic and political liberalism'. A public ideology indistinguishable from the United States – with liberal democracy, the cultural ethos of the pursuit of individual happiness, free-market capitalism and the rule of law – was the fate of the world: 'the universalization of Western liberal democracy as the final form of human government'. Not only was the US the telos of European idealism – a message that Henry Steele Commager had given in *The Empire of Reason: How Europe Imagined and America Realised the Enlightenment* (1978) – but the US had left history (something that 'the vast bulk of the Third World remains very much mired in') behind. Large-scale military conflict would now only occur between states 'still in the grip of history'; it was for others to catch up; it was for US political and economic doctrine and will to make those still stuck in history free.

Note the subtle consequences: abandon the utopian search for social justice – there was no point in challenging international capitalism or liberal, expressive individualism. The game was settled and required realism; the key players were clear and those who could not live with the rules were losers, not victims.[1] Internationally, organisations such as the International Monetary Fund and the World Bank could impose stringent conditions (e.g. adopting policies of privatising state-owned entities or introducing free-market orientated reforms) as the price of help for weaker nations, while internally, a new punitiveness emerged in several Western nations, often intertwined in a mixture of popularism, declining state sovereignty and declaring 'war' on crime and drugs (Pratt *et al.* 2005). Balance and adaptation must replace utopian idealism.

The celebratory tone, however, was not to last. History was not finished with the US and the US was not a global us; on September 11, 2001, Osama bin Laden's al-Qaeda network, the outgrowth of a disparate Islamic International brigade financed and encouraged by a variety of sources – but most graphically the US – to fight the Soviet occupation of Afghanistan, launched a devastating attack upon key targets in the US.

If few appreciated the complex networks of linkages, September 11, 2001 upset Western notions of personal and collective security and identity. Notions of civilised spatial integrity and identity that took further blows with related bombings on 'Western' targets in Bali (with tourists as targets), Madrid (where the lead bomber escaped suspicion as he had been labelled a petty criminal due to his 'un-Islamic' history of drug dealing and pimping), Turkey (HSBC building and British Embassy) and later London (where home-grown suicide bombers had moved freely around the globe receiving religious indoctrination and practical training) and Egypt (with domestic and foreign tourists as targets) as well as a number of bombings in Islamic countries notably Morocco, Pakistan, Saudi Arabia and Bangladesh. Security now was without doubt a global issue, but accepting the local and the global as intertwined did not settle on what terms, or with what degree of reflexivity, did the interactions need to be rethought.

Thus the creation of this book: I write as a representative of Western modernity whose ancestors left their marginal status in the primary Europe of Ireland, Scotland and, by repute at least, Russia, to travel to what was intended to be a new Europe – the 'new world', specifically in their case New Zealand. There, many envisaged, they and others like them would supplant the indigenous natives and civilise the land. The globe was to be Europeanised in the name of humanity, civilisation, progress and the dual tropes of modernity and the rule of law. We inhabit the consequences; we now appreciate that this all-encompassing process did not bring global peace and stability, albeit not for trying, even at the cost of employing genocide as a key tactic. Today, partly as a result of the contingencies of personal history and partly owing to a job that involves substantial 'international' travel, I live globally. In a variety of locations, certainly not all of them Western, I consume (mostly in English) the discourses and media projections of the 'globalised' West that assumes 'we' speak the languages of (Western) modernity even as the claim is made that

that modernity either has been flawed or incomplete and its accommodations must be superseded. In airport after airport and a mixture of hotel rooms, restaurants, homes and bars, a veritable bauble of opinions seems to dislocate modernist discourses from their power base and their performability. That CNN, FOX and BBC, for example, use English only serves to render the notion that they are presenting a common reality astonishing, yet each holds itself out as presenting the real. They are, moreover, but key examples of the mainstream, established media, and beyond them lies other realms of the Internet and alternative media, sites for voices offering no shortage of conspiracy theories, shadow governments and/or takes on 'Zionist Anglo-American empire meltdown', where one can listen to the need to rid the world of Jews/Muslims/liberals/lefties/traitors...[one is free to insert one's favoured agent of the worlds problems]. The dreams of purity remain.

Modernity was a global phenomenon that often avoided this description. It was depicted instead in terms of social geographies of bounded territorial integrities where two sets of discourses were tasked with rationalising security; those of war in the international arena, and those of law and order or criminology in the domestic. In rationalised forms these were to give assurances to the (Western) populace that the exercise of power was, at least in principle and perhaps always as a project yet to be accomplished, capable of being understood and guided by reason, subjected to expertise and open to relative transparency. The result was a comforting but ultimately irrational division: a land of peace and police and an outside of bombs.

The irrelevancy of criminology: itself an excluded?

Criminology[2] – in the guise of a response, that of defining the events of September 11, 2001 as an international crime, of asking for an international arrest warrant, of constituting an international legal order with a due process and a international court, with then, perhaps, an analysis of the social, political and economic factors giving rise to the actions – was an unwelcome guest in the discourses guiding power after September 11. The American social commentator and former member of the State Department, Robert Kaplan (2001, 2003) provides a point of reference for what became the mainstream Western approach. Kaplan demanded a clear use of power to resolve the ambiguities and subtlcties seemingly plaguing a postmodern world; September 11, 2001 demonstrated a disordered 'world of collapsed distances' in which the domestic and the international lie intertwined. Those who exercise power in the advanced countries of the West must chose their politics carefully; either they adopt the realism of a globally orientated 'warrior politics' or immerse themselves in an ineffectual 'civilian politics'. The latter, however, mistook the nature of the world and its language usages. It relied upon discourses of moral and social universalism and abstraction in an attempt to gain guidance and predictive ability but, misunderstanding the real conditions of the world, these only result in advocating actions (or inaction) more 'nice than wise'.

Was September 11 a radically new event that changed the nature of the world? Quite the contrary, Kaplan warns; rather it was a rebuff to all those social commentators who had obscured how many fundamental aspects of the human condition, social interaction and politics remained similar throughout the ages. We are neither in a coherent modernity nor in a chaotic postmodernity awash in relativism; we need rather to appreciate the continual existence of themes dating from the ancient world that persist in the modern and will continue in the future. Instead of inhabiting a global relativist morass, we are simply differentially located in geography and culture. We should read the long record of history in order to properly appreciate our position and move wisely within the constraints such a reading reveals. A pagan ethos will serve us well; one that treats any claims to universality on behalf of liberal moral and political principles as an abstract idealism while moving strategically on a different terrain, sometimes espousing idealism, often choosing the less bad option or keeping actions invisible from the world media.

I have, of course, skated over this writer's scene setting for the US taking an imperial role. He argues that the US must accept the task of furthering the civilising process on a global scale as a reluctant realist rather than a romantic enthusiast: the 'prize for winning the Cold War' was that

> We and nobody else will write the terms for international society … A century of disastrous utopian hopes has brought us back to imperialism, that most ordinary and dependable form of protection for ethnic minorities and others under violent assault. (Kaplan 2002: 147)

An American-led globalisation, under a variety of guises – such as 'democratic' or 'liberal imperialism'[3] – must redevelop discursive and institutional frameworks. The US is thus the only 'credible force' that can stand for individual freedom, democracy and economic development, at least for several decades while it creates the conditions for its own obsolesce.

Distance collapsed: thus 'active engagement and realism' should replace 'isolationism and idealism'. A realism structured by the understanding 'that international relations are governed by different moral principles than domestic principles'. But how honest is this realism? Take, for example, what Kaplan means by telling us to learn from history and differences in geography. He draws this particular message from reading Churchill's account in *The River War* of the British retaking of the Sudan in the 1890s via the victory of the battle of Omdurman. Kaplan refers to this battle as 'one of the last of its kind before the age of industrial war: a panoramic succession of cavalry charges in which the young Churchill, an officer in the 21st Lancers, took part' (2002: 20). In Chapter 7, I offer a rather different interpretation, closely based on Churchill's actual account, in which the battle was a one-sided killing field of mechanised slaughter that had largely devastated the enemy before the 21st Lancers charged. Rather than realism, Kaplan offers what he takes to be an uplifting and inspiring message, reframing that particular story of British imperial endeavour as one where 'an intractable physical and human landscape becomes the obstacle that moral men surmount. The more hopeless the history and geography appear to be and the more unpromising the human material, the more prolific the opportunities for heroism.' Thus we are to be the (reluctant) inheritors of a grand vision:

> Churchill saw in the United States a worthy successor to the British Empire, one that would carry on Britain's liberalising mission. We cannot rest until something emerges

that is just as estimable and concrete as what Churchill saw when he gazed across the Atlantic. (Kaplan 2003: 83)

It is best for the message that this is, of course, an allegorical, or, at best, mediated, sense of seeing. For even if we were to grant Churchill the eyesight of a Hercules, from most of the places where he could have stood to see across the Atlantic to the US, his vision would have been obscured by Ireland, for so long a distressing image of empire's property.

Witnessing enlightenment: mediated visuality, the normal and the exceptional

The new, global media think in terms of abstract universal principles – the traditional weapon of the weak seeking to restrain the strong – even as the primary responsibility of our policymakers must be to maintain our strength ... The enormous anti-war demonstrations on several continents last February revealed that life inside the post-industrial cocoon of Western democracy has made people incapable of imagining life inside a totalitarian system. With affluence often comes not only the loss of imagination but also the loss of historical memory ... the peace demonstrators ... appeared to have no idea whatsoever that their very freedom to demonstrate had been won by war and conquest in the service of liberty – precisely what the US and British governments were proposing to do in Iraq. Of course the masses are uninterested, as Ortega noted: 'Since they do not see behind the benefits of civilisation ... they imagine that their role is limited to demanding these benefits peremptorily, as if they were natural rights.' (Kaplan 2003: 80–1)

Vision, images, mediated and constituted reality: how does one see behind the benefits of civilization? what is the appropriate historical memory? Kaplan does not enter into reflexive questioning; rather he warns that in the new struggle the 'most important front ... may be the media'. While the US government operates in a world of nation states it will be judged by 'a media that already exists in a universal, post nation-state world'. We are presented with a disjuncture: on the one side media images with associated universalistic concepts of international law, human rights and appeals to moral judgements thus calculated; on the other side pragmatic demands of exercising power in a nation state world. In constructing a new global civil society, the US and allies will have to be 'especially devious', and 'operate nimbly, in the shadows and behind closed doors' (2003: 70).

Conversely, to the journalist John Pilger the peace demonstrations were an expression of public morality aroused in part by the secondary media (such as the web): 'never in my lifetime have people all over the world demonstrated greater awareness of the political forces ranged against them and the possibilities for countering them' (2004: xxix). Against the 'power of the military plutocracy' he cast 'the power of public opinion', while warning that trust in the official media is weakened by the tactics of 'information control' exercised by a coalition of government powers and media owners.

Who then are we to trust and how are we to see properly? Plato presented the 'classical' metanarrative of trust, vision and witnessing in his *Republic* (written *c.* 372 BC), a treatise on education and governance which has served to ground narratives of core and periphery, internal and external, form and substance, appearance and reality, organised and disordered, civilised and barbaric. Therein Plato offers a strategy for the training of his ideal ruling elite – the philosopher-kings. The text is structured around dialogues lead by Socrates and is replete with allegories or similes. Perhaps the most crucial is the allegory of the Cave (514a–517c), 'an analogy for the human condition' and our 'education or want of it'.

We are a group of human beings living in a deep and vast cave at the far end of which is an entrance to the outside world that we cannot see. From childhood we have been bound and positioned in such a way that we can look only ahead; we have grown up in a world of mediated and controlled visibility. Behind us a fire burns, between ourselves and the fire is a path along which different artefacts – human and animal models and all kinds of other materials – are carried. Having only seen from birth the shadows cast by the fire from the objects carried along the path and heard only the sounds of the carriers, we believe that these shadows and echoes – 'the only reality' we 'could recognise' – are indeed reality. We have become adept at distinguishing among the various shadows with prestige, honours, praises and prizes for those of us who are sharpest at making out the things that go by. Our language is based on the idea that it faithfully represents and reflects the objects, the reality, we perceive.

What, however, if one or more one of us is 'set free' and are made to stand up, to turn our heads and walk and to look towards the firelight? If we are told that the things we had been seeing and giving value to all this time had 'no substance' and that we are now closer to reality we would be 'bewildered'. In fact, we would think that there was more reality in what we'd been seeing before than in what we were now shown and reject this new awareness.

Deliverance – enlightenment – comes with being led outside. Someone must drag us up the step path to the entrance and pull us out into the sunlight. This treatment will cause pain and distress; disorientated, we would not be able to discern reality, since the sun's rays would overwhelm our eyes. But, gradually we would learn to distinguish shadows from real things, while we would next 'feast' our 'eyes on the heavenly bodies and the heavens themselves, which would be easier at night'. At last we would gaze upon the sun and in turn we would be witness to enlightenment. We realise that the sun linked together all of visible reality and made possible the seasons, growth and decay. This 'sun' is the image of the good, and Plato argues that only by an analysis of the good can we come to see the nature of particular entities: 'the sight of the character of goodness leads one to deduce that it is responsible for everything that is right and fine, whatever the circumstance'.

But what of language? How can this witness to enlightenment speak and communicate? If we, enlightened ones, were to return to the cave it would take time for our eyes to get used to the darkness. If we had to compete with those of us who had stayed in the cave in the activities of everyday life therein, we would make a fool of ourselves and the others would say the journey had ruined our eyes and it was not worth trying to follow our lead. Moreover, they would resist anyone who tried to set them free, even to the point of killing us. However, it is the duty and the destiny of those of us who have been enlightened to return to the cave and act, perhaps to rule. There we must act to resolve the misery of the conditions we are now conscious of. Our sight of goodness gives us an enlightened education or 'art of orientation', using which we can direct the inhabitants of the cave into a 'well-governed community'.

La Caverne de Platon. — Composition et dessin de Chevignard.

Figure I.1 Etching of Plato's allegory of the cave (image: MEPL; Original source: Chevignard in *Magasin Pittoresue*, July 1855: 217). This romantic European representation begs the question why the prison was allowed to go on for so long and what of the interests of those who manufactured the 'reality' that had been presented to the prisoners. The trope of encountering 'reality' and enlightenment has contemporary sceptics, and much of what goes under the name of postmodernism can be seen as a rejection of it. The trope, as argued throughout this text, has brought on many outrages, for which the image of the suicide bomber brought up in Leeds, England, but finding the truth under instruction in Pakistan, to return and bomb London, is only a contemporary manifestation. But much of the postmodern position, though well intentioned it may be, is self-denying and/or ineffectual. In mainstream philosophy, Richard Rorty, a pragmatic philosopher who seems genuinely concerned to create a more caring and just world, and at times gets across an uplifting and humanity-embracing message, argues against the idea that knowledge is based on 'seeing' the truth or that this event provides foundations for a systematic and coherent organising of our beliefs. The Platonic 'analogy between perceiving and knowing' is said to have given rise to a model of 'systematic philosophers' who, dominated by the metaphor of knowledge as vision, think of 'having our beliefs determined by being brought face to face with the object of the belief' (1989: 163). Thus agreement is determined by 'confrontation', by acts of seeing that gives 'justified true beliefs, or, better yet, beliefs so intrinsically persuasive as to make justification unnecessary' (p. 366). For such a person true knowledge is as unavoidable 'as being shoved about, or being transfixed by a sight which leaves us speechless' (p. 376). By contrast 'edifying philosophers' will be those who see themselves as but one voice in 'the conversation of mankind'. Conversation, rather than vision, is the appropriate metaphor and in this scheme to know is to have 'a right, by current standards to believe' (p. 389). In this pragmatic philosophy, an objective truth is only really that about which there is general agreement (p. 337); our aim is to participate in 'the conversation of mankind' and we must be sceptical of the alternative conceptions of knowledge that seek to close off the conversation. Rorty may, however, not escape Plato's reach: not only does he have an almost child-like faith in this conversation being open and freely engaged in, but also in a conversation that is addressed to real problems, real political and social concerns, orientates itself by the notion that somewhere, even if the conversationalists do not reach it, there is a truth that will enable one to criticise suggestions, correct assertions, reach agreement and discount propositions.

Vattimo (1992) recasts the narrative as the dream of a transparent society. This is at the end in his narrative, destroyed not by our inability to see, but by our creation of technologies that shower us with a multitude of images and spectacles (or in intellectual terms, a multiplicity of paradigms). How could we arrive at an understanding of a 'reality' as an 'objective given lying beneath, or beyond, the images we receive of it from the media'? Thus the idea of emancipation modelled 'on lucid self-consciousness, on the perfect knowledge of one who knows how things stand', should be replaced 'by an ideal of emancipation based on oscillation, plurality and, ultimately, on the erosion of the very "principle of reality"' (p. 7), to be replaced by an ethic of interpretation. But who is to teach us the art of interpretation?

Nor has the Platonic tradition been without commentators who have reversed its division of the internal and the external, or darkness and light. The Greeks also warned of a sight so terrible that we could not survive seeing it: the Gorgon. (The Gorgon were three mythical sisters, originally beautiful priestesses serving Athena, the goddess of wisdom and war. After the only mortal among them, Medusa, was raped by Poseidon, they took their revenge by torturing men passing Athena's temple. An outraged Athena turned the sisters into hideous creatures whose image of 'hate, violence and onslaught ... chills the blood': *The Iliad*, 5.741.)

Pascal provided another 'image of the human condition': 'imagine a number of men in chains, all under sentence of death, some of whom are each day butchered in the sight of other; those remaining see their own condition in that of their fellows, and looking at each other with grief and despair await their turn' (Pascal, *Pensees*, 1950). In Tavvernier's film *Life and Nothing But*, a film set in the industrial killing of World War I, a focal point is a tunnel blown up by the retreating Germans as a train was passing through it. The families of the soldiers entombed within the tunnel/cave are gathered outside, sometimes entering the tunnel or waiting for items to be brought outside by the search party and rejoicing when they can recognise them as belonging to their dead soldiers. In this depiction, the tunnel – which also stands for all that which is extracted from the routines of normal life – contains the truth of victimhood, of suffering and death.

Yet the hope for a transcendental point beyond relativism seems intrinsic to hopes for inter-subjective agreement, objectivity and ethics. But on what and on whose terms? Reflexively, in the Platonic narrative, we must put the role of the elite who organised the freeing of the individual and introduced him into seeing correctly paramount.

The cave allegory has great and enduring appeal. It cannot be confined to technical arguments concerning Plato's invocation of the realm of the intelligible or divine as opposed to the various worlds of images, objects or forms. The set of distinctions, such as between the internal and the external, darkness and light, convention and reality, technical powers and real knowledge, chaos and order, continue to underpin not only arguments about meaning in everyday life but also technical issues in theory development. The grand narrative of Western secular enlightenment follows the pattern of being brought to see the 'truth'. In the techniques of specific theory development, the notion of knowledge as a matter of seeing (control of observation) remains basic. The two are intertwined: we have difficulty in seeing properly in the space inhabited by conventional assumptions and need to undertake the journey to enlightenment. Moreover this is a social condition, progress and freedom for the inhabitants comes with the enlightenment of the rulers.

The model mixes vision-led journey combining knowledge, freedom and progress; the goal is emancipation based on lucid self-consciousness, on the full knowledge of one who has seen the good and knows how things stand in this light, how things are related in their totality. The image underpins the conventional accounts of the enlightenment.

This is the tradition of the civilising process; European-led training in visualising the nature of things and their civilised order. Thus another definition of modernity: the Europeanisation of the world. In questioning this tradition, postmodernity is the rise of scepticism as to coherence and authority. Trust becomes problematic, cynicism abounds. What then of the person who commanded the prisoner to get up and led him to see, or of the person who returns as the witness to enlightenment, who is not initially accepted, but must forcibly drag up his fellows to see the light? Perception, reality and self-interest are played off against each other.

Figure I.2 The frontispiece of the *Encyclopédie* (from the complete edition, vol. 1, first published in 1751 edited by Diderot and d'Alembert) portrays reason pulling away the veil from truth, while clouds withdraw to open up the sky to light. (Engraving by B.L. Provost after a 1764 drawing) As Condorcet put it 'The time will come when the sun will shine only on free men who have no master but their reason', but this is a particular representation of enlightenment: the person ascending is unmistakably in the image of European beauty (Figure I.2). As Wolf reflected from his late-twentieth-century American perspective:

> We have been taught, inside the classroom and outside of it, that there exists an entity called the West, and that one can think of this West as a society and civilization independent of and in opposition to other societies and civilizations. Many of us even grew up believing that this West has a genealogy, according to which ancient Greece begat Rome, Rome begat Christian Europe, Christian Europe begat the Renaissance, the Renaissance the Enlightenment, the Enlightenment political democracy and the industrial revolution. Industry, crossed with democracy, in turn yielded the United States, embodying the rights to life, liberty, and the pursuit of happiness. (Wolf 1990: 5)

The image was to point to a utopia of truth and then a settled world, a world under the control of Western culture and Western notions of legitimacy and objectivity. The late-modern or postmodern era is defined as the undercutting of those assumptions and the realisation of their unanticipated consequences

Primo Levi (1986: 35) provides an extreme instance of this being used to get people to do what they would otherwise not in accounting for the way in which the SS managed to get Jewish transportees to become members of the Special Squads by controlling 'the crucial moment of stepping off the train, when every newly arrived person truly felt on the threshold of the darkness and terror of an unearthly space'. To process human life into corpses, Nazi administration relied upon creating a 'grey zone' of moral and personal ambiguity; one result was that the Jewish *Sonderkommandos* were drawn into doing the most physically dirty work for the Nazis in managing the gas chambers and crematoria (Figure I.3). They led naked prisoners to their death and organised them in the chambers, after the gassing they removed the bodies, now stained from the cyanotic acid and human excrement, washed them with water, checked that no valuable items were hidden in the bodily orifices, took out any gold from their teeth, cut the women's hair and washed it with ammonia chloride, took the corpses into the crematoria and burnt them, before emptying out the ovens of the ash that remained and cleaning the gas chambers for the next batch. A horrific process in which the 'long chain of conjunction between victim and executioner' came lose, where the identities of oppressor and oppressed lacked stability, providing a state of exception within the exceptional, leading to a crime within a crime: 'Conceiving and organising the squads was National Socialism's most demonic crime' (p. 53).

'The intrinsic horror of this human condition has imposed a sort of reserve on all the testimony, so that even today it is difficult to conjure up an image of "what it meant" to be forced to exercise this trade for months' (p. 52). Where did this occur? One of the very few who survived as a member of the last 'special team' of Auschwitz, recalled taking part in a soccer match between the SS and representatives of the *Sonderkommando*: 'Other men of the SS and the rest of the squad are present at the game; they take sides, bet, applaud, urge the players on as if, rather that at the gates of hell, the game were taking place on the village green' (p. 55).

This great state of exception – appearing as an affront to civilised normalcy – demands surely to be given a particular place, outside the civilised; Levi a survivor, however, finds he cannot repress it, experiencing:

> A dream within other dreams, which varies in its details but not in content. I am seated at the dinner table with my family, or with friends, or at work, or in the countryside – in a surrounding that is, in other words, peaceful and relaxed, apparently without tension and suffering. And yet I feel anguish, an anguish that is subtle and deep, the definite sensation of some threat. And, in fact, as the dream continues, bit by bit or all of a sudden – each time its different – everything falls apart around me, the setting, the walls, the people. The anguish becomes more intense and pronounced. Everything is now in chaos. I'm alone at the centre of a grey, cloudy emptiness, and at once I *know* what it means, I know that I've always known it: I am once again in the camp, and nothing outside the camp was true. The rest – family, flowering nature, home – was a brief respite, a trick of the senses. Now this inner dream, this dream of peace, is over; and in the outer dream, which continues relentlessly, I hear the sound of a voice I know well: the sound of one word, not a command, but a brief, submissive word. It is the order at dawn in Auschwitz, a foreign word, a word that is feared and expected: 'Get up', Wstawac. (Levi 1988: 245–55)

Then a light may shine, illuminating a scene that ought never to have been visible, which ought never to have occurred – a counterfactual to the dream of European enlightenment.

Figure I.3 The emaciated bodies of concentration camp prisoners lie on the floor of a building in the newly liberated Nordhausen camp (Thuringia, Germany, April 1945). The scene is only visible since both the SS and the squads have ceased to function and no clean-up has occurred. (Credit: USHMM)

Who then can bear witness? For Levi only those who can not could be

> ... we the survivors, are not the true witnesses ... We survivors are not only an exiguous but also an anomalous minority; we are those who by their prevarications or abilities or good luck did not touch bottom. Those who did so, those who saw the Gorgon, have not returned to tell about it or have returned mute, but they are ... the complete witnesses, the ones whose depositions would have a general significance. (Levi 1989: 83–4)

Chapter 1:
September 11, Sovereignty and the Invasion of 'Civilised Space'

The World Trade Center was the eye of a needle through which global capital flowed, the seat of an empire. However anonymous they appeared, the Twin Towers were never benign, never just architecture. (Sorkin and Zukin 2002a: xi)

A very tall building absorbs a plane and collapses after 105 defiant minutes, having watched its twin suffer the same fate. Everyone sees it. Again and again. It captures every eye and ear in stunned amazement. When the towers fell, the world shook. Nobody could accept what they saw. Such a vertical drop seemed impossible. And no amount of analysis of the mechanics of the collapse, the simple way the attack was carried out, or the strategic mission of the attackers can ease the incredulity. The event remains unbelievable, surprising even to those who initiated it. (Wigley 2002: 69)

With an extraordinary range of emotions, the world watched in disbelief as a power unanticipated pierced a power that thought itself invincible. (Smith 2002: 99)

By the standards of spectacle, September 11 had to be close to the greatest show on earth. (Harvey 2002: 64)

In purely military terms – as defined by U.S. strategy doctrine since at least as early as 1942 – the attacks were widely successful. (Ward Churchill 2003: 31, n. 92)

Prologue, the demands of surprise

There are many types of cave. A common image after September 11, 2001 was that of Osama bin Laden inhabiting a cave in Afghanistan, directing and influencing events in the outside word via a combination of primitive and technologically advanced modes of communication, or simply providing an ideological focal point. In response, the US military utilised an array of 'cave busting' bombs that were intended – unsuccessfully – to bring a deadly reality to him: the depth and extent of the cave complexes of Tora Bora became required reading.[1] Bin Laden slipped away and as of mid-2005 remained at large with the campaign he inspired very much alive and linked to ongoing and extensive insurgency in Afghanistan and Iraq. Tora Bora was transformed into a symbol and a metaphor: revealing contrasting resources and military powers, yet also an ineffective reliance on high technology to achieve a result that required greater human interaction. While the US reliance on bombing, generally in Afghanistan (and later in Iraq), showed differing perceptions as to victim-hood; it also reflected a confusion of tactics stemming, partly at least, from defining bin Laden as a terrorist and downplaying his politics, rubbishing his appeal, ignoring his aims, refusing to acknowledge his support and misunderstanding his tactics. While for Western consumption he was successfully labelled a terrorist in charge of a terror group given refuge by a 'rogue state' that appeared as if it could be easily toppled and conquered, for all the protestations of victories and talk of spreading democracy in developing a new world order by the US and other governments (in particular the UK and Australia), the outcome of the 'war on terror' declared after September 11, 2001 looked in early 2006 dubious, both in terms of specific campaign objectives and wider effects on international rules and institutions, as well as attacks on civil liberties in Western countries.[2] What was Tora Bora: an act of war, a policing operation, an assassination attempt on a political opponent or the attempted removal of a terrorist? Who had the power to define these events and whose reality was at stake?

New York – temple of modernism, may have been a different kind of cave. The events of September 11, 2001, provided a spectacle that astonished; perhaps they should not have. Not only have a number of commentators in the last decades of the twentieth century been sketching out theses on the changing nature of war and security,[3] but with hindsight many consider that American intelligence services had enough warnings to have prevented the actions,[4] and had either downplayed them, or had not been listened to by their political masters (for the latter charge see Anonymous 2002 and 2004). Yet the overwhelming response to the events was bewilderment. They were quickly presented as a wholly exceptional event, a disruption to progress and stability, an eruption of irrationality and evil. They needed to be put in context for them to be understood, rendered safe; but there was a confusion of contexts, or rather the process of contextualising the events divided along social, political, religious and national grounds.[5] An event rendered global by communication networks; understandings local and fragile.

My contention: September 11, 2001 – not an exception to the governing strategies of modernity, rather an event that reveals entrenched historical paradigms that have constrained understanding as much as they constituted them on the relationship of the local and the global, of pain and its distributions, of labelling 'crime' and its causality. Three images may illustrate: the first was presented by the English political theorist Thomas Hobbes in 1651 as the frontispiece of the *Leviathan* (Figure 1.1), the second is the image, or indeed the images of the events of September 11 themselves, which were broadcast live via the Internet and TV, as well as providing the front covers of newspapers, and magazines (such as *The Economist* for 15–21 September 2001, which simply stated *The Day the World Changed*) worldwide. That the paradigm may have changed is reflected in another *Economist* front cover of 30 November 2002 depicting the globe as a human skull: terror, it was said, was now global.

Hobbes's paradigm of modernity: civilised space, territorial space …

Hobbes's *Leviathan* is most often associated with the depiction of the natural condition of mankind as a state of 'warre' of all on all, where reason has little chance against the violent passions of man, and the life of man is solitary, poor, nasty, brutish and short. Humanity is rescued from this condition by *fear*. Fear of death drives man to act rationally and combine, forming a strong, even

Figure 1.1 The frontispiece of the *Leviathan*. Herein we are presented with a visualisation of sovereignty and the territorial state – it concerns both protected (civilised) space and embodiment. Note that the body of the sovereign is composed of the bodies of the subjects and the reality of body limitation, of the vulnerability of all humans to pain and death, provides a key element in Hobbes's narratives that legitimates men coming together and founding the sovereign body. 'If we look at adult men and consider the fragility of the unity of the human body (whose ruin marks the end of every strength, vigour, and force) and the ease with which the weakest man can kill the strongest man, there is no reason for someone to trust in his strength and think himself superior to others by nature. Those who can do the same things to each other are equals. And those who can do the supreme thing – that is, kill – are by nature equal among themselves' (Hobbes *De cive*, p. 93). Men are to be conceived as autonomous, relatively equal and competitive, a problematic situation which must be reconciled through some representation of commonality. The image reflects a process whereby the vulnerability which all human beings possess as embodied subjects is recast in terms of strength. One escapes the irrational chaos of the natural condition by combining through contract and agreeing on government, enforced by public power. Yet this is a spatially bounded strength, within the protected space civilising processes (creating civil society, political society) are at work; outside lies a chaotic realm which is a relationship whereby the security of the protected space (internal to the State) is dependent upon the State responsible for the space being more powerful than other 'States'

totalitarian government, through accepting that power – might – lies at the heart of all social organisation and that whoever possesses power has both the ability and the right to dominate. That overly simplistic and reductionist reading obscures the radical and complex interpretation Hobbes offers for the human condition. It is, however, correct in two aspects: the extent to which he places the achievement of security – the pacification of violence – before all else and the extent to which performability (the power to enforce or to make a predictable, repeatable occurrence) is given a practical epistemic warrant.

Reading Hobbes today it is easy to gloss over how astonishingly *secular* his message was, even though he had officially presented it as a bargain between secular and ecclesiastical power.[6] As the frontispiece illuminates, the *Leviathan* concerns the creation of civilised space, a realm of civil society where a civilised humanity can flourish beneath the watching gaze of the sovereign. At stake was the control of social violence, the widespread nature of which in the early seventeenth century could hardly even be described as the waging of 'war', and was justly termed by one later commentator simply as *melee* (Clark 1958). On the page an interlocking set of images give a visual presentation of the benefits of security and stability; in effect an existential world picture. For us of course this is a classical text: we cannot recreate the experience of encountering it in the times of its writing. We acknowledge that it was written at the time of the passing of the superordinate authority of the Christian church, where religious authority, instead of being a binding force, had itself become a major source of conflict in Europe. What should replace the claims to loyalty of religious brotherhood or localised relations? The Thirty Years' War, the bitterest European campaign yet seen, had laid waste to much of central Europe and drastically reduced the German-speaking population. Few people thought globally as we mean it; but, using our current language, the major blocs of that time appear as a divided European Christendom, with the strongest other powers being the Chinese Empire, localised in its concerns, and the Islamic Ottoman Empire somewhat at odds with Islamic Persia. For centuries Islam, not Christian Europe, had been the place of learning: 'a world civilization, polyethnic, multiracial, international, one might even say intercontinental' (Lewis 2002: 6). But a grand European project was to change that world. Christian Spanish forces destroyed the last Muslim (Moorish) enclave – the Emirate of Granada – in 1492, in the aftermath of which Columbus was allowed to sail in search of a new route to India. From that time, the ships and military power of Europeans entered into the wider realms of the globe, overwhelming cultures and peoples that could not withstand the onslaught, creating new social and territorial relations in their image. Driving this world shift in power was an existential perspective on life itself. Hobbes postulated the basis of the social bond – in place of dynasties, religious tradition or feudal ties – as rational self-interest exercised by *calculating individuals*. As bearers of subjective rationality, individuals were depicted as forming the social order and giving their allegiance to a government, a sovereign, because it was in their rational self-interest to do so and the metaphor for the social bond was contractual, not traditional. The sovereign was now to have a particular *territory*, which many have rather loosely termed the 'nation-state',[7] wherein he was the representative of a people and was ultimately composed of the people who occupied that territory. To ensure security and maintain peace, Hobbes knew the sovereign must be well armed. The armaments he gave him were dual: the public sword and the weapons of the military; but there are also the weapons of metaphysical awe, the emblems of the church.

The orderly and ordered town and the countryside flourish in the protected realm of the sovereign. The rolling hills of the countryside are dotted with small villages, each with its church, while the town has neat rows of substantial houses and a cathedral, the spire of which is the highest building in the land.

This representation of inhabitable space, an ordered territory, I term civilised space. Beneath, Hobbes gives two columns in balance. On the one side is the imagery of war and military power that gives the territory secular security against attack from external forces: the castle, the crown, the cannon, the regimental flags and the confrontation of forces in battle. On the other, we have metaphysical security: the church, the bishops, the emblems of religious office and the clergy in service.

This paradigm of civilised space is also a duality. Within the civilised space granted by the power of the sovereign the necessary reference points for social intercourse – expectations, contracts and the truth of speech – are secured in a space of inclusion. Outside may lie a world of darkness. Beyond the reach of the sovereign's guarantees, lies the land of the 'other'. But we do not see it. It is however, an invisible presence. Contained in fear, in dreams, in stories told by travellers, the realm of the other is there but unacknowledged. It is the source of danger, of possible intruders, of differences that can upset the balances of the civilised. It is to be mastered or kept at a safe distance.[8]

This short interpretation of the *Leviathan* – in which mankind is placed in the centre – is of course, completely 'modern'. It ignores the range of religious issues that Hobbes's small group of intended readers would have been concerned to find; and concerned they became. They were angry when they found a text that contained many of the standard references to church and God, but was written in a language where the grammar – the meaning – denoted something else.[9] It was not just that Hobbes wrote in English, the vernacular language of a 'national' commonality and was concerned to communicate within that arena, rather than writing in Latin to preserve and acknowledge the traditions of the past and to communicate with pan-European elites. There were more unsettling features. All the standard tropes were there (including many contained in Latin phrases), but something was wrong ... there was a difference. They seemed to be presented as instruments of human projects – along with demands for reasoned strategies – and always conscious of human desires, hopes and fears.

In its structure the text was still two realms; the Commonwealth was *Civill and Ecclesiasticall*, but in reality political theory had become secular; features immanent to the human condition provided the foundation to Hobbes's 'natural law'. He had given it away in the opening sentence of 'The Introduction' when he had put his reference to God in brackets: 'Nature (the Art whereby God hath made and governs the World) is by the Art of man. . . . also imitated, that it can make an Artificial Animal'. Effectively, Hobbes rejected the persuasive power of Gnosticism, with its notion of this world as a prison to be endured with death an escape to be welcomed for it took one into the realm of the divine, by embracing a programme of (pragmatic) self-assertion. In a disenchanted world, devoid of the comfort of God's promise of eternal salvation, Hobbes wanted to push off death as far as possible: the foundational desire of man was the preservation of his life and its continuance; the ultimate basic right was that of self-preservation and self-defence. This life, in our localities, was the true realm for our concerns, where we may find happiness, or at least, play the games of desire and find (perhaps, temporal) satisfaction. Inside the protected territory, man's task (perhaps his doom) was the pursuit of success, of *felicity*, a movement of desire and fulfilment of desire. This was a game without end, for each satisfaction of desire led onto another act of desiring. The social order was constituted as contractual; to the Sovereign was given the power to rule and to the subject(s) obedience, but in effect only for so long as the ruling power ensured that the conditions necessary to promote felicity were secured.[10]

Hobbes was modern, even if he did not intend to be.[11] It was his fate. To pacify violence one must find appropriate language and representation, language that disciplined violence, representations that fostered feelings of security and the sovereign must control their use.[12] In turn the sovereign body must also remember it was composed of the people. The death of the sovereign, the collapse of sovereignty, would result from the lack of security of the people and a lack of understanding by the people of his exercising of sovereign power. The power that gave sovereignty effectiveness was itself constituted discursively and symbolically. The social bond being founded on individual self-assertion, subjective rationality cannot be turned into agreement by violence, but only by reason and symbolic attachment.[13] Reason that can be taught or rationally re-constructed, communicated and shared. This shared discourse must enable performability. Not only must sovereign and people be linked in communication and representation, those processes must result in practical projects, increasing wealth and power.[14] To the extent that these processes depended on the self-understanding of those interacting in the 'society', understandings disruptive of the sense of 'justice' and social interaction must be suppressed or denied any epistemic authority. We are to 'prove things after [our] own sense'.

The images of September 11 occur 250 years after the *Leviathan*. It has been presented as the day of the exception (*The day that shook the world* [BBC 2001], was but one representative title), when the instruments of civilised hyper-modernity – civilian planes, box cutters, mobile telephones – became weapons of great destructive power in the hands of a group of determined individuals. Individuals that were members of a loose grouping called al-Qaeda, who chose to create terror through a suicide mission, ostensibly in the name of religious belonging: fundamentalist Islam.[15] The targets that were hit were located in two American cities: one was a modern castle – the Pentagon, headquarters of the largest military complex in the world – and the other was the twin towers of the highest building in the mega-city of New York, the World Trade Center.

The twin towers were dominant points of New York's skyline. In their symbolism of late modernity the church had given way to the economy, the market, mass communication networks and individual consumption as focal points. Instead of the spires of the Cathedral reaching up to the heavens as symbols of mankind's servitude to God, the twin towers of the World Trade Center represented humanity's technological virtuosity, global trade and power over the forces of nature. They reflected an ability to escape from what had seemed the constraints of nature through applying technical knowledge of nature's forces.

On September 11, 2001, the towers came crashing down. Civilised space became invaded. And it happened in the centre of the greatest nation on the globe – the one *superpower* – the contemporary *Leviathan*: the US. Images of fear and unknown risks replaced those of modern civilised space.

A paradigm in pieces, analysis ... or the chorus to new acts of power?

Since September 11 there have been many speaking parts ... and confusion. What really happened, what actually changed? Who was responsible, what were the causes, what was the real target ... Did it have a message, was it a political act or was it 'senseless' terrorism? Was it a *crime* with a specific target, a specific act for gain or was it an expressive gesture directed at modern civilised values? Or was it an act of *war*, if so who was the agent waging war and who would be the party to engage with (and ultimately to defeat or make peace with)? Or was it some combination, moreover, an act providing evidence of a 'clash of civilisations'?[16] Was the response to wage war or launch a quasi police action or simply assassinate the leaders of the 'terrorist' group?[17] In either case who or what were the targets and were there institutions to work within and rules to abide by? Did analysis proceed with the language of *realpolitik* international relations or a neo-criminological language of an international 'crime' and legal order, that is, the legal order of some imagined 'international community'? A few voices tried the latter. In the immediate aftermath, for example, the highly experienced Middle East correspondent of the *Independent* (a leading UK newspaper) Robert Fisk (*Independent*, 16 September 2001) warned in expressly criminological terms:

> Retaliation is a trap. In a world that was supposed to have learnt that the rule of law comes above revenge, President Bush appears to be heading for the very disaster that Osama bin Laden has laid down for him ... [September 11] was a crime against humanity. We cannot understand America's need to retaliate unless we accept this bleak, awesome fact. But this crime was perpetrated ... to provoke the US.

In words that could have been lifted from numerous criminological articles addressing domestic crime policies, Fisk highlighted the type of questions asked:

> Every effort is being made to switch off the 'why' question and concentrate on the who, what and how ... No wonder we have to refer to the terrorists as 'mindless'. For if we did not, we would have to explain what went on in those minds ...
>
> I repeat: what happened in New York was a crime against humanity. And that means policemen, arrests, justice, a whole new international court at The Hague if necessary. Not cruise missiles and 'precision' bombs and Muslim lives lost in revenge for Western lives. But the trap has been sprung. Mr Bush – perhaps we, too – are now walking into it.[18]

Yet others, seemingly more in tune with neo-conservative opinion specifically decried any criminological language: 'This is not crime. This is war ... Secretary of State Colin Powell's first reaction to the day of infamy was to "pledge to bring those responsible to justice". This is exactly wrong' (wrote the syndicated columnist Charles Krauthammer on 12 September, later arguing that 'Capturing Osama Bin Laden is not enough. We also have to target the Taliban, then Syria, and finally Iran and Iraqi': both pieces appeared in over 150 newspapers on 12 September entitled 'Our Goal: Overthrow Regimes' and 28 September, entitled 'Congress Should Declare War').

But even if under the heading of pursuing justice, whose justice was it a fight for? Could this lead to a global coalition for a global justice with a global analysis of problems of law and order, of rights, status and principles of intervention?[19] Or would the response be 'the justice of this nation': to take the words of the American President George W. Bush?[20] Bush's own strategy was clear, as he stated in his 2004 State of the Nation address, this was war – not crime – and the energies of the state were directed not at 'law enforcement' but at waging 'war'.

Objects, objectivity and nothingness

On September 11, 2001, the World Trade Center became Ground Zero. An object, with thousands of human lives, became transformed into something that was symbolised by the numerical referent for nothing. An object became nothingness; except of course the symbolic meaning to both was uncertain.

First, what was the World Trade Center?

In *site specific, material terms* it was a building 110 stories, 1,353 feet (412 metres) tall comprised 'twin towers' with an acre of rentable space on each floor. This provided about 10,000,000 square feet of rentable space, occupied by about 50,000 people.

It was owned and operated by the Port Authority of New York and New Jersey and was the world's tallest building for a short time, taking over from the Empire State Building, and then surpassed by the Sears Tower.

It was on a site comprising 16 acres in lower Manhattan, with buildings grouped around a five-acre central plaza, about three blocks north of the New York Stock Exchange. It contained an observation deck on the South Tower, WTC 2, floor 107 where visitors could gaze on the city below and besides (summer hours opening 9:30 AM to 11:30 PM). It contained 'skylobbies' on floors 44 and 78 served by high speed elevators. There were seven underground levels including services, shopping and a subway station.

Two nine-story Plaza Buildings flanked the main entrance to the complex from Church Street, with WTC 4 on the south and WTC 5 on the north. Groundbreaking for construction took place on 5 August 1966. Steel construction began in August 1968. First tenant occupancy of WTC 1 was December 1970, and occupancy of WTC 2 began in January 1972.

What happened? On Friday, 26 February 1993, a massive bomb was exploded in the Center's public parking garage, but the Towers survived. On Tuesday, September 11, 2001, at 8:46 AM New York local time, WTC 1, the north tower, was hit by a hijacked 767 commercial jet airplane, loaded with fuel for a trans-continental flight. WTC 2, the south tower, was hit by a similar hijacked jet 18 minutes later at 9:03 AM. (In separate but related attacks, the Pentagon building near Washington DC was hit by a hijacked 757 at 9:43 AM, and at 10:10 AM, a fourth hijacked jetliner crashed in Pennsylvania, almost certainly as the result of actions of crew and passengers against hijackers.) The south tower, WTC 2, which had been hit second, was the first to suffer a complete structural collapse at 10:05 AM, 62 minutes after being hit itself, 80 minutes after the first impact. The north tower, WTC 1, then also collapsed at 10:29 AM, 104 minutes after being hit. WTC 7, a substantial 47-storey office building in its own right, built in 1987, was damaged by the collapsing towers, caught fire, and later in the afternoon also totally collapsed. The final list of collapsed buildings included all seven buildings of the World Trade Center complex – including WTC 6, the US Customs House to the north; WTC 3, the 22 story Marriot World Trade Center hotel just west of WTC 2; and WTC 4 and 5, the Plaza Buildings to the east. Other nearby buildings were significantly damaged, including the St Nicholas Greek Orthodox Church, and One Liberty Plaza, a 54 floor, 743-foot tall building across Church Street to the east.

About 2,800 people died on the site; many more could have.[21] At the time the recovery and site clearing process officially concluded on 30 May 2002, about 1,796 people remained unrecovered. Debris weighing 1.8 million tons had been removed from the disaster site. Images of the site continued to play a major role in world news.

As an *existential site*, the World Trade Center was a place of civilised space, a testament to modernity and the ability to define out violence from urban life and define in functionality and modern, urban civil society. Its destruction, televised live throughout the world, transformed it into an icon with great symbolic and rhetorical power. But who actually lived and worked in this space and who was excluded and by what means and on what terms did the processes of inclusion and exclusion operate? As knowledge of the events, the victims and working practices of the World Trade Center were pieced together, they seemed to mix the premodern and the modern in ways that showed up the fissures and contradictions of a globalising world, in which inequality and exclusion underlay the rhetoric of world trade and progress. For the World Trade Center was a site of power and a medium of communication that was structured through processes of inclusion and exclusion. New York also contained the symbol of freedom and the American Dream, the Statue of Liberty, a beacon to the dispossessed the world over (and reproduced in scale models in various refugee camps[22]). But the World Trade Center gave access to employment or its services depending on one's skills or investment capital. The rewards it allowed flowed according to how one was keyed into the game of international finance, or – as in the case of the cleaners or coffee shop employees – serviced those who were. Within its lived space, from the depths of the underground station to the heights of the towers, the World Trade Center filtered, distinguished, judged and enabled; processes not part of its official story.

That the World Trade Center was a symbolic site went without question, but who owned the technological power and symbolism of the World Trade

Center? The World Trade Center was itself a product, a consequence of the pursuit of rational knowledge concerning the construction of buildings. In texts produced by architects, the World Trade Center was celebrated for its technological breakthroughs and was said to achieve a balance between the demands of office space, shops, exhibition centres, hotel and mass transport.

> Yamasaki's commission to design the World Trade Center with the New York firm of Emery Roth and Sons ... house(s) anyone and anything connected with world trade. The program presented to Yamasaki, who was selected over a dozen other American architects, was quite explicit: twelve million square feet of floor area on a sixteen acre site, which also had to accommodate new facilities for the Hudson tubes and subway connections – all with a budget of under $500 million. The vast space needs and limited site immediately implied a high-rise development that ... make(s) the adjacent drama of Manhattan's business tip seem timid in comparison. ...
>
> The twin towers, with 110 floors rising 1,353 feet, ... (are) the tallest in the world. From observation decks at the top of the towers it ... (is) possible to see 45 miles in every direction. ... One distinct advantage of the project's enormity is the architectural opportunity to advance the art of building.
>
> Yamasaki re-examined the skyscraper from the first principles, considering no ground so hallowed that it could not be questioned, especially in view of the potential of modern technology. The usual economic prohibition on 'custom-made' was out, as virtually anything made for the Center would automatically become a stock item. 'Economy is not in the sparseness of materials that we use,' said Yamasaki of his $350 million estimated cost, 'but in the advancement of technology, which is the real challenge'. ...
>
> From the outset, Yamasaki believed that there should be an open plaza from which one could appreciate the scale of the towers upon approach. There is little or no sense of scale, for instance, standing at the base of the Empire State Building. Yamasaki's plaza ... [is] sheltered from the river winds and contained by five-story buildings which ... house shops, exhibition pavilions and a 250-room hotel. (Heyer 1966: 194–5)

The buildings were intended as symbols of human peace and dignity. To look for inspiration to the cathedrals and palaces of Europe would be a mistake, given the different purpose that large 'public' buildings today have.

> There are a few very influential architects who sincerely believe that all buildings must be 'strong'. The word 'strong' in this context seems to connote 'powerful' – that is, each building should be a monument to the virility of our society. These architects look with derision upon attempts to build a friendly, more gentle kind of building ... Although it is inevitable for architects who admire [the] great monumental buildings of Europe to strive for the quality most evident in them – grandeur, the elements of mysticism and power, basic to cathedrals and palaces, are also incongruous today, because the buildings we build for our times are for a totally different purpose. ...
>
> I feel this way about it. World trade means world peace and consequently the World Trade Center buildings in New York ... had a bigger purpose than just to provide room for tenants. The World Trade Center is a living symbol of man's dedication to world peace ... beyond the compelling need to make this a monument to world peace, the World Trade Center should, because of its importance, become a representation of man's belief in humanity, his need for individual dignity, his beliefs in the co-operation of men, and through co-operation, his ability to find greatness. (Minoru Yamasaki, in Heyer 1966: 186 and 194)

By contrast with the Empire State Building, which earlier had been the tallest building in the world, Yamasaki sought to position the World Trade Center in an anti-Imperial frame. As Mumford (1955) describes well, the Empire State Building was specifically monumental in style and scale. The World Trade Center, conversely, was to present strict modernism with its functionality and utility, while providing a space for co-operative development in trade and finance. Yet the building was only possible by an almost-imperialist use of power directed at the diverse interests already occupying the urban space it replaced. The story of the WTC construction was one of the destruction of a mixed urban community of residential and light industrial use and the shady dealings of property speculation (see the aptly entitled *Divided We Stand: A Biography of New York's World Trade Center* (Darton 1999)). In his research on the towers planning and construction by a semi-public agency, The Port Authority of New York and New Jersey (which purchased the existing buildings at below market price), Darton drew parallels in terrorism between the construction of the building and the earlier attempt to bomb it:

> You need only to stand for a moment in the Austin Tobin plaza to become immediately and keenly aware of how Yamasaki's abstract sculptural ethos achieved a kind of chilling perfection in his World Trade Center design. Here you find yourself in the presence of two monumental structures whose formal relationship gives us no indication of their purpose or intent. You know they are office buildings, yet their design makes it nearly impossible to imagine that they are full of *people*. It is at this point that – even without invoking the optical trick of standing at a towers's corner and looking upward – you realise the trade towers disappear as sites of human habitation and reassert their power at the level of an esthetic relationship. And it is through recognising this process that you become uncomfortably aware of a kindred spirit linking the apparently polar realms of skyscraper terrorist and skyscraper builder.
>
> This analogy between those who seek to destroy the structures the latter thought it rational and desirable to build becomes possible by shifting focus momentarily to the shared, underlying predicate of their acts. To attempt creation or destruction on such a immense scale requires both bombers and master-builders to view living processes in general, and social life in particular, with a high degree of abstraction. Both must undertake a radical distancing of themselves from the flesh and blood experience of mundane existence "on the ground". …
>
> For the terrorist and the skyscraper builder alike, day-to-day existence shrinks to insignificance – reality distills itself to the instrumental use of physical forces in service of an abstract goal. Engulfed by their daydream, they are 'no longer aware of the outside universe'. (Darton 1999: 118–19)

Power attracted power.[23] The Twin Towers were the product of a legislating and arranging power from above that organised the sweeping away of community and the construction of a starkly *modernist* edifice.[24]

> Ugly, awkward, functional – like the city itself – the Twin Towers made their great impression by sheer arrogance. They took over the skyline, staking their claim not only as an iconic image of New York but as the iconic image of what a modern city should aspire to be: the biggest, the mightiest, the imperial center. Once we gazed upon this site as a landscape of power, but since September 11, we have viewed it in sorrow – as if it holds both the dark side of grandeur and our unspoken fears of decline. (Zukin 2002: 13)

Its destruction demonstrated the weakness of that sovereign power to achieve a building that combined functionality, stability and community acceptability.[25] As indeed had the changing use of the Towers themselves. Devised in the early 1960s they were conceived in a time of high modernism; when completed they stood in a 1970s mired by recession and the oil crisis brought about by OPECH's increase in prices. The technical bankruptcy of New York City in 1975 was only one aspect as New York became an imaginary place of decline, of defunct urban organisation and increasing crime levels. Then, in the late 1980s, a transformation occurred. 'Zero tolerance' became the catchword of the official New York story in fighting crime and making the streets secure (the reality may be better told in terms of the decline of the crack-cocaine epidemic and changing patterns of gang behaviour). New York enjoyed massive inflows of capital and the growing communication technologies made observing the New York Stock Exchange and currency trading part of the daily routine of the global business network. In a global economic environment, the

> Twin Towers symbolized the era of neoliberal globalization and the role of New York financial markets in particular and the U.S. in general in forcing a certain pattern of political-economic development (at one point known as 'the Washington consensus') upon the rest of the world. They marked in towering glass and steel the moment of transition from Fordism to flexible accumulation led by financialization of every-thing. They symbolized the new-found dominance of finance capital over nation state policies and politics. By the time of the Clinton presidency, it was clear that even the federal government had to submit to the discipline of New York bond markets. (Harvey 2002: 58)

If the fear of the Hobbesian civilised space was that of the over-controlling big-brother (together with specifically modern technological abilities), was the developing world order one in which it was difficult to locate who was in control, who or what to fear? If the benign Hobbesian imagery – imagery designed to enable but contain power – was that of a bounded territorial security, a protected realm of rationality, common sense and efficiency for a humane modernity to develop, was September 11 'an out-of-geography experience'? (Booth and Dunne 2002: 1)

Geography and experiencing the events: symbolic and real

Security, geography, identity, modernity: who was protected and who feared? How was power organised to facilitate life? Although some thought that understanding September 11 needed the big picture to be rethought and understood more generally, the immediate response was structured by the appeals of victim-hood and the need for a calculated, powerful and awe-inspiring response. The events had local victims – although the list of nationalities among the victims was impressive – with global significance. In the immediate aftermath expressions of sympathy were made worldwide with many asserting that today 'we are all Americans'.[26] Many could share in the attempt of the New York writer, Don DeLillo in an article entitled 'In the Ruins of the Future', for the leading UK newspaper *The Guardian* (22 December 2001; first published by Harper's Magazine in the US, December 2001) to express 'what this day has done to us'. Language, 'inseparable from the world that provokes it', could only take its starting focus 'in the towers, trying to imagine the moment, desperately. Before politics, before history and religion, there is the primal terror. People falling from the towers hand in hand.' These imagined scenes offer a 'counter-narrative': one of 'hands and spirits joining, human beauty in the crush of meshed steel'. Moving outwards 'every basis for comparison' is lost, 'the event asserts its singularity. There is something empty in the sky'. The writer tries to give 'memory, tenderness and meaning to all that howling space'. Yet understanding technology and modernism bridges the void of the existential space of destruction and the human actions in the death-giving event.

> Technology is our fate, our truth. It is what we mean when we call ourselves the only superpower on the planet. The materials and methods we devise make it possible for us to claim our future. We don't have to depend on God or the prophets or other astonishments. We are the astonishment. The miracle is what we ourselves produce, the systems and networks that change the way we live and think.
>
> But whatever great skeins of technology lie ahead, ever more complex, connective, precise, micro-fractional, the future has yielded, for now, to medieval expedience, to the old slow furies of cut-throat religion.
>
> Kill the enemy and pluck out his heart.
>
> If others in less scientifically advanced cultures were able to share, wanted to share, some of the blessings of our technology, without a threat to their faith or traditions, would they need to rely on a God in whose name they kill the innocent? Would they need to invent a God who rewards violence against the innocent with a promise of "infinite paradise", in the words of a handwritten letter found in the luggage of one of the hijackers? … We like to think that America invented the future. We are comfortable with the future, intimate with it. But there are disturbances now, in large and small ways, a chain of reconsiderations. … the event has changed the grain of the most routine moment.
>
> We may find that the ruin of the towers is implicit in other things.

The attacks posed a challenge to the technological supremacy of the West, yet DeLillo seemed to resent above all the transformation in time and space that had occurred, for the events had made this *First World* site 'third-worldish'.

> Six days after the attacks, the territory below Canal Street is hedged with barricades. There are few civilians in the street. Police at some checkpoints, troops wearing camouflage gear and gas masks at others, and a pair of state troopers in conversation, and 10 burly men striding east in hard hats, work pants and NYPD jackets. A shop owner tries to talk a cop into letting him enter his place of business. He is a small elderly man with a Jewish accent, but there is no relief today. Garbage bags are everywhere in high, broad stacks. The area is bedraggled and third-worldish, with an air of permanent emergency, everything surfaced in ash.

It was as if history was disturbed – was it not meant to be linear with New York as symbol of progress? The imagery of transformation resounded. On the deepest personal level, the buildings that offered a civilised work environment for thousands of individuals had in its collapse reduced many of those individuals to dust and ash in a matter of seconds. There was no way of physically differentiating building dust, human dust, airline dust or of that which had been 'internal', from that which had come in from the outside. These personal tragedies spoke for the universal fragility of the human condition. Institutions also seemed fragile, security problematic, the everyday was no longer to be taken for granted but scanned for potential threats.[27] Yet in moving from the deeply personal – by its nature universally human – to considerations of the actual space invaded, empathy became mixed with the political and the situational ethics of the powerful and the dispossessed. Many dispossessed could grieve for the human lives lost but enjoy the spectacle of a power invaded.[28] On a 'global' level, the buildings were interpreted as symbols of a particular 'civilisation', that of modern capitalism and its global reach, and their destruction provided a metaphor for its fragility. If a number of commentators saw in the events a clash of civilisations, for others it necessitated a rethinking of the assumptions of progress and direction of the 'West'.[29] Some residents of New York now reacted to the destruction of the buildings as if they were symbols of an overdetermination of their daily life. They hoped the replacements would be more humane.[30]

Thus the external came to transform the civilised space of this locality of modernity. Paraphrasing Darton (1999: 119), forcibly awakened from their daydream, the residents of this place of power and security were now only too aware of the outside universe.

Visualising the new globalisation?

How did one present a post-September 11, awareness of the global? In its front covers *The Economist* magazine created a set of images for a new reality. The cover of the 19–25 October 2002 edition, under the heading *A World of Terror*, was of a small figure standing before a forest of tall sticks of dynamite with their fuses lit. For the 30 November–6 December 2002 edition, under the heading of *Preparing for Terror*, the globe was now one human skull.

Since its creation in the nineteenth century, *The Economist* had premised its journalism on a notion of global trade, liberalism and predictable rules of engagement. It now seemed to say that the 'world picture' was one of terror, fear, mistrust and death. To others, these images were only a realisation by the powerful of the terror that many in the world already lived with on a daily basis.[31] Then there was the question of interdependency. To what extent had the lack of violence in 'civilised space' been the consequence of pushing violence somewhere else? Was the peace and security of the internal a consequence of forcing violence and insecurity on the external? Was the event evidence of the dislocation of that divide?

A changed geography of security had an existential effect not only in New York but also throughout America and the West: already in the reporting of the first attack in 1993, the notion of the collapse of safe space was present. Terrorism had moved from being something that happened somewhere else – and that somewhere else a safe distance over the horizon.[32]

The insecurity of New York's space could be a metaphor for any space of what has loosely been termed the West (56 nationalities were among the dead); later seen in the bombings conducted by groups related to al-Qaeda in the holiday resort on Bali (where the main targets were tourists: Australians, British and New Zealanders), Madrid (where around 200 rail commuters were killed) and London (where bombs on the underground and bus services killed 56 with 700 injured; the first person identified as killed by the bombers was Muslim).[33] But none could turn to such an array of military and quasi-police forces, not to mention intelligence services, as the US could. In the immediate reactions to September 11 it could be felt as 'an attack on us all' (contested as translating to in reality the global elite), but only the US could combine vast military power with acute sense of vulnerability.[34] This new existential

Figure 1.2 One collection of the skulls of the 1994 genocide in Rwanda (photo: Brian Sayer, 2003, taken at a site museum). *The Economist* cover for 30 November–6 December 2002 under the title *Preparing for Terror* depicted the globe as one human skull, whose skull was this? If *The Economist* could now assert that the world had changed and terror had come upon us, what of the terrors of the so-called Third World? The genocide of Rwanda, perhaps the easiest of the great massacres of the twentieth century that could have been stopped, resulted in over 800,000 deaths. William Rubinstein's words (2004: 291) seem brutally apt:

> While overt racism certainly played no part in the attitude of the Western world towards the Rwandan genocide, it is difficult to believe that many people in the West really cared whether 100,000 or 500,000 or 800,000 perceived as illiterate savages who had contributed nothing to the world's stock of achievement and culture lived or died. An interesting experiment in fact suggests itself. If two collectors had been stationed in any shopping mall in the Western world at the time of the genocide, one raising money to stop 100,000 Tutsi children from being murdered by Hutus, the other raising money to stop 100 elephants from being slaughtered by poachers, which would collect more? If you had bet on the elephants, it is safe to say you would have put some change in your pocket.

insecurity for America was only one locality in the global imbalance in military force. The American social commentator Noam Chomsky asked his listeners to understand that much of the media was engaged in an ill-founded labelling process.

> To quote the lead analysis of *The New York Times* (16 Sept. 2001) 'The perpetrators acted out of hatred for the values cherished in the West as freedom, tolerance, prosperity, religious pluralism and universal suffrage.' US actions are irrelevant, and therefore need not even be mentioned. Such views are seduced by self-adulation and uncritical support for power. (2001: 31)

Conversely, for Chomsky, the event was historic not in its scale, for while it was 'probably the worst instant human toll of any crime' the change came in the

> direction in which the guns were pointed. That's new. Radically new ... During these close to 200 years, we, the United States expelled or mostly exterminated the indigenous population, that's many millions of people, conquered half of Mexico, carried out depredations all over the region, Caribbean and Central America, sometimes beyond, conquered Hawaii and the Philippines, killing several 100,000 Filipinos in the process. Since the Second World War, it has extended its reach around the world in ways I don't have to describe. But it was always killing someone else, the fighting was somewhere else, it was others who were getting slaughtered. Not here. Not the national territory.

To ensure the security and prosperity of the national territory was the prime concern of US sovereign power. But its actions, direct and indirect, extended around the world. In an extension of its sovereign gaze, by the Monroe doctrine of 1823 the US claimed a realm of interest and action in which it asserted a right to act unilaterally and severely in its self-interest. Beyond this realm, lay the confusions of international ordering, where the plays of power and influence must be more discrete. The results of these webs of power were complex and largely unforeseen. Notions of truth, justice, good and evil, had become overloaded with distortions or buried in silence. Thus the attacks seemed to some commentators as a return of violence formerly directed outwards to the 'other'.[35]

> The September 11 attacks were a monstrous calling card from a world gone horribly wrong. The message could have been written by Bin Laden ... but it could well have been signed by the ghosts of the victims of America's old wars. The millions killed in Korea, Vietnam and Cambodia, the 17,500 killed when Israel – backed by the U.S. – invaded Lebanon in 1982, the 200,000 Iraqis killed in Operation Desert Storm, the thousands of Palestinans who have died fighting Israel's occupation of the West Bank. And the millions who have died, in Yugoslavia, Somalia, Haiti, Chile, Nicaragua, El Salvador, the Dominican Republic, Panama, at the hands of all the terrorists, dictators, and genocidists whom the American government supported, trained, bankrolled and supplied with arms. And this is far from being a comprehensive list.
>
> For a country involved in so much warfare and conflict, the American people have been extremely fortunate. (Roy 2001)

Or as Smith (2002: 103) put it:

> No other country has been so immune to the terror that made the twentieth century the most violent in history yet so implicated in it. Nowhere else has a populace had the luxury of deluding themselves that geography is salvation, that geography protects power.

Yet as Hywel Williams (2001) pointed out, on September 11 'America's boundaries may have been violated but not her sense of superiority – a combination of military might and imagined virtue'. Behind this sense of superiority lay calculations as to military power. A report of the US Space Command overseen by US Defence Secretary Donald Rumsfeld published in 2000 outlined how a 'synergy of space superiority with land, sea, and air superiority', which would come with missile defence and provide the US an 'extraordinary military advantage'. This advantage would 'protect US interests and investment', in a globalising process likely to produce a further 'widening between haves and have-nots'.

The discursive co-ordinates of locality within globalism ... crime, war and the need for sovereign guarantees of meaning

> I know that some people question if America is really in a war at all. They view terrorism more as a crime, a problem to be solved mainly with law enforcement and indictments ... [But I state] The terrorists and their supporters declared war on the United States, and war is what they got. (George W. Bush, 2004 State of the Nation address)

For all Bush's attempts to dictate the terminology of description and analysis, post-September 11 the language of crime and war appeared without stable epistemic co-ordinates. The *Time* (27 May 2002: 25–6) special report on what the US President knew identified the shifting boundaries and language of security:

> The intelligence services were built to fight the cold war, not an enemy that flits from Afghan caves to apartments in London. The division between domestic and international security made sense when the former was concerned with what criminals did and the latter with foreign countries. But some criminals are now as powerful as countries, and some countries are run by criminals.

Who has the power to determine that these rulers of 'foreign' countries are indeed criminals?[36] What processes drive the collapse of the distinction between state functionary and criminal? With what effects? The Israeli military historian Van Creveld had warned a decade earlier:

> If low intensity conflict continues to spread, then the place of bureaucratic war-making organisations will be taken by such groups as are constructed on personal and charismatic lines. This will cause present-day distinctions between leaders and the political entities that they head to disappear or become blurred. Reflecting the new realities, the war convention will change. Over the last three centuries or so attempts to assassinate or otherwise incapacitate leaders were not regarded as part of the game of war. In the future there will be a tendency to regard such leaders as criminals who richly deserve the worst fate that can be inflicted on them. (1991: 200)

In this post-September 11 context, Kaplan (2001: 123) asked concerning the 'humanitarian war' over Kosovo: 'Would it have been more humane to assassinate Milosevic and his inner circle rather than bomb Serbia for ten weeks? In the future, such assassinations will be possible.'[37] If the terms and distinctions between war and crime come out of the modernist legal monopoly on armed force enjoyed by what has been labelled as the nation state, the collapse of control over the internal–external spatial division rendered these discourses porous and unstable. Yet the co-dependency involved in separating war and crime has often been misunderstood. Hobbes and Elias may provide convenient references.

Hobbes experienced the social scene also described by the Dutch international writer Grotius (a father figure of international law) who related 'throughout the Christian world a license in making war of which even the barbarous nations would have been ashamed ... as if men were thenceforth authorised to commit all crimes without restraint'. Beneath a confusion of religious discourses, these wars were largely fought by paid mercenaries in situations where commerce and plunder were virtually indistinguishable categories. Separating out the discursive categories allowed one to control war by tying it to purposes and ideas that provided communicable rationales of secular gain and territory.

Hobbes emphasised the need for stability in language usage, which objective constrained the otherwise chaotic effects of subjective rationality. There is no correspondence theory to give some natural or pure meaning to words; meaning is given by reference to agreed social conventions.[38] These social conventions become encoded, and positive enacted law, enforced by sovereign power, is a prime case. Since the primary reason for the social contract is the preservation of the security of the individuals within a territory, the sovereign must not act so as to threaten the lives of those within that territory. An agreed discourse must enable the subjects to understand the actions of the sovereign powers and legitimate the spectacle of pain and suffering which may attach to actions. In this way social interaction can proceed within the protected territory free from fear of the arbitrary use of force by other 'subjects' *and* the sovereign powers. Stabilised in this way the terms justice and injustice attain agreed meanings and crime and punishment can be accepted as concepts existing in logical relation with punishment a necessary 'evil inflicted by publique Authority' (Hobbes, *Leviathan*, chapters 27 and 28). Although not specifically articulated in these terms in Hobbes's writings, this demarcates the use of the military, which cannot be used to wage war upon the population internal to the territory, from what came to be called 'policing' crime and disorder. Some 300 hundred years later, Norbert Elias developed a 'process sociology' that looked back from the vantage of the mid-twentieth century and depicted a 'civilising process' in terms of a change in behaviour of everyday actions and the relationship of the everyday and violence. Elias offers a way in which the seeming paradox of the Hobbesian state – namely, that the peace of the territory depends on the possession by the sovereign powers of violence, *the publique Sword* – is explained. For Elias the concentration of force in the hands of the state and state-sponsored institutions along with the civilising change of behaviour gave a situation where physical violence 'is no longer a perpetual insecurity ... but a peculiar form of security'. Violence is in reserve and is not apparent in the routines of civilised space, but a 'continuous, uniform pressure is exerted on individual life by the physical violence stored behind the scenes of everyday life' (1982: 236 and 238).[39] Moreover, if the threat of actual violence now recedes in the territory of civilised space, what Elias calls the area of the forming of a 'good society', other forces, giving rise to continuous calculations of worth, take its place. For both Hobbes and Elias communication and the symbolic grow in importance in drawing the diverse subjective reasoning of people into a lose collectivity; a process heavily influenced by the social elites.

Among factors currently destabilising this nexus can be mentioned technological advancements in what may create harm and a multiplication in the amount of perspectives. As noted before, one current assessment is that 'impending technologies such as bullets that can be directed at specific targets the way larger warheads are today, and satellites that can track the neurobological signatures of individuals, will make assassinations far more feasible, enabling the US to kill rulers like Saddam Hussein without having to harm their subject populations through conventional combat' (Kaplan 2003: 79).

Locked in an old, cold war mentality, we are told that the institutions of international 'order' are unsuitable for the challenges: 'international law ... has meaning only when war is a distinct and separation condition from peace'. But now war grows unconventional, often undeclared, unsymmetrical, with surprise as a dominant variable: thus 'the sanction of the so-called international community may gradually lose relevance, even if everyone soberly declares otherwise' (p. 79).[40] What then of the imagery, discursive appeal, and symbolism of a challenge to the 'international community'?

> Round the world, 11 September is bringing governments and people to reflect, consider and change ... There is a coming together. The power of community is asserting itself. We are realising how fragile are our frontiers in the face of the world's new challenges. (British Prime Minister, Tony Blair, at his Party conference October 2001)

September 11 showed the need for 'strength of common endeavour': 'This is a moment to seize. The kaleidoscope has been shaken. The pieces are in flux. Soon they will settle again. Before they do, let us reorder the world around us.' If this was both 'evangelical' and 'Kantian' (Booth and Dunne 2002: 17), it brought into question who was the 'we' and on what terms was the 'strength of common endeavour' to be constituted and to what ends was it to be directed. Creating an image of a coherent 'we' was a staple of the communications media in the US and Britain, to name but two arenas, around which images of victim-hood, potential threats, discourses of crime and war revolved, and invocations of powerful sovereign power resonated.[41] But which territory, institutions or justice was invoked?

Reasserting sovereignty: beyond civilised space?

> In the struggle of Good and Evil, it's always the people who get killed. (Eduardo Galeano, 2002: 9)

At the time of the September 11 attacks, the US President, George W. Bush, who had been in office some 12 months, was considered by many as a politically compromised, if not illegitimate, President. Elected by a minority of the popular vote, his presidency was only granted by a divided decision of the Supreme Court on the legality of recounting the vote in Florida (a state governed by his brother), with the judges that gave him his presidency themselves nominated either by the previous Republican Presidents of Ronald Regan or Bush's father George Bush. As the events of September 11 unfolded he looked anything but a capable sovereign. But at the National Cathedral a few days later he declared a 'responsibility to history' to 'answer these attacks and rid the world of evil'; then on a visit to what was now termed 'ground zero' he was symbolically repositioned:

> He stood on a pile of rubble, his arm draped around a retired fire-fighter. Someone handed him a bull-horn and he began to address the crowd. 'We can't hear you', shouted some members of the audience. 'We can hear you', Mr Bush replied. It was a moment that summed up, with simple eloquence, the nation's gratitude to those men and women. (Lexington, *The Economist*, 22–28 September 2001, under the title *A Leader is Born*)

Images of Bush standing tall, holding an American flag in one hand, a megaphone in the other appeared on Television, in newspapers and magazines around the world. These were images that resonated with the sovereign imagery of Hobbes's *Leviathan*, but now this sovereign representative stood amidst ruins, while he promised rebuilding and a powerful response. The flag and the megaphone: nationalism and communication technologies. Beyond this imagery military power and religious belonging were assumptions of American identity, assumed presences that were open to varying perception by external audiences.[42]

The early chance to assert the image of command and direction was the State of the Union address of 29 January 2002. Again images of a sovereign use of language resonated. The world now divided into those that were for 'us' (inhabitants of a land of 'freedom') and those that were against 'us'. Behind the terrorists lurked an array of forces, including some States, joined in a common 'hatred' of Western democracy and way of life. Iran, Iraq and North Korea were named: 'States like those constitute an axis of evil, arming to threaten the peace of the world.'[43]

A world divided up, good and evil, we and them: a speech directed in its assumptions and rhetorics to a division of discourses between 'our-selves' and 'others'. Come September 2002, exactly one year after September 11, in a speech to the UN General Assembly Bush (BBC, online) declared that

> our principles and our security are challenged today by outlaw groups and regimes that accept no law of morality and have no limit to their violent ambitions ... in cells and in camps, terrorists are plotting further destruction and building new bases for their war against civilisation. And our greatest fear is that terrorists will find a shortcut to their mad ambitions when an outlaw regime supplies them with the technologies to kill on a massive scale.

Iraq was the named 'outlaw' regime. A choice was called for:

> We must choose between a world of fear and a world of progress. We cannot stand by and do nothing while dangers gather. We must stand up for our security and for the permanent rights and the hopes of mankind.

By March 2003, with military action in Afghanistan declared 'successful', Iraq would be the target of war; officially to pre-empt dangers to the homeland from this foreign regime's possession of weapons of mass destruction. The 'we' that provided a unanimous resolution at the United Nations Security Council requiring 'full and immediate' Iraqi compliance with UN resolutions regarding disarmament, would prove difficult to sustain.[44] Between the fact of a resolution and the subsequent declaration of military action analyses differed: whether as effect of consequence of international media and politicians being divided, power demanded to be exercised – theatricality – to ensure that the entire world was in awe of the military power of the super-leviathan, the US, and induced to share in its power to define the identity of events and their responses. With hindsight many commentators stressed the feeling in Washington that 'a tin-pot dictator was mocking the president [of the US]. It provoked a sense of anger inside the White House. After that point, there was no prospect of a diplomatic solution' ('Comment and Analysis', *Financial Times*, 27 May 2003). 'The exemplary nature of the whole exercise is well recognised by the rest of the world, after Iraq' wrote the Harvard-based middle-east historian Roger Owen (*Al-Ahram Weekly*, 3 April 2003): people will have to change their idea of world order 'from a view based on the United Nations and International Law to one based on identification' with Washington's agenda.

Not just oil, not even just a distorted interpretation of the demands of homeland security, but global hegemony is the claim (Chomsky 2003). Controlling the production of images was crucial; these must be the images of a moral power, buttressed by firm conviction, even if not secure knowledge.[45] For many, even before the specifically labelled 'shock and awe' of the military campaign with Iraq, this seemed a new *Imperium*. In the US 'empire' was now a term in fashion,[46] but while conservative American commentators may see the situation in terms of a 'uniquely benign imperium', others wondered about the consequences.[47] Some social theorists had been describing the globalisation processes as a new empire, but not one where a superpower headed it. Their descriptions were of international capital, global communications networks and consumer culture, as well as the dread of the 'bomb'.[48] But now it seems that the opaque power residing in the World Trade Center was replaced by a more visible presence:

> Globalisation would seem to require some sort of global state, and it is increasingly clear that the United States covets that role for itself. After [victory in] Afghanistan, the state apparatus scans the world – defining, judging, sentencing – to determine where and how a new intervention can best clear the decks for its own globalism. (Smith 2002: 107)

Neo-conservative writers prepared the way for a war on terror that knew no territorial boundaries and no time limits. George Will (*Newsweek*, 1 October 2001: 70), for example, linked American identity with the on–off presence of war:

> America, whose birth was mid-wived by a war and whose history has been punctuated by many more, is the bearer of great responsibilities and the focus of myriad resentments. Which is why for America, there are only two kinds of years, the war years and the interwar years.

Bush was clear that the wars would not be fought on the home land: 'There's no telling how many wars it will take to secure freedom in the homeland' (cited Anthony Shadid, *Boston Globe*, 6 August 2002). Was creating a language pattern in which issues of war, crime and legitimacy could be discussed in a new world order to be seen as a matter of power and a new imperial reach?[49] Nostalgia appeared fashionable: the British military historian Sir Michael Howard (in an article for the *Financial Times*, 7 September 2002) mixed together the imagery of the American west in posing the realistic question – 'If the Americans do not badge themselves as sheriff and hunt down the bad guys, who will?' – while paraphrasing (but warning against) the appeal of empire as the stage for global 'justice': 'If this means the assertion of hegemonial or imperial rule, so be it. There are worse things than empires. After half a century the White Man's burden must be taken up again'. What then of achieving a consensus conferring widely accepted legitimacy, or could a globally powerful (secure state) modelled after *Leviathan* do without this? Hobbes appeared pressed into service in favour of unilateralism and global realism: but this is a misreading. In both Hobbes's and Elias's accounts we have a duality, a reciprocal relation of powers. In Hobbes this is between the security of the people and the ability of the sovereign, and that of the internal and external to a secured territory – a global justice must rethink the poles of external and internal.[50] Elias argues that the formation of individual conscience is co-dependent with social structure; civil actions require a shared language of civility. Thus global civility may require a commensurability of local languages of justice and a shared perception as to human vulnerability and exercise of power, rather than the imposition of a supra-language of 'justice' developed within one set of civilised spaces.

To some this is not the situation. For Kaplan the US must exercise its power globally, but this is not to be feared since the US

> *Is* a behemoth with a conscience ... The U.S. is a liberal progressive society through and through, and to the extent that Americans believe in power, they believe it must be a means of advancing the principles of a liberal civilization and a liberal world order. (2003: 41)

Conversely, those conscious of the Nazi theorist Carl Schmitt's analysis – of the necessity of the included/excluded division – may find confirmation for their scepticism in the US domestic imprisonment rates and propensity to use the language of war to engage with social problems, such as drug usage.[51] A combination of factors – of which three are military might, definitional skill and the sense of moral superiority in large part created by mythologies of historical development – in combination give that understanding of moral and political legitimacy that makes it possible to talk of the legal monopoly over violence. Simply put, in a new world order – following technological developments or the decline of 'states' – the modernist distinctions between war and crime will break down.[52] On the up side, the regimes that rule certain states may be declared as criminal and war waged against them in the name of ridding the world of mega-criminals and restoring 'world peace'. Concomitantly, in responding to the low-level 'wars' of terrorism or major drug trafficking, the distinction between military action and policing may disappear. What then to stabilise language or confer legitimacy, or must one proceed as if modernist terms worked while ignoring them in practice?

The language of double standards

A central theme in Osama bin Laden's argument for a new jihad was the tactical message of ridding the Middle East of US troops and demanding an end to US support for Israel. He also made a broader claim that American policy was replete with double standards and specifically that the sanctions against Iraq were killing up to one million children; thus polices that were stated as necessary to protect innocent individuals were killing innocents. He has been consistent in these messages. In a video-tape of October 2001, he stated: 'A million innocent children are dying at this time as we speak, killed in Iraq without any guilt'. In the text of the 1998 *Fatwa* he described 'the great devastation inflicted on the Iraqi people by the crusader Zionist alliance, and ... the large numbers of those killed, in excess of 1 million'. Independent sources depicted those numbers as exaggerated but agreed that many deaths were occurring.[53] In addition: 'All recent food and nutrition surveys have reported essentially the same story: malnourished children ... increased mortality, and a general breakdown in the whole fabric of society'. Many found this imbalance disturbing and evidence that the West engaged in systematic double standards around the world.[54] Others agreed on the tragedy of the children, but disagreed on the causes or on the remedy. But what was surprising was a new reality of dealing with the claim of double standards. The British diplomat and ex-adviser to Tony Blair, Robert Cooper (*The Observer*, 7 April 2002) put it clearly: 'the need for colonialism is as great as it ever was in the nineteenth century'. The postmodern world order required a combination of 'liberal imperialism' and 'double standards':

> The challenge to the postmodern world is to get used to the idea of double standards. Among ourselves, we [Europeans] operate on the basis of laws and open cooperative security. But when dealing with more old-fashioned kinds of states outside the postmodern continent of Europe, we need to revert to the rougher methods of an earlier era – force, pre-emptive attack, deception, whatever is necessary to deal with those who still live in the nineteenth century world of every state for itself. Among ourselves, we keep the law but when we are operating in the jungle, we must also use the laws of the jungle.

Kagan (2003), drew approvingly upon Cooper's analysis depicting a militarily weak Europe striving for a Kantian world of 'soft' power and regimes of law, while the US still recognised that large areas of the world order were Hobbesian and required the decisive use of 'hard' power. Double standards would be inevitable; rules that the West played by inside its protected and civilised space *would and should* not bind it outside.[55] But what and where are the boundaries, or put slightly differently, what is the realm of this acceptance of double standards? Cooper later responded paraphrasing Kagan as explaining that power needed to be applied to determine the terms for a new world order: 'The United States is unilateralist because it has the strength to act on its own; Europe's attachment to treaties, the rule of law and multilateralism comes from weakness and wishful thinking' (2003: 155). Others could give a different interpretation of this imbalance: the possession of great military power seduced the holder into using it in circumstances where it was inappropriate and ill-advised in any other than in the immediate short term.[56] Kagan and Cooper also misread Hobbes, who had placed no man as so strong that he could not be brought down by others, thus arguing the need for a norm of objectivity, to constrain subjective rationality, in part to demarcate rational demands from the ploys of political manipulation (the distinction may be put thus: we can accept a theory of politics but not a politicised theory). Is the collapse of this distinction the fate of postmodern reason? And is this to recognise a truth obscured in modernism or a collapse of one of modernisms ideals? What is then the status of claims to legitimacy of discourses such as those of international relations and criminology, discourses separating war and crime? Is their status such that those who share 'defended' civilised space actually understand them simply as a smokescreen for the plays of demarcations, distinctions, labelling processes and use of coercive and military power that have no objective justification? Does any acceptance of double standards destroy the notions of reproducibility and universalism that a social science relies upon? What then of talk of global justice and injustice? Can some dream of an authentic coherence to justice covering both civilised space and the 'dark corners' of the world still be held? What do we learn from the 'methods of an earlier era', and our memories of them? Was modernist language and symbolic representation really a cover for 'force, pre-emptive attack, deception, whatever is necessary'?

Chapter 2:
Relating Visions: Patterns of Integration and Absences

[T]he last thing to be seen – and it isn't easy to see either – in the realm of knowledge is goodness; and the sight of the character of goodness leads one to deduce that it is responsible for everything that is right and fine, whatever the circumstances, and that in the visible realm it is the progenitor of light and of the source of light, and in the intelligible realm it is the source and provider of truth and knowledge ... the sight of it is a prerequisite for intelligent conduct either of one's own private affairs or of private business. ...

So each of you must, when the time comes, descend to where the rest of the community lives, and get used to looking at things in the dark. The point is that once you become acclimatized, you'll see infinitely better than the others there; your experience of genuine right, morality and goodness will enable you to identify every one of the images and recognise what it is an image of. And then the administration of our community – ours as well as yours – will be in the hands of people who are awake. (Plato, *The Republic*, 518*c* and 521*c*)

The black and while working men spoke the same regional dialect and shared the same political attitudes, all of which had been taught them by others. They denigrated liberals, unions, and the media, considered the local Wal-Mart store a blessing, and regularly gave their money to the Powerball lottery and casinos that had the architectural charm of a sewer works. They were frightened by the larger world and found comfort in the rhetoric of politicians who assured them the problems were the world's not theirs. (The popular American crime novelist James Lee Burk, setting a local scene in *Last Car to Elysian Fields*, 2003: 230)

These [the Iraqi 'insurgents'] are the worst scum of the earth that we are facing. (Senator John MacCain, who had lost the Republican primary campaign to George W. Bush, 'Meet the Press', *NBC News*, Sunday, 21 November 2004)

Our descendants, if humankind can survive the violence of our age, might consider us as late barbarians. (Elias 1991: 146)

Organising a discursive tradition: presence and absence

On 15 November 2004, CBS News, a leading US broadcasting company, announced that it had fired the producer who had directed that normal screening of *CSI: NY (Crime Scene Investigation: New York)* be interrupted for a special report on the Palestinian leader Yasser Arafat's death. The news report had broken into the last section of the 'reality' crime investigation programme, the Wednesday before, prompting viewer complaints and leading CBS to repeat the show on Friday. The producer responsible had made a mistake in thinking that the death of Arafat was so important that it was not necessary to contact a senior executive to authorise the interruption. What can we make of this?

One contention is almost banal in its simplicity: that a 'neo-reality' crime show was superior in local concerns to 'real' news concerning the Israeli–Palestinian conflict that many professional commentators considered to be at the root of the new security threats to the 'real' New York is evidence of the great divide between civilised space and its discourses and the external.

The discourse of the security of civilised space – criminology – is a discourse that operates within the territory of nation-state power. Thus it was an *a priori* that understanding September 11 would belong to the mass media, the contestable appeals of the rhetoric of political elites and a loose realm of subjective labelling and not some (semi-stable) discourse of crime: criminology. At work is the great division; inside lies civilised space and the logos of domestic security, outside – realpolitik. To quote a theorist from the field of international relations:

> Domestic society and the international system are demonstrably different. The latter is a competitive anarchy where formally similar states rely on self-help and power bargaining to resolve conflict. Domestic society (not system) is, by contrast, rule based. (Caporaso 1997: 564)

In contrast to optimists on global rules – such as Philippe Sands (2005) – generalist scholars in international relations as well as those who hold 'realist' positions in international law are with Hobbes and Austin as to the status of international law; international law is a set of rules, which bind by moral persuasion rather than through some enforcement agency.[1] Taking the model advanced by Hobbes to constitute sovereignty inside civilised space, a question is posed: without some supra national sovereign to enforce observance what is the point in terming these rules law?

Yet there is a devastating epistemological illogicality at the basis of this distinction. For to accept that this is anything other than a descriptive statement of a failure or incompleteness in the modernising or civilising process, would confine the discourses of security of domestic society to a status where they had no objectivity or ontology, other than that gifted by particular and contingent sovereign powers. Thus a great deal of the history of criminology, for example, is of attempting to free itself from a status where the law of the nation-state determined, in temporary and relativist terms, the ontological categories of its basic subject mater, that is, that crime was defined as whatever the state defined it as. Usually, however, these attempts result in logical discussions involving (even if not phrased as such) undercutting the epistemological foundations of the subject that must then be held in abeyance while sensible, useful, study – with (assumed) practical consequences – is engaged in. Chapter 1 ended with the suggestion that the paradoxical outcome of the espousal of the new realists of a warrior politics of double standards is to destroy the legitimacy of those discourses relied upon to sustain the domestic ('homeland'), or indeed, to wage war. Is criminology then a gift from Machiavelli (i.e. and admittedly negatively put, a lesson to the elites in tactics of manipulation), rather than, as is usually presented in its own texts, founded upon the appeals of reason to guide human affairs in the line of

Hobbes, Bacon and Kant? Elites (irrespective of their economic position) are of course essential in modernist narratives, but these are to be ethically committed and experienced in the interpretation of scientific findings. In the classical Platonic narrative of enlightenment that was used in the introduction as an organising point, 'civilised space' is the contained and socialised territory of rules and social trust predicated on the ruling Elites reception of reason and wisdom: enlightened power of organisation. Granted that this is a very human space, Plato's narrative was imbued with the necessity of certain kinds of understanding of human character to give it sense. His invocation of vision as the path to true reality required active tutoring; left untutored, vision could not be trusted. The language of the cave, a language accepted as a series of representations of the images presented to view, could not be accepted. That language needed to be corrected and replaced by one developed as a consequence of journeying outside the cave, where having been enlightened – having seen the good – theory is to disturb and modify drastically the view of reality therein. Thus theories which simply build upon representations of common sense perceptions of reality will reinforce mistaken perceptions and must be replaced. Plato's issue was how to move beyond the given array of visual facts and contemporary language to discern true reality. There were two elements in his answer: the role of the tutor ('who lead them up to the light') and the realm of the divine or the intelligibles. The realm of the divine allowed true vision since one was guided in seeing the good by the supposition that the totality cohered and one assumed was the object of a stabilising ordering.

For centuries it was assumed, and still is by perhaps the majority of the world's population, that what provided this ordering, and ultimately enabled man to see reality in the light of goodness, was the fact that the world and humans' place in it were part of God's creation. This provided a transcendental frame of reference, an invisible context by which to interpret the visible. As the catholic philosopher Joseph Pieper (1957: 96) states this did not guarantee that all would be revealed to our sight, but that we should not grow disheartened if we could not make certain things out, since reality was indeed bathed in light from God:

> Because things come forth from the eye of God, they partake wholly in the nature of the Logos, that is, they are lucid and limpid to their very depths. It is their origin in the Logos which makes them knowable to men. But because of this origin in the Logos, they mirror an *infinite* light and therefore cannot be wholly comprehended. It is not darkness or chaos which makes them unfathomable. If a man, therefore, in his philosophical inquiry, gropes after the essence of things, he finds himself, by the very act of approaching his object, in an unfathomable abyss, but it is an abyss of *light*.

In his understanding, reality and humanity exist because of God's creation and humans inhabit a world in the presence of God. The world, and the events in it, was to be read and interpreted for the messages they could give us as to the intentions of God and thus the meaning of the world for us and our place in it, in other words 'justice'. Yet one cannot through human endeavour alone understand all: the gift of grace is necessary. The ultimate symbols of goodness are gifts from God. In the Christian tradition, for example (an example that occupies a different position in the Islamic and Judaic traditions), the fundamental challenge in reading signs of God's will and the nature of good lies in understanding the fate of Jesus, the Son of God made man. On the Friday, the accused Jesus is denied authentic trial and handed over to be crucified along with common criminals. The body of the dead Jesus having been buried, the Saturday is spent in the absence of God; in a time of mourning the prospect of God having abandoned the world must be faced. The resurrection on the Sunday denotes the return of hope and the promise of continual transcendence, humanity's ability to move between the realms of the finite animal and that of the divine.

There is therein a unifying narrative. In writing we lay out accounts of God's message and practical interpretations of ethics and morality, such as the Bible and the Torah are not a simple mirror of God's will; we actively interpret. As Abraham Heschel (1955: 59) describes the status of the Torah:

> The Torah, we are told, is both concealed and revealed, and so is the nature of all reality. All things are both known and hidden, plain and enigmatic, transparent and impenetrable. 'Hidden are the things that we see; we do not know what we see.' The world is both open and concealed, a matter of fact and a mystery. We know and do not know – this is our condition.

But there is no despair, for interpreters imbued with faith have confidence in the existence of God, the central ontological being around which creation coheres and is ordered.

By contrast, for the vast majority of 'modern' (western?) scholars, whatever views they hold in their private lives, the world is to be analysed as if there was no such presence(s). What then guides proper vision? What ensures that what we include in theory is not some simple reflection of observation but something that we understand as the resultant effect of a process for making things visible and signifying them? Put another way, in a disenchanted world, devoid of faith in God's (albeit complex and mysterious) guidance, how do we read images and whom do we trust to explain them?

The answer is normally disciplinary practice and scholarly integrity.

The challenge of modern social theory

> [T]he time has come for sociology to renounce worldly success, so to speak, and take on the esoteric character which befits all science. Thus it will gain in dignity and authority what it will perhaps lose in popularity. For as long as it remains embroiled in partisan struggles and is content to elaborate, with indeed more logic than is commonly employed, common ideas, *and in consequence presumes no special competence*, it has no right to speak authoritatively enough to quell passions and dispel prejudices. Assuredly the time is still remote when it will be able effectively to play this role. Yet from this very moment onwards, we must work to place it in a position to fulfil this part. (Emile Durkheim, the 'father' of Academic Sociology, conclusion to *The Rules of Sociological Method*, 1982: 163)

Sociology could then become a meta-language; it could provide a language of explanation and necessarily bring religion down to earth. Durkheim may or may not have been conscious of paraphrasing Plato in laying out a mission and warning of the dangers in building theory on the basis of representation of 'common ideas'. He did, however, offer a challenge: the new science he championed must find ways of invoking presences that are absent, of bridging the gap between the observable and the invisible yet real. The social theory of a disenchanted world (i.e. one without God) contains both an inherent epistemological and ontological advantage and a crisis. That is, it must, in large part at least, be humanity and the interpretations that humans make of other human's actions, collective interaction and projects that provide both the material for understanding and the guarantee that they can be ultimately understood. Yet positivist sociology can only speak about what can be said; it leaves the world of divine intelligibles to the believers. Between positivist sociology and religious belief lies an existential gulf.

So criminology: the logos of crime; it must, for example, translate the actions of the believer – the suicide bomber – into status frustration, fanaticism, extremism, the subject of 'brain washing'. But this may be doomed to fail. Positivism needs normativism, it needs transcendence of some form; without that it is mere sterile fact.

We may find warnings in applying the narrative: first, vision-led representation needs something to transcend the visible in order to make it 'truly' visible. Second, without constant attention to its guiding sense of mission and the issue of what guides vision and understanding, particular social science disciplines are likely to be mistaken as to their own conditions of history. And, third, as the rest of this chapter argues, the particular result for criminology is that its activities miss huge areas of human activity that 'should' (normatively, but also as a logical extension of its own definitions) come within its scope of analysis. Now the hope: fourth, if such a reappraisal occurred it may gain an edge of relevancy to contemporary times and be able to appraise ordinary discourse of crime that it currently lacks.

Criminological theory and its unifying sense of mission

Criminological texts are not usually opaque as to their assumptions and sense of mission. Consider the classic internationally successful American text Vold's *Theoretical Criminology*.[2] It put forward an explicit rationale, namely: that there is a correct way to use the words that are loosely associated with the term crime, that theoretical criminology should be a realm of discourse and argument in which a considered, reflective, discourse concerning crime, criminality and punishment is constituted, and that the product of that reflection should be considered as superior, as corrective, to the emotive and unconsidered expressions of everyday life, and, consequently, that a scientific criminology, properly based on observed facts, should guide policy, influence action, and, when this occurs, the world will be a better place. Moreover, criminological theory could be presented in a linear history. The expansion in perspectives was due to a progressive advancement in claims to knowledge. These claims, however, still need to be corrected by a more sustained and consistent grounding of the discourse (including 'definitions of crime and criminal behaviour' and contrasting sets of 'explanations') in 'the observable world of facts'. The resultant theory would greatly aid in dealing with the problem of crime and improving the conditions of life in organised political society.

To the readers of that text, the connection between the criminological enterprise and civilisation seemed to need little introduction. The history of the enterprise (Vold 1958, with Bernard as ed. 1979, 1986) is presented in a narrative that begins with 'spiritual' explanations, which are replaced by varieties of 'modern thought that calls itself scientific'. Modern criminological theory is premised thereby on the condition that adherence to the rules of scientific endeavour will give an objective and authoritative language that will enable social problems to be resolved in a civilised manner. The text seemed to aptly reflect the self-confidence of those who worked in the discipline (perhaps a necessary feature for a text to be a commercial success). The theme of contributing to a civilizing process was, and still is, accepted as the core mission as it was to those who began the writings usually associated with the birth of modern criminal justice reform. The writers who produced the ideas loosely referred to as 'classical criminology' (a set of writings in which Beccaria, Bentham and Howard are iconic figures) self-consciously so located their work. Albeit with differing personal motivations, each contrasted actual operating conditions in the society they inhabited with an image of an organised society under law with opportunities for a range of commerce and personal freedoms. In an age of gentleman scholars, they did not need to define the disciplinary category of their work. But, in so far as they took as their task as commenting on contemporary conditions and writing proposals for rationalising and humanising the link between the power(s) of the state and the life of the subject (later 'citizen') – in particular concerning the power to investigate activities covered under the ascription 'crime' and 'punishment', as well as the degree of penalty to be applied – they 'pre-figured' a certain intellectual space that developed with modernity.[3] That space is now inhabited by textbooks and journals with the title *Criminology* or other titles that are recognised as making up a related field of discourse and study. It is sometimes the subject of academic debates as to whether it is best seen as a multidisciplinary arena of exchange and interaction or as one that should cultivate and defend its own territory. But few doubt its existence or themes that give hegemony and define its 'mainstream'. Loosely defined, it is that realm of discourse that takes its subject matter as understanding crime and guiding the state's reaction to crime.[4] That it was a modern enterprise contributing centrally to a civilising process its proponents had no doubts. As Wines, quoting from Victor Hugo, put it (1910: 3):

> Is the under-world of civilization, because it is deeper and more gloomy, less real and important than the upper? Can we know the mountain, if we know nothing of the caverns?

In his lectures advocating the introduction of criminological study in the United States, delivered in 1893 and 1895 (published, 1895, 1910, revised edn 1919), Wines laid out a platform of continual critical study guided by an understanding of the good (specifically, 'Christian civilisation'). Crime and criminality, punishment and the justice delivered by the state, were to be 'judged by a higher criticism' as befitting the advancing stages 'of Christian civilisation'. Individual projects were to be guided by a grasp of the history of the field of study and philosophical perspective.[5]

For much of the twentieth century various master tropes of a shared history positioned study: enlightenment; progress; rational humanism and scientific commitment. One could argue over particular structures of 'modern society', though most seemed to accept a narrative of the replacement of custom, tradition and despotism by a liberal and democratic governance (rather than socialism). And accepting scientific positivism as a methodology seemed to imply a change from a religious metaphysic to committed secularism; from the view of human existence as a chain of being to a separation of the spheres of the religious, the political, the artistic and the scientific. These histories either invoked 'a distinguished Enlightenment past and a progressive scientific mission' (Garland 2002: 10) or provided a foil against which to argue for a new beginning (as in the case of Matza 1964, or Talyor *et al.*, 1973). Traditional or mainstream criminology had a clear sense of mission focused around the understanding that the concept 'crime' related to a particular social problem. The task was to find real, empirically based, knowledge, knowledge that could be verified by relation to observation or directly traceable to it, that explained why crime was committed and the state could take measures to combat it.[6] Most texts stressed the need to be 'value free' when one operated as a scientist, but sometimes the object of the discipline was expressed in broader terms, that of reducing 'the amount of pain and suffering in the world'.[7] How to achieve that varied with the view the writers took as to the driving force of human suffering. The authors of a well known 'radical' approach, for example, argued for transgressing the norms of 'a discussion of what were previously technical issues' by dealing 'with society as a totality'. In this *New Criminology* the criminological task was presented as a subset of a holistic vision, of creating 'a society, in which the facts of human diversity, whether personal, organic or social, are not subject to the power to criminalise' (Taylor *et al.*, 1973: 278, 282). Yet the boundaries or border conceptions between civilised space and the global were not directly addressed. Moreover, while the 'radical' vision sought a normative direction against the operating ethos of the capitalist nation-state to focus upon, it lacked performability: mainstream criminology strengthened an administrative ethos that ensured it flourished. And as crime rates – now the accepted, democratic, objective, reproducible 'picture' of crime – rose throughout the western world in the 1970s, 1980s and early 1990s, it expanded with a task seemingly even more complex and essential.

Conversely others thought this link between rising crime and the spread of criminology paradoxical, an affront to the supposed practicality of the discipline. For if criminology was the servant of the civilising process, and if the civilising process was progressive and led by the organised political societies of the (predominantly European) West, which in their diverse ways represented the good (society), why was there more crime and why did criminology appear not to have much policy impact? Under the influence of Foucault and others, the assumed history of the progressive development of criminology became complicated by critical and revisionist accounts of the production and self-sustainability of core discourses; however, these self-critical and reflexive 'histories' did not seem to upset the operational basis for mainstream criminology.[8] If the underpinnings of traditional criminology were provided by the metanarratives of modernity as a progressive civilising process, and late- or post-modernity implied that these narratives no longer had persuasive grip, then the coherence of the criminological enterprise should deconstruct. The assumed progressive march of criminology and civilisation would have to be radically rethought; in the utopias of the post-modernists there would be a flowering of perspectives and different approaches to crime and social interaction.

Does criminology without metanarratives have a history? Does it need one?

In the last decade of the twentieth century and into the twenty-first practical 'reality' seemed opposite such hopes. Penal policy, mainstream criminological theorising increasingly obsessed with cost-effective policing and the rise of zero tolerance seemed exactly counter to those 'post-modern' hopes. Disorientation there may have been, but it appeared to offer more scope for symbolically strong exercises of sovereign power than a flourishing of interpretative perspectives and social tolerance. Outside academia and certain areas of cultural production the collapse of metanarratives was either ignored or repackaged into marketable commodities. If Fukuyama (1989, 1992) could announce that his end of the competing metanarratives of history was simply the victory of one set of organising structures, it would be easier to identify the basic conditions for organising social life. In these new conditions there was a greater need for criminology, or at least for a mundane and applied criminology that saw its task as providing technologies and training for a 'culture of control' (see the contrasting analyses of Christie 1993, 1994, 2000 and Garland 2001). Or, given a reduction in the narrative complexity of the political context, to observe the facts and create strategies that would offer protection from criminal activity in the daily context of routine activity within the localities of a now settled capitalist future (Felson 1998; Clarke and Felson 1993). This criminology had little need for the orienting guides of a progressive enlightenment history, critical philosophy or theoretical sophistication. It now seemed that policy determined the acceptability of theory, or at least its marketability. To Garland these developments in crime control and criminal justice involved a

> sudden and startling reversal of the settled historical pattern. They display a sharp discontinuity that demands to be explained. The modernising processes that until recently, seemed so well established in this realm – above all the long-term tendencies towards 'rationalisation' and 'civilisation' – now look as if they have been thrown into reverse. (2001: 3)

To try to explain this, Garland concentrated upon changing forms of culture in which criminal justice and penalty operated since the mid-nineteenth century. The 'present' was characterised by a return of emotivism, a new popularism, politicisation, a sense of crisis, a sense of the normalcy of high crime rates, a new relationship of crime and the mass media, a loss of trust in social-welfare expertise.

Assessing the operational basis of modern criminology

Garland suggests there may a reorganisation of the existential role of crime: from that of a problem to be resolved and remedied with appropriate expert knowledge to that of an everyday and continual event of social life that needs to be controlled and managed. Criminological modernism, defined as the period from the late nineteenth century until the 1970s, is presented as a historically distinctive *episteme* adapted to the individualising processes of criminal justice and the social rationality of the welfare state. By contrast, control theories now shape official thinking and action that both imply a different social politics and a different relation to the everyday. 'Where the older criminology demanded more in the way of welfare and assistance, the new one insists upon tightening controls and enforcing discipline' (2001: 15). The 'criminologies of everyday' life require 'no special motivation or disposition, no pathology or abnormality', crime is simply 'an event ... written into the routines of contemporary social and economic life' (p. 16).

We have therein a supposition of contingent and dependent foundations. In this narrative, criminology as a discipline has no independent epistemological resources that enable it to survive the demands of the everyday or give it that authority Durkheim dreamed of for sociology. Few would dispute that the production of criminological theory is dependant upon its context. Indeed it is a staple of the philosophy of scientific positivism, that the context of scientific discovery is one thing, and the subsequent replication of the research leading to that discovery, the opening up of the theory to falsification, the justification for the theory continuing to be held is another.[9] Epistemology – the process of ascertaining the truth of claims – is a separate process from that of describing the context of the claims being made – which is the task of sociology, psychology or history. Such purity has proved hard to reproduce. Indeed, philosophical positivism did not succeed in establishing an indubitable base for empirical science or eradicate the metaphysical elements from scientific theories. This led to the notion of the closed scientific community as the final arbiter and source of authority. Similar processes have occurred in the social sciences, where the interpretative turn has transformed the nature of debate over the epistemological strength of theoretical claims.

Criminological theory has an especially disputed status and ironic practicality. The greater the attention paid to epistemological purity and the foundational security of the discipline, the weaker they appear; but this has no effect upon the practical acceptability of parts of the discipline.[10] With an array of competing theoretical claims (many of them mutually incompatible) policy makers can choose a suitable perspective to lend theoretical support to the programmes they desire.

One common response to this lack of epistemological security is to call for a renewed scientific commitment. To produce more focussed empirical research, to use facts to move policy. But this very lack of security forces us to ask if the history of criminology actually has been an attempt to develop theories based on the foundation of a 'world of observable facts'? How is such a world laid out?

This issue is traceable in the debates over positivism within the discipline. For all the flowering of radical, critical, feminist and social interactionist projects, 'most contemporary criminological work, whether mainstream inquiry or radical-Marxist efforts, is based, at least loosely, on neo-positivist foundations' (Gibbons 1994: 159). We begin to get an indication of the problem to follow if we also accept an often repeated refrain namely that 'for positivists, a proposition … is true if it accords with certain institutional facts'. For it then follows that this 'criminology' is constituted

by the history of its institutional underpinnings that allow those facts to be visualised which are accepted as relevant and demarcates acceptable and unacceptable research methods and findings.

Such is the story of the constituting of criminology provided by David Garland (1985a, 1985b, 1988, 1992, 1994, 2001, 2002), perhaps the most articulate presenter of a revisionist history of criminology, specifically labelled as 'a history of the present'. The problem is that this 'history of the present', a history of those discourses and practices that have been 'successful' as criminology, is in the grip of a representational methodology that thereby accepts that the discipline is indeed what is has been limited to. In this case, the worry is that in escaping from the grip of 'traditional' histories, which present an image of 'steady progress and refinement' of a core object of study (and fall in the trap of a context-free positivism of 'facts'), one's account becomes a *neo-positivist* history (in which the context is read as that which explains the 'facts' of the texts and their strategies).

The history of the present: still in the grip of positivist vision?

Through rethinking narratives of enlightenment, Foucault helped create a new way of writing the history of institutions, disciplines and intellectual practices. Previous history attempted an all-encompassing 'encyclopaedic' account that sought to produce chronological, incremental descriptions of 'development'. The result was versions of a safe and uncontentious history, usually with an underlying metanarrative of progressive humanism, greater freedom and enlightenment. These particular accounts lacked critical bite and either a consensual view of social interaction or one of limited political conflict tended to be assumed. The identity of institution or intellectual practice was accepted as it presently was recognised at the time of presenting the history. The history was then an account of how things had developed into the present, but what was assumed was a relative continuity of progressive identity.[11] Foucault displaced this identity. Thus in *Discipline and Punish* the focus was not 'punishment' but practices of discipline and correction and the effects envisaged; in the *History of Sexuality*, the focus was not sexuality per se, but the regulatory practices governing the sexuality of men, women and children inscribed in the discourses of the medical, pedagogical, psychiatric and economic fields.

These new histories, however, were located by archives. The history of a discipline must be related to a set of texts and discursive practices that can be recognised as constituting the field. Yet the investigation is to move beyond what is visible in 'studying statements at the limit that separates them from what is not said' (Foucault 1969: 119). The materials are the positive starting-point for a wider interrogation, an interrogation that seeks to link the discourse with strategies of knowing and governing human life (which Foucault loosely refers to as bio-power) that have both productive and constraining power-effects. Texts that present the social sciences are both literature (and able to 'be far from reality') yet wedded to truth (and under pressure to disclose reality) and produced in complex social processes relating to political and economic relations (that are not present to view in the actual discourses produced). In seeking to persuade, such texts must conjure up both the exceptional and the transgressive (to convince of something 'new'), yet not destroy faith in the regular (but encourage us to think of a new regularity in the variation) as well as assuring the audience they are contributing to progress.[12] In *Discipline and Punish*, for example, positioning the archive is a set of concrete events (the execution of Damiens, the writing by Bentham of his plans for a Panopticon, the creation of a timetable for a juvenile institution or reformatory) and the scholar aims to convey the regulatory forces that constitute them. Throughout his writings, Foucault suggested the duality of power and knowledge in interaction ('Two words sum up everything: power and knowledge', 1977a: 293).

Specific conditions of power make actual knowledge claims (such as those written in a document) possible; accepting specific knowledge(s) make practices legitimate and regular over time. Lemert and Gillan (1982: 39) comment:

> Power-knowledge is not an abstraction. It is practices, it is only intelligible by means of the concrete historical conditions that rule and regulate, exclude and include what is done, what is said. These are power-knowledge.

Garland showed how this was picked up in the first instance to present a reassessing criminological history that was later revised. The *contingency* of criminology is a focal theme of Garland's history of the subject. Earlier versions, such as the 'criminology-through-the-ages style of history', have serious failings. First, they distort the *meaning* of what earlier writers have said/wrote and conceal the fact that their assumptions, objectives, institutional contexts and cultural commitments were 'quite different from those of modern criminology'. Second, they give 'the false impression that criminology is our modern response to a timeless and unchanging set of questions that previous thinkers have also pondered, though with notably less success'. Thus 'criminology was seen as a science that was waiting to happen, the end point of a long process of inquiry that has only recently broken through to the status of true, scientific knowledge'. However, this

> progressivist, presentist view of things fails to recognise that criminology is, in fact, a socially constructed and historically specific organisation of knowledge and investigative procedures – a particular style of reasoning, representing, and intervening – which is grounded in a particular set of institutions and forms of life. It is a 'discipline', a regime of truth with its own special rules for deciding truth and falsity, rather then the epitome of right thought and correct knowledge. (Garland 2002: 13)

By contrast, Garland begins

> with the clear assumption that the phenomenon to be explained is a present-day phenomenon – the modern discipline of criminology – and that my task is to trace its historical conditions of emergence, identify the intellectual resources and traditions upon which it drew, and give some account of the process of its formation. (p. 14)

The resultant history further subdivides. Criminology becomes

> structured around two basic projects – the governmental and the Lombrosian – and that the formation and convergence of these projects can be traced by studying the texts and statements which constitute criminology's historical archive. (p. 16)

The governmental project is evidenced in 'the long series of empirical inquires, which, since the eighteenth century, have sought to enhance the efficient and equitable administration of justice by charting the patterns of crime and monitoring the practice of police and prisons'. The Lombrosian project 'refers to a form of inquiry, which aims to develop a etiological, explanatory science, based on the premises that criminals can somehow be scientifically differentiated from non-criminals'.

> One pole of the discipline pulls its practitioners towards an ambitious (and ... deeply flawed) theoretical project seeking to build a science of causes. The other exerts the pragmatic force of a policy-orientated, administrative project, seeking to use science in the service of management and control. (p. 8)

These projects resulted in and were themselves, in turn, the result of specific practices of investigation, recording and analysis. The governmental project utilised 'empirical data and scientific methods to improve government's grip on the population'. While the Lombrosian project, under the influence of Goring's massive study,

> would no longer depend on the clinical gaze of a Lombroso and its impressionistic identification of anomalies ... Instead it must be a matter of large populations, careful measurement, and statistical analysis, demonstrating patterns of differentiation in the mass that would not be visible in any specific individual or apparent to the naked eye unaided by statistical analysis. (p. 36)

Thus Garland identifies the emphasis on visualisation as the guiding epistemology. This underpins the project of governmentality by making visible patterns in the mass population that reveal the extent of social problems and the careful observation of individuals to reveal their abnormality. But Garland does not stop there. He now adopts visualisation as his own criteria for determining the structure of criminology itself, relegating the normative and structural discursive concerns of classical criminology to the status of non-criminology and concentrating only on what he can visibly identify as a criminological canon. 'If criminology is a specific organisation of knowledge which first emerged in the late nineteenth century, then the key problem is to describe its particularity and to explain the historical transmutation which produced this new form of enterprise'.

One danger in this account is that the distinction between history and justification loses any bite. In other words, history becomes a master-language and there is no other place for a justifying logic to stand. The past is analysed for those studies, which either are, or 'could be identified as the roots of particular ingredients in the modern criminological mix'. Consequently, only those discourses that were 'struggling to create a distinctive criminological enterprise' can be included in a proper history of the discipline (p. 23).

This faithfulness raises the problem of neo-positivism, for the history is located with reference to the materials presented as the archive. Although the materials are interrogated differently and the notion of some essential, centralised and transcendent subject is weakened if not abandoned, the history of *the present* is a history of *what is present to view*. But what of the history of the non-present, of that which is not present to view, of the marginalised or the subaltern, or that which does not appear to the routines of everyday life?[13] It is true that the Foucaultean history of the present does not remain at the level of an assumed (self-sustaining) facticity of the materials; instead it seeks out the hidden plays of power that help constitute those materials. However, the criteria of (visible) success, which Garland has elsewhere adhered to,[14] means that criminology becomes identified as *that which has successfully established itself as criminology*. But why should a history that serves to analyse concrete social practices mean a limitation to those that reveal their action, at the expense of those that are silent? Further, if the (invisible) rule that is operating is one of denial, or simply ignorance, then writing the history of the present (while offering an incisive and complex uncovering of many of the plays of power at work) will be implicated in other less visible plays, if it makes any claims to present any other history than that of a subject that has been present. This discussion may seem rather opaque. It may be clearer if an excluded is introduced.

Describing the particularity of criminology: the visible and the excluded

Norbert Elias theorised a core part of the civilising process as a rather specific interaction of the powers and sources of control of developing nation-states and individuals. Most of his analysis was specifically historical, analysing conditions and group conflicts internal to Western Europe and ending with the nineteenth century. In trying to face up to the holocaust, however, he gave hints at a more general notion of the civilising process. In a succinct passage he offered a formula for the civilising process as that which enabled people

> to satisfy their elementary animalistic needs in their life together, without reciprocally destroying, frustrating, demeaning or in other ways harming each other time and time again in their search for this satisfaction – in other words, without fulfilment of the elementary needs of one person or group of people being achieved at the cost of another person or group. (Elias 1996: 31)

Protecting individuals or groups from being the expendable material utilised for the benefit of some dominating individual, group or organised collectivity would appear a core task of those endeavours, intellectual and practical, which seek to contribute to the civilising process. And indeed, with little paraphrasing, this would cover the majority of attempts by criminological writers to express their sense of mission.[15] Yet in striving for this, the range of material included as the archive has been extraordinarily 'particular'.

In the second extract at the beginning of this chapter Elias is clear that from a future perspective we – the civilised – could be seen as later day barbarians. The twentieth century, the century of criminology's growth, can be written from different perspectives and focal concerns. It was a century of great advances in technological performance, of wonders – such as the creation of the twin towers of the World Trade Center, supersonic air travel and mass communication[16] – hardly dreamed of at its beginning: a century of huge increases in wealth and opportunity, not just for a few, but for a very significant number of people. But it was also a century of increasing poverty for many, of ecological destruction, of powerlessness. And it was a century where humans killed humans with greater readiness and increased sophisticated technological ability. In Bauman's words (1995: 193) 'what we learned in this century is that modernity is not only about producing more and travelling faster, getting richer and moving around more freely. *It is also about – it has been about – fast and efficient killing, scientifically designed and administered genocide.*'

What image of the twentieth century do authors of criminological texts choose to portray? The sociologist and scholar of genocide Helen Fein (1993: 6) states that 'between 1960 and 1979 there were probably at least a dozen genocides and genocidal massacres – cases include the Kurds in Iraq, southerners in the Sudan, Tutsi in Rwanda, Hutus in Burundi, Chinese … in Indonesia, Hindus and other Bengalis in East Pakistan, the Arche in Paraguay, many peoples in Uganda'. In this period – a fertile time of diverse criminological theorising – criminology, the discipline devoted to the study of crime – could not find space in its texts for these events. In a century literally awash with human blood and reeking with the stench of corpses, mainstream criminology seemed to inhabit another world.[17] Bauman (1995) asks if the twentieth century will be branded the 'Age of the Camps'? Has it exposed temptations for power to resort to the genocidal mode 'whenever it is impossible to alleviate accumulated human misery, or whenever the picture of future bliss is so tempting that disregard for those living in the present seems a reasonable price to pay?' Or alternatively will we build our resources for facing the future in reflecting on the 'human costs of social improvement'.

Criminology and the governmental project: the signification of civilised space

Appreciating the character and truth of the twentieth century varies with one's experience of it. Such experience varies in space and time. Criminology is a post-enlightenment endeavour, largely influenced by the hopes and fears of, first, the European intellectuals and then those of the new world (a second Europe). Most twentieth-century 'criminology' has been produced in the United States, Britain, Germany, Holland, Italy, France, and latterly Australia, Canada and New Zealand with scattered contributions from elsewhere in Europe and emerging forms in Latin America and Africa. Text after text implicitly acknowledges that the production of the criminology therein contained is geographically specific, but then continues as if the resultant 'knowledge(s)' and 'concepts' contained truths that were of general applicability. Specificity of production plays against universality of meaning. As Vold's *Theoretical Criminology* began its third edition (1986: 4):

> Criminology as a field of study has been well documented by a long line of excellent and distinguished textbooks, both European and American, going back many decades. (It then gives a long footnote containing the titles of 'readily available American textbooks in *general criminology*' [emphasis added] many of which were simply entitled *Criminology*, *Crime and Criminology*, or *Society, Crime and Criminal Behaviour*.) Most of these texts concentrate on presenting facts known about the subject of criminality. For example, they discuss such subjects as the extent and distribution of criminal behaviours in society; the characteristics of criminal law and procedure; the characteristics of criminals; and the history, structure, and functioning of the criminal justice system. Almost all texts review

the major theories about the causes of criminal behaviour, and some texts present other theoretical material such as sociology of law, philosophy of punishment or theories of correctional treatment.

There are at least two considerations here.

One is the geo-physical location for writing and research, which inevitably includes certain experiences and excludes other experiences. These processes occur in a number of ways: for example, it is clear that exclusion occurs in focussing on the particular that the location reveals, but it also occurs in excluding out features from the outside that structure the local. This 'outside' is constituted in both time and space; it is both the 'before' of the 'present' of the locality, and the exterior space. The local is always a product of the non-local.

Another consideration is the issue of extensionality in claims that explicitly or implicitly universalise from that writing or research without directly acknowledging the difficulties of doing such, indicating common linkages assumed, or are modest in their conclusions. In the above quotation, what is nationally produced is simply assumed to provide a 'general criminology'; this continues the narrative of progressive enlightenment noted earlier, only here enlightenment is associated with a particular set of nation-states and their hegemony.

This hegemony and the assumption that certain nation-states determine the production of criminological knowledge is simply institutional fact. It is reflected in the holdings of the major criminological libraries, publishing networks and teaching syllabuses. It is so persuasive that it is largely unremarked upon or seen as unremarkable.[18] Yet it is remarkable, since it assumes, without explanation, that analysis of the conditions in a particular set of locations produces what is 'general'.

To example: in 1990 one of the most distinguished names in American criminology, Travis Hirschi, published a co-authored book entitled *A General Theory of Crime* (Gottfredson and Hirschi 1990). The authors expressly argue that their theory 'can encompass the reality of cross cultural differences in crime rates' (p. 175). They also expressly state that 'a general theory of crime must be a general theory of the social order' (p. 274; although they said that lack of time and space prevented them from pursuing this later issue further). Combining 'classical' conceptions of crime, and 'positivist' analysis of criminality, the authors (Introduction) argue that

> Nearly all crimes are mundane, simple, trivial, easy acts aimed at satisfying desires of the moment, as are many other acts of little concern to the criminal law.
>
> … the offender appears to have little control over his or her own desires. When such desires conflict with long-term interests, those lacking self-control opt for the desires of the moment, whereas those with greater self-control are governed by the restraints imposed by the consequences of acts displeasing to family, friends, and the law.

Criminality is a matter of the level of self-control an individual possesses. Low rates of self-control also mean the offender is less likely to hold a steady job, more likely to have drug or other addiction problems, and more likely to be involved in accidents. Individuals differ in the amount of self-control they possess and 'self-control is presumably a product of socialisation and the current circumstances of life'. (p. 179)

There have been many attempts to apply this theory. Conversely, some critics have seized on their use of terms such as 'ordinary crime', 'the typical or standard homicide', 'the typical or standard robbery' (Gibbons 1994: 194–6) to argue that the authors standardised the facts of these crimes. But nowhere has the theory been confronted with state-sponsored massacres and genocide.

In many such cases the perpetuators have a job (in the army or intelligence services), do not get involved in accidents (which would be prejudicial to the performance of their function) and would probably score high on whatever self-control test that could be devised to empirically operationalise the theory. In some other cases they well fit the picture outlined in the theory. The theory may well benefit from such an engagement. The point is that such events are simply not regarded as providing any facts that a 'general theory of crime' should consider. Yet the figures for state-sponsored massacres or other forms of deliberate death in the *twentieth century – excluding military personnel and civilian casualties of war* – are usually regarded as between 167 and 175 million people Brzezinski 1993, who calls this the century of 'megadeath', 'organised in sanity?' and 'politically motivated carnage' (Rummel 1994; Smith 2000).

These are excluded data of equivalent time, of near time, but there is an even greater exclusion of the events of past time. Criminology does not have much space for 'subaltern' discourses, those produced by the 'objects' of (imperialist?) history, rather than by the active, powerful subjects. Bauman captures this well:

> The construction of modern nation-states was a story of violence perpetrated by the relatively few resourceful and successful ethnicities upon the multitude of incohoate, lesser and hapless ones – the 'would be' but 'never to be' nations. Histories are written by victors, and so the suppression and physical or cultural extermination of defeated minorities never given the chance to write their own histories came to be recorded and retold as an edifying and uplifting story of progress or of a civilizing process: of a gradual yet relentless pacification of daily life and purification of human interaction from violence. (2001: 215)

Given the figures involved in the pacification of the Americas, for example, it would have been more correct to have said the defeated and decimated *majorities*, for the destruction of the native inhabitants in the Americas was awesome in the numbers involved. From the perspective of the subaltern, Columbus was not the bringer of civilization. He was, rather, the instrument of genocide.[19]

There are undoubtedly understandable 'pragmatic' explanations for avoiding consideration of this enormous range of human experience. One lies in the institutional conditions of the discipline's development. That criminology and penology lie intertwined was once common sense. To provide knowledge about crime would be to provide guidance to structure responses and enable a rational and civilised penology to be constructed. And penology by definition was the discourse of the powerful, the successful and the dominant. In criminological discourse this appears – without a touch of irony – as simple, institutional fact. As late as 1959, it could be said that 'until recently the study of crime was almost exclusively concentrated on those offenders who had already become involved in the legal process' (Korn and McCorkle 1959: 5). As an activity of 'scientifically' studying crime/criminality, criminology was born in the interstices of (nation-state) criminal justice processes. It has already been emphasised that part of the sense of mission of the writers who gave it an intellectual space was to humanise and civilise those processes.[20] This linked criminology to penalty, to censure, to the application of the state's power to punish. Although there have been numerous attempts to break this linkage,[21] it continues as the most important source of data. If the state does not, or will not, punish there is no data. Descriptively true, but normatively? Certainly, in this area at least, Tappen's (1947: 47) well-known argument that criminology should accept the legal process's definition of who is a criminal, since 'adjudicated offenders represent the closest possible approximation to those who have in fact violated the law, carefully selected by the sieving of the due process of law', is simply wrong. Or put more generally, and somewhat sceptically, to paraphrase the nineteenth-century legal theorist John Austin, if the sovereign powers do not enforce a law, how can you realistically call it law? (Which is not the same thing at all, as John Austin tried to convey [1832, 1862], as questioning whether or not there should be an effective law in this area.)

A second factor is geographical. The 165–175 million dead did not die in the US, UK, Australia, Canada and New Zealand (where, however, victims of massacres died in large numbers earlier in time). And individuals from France, Germany and Italy, who would be counted in that total, were mostly victims of the holocaust, a subject that has not been taken to provide facts for criminology. (This geographical consideration upsets global causation, for, of course, individuals and processes with France, Germany and Italy as axis were responsible for large massacres which took place in their 'dependent' territories, such as the French colonial powers' massacres in Madagascar in 1947.)

A third consideration is the technologies of data collection. Gotfredson and Hirschi considered that their theory could explain 'cross-cultural crime rates', but what are these? They certainly do not mean those of the same locality under different cultural hegemonies, rather they are referring to crime rates in near time in differing locations in the globe. But consider the effect on crime as revealed in recording practices if one included 'genocide'. Three examples will illustrate: Cambodia, Rwanda and Bangladesh. In the case of Cambodia, a conservative estimate for the number killed between 1975–9 in the Pol Pot 'auto-genocide' is 2,000,000. This represented around 25 per cent of the then population. In the Interpol International Crime Statistic for 2000, Cambodia with a greatly expanded population of 11,304,084 recorded 553 'voluntary homicides' or 'murders'.[22] On these figures it would take 3,616 years of 'normal' homicide to equal 3 years of the exceptional. For Rwanda the accepted figure for the 6 months of genocide in 1994 is 800,000+ while in the 2000 Interpol statistics 3,606 voluntary homicides were recorded. Thus it would take around 222 years of 'normal' homicide to equate to 6 months of the exceptional. A figure of 1,500,000 would be a conservative figure (the Bangladesh government claims 3 million) for the numbers killed in the 9 months from 25 March to December 1971 out of a population of 75 million from the West Pakistani Military actions (widely called attempted genocide) and disease that resulted from the dislocation of the population and associated political and ethnic cleansing in what was then East Pakistan (now Bangladesh).

Three thousand and five hundred and thirty nine voluntary homicides were recorded for Bangladesh in the 1998 Interpol figures (the latest available) for a population of 127,400,000. Again it would take around 424 years of the normal for this much larger population to give 9 months of the exceptional. But these are not included in the criminological domain as data that could have any relevance in building a 'picture' of the reality of homicide!

As addressed in Chapter 3 of this text, 'the world of facts' visualised for criminology has been a very particular world picture indeed.

Registering criminological apartheid?

It is remarkably common in criminology to give a domestic history and a domestic discussion to images and events as if the domestic was self-sustaining. The entire history of European imperialism and capitalist globalism is omitted. I give two examples; both easily pass as unremarkable comments.

First, in an essay introducing concepts of globalisation into criminology, Loader and Sparks were rightly concerned to emphasis that criminology must reposition itself and 'cannot rest content only with doing the old work in the old way'. They stressed that criminology should always be seen as 'caught up irredeemably in the grander movements of social and political change'. Hence, they asked us to remember that criminology was 'originally a child of another era of massive upheavals, namely the industrial and scientific revolutions of the nineteenth century' (Loader and Sparks 2002: 103). This may be to give the commonplace version of its history. But it neglects the reality that the nineteenth century was also the century of the global European Empire(s). The *governmental project internal to the battles of the European nation-state has been read as the localised context for criminology, but that is only one aspect of the governmental projects of the nineteenth and twentieth centuries.* Tocqueville's comment that 'the physiognomy of government can be best detected in their colonies, for there their features are magnified and rendered more conspicuous' needs sustained research. The imperial governmental project was both home and overseas (as the English put it); they were united at several points, a central one was that both concerned the governance of 'strangers' ('the other'). Strangers who were increasingly moving into urban areas and becoming part of the everyday, who needed to be understood, recognised, categorised, labelled and reacted to.

This is the topic of the second example. In a recent discussion on nineteenth-century images of criminals, John Pratt (2002: 81–6) turns to Dickens's (1860) novel *Great Expectations* for 'one of the most famous literary descriptions of "the criminal", using language that was being spoken across all social groups'. The description reveals a 'set of sensitivities and ways of thinking about such individuals'. The convict in question, Magwitch, is a central presence in *Great Expectations*. Early in the story he surprises the young hero Pip and the description of Magwitch is indeed terrifying. A frightened Pip helps Magwitch by bringing him some food and a file to cut his leg irons. But Pratt is more interested in how the description reveals a change of attitude where those who were previously outlaws, living outside of 'society', have been turned into eponymous convicts. With the outlaw, 'the decision to live beyond its reach was their own, but [they] would still make periodic returns to it to take on and challenge the authorities'. By contrast, in Magwitch there is nothing to celebrate or admire: 'Marked off from the rest of society by his own appearance as dangerous and to be avoided at all costs, he can command only terror and horror'. Pratt (2002: 82–3) puts this in a context:

> In the period in which the novel was set (as opposed to when it was written), the penal system was designed to act in such a way that Pip and *the rest of society* would be spared such terrors: convicts such as Magwitch would normally face some form of *expulsion from society* whether by means of transportation or the death penalty. (emphasis added)

Pratt's narrative cannot be questioned, nor is his use of the term 'society' at all unusual. But in the above quote no one counts as being in society other than members of the population of Britain: 'the rest of society' explicitly refers to the rest of mainland Britain, and 'expulsion from society' means being physically taken from mainland Britain and being relocated in Australia. This is replicated in an 1864 quote from Mary Carpenter, who Pratt reads as expressing the same fears of the convict as Pip: 'We might desire to rid ourselves of them by sending them ... To some spot where they should be cut off from the civilised world by the mighty ocean – and where their fiend like passions should be vested upon each other, not on peaceable and harmless members of society'. Given the history of Australia, the potential for violence Magwitch may exhibit could easily have become focussed on the natives of Australia, who, in a process of distinguishing them from the European settlers who were to become 'Australians', the Europeans called 'Aborigines'. Indeed, one relatively common explanation for the massacres of Aborigines that was given was the 'low stock' of the much of the immigrants and freed transportees (Reynolds 2001).

It is difficult to escape from the process of reading otherwise diverse material criminologically, or doing mainstream criminology, only from within a national paradigm abstracted from global context. In Pick's study of the discourse of degeneracy he is concerned to demonstrate how the 'the criminal' was an emerging source of great concern in the Victorian period. In support of the image of 'a social blight which undermined the national situation as a whole' he quotes from the Saturday Review of 1862 during the 'garrotting panic':

> It is clear that we have not yet found out what to do with our criminals. We neither reform them, nor hang them, nor keep them under lock and key, nor ship them off to the Antipodes. Our moral sewage is neither deodorised nor floated out to sea but remains in the midst of us polluting and poisoning our air. (quoted Pick 1989: 178)

Concentrating on the imagery of the criminal as moral sewage, one may overlook the fact that it was quite acceptable to ship people so categorised off to the Antipodes where they could pollute and poison. Of course the fact that the people who had inhabited Australia for some 40,000 years did not count was an essential presupposition for the otherwise extraordinary event in 1788, when the officials of the 'First fleet raised the British flag over the motley collection of convicts and gaolers at Sydney Cove and took "possession of the colony in form" ' (Reynolds 1987: 7). Australia was land without a sovereign, *terra nullius*, assumed to be uncultivated land belonging to no one. It was a convenient assumption, unless you were a native, and it went largely untested legally for 200 years until *Mabo* v. *Queensland* in 1992. There were more contestable assumptions, namely that 'Aborigines' did not have a society. In the words of the father of modern sociology Emile Durkheim (1965: 54–5), society is the bearer of civilisation.

> Society transcends the individual's consciousness ... Because it is at once the source and guardian of civilization, the channel by which it reaches us, society appears to be an infinitely richer and higher reality than our own ... The more we advance in time, the more complex and immense does our civilization become. ... Each of the members of an Australian tribe carries in himself the integrated whole of his civilization, but of our present civilization each one of us can only succeed in integrating a small part.

Thus Durkheim could ascribe to Australian 'Aborigines' exactly the opposite of what we now accept as their relation to culture and heritage. The danger was even more apparent in less cautious hands for whom Durkheim's phrases '...a man is only a man to the degree that he is civilised', or deprived of what 'society has given him ... he becomes a being more or less distinct from an animal' (p. 55), could help justify seeing in the 'other' outside of the civilised space of Western arenas only an object for power to register, utilise or extinguish. *Such activities may seem extreme, but they can be seen as part of a continuum in which the unremarkable or commonplace is the fact that in analysis after analysis, when the term 'society' is used, what is meant is some image of a nation-state arena and what is overlooked is the real fact that such 'societies' are not self-sufficient but part of global processes.*

That the connections and flows of power are not visible to view does not mean that they are not real. Some Australian writers, notably Robert Hughes and Paul Carter, have incorporated *Great Expectations* into their revisionist narratives of Australian history trying to unpick the webs of illusion that sustained the 'white' imperialist project. There are many illusions at work in *Great Expectations* and the fantasy of Pip that he can escape his class origins and attain higher status is a central one. Underlying the text is a complex relationship between England and its overseas territories, an imperial and modernist relationship.[23] The convict is to be expelled from the civilised space, yet the border is transversed in various ways in the novel. In criminological terms Magwitch is potential violence. This potential for violence is dispersed to the colony; however, there is more at play than simply expulsion. *Great Expectations* is structured around a series of interlocking flows of humans and capital in which the overseas possessions are terrain to be used, a lesser world to be imposed upon, to be developed in the image of the home.[24] Magwitch is expelled to Australia; in that land he succeeds in transforming his economic status and in time he sends capital back from Australia. The source of this capital is kept secret from Pip, the beneficiary, who mistakenly believes it has a domestic source. Magwitch 'illegally' returns from Australia (the grand transgression for which there is no discretion, he must pay the price of death), Pip is initially repulsed by him but learns the truth of his previous good fortune and is reconciled to the dying Magwitch. Pip collapses into illness, but recovers and starting afresh builds his future by moving overseas to take a position in a trading business in the Orient. We are not provided much detail of the nature of those operations, apart from being told that while Pip and his partners were 'not in a grand way of business', 'we worked for our profits, and did very well'. By travelling to the overseas territories, Pip, as Magwitch before him, escapes his class position and becomes economically independent. Unlike Magwitch, Pip may return freely, but probably will not, at least during his productive life.[25] Pip's life is thus transformed twice by imperialism, and overseas lands change the opportunities of those who by illusion think they inhabit a self-sustaining metropolis.

What then, in place of this misunderstood term 'society'? Perhaps we cannot yet know … but material to work with will include acknowledging it was conceived of within processes of colonial globalisation with diverse sets of localities, presences and absences (and it must be acknowledged that there was never 'one' colonial process, but almost as many colonialisms as there were territories). Presences and absences structured by the empowering and constraining effects of political, economic and cultural relations. What is clear, however, is that in these times where a new imperialism is embraced, a discipline founded on such a politically partial constituted 'world of facts' as mainstream criminology has been can indeed be safely ignored; moreover, without reform it *ought* to be so ignored.

Chapter 3:
Criminal Statistics, Sovereignty and the Control of Death: Representations from Quetelet to Auschwitz

... statistics are to industrialism what written language was to early civilisation: at once its product and its means of expression. (Perkin 1969: 326)

WE ARE BEGINNING TO DETECT A SHORTFALL IN ... OUR DATA BASE. (Cable sent by the UN Special Representative in the Balkans, Yasushi Akashi, on 13 July 1995, two days into the genocidal massacre at Srebrenica, Bosnia, quoted Danner 1998: 69)

Part I

Statistics: the measuring of crime and the power of the nation-state

The previous chapter ended with the charge that criminology is an extremely partial discourse, constituted around a politically confined 'world of facts'. This is not the idea we are presented with in its professed dedication to scientific endeavour. It is important to realise the hope inscribed in that dedication and its weaknesses.

Modern science promised enlightened vision, that is, neutral and trustworthy 'knowledge of what is observable'.

> *Science* and *scientific*, then, are words that relate to only one kind of knowledge, i.e., to knowledge of what is observable, and not to any other kinds of knowledge that may exist. They do not relate to alleged knowledge of the normative – knowledge of what ought to be. Science concerns what has been, is, or will be, regardless of the 'oughts' of the situation. (Van Dyke 1960: 192)

Against the context of the breakdown of status or feudal relations, one way in which social science aims to reconstruct its target of analysis – such as crime, the 'criminal' and criminality – is on the basis of a picture of social reality presented as categorical grids, tables and other representations of brute data. Unencumbered by value positions we were to be presented with that which simply 'is'. Analysis of this realm of facticity, however, was to do more. It offered a way into understanding what is otherwise hidden; the visual representation provides the route to visualising the invisible but real – the truths of social relations. A grounding was laid for this in 1827, 1833 and 1835 when first the French statistician Guerry and then the Belgium Quetelet provided templates for the collection and analysis of social statistics, or, as they put it, 'moral statistics'. They draw maps of their studied territories (France, the Low Countries and the Duchy of the Lower Rhine) in terms of crime rates and concentrations of other indices (A.M. Guerry 1833; Quetelet, English translation 1842, plates 5, 6 and 7).[1] As Guerry explained:

> In order to make our results more striking, we have resorted to the use of graphical illustrations. Without excluding the enumerations which the reader can make if he so chooses, these illustrations have genuine advantages. The shades of color of our maps provide instant geographical images which tend to be lost in a long series of numbers; relative quantities can be expressed with precision through contours which leave a visible and lasting impression on the eye. (1833: 3)

Data tabulated in tables, graphs or maps serve as particular visualisations – representations – which read properly, allow correlations and thus may indicate casual forces and determining causes. In the classical urban sociology of the Chicago School, for example, they provided the basis for making distinctions and locating the criminogenic factors of 'delinquency areas' and patterns of 'social disorganisation' in urban environments (Shaw and McKay 1969). Other scholars have noted the tautology of much of the conceptualisations involved in the process of collection of data, creation of representations of the spread of activity as revealed by that recorded data to criminological explanation.[2] It is common, however, for the statistical picture to be accepted as identifying the factors to be analysed.[3] For example, having acknowledged criticisms of the Chicago School, Vold and Bernard accepted that their statistical analyses raised what 'remains a central issue in criminology: how to provide a theoretically sound explanation of the high crime rates among the lower classes' (Vold 1986: 199). A claim that takes it origins from Quetelet's analysis of the first official criminal statistics, the French *Compte* of between 1826 and 1829, which revealed to Quetelet that young males, the poor, those without employment or in the lowest-paid jobs had a greater probability to commit crimes and be convicted of them; but did this really mean that they had a greater propensity to commit crime, and was identifying that propensity the key to understanding criminality?

Objectivity is the aim; a clarity of vision around which discussion by interested parties can cohere. Images of statistical distribution are held out as pictures reflecting reality, revealing, among other things, neutral or observer-independent questions for research. As Quetelet explained:

> My aim is not to defend systems, or bolster up theories; I confine myself to the citation of facts, such as society presents to our view. If these facts be legitimately established, it follows that we must accept and accommodate our reason to them. (Quetelet 1842: vii)

For Quetelet they promised (at some time in the future if not at present) to reveal the type and spread of normal or average crime and by linking this to the characteristics of a concept he came to put forward as his central organising motif – that of the 'average man' – we would come to see the characteristics of criminality. This has subsequently been a constant aim for the positivist tradition; namely that through technologies of reproduction, we can see the underlying structure of our problem, and, perhaps, the solution.

The dream is that of becoming a successful applied science working towards … [utopia, the grand society, peace or homogeneity are concepts put at some time as the end]; the history of the twentieth century has also shown it as a nightmare.

Quetelet, moving from individual consideration to aggregate social laws: the first criminologist of bio-power?

Quetelet – 'the first social criminologist' (de Quiros 1911: 10) – laid out the template for quantitative analysis in positivist criminology. 'It is due to him that criminal statistics have become such an aid to criminal sociology. It was also due to his work that criminality was shown, for the first time, to be a social fact' (Bonger 1936: 50).

What consequences flow from this power to display 'criminality as a social fact'? Into which distribution of powers does it fit?

Consider Figure 3.1. The text of the pie charts reads (clockwise from the top): Jews were 42% of all physicians, 52% of all insurance physicians, 45% of all hospital directors, 35% of all dentists, 28% of all pharmacists, 48% of all doctors, 56% of all notaries and 80% of all directors of theatres. The phrase at the bottom reads: 'The Jews are our misfortune'.

The poster denotes a complex interaction and a certain aesthetic modernism. It appears a simple representation, yet it is structured by a strange redemptive appeal; the percentages reveal the cause of 'misfortune', that a reduction in those percentages gives benefits: the fortunate people will be without Jews.

This product of ideology works through modernist representation: its seductive appeal mixes the redemptive appeal of anti-Semitism and modernist scientific legitimacy. Baumann claims one of the contributing factors that allowed the Nazi holocaust of European Jewry to occur was the application of the modernising scientific spirit; modern in that a solution to problems was to be achieved by 'design, manipulation, management, engineering'

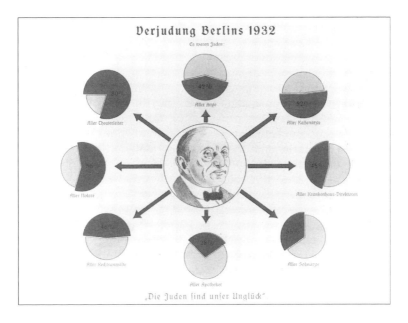

Figure 3.1 Eugenics poster, *The Judaizing of Berlin 1932*. (Credit: USHMM # 94185)

(Bauman 1991b: 7). While this claim is made at a great level of generality (contentious in itself) as well as containing inherent and possibly open-ended questions about the interaction of scientific and administrative method, its control and aims, it focuses upon the 'downside' of modernity. The features of modernity that Bauman emphasises were meant, according to the narratives of enlightened rational modernism, to improve human life; yet under Nazi Germany, they destroyed it. How was this possible?

One, perhaps the most comforting, line of explanation (and not Bauman's) holds that in Germany a terrible distortion took place in the heart of modernity – a criminal gang took over the power-centre of one of Europe's states and turned all the agencies of the state into the opposite of what they normally functioned as. The state became in reality a non-state, with pseudo-law and the abuse of expertise by pseudoscientists and pseudo-doctors. In mainstream Anglo-American legal theory, for example, Lon Fuller exerted great energy in trying to show that a properly functioning and true 'legal system' has certain essential features that the Nazi regime had destroyed; thus they were not operating with a 'real' legal system. Certain German writers, such as Radbruch, writing after World War II tried to label the jurisprudential approach known as legal positivism as a mode of thought that led to German officials accepting as legal something that was not. Thus the main fault was not distinguishing real law from pseudo-law. There is in turn a certain redemptive appeal to this line of argument, for if proper law would not have allowed the state to have been taken over by the Nazis and would have protected the Jews then 'real' law and real 'state-hood' is the solution to modernity's problems. Yet the status of the Jews is still ambivalent in this line of thought for as Wistrich has recently catalogued (2001: especially chapter 6), not only was the Jew only too easily stripped of the protection of law from the beginning of the holocaust in Germany but in the course of the late 1930s and early 1940s most of the countries within the German hegemony passed all too quickly anti-Jewish legislation stripping them of their civil rights, dispossessing them of their property and in most cases actively collaborating in their elimination. The Jews, as a people (and neglecting the differences that existed intra-Jews), occupied a particular place in the European (and Christian) cultural imagination that gave them characteristics of non-integration, of not belonging, no matter how much in fact they were 'assimilated'. Jews were able to be conceived as non-nationals and thus devoid of the security of a territorial state and a sovereign that was their own, represented as a cotangent, or as the invisible power behind all too visible problems, or as the weeds of the garden with the consequence that their elimination became a logical extension of the legitimate problem-solving ethos of modernity. This very process, however, shows the weakness of the refrain: 'If only they had the protection of law ...' This narrative form, impliedly at least, seems to provide an explanation for the absence of the holocaust from criminology, for law did not cover the matter and thus criminology as a subject that comes after the law could not conceive of this. But in the end it can only give us a strange absence at the heart of the interaction: Nazi criminals dealing with non-citizens. But the *Nazis were the State* ... this attempt to push law away from being part of the problematics and able to come in as a saviour, makes us instead adrift in the a priori of law. Yet, reflexivity is usually not entered into on this issue and it is more common to use the example as a trope in a story containing an optimistic path for the future; in which, in building a new world order, one that would be post-holocaust, law would extend to all, globally, and the holocaust would become an object of legal prohibition (genocide) and any such future actions would be material for proper functioning of laws.

Another version holds that the entire period of Nazi rule 1933–45, was criminal: thus Bauer (2001: 113, interpreting with favour Friedlander 1997), 'the crucial issue was the criminal nature of the regime, its crimes against humanity, against target populations, first and foremost the Jews … the extraordinary character of Nazism … lay in its criminality'. Thus the Nazis were truly extraordinary, but this extreme can still be captured in our intellectual discourses: a criminal regime, a criminal state. This line then raises the reflexive issue: if this truly was a criminal regime and a criminal state, then it should be at the very core of any studies in criminology; it should serve as the foundational reference point to distinguish 'normal' and 'extraordinary' states (at least in post-enlightenment modernity). Again, this provides an illusive issue for there does not seem to be any text in which this has occurred.

But what if the holocaust was included in law, not in the sense of some post-event rationalisation and attempted punishment of the perpetrators – partial as that may be – but was legal? To be specific: what if the holocaust was simply the end result of a path of legitimate powers, that is, a normal (albeit terrible, immoral, Gorgon) extension of the powers of the sovereign? In this line (vaguely hinted at in Hart 1961; explicit in Fraser 2005[4]), we should note that we are dealing also with the conditions that created a genocidal consensus: an issue that concerns professional responsibility, that of the array of lawyers, social scientists, designers and so forth, who saw in the new context opportunities for career advancement, research grants and/or opportunities for simply doing things (such as medical experiments) that were denied before by the political–ethical–social nexuses. In this characterisation, the Nazi period was a modernism that destroyed the constraining factors – the compromises – of the German version of liberal modernity.

We are looking at a certain aesthetic presentation and a mandate. Namely that life can be addressed through aesthetic presentation that makes (an independent) morality redundant.

In that case the exception – the holocaust – was not some great opposing force to normal modernity but a must-be-repressed expression of trends inherent in the normal. This is one possible reason why genocide must be excluded from the materials that constitute the data of normal criminology; for to consider it brings into question the ethos of the applied science branch of the discipline. In this line of explanation the story told would be one where the Jew became the legally excluded, but we should be conscious of the situation that since they were excluded by the operation of law they were always within the power of the law. We should also be clear that this is a law that linked with other powers and which gained legitimacy for its decisions from other modes of representation, specifically those of mathematical calculations of life, or what Foucault has called *bio-power*.

Quetelet, closely observed, reveals a path for bio-power as he works within an early modern concern with policing. To achieve effective policing we must

Figure 3.2 The Reichstag and the Temple of Law (image: MEPL). Bauer (2001) considers Nazism in terms of a certain ideological approach taken by an elite group attained rule over a modern industrial society. Nazi modernism was in his opinion, irrational, but (using Bauman) was modernist in appearance. It was actually an anti-modern modernism because it was guided by a reactionary ideology – a combination of technology and irrationality not inherent to modernity, capitalism, or the enlightenment but rather peculiar to an authoritarism, anti-liberal and enlightenment-less nationalism.

The destruction of the Reichstag and its rebuilding was both symbolic and central to the jurisprudence of the Nazi era. The chronology of events went as follows: on January 30, 1933 Weimar Republic President Paul von Hindenburg appoints Hitler Chancellor. On February 27, 1933 the Reichstag burns down – a dazed Dutch Communist named Marinus van der Lubbe is found at the scene and charged with arson. [He is later declared guilty and executed.] On February 28, 1933 President Hindenburg and Chancellor Hitler invoke Article 48 of the Weimar Constitution, which permits the suspension of civil liberties in time of national emergency. This

picture the problem, visualise the link between bodies and the health of the social state. Quetelet used three discrete models of representation. One, *maps*, illustrating the spread and distribution of crimes – interactions of bodies, time and place – and then correlated with maps of various other factors that has already been commented upon. The second, that of *tables of offences*, divided by age or gender, has served in providing basic data for building criminological theories of criminal involvement, and has survived almost unaltered and has given rise to the continual quest for the 'dark figure' of crime (the proportions in criminal involvement he revealed from the statistics as between males and females have largely survived). In Quetelet's hands it also provided a visible demonstration of the need to go beyond individualist explanations for crime. The third – *the bell curve* – demonstrated, according to Quetelet, that there was a strict lawfulness that governs individual variation in human beings. The bell curve represented faithfully this variation and helped explain a finding of his statistical data, namely that crime, external conditions being relatively constant, had a regular pattern. The bell curve showed the variable composition of the basic material: 'the human material, with which society has to work' (Bonger 1936: 123).

If 'facts are legitimately established, we must accommodate our reason to them': Quetelet. By extension, thinking aggregately, the problem may be solved by changing the composition of the aggregation … And, normatively, if one is committed to solving the problem … then surely one 'ought' to … The metaphysic is one of progress and taking control of the social environment:

> one of the principal facts of civilisation is, that it more and more contracts the limits within which the different elements relating to man oscillate. The more knowledge is diffused, so much the more do the deviations from the average disappear; and the more, consequently, do we tend to approach that which is beautiful, that which is good. The perfectibility of the human species results as a necessary consequence from all our researches. Defects and monstrosities disappear more and more from the physical world; the frequency and the severity of diseases are combated with more advantage by the progress of medical science; the moral qualities of man experience not less sensible improvements; and the farther

Decree of the Reich President for the Protection of the People and State abrogates several constitutional protections, namely free expression of opinion; freedom of the press; right of assembly and association; right to privacy of postal and electronic communications; protection against unlawful searches and seizures; individual property rights; States' right of self-government. A supplemental decree creates the SA (Storm Troops) and SS (Special Security) as Federal police agencies.

There is no agreement on who is actually responsible for the Reichstag Fire: van der Lubbe acting alone, or a Communist plot, or the Nazis themselves in order to create an incident. Regardless of who actually planned and executed the fire, it is clear that the Nazis immediately took advantage of the situation to declare a state of emergency and centralise and enlarge their power. The Decree enabled the Nazis to ruthlessly suppress opposition in the upcoming national election of March 5, 1933 which gave the Nazis 44% plurality in the Reichstag. Herman Göring then declared there was no further need for State governments. Over the next few weeks, each of the lawful Weimar State governments fell for the same ruse: Local Nazi organizations instigate disorder; the disorder is quelled by replacing the elected state government by appointed Nazi Reich Commissioners. On March 24, 1933 The Reichstag passes the Law for Terminating the Suffering of People and Nation – also known as the Enabling Law – essentially granting Hitler sole legitimate power.

we advance, the less are great politic overthrows and wars (the scourges of humanity) to be feared, either in their immediate effects or in their ultimate consequences. (Quetelet 1842: 108)

Observation of the visible and aggregation of the visible and invisible

'Moral statistics' were to be gathered and dealt with in the same way as statistics derived from the application of the scientific method elsewhere. As if following Plato's scheme for education, mathematics was Quetelet's first love and gave him a method of calculation (probability theory) he subsequently used to discern gaps in his observations, anticipate where interesting questions should be asked and test the accuracy of his visual impressions. If he is remembered for the contribution he made to the study of 'moral statistics' he entered into this study of the good having 'feasted his eyes on the heavenly bodies and the heavens themselves, which would be easier at night'. Teaching mathematics in Brussels from 1819 he founded and directed the Royal Observatory, having studied astronomy and probability in Paris in 1824. Quetelet's strategy for progress in astronomy (and weather prediction, a crucial practical application of observation and probability) was twofold: first, to increase the number of observatories and improve the techniques of observation; second, to creatively use probability theory to direct observation into areas of space where there was as yet no observable phenomenon but where mathematical calculation suggested that there should be.

From 1830, he sought different ways to apply probability theory to understanding human action.[5] That properly developed scientific knowledge should guide policy and would improve the human condition was simply assumed. Moreover, statistical analysis of social life would offer a whole new way of understanding; one that would be democratic in nature, unable to be manipulated by elites and available for all to see in objective fashion. One effect would be the replacement of individual or philosophical understandings of worth and man by aggregations.

> Man is born, grows up, and dies, according to certain laws which have never been properly investigated as a whole or in the mode of their mutual relations.

These laws with which Quetelet began his most well-known work *Sur l'homme, et le development de ses facultes* (published in Paris in 1835, translated into English as *A Treatise on Man* in 1842), are not that of the politically choosing sovereign, but those of bio-power that the sovereign must then adopt if he was to be scientific. Both man's individual, physical composition and his social relations must be understood as governed by certain laws. We identify these by the interpretation of statistical facts that reveal man's position in a 'system of social physics'.

> Experience alone can with certainty solve a problem which no *à priori* reasoning could determine. It is of primary importance to keep out of view man as he exists in an insulated, separate, or in an individual state, and regard him only as a fraction of the species. In thus setting aside his individual nature, we get quit of all which is accidental, and the individual peculiarities, which exercise scarcely any influence over the mass,

become effaced by their own accord, allowing the observer to seize the general results. (p. 5)

Studying man 'too closely' it becomes impossible to apprehend the laws that affect the human species, the observer seeing only 'individual peculiarities, which are infinite'. By observing only individuals we limit ourselves to 'a series of incoherent facts'. General laws can be found by collecting 'a sufficient number of observations' that 'bring out what is constant', and 'set aside what is purely accidental'.

We might assume that human action would vary as widely as human caprice; but careful study of regularities – observable in 'the statistics of tribunals' – confounds our expectations. In respect of crime, what do we 'in reality observe'?

> [T]he same numbers are reproduced so constantly, that it becomes impossible to misapprehend it – even in respect to those crimes which seem perfectly beyond human foresight, such as murders committed in general at the close of quarrels, arising without a motive, and under other circumstances to all appearance the most fortuitous or accidental: nevertheless, experience proves that murders are committed annually, not only pretty nearly to the same extent, but even that the instruments employed are in the same proportions. (p. 6)

This constancy to the statistics of crime pointed to an underlying law of averages or repetition. Quetelet's analyses of crime in France and Belgium drew upon the first national statistical tables on crime, the annual *Compte general* (General Account), commissioned by the French government in 1825, and published after a winter during which crime and death rates both increased and public concern with crime had been heightened. The tables made clear a 'remarkable constancy with which the same crimes appear annually in the same order, drawing down on their perpetrators the same punishments, in the same proportions', This was 'a singular fact, which we owe to the statistics of the tribunals'. They constituted a social budget,

> which we pay with frightful regularity – it is that of prisons, dungeons, and scaffolds. Now, it is this budget which, above all, we ought to endeavour to reduce ... there is a tribute which man pays with more regularity than that which he owes to nature, or to the treasure of the state, namely, that which he pays to crime. Sad condition of humanity! We might even predict annually how many individuals will stain their hands with the blood of their fellow men, how many will be forgers, how many will deal in poison, pretty nearly in the same way as we may foretell the annual births and deaths. (p. 6)

Despair is not appropriate, for as Quetelet responded to a statement of the author of *An Essay on the Moral Statistics of France*, who had read Quetelet as if he was stating an invariability of the amount of crime: 'I never considered the number of crimes invariable. I believe, on the contrary, in the perfectability of the human species.' Statistical representation and the tracing of probable effects behind the distributions, leads us to understand causes, which we then can tackle.

> Society includes within itself the germs of all the crimes committed, and at the same time the necessary facilities for their development. It is the social state, in some measure, which prepares these crimes, and the criminal is merely the instrument to execute them.

Every social state supposes, then, a certain number and a certain order of crimes, these being merely the necessary consequences of its organisation. This observation, so discouraging at first sight, becomes, on the contrary, consolatory, when examined more nearly, by showing the possibility of ameliorating the human race, by modifying their institutions, their habits, the amount of their information, and, generally, all which influences their mode of existence. (p. 6)

Analysis relied upon a 'fundamental principle':

the greater the number of individuals observed, the more do individual peculiarities, whether physical or moral, become effaced, and leave in a prominent point of view the general facts, by virtue of which society exists and is preserved. (p. 6)

Aggregate knowledge must be distinguished from individual accounts. This new understanding, this 'social physics', 'never can pretend laws, which verify themselves in every particular, in the case of isolated individuals' (p. x). Instead, they relate to 'the social body'. Owing to the infinite causes of individual action, the laws of general phenomena apply to individual cases 'only within certain limits', in the same way that we could not 'determine the precise period of a person's death by looking into the tables of mortality'.

The particularity of 'criminal statistics' and the rise of the dark figure

Criminal law has traditionally been a particularly individualising form of knowledge carrying assumptions such as free will, individual motivation and responsibility. Many criminological histories give Quetelet pride of place as helping break this metaphysic and bringing on real criminology with his promise of an aggregate knowledge that holds the promise of discarding the legal methodology of governing.

We must give credit to this power of visualisation that was offered; a mathematically grounded scientific framing power, a power to represent. This is not a method only, pure instrumental rationality, but one that Quetelet assures us must always be tied to the assumption of human improvement: the social and individual perfection of the human race. *This is power not to confine, or to determine limits, but to govern an enhancement of life.* What is nature? Nature is not an assumed ordering of pre-existing hierarchies or status-rankings, but neither is it to be viewed as a Hobbesian realm of relativism and individualism. It can be know via the representations of graphs, bell curves (Figure 3.3) and tables. Quetelet announces:

every thing which pertains to the human species considered as a whole, belongs to the order of physical facts: the greater the number of individuals, the more does the influence of human will disappear, leaving predominance to a series of general facts, dependent on causes by which society exists and is preserved. (p. 96, original emphasis)

What of individuality? Does it follow that the individual must disappear as an operative concept, to be replaced by another object, that of a 'part' of the social body?

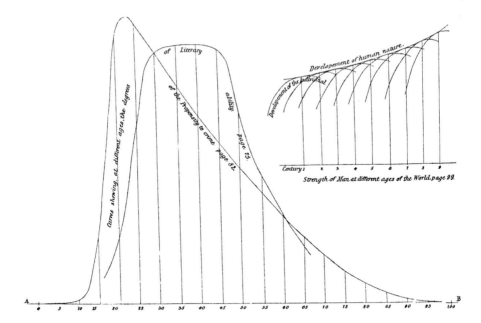

Figure 3.3 Representation of the bell curve To what extent does this establish a meta-semantics of presentation? The location of the individual on the curve determines its identity, its worth. This is not a relativist, individualist articulation of individuality – any statement about an individual therein represented is located, given its placement within an overall representation of existence. (Source: Quetelet, 1842).

Quetelet's average man

> The determination of the average man is not merely a matter of speculative curiosity; it may be of the most important service to the science of man and the social system. It ought necessarily to precede every other inquiry into social physics, since it is, as it were, the basis. The average man, indeed, is in a nation what the center of gravity is in a body; it is by having that central point of view that we arrive at the apprehension of all the phenomena of equilibrium and motion. (p. 96)

Individuality can only be scientifically comprehended by the relation of the particular person to the average man of that race or nation. Thus while it was not feasible to demonstrate the determining effect of social laws upon the actual and diverse choices of individuals, it would be possible to demonstrate how the social laws determined the actions and behaviour of the average man of that race or nation. Particular individuals would then be located in varying sections on the curve representing the spread of probabilities for particular actions or characteristics. One, for example, was crime.

If the investigator took care to ensure that they had obtained accurate measurements of sufficient individuals belonging to a particular race or nationality, it would be possible to determine any unknown physical or intellectual aspect of the population under investigation. These could be viewed in relation to what became his central concept: the average man. To his critics who thought the idea absurd, Quetelet replied that the apparent absurdity 'only proceeds from the want of a sufficient number of accurate observations'. His own research agenda was simple: to attempt 'to determine the laws of development of the physical powers' as well as 'the moral and intellectual qualities' of the average man (p. 74). Quetelet appears seduced by the representational ability of his statistical analysis, the 'average man' replaces the individual as the focus: 'The constitution of the average man serves as a type to our kind' (p. 99). There is debate as to what exactly he meant by the average man, but there is ground to believe that Quetelet thought of 'average' physical and mental qualities as real properties of particular people or races awaiting discovery and not just abstract concepts. The conception of the average man became the central value about which measurements of a human trait are grouped according to the normal curve.

The concept of the average man may have begun as a simple way of summarizing characteristics of a population, but it took on the function of an actual ideal type towards which nature was working, and deviations from this target were errors.[6] Deviation from the mean and the distribution of all the non-physical qualities of man was in a determinate order. The criminal propensities of the average man rarely translated into criminal actions, but against those characteristics was the criminality of vagabonds, vagrants, primitives, gypsies, the 'inferior classes', certain races with 'inferior moral stock' and 'persons of low moral character'. In the 1840s, quasi-medical metaphors became common in his writings and biological and phrenological defects were given a causal role in the genesis of crime. Crime became 'a pestilential germ ... contagious ... (sometimes) hereditary' (quoted with commentary in Beirne 1993: 88–90).

Quetelet's metaphysic of science and progress

'How little advanced [i]s the study of the progressive development of man' (Quetelet). The faculties of particular men may be established from observations represented in tables and charts. We can ascertain the values of those things we can observe and fit them within the tables of limits already established and establish their relationship to the average man, the 'ideal type'.[7] Research will enlighten governments by distinguishing deviant individuals from the average man. As the rate of human growth can be measured and the physical characteristics of man vary with the degree of civilisation, we can change (future) history. If the progress of civilisation does indeed reduce 'the limits within which the different elements relating to man oscillate', then we can make 'deviations from the average disappear' and 'consequently' we may 'approach that which is beautiful, that which is good. The perfectibility of the human species results ...' The counter measure, Quetelet assures us, is that nature will provide against humanity amalgamating into one common type for it 'will always be so prodigiously varied': but it is up to us to act so that we 'bring out treasures unknown to [our] predecessors' (1842: 108).

We are offered a new governing rationality, not a social contract but of a table of weights and measures, of costs and benefits:

> Since the price of grain is one of the most influential causes operating on the mortality and reproduction of the human species, and since, at the present day, this price may vary

within the widest limits, it is the province of the foresight of governments to diminish as much as possible all the causes which induce these great variations in prices, and consequently in the elements of the social system.

This is only one practical, but minor, aspect of the new power that this reasoning would give to the Sovereign.

since the crimes which are annually committed seem to be a necessary result of our social organisation, and since the number of them cannot diminish without the causes which induce them undergoing previous modification, it is the province of legislators to ascertain these causes, and to remove them as far as possible: they have the power of determining the budget of crime, as well as the receipts and expenses of the treasury. Indeed, experience proves as clearly as possible the truth of this opinion, which at first may appear paradoxical, viz., that society prepares crime, and the guilty are only the instruments by which it is executed. Hence it happens that the unfortunate person who loses his head on the scaffold, or who ends his life in prison, is in some manner an expiatory victim for society. His crime is the result of the circumstances in which he is found placed: the severity of his chastisement is perhaps another result of it. However, when matters have come to this point, the punishment is no less a necessary evil, were it only as a preventive means: it would only be desirable that the other means of prevention might afterwards become sufficiently efficacious for us not to be obliged to have recourse to the former severe means.

A challenge and a promise: understand causality, remove the determining factors and attain a new budget. Above all, do not be constrained by an individualist account of social relations, the aggregate is to be the frame of reference.

Excursus: can criminological texts cope with attempts at a 'law of social development'?

Karl Popper has many backers to be considered the leading philosopher of science writing in the English language during the twentieth century. After leaving the growing anti-Jewish environment of Austria in the 1930s he witnessed World War II from his teaching position in Otago University in the South Island of New Zealand. There he penned *The Open Society and its Enemies* (1945) and laid out the framework for *The Poverty of Historicism* (1957). The latter he dedicated to the 'memory of the countless men and women of all creeds or nations or races who fell victims to the fascist and communist belief in inexorable Laws of Historical Destiny'. Popper's underlying target was those who claim 'the existence of sociological laws or hypotheses which are analogous to the laws or hypotheses of the natural sciences' (1957: 62), and claim that policy must be redesigned so as to fit with those laws.

In criminology few theorists feel confident enough to state their theories in terms of clearly written theses similar to the laws of the natural sciences. One exception was Sutherland. Sutherland's first full formulation of his theory of differential association (1939: 4–8) expressly, albeit unnoticed, followed the Quetelet structure of variation and attraction. In a society with cultural diversity and cultural conflicts an individual interacts in patterns discernible by their 'frequency' and 'consistency'. Individual differences are only important to the extent that they affect the frequency or consistency of the association with criminal patterns that result in 'systematic criminal behaviour', which 'is determined in a process of association with those who commit crimes ...'[8] Here we have the defining characteristic of continued criminal behaviour, the staticity or constancy Quetelet favoured. By the 1947 edition, however, this notion of 'systematic' behaviour no longer confines the theory, which now seems to be a general theory. Thus, he lays out various points, including

> 6. A person becomes delinquent because of an excess of definitions favourable to violation of law over definitions unfavourable to violation of law. This is the principle of differential association ...
>
> A person becomes delinquent because in his association with others he learns an excess of definitions favourable to violation of law over definitions unfavourable to violation of law, and thus differential association is the case of criminal behaviour. (Sutherland 1947: 9)

Korn and McCorkle (1959: 299) were not alone in pointing out that this ignored problems of personality, motivation, individual differences, individual meanings and interpretations; in short all those subjective grounds for individual choice. Perhaps in response to the critics in the discussion presented in the 2nd edition of Vold's *Theoretical Criminology* (Vold and Bernard 1979: chapter 11), the terrain on which the theory is to work seems to have moved. For, while opining that differential association seemed to offer much more than it could deliver, Vold and Bernard traced various writers' usage of the terms that widened the terminology beyond Sutherland's original formulation with the effect that it became used as a central example of normal learning theory. The basis for this changed terrain is simple, criminal behaviour can no longer be fitted into particular aspects of the spread of a bell curve in which we hold steady a certain social consensus over crime and normal behaviour. Rather criminal behaviour is spread throughout the social body. 'The theory of crime as consisting primarily of ordinary, everyday learned behaviour of normal people has as its principal reason for being, as well as its principal type of supporting data, in the overall frequency and distribution of facts known about those individuals who become involved in criminality' (1979: 247). In light of the information, provided by self-report and victim surveys, that they include a significant part of the total population (thus 'delinquent behaviour is widespread in all social classes'[9]), then

> just as it makes little sense in political discussion to try and convict an entire people of treason, so in criminology, it is meaningless to look for abnormality ... as the explanation of behaviour that includes individuals in every segment and group ...

In a text that makes no mention of genocide or state-sponsored massacres as data for criminology, the last sentence was revealing. For it was precisely this type of claim that Daniel Goldhagen made in 1996 concerning the willingness of ordinary Germans to participate or tolerate the holocaust. But seemingly oblivious to actual examples of political organisation linked to the great killings of the twentieth century, Bernard went on:

> If criminal behaviour, by and large, is the normal behaviour of normally responding individuals in situations defined as undesirable, illegal, and therefore criminal, then the basic problem is one of social and political organisation and the established values or definitions of what may, and what may not, be permitted ...

Crime, in this sense, is political behaviour, and the criminal becomes in fact a member of a 'minority group' without sufficient public support to dominate and control the police power of the state.

Later in the chapter Bernard's editing stressed that this perspective was at odds with that of the positivist tradition, but he succeeded only in reducing it to a form of positivism. Having stated that 'crime is rather obviously a melange of nearly every kind of behaviour, having only one thing in general (in common) namely, that it violates the criminal law' (Ibid.: 246), all that this criminology textbook can offer us is a reduction of theory to the domain of nation-state power. And on this basis, as Rubenstein (2000: 296) states, 'National Socialist Germany probably committed no crime at Auschwitz': remembering that it was the Nazi state, not extra-state criminals that ordered the destruction of the Jews. They used generally accepted methodologies to define Jews, Roma and others, as life forms that were deviant and not deserving of continuing. This could be the avenue to explore important issues in *Theoretical Criminology*, yet Bernard seems oblivious even to what is in the text he is responsible for. His editing seems orientated towards a general theory of *Theoretical Criminology* as covering the problems of the discipline, but the work has no bite. Perhaps Bernard's type of sloppy theorising is simply a reflection of deep intellectual structures that ensure that criminological theory gets no grip on the big issues. First, if his ascription of crime as political behaviour is meant as anything more than the most banal description of a labelling process, it is theoretical incoherence hiding under the image of seeking multiple perspectives. Certainly agreeing that all the behaviour so labelled by the state is crime, it is not at all what the majority of the writers who were to be placed in that category were actually asserting. They were, conversely, trying to show the difference between crime and politics and denying the legitimacy of the criminalisation by the state of the behaviour they defended.[10] Second, this sloppiness takes us on the road to relativism and criminological nihilism. For even if we were to accept, for example, that the mass killings of defenceless Jewish men, women and children carried out by Reserve Police Battalion 101 in occupied Europe from 1940 to 1943 were indeed the 'normal learned behaviour' of either 'ordinary Germans' or 'ordinary men' (to give an example from the discussion of Chapter 8 of this book), it does not follow that the fact that we now call their actions 'crimes' and the individuals concerned as 'criminals' (although, as it must be repeatedly stressed, the majority were not punished and many went back to careers as ordinary policemen in post-war Germany) is simply a political decision. *The fact that it is a political decision, and the fact that if the Nazis had succeed in world domination then both the Jews and the question may have disappeared from the history books or be only a set of exhibits in the museums of the victors, does not effect the normative status of the allocation of the terminology of crime and criminals.* Politics, strangely, may sometimes be right even if we have difficulty in explaining why.

It should be noted again that much of what is routinely accepted as relativism is simply a consequence of not setting the parameters of the discussion wide enough and paying careful attention to the actual meaning that supposedly similar behaviours with differing outcomes have to the participants involved. As Peter Grey has pointed out (1968), in the political conditions of the liberal Weimar Republic, with its sceptical, experimental culture, the outsider became the insider. The minority National Socialist Party, through a combination of circumstances, did after 1933 come to dominate and control the police (as well as the military and secret security) power of the state and scholars in a range of disciplines are still trying to understand how much popular support they had in carrying out a range of actions that at its extreme constituted the holocaust. If the holocaust is now called the crime of the twentieth century, a label that surely is done an injustice to if it is said that it was only the result of a successful act of cultural definition by a political group, although descriptively, of course, it is that. But the fact that we can describe how a label came to be applied, and can imagine circumstances in which history could have been different and the label not so applied, does not mean that the label *is only* a political contingency. Given the task of upgrading and updating a famous text from the late 1950s (the 1st edition of Vold being 1958) Bernard reconstructs the text oblivious to the major crimes of the twentieth century. Moving only within the confines of a disciplinary imagination constituted largely by reference to American work on the geo-social relations within the US, Bernard seems happy to lead on to an amoral criminology. And the refusal to see a big picture is not confined to one chapter; seemingly trying to escape from criminological positivism's acceptance of the power of the state to define the ontology of crime, he refuses any reference to human values or attempted universalism, turning instead, in true textbook fashion, to the then recent discourses of critical criminology with its group conflict and other perspectives. But there, avoiding any espousal of value position (again in counter-distinction to many of the writers referred to) we encounter a relativist morass. His summary of group conflict theory tells us that there are probably 'many situations in which criminality is the normal, natural response of normal, natural human beings struggling in understandably normal and natural situations for the maintenance of the way of life to which they stand committed' (1979: 296). Again we have the reduction of an anti-positivist strand to positivism, nor are we offered any material by which we could have criteria to judge the justness or otherwise desirability of the struggles and conflicts that a group conflict theory of 'crime' might encourage us to learn from. For much of the discourse of genocide concerns actions that outsiders find shocking, bewildering and far beyond the normal, but were engaged in by otherwise normal and 'law-abiding' individuals following, in the case of Germany or Pakistan, to give what appears as differing examples, the state. And many of those who engaged in behaviour we may now call genocide, stated (and there is more to this language than a pun) that they were engaged either in the promotion of (then) accepted civilised values (which unfortunately it seems that they often were), or in the defence of a way of life to which they were committed and the others not. Reading *Theoretical Criminology* with accounts of genocide in mind, it seems quite clear why genocide could not be a subject providing data for the criminology that was represented in the text that Bernard edited. For it appeared that he lacked either the inclination or the ability to impose any normative ordering on the practical and discursive practices that constituted the criminology he termed theoretical. Recourse to a sterile positivism – without acknowledging even that that was the result – was certainly intellectually lazy; but it was also just normal criminology.

What is the purpose of such texts and what are their effects? It has become a staple of so-called postmodern accounts of social theory that social theory is to be read as projections of social power. In some accounts, such as Foucault, this is linked to regimes of governance and epistemic transformation; in others we have varieties of Marxist-influenced class relations. From the 1920s, Walter Benjamin argued that particularistic knowledge generated by a dominant class is presented as if it were disinterested, objective and universal by projecting its focus of production outside of class or historical location. Education, we are told, is never disinterested but an instrument of transmitting central fictions, on which a 'reality' is predicated and core institutional values, distinction and identities are rationalised. It is here that one comes back to Popper's fears. For the use of the word predicated in the above sentence, although growing in usage, is actually technically incorrect. The proper word should be 'predicted' – meaning that which is predicated on the subject. To predict is to give a property or attribute of the subject. But predict also bears the common meaning of foretelling, to engage in prophetic action. Thus the bind, or the dream. In predicting in meaning, we predict. The type of criminology presented here offers no resources to do anything but join in the state's predicting power; the student is left only the role of functionary.

Of course to write a textbook is not to convey the full theoretical insights or projects of the scholars noted, but we should not be ignorant of the wider costs of the projects. For to return to the main subject of this chapter, Quetelet developed not only particular modes of representation but championed a language of determinist laws of social development that held out the promise of problem solving by changing social policy; a legacy that fitted into a particular social atmosphere that supported the events that Popper, quite rightly, reacted against.

To return to bio-power: from the law of the bell curve to genocide?

Having presented the propensity to crime in a bell curve, the dream is to simply change the location of the curve through a society-wide programme. As the Dutch criminologist Bonger speculated on practical action to change the social location for Quetelet's bell curve of criminal propensity:

> the general character of the curve in question does not alter. That is not to say, however, that its level is of necessity always the same. It may be possible, by means of selection, to change it to some extent. If for instance, only plus-variants were allowed to reproduce themselves the general level would be raised; the average comes on a higher level, the maximum higher, and the minimum less low. Both fauna and flora have thus been improved by human interference. Eugenists imagine this to be possible also for humanity. Theoretically it must be admitted that this possibility exists. In regard to the practicability of such a measure, however, I maintain an extremely sceptical attitude … even the elimination of minus-variants from reproduction would entail the most tremendous difficulties; and even this would have to be done on a fairly large scale, if one wished to achieve any practical result …
>
> … there seems to be no chance of any radical eugenic measures; but perhaps time will bring changes here, too. (1936: 125–6)

How much culpability must Bonger carry for this blindness to historical trends? His text was published in Holland when the views of Hitler ought to have been known even before the promulgation of the Nazi Nuremberg Laws of September 1935.[11] Was Bonger an outsider who did not see all the game – to paraphrase Fraser's chapter title surveying the widespread acceptance of key elements in the Nazi social and legislative strategies of the 1930s (Fraser 2005: chapter 4) – or was it more the case that the Nazi era seized ambitions others only hinted at? As commentators on those laws noted (the best known of a general programme), they were legislative acts that had turned their backs upon tradition; instead they reflected a specifically 'modern' and anti-individualist legislative power that made law an instrument in the shaping of a new social order. But we need to recognise that this was not a total break with the past, this did not make the outlook counter-law; rather it defined it as *modern* law. Nor could this be argued as confined to civil law jurisdictions: in the Anglo-American legal world the English Jurisprudent John Austin had tried to break the hold of the common law tradition by declaring in the late 1820s and early 1830s that Law was the command of the central political power directed to political inferiors and backed by the coercive power of the state. This criterion, this definition, gave the minimum condition for its identification, but Austin also argued it should also be rational. It should, in other words, align itself with knowledge (in his case he believed in the truths of political economy and utilitarianism, Austin 1832 and 1864 Lecture 3, see generally Cotterrell 1989 and 2003: chapter 3; and Morrison 1997: chapter 11). Modern 'positive law' was law when it came from a recognised sovereign power and was backed by the state's apparatus of enforcement, but it was rational law when it followed the dictates of scientific knowledge. Why are we surprised then that Hitler saw in this combination of knowledge and political superiority a legislative ambition beyond the confines of the nation?

> The conditions of the time compelled me to begin on the basis of that conception. But I realized from the first that it could have only transient validity. The 'nation' is a political expedient of democracy and Liberalism. We have to get rid of this false conception and set in its place the conception of race, which has not yet been politically used up. The new order cannot be conceived in terms of the national boundaries of peoples with an historical past, but in terms of race that transcends those boundaries. All the adjustments and corrections of frontiers and regions of colonization are like plowing on sand.
>
> Do you understand what I mean? I have to liberate the world from dependence on its historical past. Nations are the outward and visible forms of our history. So I have to fuse these nations into a higher order if I want to get rid of the chaos of an historic past that has become an absurdity ... With the concept of race. National Socialism will carry its revolution abroad and recast the world. (Adolf Hitler, quoted in Rauschning 1940: 232)

Segregation addressed to the Jews was the early instalment of legislative rationality in the service of a racial ideology, the practical implementation of which meant by 1946 no one should have been in a position to argue that not only had the possibility of a grand eugenic 'experiment' existed, but also that it had been grasped. The Nazi conception of *Lebensunwertes Leben* literally meant that some *life was unworthy of life* (as initially formulated in the 14 July 1933 Law for the Prevention of Hereditarily Diseased Offspring). And we should not escape the consequences of this by asserting that this was solely the result of some dictatorship. While we may learn much from the jurisprudence of Carl Schmitt and the state of exception (and its roots in colonial administration) as explaining key elements of sovereignty as exercised or established therein, we may also be in the grip of a relatively popular movement, albeit one that is subject to the constituting powers of the media. Nazi political order was constituted in part by the public[12] who were invited to share in this project through, for example, realising the costs that the legislature needed to consider in a budget of the social order, as in Figure 3.4.

The 1933 Law was co-authored by Ralk Ruttke, a lawyer, and Authur Gutt, a physician and early leader of the German racial hygiene movement. Men and women were subjected to this law if they 'suffered' from any one of nine conditions assumed to be hereditary: feeble-mindedness, schizophrenia, manic-depressive disorder, genetic epilepsy, Huntington's chorea (a fatal form of dementia), genetic blindness, genetic deafness, severe physical deformity and chronic alcoholism. Special hereditary courts were to oversee any decisions, but they appear to have been routine. Is it really shocking to realise that many of the well-known geneticists, psychiatrists and anthropologists sat on the courts at one time or another, mandating the sterilizations of an estimated 400,000 persons? Was this not just modernism (and a social-modernism's justice)? Sterilisation was widely supported in eugenic circles and elsewhere as a rational means of reducing social costs; rates of sterilisation climbed in some US states during the depression and new laws were adopted in Finland, Norway and Sweden (the latter continuing until the 1970s). In some accounts only Catholic opposition blocked a proposed law in the UK.

Figure 3.4 Propaganda slide produced by the Reich Propaganda Office in 1936 showing the opportunity cost of feeding a person with a hereditary disease. The illustration claims that an entire family of healthy Germans can live for one day on the same 5.5 Reichsmarks it costs to support one ill person for the same time (Credit USHMM)

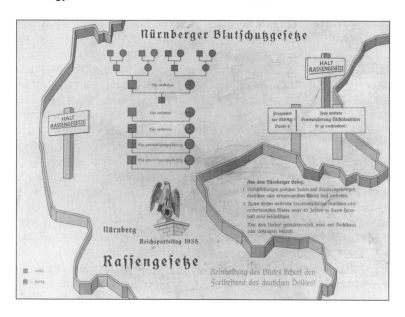

Figure 3.5 Poster number 70 in a series called 'Erblehre und Rassenkunde' (Theory of Inheritance and Racial Hygiene), published by the Vergag fur nationale Literatur (Publisher for National Literature), Stuttgart *c.* 1935. Credit USHMM. Paraphrasing Bauer's general thesis (2001), this poster expresses the victory of volk instincts over liberal morality, the racial soul presented in aesthetically conceived modernist, scientific form. Entitled 'The Nuremberg Law for the Protection of Blood and German Honor', the poster is a stylised map of the borders of central Germany on which is imposed a schematic of the forbidden degrees of marriage between Aryans and non-Aryans, point 8 of the Nazi party platform (against the immigration of non-Aryans into Germany) and the text of the Law for the Protection of German Blood. Civilised space was to be protected. The Nuremberg Laws – The Reich Citizenship Law and the Law for the Protection of German Blood and Honour – were announced at the annual party rally, the law revoked Reich citizenship for Jews and prohibited Jews from marrying or having sexual relations with persons of 'German or related blood'. This was termed 'racial infamy' and was made a criminal offence. A 'Jew' was defined as someone with three or four Jewish grandparents. Consequently, the Nazis classified as Jews thousands of people who had converted from Judaism to another religion, among them even Roman Catholic priests and nuns and Protestant ministers whose grandparents were Jewish. On October 18, 1935, new marriage requirements were instituted under the 'Law for the Protection of the Hereditary Health of the German People'; this required all prospective marriage partners to obtain from the public health authorities a certificate of fitness to marry. Such certificates were refused to those suffering from 'hereditary illnesses' and contagious diseases and those attempting to marry in violation of the Nuremberg Laws. On November 14, 1935 the Nuremberg Law was extended to other groups by supplemental decree. The prohibition on marriage or sexual relations is extended between people who could produce 'racially suspect' offspring. A week later, the minister of the interior interpreted this to mean relations between 'those of German or related blood' and Roma (Gypsies), blacks or their offspring. This civilised space was no longer to be considered in terms of citizens, but in terms of race. . . . This racial awareness was to take control of the history of the land, to make the ploys of past colonialism irrelevant – to transform history. The Jews were a unique target embraced not only by a traditional anti-semitism that had become scientifically racist, but by the appeal of the redemptive claims of purity and power to be achieved by their elimination

Stylistically represented, the Jews were thus a distortion of the average German and their impact upon the bell curve must be corrected. Central to German anti-Semitism was the idea of a return to the authentic essence of Germaness. Lagarde was certainly not alone when in the 1880s he argued that the Germans needed to express their character as a nation, which entailed that there was no place of the Jews. His cry that 'Germany must become full of German people and German ways ... To the degree that we become ourselves, the Jews will cease to be Jews' found fertile ground and (seeming) scientific support.

This was redemptive ... we now see it as a dangerous dream, but under the eugenic philosophy of the 1930s the metaphorical elements of the myth of German Judaization were fused with that of the racial (Aschheim 1996). The Nazi history of the social body made the Jew the physical embodiment of the presence of evil and corrupting powers. The greater true German expression would be felt, the less the cotangent would be present. Now the Jews could be 'scientifically' re-presented.

John Jay Lifton depicts Nazism as the 'medicalism of killing'. A biomedical vision combined with a vast, programmatical task of racial and eugenic hygiene. It took control of the human biological future, granting a healthy future to 'positive racial stock and purging humanity of its sick, degenerative elements'. Its vision was that of a 'violent cure' and its policies constituted a 'therapeutic imperative' (Lifton 1987, esp.: 15–27 and chapter 21; see also Aziz 1976; for the argument that the final solution flowed from a similar logic to euthanasia see Friedlander 1995; for other views on the 'murderous science' see Muller-Hill 1988; and Proctor 1988). Bauman explains it as 'an outcome of a unique encounter between factors by themselves quite ordinary and common', an extension of 'everything we know about our civilisation, its priorities, its immanent vision of the world' (1989: 8). Yet in his narrative, is it possible for us to refer to 'the murder of the Jews', for is this now simply extermination, not a 'matter of [social] pathology' representative of a criminal milieu, but an activity to be seen within 'the context of cultural tendencies and technical achievements of modernity' (see also Biaglioli 1992, for another argument concerning the links between 'science, modernity and the "final solution"'). For the historians Aly and Heim, the holocaust is not to be understood in terms of pathology or political irrationality, but it was a 'sensible' outcome of rational utilitarian-economic and power-political considerations and was the outcome of specialised studies and proposals on economics, geographers, carried out by a variety of relatively low-level 'experts' and planning officers. These experts 'did not revel in myths of blood and race, but thought in categories of large scale economic spaces, structural renewal and overpopulation with its attendant food problems; and they were resolved to effectuate more rational methods of production, standardize products, and improve social structures'. The Germanic development simply could be achieved faster 'if they found a way to eliminate the sizeable Jewish minority from the population' (published in German, discussed in Aschheim 1996: 132–3, who notes that they expressly saw this as a part of the expansion of capitalism, a simplifying tendency; see also Aly, Chroust and Pross 1984).

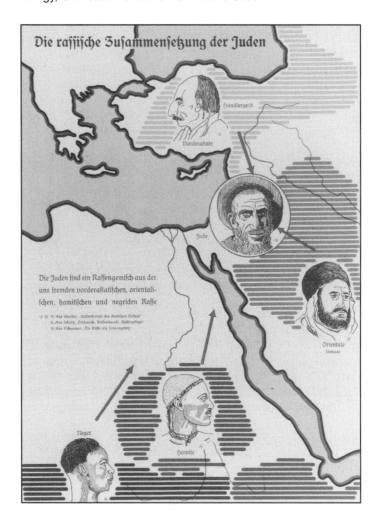

Figure 3.6 Eugenics poster entitled 'The Racial Composition of the Jews'. Credit USHMM. The German text reads: 'The Jews are a mixture of alien Near Eastern, oriental, Hamite and Negroid races'. Poster number 55 in a series entitled 'Erblehre und Rassenkunde' (Theory of Inheritance and Racial Hygiene), Stuttgart. Before Jews could be recognised as the contimant the they had to be constituted by the scientific gaze, their corrupting abilities displayed

As the territory expanded so did the terrain of representation. Consider Figure 3.8. Here the pie charts represent changes as a result of the actions undertaken.

The message is chilling.

There are a host of more particular factors to be addressed. Some shall be touched upon in Chapter 8. But let us not escape from another question, that

Figure 3.7 The perfect Aryan family (Reproduction of an oil painting by Wolf Willrich MEPL/Weimar Archive). The Nazi state stayed faithful to the injunction that the State organise life. Hitler counted the Jew as the greatest danger: 'The same battle that Pasteur and Koch had to wage must be waged by us today. Countless illnesses have their cause in the one bacillus: the Jews! ... We will recover our health when we eliminate the Jews' (dinner conversation with Himmler, February 22, 1942, quoted, Jochmann 1980: 293)

which Fraser (2005: 418) poses in relating 'a perverse and bizarre' interaction of man and law, under which:

> [This man] was really little more than a police officer. He did his job and his job included killing Jews. The killing of the Jews of [occupied Eastern Europe] took place in a context of legitimate police action against lives [deemed by state sponsored law and medicine] unworthy of living, of the death but not the murder [as within the law], of the extra-legal subject of law, *homo sacer*. This is the truth which all the [subsequent] legal proceedings ... have had to ignore if they are to remain in our shared and inaccurate understanding of law after Auschwitz. We simply could not, nor can we today, accept the possibility that [this man] and untold others were in fact simply "following orders", lawful orders based in an underlying set of commonly accepted legal norms and practices.

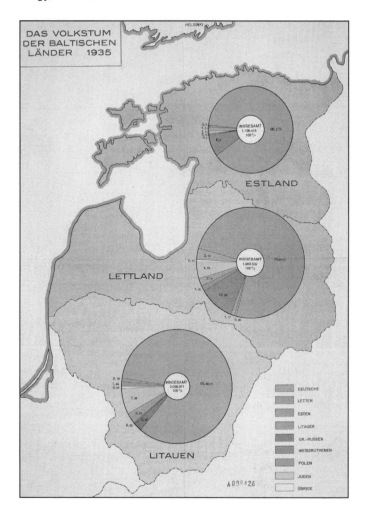

Figure 3.8 Credit USHMM 89046c. A pie chart indicating the populations of Estonia, Lativa and Lithuania by ethnic group that accompanied the report of SS-Brigadier General Stahlecker to the Reich Security Main Office, Berlin. The chart, entitled 'The Population of the Baltic States 1935', shows that in 1935, 7.58 per cent of Lithuanians were Jews. In 1939, the proportion of Jews increased to nearly 10 per cent after the contested Vilna region was returned to Lithuania. The Stahlecker report contains, among other things, the following information

> In Kovno a total of 7,800 have now been killed – a portion through the pogrom, a portion short by Lithuanian commandos. All corpses have been disposed of. Continued mass shootings are no longer possible. Instead I explained to a committee of Jews that up to now, we have not had reason to intervene in the internal conflicts between Lithuanians and Jews. The conditions to undergo reorganisation are: Establish a Jewish ghetto ... The town of Viljampole has been designated to be the ghetto.' Report for 15 October 1941–31 January 1942.

Consider Bauer (2001: 104): 'It appears that when an intellectual or pseudo-intellectual elite with a genocidal programme, whether explicit or implicit, achieves power in a crisis-ridden society for economic, social, and political reasons that have nothing to do with the genocidal program, then, if that elite can draw the intellectual strata to its side genocide will become

Those lawful orders demanded the killing of millions. The price of law is a high one. The debt to justice remains, as it must, unpaid.

Among Fraser's points is the shuffling off of the weight of moral decision-making and the need to see beyond the legal into the ideological reasoning of the directors. The need, I would paraphrase, to put the mystery of ethics above all ontology, all representation.

possible'. By intellectual strata he referred to upper-class social groups, army officers, church leaders, bureaucrats, doctors and lawyers, industrial and commercial elites and especially the university professors who provided the rest with the necessary ideological tools but how this translates to the actuality of Figure 3.9, with its different visuality is a process that cannot be blamed on such all-embracing concepts as capitalism, the spirit of modernity or such like.

Figure 3.9 A German police officer shoots Jewish women still alive after a mass execution of Jews from the Mizocz ghetto, 14 October 1942 (Credit: USHM 17878). According to the Zentrale Stelle in Germany (Zst. II 204 AR 1218/70), these Jews were collected by the German Gendarmerie and Ukrainian Schutzmannschaft during the liquidation of the Mizocz ghetto, which held roughly 1,700 Jews. On the eve of the ghetto's liquidation (13 October 1942), some of the inhabitants rose up against the Germans and were defeated after a short battle. The remaining members of the community were transported from the ghetto to this ravine in the Sdolbunov Gebietskommissariat, south of Rovno, where they were executed. Information regarding this action, including the photos, were acquired from a man named Hille, who was the Bezirks-Oberwachtmeister of the Gendarmerie at the time. Hille apparently gave the five photos (there were originally seven) to the company lawyer of a textile firm in Kunert, Czechoslovakia, where he worked as a doorman after the war. The Czech government confiscated the photos from the lawyer in 1946 and they subsequently became public. That the photos indeed show the shooting of Jews in connection with the liquidation of the ghetto was also confirmed by a statement of Gendarmerie-Gebietsfuehrer Josef Paur in 1961.

This territorial state had looked outward and embraced a territory to be conquered; this territory was to be cleansed on many of its inhabitants, rendered suitable for the development of German life. This was nothing short of the biological reorganisation of European living space (and, we should note, by extension a new biologically engineered world order). This ordering of space shows the actual exceptional identity of the holocaust for this was not simply a taking of land – as occurred in Australia, the Americas, or Africa – but a taking of what was outside – exterior to the civilised space and incorporating it in a new order. This was a very modern expression of that which was fundamental to modernity's growth: colonisation. A process which has always demanded the greatest of European values: fortitude and a little absence of visualisation – as Himmler extolled his men: 'Most of you know what it means when 100 corpses lie there, or when 500 corpses lie there, or when 1,000 corpses lie there. To have gone through this and – apart from a few exceptions caused by human weakness – to have remained decent, that has made us great. That is a page of glory in our history which has never been written and which will never be written.' (Himmler, 4 October 1943, quoted Hilberg 1979: 648)

Part II

Criminal statistics outside of the nation-state: acknowledging 'genocide'

Two of the many legacies derived from Quetelet concern the ongoing search for the dark figure of crime (that is crime that does not appear in the official criminal statistics), a concept that has spanned a series of alternative indices of crime, such as self-report and victim surveys (such as the British Crime Survey), and the concept of the normal rate of crime.

As critical correctives of the official criminal statistics, the alternative indices of victim reports and self-report studies had understandably localised modes of production and concerns. Both have largely occurred in partnership with the epistemic gaze of the nation state. In Chapter 2, it was claimed that the figures of death and destruction of property and ways of life that have occurred by state-sponsored action – with genocide as their culmination – for the twentieth century may be between 170 and 190 million. This vast range of activity has been, and continues to be, excluded from the database; it is not part of the normal crime rate; but if we include this data of the 'exceptional', rather than the average rate of crime, our picture of crime and range of observable facts changes dramatically. It was also stated that in the vast majority of cases there has been and continues to be no criminal justice process that in practice covers genocide, and by extension, no criminology. Absent such discourse we have the incoherence of the great divide.

Criminology follows official criminal statistics, albeit by attempting to fill in their shadows or dark figure. Creating new criminal offences seems linked to notions of individual responsibility and mobilizing penalty. As discussed in Chapter 7, the most important of the post-World War II cases in Europe were the trials of those of the International Military Tribunal now often referred to as the Nuremberg trials.

In 1946 the General Assembly of the United Nations adopted resolution 95 (1), which incorporated the judgment of the Nuremberg court, or, in language derived from the common law tradition that provided much of the legitimacy for the trials, the Nuremberg principles, into international law. Nuremberg has become associated in the popular mind with establishing liability for 'crimes against humanity'; this established a mythology of accountability which needs to be properly understood. In reality – as expanded in Chapter 7 – the most important element of these trials was thought to be the principle that a state that wages *aggressive war* commits the supreme international crime, punishable by any state able to bring that state's planners to justice. Its leaders incurred criminal responsibility – arising directly under *international* law – for their conduct that causes the state to be liable under international law. But we must be clear as to the limits imposed: they may be tried and punished for their participation in the unlawful use of force against other states and actions deemed criminal *associated with that.* When the trials established that an individual can be the subject of international law – the Nuremberg tribunal specifically rejected the notion that international law covers only the actions of states; concluding that crimes against international law are committed by men, not by abstract entities and thus the provisions of international law were to be enforced by punishing individuals who commit such crimes – it was a particular, state-orientated version of law that was upheld. The fact that the Nazi defendants claim – namely that they had no obligations under international law and their only duty was to the Nazi state, which, in turn, would bear responsibility under international law – was denied and the court firmly established that individuals had international duties that transcended the national obligations of obedience imposed by the individual state, should not blind us to the fact that Nuremberg and Tokyo actually reinforced a state-orientated vision.

All charges that the defendants faced were orientated around the central one of waging aggressive war. Notions of *war crimes* were expanded with the terminology of crimes against humanity, but there was no effective, free standing category of 'crimes against humanity', nor was there a separate conceptualisation of the holocaust as genocide (nor was there, apart from a later minor Polish court, a judgement that ordered punishment for genocide, as discussed in Chapter 7 of this book).[13] In fact, as Donald Bloxham, among others, has demonstrated (2001), while the IMT did give a narrative of the extraordinary persecution of Jews there was little effort to recognise or punish crimes against Jews as a specific category. If there was anything their fate was played down. The trials did not bring out the unique horror of the holocaust, nor did they fully face up to the issue of genocide. While the term was used in a charge and in closing argument, it did not appear in the final judgement. The term genocide is largely the result of the work of Raphael Lemkin, a Polish–Jewish specialist in international criminal law. Lempkin documented for the US State Department the various violations of the international laws of war committed by the German armed forces occupying various European countries. His problem was that no adequate terminology of crime covered the data he was receiving. The traditional doctrines of the laws or war were based on the notion that wars were fought between states while the German state was waging a war against peoples under an ideology of biological superiority and racial cleansing and restructuring of Europe. The Nazi aim was not merely the military defeat of enemy states but the biological reorganisation of Europe and later the establishment of a new world order.

Lemkin re-conceptualised the German actions as a crime against certain fundamental principles underlying international law. We must be clear of his limitations however, for while he made it not only a crime against the rules of war but also a crime against humanity itself – affecting not just the individual or nation in question, but humanity as a whole (Lemkin 1944) – Lemkin was a product of modernity; the focus point for the new concept – *genocide* – was to see it as a crime against nationhood. *Nations* were bearers of culture and value and the destruction of nations was a kind of *inter-national* vandalism. This reliance upon nations impliedly came into conflict with the assertion that genocide was also a violation of individual human rights (as well as a violation of the principles of just-war theory, which required armies not to attack non-combatant populations in the absence of military necessity). He did not understand – as we do with the benefit of decades of historical research – the full impact of the racial/biological reorganisation. He could only work with the data he had, which showed that particularly in the east, German occupation policies were a deliberate targeting of civilians. Thus, still optimistically – without putting modernism or modernity on trial – he constructed the term *genocide* from the Greek word *genus* (race, tribe) and the Latin word *cide* (killing) denoting

> a coordinated plan of different actions aiming at the destruction of essential foundations of the life of national groups, with the aim of annihilating the groups themselves. The objectives of such a plan would be the disintegration of the political and social institutions of culture, language, national feelings, religion, economic existence, of national groups and the destruction of the personal security, liberty, health, dignity, and even the lives of the individuals belonging to such groups ... Genocide is directed against individuals not in their individual capacity, but as members of the national group. (Lemkin 1944: 79)

Lemkin visualised two phases: the destruction of the national patterns of the oppressed group and after the imposition of the national patterns of the oppressor. The Nazi state carried out genocide in seven areas: social, physical, cultural, economic, biological, religious and moral. An international, multilateral treaty prohibiting genocide should be produced, which would then be incorporated into the constitutional and criminal codes of the nation-states party to the treaty. Moreover, an international tribunal should be established to examine allegations of genocide brought against government leaders. Finally, an international non-governmental organization, such as the Red Cross, should be charged with supervising the treatment of civilians in time of war.

Genocide provided a formative concept; it was an analytical and normative category as well as descriptive. While concerned to cover the treatment of the Jews, Lemkin was reacting to the whole policy towards the Poles, Serbs, Czechs and others of Eastern Europe. For him genocide did not require physical annihilation; a programme of cultural destruction was enough. Since he believed that the essence of a nation was its culture, the destruction of a national culture (through attacks on its religion, language, cultural leadership and economy) was genocide. A theme of Chapter 9 was the 'preservation of the integrity of a people'. The target of genocide was 'national groups as distinguished from states and individuals':

> The idea of a nation signifies constructive co-operation and original contributions, based upon genuine traditions, genuine culture, and a well-developed national psychology. The destruction of a nation, therefore, results in the loss of its future contributions to the world. Moreover such destruction offends our feelings of morality and justice in much the same way as does the criminal killing of a human being: the crime in the one case as in the other is murder, though on a vastly greater scale. Among the basic features which have marked progress in civilization are the respect for and appreciation of the national characteristics and qualities contributed to the world culture by the different nations – characteristics and qualities which, as illustrated in the contributions made by nations weak in defence and poor in economic resources, are not to be measured in terms of national power and wealth. (1944: 91)

Genocide was a form of cultural destruction and prevention of potential being realised. It was also the most extreme form of an abuse of power, for a successful genocide replaced the culture and being of a nation with the image of the perpetrator. Committed to a narrative of enlightened progress and this progress being led by civilised ideals, Lemkin thought of the German actions as a specific, modern form of an ancient, generic type of military or quasi-military action. Wars of extermination were known in antiquity, what gave the German programme its specific substance was its occurrence in the centre of the modern 'civilised' world. The modern era should have moved on from the barbarism of the Middle Ages and we largely thought that we had reached a stage of enlightened humanitarianism, manifested in international law itself. The German actions were thus a shocking recurrence of a type of behavior well known to history that modern conditions should have rendered impossible.[14] It was unique for three reasons: it was carried out in the centre of the civilised world, it was carried out with technical efficiency possible only in modern society and it was carried out on the basis of a genocidal will that had been adopted by a modern state.

Genocide: definition and controversies

Although he could not foresee either the extensiveness or the character of the exterminatory practices subsequently carried out under the auspices of the Third Reich, Lemkin had in 1933 submitted to an International Conference for Unification of Criminal Law a proposal to declare the destruction of racial, religious or social collectivities a crime in international law. After the war he waged an intensive lobbying campaign of United Nations' officials and representatives to secure a resolution by the General Assembly affirming that 'genocide is a crime under international law which the civilised world condemns and for the commission of which principals and accomplices are punishable'. The matter was referred for consideration to the UN Economic and Social Council, their deliberations culminating with the signing of the 1948 United Nations Convention on Genocide (though several nations, most particularly the US did not ratify it until much later). The definitional article included in the 1948 convention stipulates at Article II:

> In the present Convention, genocide means any of the following acts committed with intent to destroy, in whole or in part, a national, ethnical, racial or religious group, such as:
> 1 Killing members of the group;
> 2 Causing serious bodily or mental harm to members of the group;
> 3 Deliberately inflicting on the group conditions of life calculated to bring about its physical destruction in whole or in part;
> 4 Imposing measures intended to prevent births within the group;
> 5 Forcibly transferring children of the group to another group.

In terms of accountability under the convention the critical element is the presence of an 'intent to destroy', which can be either 'in whole or in part', groups defined in terms of nationality, ethnicity, race or religion. Policies implemented during the Third Reich respecting Jewish, Roma and Sinti groups were clearly genocidal in terms of this article as there was a clearly stated policy indicating the presence of intent to destroy them. Members of all these groups were subjected to mobile killing squads, rounded up and processed in certain extermination camps, were subjected to serious bodily and mental harm, and had conditions inflicted upon them intended to bring about their physical destruction, including starvation in ghettoes, and had measures applied to them intended to prevent births within the group (sterilisation).

These criteria have been criticised; they may not be sufficiently broad. For instance, the definition excludes the physical destruction of certain sub-groups that have regularly been the victims of extensive killing programs. Furthermore, the definition focuses on the physical destruction of the group. There have been many instances in which the group has physically survived but its cultural distinctiveness has been eradicated. These and other deficiencies need to be understood in the context of the background to the passage of this convention that involved considerable political bargaining (on this see e.g. Leo Kuper 1981: chapter 2; Schabas 2000: chapter 2).

There are considerable disagreements among experts concerning whether a specific complex of behaviours merits the designation genocide, even leaving aside clear-cut instances of attempts at moral appropriation of the concept. There are various reasons for this variation and imprecision.

First, is the conflict between sociological and legal structures of knowledge, each with their own strategies of concept formation. The convention is a legal instrument, which creates a form of legalist truth that requires a process of autopoetic hegemony for its concepts to develop as practical entities. In other words, a legal definition requires processes of enactment, prosecution and judicial-practical debate as to the meaning of the terms and whether specific behaviour fits them (the binary of guilt-innocence), which in turn becomes the material for subsequent academic commentary. In the case of genocide all this has not taken place: there has been no prosecution until recently. The legal understanding of a concept is a question of the terms of definition; the world is brought to the appropriate forum and activities are fitted into the definition or not as the case may be. The strictly positivist social sciences, such as behavioural sociology, by contrast, takes the meaning of its terms from observing patterns of behaviour in the world and then deducing definitional relationships from those patterns. It can hardly be expected that they agree.

Second, the convention, as with any legislation, was the outcome of negotiations between parties that held conflicting views as to the proper scope of its constituent parts. Although Article IX allows for disputes between parties to be adjudicated by the International Court of Justice, because accusations of genocide are invariable made by one state against another, this has never occurred. Consequently, while the fact that there is no body of international law to clarify the parameters of the convention that can be seen as a systems failure in terms of creating clarity, it is clearly a political convenience.

A third reason for uncertainty as to how the concept can be fitted to particular complexes of behaviour derives from the fact that it is assumed that the ideal–typical genocidal complex Lemkin had in mind was the Nazi policy of reorganising Europe on racial grounds.[15] However, as hinted at before and contrary to what many now take as common sense, he did not create the term principally to fit the destruction of European Jewry; working within accepted concepts of international law he was concerned to distinguish the Nazi actions from those of a just war and limit the conduct and conditions of war.[16] If

Lemkin saw genocide as a generic concept, the Nazi policy was but a particularly devastating reoccurrence of a pattern of behaviour that he had hoped to have been made redundant with the progress of civilization. He clearly included cultural destruction; but this was lost in the Convention definition. With greater knowledge of the Nazi programme, an interpretation of the Jewish experience was available to those who drafted and negotiated the UNCG. Perhaps (but this may be an overly generous interpretation) because this particular instance was so near to the genesis of the UNCG, its application to other situations has been problematic.

Genocide has not been an easy topic for study. This statement may rightly invoke almost a sense of revulsion; how, or why, should such a topic, event (language seems not to do it 'justice') be related to? To say that social scientists have different definitions of genocide from each other and from the definition in international law (the UN Genocide Convention) is an understatement almost banal in its descriptive ability but totally inadequate in dealing with the normative chaos (for a study of the different concepts see Stein 2005). Yet it is understandable, for these differences stem from the differences between generic concepts and legal definition, differences in purpose of the definer and because of the political and group processes involved in drawing up an international convention. In addition, genocide is an inherently problematic topic of study; some scholars, such as Rummel, try to provide supplementary concepts to distinguish and/or cover a wider range of state-sponsored massacres. His term 'democide' covers both genocide and other forms of 'government mass murder'. But there is another reason: genocidal activity has simply been a key element in the processes we now call globalisation, how can the social sciences born and linked into those processes do anything more than try to describe this, while law may be trapped in circles of prescription and ethical accountability for processes in which it is actually a constituting part?

International criminal statistics?

This chapter began with two short quotes. One stressed the role of statistics as the language of modern industrialised civilisation, the other was the cryptic cable sent by the UN Special Representative in the Balkans two days after the Bosnian Serbs had massacred up to 7,000 defenceless civilians at the supposedly UN safe area of Srebrenica (a 'fact' finally only made 'real' to the majority populace of Serbia and Greece due to a home-made video of some of the killings put on state media in mid-2005). The latter talked of elements of the database missing. The cable is chilling and an apt signifier of genocide and government-sponsored mass murder as the real dark figure of modern criminal statistics.

Criminological positivism sought to replace the categorisation of law with alternative indices guaranteed not by state power, but by replicable methodological injunctions. In this field however, it has been difficult to escape the defining power of the territorial state.

To return to Hobbes, it is one of the privileges of power to define the terms in which social reality is discussed. It is one of the privileges of Westphalia sovereignty that there are no official international criminal statistics that creates maps, pictures and lists of government-sponsored killings. To compile a global set of statistics for genocide and other mass killing has been the projects of concerned individuals. Their work, such as that of Elliot in his aptly titled *Twentieth Century Book of the Dead* (1972), attempts to count the results of governmental mass killing not directly related to war. In his work the mediating effects of technology and dehumanisation by the killers of their victims are influential considerations. Rummel (1990; 1991; 1992; 1994) provides the paradigm of these attempts, particularly his two texts of *Death by Government*. There, in table after table, in list after list, are totalled numbers derived from an impressive array of sources; source after source is acknowledged, compared and in true pragmatic fashion a middle figure extracted; it is a chilling and yet impassive cataloguing.

There are no state-operative agencies dealing with this 'reality'. Thus our figures are debatable. To witness: consider the following table representing some of the leading events, which are represented as major genocidal acts during the twentieth century by genocide scholars.

Year	Victim	Main Perpetrator	UN recognised
1885–1908	Native Congolese of the Congo Free State *c.* 8 million	Regime of Léopold II of Belgium	No
1904	Hereros of southern Africa 65,000 out of 80,000 killed	German Government	Yes
1915–22	Armenians of Turkey 1.5 million	New Turks (collapse of Ottoman Empire)	Yes
1918–21	Jews living in the Ukraine 100,000–250,000 by pogroms	Ukrainian	Yes
1932–33	Ukrainians 38 million by imposed famine	USSR Government	No
1936–39	Soviet political dissenters 400,000–500,000	USSR Government	No
1939–45	Jews of Europe 6 million Jews	Nazi Government of Germany	Yes
(5 million others including Gypsies, handicapped, homosexuals and others)			
1950–59	Buddhists in Tibet	Chinese Government	No
1965	'Communists' in Indonesia 600,000 political opponents	Indonesian Government	No
1965–72	Hutus in African Nation of Burundi 100,000–300,000	The Tutsi	Yes
1965–92	Guatemalan Indians	Government Troops	No
1966	Iho people of N. Nigeria	Government Troops	No
1971	Bengalis in East Pakistan (now Bangladesh) 2–3 million	Pakistani Government	No

Continued

Year	Victim	Main Perpetrator	UN recognised
1972	Ache Indians of Paraguay	Paraguayan Government	Yes
1975–79	Cambodians 2 million	Khmer Rouge Government	Yes
1975–2000	Citizens of East Timor 200,000+	Indonesian Troops	No
1980–94	Members of the Baha'i religion in Iran	Government of Ayatollah Khomeini	Yes
1991–94	Kurds of Iraq	Iraqi Government	No
1992–98	Muslims of Bosnia	Croats and Serbs	Yes
1994	Tutsi of Rwanda 800,000+	Hutu militia and government soldiers	No

For most of these the term genocide is contested and the subject of a politics of naming.[17] As the defence minister of Paraguay retorted to the use of the term: 'Although there are victims and victimizers, there is not the third element necessary to establish the crime of genocide – that is "intent". Therefore, as there is no "intent", one cannot speak of genocide' (quoted Kuper 1981: 110). In the case of Rwanda 1994, the fact that there was and is a legal obligation on those who have ratified the convention to take action against genocide, provided a reason for the US and the UN Security Council to avoid using the term, preferring to withdraw the bulk of the troops already there, engage in agonised inaction and humanitarian aid rather than any interventionist police action. (The fact that France had been the major military supplier to the forces instigating the actions can be seen as an example of counterproductive intervention.)

In addition there is an array of what might properly be called government-sponsored mass killing or 'administrative massacre', such as in nationalist China under Chiang Kai-shek, or the well-known disappearances that occurred under the Military Junta in Argentina which claimed around 30,000 lives and those in Chile perhaps 6,000–10,000. Many others can be added to the names of Burundi, Sudan, Somalia, Azerbaijan, DR Congo and Chechnya. There are problems of identification and boundary drawing: when, for example, does a process, such as 'ethnic cleansing' become genocidal in intent and reality? Was Srebrenica to be the extreme event or would it have become the norm if the Bosnian Serbs had been allowed to continue in their activities? What of intent? Was there a plan, for example in relation to Bosnia, either consciously formulated or evolving, which involved the top Serbian political figures, particularly Milosevic? Here the legal back hole into which the investigation of the Katyn massacre in 1940 (specifically the Russian refusal to release the results of their own internal investigation), in which Stalin's secret police murdered *c.* 21,700 Polish military officers, intellectual leaders and clergy, is illustrative. Pursuant to the non-aggressive pact between Hitler and Stalin reached in August 1939, a month before Germany began World War II by invading Poland, when Hitler invaded Stalin seized eastern Poland and 9 months later the Baltic republics. After seizure the commands elite of the Polish Army along with intellectuals and churchmen 'disappeared': mass graves were later uncovered. At the Nuremberg Military Tribunal the Soviets tried (unsuccessfully) to blame this on the Nazis and continued to maintain this stance throughout the cold war. The Polish Parliament in March 2005, declared that 'only the disclosure of the whole truth about the crime and the condemnation of the perpetrators can heal the wounds and lead to good relations between Poland and the Russian Federation'. While the Polish authorities call this a war and an act of genocide, the Russian position is that since the Soviet Union was not at war with Poland this cannot be a war crime, and as there was no intent to exterminate there was no genocidal intention.

Can we globalise criminal statistics? If part of the aim of the statistical analysis of Quetelet was to gauge the normal rate of crime in a society and thus determine risk, how does one move into a statistical image of a world risk society?

Following the lead of national criminal statistics to create a statistical reality of global crime would require an international bureaucracy, an array of managers of processes and checkers on the results of those processes. But could such an international bureaucracy be trusted?

Leo Kuper highlighted the difficulty for a body composed of sovereign states policing the activities of other sovereign states usually within their territorial boundaries. Indeed he went so far as to propose a thesis

> that the sovereign territorial state claims, as an integral part of its sovereignty, the right to commit genocide, or engage in genocidal massacres, against peoples under its rule, and that the United Nations, for all practical purposes, defends this right. To be sure no state explicitly claims the right to commit genocide – this would not be morally acceptable even in international circles – but the right is exercised under other more acceptable rubrics, notably the duty to maintain law and order, or the seemingly sacred mission to preserve the territorial integrity of the state. And though the norm for the United Nations is to sit by, and watch, like a grandstand spectator, the unfolding of the genocidal conflict in the domestic arena right through to the final massacres, there would generally be concern, and action to provide humanitarian relief for the refugees, and direct intercession by the Secretary-General. (1981: 161)

The response of the United Nations to genocide, according to Kuper in a later work, 'is as negative as its performance on charges of political mass murder. There are the same evasions of responsibility and protection of offending governments and the same overriding concern for state interests and preoccupation with the ideological and regional alliances' (1985: 160). National interests prevented action to prevent the genocide of Rwanda; currently they prevent action in the Darfur region of the Sudan (see e.g. 'The World has turned away – but Darfur's misery goes on', *The Observer*, 31 July 2005; see also Hagan, Rymond – Richmond and Parker 2005, in an article in the mainstream journal *Criminology*, which may denote a change in at least one corner of a discipline's concerns).

At a scholarly level we are also left with another consequence of the great divide. The statistics that map the non-recognised 'crimes' of states and state-sponsored actors lack the validation process of state-sponsored processes of collection and recognition. In his work Rummel warned that his own figures could not be other than partially incorrect and that he would be amazed if future research came up with figures within even 10 per cent of his:

> Regimes and their agents usually do not record all their murders, and what they do record is secret. Even when such archives are available, such as after defeat in war, and even when they are kept by the most technologically advanced of regimes with a cultural propensity for record keeping and obedience to authority, and a bureaucratic apparatus that systematically murders, the total number of victims cannot be agreed upon. (1994: xviii)

What is the impact of these figures on our conception of the twentieth century? Writing in 1987 Rummel states

> during the first eighty-eight years of this century, almost 170 million men, women, and children have been short, beaten, tortured, knifed, burned, starved, frozen, crushed, or worked to death; buried alive, drowned, hung, bombed, or killed in any other of the myriad ways governments have inflicted death on unarmed, helpless citizens and foreigners. The dead could conceivably be nearly 360 million people. It is as though our species has been devastated by a modern Black Plaque. And indeed it has, but a plague of Power, not germs.
>
> The souls of this monstrous pile of dead have created a new land, a new nation among us. In Shakespeare's words, 'This Land be called The Field of Golgotha, and dead men's Skulls'. And it is clear … this land is multicultural and multiethnic. Its inhabitants followed all the world's religions and spoke all its languages. Its demography has yet to be precisely measured. (1987: 9)

How can this land be conceptualised? We are in a realm where the seductions of statistics only deaden our grasp. Perhaps only irony or satire, irreverent though these forms are, can by a strange twist confer proper reverence; Mark Twain in his commentary upon King Léopold II, the subject of Chapters 5 and 6, may be a guide. He wrote an ironical deconstruction of Léopold's regime of truth and campaign against those who tried to expose the horrors of his rule of the Congo (1884–1908) by putting words into Léopold's mouth; a fit ending to this chapter may be the section where he has Léopold' reference to a madman's scheme to create a monument to the dead whose labour had created the wealth that Léopold took to create the grand monuments of Brussels (see Chapter 6):

> Another madman wants to construct a memorial for the perpetuation of my name, out of my 15,000,000 skulls and skeletons [Mark Twain takes the highest estimated total of deaths caused by Léopold's rule, the real figure is probably 8,000,000], and is full of vindictive enthusiasm over his strange project. He has it all ciphered out and drawn to scale. Out of the skulls he will build a combined monument and mausoleum to me which shall exactly duplicate the Great pyramid of Cheops, whose base covers thirteen acres, and whose apex is 451 feet above ground. He desires to stuff me and stand me up in the sky on that apex, robed and crowned, with my 'pirate flag' [the flag of the Congo Free State] in one hand and a butcher-knife and pendant handcuffs in the other. He will build the pyramid in the center of a depopulated tract, a brooding solitude covered with weeds and the mouldering ruins of burned villages, where the spirits of the starved and

murdered dead will voice their laments forever in the whispers of the wandering winds. Radiating from the pyramid, like the spokes of a wheel, there are to be forty grand avenues of approach, each 35 miles long, and each fenced on both sides by skulless skeletons standing a yard and a half apart and festooned together in line by short chains stretching from wrist to wrist and attached to tried and true old handcuffs stamped with my private trademark, a crucifix and butcher-knife crossed, with motto, 'By this sign we prosper'; each osseous fence to consist of 200,000 skeletons on a side, which is 400,000 to each avenue. It is remarked with satisfaction that it aggregates three or four thousand miles (single-ranked) of skeletons – 15,000,000 all told – and would stretch across America from New York to San Francisco. It is remarked further, in the hopeful tone of a railroad company forecasting showy extensions of its mileage, that my output is 500,000 corpses a year when my plant is running full time, and that therefore if I am spared ten years longer there will be fresh skulls enough to add 175 feet to the pyramid, making it by a long way the loftiest architectural construction on the earth, and fresh skeletons enough to continue the transcontinental file (on piles) a thousand miles into the Pacific. The cost of gathering the materials from my 'widely scattered and innumerable private graveyards', and transporting them, and building the monument and the radiating grand avenues, is duly ciphered out, running into an aggregate of millions of guineas, and then – why then (– – !! – – !!), this idiot asks me to furnish the money! [Sudden and effusive application of the crucifix] He reminds me that my yearly income from the Congo is millions of guineas, and that only 5,000,000 would be required for his enterprise.

Every day wild attempts are made upon my purse; they do not affect me, they cost me not a thought. But this one – this one troubles me, makes me nervous; for there is no telling what an unhinged creature like this may think of next. ...

Indeed ...

Chapter 4:
The Lombrosian Moment: Bridging the Visible and the Invisible, or Restricting the Gaze in the Name of Progress?

Part I

Visualising criminality

Visitors to the Palazzo delle Belle Art, in Rome in the autumn of 1885 became the witnesses of a most unusual spectacle. On display in one hall was a huge array of objects including well over three hundred skulls and anatomical casts, probably several thousand portrait photographs and drawings of epileptics and delinquents, insane and born criminals, and maps, graphs and publications summing up the results of research in the new scientific discipline of criminal anthropology. The exhibition was displayed for only one week next to the assembly hall in which some 130 European criminologists, anthropologists, psychiatrists, jurists and physicians had convened for the first international Congress of Criminal Anthropology between 16 and 20 November. The sight of the place must have been dizzying. Forty-three exhibitors, most of them Italian some French, German, Hungarian and Russian, showed their personal collections which characterised their individual achievements in the field. Laid out on tables and shelves were series of skulls, demonstrating the typical features of epileptics, street robbers, or suicidels, and individual specimens of special cases: megalocephalics, prostitutes, murderers; brains conserved in alcohol or, after a special method invented by Giacomini in gelatine, which allowed the fine slicing of the brain for microscopic examination; plaster casts of heads skulls faces, ears, and no less than five completely conserved heads, two of nihilists, two of delinquents, and that of the infamous bandit Giona La Gala, which was there in the exhibition of the Genoa penitentiary, complete with his brain, tattoos, and gall bladder stones found during the autopsy.

Maps, diagrams and other graphic displays hung on the walls, illustrating the geographical distribution of various sorts of crimes, the rapport of growing suicide and insanity rates with the rise of crime, or the influence of variations in temperature and grain prices on Italian criminality. Clay and wax figures made by prisoners and mental patients, examples of their writings and drawings, an album with copies of two thousand tattoos, all illustrating aspects of criminal or insane creativity. And in many of the individual collections, second only to skulls, were portraits of criminals, drawings as well as photographs. (Broeckmann 1995: 3)

Positivist criminology strives to render criminality a visible presence. It should be no surprise that the first Congress of Criminal Anthropology of 1885 presented such a diverse exhibition of material culture.[1] In walking through the hall delegates lived, physically experienced through the senses of sight and touch, the interaction between personal desire, classification system and material collection.[2] Although organised and hosted in Rome, and reflecting many of the concerns of a group of individuals loosely referred to as the Italian school, the 1885 Congress provided an interdisciplinary arena populated by dilettantes with a range of personal and institutional training. The meeting offered them expert status in laying out a new terrain: one that came to be labelled the science of criminology.[3] The field was contested, and it has generally been considered that the clearest division was between the French social statistical approach championed by Lacassagne – which emphasised that the process of reading statistical regularities and the mapping of crime showed the influence of the social environment – and the anthropological epitomised by Lombroso. Quetelet's influence is normally read as favouring Lacassagne – even allowing for subtle differences in emphasis amongst each camp's sympathisers – and Lombroso's group is now relegated to the status of quasiscience (e.g. Gould 1981; but contrast Taylor (1981) for an espousal of the biological basis of crime). This dismissal overlooks a key element to Lombroso's science, namely the desire to find a stable way of recognising the propensities that were revealed in statistical aggregations. Lombroso's move to a multifactor analysis is a complicated path from his original supposition that Quetelet had revealed that the average man and the contrasting men at the extremes of the bell curve were different; different constitutionally, reflecting differences in underlying reality.

This had clear practical policy implications. The school of thought we now refer to as classical criminology used penal law as a strategy of control; Lombroso's argument was that the penal law relied upon assumptions – such as rational choice – that reflected our self-understanding, but while they may work for the average man, or the ordinary man, society was not composed of such alone. A visuality that differentiated types would allow a scientific response tailored to each.

Drawing out Lombroso's intellectual foundations appears difficult, partly because, as this Congress demonstrated, we are faced with a freedom of experimentation, a social space governed only loosely by a relatively unstable set of disciplinary norms where individuals and groups sought to make an impact, to demonstrate their science through invoking presence and through their scientific discourse to allow the objects to communicate, to demonstrate answers to questions and to reveal identities. Lombroso brought the largest, at first sight eclectic, collection to display:

> There were seventy skulls of Italian delinquents, another thirty of epileptics, and the only complete skeleton in the whole exhibition, that of a thief. Further anatomical evidence of criminality was provided by two plaster casts of delinquent heads, and a set of specimens of conserved skin with tattoos. There were three hundred photographs of epileptics and, collected in an album, another three hundred photographs of German criminals. Of twenty-four Italian and foreign criminals, Lombroso showed life-size portrait drawings, complete with biographies. Among the results of criminal creativity in Lombroso's collection was a jug with graphic scratchings made by Cavagilia, a suicidal murderer and thief. Furthermore, there were graphological samples from delinquents, and two hundred manuscripts and graphics by mental patients and finally, some graphic tables and publications as proof of Lombroso's own scientific endeavours. (Broeckmann 1995: 3)

The collection was not without focus – it cohered around tactics of reading the body and the handicrafts of the deviant in search of similarity underlying the appearance of diversity. The presentation of the skulls along with products of the mind of the insane and the criminal displayed a confidence in a particular method of moving from the material and visible to conjectures of an invisible structuring. The theoretical movement was a passage from confusing appearance to a more certain reality made possible by the *expert*. Anthropology could demonstrate the natural contours of criminality while sociology could reveal the conditions in which criminality expressed itself (as he was to state at the Second Congress in 1889: 'it is not the opportunity that makes the thief, it is the opportunity which makes the individual predisposed to steal commit a theft'. (quoted Broeckmann 1995: 3)

Yet this demarcation between criminal anthropology and sociology – with their differing systems of classification and collection – shared the common heritage of statistical regularities. They differed in relating the statistical representations to the narratives of the civilising process. This all-too-human organisation was obscured, simply assumed as unproblematic. At the 1885 Congress many delegates appeared to believe that these collections of objects could speak for themselves (positivism); however, Jean Baudrillard's question cannot be so easily escaped (1994: 24): can objects 'ever institute themselves as a viable language? Can they ever be fashioned into a discourse orientated otherwise than to toward oneself?' Lombroso's project was a complex of activities that were founded on the reading of statistical data, new technologies and places of measurement (e.g. the volumetric glove, pelvimeter, craniograph anfossi, see Lombroso 1911: Part II, chapter 1; and the prison, the clinic and the asylum), a selective understanding of the emerging Darwinianism and, above all, confidence in the location of the observer (e.g. Lombroso) in the civilising process. Ultimately, the project fails, not because of a lack of scientific effort or application of accepted norms, but because without a reflexive understanding of the position of the observer in 'the civilising process' the materials are indeed bound together by the interests and technologies employed by the observer.

The events must be contextualised, for a simple dismissal of the project as pseudoscience makes it possible for criminological texts – among other sciences – to avoid acknowledging how the project to make the criminal's body visible, to make the deviant recognisable, to render pathology transparent, relied upon a prioritising of the reference point of the observer and his interests, and had the potential to be taken up in practices of exclusion that have at their logical extremity extermination. This reflexive blindness was part of the constituting process of the European (then globalising) scientific project. The science of rendering the 'deviant' as an observable pathological entity, a project in which the aim was for the general populace to see as equally well as the scientist, was allowed by the history of European technological power over non-European others (including the bio-social power of resistance to germs, which, when introduced elsewhere in the globe, kill) who could be exterminated; and because of the fact of their extermination they were inferior. Tied to an image of the civilising process in which the 'inferior' were to be removed in the process of globalisation, it followed that the pathologically deviant were in part a remnant of the debris of the civilising/evolutionary process.

The mainstream story of visualising the criminal body: an intellectual revolution?

The writers of criminological texts that seek to be understandable by more than a tiny handful of specialists usually contextualise the development of what is referred to as an Italian school, by reference to Lombroso – the 'father' of scientific criminology – as if criminology was the product of certain 'pioneers'.[4] The context for these pioneers' thoughts is presented as a break away from legalism and the social contract assumptions of Beccaria to the biological evolutionism of Darwinism as providing a new intellectual milieu. More detailed studies now stress continuities, rather than dramatic oppositions,[5] but the summary of Vold and Bernard (*Theoretical Criminology*, 2nd edn 1979: 35–6[6]) is characteristic of textbook history. The century between Beccaria and Lombroso was said to constitute an 'intellectual revolution', methodologically and existentially. 'The logic and basic methodology of objective, empirical, and experimental science became well established', while many looked to Darwin to supply the 'answers to the old, old question. What sort of creature is man?' and found them – we are told – in his *Origin of Species* (1859) and *Descent of Man* (1871). 'Man was beginning to appear to science as one of many creatures, with no special link with Divinity … as a being whose conduct was determined by his biological and cultural antecedents'.

Lombroso's classic work *L'uomo dilinquente* (1876) is taken as the foundational text for positive criminology (in part for the massive study by Goring (1913) it stimulated).[7] It is sometimes today placed in the camp of degeneration literature, reflecting both the fears of nineteenth-century gentlemen-intellectuals of social and biological decline within an otherwise progressive western civilisation, and the idea of being able to visualise and identify 'types', thus enabling one to differentiate the progressive from the regressive. The techniques of representation in Lombroso's text span the gap between physiognomic anthropology and clinical criminology, directly utilising the representational methodologies of the cousin of Charles Darwin, Francis Galton.[8] Galton had developed a photographic methodology of composite photography that was held to reveal 'types'. Lombroso argued that phrenology and physiognomy demonstrated that criminality was the sign of a primitive form within modern society. This was an active semiotics, a positive methodological invocation of presence. *L'uomo dilinquente* not only contained several pages of photos of offenders ('Faces of criminality') that the reader was invited to scan (and with guidance thus to share in Lombroso's methodology) but it also presented several series of composite photographs of 'criminal skulls' that were held to demonstrate their anachronistic structures. Photography seemed to be able to demonstrate both the 'stigmata' of atavism (empirical evidence of the primitive condition of the subject) and, by means of composite portraits, to reveal the underlying features of those individuals who could be assigned to one or other 'criminal type'. Criminal types could be revealed in large tables containing photographic portraits of convicted criminals. By implication, Lombroso argued, it would be possible to establish, through the direct observation of 'stigmata', whether someone accused of a crime was the perpetrator. This was no allusion or metaphor, but direct inference; it was intended to a tool of a practical investigative criminology.[9]

Locating criminality within a lens of degeneration opens up the subject for interdisciplinary study and had distinct political overtones; criminal anthropology could play an important role in the defence of society and help identify causes of problems for social integration.[10] A northern Italian, Lombroso's training and early service as a medical doctor took place in the context of the unification struggle to build an Italian nation state. In the field of social medicine he was particularly interested in the prevalence of pellagra and cretinism in Calabria. From 1862 he conducted large-scale research into the ethnic diversity of the Italian people, using emerging anthropometric methodologies. He depicted crucial problems for unification lying in the racial diversity of the peoples that were to make up the new nation state and seemed to offer a scientific basic for the claims of 'atavism' or backwardness of the peoples of the south or *Mezzogiorno*. The differential spacial location and associated identity must be noted. Niepce Nicefore, a follower of Lombroso, would express this clearly in a 1901 book entitled *Northern Italians and Southern Italians*:

> Not all the parts which compose [Italy's] multiple and differentiated organism have progressed equally in the course of civilisation; some have remained behind, due to inept government or as the sad result of other factors and are unable to advance except at great effort, whilst the others have progressed dynamically. The Mezzogiorno and the Islands find themselves in the sad condition of still having the sentiments and customs, the substance if not the form – of past centuries. They are less evolved and less civilised then the [society] to be found in Northern Italy. (quoted Pick 1989: 114–15)

Responsible for mental patients in several hospitals in the North from the 1860s, Lombroso took a chair in legal medicine and public hygiene at Turin University in 1876. In the Introduction to *Criminal Man*, an English edition of his work prepared by his daughter and collaborator, Gina Lombroso Ferrero, published in 1911,[11] Lombroso set out how he arrived at the 'two fundamental ideas' underlying his work: namely,

> an essential point [is] the study not of crime in the abstract, but of the criminal himself; and
> the congenital criminal [is] an anomaly, partly pathological and partly atavistic, a revival of the primitive savage.

These ideas 'did not suggest themselves ... instantaneously under the spell of a single deep impression, but were the offspring of a series of impressions'. First, he 'was struck by a characteristic that distinguished the honest soldier from his vicious comrade: the extent to which the latter was tattooed and the indecency of the designs that covered his body'. Second, he resolved 'to make the patient, not the disease, the object of attention', consequently, in studying the insane, he 'applied to the clinical examination ... the study of the skull, with measurements and weights, by means of the esthesiometer and craniometer'. Moving to the study of crime, Lombroso realised 'that the a priori studies on crime in the abstract, hitherto pursued by jurists, especially in Italy, with singular acumen, should be superseded by the direct analytical study of the criminal, compared with normal individuals and the insane.' He began to study 'criminals in the Italian prisons', whereupon he reports a moment of true enlightenment (Figure 4.1):

> I made the acquaintance of the famous brigand Vilella. This man possessed such extraordinary agility, that he had been known to scale steep mountain heights bearing a sheep on his shoulders. His cynical effrontery was such that he openly boasted of his crimes. On his death one cold grey November morning, I was deputed to make the *postmortem*, and on laying open the skull I found on the occipital part, exactly on the spot where a spine is found in the normal skull, a distinct depression which I named *median occipital fossa*, because of its situation precisely in the middle of the occiput as in inferior animals, especially rodents. This depression, as in the case of animals, was correlated with the hypertrophy of the *vermis*, known in birds as the middle cerebellum.

Figure 4.1 The Skull of Vilella, preserved in a glass presentation box, on Lombroso's desk. (Photo: Wayne Morrison) Lombroso had continued his account: 'I was further encouraged in this bold hypothesis by the results of my studies on Verzeni, a criminal convicted of sadism and rape, who showed the cannibalistic instincts of primitive anthropophagists and the ferocity of beasts of prey.' Horn (2003: 31) considers that this account, at the end of Lombroso's life, possesses 'a mythic quality', but also relates that in his original 1871 article Lombroso had already stressed how important that particular skull was and that the anomaly observed was 'unique in the natural and pathological history of man'. The skull was put in a glass presentation case and permanently displayed on Lombroso's desk, where it remains in his reconstructed study in the *Museo de Criminal Anthropology* (Lombroso), Turin (see Morrison 2004b)

This was a revelation following the terms of Plato's simile of the Cave – Lombroso was confronted with a reality that held him in its grip.

> At the sight of that skull, I seemed to see all of a sudden, lighted up as a vast plain under a flaming sky, the problem of the nature of the criminal – an atavistic being who reproduces in his person the ferocious instincts of primitive humanity and the inferior animals. Thus were explained anatomically the enormous jaws, high cheek-bones, prominent superciliary arches, solitary lines in the palms, extreme size of the orbits, handle-shaped or sessile ears found in criminals, savages, and apes, insensibility to pain, extremely acute sight, tattooing, excessive idleness, love of orgies, and the irresistible craving for evil for its own sake, the desire not only to extinguish life in the victim, but to mutilate the corpse, tear its flesh, and drink its blood.

Not only can he now see certain clear signs of the criminal (stigmata), but also the meaning of these are situated in an order of being beyond the visible: a realm of progress and of reversion that locates ourselves and the 'others'. Lombroso relates this in terms of the progress of civilisation towards true enlightenment. But how is this access to a second order of visibility achieved? And how is this progress therein made apparent?

The visible and the invisible: reducing the other

Lombroso's work involves techniques of reading and making visible an 'other', and the imposition of a structure of power on that 'other' to position and capture him for techniques of theoretical reproduction. There are levels of location: north (civilised/Lombroso) versus south (degeneration), viewer/object and differential positioning within evolutionary progress. Tracing the maps of crime and other factors for Italy, Lombroso saw differences in civilisation. Thus a uniform rule of law in the shape of a penal code would be a mistake for in many regions 'an almost medieval barbarism still reign supreme'. Law was appropriate for people who had reached the same stage of civilisation. But upon 'examination' we find that the 'criminal population' is to be 'distinguished from the average member of the community' by physical signs, discernable to the trained observer.[12] *The Female Offender* (1895), for example, begins with the study of 'normal women' to which the deviations are compared (In political terms Lombroso was a liberal and he argued against the 'tyranny' to which women were subjected and against their exclusion from higher education).

There are two linked methodological patterns at work: the first is the allocation of stigmata and the reading of the skull, aided by the composite portrait to establish the criminal type; the second is the transference of the visual into the meta-object, the grand narrative of evolutionary progress and social hygiene.

First the dream of immediate transference, or a semiotics that allowed criminality to be revealed.

This was both a reflection of power and a consequence of global social divisions.

At least two types of power/knowledge production lie intertwined. One is the power of the institution, in this case the dissecting room, to produce knowledge out of its practices, epitomised by the phrenological heritage of Gall. The second was a mobile power to distinguish, to locate types in an evolutionary sequence. This power was harnessed to the specific problem of governance, but was also the product of a governing mentality. We must be careful to note this duality: the power to distinguish is itself a product of a distinguishing mentality.

The phrenological heritage. The belief that facial indicators reflected more fundamental proclivities and the systematic study of their underlying mechanisms would tell science more about the basic constitution of the human being was relatively widespread earlier in the nineteenth century. The phrenology of the brilliant anatomist Franz Gall, and his disciple Juergen Spurzheim reached its height in the third decade of the century.[13] Theories of Gall and Spurzheim seemed fully in keeping with the universalistic claims of enlightenment methodology: namely, that there was 'throughout all of nature, a general law that the properties of bodies act with an energy proportional to their size, the form and size of the brain regulate the form and size of the skull' (1812: 226). In empirical studies of human and animal brains and crania, Gall and Spurzheim related skills, talents and character dispositions to cranial structures, locating over 33 'traits' in specific parts of the brain. These traits were initially located visually through illustration or sculpture, but the development of photography seemed to promise a greater objectivity. Cowling relates that 'reading the bumps' became a popular craze in the early Victorian era but this popularisation meant acceptance of claims that far exceeded the neurological value envisaged by its founders. However, this 'played an important part in focussing the attention of anthropologists on the cranium, which, throughout the century, was to remain the prime index of mental capacity and racial identity' (Cowling 1989: 40).

The composite portrait. The composite portrait was largely the result of Galton's attempts to accurately measure the 'other' and locate types of the human races. The trope of his desire is usually traced to certain events on his expedition in South West Africa in 1852–4 when he encountered a striking African woman. In his account of his expedition, Galton referred to a Nama woman, the wife of one of his host's servants, as a 'Venus among Hottentots'. He described himself as being 'perfectly aghast at her development'; of course, as a 'scientific man', he was 'exceedingly anxious to obtain accurate measurements of her shape'. However, the circumstances were difficult and Glaton reported that he 'felt in a dilemma as I gazed at her form'. Galton was proud of the solution he devised, namely, taking a series of observations 'upon her figure' with his sextant, making an outline drawing while she stood at a distance under a tree. Then he 'boldly pulled out' his measuring tape to calculate the distance and worked out the results using trigonometry and logarithms.[14] This passion for measurement of the 'other' was soon to take a particular technological form:

> Galton came home to England and turned his insatiable desire for numbers and measurements increasingly towards domestic 'problems' of inheritance and anthropometry informed by Darwinism. He suffered a succession of 'maladies prejudicial to mental effort', culminating in a breakdown in 1866; amongst other disappointments, it was in this period that it became apparent that his own marriage was

likely to prove infertile; he became ever more fascinated by the evolution and inheritance at large, urging Britain's transformation from 'a mob of slaves, clinging together, incapable of self-government and begging to be led' ... into a new race of 'vigorous self-reliant men' ... In Galton's work, deeply troubling questions about the nation's level of social and political maturity, and specifically about the effects of a changing and widening electoral constituency after 1867, were deflected onto the problem of the racial body and mind; politics was dissolved into mathematics and biology. (Pick 1989: 197)

The methodological breakthrough came with the combination of Quetelet's statistical conception of the normal and the application of photography. After 1865 Galton employed photographic devices in order to capture and display a physiognomic record of 'degenerate mental types' and criminals. The Inspector of Prisons, Edward du Cane, provided photographs of prisoners and Galton attempted to identify the common features of violent criminals, felons and sexual offenders (as already mentioned, a collection of such photographs appeared in Lombroso's major text under the title 'The faces of criminality'). Quetelet's statistical averaging pointed him to experimentally find 'average' physical characteristics in a single image, so that a normal distribution of characteristics could be observable in the same way as a graph might indicate the relation of a populations characteristics to their statistical mean, a bell-shaped curve. To create a composite image, Galton re-photographed subjects on the same plate by successive multiple exposures. This provided the 'photographic mean' of the subject 'type'. These types meshed with the 'different physiognomic classes'. The finished images gave a new presence. 'The special villainous irregularities in the later [individual portraits] have disappeared, and the common humanity that underlies them has prevailed. They represent, not the criminal, but the man who is liable to fall into crime' (Galton 1878: 135). The composite image was achieved by taking a series of very short multiple shots; it produced a synthesised image that was held to transform the diverse appearances of the individuals who formed a particular class or race into an 'average' or truly representative characteristic physiognomy.

> It is the essential notion of race that there should be some idea typical form from which the individuals may deviate in all directions, but about which they chiefly cluster. Now there can hardly be a more appropriate method of discovering the central physiognomical type of any race or group than that of composite portraiture. (Galton 1882: 26; quoted Hamilton and Hargreaves 2001: 98)

This methodology could be used to ascertain the 'condition of the race' and fitted into the philosophy of eugenics. The residuum of the population could be observed, identified and measures taken to separate them out from the rest of society.

But what do these images actually represent? In *L'uomo dilinquente* Lombroso presented composite portraits of skulls specifying that these showed various types of criminals. The suspicion that Lombroso relied upon a notion of direct and unmediated transference lay at the heart of the criticism of Lombroso's use of photography by the French experimental photographer Arthur Batut and others. For Batut, the resulting composite was actually an invocation of something other, which lay beyond the visible. The composite was a form of virtual reality, an allusion or 'image of the invisible' that was always open to interpretation, whereas Batut suspected, Lombroso made direct, physiognomic links between physical characteristics (stigmata), mentality and 'criminal' type. At the Paris Congress of 1889 Lombroso defended his thesis, asserting his was a careful statistical study and that his criminal types were revealed through the clarity of Galtonian photography:

> Furthermore, in other to be safe from all reproaches, I have in recent years, applied Galtonian photography to the study of the criminal type, and *the irreproachable testimony of the sun has responded to me much better than that of men*; one can, then, see here that there really are criminal types which are divided into sub-groups: CROOKS, THIEVES, and MURDERERS, in the latter of which all the features accumulate, while in other they are less developed. (*Proceedings*, quoted Broeckmann 1995: chapter 1, emphasis added)

The characteristics of criminal types were revealed by the 'unquestionable mediation of the sun' – issues of culture or narrative positioning need not be engaged with.

Part II

The Darwinian imagination: moving from the social to the technical

By the time of Darwin's death in 1882 it was becoming commonplace to describe the times as the century of Darwin and to claim that Man's place was to be understood through theses of biological evolution. But what was the relationship in developing a criminological imagination?[15] How could crime in its totality be grasped, what effect was there on Hobbes' invocation of power and the epistemological warrant of the sovereign as the defining entity? In our specific context is the assumption that Lombroso reflected, albeit poorly, a new Darwinian-intellectual world picture correct, or is his name now justly used as 'a kind of metaphor for an aberrant tradition'? (Pick 1989: 111)

Darwin is best remembered for his 1859 *Origin of the Species*, outlining a picture of life (including human) being embedded in the processes of an always-changing natural environment. In large part because of our contemporary common sense of what is taken to be 'Darwinianism', few now read Darwin's original texts. His later work, *On the Descent of Man* (1871), is assumed to follow on from the *Origin of the Species*, simply fitting humanity more fully into the original theoretical framework. This is a mistake. We now accept the views outlined in the *Origin* of 'natural selection'. It is crucial to recognise that natural selection is a relativist process: evolution occurs through countless small variations of a species, some of which fit better with the environment. The theory is both relativist (environments are simply different, complex and themselves subject to change) and specifically rejects that the notion of stages of development, or a hierarchy of evolution, can be cast in moralist terms. The social evolution of Spencer and the hierarchical sociology he created – at odds with the views in Darwin's *Origin* – highly popular in his time, have today little currency. However, when Darwin came to deal specifically with humanity in *On the Descent of Man*, he presented 'a view so precisely opposed' (Ingold 1986) to that outlined in *The Origin of Species* that it is as if there were two Darwins. In fact there were: there was Charles Darwin, an educated middle-class male, the inhabitant of a particular locality – the 'civilised space' of England – and Darwin the traveller–explorer; a person who not only explored and transgressed the boundaries of conventional theory, but who had also physically traversed the Globe.

There is a popular image of Darwin enclosed in his Victorian study obsessed with the study of barnacles. The image conveys intellectual concentration, a filtering out of the extraneous and the irrelevant, as well as the virtue of remaining immersed and faithful to the material in front of the observer. These are key elements of the appeal of scientific positivism. Positivism requires control over the process of observation and recording, since the key to accepting the process as scientific will be reportage and replication of results. The ideal location is the laboratory and such an environment needs to be constructed, while it is essential to build in barriers preventing contamination. Yet theory is a way of seeing and depends upon a heritage of interpretation. One brings into the laboratory (or the clinic, etc.) a training in seeing. Even a representational theory of language usage – i.e. that the resulting report is true if it accurately restates the 'facts', and these are the facts of some 'independent reality' – must accept that the process involves a practice. Varieties of representational theory strive to make the practice transparent so that such practice can be controlled for and said not to influence the result. The fact that we share a common world, and this world is commensurable, allows the results to be open to replication and attempted falsification. But there is a fallacy in this notion. It is clear that we share a common world, but in another sense it is clear that we do not share our world in common. Indeed we may have a common world only to the extent that we understand how we variedly but commonly participate in the multivarious activities that constitute this changing world. The essence of understanding may then lie with realising how we participate in those activities. In recording the world of facts, what then is the role of the recorder in the activities that constitute this world? Or, in the total theory that Darwin was later to set out, where did human action fit? And what was the position of Darwin himself?

Although the result of protracted study, the ideas systematised in Darwin's two contrasting works (separated by a decade) were the product of merging diverse intellectual remnants and the empirical observations Darwin undertook during the voyage of HMS *Beagle* (lasting from 27 December 1831 to 2 October 1836) round the world. His journal was published in 1839 under the popular title of *Darwin's Voyage in the Beagle.*[16] Darwin called this voyage 'by far the most important event' of his life, for it 'determined' his 'whole career'. The author of the biographical introduction to the later editions of the journal argues that Darwin's discovery was not the simple proposition that 'species became changed in time', but to present 'a reasonable mode by which such changes could be supposed to come about, supporting it by a multitude of skilfully arranged facts' (p. viii).

Life and death – creation and destruction – were common themes: 'Certainly, no fact in the long history of the world is so startling, as the wide and repeated extermination of its inhabitants' (p. 126). What of the actions of humankind on other species? And Darwin's personal understanding? At the time of his voyage Darwin was in his early thirties. The journal is dedicated to Charles Lyell with thanks for Lyell's 'admirable' *Principles of Geology*, the major reference text that accompanied Darwin. There are numerous references to the *Principles* in the journal, but Malthus is another presence felt, and refuting the French theorist Cuvier's thesis of sudden catastrophes determining the fate of species is a theme. For all the technical issues and observations on fossils, however, Hobbes' question – without being explicitly stated – pervades the journal:

> is there justice in nature? Or is justice simply a matter of our language usage? Or a specific human use of language?

Darwin never satisfactorily answered it.

It would be dangerous to draw out Darwin's intellectual grasp and the movement in his observations from social concerns to natural history and geology by presenting short quotes only, rather extended readings allow us to have more confidence that it truly is his voice presented. The intellectual current in Europe should also be borne in mind. While Darwin was on his voyage, for example, John Howison in 1834 published his critique of European Colonialism specifically adopting a tactic of multiple view points.[17] Herbert Spencer, who probably would have read Darwin's journal, wrote 19 years after Darwin began his journey, a clear summary of a position many had held for some decades:

> The forces which are clearing out the great scheme of perfect happiness, taking no account of incidental suffering, exterminate such sections of mankind as stand in their way ... Be it human or be it brute – the hindrance must be got rid of. (1967 [1850]: 416)

Spencer was to present the fashionable view, but there was another argument, namely, it was necessary to control colonial administrations and settlers. In his 1838 lectures at Oxford on *Colonization and Colonies*, delivered 1839, 1840 and 1841, published 1861 (reprint 1967), Herman Merivale rejected the argument that the white was 'destined to extirpate the savage'. The main reason for the destruction of the natives was simple: the behaviour of the powerful. Beyond the shores of the civilised space of Europe, 'civilisation' was in the hands of 'the trader, the backwoodsman, the pirate, the bushranger', who were free to act as they wished, often aided by the authorities:

> The history of European settlements in America, Africa and Australia, presents everywhere the same general features – a wide and sweeping destruction of native races by the uncontroled violence of individuals, if not of colonial authorities, followed by tardy attempts on the part of governments to repair the acknowledged crime.

This, Darwin encountered for himself. As he recounts of his time in South America in 1833[18]

> During my stay at Bahia Blanca, while waiting for the *Beagle*, the place was in a constant state of excitement, from rumours of wars and victories, between the troops of Rosas and the wild Indians. One day an account came that a small party forming one of the postas on the line to Buenos Ayres, had been found all murdered. The next day three hundred men arrived from the Colorado, under the command of Commandant Miranda. A large portion of these men were Indians (*mansos*, or tame), belonging to the tribe of the Cacique Bernantio. They passed the night here; and it was impossible to conceive anything more wild and savage than the scene of their bivouac. Some drank till they were intoxicated; others swallowed the steaming blood of the cattle slaughtered for their suppers, and then, being sick from drunkenness, they cast it up again, and were besmeared with filth and gore ...
>
> In the morning they started for the scene of the murder, with orders to follow the 'rastro', or track, even if it led them to Chile. We subsequently heard that the wild Indians had escaped into the great Pampas, and from some cause the track had been missed. ...
>
> A few days afterwards I saw another troop of these banditti-like soldiers start on an expedition against a tribe of Indians at the small Salinas, who had been betrayed by a prisoner cacique. The Spaniard who brought the orders for this expedition was a very

intelligent man. He gave me an account of the last engagement at which he was present.

Some Indians, who had been taken prisoners, gave information of a tribe living north of the Colorado. Two hundred soldiers were sent; and they first discovered the Indians by a cloud of dust from their horses' feet, as they chanced to be travelling. The country was mountainous and wild, and it must have been far in the interior, for the Cordillera were in sight. The Indians, men, women, and children, were about one hundred and ten in number, and they were nearly all taken or killed, for the soldiers sabre every man. The Indians are now so terrified that they offer no resistance in a body, but each flies, neglecting even his wife and children; but when overtaken, like wild animals, they fight against any number to the last moment. One dying Indian seized with his teeth the thumb of his adversary, and allowed his own eye to be forced out sooner than relinquish his hold. Another, who was wounded, feigned death, keeping a knife ready to strike one more fatal blow. My informer said, when he was pursuing an Indian, the man cried out for mercy, at the same time that he was covertly loosing the bolas from his waist, meaning to whirl it round his head and so strike his pursuer. 'I however struck him with my sabre to the ground, and then got off my horse, and cut his throat with my knife.' This is a dark picture; but how much more shocking is the unquestionable fact, that all the women who appear above twenty years old are massacred in cold blood! When I exclaimed that this appeared rather inhuman, he answered, 'Why, what can be done? They breed so!'

Every one here is fully convinced that this is the most just war, because it is against barbarians. Who would believe in this age that such atrocities could be committed in a Christian civilised country? The children of the Indians are saved, to be sold or given away as servants, or rather slaves for as long a time as the owners can make them believe themselves slaves; but I believe in their treatment there is little to complain of.

In the battle four men ran away together. They were pursued, one was killed, and the other three were taken alive. They turned out to be messengers or ambassadors from a large body of Indians, united in the common cause of defence, near the Cordillera. The tribe to which they had been sent was on the point of holding a grand council; the feast of mares' flesh was ready, and the dance prepared: in the morning the ambassadors were to have returned to the Cordillera. They were remarkably fine men, very fair, above six feet high, and all under thirty years of age. The three survivors of course possessed very valuable information; and to extort this they were placed in a line. The two first being questioned, answered, 'No se' (I do not know), and were one after the other shot. The third also said, 'No se'; adding, 'Fire, I am a man, and can die!' Not one syllable would they breathe to injure the united cause of their country! The conduct of the above-mentioned cacique was very different: he saved his life by betraying the intended plan of warfare, and the point of union in the Andes. It was believed that there were already six or seven hundred Indians together, and that in summer their numbers would be doubled. Ambassadors were to have been sent to the Indians at the small Salinas, near Bahia Blanca, whom I have mentioned that this same cacique had betrayed. The communication, therefore, between the Indians, extends from the Cordillera to the coast of the Atlantic.

General Rosas's plan is to kill all stragglers, and having driven the remainder to a common point, to attack them in a body, in the summer, with the assistance of the Chilenos. This operation is to be repeated for three successive years. I imagine the summer is chosen as the time for the main attack, because the plains are then without water, and the Indians can only travel in particular directions. The escape of the Indians to the south of the Rio Negro, where in such a vast unknown country they would be safe, is prevented by a treaty with the Tehuelches to this effect; – that Rosas pays them so much to slaughter every Indian who passes to the south of the river, but if they fail in so doing, they themselves are to be exterminated. The war is waged chiefly against the Indians near the Cordillera; for many of the tribes on this eastern side are fighting with Rosas. The general, however, like Lord Chesterfield, thinking that his friends may in a future day become his enemies, always places them in the front ranks, so that their numbers may be thinned. Since leaving South America we have heard that this war of extermination completely failed.

Among the captive girls taken in the same engagement, there were two very pretty Spanish ones, who had been carried away by the Indians when young, and could now only speak the Indian tongue. From their account they must have come from Salta, a distance in a straight line of nearly one thousand miles. This gives one a grand idea of the immense territory over which the Indians roam; yet, great as it is, I think there will not, in another half century, be a wild Indian northward of the Rio Negro. The warfare is too bloody to last; the Christians killing every Indian, and the Indians doing the same by the Christians. It is melancholy to trace how the Indians have given way before the Spanish invaders. Schirdel says that in 1535, when Buenos Ayres was founded, there were villages containing two and three thousand inhabitants. Even in Falconer's time (1750) the Indians made inroads as far as Luxan, Areco, and Arrecife, but now they are driven beyond the Salado. Not only have whole tribes been exterminated, but the remaining Indians have become more barbarous: instead of living in large villages, and being employed in the arts of fishing, as well as of the chase, they now wander about the open plains, without home or fixed occupation.

So Darwin can recount a narrative of extermination in which man is the active agent. We may not know how much he realised before he undertook his voyage that the progress in civilising the 'Americas' and the reduction in the state of the natives was the consequence of European action aimed at 'extermination'. But we can note his perception as to the future. For, although Darwin relates that he subsequently heard that 'this war of extermination completely failed', it was ongoing. Later actions, such as those of General Julio Roca in 1897, cleansed much of the land (Patagonia) below the Rio Negro of the Araucano Indians in what was called a 'civilising mission'.[19] Such speculation takes up only a fraction of his chapter, indeed, in the midst of this 'melacolony' story, he finds a pleasing aesthetic.

I heard also some account of an engagement which took place, a few weeks previously to the one mentioned, at Cholechel. This is a very important station on account of being a pass for horses; and it was, in consequence, for some time the head-quarters of a division of the army. When the troops first arrived there they found a tribe of Indians, of whom they killed twenty or thirty. The cacique escaped in a manner which astonished every one. The chief Indians always have one or two picked horses, which they keep ready for any urgent occasion. On one of these, an old white horse, the cacique sprung, taking with him his little son. The horse had neither saddle nor bridle. To avoid the shots, the Indian rode in the peculiar method of his nation; namely with an arm round the horse's neck, and one leg only on its back thus hanging on one side, he was seen patting the horse's head and talking to him. The pursuers urged every effort in the chase; the Commandant three times changed his horse, but all in vain. The old Indian father and his son escaped, and were free. What a fine picture one can form in one's mind, – the naked, bronze-like figure of the old man with his little boy, riding like a Mazeppa on the white horse; thus leaving far behind him the host of his pursuers!

Darwin does not dwell too long on these matters; his attention is soon drawn back to science. He ends the chapter by recounting an item of archaeological importance:

> I saw one day a soldier striking fire with a piece of flint, which I immediately recognized as having been a part of the head of an arrow. He told me it was found near the island of Cholechel, and that they are frequently picked up there. It was between two and three inches long, and therefore twice as large as those now used in Tierra del Fuego: it was made of opaque cream-coloured flint, but the point and barbs had been intentionally broken off. It is well known that no Pampas Indians now use bows and arrows. I believe a small tribe in Banda Oriental must be excepted; but they are widely separated from the Pampas Indians, and border close on those tribes that inhabit the forest, and live on foot. It appears, therefore, that these arrow-heads are antiquarian relics of the Indians, before the great change in habits consequent on the introduction of the horse into South America.

How did Darwin view the 'other' that he was coming across?[20] It is clear from the journal that he felt able to rank different varieties of 'savages'. When the Beagle spent time at the bottom of South America, at Tierra del Fuego he met species he placed at the bottom of the ranking:

> While going one day on shore near Wollaston Island, we pulled alongside a canoe with six Fuegians. These were the most abject and miserable creatures I anywhere beheld. On the east coast ... the natives have guanaco cloaks, and on the west, they possess seal-skins. Amongst these central tribes the men generally have an otter-skin, or some small scrap about as large as a pocket-handkerchief, which is barely sufficient to cover their backs as low down as their loins. It is laced across the breast by strings, and according as the wind blows, it is shifted from side to side. But these Fuegians in the canoe were quite naked, and even one full-grown woman was absolutely so. It was raining heavily, and the fresh water, together with the spray, trickled down her body. In another harbour not far distant, a woman, who was suckling a recently-born child, came one day alongside the vessel, and remained there out of mere curiosity, whilst the sleet fell and thawed on her naked bosom, and on the skin of her naked baby! These poor wretches were stunted in their growth, their hideous faces bedaubed with white paint, their skins filthy and greasy, their hair entangled, their voices discordant, and their gestures violent. Viewing such men, one can hardly make oneself believe that they are fellow-creatures, and inhabitants of the same world. It is a common subject of conjecture what pleasure in life some of the lower animals can enjoy; how much more reasonably the same question may be asked with respect to these barbarians! (p. 154)

Darwin's account of 'these barbarians' is somewhat different from that of Johann Reinhold Forster's observations (quoted Thomas 1994), made in another publication resulting from a voyage round the world, namely, his participation in Cook's second voyage to the Pacific of 1772–5.

> We found them [the inhabitants of Tierra del Fuego] to be a short, squat race, with large heads; their colour yellowish brown; the features harsh, the face broad, the cheek-bones high and prominent, the nose flat, the nostrils and mouth large, and the whole countenance without meaning ... Their women are much of the same features, colour, and form as the men, and generally have long hanging breasts, and besides the seal-skin on their backs, a small patch of the skin of a bird or seal to cover their privities. All have a countenance announcing nothing but wretchedness. They seem to be good-natured, friendly, and harmless; but remarkably stupid, being incapable of understanding our signs, which, however, were very intelligible to the nations of the South Sea.

Foster had, however, provided a template for recording observations in which behavioural characteristics ascribed to 'varieties' of mankind and natural history are run together. One of Forster's key sections dealt with 'the Varieties of the Human Species, relative to Colour, Size, Form, Habit, and Natural Turn of Mind in the Natives of the South-Sea Isles'. He opens with a characteristic statement of his ability to relate natural 'history' and particular behavioural characteristics.

> The varieties of the human species are, as everyone knows, very numerous. The small size, the tawny colour, the mistrustful temper, are as peculiar to the Esquimaux; as the noble and beautiful figure, and outline of the body, the fair complexion, and the treacherous turn of mind, to the inhabitant of Tcherkassia. The native of Senegal is characterized by a timorous disposition, by his jetty black skin, and crisped wooly hair.

Foster's gaze could recognise and discern types, consisting both of physical features and a 'natural turn of mind'. Culture was not an intermediate factor, nor did the different locations lead him to cultural or social relativism:

> dispositions were instead rendered natural and peculiar to a type of humanity that could be clearly distinguished from its neighbours. The 'variety' of humankind, sometimes a sub-category of a 'nation' or 'race', at other times a loose equivalent, was thus not something that might be stereotyped in an unscientific manner, but a unitary entity which could be known, that stood as the referent for a certain kind of truth. (Thomas 1994: 84–5)

Thomas observes a constant conflation in the epistemic gaze of these travellers/explorers: the experience and perceptions of the knower are taken not merely to express his response to the other, but as well to capture the essential nature of the 'other'. The viewer does not implicate himself into this act of viewing but takes the other person as something to be seen, rather than as an actor of the same kind as himself. And behind the power to identify the other there is the narrative of progressive evolution to a civilised state. Foster wrote of the Tongans: 'the character of these people is really amiable; their friendly behaviour to us, who were utter strangers to them, would have done honour to the most civilised nation'.

What of the behaviour of the European in these new social settings? Darwin was on a voyage into relativity of language usage and experiences. In April 1832, inland of Rio de Janeiro, he had passed a spot 'notorious for having been, for a long time, the residence of some runaway slaves'. When discovered, a party of soldiers had seized the lot with the exception of an old woman, 'who sooner than again be led into slavery, dashed herself to pieces from the summit of the mountain. In a Roman matron this would have been called the noble love of freedom: in a poor negress it is mere brutal obstinacy' (p. 14). He marvelled at the abundance of food provided for their dinner on a slave-operated estate owned by a relative of one of his party, but seemed oblivious to the complex global flows of capital and people that sustained it: 'As long as the idea of slavery could be banished, there was something exceedingly fascinating in this simple and patriarchal style of living: it was such a perfect retirement and independence from the rest of the world' (p. 17).

Darwin related an incident where he found himself with 'feelings of surprise, disgust, and shame'. Trying to make a Negro ferry operator, 'who was uncommonly stupid', understand his instructions, he shouted and waved his arm close to the man's face, whereupon the man thinking Darwin was going to strike him, 'instantly, with a frightened look and half-shut eyes ... dropped his hands'. Darwin was shocked at 'seeing a great powerful man afraid even to ward off a blow, directed, as he thought, at his face. This man had been trained to a degradation lower then the slavery of the most helpless animal' (p. 18). In Chile, he noted 'many robberies are committed, and there is much bloodshed: the habit of constantly wearing the knife is the chief cause of the latter'. These robberies were 'a natural consequence of universal gambling, much drinking, and extreme indolence'. Asking two men why they did not work, one 'gravely said the days were too long; the other that he was too poor. The number of horses and the profusion of food are the destruction of all industry' (p. 113). The 'police and justice' were quite inefficient': 'If a man who is poor commits murder and is taken, he will be imprisoned, and perhaps even shot; but if he is rich and has friends, he may rely on it no very severe consequence will ensue'. Darwin found it 'curious' that 'the most respected inhabitants of the country invariably assist a murderer to escape; they seem to think that the individual sins against the government, and not against the people'. A traveller had 'no protection besides his firearms', and must carry them at all times. Even the 'higher and more educated classes' in the towns were 'stained by many vices':

> Sensuality, mockery of all religion, and the grossest corruption, are far from uncommon. Nearly every public officer can be bribed. The head man in the post-office sold forged government franks. The governor and prime minister openly combined to plunder the state. Justice, when gold came into play, was hardly expected by any one. (p. 113)

What of a global perspective on the events he was observing? What hints are present of the metatheoretical grasp Darwin was later to accomplish? By 1833 Darwin was confronting the reality of 'civilised' man's destruction of other humans, was a concept of justice applicable? Darwin comforts himself by reminding the reader of principles of interaction, such as those of Malthus,[21] before following comments from Lyell's *Principles*:

> In the cases where we can trace the extinction of a species through man, either wholly or in one limited district, we know that it becomes rarer and rarer, and is then lost: it would be difficult to point out any just distinction between a species destroyed by man or by the increase of its natural enemies. (p. 127)

Convinced that change in species was gradual and hardly noticeable, observations of change become relative: 'why should we feel such astonishment at the rarity being carried a step further to extinction?' Indeed, we may be too quick in seeking human action to blame, or to 'call in some extraordinary agent'. 'Why', asked Darwin, 'when we accept that sickness is the prelude to death and are not surprised at sickness', do we "wonder" when the sick man dies and "believe that he died through violence"'?

But identifying violence is the normative question. Such identification requires understanding complex chains of activities, events and interdependencies. The possibility of distinguishing violence due to human action and sickness from avoidable disease as well as consequences of the social and cultural destructions of subjugation; then subjecting those processes to rational control, is a motivation for those who espoused what has become the human rights movement. But such distinguishing entailed empathy and a different form of seeing than the mere recording of 'facts' seen as completely independent of human activities. As J.C. Prichard put it in his 1838 lecture in Oxford *On the Extinction of Human Races*, it was plain that the 'savage races' were beyond saving. The role for the scientist lay in collecting as many facts and examples of their physical and moral characteristics as possible. Sven Lindqvist (1997: 123) offers a scathing summary: 'The threat of extermination provided motivation for anthropological research, which in exchange gave the exterminators an alibi by declaring extermination inevitable'.

Not all shared the view that the 'savage races' were doomed; what if they could be quickly 'civilised'? When the *Beagle* visited New Zealand, Darwin's gaze was simultaneously epistemic and governmental. First the epistemic:

> Looking at the New Zealander, one naturally compares him with the Tahitian; both belonging to the same family of mankind. The comparison, however, tells heavily against the New Zealander. He may, perhaps, be superior in energy, but in every other respect his character is of a much lower order. One glance at their respective expressions brings conviction to the mind that one is a savage, the other a civilised man. It would be vain to seek in the whole of New Zealand a person with the face and mien of the old Tahitian chief Utamme. No doubt the extraordinary manner in which tattooing is here practised, gives a disagreeable expression to their countenances. The complicated but symmetrical figures covering the whole face, puzzle and mislead an unaccustomed eye: it is moreover probable, that the deep incisions, by destroying the play of the superficial muscles, give an air of rigid inflexibility. But, besides this, there is a twinkling in the eye which cannot indicate anything but cunning and ferocity.[22] Their figures are tall and bulky; but not comparable in elegance with those of the working-classes in Tahiti. (p. 306)

This epistemic ranking and allocation, a dissection of the signs of the face, is complemented by his realisation of the powers of European civilisation to transform the land, verily an 'enchanter's wand'. Darwin recounts how he travelled to a small village of missionaries.

> At length we reached Waimate. After having passed over so many miles of an uninhabited useless country, the sudden appearance of an English farmhouse, and its well-dressed fields, placed there as if by an enchanter's wand, was exceedingly pleasant. Mr. Williams not being at home, I received in Mr. Davies's house a cordial welcome. After drinking tea with his family party, we took a stroll about the farm. At Waimate there are three large houses, where the missionary Gentlemen, Messrs. Williams, Davies, and Clarke, reside; and near them are the huts of the native labourers. On an adjoining slope, fine crops of barley and wheat were standing in full ear; and in another part fields of potatoes and clover. But I cannot attempt to describe all I saw; there were large gardens, with every fruit and vegetable which England produces; and many belonging to a warmer clime. I may instance asparagus, kidney beans, cucumbers, rhubarb, apples, pears, figs, peaches, apricots, grapes, olives, gooseberries, currants, hops, gorse for fences, and English oaks; also many kinds of flowers. Around the farmyard there were stables, a thrashing-barn with

its winnowing machine, a blacksmith's forge, and on the ground plough-shares and other tools: in the middle was that happy mixture of pigs and poultry, lying comfortably together, as in every English farmyard. At the distance of a few hundred yards, where the water of a little rill lad been dammed up into a pool, there was a large and substantial water-mill.

All this is very surprising, when it is considered that five years ago nothing but the fern flourished here. Moreover, native workmanship, taught by the missionaries, has effected this change; — the lesson of the missionary is the enchanter's wand. The house had been built, the windows framed, the fields ploughed, and even the trees grafted, by the New Zealander. At the mill, a New Zealander was seen powdered white with flour, like his brother miller in England. When I looked his whole scene, I though it admirable. It was not merely that England was brought vividly before my mind; yet, as the evening drew to a close, the domestic sounds, the fields of corn, the distant underlating country with its trees might well have been mistaken for our fatherland: nor was it the triumphant feeling at seeing what Englishmen could effect; but rather the high hope thus inspired for the future progress of this fine island. (pp. 309–10)

Progress, is a product of the transformation of the island through adopting the customs and products of England. The landscape has been radically reformed, the New Zealander turned into a productive being and even practices of enjoyment developed:

Several young men, redeemed by the missionaries from slavery, were employed on the farm. They were dressed in a shirt, jacket, and trousers, and had a reasonable appearance … These young men and boys appeared very merry and good-humoured. In the evening I saw a party of them at cricket: when I though of the austerity of which the missionaries have been accused, I was amused by observing one of their own sons taking an active part in the game. (p. 310)

And he notes approvingly that the bodies of some Maori were adopting more civilised forms:

A more decided and pleasing change was manifested in the young women, who acted as servants within the houses. Their clean, tidy, and healthy appearance, like that of dairy-maids in England, formed a wonderful contrast with the women of the filthy hovels in Kororadika. The wives of the missionaries tried to persuade them not to be tattooed; but a famous operator having arrived from the south, they said, 'We really must just have a few lines on our lips; else when we grow old our lips will shrivel, and we shall be so very ugly'. There is not nearly so much tattooing as formerly; but as it is a badge of distinction between the chief and the slave, it will probably long be practised. So soon does any train of ideas become habitual, that the missionaries told me that even in their eyes a plain face looked mean, and not like that of a New Zealand gentleman. (p. 310)

Yet, in dreaming of overcoming local customs and producing civilised space, Darwin could not forget the context of the surrounding environment. As Darwin explains when he arrived at the house where he was to spend the night:

I found there a large party of children, collected together for Christmas-day, and all sitting round a table at tea. I never saw a nicer or more merry group; and to think that this was in the centre of the land of cannibalism, murder, and all atrocious crimes! (p. 310)[23]

Excursus: on photography and typologising

Figure 4.2 Photo of Maori male with full Te Moko, late nineteenth century. Courtesy of Alexander Turnbull Library, Wellington, New Zealand. The late New Zealand historian Michael King (1996: 4) speculates 'why Maoris should have better survived the "fatal impact" of the industrialised West than coloured races in other colonized countries.' His answer involves a role for photography, not used to reveal the Maori as a vanishing type, but as an emphatic subject: 'They retained a large (though greatly reduced) share of their lands; they were paid for much of what they relinquished; they conserved and indeed strengthened many aspects of their culture; and they were by the 1980s taking a confident and forceful part in the national life. If credit is to be assigned for survival on this scale in the face of rampant cultural and technological imperialism, then most of it must go to Maoris themselves for their adaptability and their resilience; and to the fact that when the feelings of Europeans were running highest against Maoris during the wars of the 1860s, annihilation of the adversary was clearly impossible because of the vast and rugged areas of the North Island controlled by armed Natives. The fact that Te Kooti Rikirangi was able to attack settlements and then escape again and again into the hills, defying capture for 15 years until his eventual pardon, had wider significance. It meant simply that large tracts of the country were ungovernable without Maori cooperation. It was not a situation that would allow genocide.

Nevertheless, part of the credit for Maori survival must go to their allies among the European settlers. The growth of European pre-eminence in New Zealand was always tempered in some degree by the exercise of liberal and humanitarian consciences. This was by no means apparent on the part of all Europeans; but it was true of a sufficient number to demand a justice accounting for race relations policies. This acted as a brake on the more unscrupulous agents of white supremacy, even when those agents seemed to control the organs of settler government.

And in this context, part of the credit for fostering humanitarian feelings for Maoris among Europeans must go to the advent of photography. In case anybody doubted it, especially anybody not in regular association with them, photographs emphasised that Maoris were human. And they were humans capable of displaying – in photography as in life – grace, beauty, dignity, courage, as well as a capacity to suffer pain and degradation. Photography gave Maoris real faces in the eyes of their adversaries at a time when they could have been reduced to mere stereotypes of enemies and 'savages'

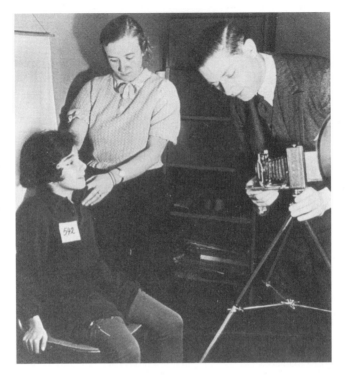

Figure 4.3 A Jewish child being photographed by the Institute of Racial Research, so that they can be classified under 'racial types' in the Third Reich, mid-1930s (image: MEPL/Weimar Archive). The project of classifying race penetrated deep into everyday consciousness. '... Gregor recognised the face at once: it was one of those young Jewish faces of a kind he had often seen at the Youth Association in Berlin or Moscow. This was a particularly fine specimen of such a face .... A black-haired young girl ... with a beautiful, tender and alien face showing the features of her race .... (Character in the kitsch novel of Alfred Andersch, *Sansibar oder der letzte*)

Darwin landed at Sydney Cove on 12 January 1836:

> At sunset, a party of a score of the black aborigines passed by, each carrying in their accustomed manner, a bundle of spears and other weapons. By giving a leading young man a shilling they were easily detained, and threw their spears for my amusement. They were all partly clothed, and several could speak a little English: their countenances were good-humoured and pleasant, and they appeared far from being such utterly degraded beings as they have usually been represented.[24] In their own arts they are admirable. A cap being fixed at thirty yards distance, they transfixed it with a spear, delivered by the throwing-stick with the rapidity of an arrow from the bow of a practised archer. In tracking animals or men they, show most wonderful sagacity; and I heard of several of their remarks which manifested considerable acuteness. They will not, however, cultivate the ground, or build houses and remain stationary, or even take the trouble of tending a flock of sheep when given to them. On the whole they appear to me to stand some few degrees higher in the scale of civilization than the Fuegians.

It is very curious thus to see in the midst of a civilised people [the English settlers of Sydney Cove], a set of harmless savages wandering about without knowing where they shall sleep at night, and gaining their livelihood by hunting in the woods. As the white man has travelled onwards, he has spread over the country belonging to several tribes. These, although thus enclosed by one common people, keep up their ancient distinctions, and some-times go to war with each other. In an engagement which took place lately, the two parties most singularly chose the centre of the village of Bathurst for the field of battle. This was of service to the defeated side, for the runaway warriors took refuge in the barracks.

The number of aborigines is rapidly decreasing. In my whole ride, with the exception of some boys brought up by Englishmen, I saw only one other party. This decrease, no doubt, must be partly owing to the introduction of spirits, to European diseases (even the milder ones of which, such as measles, prove very destructive), and to the gradual extinction of the wild animals.[25] It is said that numbers of their children invariably perish in very early infancy from the effects of their wandering life; and as the difficulty of procuring food increases, so must their wandering habits increase; and hence the population, without any apparent deaths from famine, is repressed in a manner extremely sudden compared to what happens in civilised countries, where the father, though in adding to his labour he may injure himself, does not destroy his offspring.

Besides these several evident causes of destruction, there appears to be some more mysterious agency generally at work. Wherever the European has trod, death seems to pursue the aboriginal. We may look to the wide extent of the Americas, Polynesia, the Cape of Good Hope, and Australia, and we find the same result. Nor is it the white man alone that thus acts the destroyer; the Polynesian of Malay extraction has in parts of the East Indian Archipelago, thus driven before him the dark-coloured native. The varieties of man seem to act on each other in the same way as different species of animals – the stronger always extirpating the weaker. It was melancholy at New Zealand to hear the fine energetic natives saying, that they knew the land was doomed to pass from their children. Every one has heard of the inexplicable reduction of the population in the beautiful and healthy island of Tahiti since the date of Captain Cook's voyages: although in that case we might have expected that it would have been increased; for infanticide, which formerly prevailed to so extraordinary a degree, has ceased, profligacy has greatly diminished, and the murderous wars become less frequent. (pp. 315–16)

So 'the varieties of man seem to act on each other in the same way as different species of animals – the stronger always extirpating the weaker'. We may speculate if this was to influence Spencer to coin the phrase 'survival of the fittest', which he first used in 1852 and which Darwin was later to be convinced to adopt (Ingold 1986: 4). Ingold is clear that Darwin's biological evolutionism does not imply that the 'fittest' were those who 'managed – with "tooth and claw" – to eliminate their rivals in a direct competitive struggle' but simply 'those who left relatively more offspring'. But in his journal, Darwin is recounting the facts, albeit ones he finds 'melancholy', that those groups lower on the ranking of 'civilisation' will be exterminated by the actions, direct and indirect, of those higher in the rankings of the 'civilised' who have entered into the territory of the 'aboriginal' possessed of superior force and bringing the gift of death.[26] By 22 January Darwin felt able to speculate on the future of Australia. Before arriving he had been interested most in 'the state of society amongst the higher classes, the condition of the convicts, and the degree of attraction sufficient to induce persons to emigrate'. He was now disappointed in the state of society.

> The whole community is rancorously divided into parties on almost every subject. Among those who, from their station in life, ought to be the best, many live in such open profligacy that respectable people cannot associate with them. There is much jealousy between the children of the rich emancipist and the free settlers, the former being pleased to consider honest men as interlopers. The whole population, poor and rich, are bent on acquiring wealth: amongst the higher orders, wool and sheep-grazing form the constant subject of conversation. There are many serious drawbacks to the comforts of a family, the chief of which, perhaps, is being surrounded by convict servants. How thoroughly odious to every feeling, to be waited on by a man who the day before, perhaps, was flogged, from your representation for some trifling misdemeanour. The female servants are of course much worse: hence children learn the vilest expressions, and it is fortunate if not equally vile ideas. (p. 323)

The drawcard was the promise of wealth: 'the capital of a person, without any trouble on his part, produces him treble interest to what it will in England; and with care he is sure to grow rich'. Subsequent economic history would show Darwin was not a good judge of the natural capabilities of the land, as he argued that because of the poor water supplies agriculture could 'never succeed on an extended scale'! 'Therefore … Australia must ultimately depend upon being the centre of commerce for the southern hemisphere, and perhaps on her future manufactories.' He noted that coal was available and 'from her English extraction, she is sure to be a maritime nation.' However, his original hopes that 'Australia would rise to be as grand and powerful a country as North America' now seemed to him dashed: 'such future grandeur is rather problematical'. He then turned to the conditions of the 'convicts'.

Darwin was keen to observe the great 'penal experiment' of transportation; at the time he visited some 4,100 convicted transportees were arriving each year. Transportation of convicted offenders to America from Britain – called by the Webbs 'virtually a branch of the slave trade' – had begun early in the seventeenth century. By the mid-eighteenth century it had become 'the standard punishment for about 90% of convicted felons' (Sellin 1976: 97; following quotes and discussion from chapter 8; see also Radzinowicz and Hood 1990: chapter 14). The loss of the American colonies created a practical problem in part addressed by the 1779 Act (19 Geo. III, *c.* 74), initially drafted by William Blackstone and Eden with assistance from John Howard, which created two national penitentiaries to hold 600 males and 300 females. The drafters hoped 'if any offenders convicted of crimes for which transportation has been usually inflicted were ordered to solitary confinement, accompanied by well-regulated hard labour, and religious instruction, it might be the means, under Providence, not only of deterring others, but also of reforming the individuals, and turning them to habits of industry'. The Act also created the new punishment of 'imprisonment in the hulks', or convict ships. The Act was not properly implemented and Penitentiaries were not built until the 1840s with Pentonville (by itself designed to be the 'portal' for the penal colony, where offenders would spend 18 (actually reduced to 9) months before leaving for Australia). In 1787, it was decided to establish a penal settlement at Botany Bay in what is now New South Wales on the eastern shore of Australia. A total of 163,000 transportees had left the UK for Australia by the time transportation was stopped in 1867 (Van Diemen's Land ceased receiving transportees in 1852, Western Australia was the last state stopping in 1867).[27]

With respect to the state of the convicts, I had still fewer opportunities of judging than on the other points. The first question is whether their condition is at all one of punishment: no one will maintain that it is a very severe one. This, however, I suppose, is of little consequence as long as it continues to be an object of dread to criminals at home. The corporeal wants of the convicts are tolerably well supplied: their prospect of future liberty and comfort is not distant, and after good conduct certain. A 'ticket of leave', which, as long as a man keeps clear of suspicion as well as of crime, makes him free within a certain district, is given upon good conduct, after years proportional to the length of the sentence; yet with all this, and overlooking the previous imprisonment and wretched passage out, I believe the years of assignment are passed away with discontent and unhappiness.[28] As an intelligent man remarked to me, the convicts know no pleasure beyond sensuality, and in this they are not gratified. The enormous bribe which Government possesses in offering free pardons, together with the deep horror of the secluded penal settlements, destroys confidence between the convicts, and so prevents crime. As to a sense of shame, such a feeling does not appear to be known, and of this I witnessed some very singular proofs. Though it is a curious fact, I was universally told that the character of the convict population is one of arrant cowardice: not unfrequently some become desperate, and quite indifferent as to life, yet a plan requiring cool or continued courage is seldom put into execution. The worst feature in the whole case is, that although there exists what may be called a legal reform, and comparatively little is committed which the law can touch, yet that any moral reform should take place appears to be quite out of the question.[29] I was assured by well-informed people, that a man who should try to improve, could not while living with other assigned servants; – his life would be one of intolerable misery and persecution. Nor must the contamination of the convict-ships and prisons, both here and in England, be forgotten.[30] On the whole, as a place of punishment, the object is scarcely gained; as a real system of reform it has failed, as perhaps would every other plan; but as a means of making men outwardly honest, – of converting vagabonds, most useless in one hemisphere, into active citizens of another, and thus giving birth to a new and splendid country – a grand centre of civilization – it has succeeded to a degree perhaps unparalleled in history! (p. 324)

Each phrase Darwin records is heavy with contestable assumptions and inferences. In 1838, a House of Commons Select Committee on Transportation would report that 'as the lot of a slave depends upon the character of its master, so the condition of the convict depends upon the temper and disposition of the settler to whom he is assigned ... the condition of a transported convict is a mere lottery' (cited Radzinowicz and Hood 1990: 470, who state that assignment was 'a system which offered the extremes of opportunity and of abuse. The more fortunate convicts might find themselves working for masters who treated them with humanity and with whom they could learn real skills, going on to become prosperous landowners in the new colonies. The less fortunate could find themselves ruthlessly exploited and virtually destroyed.').

The Australian-born journalist, John Pilger, gives an account of the factors that had caused his great-great grandfather to be transported on the *John Barry*.

The John Barry carried mostly political prisoners from Ireland, the 'inflammable matter', as Queen Victoria called them; and my great-great-grandfather was one of them. His name was Francis McCarthy and he had been convicted of 'uttering unlawful oaths' in his native County Roscommon. This was a charge interpreted in the English courts at that time as 'making political agitation' or 'taking part in seditious conspiracy'. McCarthy was sentenced to transportation to a penal colony for fourteen years, which was double the sentence handed down to the six Tolpuddle Martyrs for the crime of seeking to form a trade union.

To be guilty of objecting to enforced degradation and starvation in Ireland during the first half of the nineteenth century was to be a political criminal. Even before the potato famine, nowhere else in what the Victorians called 'the civilised world' did such uncivilised conditions exist. Absentee English landlords controlled the Irish peasantry; and those Irish people who could not afford a tenancy, or were evicted, were forced to live in holes in the bog: caves of mud without beds or chairs, in which infants lay where animals defecated. Food was dried potatoes and death and disease were on a scale scarcely believable. To these was added the constant menace of English terrorism; if you were convicted or if your crops failed, the Redcoats would arrive to drag away your animals, your last means of survival, and any recalcitrance would lead inevitably to a bloody arrest. (1986: 4–5)

Is Pilger overstating? In 1839, Gustave de Beaumount, having travelled throughout America, visited Ireland.

I have seen the Indian in his forests and the Negro in his irons, and I believed, in pitying their plight, that I saw the lowest ebb of human misery; but I did not then know the degree of poverty to be found in Ireland. Like the Indian, the Irishman is poor and naked, but he lives in the midst of a society which enjoys luxury, honours and wealth ... The Indian retains a certain independence which has its attraction and a dignity of its own. Poverty-stricken and hungry he may be, but he is free in his desert places; and the feeling that he enjoys this liberty blunts the edge of his sufferings. But the Irishman undergoes the same deprivations without enjoying the same liberty, he is subjected to regulations: he dies of hunger. He is governed by laws; a sad condition, which combines the vices of civilization with those of primitive life. Today the Irishmen enjoys neither the freedom of the savage nor the bread of servitude. (quoted Mansergh 1965: 23)

In the year after the publication of Darwin's *Origin of the Species*, Charles Kingsley could find a new language to describe what he has seen in Ireland on his 1850 visit to Sligo:

I am haunted by the human chimpanzees I saw along that hundred miles of horrible country. I don't believe they are our fault. I believe ... that they are happier, better, more comfortably fed and lodged under our rule than they ever were. But to see white chimpanzees is dreadful; it they were black, one would not feel it so much, but their skins, except where tanned by exposure, are as white as ours. (Charles Kingsley, cited in G.J. Watson 1989: 17)

Radzinowicz and Hood uncompromisingly refer to transportation as virtual slavery, an economic resource for colonisation:

It was indeed to the economic advantage of the colony, particularly in its early stages, to have a large supply of what was virtually slave labour, both to assist free emigrants in developing farms and other resources and to build the infrastructure of roads, harbours and other public works. At the home end these developments were important in fostering the expansion of trade. It was only when this arrangement ceased to be necessary in these colonies (though still desirable in the eyes of the home country) that the system of transportation broke down. (1990: 473)

They find an explanation for the ambiguity with which it was viewed – as horror by some, but an opportunity by others – in the actual condition of farm labourers and urban poor of the early nineteenth century. In *The Edinburgh Review*, Charles

Grey wrote that the worst that could be said about transportation might appear 'anything but terrible to labourers in England – least of all those who in the southern counties, find themselves, by the operation of the Poor Laws, reduced to a condition but little removed from slavery and which they have scarcely a hope of improving' (quoted Radzinowicz and Hood 1990: 476). Extreme terrors were often devised to render the transportees controllable. Pilger relates that when the convicts were unloaded in Sydney they were divided into 'intractables' and those 'prepared to knuckle under'. The intractables were taken to Goat Island, a place of great reputation for the cruelty practised there. As they arrived they saw an image of the power to punish.

> In a cleft in the rock face there appeared to be a coffin. It had a wooden cover and at one end the upright head of a man was visible. His name was Charles 'Boney' Anderson and he had been transported for theft and drunkenness, even though previously he had been wounded in a naval battle and had suffered a mental disability. On arrival in Sydney Anderson was sent to Goat Island for two months. He escaped, was caught and given one hundred lashes, and another one hundred lashes every month for offences such as 'looking up from work' and 'looking at a steamer on the river'. Again he escaped, and again caught. This time he was given two hundred lashes, and for the next two years he was chained to a rock by a twenty-six-foot chain fastened to his waist. His food was pushed to him at the end of a long pole and at night the wooden cover, with its few air holes, was clamped over him. During the summer months he became something of an early tourist attraction; boat trippers would sail by and throw him bread and dry biscuits. In all, he was given 1,700 lashes. He died insane. (Pilger 1986: 5–6)

Conditions for those prepared to knuckle under were harsh. Floggings were common and there was a home spun name for the apparatus that people were tied to when flogged: the 'three sisters'.[31] Moreover, 'the children of the first great property owners observed the treatment of those who worked in chains for their parents, and, inspired by such ruthlessness, played at flogging a tree 'as children in England play at horses'. Those to whom the convicts were assigned, the 'squatters', accumulated wealth 'without the drawback of labour costs and the stigma of Negro slavery'.

> My great-great-grandfather was 'assigned' to a Mr Robertson, whose land included part of what is now skyscraper Sydney. He was fortunate, for Robertson was a benevolent man, perhaps not unlike the most paternalistic of the slave-owners in the American Deep South. What was certain was that 'assignment' was slavery by another name, although … historians … seldom made mention of slavery, just as the early colonial artists never portrayed such a hell, preferring to contrive idyllic scenes of incongruent gentility from out of the most primitive and harsh landscape in the world. Real Australia and its stains on 'civilization' did not exist, as if Victorian middle-class England was just over the brow.

For Pilger this was the beginning of 'the great Australian silence' that emasculated the truth of the past and distorted the way in which Australian would come to regard themselves and their nation for a numerous school account of confronting the silence, see Henry Reynolds (1999) *Why Weren't We Told? A Personal Search for The Truth about Our History*.

Having recorded his impressions of the convict situation, Darwin recounts his time in Tasmania (Van Diemen's Land). In 1851, Earl Grey, speaking in the British Parliament felt the need to recount the history of this island's settlement as the authorities were now refusing to take more convicts: 'Van Diemen's Land was a colony which owed its creation to the penal system ... It had been the establishment of the convict system that created the whole wealth and material prosperity which now existed in the colony' (quoted Radzinowicz and Hood 1990: 483–4). But as convicts were expelled from Britain to provide labour for this colonising process, the authorities had not found an empty land, although the whole legal basis of their occupation was said to be that of *terra nullius* (cf. Reynolds 1987).

> January 30th, – The Beagle sailed for Hobart Town in Van Diemen's Land ... I was chiefly struck with the comparative fewness of the large houses, either built or building. Hobart Town, from the census of 1835, contained 13,826 inhabitants, and the whole of Tasmania 36,505.
>
> All the aborigines have been removed to an island in Bass's Straits, so that Van Diemen's Land enjoys the great advantage of being free from a native population. This most cruel step seems to have been quite unavoidable, as the only means of stopping a fearful succession of robberies, burnings, and murders, committed by the blacks; and which sooner or later would have ended in their utter destruction. I fear there is no doubt that this train of evil and its consequences, originated in the infamous conduct of some of our countrymen. Thirty years is a short period in which to have banished the last aboriginal from his native island, – and that island nearly as large as Ireland. The correspondence on this subject, which took place between the government at home and that of Van Diemen's Land, is very interesting. Although numbers of natives were shot and taken prisoners in the skirmishing which was going on at intervals for several years, nothing seems fully to have impressed them with the idea of our overwhelming power, until the whole island, in 1830, was put under martial law, and by proclamation the whole population commanded to assist in one great attempt to secure the entire race. The plan adopted was nearly similar to that of the great hunting-matches in India: a line was formed reaching across the island, with the intention of driving the natives into a *cul-de-sac* on Tasman's peninsula. The attempt failed; the natives, having tied up their dogs, stole during one night through the lines. This is far from surprising, when their practised senses and usual manner of crawling after wild animals is considered. I have been assured that they can conceal themselves on almost bare ground, in a manner which until witnessed is scarcely credible; their dusky bodies being easily mistaken for the blackened stumps which are scattered all over the country. I was told of a trial between a party of Englishmen and a native, who was to stand in full view on the side oft a bare hill; if the Englishmen closed their eyes for less than a minute he would squat down, and then they were never able to distinguish him from the surrounding stumps. But to return to the hunting match; the natives, understanding this kind of warfare, were terribly alarmed, for they at once perceived the power and numbers of the whites. Shortly afterwards a party of thirteen belonging to two tribes came in, and, conscious of their unprotected condition, delivered themselves up in their despair. Subsequently by the intrepid exertions of Mr. Robinson, an active and benevolent man, who fearlessly visited by himself the most hostile of the natives, the whole were induced to act in a similar manner. They were then removed to an island, where food and clothes were provided [to] them. Count Strzelecki states, that 'at the epoch of their deportation in 1835, the number of natives amounted to two hundred and ten. In 1842, that is, after the interval of several years, they mustered only fifty-four individuals; and, while each family of the interior of New South Wales, uncontaminated by contact with the whites, swarms with children, those of Flinders' Island had during eight years, an accession of only fourteen in number!'
>
> The Beagle stayed here ten days, and in this time I made several pleasant little excursions, chiefly with the object of examining the geological structure of the immediate

neighbourhood. The main points of interest consist, first, in some highly fossiliferous strata, belonging to the Devonian or Carboniferous period; secondly, in proofs of a late small rise of the land; and lastly, in a solitary and superficial patch of yellowish limestone or travertin, which contains numerous impressions of leaves of trees, together with land-shells, not now existing. It is not improbable that this one small quarry includes the only remaining record of the vegetation of Van Diemen's Land during one former epoch. (pp. 324–6)

Thus Darwin could acknowledge the presence of massacre and activities now viewed by many as genocide, but not linger on it too long. It was not after all his place or his concern. Both scientific rationality and personal pleasure drew him to 'the geological structure of the immediate neighbourhood'. He did, however, comment further on the ability of the island to sustain advances in civilisation: 'The climate here is damper than in New South Wales, and hence the land is more fertile. Agriculture flourishes; the cultivated fields look well, and the gardens abound with thriving vegetables and fruit-trees. Some of the farmhouses, situated in retired spots, had a very attractive appearance' (p. 354). For all the ambivalence of his personal asides, his was the gaze of power and it appreciated the productive ability of European dominance.

Consider three images that tell a narrative of settlement of the civilizing of Van Diemen's Land (now the state of Tasmania).

Images of land usage and the status of the native inhabitants were crucial to constructing a narrative of civilizing a place, rather than dispossessing a community. This was a place outwith the law of sovereignty as there was no recognizable sovereign and no discernable practice of land cultivation (at least to European eyes). George Arthur's Proclamation published on 19 April 1828 in the Hobart Town Gazette states on the one hand that 'humanity and natural equity, equally enforce the duty of protecting and civilizing the Aboriginal inhabitants', and on the other, that 'the Aborigines wander over extensive tracts of Country, without cultivating, or permanently occupying any portion of it'. This Proclamation announced a dual policy of legislating to 'restrict the intercourse between the White and Coloured inhabitants' and negotiating 'with certain Chiefs of Aboriginal Tribes' and reflected and expressed the doctrine of terra nullius or 'no man's land'; the Aboriginal occupants of the Island had claims to an equitable treatment, but lacked sovereignty and thus constitutional existence.

This Proclamation was issued at a time of frequent violence between Aboriginal and European people in country districts. Although Aboriginal numbers were by then reduced to a few hundred, there was serious doubt in Arthur's mind whether European inland occupation was viable. In September 1828 Arthur declared martial law in these districts. In 1832, after remaining Aboriginal people had been removed to Flinders Island,
Arthur opined:

'It was a fatal error in the first settlement of Van Diemen's Land that a treaty was not entered into with the Natives, of which Savages well comprehend the nature – had they received some compensation for the territory they surrendered, no matter how trifling, and had adequate laws been from the very first introduced and enforced for their protection, His Majesty's Government would have acquired a valuable possession without the injurious consequences which have followed our occupation and which must ever remain a stain upon the Colonisation of Van Diemen's land.

Figure 4.4 Pictorial proclamation issued by George Arthur, the lieutenant-governor of Van Diemen's Land from 1824 to 1837 issued in the year he declared martial law. The upper sections display images of intercultural mixing and friendship; the lower ones indicate the sanctions for violence and the power of the new authority. The lieutenant governor appears in full ceremonial dress, the embodiment of colonial power and authority. Attribution to Governor Davey is incorrect; it was issued during the administration of Governor Arthur and is believed to have been designed by George Frankland. Image courtesy Tasmanian museum and Art Gallery. The mistaken attribution to Thomas Davey, the first administrator of the whole island is probably due to the fact that in 1814 he issued a proclamation to treat aborigines kindly; yet in April 1815, in the face of an escalation of 'bush ranging' by the colorists and Aboriginal resistance, he declared martial law. Arthur repeats this process

Figure 4.5 *The Conciliation*, by Benjamin Duterrau, 1840 (Tasmanian Museum and Art Gallery). Benjamin Duterrau was an English painter, printmaker and sculptor who was born in London, 1767 and died in Hobart, Tasmania, 11 July 1851. Arrived in Hobart, Tasmania, in 1832 where at the Hobart Mechanics' Institute in 1833 he delivered the first lecture in Australia on the subject of painting. His major work, *The Conciliation* (1840), represents the so-called conciliation between Aborigines of the Big River and Oyster Bay tribes and the European colonists, and was called by the art historian William Moore (1868–1937) 'the first history painting attempted in Australia'. The central figure is George Robinson, a Christian missionary and local trader who worked with Aboriginal people in Van Demians land and was commissioned by Lieutenant Governor Arthur to persuade the remaining Aborigines to settle on a reserve. Paffen (2001) argues that in composing the painting Duterrau was guided by principles of taste, which were shaped by British views concerning history painting and British theories of moral sentiment. Duterrau applied to his representation of Tasmanian Aborigines expressions in keeping with principles of expression embodied in Raphael's tapestry cartoons to sustain British nationalist and aesthetic interests in a colonial context. Duterrau did not draw or paint in the actual places Aborigines lived; instead when the Aborigines arrived in Hobart, Robinson would take them to the studio where Duterrau used them as models and also made etchings and plaster sculptures of them. While the subject of the picture presents conciliation as an historic fact, Duterrau's treatment suppresses the fact that the Tasmanian Aborigines were finally evicted from Van Diemen's Land between 1830 and 1834 by a process of intimidation rather than conciliation. Robinson became overseer of Wybalenna on Flinders Island in Bass Strait, a 'resettlement' of the Tasmanian Aboriginals where more than half died in the first 5 years. Atkinson and Aveling (1987: 306) note that 'Robinson never wavered from his belief that it was better for the Aborigines to die on the threshold of British civilisation than to live as savages in their own'. (there was no total physical) By contrast the surviving Aborigines were returned to a reserve near Hobart in 1847. The governors of New South Wales preferred the idea of incorporation to segregation and appointed white protectors to help relations with whites; Robinson became chief protector of Aborigines in the Port Phillip District

Figure 4.6 John Glover, Great Britain/Australia, 1767–1849. A view of the artist's house and garden in Mills Plains, Van Diemen's Land, 1835, Deddington, Tasmania. Oil on canvas 76.4 × 114.4 cm. (Morgan Thomas Bequest Fund 1951: Art Gallery of South Australia, Adelaide.) The successful English painter John Glover settled in Australia in 1831 buying 3000 hectares to construct his pastoral residence. Here the landscape has been civilised in the fashion that Darwin found so comforting; the original has been transformed, trees and scrub cleared and European plants make up the land near the house with the native forest a brooding presence, still to be cleared in the background

One interpretation of the contrast between what is sometimes referred to as 'the hopeful Proclamation of April 1828, and the despairing declaration of martial law a few months later' is that they reveal the 'contradictory policies' under which Arthur hoped that bloodshed would be checked 'as much as possible'. The complexity and the real presence of conflicting and various perceptions, ideals, hopes and interests in actual situations must be noted, but Julie Evans points out the regularity with which Martial Law was declared in colonial conditions. The civilizing process was accompanied by the rhetorical companion of the spread of the rule of law; yet the denial of the 'savage' the right to contract meant that the recognition and possession of the rule of law was always one-sided. Arthur never doubted his sovereignty under the land of this island yet he could only impose it by recourse to martial law – the state of exception to any rule of law. This state of exception however was a frequent state of affairs at the 'point of inclusion/exclusion in the developing normal order when colonial laws relation to Indigenous peoples was at its most unstable' (Evans 2005: 60). Evans (2005: 69) seeks guidance from the European writers of exception – Schmitt and Agamben: 'Both Schmitt and Agamben assume a European origin impossible to localize in specific temporal or spatial terms, a "time immemorial". But in the colonies, in the critical formative stages of establishing state power ... we encounter native society as the origin that has to be suppressed – through the constitution of the law that at once presupposes and authorizes its suppression.'

Thus colonised peoples were 'brought both within the reach of the law and yet denied its protection' (Anghie (1999: 103); in mid-twentieth century Europe, Jews were very much within the reach of the law as they were systematically stripped of rights and converted into the status of life unworthy of life.

[In 1995 Tasmania passed the Aboriginal Laws Act 1995 (*Tas*). This accepts that Aboriginal people were not totally eliminated from Tasmania and acknowledges the dispossession of Tasmania's Indigenous people and recognizes certain rights of Tasmanians of Aboriginal descent. It is the first such legislation in Tasmania, where the assumption that no Aboriginal people remained after the first 50 years of the Colony meant the issue of reconciliation in law was ignored. The Act provides for the establishment of an elected Aboriginal Land Council to own and manage lands of historical and cultural significance.]

Part III

Reconciling Darwin and Lombroso

The journal reveals Darwin the gentleman traveller. Herein lay a divided vision. Concerned only with 'nature' he was the detached observer, absolutely absorbed and radically inquiring. But when he was concerned with the interaction of Europeans and Natives, he was an involved representative of a civilised space that had ascended the steps of progress and power, a man who could make confident epistemic and aesthetic judgements on social relations. This difference is apparent in the distinction between the theory of the *Origin* and that of the *Descent*. As Ingold (1986: 47–8) describes the Darwin present in the *Descent*: 'The wondering curiosity of the naturalist is still there, but it is thickly blended with the ponderous morality of the Victorian gentleman … committed to a view of the progressive enlightenment of mankind that was, for its time, thoroughly conventional. He had no qualms about comparing the various grades of general advancement to the stages of maturation of the human individual from infancy to childhood.' The Darwin of the *Descent* 'accepted quite uncritically … that existing "savage" and "barbarous" tribes represent the successive steps of a gradual and uniform ascent already trodden by the ancestors of "civilised" nations. And yet in the *Origin* … Darwin had decisively rejected all notions of predetermined, orthogenetic advance in the world of nature.'

Ingold tries to reconcile the 'compromise' of principles by reference to the position of Darwin himself as author of the works. In the *Origin*, Darwin

> touched only incidentally on man, yet *as a man*, he placed himself – the observing scientist – outside the spectacle of nature. His own absolute superiority (and by extension, that of his kind) *vis-a-vis* the rest of the animal kingdom was something he never thought to question. For the fact remains that no animal whose project is precisely inscribed in the materials of heredity could have written *The Origin of Species*. But conversely, an animal capable of performing this feat, or any other that involves conscious reflection on the material conditions of existence, must also be able to bend the course of evolution to its purpose. (pp. 48–9)

However, in writing the *Descent*, Darwin could not adopt some position outside the world but took up position inside it. Thus he gave a picture of the human condition that came from his own understandings, implicit and explicit, of his own position within it as the representative of the civilised.[32]

There was even a form of natural selection for those who were morally 'well-endowed'. Darwin can now give a naturalist explanation for the escape of the natural state of 'warre' Hobbes had postulated man achieved by rational acceptance of the need for a pragmatic political solution. 'Fidelity and courage' were 'all important in the never-ceasing wars of savages'. Through natural selection those individuals and tribes that possessed 'a high standard of morality', namely, 'the spirit of patriotism, fidelity, obedience, courage and sympathy' would be successful. Since they would be always 'ready to aid one another' or sacrifice themselves for the common good', they would thus be 'victorious over most other tribes; and this would be natural selection' (Darwin 1874: 203–4; discussed in Ingold 1986: 52–3) The advance of civilisation 'depends on the increase in the actual number of a population, on the number of men endowed with high intellectual and moral faculties, as well as on their standard of excellence' (1874: 216). As a matter of history, 'tribes have supplanted other tribes' and 'civilised nations are everywhere supplanting barbarous nations', with the victorious groups having a higher proportion of (morally) 'well-endowed men' (1874: 197). Moreover Darwin was a materialist. The brain housed the mental faculties and the skull reflected this.

Hence Lombroso: far from being aberrant, Cesare Lombroso similarly accepted his own superiority, his ability to make epistemic and aesthetic judgement. He followed this second Darwin in his materialist conception of the mind and the assumed parallel of social development with that of the child to adult. In explaining her father's work to an American audience, Gina Lombroso-Ferrero (1911: 49) set out the aesthetic acceptability of criminal anthropology:

> Just as a musical theme is the result of a sum of notes, and not of any single note, the criminal type results from the aggregate of those anomalies, which render him strange and terrible, not only to the scientific observer, but to ordinary persons who are capable of an impartial judgement.
>
> Painters and poets, unhampered by false doctrines, divined this type long before it became the subject of a special branch of study ...

Not only can we, suitably cleansed of 'false doctrines', observe in them their differences but they reveal it in what they say and do. Their love of tattoos recalls primitive tribes as does their use of 'slang' resemble the languages of primitive peoples. Physiogenically, stigmata are indicators of stunted mental facilities. When we listen to their explanations we realise that 'the notions of right and wrong appear to be completely inverted in such minds'. 'Many criminals do not realise the immorality of their actions ... A Milanese thief once remarked to my father: "I don't steal. I only relieve the rich of their superfluous wealth" ... Murderers, especially when actuated by motives of revenge, consider their actions righteous in the extreme' (p. 29). Today, we may wonder at the absence of any cultural explanation, no 'techniques of neutralisation' (as per Sykes and Matza 1961), nor any awareness of *The Moral and Sensual Attractions of doing Evil* (Katz 1988); alternatively, some may think that the 'criminals' understood the justice of their societies better than Cesare or Gina. As for their art:

> In spite of the thousands of years which separate him from prehistoric savages, his art is a faithful reproduction of the first, crude attempts of primitive races. The museum of criminal anthropology created by my father contains numerous specimens of criminal art, stones shaped to resemble figures, like those found in Australia, rude pottery covered with designs that recall Egyptian decorations or scenes fashioned in terra-cotta that resemble the grotesque creations of children or savages. (Lombroso-Ferrero 1911: 132)

We have an anthropological 'control' theory. The faces and bodies with signs of 'criminality' could be recognised and separated. This is the gaze of power, sure of its organisational ability, oblivious of an ethical need to appreciate the culture of the other.[33] Over time criminality could be bred out as children are suitably controlled and 'influenced by moral training and example'. In Australia such a control theory was put into practice to breed out the 'aboriginal' in the children. A largely theoretically incoherent policy since the offending 'aboriginal' characteristics were themselves a creation of the European gaze.

Henry Reynolds (2001: chapter 10) relates that the 1997 report of the Human Rights Commission into the separation of Aboriginal and Torres Strait Islander children from their families, *Bringing Them Home*, found that the policies pursued by Australian governments from the early twentieth century to the 1960s constituted crimes against humanity. Note the report's words on the issue of genocide:

> The policy of forcible removal of children from indigenous Australians to other groups for the purpose of raising them separately from and ignorant of their culture and people could properly be labelled 'genocidal' in breach of binding international law from at least 11 December 1946 ... The practice continued for almost another quarter of a century.

The reasoning was as follows: First, the children were removed because they were seen as being members of a distinct group who, if they remained with their own people, would acquire their culture and traditions. Second, among policy-makers and administrators there was an intention to destroy the group 'in whole or in part'. (The predominant aim of child removals was the absorption or assimilation of the infants into the wider, non-indigenous community in order that 'their unique cultural values and ethnic identities would disappear, giving way to models of Western culture'.) Third, the fact that the policy was driven by a mixture of motives and good intentions did not mean that the convention did not apply. The authors of the report observed:

> a key objective of the forcible removal of indigenous children was to remove them from the influence of their parents and communities, to acculturate them and to socialise them into Anglo-Australian values and aspirations. Other objectives included education of the children to make them 'useful' and 'worthy' citizens, their training for labour and domestic service, their protection from malnutrition, neglect or abuse, the reduction of government support for idle dependants and the protection of the community from 'dangerous elements'.

The commissioners reviewed the differing objectives involved in the removal policies over the years and concluded that diversity of aim did not necessarily undermine the charge of genocide.[34]

Historical recall: a failure in the civilising process or genocide?

How does history relate the fate of the 'aboriginals' in the civilising process of Australia? John Pilger, provides a voice of angry liberal Australia (note also that he does not use the term 'aboriginal').

> Growing up, I was given to understand that we whites were merely innocent bystanders to the slow and 'natural' death of people whose time had come, rather than the inheritors of a past as bloodthirsty as that of the United States, Spanish America and colonial Africa and Asia. That the jolly swagman was not especially jolly was unmentionable; that genocide was all but colonial policy in Australia was a secret. (Pilger 1986: 546)

The impression he had of Van Deminan's land was just one piece of a collective mythology that he learned to unpick. Later he came across native oral histories of death, rape and torture. But 'growing up in Australia I knew nothing about this; none of us did. Our history was one of suppression, omission and lies.' The historian Henry Reynolds, called by Pilger, 'one of Australia's new wave historians', argues that 'the barriers which for so long kept Aboriginal experience out of our history books', were not principally those of source material or methodology but rather of perception and preference. The social space in which Australian history was written was too polite, too civilised to accept this other history.

> Much of the material used in this book [*The other side of the frontier: Aboriginal Resistance to the European Invasion of Australia*, 1981] has been available to scholars for a century or more. But black cries of anger and anguish were out of place in works that celebrated national achievement or catalogued peaceful progress in a quiet continent, while deft scholarly feet avoided the embarrassment of bloodied billabongs. (Reynolds 1981: 163)

In 2001 Reynolds published *An Indelible Stain? The question of genocide in Australia's history*. Reynolds argument centred on the applicability of the UN Convention on Genocide to the Australian context. The principle instances for investigation he outlined were: the small pox epidemics; the fate of the natives

MOUNTED CONSTABLES WILLSHIRE AND WORMBRAND WITH NATIVE POLICE
IN CENTRAL AUSTRALIA, MAY 20TH, 1887.

Figure 4.7 The official presentation of peaceful settlement and nation building? 'Mounted police Constables Willshire and Wormbrand with Native Police in Central Australia, 20th May 1887' is an example of the officially constructed visual narrative of cooperation and achievement of a well-ordered society. The use of Native Police varied between States, but while it may appear as a sensible measure to build bridges between the settler forces and the natives being policed, in practice it was often extremely hostile towards the tribespeople of the area 'policed'. See Peterson, 1989 for analysis of this image (RAI 35530)

of Tasmania; policies of dispersement and use of native police in Queensland; massacres of retribution and the removal of aboriginal children and forced assimilation policies. Of the radical decline in the native numbers, of the 'fact' that this decline was in large part the consequence of the actions of the settlors, there was little dispute, but what of 'intention'? Intention is the issue that Reynolds, like many other scholars investigating genocidal consequences, finds ambiguous and ultimately irresolvable.

The visual and the criminal

Speaking during the closing session of the Rome Congress, the Parisian psychiatrist August Motel drew attention to the visual power of the skulls in Lombroso's exhibition. Here, he thought, criminality showed its immediate presence.

> I do not know anything more interesting than these hundred skulls, 70 of which are from non-insane criminals who have died in prisons, while 30 are of epileptic criminals. You will find all the cranial malformations, all the exaggerations, all the diminutions of volume. Carefully consider these enormous scaphocephalies, these oxycephalies; look at this skeleton of a criminal, solid structure for a vigorous muscular system, and compare to this forceful animality this minuscule head, container of a brain that had no command over acts other than those guided by instincts. (*Proceedings*, quoted Broechmann 1995: 37)

Who were the individuals whose skulls now provided the material culture of positivist criminology? About some there were individual stories, but silence covered how most were caught in the webs of power. Throughout the civilising world, skulls were being collected.

Each may have had complex narratives of existential anguish, despair or resistance. We do not know, as in the hands of the criminal anthropologists and physicians, the powerful did the speaking.[35] The final ethnic cleansing around the Sydney basin was achieved in a series of skirmishes between 1797 and 1805. These were partly aimed at destroying the armed resistance led by a rarity in the story of the Aboriginal decline: a quasi-military leader named Pemulwuy who had succeeded in organising a group of around a hundred Aborigines to engage in hit and run attacks upon settlers in 1797. While at first evading a military party sent to capture him, he challenged it to see five of his party killed by rifle fire and himself wounded in the head. Taken to hospital in chains he escaped with the iron still around his leg. After more raids in 1801 a reward was placed on his head, and in '1802 he was killed by two settlers, decapitated, and his head sent to Sir Joseph Banks in England' (Elder 1998: 11–12). Other skulls were to follow into 'scientific collections'.[36]

Sometimes they were joined by full skeletons. Those who mistakenly define the case of the Aborigines of Tasmania as a completed physical genocide describe Truganini (Figure 4.8) (commonly spelt Trucanini in European publications) and William Lanney as the last female and male of the tribe. When William Lanney died on 3 March 1869, his grave was plundered and his skeleton removed for prosperity. As this was a breach of native custom Truganini lived on for another 7 years of desperate loneliness and 'fearful that she would meet the same fate, Truganini pleaded with the colonists on her death bed, "Don't let

Figure 4.8 Trucanini, 1866 Photograph by C.A. Woolley (RAI 687). This became the standard, tragic, image of the Australian 'Aborigine'. Woolley photographed what were thought to be the remaining five Tasmanians when Trucanini was age 54, fearful of the death of her remaining companions and her being left alone. The image taken became the iconic representation of a vanished race. See discussion in Rae-Ellis (1992), who points out that Woolley posed his subjects in European clothes suggesting that they were successfully christianised and civilised, when 'nothing could have been further from the truth'. The only indication of indigenous culture in these images is the shell necklace made and worn by Trucanini. This photograph which portrays her as a Black European has been replicated in official publications; it was selected for an Australian stamp, in preference to earlier images from watercolours, which showed her in more natural light

them cut me up. Bury me behind the mountains". Her pleas were ignored. For years her skeleton hung on public display in the Tasmanian Museum' (Elder 1998: 47–8).[37]

In 1908, as a final sign of his intellectual commitment, Lombroso commanded in his will that his skeleton, brain and the skin from his head should be placed in the collection of the *Museo* (now located in Tourin, Northern Italy). They are still housed there exerting their exhibitory presence, but are now trapped in the ambivilance of history (Morrison 2004b).

Today there are other museums containing skulls and human remains. In certain museums of Bangladesh, Cambodia and Rwanda rows of skulls and other human remains speak to another presence (see Figure 1.4).[38] A presence that criminology never placed within its domain and following the technological imperative of Darwin's legacy chose to ignore or treated as 'some mysterious process', outside the ongoing institutional emphasis on studying the 'criminal' in the service of the state. There would soon be too many skulls to collect and send to the civilised displays of Europe, for while individuals were busy constituting a criminological imagination, the European nation states had turned to 'civilising Africa'. 1885 was also the date for the Berlin Conference, where the major European nations, in the presence of a delegation from the US, drew upon one of the European constructed maps of Africa and decided which parts each would have legitimate domination over. European power – European measurements – would now determine the political boundaries of a continent. Those who occupied the lands were deemed to have given their consent or to have no reasonable (read 'powerful') presence to count. Few would hold the actions of the globalising powerful to account, least of all see what was happening as an action that could provide material for criminology. Subjection and genocide were finding a very modern arena of action, safely outside the confines of criminology's developing institutional imagination.

Chapter 5:
Civilising the Congo, Which Story, Whose Truth: Wherewith Criminology?

Part I: Léopold II and the civilising of the Congo

Our refined society attaches to human life (and with reason) a value unknown to barbarous communities. When our directing will is implanted among them its aim is to triumph over all obstacles, and results which could not be attained by lengthy speeches may follow philanthropic influence. But if, in view of this desirable spread of civilisation, we count upon the means of action which confer upon us dominion and the sanction of right, it is not less true that our ultimate end is a work of peace. Wars do not necessarily mean the ruin of the regions in which they rage our agents do not ignore this fact, so from the day when their effective superiority is affirmed, they feel profoundly reluctant to use force. The wretched negroes, however, who are still under the sole sway of their traditions, have that horrible belief that victory is only decisive when the enemy, fallen beneath their blows, is annihilated. The soldiers of the State, who are recruited necessarily from among the natives, do not immediately forsake those sanguinary habits that have been transmitted from generation to generation. The example of the white officer and wholesome military discipline gradually inspire in them a horror of human trophies of which they previously had made their boast. It is in their leaders that they must see living evidence of these higher principles taught that the exercise of authority is not at all to be confounded with cruelty, but is, indeed, destroyed by it. I am pleased to think that our agents, nearly all of whom are volunteers drawn from the ranks of the Belgian army, have always present in their minds a strong sense of the career of honour in which they are engaged, and are animated with a pure feeling of patriotism; not sparing their own blood they will the more spare the blood of the natives, who will see in them the all-powerful protectors of their lives and their property, benevolent teachers of whom they have so great a need. (King Léopold, II, Sovereign of Belgium and the Congo Free State, 1885–1908, quoted Guy Burrows 1898: 286.)

After one has talked with the men and women who have seen the atrocities, has seen in the official reports that those accused of the atrocities do not deny having committed them, but point out that they were merely obeying orders, and after one has seen that even at the capital of Boma [then capital of the Congo] all the conditions of slavery exist, one is assured that in the jungle, away from the sight of men, all things are possible. Merchants, missionaries, and officials even in Léopold's service told me that if one could spare a year and a half, or a year, to the work in the hinterland he would be an eye-witness of as cruel treatment of the natives as any that has gone before, and if I can trust myself to weigh testimony and can believe my eyes and ears I have reason to know that what they say is true. I am convinced that to-day a man, who feels that a year and a half is little enough to give to the aid of twenty millions of human beings, can accomplish in the Congo as great and good work as that of the Abolitionists …

Three years ago atrocities here were open and above-board. For instance, in the opinion of the State the soldiers, in killing game for food, wasted the State cartridges, and in consequence the soldiers, to show their officers that they did not expend the cartridges extravagantly on antelope and wild boar, for each empty cartridge brought in a human hand, the hand of a man, woman or child. These hands, drying in the sun, could be seen at the posts along the river. They are no longer in evidence. Neither is the flower-bed of Lieutenant Rom, which was bordered with human skulls. A quaint conceit.

The man to blame for the atrocities, for each separate atrocity, is Léopold. (Richard Harding Davis 1907: 44–7)

UN investigators have confirmed reports of human rights violations committed by rebel troops during recent fighting in the Democratic Republic of Congo (DR Congo) including rape, torture, arbitrary executions and cannibalism.

The UN mission in DR Congo says soldiers from the Ugandan-backed Movement for the Liberation of Congo (MLC) and two smaller factions were responsible for the atrocities which took place between mid-October and the end of December in north-eastern Congo.

More than 350 witnesses and victims interviewed by the UN rights investigators confirmed earlier allegations that rebels from the MLC had committed widespread human rights violations during their recent advance on the town of Beni.

In one case, investigators heard how a young girl was cut into small pieces by the soldiers and then eaten. In others, how hearts and other organs were cut out of victims and forced on their families to eat.

The rights investigators heard that the soldiers systematically raped women and looted houses in the town of Mambasa and in villages along the road towards Beni.

Members of the minority Pygmy community, forced to flee their forest homes for the first time anyone can remember, were among those targeted. The Pygmies say they have been targeted by the violence.

The UN spokesperson in Kinshasa described the rebel soldiers as 'freaks' who were out of control and said that abusers of human rights wherever they were in Congo, should be brought to justice. She said a copy of the investigators' findings had been given to the UN Security Council. (BBC News Online, Wednesday, 15 January 2003, 'UN confirms DR Congo cannibalism', by Mark Dummett BBC, Kinshasa [Congo])

Introduction: visualising a terrain

In 2003, while visiting the Royal Museum of Central Africa, in Turven, Belgium (an institution of display and spectacle that is the subject of the following Chapter 6) devoted to the exploration of the large area of Africa, what Europeans came to call the Kongo (later changed to Congo), I noticed in one of the glass display cases a book opened to reveal a fold out engraving (Figure 5.1). The scene is a representation of the first Portuguese explorers and officials being received at the Court of the King of the Congo. A group of Portuguese soldiers in armour, nobles in finery and priests approach a stage upon which the King is seated on a throne accompanied by several attendants with well-dressed women at the side. Before the King, some of his subjects lie prostrated on the ground while several raise their arms in praise; in the background natives queue to receive the Christian message. The stage and the large building behind it appear as if of European construction and the Congolese are depicted with European features. This may be the representational high point of interaction between Congolese and Europeans conferring upon the Congolese a status that subsequent European ideology never accepted and tragically reinterpreted from the vantage point of possessors of power.

Figure 5.1 Early engraving as presented at the RMCA, image Wayne Morrison

The Portuguese may well have treated the discovery of the mouth of the vast Congo River in 1482, followed by the first visit to the Court of the Kingdom of the Congo in 1491, as an opportunity for cooperative development. The Congolese court offered expressions of mutual respect and accepted Christianity. Nzinga Mbemba Affonso, who reigned for nearly 40 years from 1506, embodied what could be achieved by enlightened interaction. As a provincial chief he had taken to the Portuguese, accepting advisors, converting to Christianity and immersing himself in religious study. One priest wrote to the King of Portugal that he would be astonished to meet Affonso for 'he speaks so well and with such assurance that it always seems to me that the Holy Spirit speaks through his mouth' (quoted in Hochshild 1998: prologue). When King Affonso sought the advantages of European learning, goods and weapons, he asked for technical expertise in the form of craftsmen and builders to come from Portugal while he sent many of his relatives and others to study in Portugal.

He was also to see his hopes dashed by a process we have only recently given the term globalisation. For in 1500 a Portuguese expedition came upon Brazil and within a few decades a huge demand for slave labour had grown up. Slavery was widely practised in Africa with most slaves having been captured in warfare, while some were put into slavery as a consequence of committing offences or causing serious trouble or given away by their families as part of dowry settlement. Slaves were utilised in symbolic rituals. They could be sacrificed on special occasions, such as the ratification of a treaty between chiefdoms with the slow death of an abandoned slave with his bones broken symbolising the fate of anyone who violated the treaty. But they were also an integral part of the social fabric of the society; some would intermarry and they were often seen as part of the extended family. Yet the fact that some humans were treated in this way was to provide a destructive historical burden, for it meant that there were plenty of Africans ready to trade slaves for the goods Europeans offered.

In a series of letters written to the King of Portugal, Affonso's growing unease and sense of despair is apparent.

> Each day the traders are kidnapping our people – children of this country, sons of our nobles and vassals, even people of our own family. … This corruption and depravity is so widespread … We need in this kingdom only priests and schoolteachers, and no merchandise, unless it is wine and flour for Mass. … It is our wish that this kingdom not be a place for the trade or transport of slaves. (1526)

Later that year he refers to the seductive power of the consumer goods brought into the kingdom.

> Many of our subjects eagerly lust after Portuguese merchandise that your subjects have brought into our domains. To satisfy this inordinate appetite, they seize many of our black free subjects … They sell them. … As soon as the captives are in the hands of white men they are branded with a red-hot iron.

His letters revealed a growing dependency and obscene addition.

> These goods exert such a great attraction over simple and ignorant people that they believe in them and forget their belief in God … My Lord, a monstrous greed pushes our

subjects, even Christians, to seize members of their own families, and of ours, to do
business by selling them as captives.

In 1539, towards the end of his life, he learnt that 10 of his own relatives that
he had sent to Portugal for religious education had disappeared, probably
traded into slavery by the Portuguese he had entrusted them to. Trust was
declining; even missionaries took slaves and often financed their missions by
trading. The slave trade became the consuming disease militating against
social and political organisation. The European slave traders had an interest in
ensuring that native Chiefs played each other off, as any local dispute that
resulted in conflict provided more captives for the endless demands of Brazil
and then the Caribbean and the Americas for imported labour. The decline of
the Kingdom of the Congo was just part of a cyclic process of intervention,
destruction and justification. The fact that European intervention effectively
undercut the possibilities of large social units was conveniently overlooked,
since the fact that there were no large-scale and militarily resistant units was
put forward as evidence of their lack of social advancement. In time that very
lack was held sufficient reason for the need to intervene and place the areas
under the civilising influence of European power.

There are many competing accounts of the colonisation of Africa, but of
the acts of colonial governementality none was designed by its backers to have
as particular an image for public consumption as that of the Congo. Basically
seized as a personal state by Léopold II, King of the Belgians, a narrative of
humanitarian intentions and the civilising of the Congo was constructed that
bathed an imagined desolate and slave ridden area with the glow of
enlightened rule. Conversely others asserted, and most scholars who have
looked at the question today accept, that the reality was the institution of a
system of exploitation and neo-slave labour, as well as mass atrocities, that was
captured by coining the phrase 'crimes against humanity'.

From the African perspective the 'discovery' of Africa is a misnomer: as
African leaders are fond of stating, Africans were there all along. Discovery
meant rather Europeans coming upon a land, which they assessed for benefits
to them and prospects of future development as they defined it. Central Africa
is a diverse and historically fertile area, rich in mineral deposits. After AD 1000,
in what is referred to as the 'late iron age', a number of states emerged with
sophisticated metal working techniques. To the East, between the rivers
Zambezi and Limpopo, the grassland zone was rich in cattle and gold. A
distinctive and elaborate form of pottery was made. By the thirteenth century
an empire known as Great Zimbabwe emerged, and today it is still possible to
see stone ruins of what must have been a spectacular fortified palace. By the
fifteenth century when the Portuguese arrived this empire had collapsed,
taken over by the Mutapa rulers. The Portuguese were soon trading across the
width of southern Africa, from what is now Angola in the west, to Mozambique
in the east. Any potential benefits of the Portuguese arrival were soon lost as a
consequence of their desire for gold and slaves. Although technologically
superior in armaments they encountered a number of powerful kingdoms.
The Kingdom of the Congo in the west occupied part of present day northern
Angola and part of DR Congo, in the centre was the decentralised and flexible

state of Lunda, while the Lundu Kingdom in the east cultivated cassava and maize which the Portuguese successfully imported. Also in the east Monumutapa, under Mutapa rule, resisted all attempts by the Portuguese at subjugation and, although it was reduced in size, it maintained its vigour under the military dynasty of Changamires into the eighteenth century. The Congo kingdom, however, was by the seventeenth century devastated by the slave trade, which had not necessitated the Portuguese to try and force their way into the interior. The tribes and kingdoms of the interior confined their dealings to middlemen in search of ivory, slaves and gold for sale to coastal traders, both African and European. By the mid-nineteenth century European eyes turned to a new governmental project – carving up Africa. In accordance with enlightenment principles, this would be conducted legally – by contract and international agreement – and guided by the desire for progress. Today historians call this the scramble for Africa and the key explorer in the Congo's story was Henry Stanley.

Stanley: from a bastard birth to burial in Westminster Abbey

Stanley's official story represents a great triumph of the human spirit over humble beginnings and adversity. Originally named John Rowlands, Stanley was born a bastard on 28 January 1841, at Denbigh, Wales. He was soon placed in a school for unwanted children and his upbringing is a tale of constant misery. When 18 he sailed as a cabin boy to New Orleans, Louisiana, where he gained employment under an American merchant named Henry Morton Stanley, whose name he adopted. During the American Civil War he was served in the Confederate army and in 1862 was captured at the Battle of Shiloh. As an escape from the appalling conditions in which he was held, he was transferred to the federal service but was discharged, ostensibly because of ill health. He joined the Union Navy in 1864 and became a ship's clerk on the frigate Minnesota and when the ship bombarded a Confederate fort in North Carolina, Stanley became one of the few people to see combat on both sides of the civil war. He deserted in 1865 and started a new role as a part-time journalist, sending back accounts of the western frontier towns. Stanley travelled to Turkey in search of interesting stories, but returned and received his break when covering the Indian Wars, having dispatches published not only in St Louis but East Coast newspapers as well. The style was settled; it did not matter that there was little action to report on; Stanley could make it up and present it with a flourish that attracted readers. He caught the attention of the flamboyant James Gordon Bennett, publisher of the New York Herald, who hired him as a special correspondent to cover the British punitive expedition that was being organised under Napier against the Ethiopian king Theodore II. According to some accounts (Hochschild 1998: 26) Stanley bribed telegraph officials to ensure that he was the first to relay the news of the fall of Magdala, then the capital of Ethiopia. Whatever the truth, Bennett understood Stanley's ability to court publicity and to sell copies and in 1869 he dispatched Stanley to find the Scottish missionary and explorer David Livingstone from whom little had been heard while he was searching for the source of the Nile. After being delayed by other assignments, Stanley reached the island of Zanzibar off the eastern coast of Africa on 6 January 1871 and crossed over to the mainland with about 2,000 men and left for the interior on 21 March. On 10 November he met the ailing Livingstone at Ujiji, a town on Lake Tanganyika, and is said to have greeted him with the now famous phrase: 'Dr Livingstone, I presume?'

The only accounts of the journey were those Stanley sent since his white travelling companions had died. In his narrative, Stanley nurses Livingstone back to health and they become good friends, going on to explore the northern end of Lake Tanganyika. Perhaps fortunately for Stanley's reputation, Livingstone stayed on in Africa and died the next year. Stanley returned to Europe in 1872, and the following year was sent by the Herald to west Africa to report on the British campaign against the Ashanti of what is now Ghana. The New York Herald and London Daily Telegraph shared the cost of Stanley's next expedition, planned to continue the exploring work of Livingstone whose body had been returned to London with Stanley being one of the pall-bearers at the burial. In November 1874, Stanley left Zanzibar for the interior accompanied by 359 persons. He visited King Mutesa of Buganda and then circumnavigated Lake Victoria, becoming involved in several skirmishes with the inhabitants of the lakeshore. He then went south, circumnavigated Lake Tanganyika, and headed west to the Lualaba River, a headstream of the Congo River, navigated down the Lualaba and Congo rivers as far as a large set of falls he named after Livingstone. Finally he continued overland for a short distance to the Atlantic Ocean, which he reached in August 1877. This was certainly a great journey of discovery; at its end less than half his original party were alive.

Stanley returned to London in January 1878, rather ill but an international celebrity receiving honours and invited to make speeches around Europe. At great risk to his health he undertook writing assignments, public meetings of various kinds and a lobbying campaign to 'pour the civilisation of Europe into the barbarism of Africa'. Stanley was clear that he really referred to 'the boundless opportunity for commercial exploitation' of the lands he had explored and mapped for European consumption. Beyond the rapids that had marked the limits of the penetration up the Congo River:

> There are 40,000,000 naked people and the cotton-spinners of Manchester are waiting to clothe them ... Birmingham's factories are glowing with the red metal that shall presently be made into ironwork in every fashion and shape for them ... and the ministers of Christ are zealous to bring them, the poor benighted heathen, into the Christian fold.

It is almost certain that Stanley's estimate was a tactical exaggeration to encourage the reader into images of profitable trade. In later work he downgraded his estimate to *c.* 28,000,000 and this figure has reasonable acceptance in the literature as a rough estimate. If this later figure was at all an accurate guess, the administration he was to help found would take the lives of over half in a campaign of ruthless exploitation using neo-slave labour, which resulted in the first use of the term crimes against humanity.[1] For while the British government was not at all keen to take on another colonial territory, Léopold II, King of Belgium, a country not long independent, was desperate for a colonial territory to exploit.[2] Léopold convinced Stanley to return to the Congo under his sponsorship on another expedition, which lasted for five years. During this period he constructed a road from the lower Congo to Stanley Pool (now called Malebo Pool) and laid the foundations for the establishment of the Independent State of the Congo. In January 1887, Stanley was placed at the head of an expedition to assist the German explorer Mehmed Emin Pasha, officially titled governor of the Equatorial Province of the Egyptian Sudan, who was surrounded by rebellious Mahdist forces. In 1888 Stanley reached Emin Pasha who refused to return to Egypt. During this expedition, Stanley found the Ruwenzori Range, the so-called Mountains of the Moon, and found that the Semliki River linked Lake Albert to Lake Edward. In 1889, Stanley finally succeeded in bringing Emin Pasha back to the coast. In 1890 Stanley married Dorothy Tennant, who later edited his autobiography (1909). He had been naturalised a US citizen in 1885, but in 1892 again became a British subject. From 1895 to 1900 he sat in parliament as the Liberal Unionist member for North Lambeth. Stanley's last visit to Africa was in 1897, and in 1899 he was knighted. He died in London on 10 May, 1904, and was buried in Westminster Abbey. His books narrating his adventurous life were commercial successes, among them *How I Found Livingstone* (1872); *Through the Dark Continent* (1878); *In Darkest Africa* (1890); *My Early Travels and Adventures in America and Asia* (1895); *Through South Africa* (1898); and *Autobiography* (edited by his wife, 1909).

So reads the success story. Having laboured to create his own personal narrative and control the representational truth of his life, Stanley was rewarded with commercial success and increased status: the bastard came to serve in Parliament and be buried in Westminster Abbey, the final resting place of the British elite.

Throughout his travels Stanley provided a conduit for power and images. For those who lived on the East Coast of the US and later Europe, Stanley's writings relayed a journey of a man possessed of great personal courage, carrying western truth and superiority into a realm of chaos and darkness (note the titles of his works, *Through the Dark Continent* (1878); *In Darkest Africa* (1890)). The accounts not only provided evidence, usually accompanied by various images, of the primitive state of the other, they also reinforced notions of the civilised space the reader inhabited. As the *Anti-Slavery Reporter* put it:

> From the untracked depths of one of Nature's densest and most deadly forests, saturated with the tropical rains of countless ages, and alive with malignant pigmies, skilled in the use of poisoned arrows, Stanley like a hero of Romance, has once again emerged into the light of civilisation. (September–October 1889: 269)

Stanley's journeys were certainly triumphs of personal drive and testament to his acceptance of great personal hardship; they also revealed an easy resort to violence and use of any technological superiority he would muster. By contrast to the paternalistic Livingstone, who travelled without a retinue of heavily armed followers, Stanley was a harsh and brutal taskmaster. His published accounts were rewritten with an eye to the civilised sensibilities of the audience but they still showed the human cost of his journeys and his intolerance of anything other than total commitment to the point of death from his fellow travellers and porters. Stanley drove his men up hills and through swamps without let up and often subjected them to his violent rages: 'When mud and wet sapped the physical energy of the lazily-inclined, a dog-whip became their backs, restoring them to a sound – sometimes to an extravagant – activity'. The fact that he had himself deserted from the US Navy may have affected his desire to ensure that 'incorrigible deserters … were well flogged and chained'. It would have been difficult to distinguish his from a slave caravan, except this was also run as a military campaign: 'We have attacked and destroyed 28 large towns and three or four score villages'. No challenge to his status could be tolerated: 'the beach was crowded with infuriates and mockers … we perceived we were followed by several canoes in some of which we saw spears shaken at us … I opened on them with the Winchester Repeating Rifle. Six shots and four deaths were sufficient to quiet the mocking.' (Figure 5.2).

Towards the land and its peoples, Stanley's gaze was epistemic and opportunistic. Although he claimed a considerable population able to provide a source of labour and future consumers he depicted large parts as covered by a forest of darkness and vast thinly populated plains. Africa was scanned for the potential transformation of that 'Unpeopled country'.

> What a settlement one could have in this valley! See, it is broad enough to support a large population. Fancy a church spire rising where that tamarind rears its dark crown of

Stanley's Reisen in Afrika: Ein Kampf mit den Wilden.
(Siehe Seite 330.)

Figure 5.2 Travelling in the Congo, Stanley is challenged by natives shaking spears so, of course, he shoots them. Engraving by unnamed artist in *Neue Illustrirte Zeitung*, 17 February 1878, p. 332 (MEPL)

foliage, and think how well a score or two of pretty cottages would look instead of those thorn clumps and gum trees! ... There are plenty of ... Pilgrim Fathers among the Anglo-Saxon race yet, and when America is filled up with their descendants, who shall say that Africa ... shall not be their next resting place?

Stanley's journeys were from the beginning a relationship with diverse audiences that was supported by the military technology of the West and the punishment that such technological power allowed Western authorities to meet out on those that resisted it. In his dispatches from the 1867 Indian Wars the fact that most of the year had been devoted to peace negotiations was of no consequence, nor was there any discussion of the justice of the cause. Instead the readers were told that 'the Indian War has at last been fairly inaugurated ... the Indians, true to their promises, true to their bloody instincts, to their savage hatred of the white race, to the lessons instilled in their bosoms by their progenitors, are on the warpath'. It was the message the readers wanted. The future US President Theodore Roosevelt expressed the common sentiment in his *The Winning of the West*: 'The settler and pioneer have at bottom justice on their side; this great continent could not have been kept as nothing but a game reserve for squalid savages' (Roosevelt 1889: 90). From writing within the military protection of this internal colonisation of North America, Stanley journeyed with the British 'punitive expeditions' against the Emperor of Abyssinia and the Ashanti of what is now Ghana. The concept of a 'punitive expedition' was never the subject of analysis, justice was assumed, pride restored; conversely, today some question their legality and wonder what to do with the cultural objects taken (these events are briefly discussed in Chapter 7 of this text). Buttressed with this cultural power Stanley, himself, became a willing instrument of the power of Léopold II.

For almost six years during 1879 to 1884, Stanley worked on behalf of Léopold to survey the basin of the Upper Congo River with a view to establishing an imperial enclave in Central Africa. Léopold's previous efforts to obtain a colony had proved unsuccessful; his new plan was dressed in humanitarian rhetoric, language he implored Stanley to use.[3] Moreover, Léopold appeared to risk his own money in the service of a civilising mission having founded the supposedly philanthropic International African Association which, during Stanley's sojourn in the Congo, became the International Association of the Congo. During the years he spent in Africa, Stanley signed 'treaties' with over 450 native chiefs, thus acquiring for Léopold sovereignty over their territories in accordance with the general terms of a standard treaty in which those chiefs 'freely and of their own accord, for themselves and their heirs and successors for ever, do give up to the said Association the sovereignty and all sovereign and governing rights to all their territories ... and to assist by labor or otherwise, any works, improvements, or expeditions which the said association shall cause at any time to be carried out in any part of these territories'. The Chiefs also gave up 'all roads and waterways running through this country, the right of collecting tolls on the same, and all game, fishing, mining, and forest rights [which are now] to be the absolute property of the said association, together with any unoccupied lands as may at any time hereafter be chosen.' For their part the 'International African Association' agreed to pay to the chiefs 'one piece of cloth per month to each of the undersigned chiefs …; and the said chiefs hereby acknowledge to accept this bounty and monthly subsidy in full settlement of all their claims on the said Association' (source, Stanley, *The Congo and the Founding of its Free State* (1885), Vol. II: 195–7).

Léopold's personal ambition was the driving force behind the creation of the Congo Free State, but his enterprise also reflected the enterprise of a concerned Sovereign of a European dominion. He believed Belgium's future could only be guaranteed by Imperial possessions that offered military glory, social purpose and financial surplus.

> Surrounded by the sea, Holland, Prussia and France, our frontiers can never be extended in Europe. It is far away that we must find compensation … Our neutrality … forbids us, outside of our nine provinces, any political activity in Europe. But the sea bathes our coast, the universe lies in front of us, steam and electricity have made distances disappear, all the unappropriated lands on the surface of the globe may become the field of our operations and of our successes. (quoted in de Lichtervelds 1928: 37)

Léopold had a special relationship with his military and 'never ceased to defend the interests of an army that he regarded as a safeguard of Belgian neutrality and social order'. Yet this was not widely shared for Belgium's catholic masses did not appreciate that the 18 per cent of Belgian national expenditure spent on the military in 1880 was small compared to the 30.3 per cent in France and the 30.8 in Holland (Gann and Duignan 1979: 21). A colonial possession would provide markets and revenues to pay for strengthening Belgium's armed forces thus defending its neutrality in Europe while providing a place for social expansion and a civilising mission for the military, otherwise bored with the routines of army life in a neutral country. It would in short solve many practical problems for a country 'choking in its narrow limits' by offering 'an outlet for her surplus production of men, things and ideas'. Belgium must expand as Athens, Venice, Portugal and Holland had in the past:

> These small states which had but limited provinces in Europe, knew how to create outside possessions and relations which not only extended their commerce, but also procured them the means of paying for their military expenses and maintaining their political existence. (quoted in de Lichtervelds 1928: 33, 38 and 193)

The Berlin conference 1884–5

The Victorian social evolutionist Herbert Spencer was articulating a widespread perception when he gave the perfection of society as the goal of evolution. That perfection was the endpoint of the path of social progress; the civilising process was a movement from savagery and ignorance towards that eventual goal. Social evolution required as a simple empirical fact the displacement of less developed societies by those that had moved further along the path. This process needed to be managed on a global scale and an important feature of developed societies was their recognition of the need to minimise military conflict between them and to use their military power to absorb the weaker societies.

> [I]n a struggle for existence among societies, the survival of the fittest is the struggle of those in which power of military co-operation is the greatest, and military co-operation is

that primary kind of co-operation which prepares for other kinds. So that this formation of larger societies by the union of smaller ones in war, and this destruction or absorption of the smaller ununited societies by the united larger ones, is an inevitable process through which the varieties of men most adapted for social life supplant the less adapted varieties. (Spencer 1967: 78)

Spencer's views were inherent in the Berlin Conference of 1884–5. This key act in Africa's integral destruction was at the time dressed up as a progressive act by the great powers. In order to reduce the potential for military conflict between themselves the colonial powers superimposed territorial boundaries onto the African continent and allocated each area to one of themselves. By the time independence returned to Africa in 1950, the realm had acquired a legacy of political fragmentation that could neither be eliminated nor made to operate satisfactorily.

This was a conference with many layers of deceit, potential conflict and double-dealing. German chancellor Otto von Bismark officially called together the major Western powers to negotiate questions that caused conflict and end confusion over the control of Africa. Although the request formally came from Portugal, who wished to safeguard their own possessions from being seized by Britain or France, Bismarck also aimed to protect his recently acquired (albeit rather reluctantly) holdings and force his rivals to struggle with one another for territory. At the time of the conference, although they were increasingly claiming large chunks of land, only the coastal areas of Africa were effectually colonized by the European powers with some 80 per cent of Africa remaining under traditional and local control. The fear was that a scramble for control over the interior could result in a European war. In a hodgepodge of geometric boundaries Africa was divided into 50 irregular countries, a map for a continent that was superimposed over a 1,000 indigenous cultures and regions. These new geographical entities were artificial constructs, although the boundaries were often meant to follow recognisable divisions, such as major rivers. They divided coherent groups of people and merged together disparate groups whose only similarities often were to be their relationship with the coloniser.

This was an act of the then 'international community'. Fourteen countries were represented by a plethora of ambassadors when the conference opened in Berlin on 15 November 1884 (including Austria–Hungary, Belgium, Denmark, France, Germany, Great Britain, Italy, the Netherlands, Portugal, Russia, Spain, Sweden–Norway [unified from 1814–1905], Turkey and the US). Of these France, Germany, Great Britain and Portugal were the major players in the conference, controlling most of colonial Africa at the time.

Extending free trade was the initial task of the Conference by agreeing that the Congo River and Niger River mouths and basins be considered neutral and open to trade. Officially, the agenda concentrated on promoting free trade and free navigation in the Congo and the Niger, the formalities to be observed in the future for valid annexation of African territory, the protection of the native peoples and the suppression of the slave trade. The conference had no mandate to deal with territorial questions as such, but behind the scenes claims and counterclaims were fought out, and in practice were regarded as more important than the official business. Little time was devoted to humanitarian questions or the effect of the conference's deliberations upon the future of African peoples. The division of spoils was paramount.[4]

Territorial claims were founded upon the assumption that the treaties that both the Association and France had concluded with African chiefs were valid (and in the case of the Association, that such treaties could legally be made with a private body). Stanley recounted the Association's position at the beginning of the conference:

> The Association were in possession of treaties made with over four hundred and fifty independent African chiefs, whose rights would be conceded by all to have been indisputable, since they held their lands by undisturbed occupation, by long ages of succession, by real divine right. Of their own free will, without coercion, but for substantial considerations, reserving only a few easy conditions, they had transferred their rights of sovereignty and of ownership to the Association. The time had arrived when a sufficient number of these had been made to connect the several miniature sovereignties into one concrete whole, to present itself before the world for general recognition of its right to govern, and hold these in the name of an independent state, lawfully constituted according to the spirit and tenor of international law.

Whether African chiefs had understood the treaties to which they had affixed their marks, or if 'substantial considerations' had indeed been provided or even whether the Chiefs had any right to make the concessions they did was irrelevant.[5] It was an unquestioned assumption that the European Powers had the right to annex African territory for their own advantage, so long as the nominal consent of a certain number of African chiefs had been obtained. In taking over the Congo, what counted was the inability of the Africans to launch any full-scale resistance, their local tribal structures and the successive weakening of those Kingdoms that could have provided major resistance as a consequence of the slave trade rendered European intrusions unanswerable. As Harry Johnston noted (1895: 299–300) in 1884, African divisions accounted for Stanley's rapid success.

> What has hitherto made Mr Stanley's work so rapid and so comparatively easy has been the want of cohesion amongst the African chiefs; he has had no great jealous empire to contend with, as he would have had no farther north or father south. If one village declined to let him settle among them, the next town out of rivalry received him with open arms. There has been no *mot d'ordre*, and this had enabled him to effectually implant himself in their midst. ... Union ... would inevitably turn them with race jealousy against the white man, the entry of civilisation into the Congo countries would be hindered, and this great work made dependent upon the caprices of an African despot. The black man, though he may make a willing subject, can never rule. These people are well disposed in their present condition to receive civilisation, but the civilisation must come not as a humble supplicant but as a monarch. It must be able to inspire respect as well as native wonder, and this is what the expedition as conducted by Mr. Stanley has succeeded in doing.

The Berlin Conference was a triumph for Léopold. Bismarck had acquired substantial new holdings in south-west Africa and had no desire for the Congo, but did not want it to go to either England or France. Léopold had impressed Portugal's dreadful slavery record upon the British administration and quietly let English merchant houses know that he would, if given formal control of the Congo, give them the same 'most favoured nation' status that Portugal offered. At the same time he promised Bismark that he would not give any one nation special status, and that German traders would be as welcome as any other. Then Léopold offered France the support of the Association for French ownership of the entire northern bank, and sweetened the deal by proposing that if his personal wealth proved insufficient to hold the entire Congo (as seemed inevitable) it should revert to France. His coupe, however, was gaining the support of the US by sending President Arthur carefully edited copies of the treaties Stanley had extracted and proposing that, as an entirely disinterested humanitarian body, the Association would administer the Congo for the good of all, handing over power to the locals as soon as they were ready for the grave responsibility. France was given 257,000 square miles on the north bank (modern Congo–Brazzaville and the Central African Republic), Portugal 351,000 square miles to the south (modern Angola), and Léopold's wholly owned, single-shareholder philanthropic organisation received the balance: 905,000 square miles, to be constituted as the Congo Free State. Although the negotiations were twisted and the factual situation on the ground often at odds with what was asserted (see Ewans 2002: part III), in effect sovereignty for the Congo was transferred to himself individually. He became sole ruler of *c.* 28 million people, without constitution, without international supervision, without ever having been to the Congo, and without more than a tiny handful of his new subjects having heard of him.

Certainly there was a statement of enlightened principles of government. Under the General Act of Berlin, signed at the conclusion of the conference, the powers agreed that activities in the Congo Basin should be governed by certain principles, including freedom of trade and navigation, neutrality in the event of war, suppression of the slave traffic, and improvement of the condition of the indigenous population. In practice, the Conference's legal requirement of 'effective occupation', provided the rationale for Léopold to turn the Congo Free State into an effective instrument of colonial hegemony. Indigenous conscripts were promptly recruited into a nascent army, the *Force Publique*, manned by European officers, which reached 19,028 men under arms by 1898 (much greater than the armies of the Portuguese or German possessions). A corps of European administrators, many drawn from the Belgium army, was assembled and numbered 1,500 by 1906. A skeletal transportation grid was eventually assembled to provide the necessary links between the coast and the interior. The cost of the enterprise proved far higher than had been anticipated, however, as the penetration of the vast hinterland could not be achieved except at the price of numerous military campaigns. Some of these campaigns resulted in the suppression or expulsion of the previously powerful Afro-Arab slave-traders and ivory merchants. Léopold could only hold and exploit what became in effect and substance a personal fiefdom by the ruthless and massive suppression of opposition and exploitation of African labour and the lack of interest in Belgium in the actual operation of his programme.

The Léopoldian system: state concessions and monopolies, forced labour and atrocity

Léopold's belief that profits could be easily obtained owed much to his misunderstanding the Dutch experience based upon reading a work on Dutch colonisation called *Java, or How to Manage a Colony*, by the coincidently named author J.W.B. Money (1861). There he learnt that the Dutch had derived large profits with minimal investment by forcing their subjects to raise cash crops and transferring the accumulated surplus to the motherland. The colonies were to be exploited not by the operation of a market economy, but by state intervention and compulsory cultivation of a cash crop to be brought by and distributed by the state at controlled prices. This model, however was archaic by the time Léopold came to apply it. The enforced culture system had turned out to be inefficient and they had been largely replaced by 'free-wage' labour, which turned out to work harder than conscripts. In the so-called Liberal era in Java (*c.* 1870–1900) the Dutch largely did away with compulsory labour, state plantations gave way to private enterprise and alienation of native land to foreigners was abolished (Gann and Duignan 1979: 31).

Léopold did not look deeply into the actual conditions in Java; he was seduced by the simplicity of the model, although he was careful not to reveal the strength of his economic calculations, preferring instead to stress that concern with a financial return was necessary to pay for the civilising mission. There was, however, no escaping a problem of simple logic in the structure of the engagement in the Congo that necessitated neo-slavery. The goal of fighting slavery and bringing civilisation while at the same time making a profit for Léopold required a source of abundant labour at the cheapest possible terms and there was little incentive for the native Africans to supply it. Stanley had argued that a railroad was essential to turn the Congo into a profitable area. Without recourse to forced labour, however, the railroad could not be built; nor could the huge concessions made to private companies become profitable unless African labour was freely used to locate and transport first ivory and then rubber; nor could the resistance of African tribes be overcome without a substantial recruitment of indigenous troops. The logic of the revenue imperative left the Léopoldian system with no apparent option but to extract a maximum output of labour and natural resources from the land. At the heart of the system lay a perverse combination of rewards and penalties. Congo Free State agents and native auxiliaries (the so-called *capitas*) were given authority to use as much force as they deemed appropriate to meet delivery norms, and because their profits were proportional to the amount of rubber and ivory collected, the inevitable consequence was the institutionalisation of force on a huge scale.

Although native chiefs were expected to cooperate, the incessant and arbitrary demands made on their authority were self-defeating. Many chiefs turned against the emerging colonial state; others were quickly disposed of and replaced by state-appointed straw chiefs. Many small-scale revolts ensued, which had an immediate effect on the scale and frequency of military expeditions.

Third party expectations of the high cost of developing the Congo had been a factor in the readiness with which Léopold had been given the Free State. Many expected him to go bankrupt. He was saved only by the ruthless exploitation of labour and a new source of income, rubber and by his ability to turn to the Belgium State at crucial moments to extend loans when Léopold cleverly presented the alternative as much worse. As his costs increased, financial disaster seemed inevitable but Léopold arranged in effect a massive interest free loan from the Belgium State and declared a state monopoly on rubber and ivory. The free-trade principle that was to have been the cornerstone of the Congo Free State thus became a legal fiction, summarised by Father Vermeersche in a critical book in 1906 as 'Article one: trade is entirely free; article two: everything belongs to the State and it regrets it can only give restricted place to trade, besides there is nothing to buy or sell'. The discovery of the technological uses of rubber in 1890 transformed the financial situation, for rubber trees were growing wild in many parts of the territory. Rubber production increased from under 250 tons in 1892 to over 1,200 tons in 1896 and exceeded 1,500 tons in 1897. By 1897 Léopold believed he would prove to be financially a major winner and he expanded his building works in Brussels designed to celebrate his power and dedication to the rather fragile nation-state of Belgium. Works that were to include a baroque palace at Tervuren to house a Congo museum, linked to the city by an avenue of elm trees.

The residents and visitors to Brussels would see great works celebrating the civilising mission happening in a far away place (see Chapter 6). It was vital to prevent anything that would disturb the image of Léopold's project as a shared sense of value and purpose. However, a number of voices made troublesome contributions. Protestant missionaries were the first to alert international public opinion to the extent of cruelties visited upon the African population, and with the creation of the Congo Reform Association in England in 1904, a major campaign against the Congo Free State was launched. Not until 1908, however, did the Belgian parliament vote in favour of annexation as the most sensible solution to the flood of criticisms generated by the reform movement. The Colonial Charter provided for the government of what was thereafter known as the Belgian Congo. This charter permitted the king to retain a great deal of authority and influence over affairs in the colony through power of appointment and legislative authority, but his power was constitutional rather than personal and therein limited. The main purpose of the charter was to prevent the establishment of a royal autocracy in the colony similar to the one that had existed in the Congo Free State but it also inscribed racial differences, for while under the Belgium all citizens were equals, in the colonial charter Europeans and Natives were different legal beings.

The battle over truth

Nothing is more clear to the student of the history of Africa than the definite purpose which animated all King Léopold's legislation from the commencement of his rule over the Congo through all the changing years to the present moment. That purpose has ever been to secure the prosperity of the wide realm of the Congo and of its inhabitants. It is clearly shown and clearly observed in every decree the sovereign of the Congo has made.

All that has been done in the Congo rests on the King's sole authority. In accepting the sovereignty of the Independent State King Léopold faced the greatest problem and undertook the weightiest responsibility of our age, but he faced it unfettered. The diplomatists who sat at the Congress of Berlin seem to have looked to no more than the interests of foreign traders and, in a somewhat vague way, the protection against slavery of the native races of Africa. It is well for man-kind that the sovereign of the Congo looked farther, and that his views were wise.

King Léopold undertook to protect the native races from the raids of slave traders, and he undertook to free them from slavery; he undertook to open up Equatorial Africa to trade, and to establish a settled government in it; but these undertakings, great though they were, were but the least part of his task. Besides them, he had to regulate his government so that trade and industry would flourish profitably in the land in the future, and he had to educate and to civilise the negroes. Politicians and pamphleteers who deal only with the present moment are apt to overlook these, the main, points of King Léopold's great undertaking; but it is with regard to them, and not to any passing need, that King Léopold's rule in Africa and his legislation for the Congo must be judged. John DeCourcy MacDonnell (1905: 162–3). MacDonnell (1869–1915) an Irishman and a Celtic scholar was a Belgian civil servant.

While MacDonnell's account looks today to be propaganda, to the European elites of his time (and, one would estimate, for most Belgium citizens today) Léopold could be trusted to have honourable intentions. The Belgian administrator Liebrechts articulated the popular perception: 'Left to himself, the Negro would never have improved himself; it has taken the direct and commanding action of the European to change him' (1909: 255).

From the beginning of occupation economic calculations had to be kept from view. As Léopold wrote to the Belgium prime minister after a parliamentary debate in 1891: 'I thank you for having done justice yesterday to the calumnies spread by enemies of the Congo state, to the accusation of secrecy and the spirit of gain. The Congo state is certainly not a business. If it gathers ivory on certain of its lands, that is only to lessen its deficit'. Calling the natives to work, however, was another matter. Work was the instrument of civilisation although the methods required to ensure that the natives worked may not necessarily be those employed in Belgium. As Léopold once declared to an American Reporter: 'In dealing with a race composed of cannibals for thousands of years it is necessary to use methods which will best shake their idleness and make them realize the sanctity of work'.

In the early 1890s that work included obtaining all the ivory that could be found. Congo state officials and their African auxiliaries undertook ivory raids, shooting elephants and buying tusks from villagers for a pittance, or simply confiscating them. The peoples of the Congo region had traditionally hunted elephants, but now they were forbidden to sell or deliver ivory to anyone other than an agent of Léopold. The basis of the state sanctioned ivory-gathering method was a commission structure the king imposed in 1890, whereby his agents in the field got a cut of the ivory's market value – but on a sliding scale. For ivory purchased in Africa at 8 francs per kilo, an agent received 6 per cent of the vastly higher European market price. But the commission climbed, in stages, to 10 per cent for ivory bought at 4 francs per kilo. The European agents thus had a powerful incentive to force Africans – if necessary, by violence – to accept extremely low prices. There was no incentive to develop a sustainable economy (Figure 5.3). Gann and Duignan (1979: 141) summarise: 'The Congo Free State remains a classic example of the evils that beset a coercive economy. Private monopolies in partnership with the state proved efficient as a means of bloody oppression, but failed even on their own terms as instruments of development.'

Certainly, the Congo was not the only part of Africa where colonial administration resulted in abuse of power and atrocities, but the Congo was exceptional both in its administrative arrangements that concentrated power without formal accountability in the colonial nations government and in that the scale of the abuse was embedded into the structure of administration. The Congo Free State had deliberately and as a matter of official regulation deprived the Africans of their traditional rights in the land and its products, and had compelled them to work either for the State itself or for concessionary companies in which the State was interested. State and company agents were at one and the same time administrators and traders; their basic salaries were low, but they received large bonuses scaled according to the amount of rubber and other products that they were able to collect. There was thus no incentive to check the methods employed by their African subordinates, whose

Figure 5.3 Image of an Ivory station. One of the lantern slides used by the Congo Reform Association; the cracks in the lantern slide can be clearly discerned (source: Anti-Slavery Association)

instructions encouraged them to force the local populations to furnish ever-increasing quantities of these products. Yet this was an internationally sanctioned regime and any government that cared to follow up on the allegations soon came to understand the reality. As the British government official, Pickersgill commented after inquiring into the allegations made by the Swedish missionary Sjoblom: 'The barbarities referred to are but the natural outcome of the system of government … The amazing thing about the Congo atrocities is not that they have occurred, but that they have been so systematically denied … The loss of life has been very great.' (quoted, Ewans 2002: 183). But he and others doubted that there was any legal basis on which outside Governments could intervene.

In the account of the American historian Hochschild (1998) – a text which when translated and appearing in Belgium in 2001 has had a substantial role in raising the issue of the colonial past in contemporary Belgium – there is a successful counter movement; a campaign for international human rights. In his account, a group of dedicated individuals – the Congo Reform Association formed by Morel[6] – broke the veils of secrecy and brought out images and accounts of the evil. As a compromise to appease agitation in parliament for the British government to gather together the signing nations to the Berlin Conference and check if the Congo Free State was actually being run as agreed, the British government charged Roger Casement, an Irish British civil servant, with writing a report on the situation in 1904. His report was damming (see Ó Síocháin and O'Sullivan, 2003, for a modern edition of his report and 1903 diary). The claim of the Congo administration that it had suppressed the slave-trade was met with a damming retort:

> It has not suppressed the Slave-Trade, it has merely substituted itself for the Arab who formerly exacted service from the native.
>
> Instead of selling him it only requires him to serve it under compulsion, and to give it, for the sole benefit of far distant European speculators and financiers, whatever his soil is capable of producing.

Even without a responsibility to report, it was hard for anyone who went to the Congo to miss the signs. 'A file of poor devils, chained by the neck, carried my trunks and boxes toward the dock', a Congo state official noted matter-of-factly in his memoirs. At the next stop on his journey more porters were needed for an overland trip: 'There were about a hundred of them, trembling and fearful before the overseer, who strolled by whirling a whip. For each stocky and broad-backed fellow, how many were skeletons dried up like mummies, their skin worn out … seamed with deep scars, covered with suppurating wounds … No matter, they were all up to the job.' Without any mechanical mode of transportation across land or domestic animals to use, humans were the beasts of burden. Porters were needed most at the points where the river system was blocked by rapids, particularly – until the railroad was built – for the three-week trek between the port town of Matadi and Stanley Pool. This was the pipeline up which supplies passed to the interior and down which ivory and other riches were carried to the sea. Moving dismantled steamboats to the upper section of the river was the most labour-intensive job of all: one steamboat could comprise 3,000 porter loads. Although many involved in the

Congo defended the portage system as the only feasible way of achieving civilisation it was clear that the lower river peoples were devastated by a system which 'laid so many burdens over the years on their heads and shoulders that it finished by crushing them, so that their bones mingled with the dust of the path and the whole region was depopulated'. The lower river tribes' people did not have the technology to resist. Their only hope lay in the Europeans suffering from the very things that they themselves feared.[7] Advances in medicine however, were aiding the power of the European to survive the predations of geography. The sights of coercion and discipline were disturbing to those not used to it. To quote Edmond Picard, a Belgian senator, on a caravan of porters he saw on the route around the big rapids in 1896:

> Unceasingly we meet these porters ... black, miserable, with only a horribly filthy loin-cloth for clothing, frizzy and bare head supporting the load – box, bale, ivory tusk ... barrel, most of them sickly, dropping under a burden increased by tiredness and insufficient food – a handful of rice and some stinking dried fish; pitiful walking caryatids, beasts of burden with thin monkey legs, with drawn features, eyes fixed and round from preoccupation with keeping their balance and from the daze of exhaustion. They come and go like this by the thousand ... requisitioned by the State armed with its powerful militia, handed over by chiefs whose slaves they are and who make off with their salaries, trotting with bent knees, belly forward, an arm raised to steady the load, the other leaning on a long walking-stick, dusty and sweaty; insects spreading out across the mountains and valleys their many files and their task of Sisyphus, dying along the road or, the journey over, heading off to die from overwork in their villages.

The *chicotte* – a whip of raw, sun-dried hippopotamus hide, cut into a long sharp-edged corkscrew strip, provided the motivation to work and the usual form of punishment. The *chicotte* was usually applied to the victim's bare buttocks (and became the symbol of colonial power in the Congo, Dembour 1992: 205–25) (Figure 5.4). Its blows would leave permanent scars; more than 25 strokes could mean unconsciousness; and a 100 or more – not an uncommon punishment – were often fatal. The administrator Lefrancs was to see many *chicotte* beatings, although his descriptions of them, in pamphlets and newspaper articles he published in Belgium, provoked little reaction.

> The station chief selects the victims ... Trembling, haggard, they lie face down on the ground ... two of their companions, sometimes four, seize them by the feet and hands, and remove their cotton drawers ... Each time that the torturer lifts up the *chicotte*, a reddish stripe appears on the skin of the pitiful victims, who, however firmly held, gasp in frightful contortions ... At the first blows the unhappy victims left out horrible cries which soon become faint groans ... In a refinement of evil, some officers, and I've witnessed this, demand that when the sufferer gets up, panting, he must graciously give the military salute.

Public hangings were also frequent. Here, for instance, a station chief named Georges Bricusse describes in his diary a hanging he ordered in 1895 of a man who had stolen a rifle:

> The gallows is set up. The rope is attached, too high. They lift up the nigger and put the noose around him. The rope twists for a few moments, then *crack*, the man is wriggling on the ground. A shot in the back of the neck and the game is up. It didn't make the least impression on me this time!!! And to think that the first time I saw the *chicotte* administered, I was pale with fright. Africa has some use after all. I could now walk into fire as if to a wedding.

Figure 5.4 This photo of the *chicotte* in use is one of the collection of the Reform Association (supplied originally by Alice Harris, Baptist Missionary); writing on the back indicates that it was a posed image. The person that is supposed to be doing the whipping is clearly awaiting instructions and the person prostrate is actually not chained down (some chains are at bottom left as if the poser was debating whether to use them). It still depicts a reality where natives were coerced into their own subjugation. Another image, certainly of a real whipping, appears in Edouard Manduau's painting of 1884. This paining is on display at the RMCA and was engraved appearing in 1885 in *Le Moniteur* with the message that the *chicotte* 'acts as justice of the peace for the blacks of all AIC stations' [The AIC was a major rubber company]

The weapons of the natives were of little use against European arms and those who did not suffer at their hands immediately tried to align themselves with the superior force. Hochschild's comment is apt:

> Because so many Congo peoples had earlier fought among themselves, the *Force Publique* was often able to ally itself with one ethnic group to defeat another. But sooner or later the first group found itself subdued as well. With their forces stretched thin over a large territory, Léopold's commanders made clever use of this shifting pattern of alliances. In the end, though, their superior firepower guaranteed victory – and a history written by the victors.

The actions taken were termed *reconnaissances pacifiques* – actions taken in pursuit of security. What were these resisters – state enemies, insurgents ...

criminals? Today some resistance may seem heroic. Hochschild (1998: 124) relates how in Katanga in the far south, warriors from the Sanga people were led by a chief named Mulume Niama. Although the state troops were armed with artillery, Niama's forces succeeded in killing one officer and wounding three soldiers. Afterwards they took refuge in a large chalk cave called Tshamakele. The *Force Publique* lit fires at the three entrances to the cave to smoke the rebels out and a week later attempted to negotiate Mulume Niama's surrender. After the chief refused soldiers lit the fires again and blocked the cave for three months. 178 bodies were found when the troops finally entered. To prevent this being used as a martyrs' grave, the *Force Publique* triggered landslides to obliterate all traces of the existence of the Tshamakele cave and of the bodies of Mulume Niama and his entourage.

Léopold's edicts officially banned the slave-trade and Free State officials even went to war with the Arab slave-traders over the issue (at least that was the public reason), but the reality was different. Even the African soldiers of the *Force Publique* were, in effect, slaves. Moreover, under a system personally approved by the king, white state agents were paid a bonus according to the number of men they turned over to the *Force Publique*. Sometimes agents bought men from collaborating chiefs, who delivered their human goods in chains; in one transaction, recorded in a district commissioner's notes, 25 francs per person was the price received for a half-dozen teenagers delivered by two chiefs from Bongata in 1892. Congo state officials were paid an extra bonus for reduction in recruiting expenses – which meant in practice anything that saved the state money by kidnapping these men directly instead of paying chiefs for them.

Euphemisms clothed this neo-slave system: 'Two boats … just arrived with Sergeant Lens and 25 *volunteers* from Engwettra in chains; two men drowned trying to escape' (emphasis added), wrote one officer, Louis Rousseau, in his monthly report for October 1892. Some three-quarters of such 'volunteers' died before they could even be delivered to *Force Publique* posts, a worried senior official wrote the same year. Among the solutions to the problem of this 'wastage' he recommended were faster transport and lightweight steel chains instead of heavy iron ones. Documents from this time repeatedly show Congo state officials ordering additional supplies of chain. One officer noted the problem of files of conscripts crossing narrow log bridges over jungle streams: 'when *libérés* [liberated men] chained by the neck cross a bridge, if one fails off, he pulls the whole file off and it disappears'. White officers who bargained with village chiefs to acquire 'volunteer' soldiers and porters were sometimes dealing with the same sources that had supplied the east coast Afro-Arab slave traders.

Léopold discredited attempts to reveal the atrocities. Some accounts by Missionaries did surface. (e.g. Morrison 1903; and Sheppard, both men were arrested and sued with libel, they were acquitted on a technicality). Léopold's agents could reply that they were evidence of Protestants attempting to undercut the civilising work of Catholic Belgium.[8] That public attention was drawn to the Congo was in large part due to Edmund Dene Morel, who set up a campaigning movement and published a newspaper (the *West African Mail*) and a number of damming books (*King Léopold's Rule in Africa* 1904; *The Congo Slave State* 1904; *Red Rubber* 1906; later when the Belgium government had taken responsibility for the area, *Great Britain and the Congo: The Pillage of the Congo Basin* 1909). Morel was a clerk of a Liverpool shipping line used by Léopold to ship out Congo's wealth, who discovered on his several journeys to the Belgian port of Antwerp in the 1890s that while rubber and ivory were shipped from Congo to Antwerp, only guns and soldiers were going from Antwerp to Congo. This marked the beginning of his newspaper and lobbying campaign to expose the atrocities. He was to make a struggle for justice his life long mission; ultimately it was to cause his death.[9] After the report of Roger Casement, later to be knighted but finally executed for his activities on behalf of Irish nationalism, which indicted the whole system, the two became allies and Casement provided the initial finance for the Congo Reform Association. In his report he reveals how even the simplest request for labour had coercion behind it. Where India-rubber was tapped, the exaction's on the population was evidently disastrous causing many refugees. The people who used to inhabit the *Domaine de la Couronne*, for example, declared that

> They had endured such ill-treatment at the hands of the Government officials and the Government soldiers in their own country that life had become intolerable, that nothing had remained for them at home but to be killed for failure to bring in a certain amount of rubber or to die from starvation or exposure in their attempts to satisfy the demands made upon them.

As one of the appendices to the report, Casement included the statement of one of the refugees (obviously a literal translation) describing the kind of life rubber-collecting meant:

> It used to take ten days to get the twenty baskets of rubber—we were always in the forest to find rubber vines, to go without food, and our women had to give up cultivating the fields and garden. Then we starved. Wild beasts—the leopards killed some of us while we were working away in the forest and others got lost or died from exposure and starvation and we begged the white men to leave us alone, saying we could get no more rubber, but the white men and their soldiers said: 'Go. You are only beast your selves, you are only nyama (meat).' We tried, always going further into the forest, and when we failed and our rubber was short, the soldiers came to our towns and killed us. Many were shot, some had their ears cut off; other were tied up with ropes round their necks and bodies and taken away.

Several witnesses' accounts revealed a correlation between bullets and severed hands (Figure 5.5), for example:

> The S.A.B. on the Bussira, with 150 guns, get only ten tons (rubber) a month; we, the State, at Momboyo, with 130 guns, get thirteen tons per month.' 'So you count by guns?' I asked him. 'Partout', M.P. said. 'Each time the corporal goes out to get rubber cartridges are given to him. He must bring back all not used; and for every one used, he must bring back a right hand.' M.P. told me that sometimes they shot a cartridge at an animal in hunting, they then cut off a hand from a living man. As to the extent to which this is carried on, he informed me that in six months they, the State, on the Momboyo River, had used 6,000 cartridges, which means that 6,000 people are killed or mutilated. It means more than 6,000, for the people have told me repeatedly that the soldiers kill children with the butt of their guns.

(The Congo Reform Association could produce an array of photographs, presenting victims of the atrocities, most taken by Alice Harris, a Baptist missionary.)

Figure 5.5 This image of two mutilated young people became an iconic image of Léopold's regime. Mola's hands (seated) were destroyed by gangrene after being tied too tightly by soldiers. The right hand of Yoka (standing) was cut off by soldiers wanting to claim him as killed, source, Anti-slavery International, originally from Alice Harris.

Also attached to Casement's report was a letter written by one Rev. Whitehead of the B.M.S. station at Lukolela to the Governor General of the Congo State dated 28 July 1903, which seemed to corroborate the evidence of the refugees:

> The pressure under which they live at present is crushing them; the food which they sadly need themselves very often must, under penalty, by carried to the State post, also grass, cane string, baskets for the 'caoutchouc' (the last three items do not appear to be paid for); the 'caoutchouc' must be brought in from the inland districts; their Chiefs are being weakened in their prestige and physique through imprisonment, which is often cruel, and thus weakened in their authority over their own people, they are put into chains for the shortage of manioc bread and 'caoutchouc'.

Casement himself summarised his own impressions as follows:

> A careful investigation of the conditions of native life around the lake [Mantumba] confirmed the truth of the statements made to me both by … the local American missionary, and many natives, that the great decrease in population, the dirty and ill-kept towns, and the complete absence of goats, sheep, or fowls – once very plentiful in this

country – were to be attributed above all else to the continued effort made during many years to compel the natives to work India-rubber. Large bodies of native troops had formerly been quartered in the district, and the punitive measures undertaken to this end had endured for a considerable period. During the course of these operations there had been much loss of life, accompanied, I fear, by a somewhat general mutilation of the dead, as proof that the soldiers had done their duty.

The full report runs for 40 pages of the Parliamentary Papers to which is appended another 20 pages of individual statements gathered by the Consul, including several detailing grim accounts of killings, mutilation, kidnapping and cruel beatings of men, women and children by soldiers of Bula Matadi (the name used by the natives for the Congo Administration of King Léopold). Copies of the report and enclosures were transmitted by the British government to the Belgian government as well as to governments (Germany, France, Russia *et al.*) who were signatories to the Berlin Act in 1885. The report was not published as Casement had written it.[10] Even so, the Congo administration was forced to initiate an investigation into the atrocities detailed in the report, which led to the arrest and punishment of white officials who had been responsible for cold-blooded killings during a rubber-collecting expedition in 1903 (including one Belgian national who was given five years' penal servitude for causing the shooting of at least 122 Congolese natives (Ref.: British Parliamentary Papers, 1904, LXII, Cd. 1933; modern edition 2003). Hochschild relates this as the first great human rights campaign and uses this as an example of what can be achieved. Until recently the official story was one where Belgium set up its own enquiry in 1904, which was given the full text of Casement's report and other materials; the report of this enquiry was highly critical of the Congo Free State but also was clearer on the advantages of colonial government, after which faced with growing criticism (such as that of Cattier's 1906 *Etude sur la Situation de l'Etat Independent du Congo*) the Belgium State annexed and took on grave colonial responsibilities ushering in enlightened colonial rule, in the light of which modern day disorder is an African problem. Nelson (1994: 114) is indicative of a more recent scholarly awareness:

> In reality however, the Belgian annexation of the Congo ultimately produced no substantial departures from the policies of Léopold's Free State. Belgian public indifference to colonial affairs and the indecisiveness of the Colonial Council allowed the colony to slip into the hands of conservative bureaucrats and powerful financial groups. The concessionary system in the Congo basin was not only maintained but enlarged, resulting in ever-increasing amounts of so-called vacant African land alienated to large-scale European companies. Labour reforms proved equally illusionary: although brutally enforced labor was prohibited by law, taxes and compulsory farming quotas became new forms of labor coercion.

Even Hochschild's own message of success for human rights is not so clearly brought out by his text. Certainly, the Belgian government was forced to step in but it actually bought the Congo from Léopold in 1908. Léopold's complex revenue streams and profits were not properly investigated, nor, we should note now, was it fully realised that the rubber production was drastically declining owing to the exploitative nature of the system and the financial position of the CFS was set to decline. The deal was in reality a financial coup for Léopold: 'The Belgian government first of all agreed to assume (Congo's) 110 million francs worth of debt, much of them in the form of bond's Léopold had freely dispensed over the years to (his) favourites'. Nearly 32 million franc of the debt was owed to the Belgian government itself through loans it had given years earlier to Léopold. The government also agreed to pay 45.5 million francs towards completing Léopold's then unfinished building projects in Belgium. On top of all this, Léopold got another 50 million francs (to be paid in instalments) 'as a mark of gratitude for his great sacrifices made for the Congo'. Moreover, the funds were not expected to come from the Belgian taxpayer. They were to be extracted from the Congo itself. Hochschild finishes his book with a section he calls *The Great Forgetting*:

> From the colonial era, the major legacy Europe left for Africa was not democracy as it is practised today in countries like England, France and Belgium; it was authoritarian rule and plunder. On the whole continent, perhaps no nation has had a harder time than the Congo in emerging from the shadow of its past. When independence came, the country fared badly ... Some Africans were being trained for that distant day; but when pressure grew and independence came in 1960, in the entire territory there were fewer than 30 African university graduates. There were no Congolese army officers, engineers, agronomists or physicians. The colony's administration had made few other steps toward a Congo run by its own people; of some 5,000 management-level positions in the civil service, only three were filled by Africans. Yet on the day of independence, King Baudouin, the then monarch of Belgium, had the gall to tell the Congolese in his speech in Kinshasa: 'It is now up to you, gentlemen, to show that you are worthy of our Confidence'.

And the Congolese were not left alone to 'repay' this confidence. Not only were they informed of a national debt, but the first prime minister – whose speech at the independence day celebrations was viewed by the Belgians as rather ill mannered (in part for asking on what justification did the Congo inherit a 'national debt'[11]) – was assassinated by joint Belgium and Congolese activity (aided by the CIA and with indirect UN assistance, De Witte 2001) after refusing a neo-colonial compromise. Thenceforth the interventionist ploys of the cold war were to mean that whoever appeared to offer the West the strongest protection for their interests would be covertly and not so covertly supported (Wrong 2001). We are dealing with a certain art of forgetting and avoiding interconnection.

The contemporary Congo is a place of death, with an ongoing conflict that can not be adequately described as a civil war; it is rather a return to that state of mêlée Hobbes had tried to overcome. Again the potential wealth to be gained from the Congo is the draw card, as troops from six neighbouring countries intervene citing various justifications but in reality seeking loot and plunder. The conflict is estimated by the UNCR to have cost between three and three and a half million lives since 1994. Rwanda, for example, claimed it was perusing Hutu militiamen that had carried out the 1994 genocide and would withdraw once those had been disarmed. Observers consistently say that its government is grossly exaggerating the numbers of the Interahamwe militiamen, who carried out the 1994 Rwandan genocide before fleeing there. Instead Rwanda soldiers collaborate with the Hutu militiamen to maintain their excuse for occupying Congo and plundering a mineral-rich expanse 27 times the size of Rwanda.

Figure 5.6 The State Funeral of Léopold II, 22 December 1909, the procession of the Judges (original postcard in the collection of the author). A scandal surrounded Léopold's death; it concerned the fact that he had quickly married the last of his young mistresses. I have a certain fantasy concerning this image: it is that the Judge third from left is looking around because he is embarrassed to be processing at the funeral of the person about whom Conan Doyle (*The Crime of the Congo*) wrote had committed the greatest crime then known. But I know that is a fantasy; Léopold's death was of considerable concern to the legal profession, but only insofar that there were great amounts of work to be undertaken in sorting out the complex webs of finances he had and trying to defend the interests of his daughters or organise the private foundation he had left most of the considerable fortune he died with in order to finance more lavish buildings and their upkeep. There was, of course, no lawyers asking for the return of the vast amounts he had taken from the Congo (and interestingly he has also secretly taken substantial holdings in the concessions of the French Congo and the nearby German colonial possession).

Rwanda's soldiers and the rebels it created and controls are at the forefront of the killing, says Human Rights Watch, 'regularly slaughtering civilians in massacres'. All factions stand accused of atrocities. But because most militias were formed to resist Rwanda's occupation, Rwanda bears most responsibility, diplomats say. 'It's clear to us the killing continues because Rwanda refuses to leave Congo. Rwanda must leave eastern Congo,' said a French diplomat in Kinshasa, Congo's capital.

Congo's government has maintained the Interahamwe's threat to Rwanda by supplying them with arms. But, with its army incapable of resisting Rwanda's efficient troops – who captured Kinshasa in May 1997 and almost again in August 1998 – many diplomats in the region describe this as a legitimate military tactic.

'What should the Congolese do?' said a North American diplomat in Kinshasa. 'They're under attack ... it's the rules of war.' Rwanda says 55,000 of the Interahamwe are hiding in Congo, either in the forests of the east or the ranks of Congo's army. According to the

International Crisis Group, a privately funded organisation working to resolve conflict, the true figure is less than half that, with as few as 8,000 remaining in occupied eastern Congo. Up to 90 per cent of these were recruited from refugee camps after 1994, the group says – so only a small proportion were involved in the genocide. ('Rwandans wage a war of plunder: Witnesses say occupying troops are spinning out the violence to grab Congo's riches.' *Observer Worldview*. James Astill in Kigali, Sunday, 4 August 2002. *The Observer*)

Massacres, mutilation, forced labour, mass rape; Casement's 1904 findings are apt:

Of acts of persistent mutilation by Government soldiers ... Of the fact of this mutilation and the causes inducing it there can be no shadow of doubt. It was not a native custom prior to the coming of the white man; it was not the outcome of the primitive instinct of savages in their fights between village and village; it was the deliberate act of the soldiers of a European administration, and these men themselves never made any concealment that in committing these acts they were but obeying the positive orders of their superiors.

There may be grounds for applying Sunderland's learning theory, for the lesson of the Free State appears to have been learnt well. Ascherson (1963: 203) summed up Léopold's legacy as 'too viciously wasteful, too recklessly short-term in its conception, to deserve even the name of exploitation. It was no more than a prolonged raid for plunder'. But in the time, since Fukuyama announced the end of history, the Congo has been a largely ignored tragedy, in the contemporary ethos of humanitarian intervention by the West it does not rank highly and the UN peacekeepers who were belatedly dispatched are more in the news for sexual harassment or ignoring fighting than for peacekeeping (e.g. 'Mandate Abused: UN peacekeepers disgraced themselves in Congo', *Times on Line* 21 December, 2004; 'Two killed during riots over UN "inaction" in Congo', *Times on Line*, 3 June 2004). There are forms of institutional power at work that aid in the forgetting process and renders messages upsetting to civilised space redundant. That this was clearly known in the nineteenth century we can see next from Conrad's writing while Chapter 6 will analyse the civilised space of contemporary Brussels.

Part II

Heart of Darkness: a metaphor for the relationship between criminology and global imagination?

Heart of Darkness: a mere work of literature?

David Garland notes that theories of criminology have a basis in the stories of crime and offenders, in novels, religious accounts and popular narratives:

> Stories of how the offender fell in with bad company, became lax in his habits and was sorely tried by temptation, was sickly, or tainted by bad blood, or neglected by unloving parents, became too fond of drink or too idle to work, lost her reputation and found it hard to get employment, was driven by despair or poverty or simply driven to crime by avarice and lust – these seem to provide the well-worn templates from which our modern theories of crime are struck, even if we insist upon a more neutral language in which to tell the tale, and think that a story's plausibility should be borne out by evidence as well as intuition. (Garland 1997: 22–3)

But the stories that were to provide the 'well-worn templates' were themselves a selection. The various International Congresses' of Criminal Anthropology met and debated oblivious to what came to be called a crime against humanity. King Léopold's destructive rule was however, the subject of writing by three renowned storytellers. Joseph Conrad gave his text the graphic title *Heart of Darkness* (1899), Mark Twain was more ironical with his biting satire *King Léopold's Soliloquy: A Defense of His Congo Rule* (1905) and Arthur Conan Doyle simply called his *The Crime of the Congo* (1909). These neither impacted upon the development of the institutional discourse called criminology, nor are they seen as providing material for analysis; criminology's stories appeared limited to the local, even if they made universalistic assumptions.

Benjamin (1973: 84–5) depicts two types of storytellers, one who has come from afar, and another who has stayed at home drawing his narrative out of 'the local tales and traditions'. For Benjamin each group can be ascribed archaic representatives: 'one is embodied in the resident tiller of the soil, and the other in the trading seaman'. Benjamin finds, however, that the local is constituted by reference to filtered tales from afar. The community of a locality will combine elements of 'the lore of faraway places', with 'the lore of the past'. The locality is structured by reference to the imaginative reconstruction of the 'other', by which threats to the security of the local may be recognised. So Conrad in *Heart of Darkness* gave his narrator Marlow, a man of the sea, the task of relating his story to a small group sitting on a cruising yawl at anchor in the Sea-reach of the Thames river at dusk after a dinner hosted by the Director of Companies. Conrad clearly orientates the rhetoric of Marlow's account to a divided audience. Although members of the audience will have their own tales, Marlow is aware while relating his tale of the terrors of the exotic, that his audience is also immersed with the local concerns of a specific community. The story Marlow tells seems to centre around a man named Kurtz, what Marlow heard of Kurtz and Marlow's journey to encounter Kurtz, Kurtz's death and Marlow's return to Brussels. In the end the text has a duality: one aspect conforms to the normative expectations of that localised community (as when

Marlow lies in telling Kurtz's betrothed that Kurtz's last words were of her rather than 'the horror'), the other relativises notions of normalcy and the exception, the local and the outside, the civilised and the 'savage' other. However, the final words of the text are of a returning to normal conditions. The pause when Marlow finishes is broken by the Director, 'We have lost the first of the ebb'. The narrative is relegated to the status of a story told, something that filled in some time and now everyday business called.

Voyage into the *Heart of Darkness:* a complex criminology?

> You have shown us lubricious and ferocious orangutans with human faces; certainly, being such they can act no other way; if they rape, steal, and kill, it is invariably on account of their nature and their past. The more reason for us to destroy them as soon as one is sure that they are and will remain orangutans. On this account I have no objection to the death penalty if society finds profit in it. (Letter to Lombroso from the French theorist Taine, quoted Pick 1989: 109)

> All Europe contributed to the making of Kurtz; and by-and-by I learned that, most appropriately, the International Society for the Suppression of Savage Customs had intrusted him with the making of a report, for its future guidance. And he had written it, too. I've seen it. I've read it. It was eloquent, vibrating with eloquence ... 'By the simple exercise of our will we can exert a power for good practically unbounded', etc. etc. From that point he soared and took me with him. The peroration was magnificent, although difficult to remember, you know. It gave me the notion of an exotic Immensity ruled by an august Benevolence. It made me tingle with enthusiasm. This was the unbounded power of eloquence – of words – of burning noble words. There were no practical hints to interrupt the magic current of phrases, unless a kind of note at the foot of the last page, scrawled evidently much later, in an unsteady hand, may be regarded as the exposition of a method. It was very simple, and at the end of that moving appeal to every altruistic sentiment it blazed at you, luminous and terrifying, like a flash of lightning in a serene sky: 'Exterminate all the brutes!' (Joseph Conrad, references to the 1988 edition: 50–1)

It is an ambivalent feature of great literature that it can be analysed on many levels. In both recording and transcending our understandings of the human condition, in giving us encounters, presences and absences, it stretches our perception of reality. Conversely, that action of extension may cause us to neglect its origins as a recounting of empirical events, as striving to be faithful to what went on. A related process occurs as we label the literature as belonging to specific disciplinary areas. Thus the fact that it is almost too mundane to say that Conrad's short novel *Heart of Darkness* is criminology of acute warning may preversely provide grounds for dismissing it from consideration. Certainly it concerns power and the visualisation of governance in action. Later novelists, notably Orwell, have warned against the authoritative structuring lying in the combination of technology and desire for power inherent in the culture of control of western modernity. Conrad's narrative brings us a subjectivity of paternalistic imperialism and the complexity of racial ideology. *Heart of Darkness* can be read as solely concerning racism and power (a racism, some critics suggest, the author did not himself escape from[12]), but his message is beyond that (albeit vital) particularity. For Conrad's text is an existential warning; an encounter with a time transcendent its space, without limits, where the excluded or the 'other' is now within one's power, where one's power over the other reaches into all the constraints, the restraints of one's guilt ridden 'civilised' self. To bring us the refrain of 'a sickness, the sickness, the sickness, the horror, the horror …'

The signifier is the Congo, but that place is outside the confines of civilised space. Beyond the security of a sovereign control over definitions and language usage, we move into 'the other world', journeying upriver to meet Kurtz becomes a journey out of civilised space to encounter a different truth. Conrad may not have had Plato's allegory of the cave in mind when he wrote it, but the similarity of structure is striking. The culmination of the journey, meeting Kurtz, 'seemed somehow to throw a kind of light on everything about me – and into my thoughts' (p. 11), but the effect of this light is reversed and the resultant referential point is not of the good but of the horror. Marlow returns to Europe a changed and more knowing man. Ordinary people are now 'intruders whose knowledge of life was to me an irritating pretence, because I felt so sure they could not possibly know the things I knew'. But when he tells his new knowledge, in the end his audience ignores it; everyday life rules.

From the title we can expect the symbolism of black and white, light and dark to conform to the usual pattern of nineteenth-century narratives of the civilising process. Namely, for one side to be represented by Black/dark, death, evil, ignorance, mystery, savagery and the uncivilised; while the other is represented by White/light, life, goodness, enlightenment, the civilised and religion. In the stories of social development the Middle Ages, when science and knowledge was suppressed, are the Dark Ages out of which we are delivered by the enlightenment. Christian traditions hold that in the beginning of time all was dark and God created light. In *Heart of Darkness*, before the Romans came, England was dark. In the same way, Africa was considered to be in the 'dark stage'. However, expectations are not met in the narrative; the usual pattern is reversed and darkness denotes truth, whiteness falsehood. This reversal subverts political control of definitions and offers a counter-political experience concerning races in the Congo, a psychological revelation about Kurtz, Marlow and all of us (the possibilities within that we fear, therefore dark and obscure), and a complicating of moral positions (the trade in ivory is dark and dirty).

Heart of Darkness is narrated by Charlie Marlow, 32 years old, who has always 'followed the sea'. He travels to Brussels and takes a position as a river steamboat master in the developing Congo. Marlow is shocked and disgusted when he arrives at the Central Station on the Congo River by the sight of wasted human life and ruined supplies. He despairs at the manager's senseless cruelty and foolishness; he longs to see Kurtz – an extremely successful ivory agent hated by the company manager. More and more, Marlow distances himself from the white people (because of their ruthless brutality) embracing the dark jungle (a symbol of reality and truth). He comes to identify with Kurtz – long before he even sees him or talks to him. In the end, the affinity between the two men becomes a symbolic unity. Marlow is what Kurtz might have been; Kurtz is what Marlow might have become.

Kurtz, like Marlow, originally came to the Congo with noble intentions: each ivory station should stand like a beacon light, offering a better way of life to the natives. Kurtz' mother was half-English; his father half-French; educated in England he speaks English fluently. Kurtz is the product of all of Europe's culture and civilisation: orator, writer, poet, musician, artist, politician, ivory procurer and chief agent of the ivory company's Inner Station at Stanley Falls. A 'universal genius', but also a 'hollow man', lacking character and virtue, he is without basic integrity or any sense of social responsibility. Kurtz's experiences have turned him into a thief, mass-murderer, raider and persecutor; his dwelling is surrounded by a display of dried and shrunken severed human heads; he allows himself to be worshipped as a god. He has succumbed to all the temptations noted from the time of the first contact between the technologically powerful European and the natives.[13] Marlow can only see the final Kurtz, so emaciated by his experiences and disease that he looks more like a ruined piece of a man than a whole human being. There is no trace of Kurtz's former good looks or his former good health. Marlow remarks that Kurtz's head is as bald as an ivory ball and that he resembles 'an animated image of death carved out of old ivory'. Kurtz controls men through fear and adoration; yet his power over the natives almost destroys Marlow and the party aboard the steamboat. Kurtz is the lusty, violent devil by contrast to the manager, who although weak and flabby, exercises great administrative power. Administration that controls resources and determines practical possibilities. Kurtz is in part a victim of the manager's deliberate neglect and implicit cruelty; how could Kurtz have carried out his task virtuously in light of the manager's neglect. Kurtz may never have embraced evil if he had not been put into the situation that he had been by the manager. Yet this is simply method, empty administration, for the manager has no real ethics, neither programme of advancement or hatred of Kurtz; he simply functions, and strangely, survives because he seems immune to the diseases that have killed so many other Europeans.

The inside and the outside: the centre and the periphery

> But Marlow was not typical ... and to him the meaning of an episode was not inside like a kernel, but outside, enveloping the tale which brought it out as a glow brings out a haze ... (p. 9)

Heart of Darkness is not structured by a simple set of oppositions or by a centre where meaning was concentrated and an outside of lesser importance. In the original manuscript, the words 'in the unseen' followed the word outside in the above quotation. Thus the meaning of the events related was not to be found in the confrontation that was visualised but in an outside that was unseen and hidden from view. The meaning is not found in the centre of the book – in the Congo – but on the periphery of the book; in a Brussels being enriched from the Congo, in the measuring of Marlow's head by the doctor before he departed, on the Nellie as Marlow tells the story, and on the various audiences that do not have the knowledge bought to them and thus remain ignorant and/or indifferent.

The text conveys many messages; one is of narration, of the power of communication and representation. In the same way that Europeans and others gained their knowledge of the Congo from stories that were related to them or spectacles that were put on in their own cities – as by the Lantern Slide show of the CRA – most of what Marlow knows about Kurtz, he has learned from other people. Marlow has to piece together much of Kurtz's story from others, many of whom have good reason for not giving a truthful account. In the end we know very little more about Kurtz. What we do learn, is only through interpreting his actions by reference to what we think we already know. Reality is presented to us only through other people's accounts, many of which are twice-told tales.[14]

Dream and reality

Perhaps one reason for *Heart of Darkness* not being used in criminology is that it is pigeon holed into literature and often given a rather Freudian interpretation. Therein it is read as a night journey into the unconscious and confrontation of an entity within the self. The narrative is searched for clues as to the unconscious and these seem easy to find. Marlow insists on the dreamlike quality of his narrative. 'It seems to me I am trying to tell you a dream – making a vain attempt, because no relation of a dream can convey the dream-sensation.' It was difficult to describe the actuality of the voyage; even before leaving Brussels, Marlow felt as though he 'was about to set off for center of the earth', but this is a voyage beyond one's familiar rational world, 'cut off from the comprehension' of one's surroundings, the steamer toils 'along slowly on the edge of a black and incomprehensible frenzy'. As the crisis approaches, the dreamer and his ship moves through a silence that 'seemed unnatural, like a state of trance; then enter a deep fog'. The approach to the final truth of Kurtz's station and methods was surrounded by dangers and layers of incomprehensibility as though he had been an 'enchanted princess sleeping in a fabulous castle'. Later, Marlow's task is to try 'to break the spell' of the wilderness that holds Kurtz entranced. But can this validly be given some Freudian interpretation? Consider the narration after Marlow says that 'instead of going to the centre of a continent I were about to set off for the centre of the earth'. In his account we are led through the rhyme and rhythm of an 'enigma', at first the coast keeps him 'away from the truth of things' in a 'toil of a mournful and senseless delusion', but he is seduced by the constant whisper 'to come and find out'. This is no dream, although the narrator experiences reality as dreamlike since Conrad has wrapped him in the European ideology of Africa that now confronts something else.

> For a time I would feel I belonged still to a world of straightforward facts; but the feeling would not last long. Something would turn up to scare it away. Once, I remember, we came upon a man-of-war anchored off the coast. There wasn't even a shed there, and she was shelling the bush. It appears the French had one of their wars going on thereabouts. Her ensign dropped limp like a rag; the muzzles of the long six-inch guns stuck out all over the low hull; the greasy, slimy swell swung her up lazily and let her down, swaying her thin masts. In the empty immensity of earth, sky, and water, there she was, incomprehensible, firing into a continent. Pop, would go one of the six-inch guns; a small flame would dart and vanish, a little white smoke would disappear, a tiny projectile would give a feeble screech – and nothing happened. Nothing could happen. There was a touch of insanity in the proceeding, a sense of lugubrious drollery in the sight; and it was not dissipated by somebody on board assuring me earnestly there was a camp of natives – he called them enemies! – hidden out of sight somewhere.

This is not the technology of a 'shock and awe' campaign. It was simply killing (or attempting to) at a distance, or going through the motions of using what military power was available. Did it make sense … what criteria was there to use, what was the idea behind this civilising process? Encountering this scheme was 'like a weary pilgrimage amongst hints for nightmares'. Seeking for guidance Marlow asks what kind of man penetrates upriver but the answers are not apparent, some talk of suicides, some hint at worse things. At last he came upon the Company Station: 'mounds of turned-up earth by the shore, houses on a hill, others with iron roofs, amongst a waste of excavations, or hanging to the declivity. A continuous noise of the rapids above hovered over this scene of inhabited devastation. A lot of people, mostly black and naked, moved about like ants. A jetty projected into the river. A blinding sunlight drowned all this at times in a sudden recrudescence of glare'; thus he finds the beacon of the civilising process.

'A horn tooted to the right, and I saw the black people run. A heavy and dull detonation shook the ground, a puff of smoke came out of the cliff and that was all. No change appeared on the face of the rock. They were building a railway. The cliff was not in the way or anything; but this objectless blasting was all the work going on.' Then the sight:

> A slight clinking behind me made me turn my head. Six black men advanced in a file, toiling up the path. They walked erect and slow, balancing small baskets full of earth on their heads, and the clink kept time with their footsteps. Black rags were wound round their loins, and the short ends behind waggled to and fro like tails. I could see every rib, the joints of their limbs were like knots in a rope; each had an iron collar on his neck, and all were connected together with a chain whose bights swung between them, rhythmically clinking. Another report from the cliff made me think suddenly of that ship of war I had seen firing into a continent. It was the same kind of ominous voice; but these men could by no stretch of imagination be called enemies. They were called criminals, and the outraged law, like the bursting shells had come to them, an insoluble mystery from the sea. All their meager breasts panted together, the violently dilated nostrils quivered, the eyes stared stonily up-hill. They passed me within six inches, without a glance, with that complete, deathlike indifference of unhappy savages. Behind this raw matter one of the reclaimed, the product of the new forces at work, strolled despondently, carrying a rifle by its middle. He had a uniform jacket with one button off, and seeing a white man on the path, hoisted his weapon to his shoulder with alacrity. This was simple prudence, white men being so much alike at a distance that he could not tell who I might be. He was speedily reassured, and with a large, white, rascally grin, and a glance at his charge, seemed to take me into partnership in his exalted trust. After all, I was also a part of the great cause of these high and just proceedings.

Was this an isolated evil? Was it simply violence by officials without proper supervision? No there was something more insidious, much more complex to grasp, perhaps beyond our grasp:

> … as I stood on this hillside, I foresaw that in the blinding sunshine of that land I would become acquainted with a flabby, pretending, weak-eyed devil of a rapacious and pitiless folly. How insidious he could be, too, I was only to find out several months later and a thousand miles farther. For a moment I stood appalled, as though by a warning.

But the narrator must move on, practicalities make demands; to think is to encourage chaos and meaningless. What – in this opening up of the globe – was dream and what is reality? Marlow is there because he has always sought strange adventures. As a child he had pored over maps of the world, losing himself 'in all the glories of exploration'. The Congo had once been 'a blank space of delightful mystery – a white patch for a boy to dream gloriously over. It had become a place of darkness' (p. 12). In part this transformation was Stanley's legacy. Encountering the blank space of mystery and turning it into a heart of darkness was a visual problem from the outset, moving at 'the threshold of the invisible'. Stanley had laid out the descriptive icons for the Congo and subsequent travellers came armed with expectations based on Stanley's accounts. Both Lang and Adolphus Frederick of Mecklenburg, who led the German expedition of 1908, for example, could find no other way to describe the Congo forest than to quote Stanley:

> Imagine the whole of France and the Iberian peninsula densely covered with trees 6 to 60 metres in height, with smooth trunks, whose leafy tops are so close to one another that they intermingle and obscure the sun and the heavens, each tree over a metre in thickness. The ropes stretching across from one tree to another in the shape of creepers and festoons, or curling round the trunks in thick, heavy coils, like endless anacondas, till they reach the highest point.
>
> Imagine them in full bloom, their luxuriant foliage combining with that of the trees to obscure the sunlight, and their hundreds of long festoons covered with slender tendrils hanging down from the highest branches till they touch the ground, interlacing with one another in a complete tangle. (Mecklenburg 1913: 249)

Stanley could be said to have exaggerated, but it was exceedingly difficult to replace his words. For Stanley, the Congo could not be described in the traditional fashion, but could only be imagined; however, Stanley's imaginative description was imbued with an 'ethical' methodology: one viewed with a purpose for this was land to be subdued, to be controlled, to be manipulated, to be transformed into a land fit for European civilisation. It was difficult to break from this legacy, yet to bring light into the darkness different ways of seeing – and not seeing – were possible. Power brought its ability to turn the darkness into spectacle and visualise the terrain in terms of cost benefit analysis worked out in the daily routines of surveillance. As to the 'reality' of the civilising process, Léopold strove to control the spectacle for European and American consumption and create an administration of continual profit. If Léopold epitomised the full hypocrisy of European power, the reformers, such as Casement and Morel, who protested his regime represented another mode of imaginative visualisation. One which saw the basic material for a world of free producers, partaking in open trade premised on the assumption of the inherent dignity of the natives and their future liberty.

> Seated in an imaginary airship, which we will fancy perfected and invisible, let us take a bird's eye view of the Congo as it was 25 years ago (i.e. before the Berlin Conference and the Congo Free State), not in the spirit of the anthropologist, naturally and rightly on the lookout for strange and repulsive rites; nor in the spirit of the moralist, lamenting the aberrations of primitive man with a zeal inducing unmindfulness of civilization's sores: but in the spirit of the statesman, which presupposes both the student and the man of

broad practical sympathies, contemplating this vast new country for the first time ... The mightiest forest region in the world now unrolls before us its illimitable horizon, the primeval forest whither races of black, brown and copper coloured men have been attracted or driven for untold ages ... In these fertile villages, man has settled and multiplied. He is well represented almost everywhere on the banks of the rivers except where they are very low lying and habitually flooded. But he has made many thousands of clearings in the forest too, and has cultivated the soil to such good purposes where need was, that we shall be astonished at the number and variety of his plantations. Throughout this enormous forest region ... we shall note an intelligent, vigorous population, attaining considerable density in certain parts, digging and smelting iron, manufacturing weapons for war and the chase, often of singularly beautiful shape, weaving fibres of sundry plants into tasteful mats and cloths, fabricating a rough pottery, fishing nets, twine baskets. (Morel 1968: 17, 21)

Another visualisation was that of anthropology. Anthropology, premised on a positioned vision, was imbued with the assumptions of progress, civilisation verses savagery and the fated disappearance of the primitive. As the first report of the Lang and Frederick expedition explained, the domain of study was

The Upper Congo region, that great, steaming land of equatorial Africa shrouded in jungle ... They have seen strange places and stranger primitive peoples, of whom it is time that the world obtain complete scientific record in view of the rapid advance that civilisation must make in the Congo in the immediate future. (Dickerson 1910: 147)

Lang dedicated himself to Léopold's vision. Under the Congo Free State, he simply assumed that 11 million people had supposedly been taken from the former practice of cannibalism. To Lang, a keen and unquestioning supporter of eugenics, scientifically speaking the results were mixed: the 'horrible practice produced some fairly good results in eugenics, as in many tribes weakened people or crippled children helped to nourish their more sturdy brothers' (Lang 1915: 382). Against the 'wise decisions of a responsible government' Lang opposed the 'impetuosity of the unfortunate campaign of the reformers' (p. 380). The terrain was the site of a natural chaos and the white man's role that of the directing power: 'White Man's impetus must be the motive to progress, whereas the Negro will supply the activity to bring final order from chaos' (1919: 698).

Yet this is the crux for dissuading any interpretation of *Heart of Darkness* as that of a dream voyage. Heart of Darkness warns. If it concerns a dream it is that of the European Enlightenment. Who are the agents, what is the structure? Everything that Marlow confronts, questions and interprets lose their bearings – old women knitting black wool in the Belgian office; the phrenologist measuring Marlow's skull and warning of changes to take place inside; the tale of how his predecessor died in an uncharacteristic dispute over black hens; the Inner Station with its barrels of unused rivet and the needless blasting of a cliff as a railroad is built; its valley of death and shackled prisoners, and its gleaming white-suited Accountant, who frets over his figures while a man lies groaning his last in his office; the Central Station, rivet-less and straw-less, where the manager smiled his mysterious mean smile and the idle brick-maker (the 'paper-mache Mephistopheles') drinks champagne and lights his privileged candle in its silver holder; where a man is dragged out at random and beaten for having set a fire (regardless of whether he did or not), and where Marlow's boat is sunk; meanwhile, the Eldorado expedition passes through; the Russian himself, dressed in motley clothes, his icon which is dull text (language pored over reverently in spite of content); the 'gateposts' which become heads on poles, shrunken and dried and made to face Kurtz's house: signs not of domestic order but of terror. What is solid? What is foundational? If one looks at the Roman colonisation of ancient Britain

> They grabbed what they could get for the sake of what was to be got. It was just robbery with violence, aggravated murder on a great scale, and men going at it blind … The conquest of the earth, which mostly means the taking it away from those who have a different complexion or slightly flatter noses than ourselves, is not a pretty thing when you look into it too much.

If the civilised space Marlow leaves is itself not pure, if the people there are not awake, where is a reality to be trusted? We are protected from ourselves through our immersion in the routines of the common life with its laws and watchful neighbours and work. 'You wonder I didn't go ashore for a howl and a dance? Well, no – I didn't. Fine sentiments, you say? Fine sentiments be hanged! I had no time, I had to mess about with white-lead and strips of woollen blanket helping to put bandages on those leaky steam pipes'. But when the external restraints of society and work are removed we must meet the challenge with our 'own inborn strength. Principles won't do.' This inborn strength appears to include restraint, the restraint that Kurtz lacked and the cannibal crew of the Roi des Belges surprisingly possessed. The hollow man, whose evil is the evil of vacancy, succumbs. In their different degrees the pilgrims and Kurtz share this hollowness. 'Perhaps there was nothing within [the manager of the Central Station]. Such a suspicion made one pause – for out there there were no external checks.' And there was nothing inside the brick-maker, 'but a little loose dirt, maybe.' As for Kurtz, the wilderness 'echoed loudly within him because he was hollow at the core'.

This is classical ground: here ethics as understood as the creation of character plays off against disciplinisation and routinisation. Today Kaplan repeats Conrad's argument on character and imperial idea as necessary for the American military in their new roles: 'Effective leadership will always reside within the mystery of character' (2002: 150). But Kurtz was no isolated failing. In *King Léopold's Ghost*, Hochschild posed the question of why when colonialism involved many 'mass murders that went largely unnoticed except by their victims, why, in England and the United States, was there such a storm of righteous protest about the Congo?' His answer was that 'What happened in the Congo was indeed mass murder on a vast scale, but the sad truth is that the men who carried it out for Léopold were no more murderous than many Europeans then at work or at war elsewhere in Africa.' For Conrad: 'All Europe contributed to the making of Kurtz'. Kurtz – author of a 17-page report to the International Society for the Suppression of Savage Customs, at the end of which he scrawls in shaky hand: 'Exterminate all the brutes'. The model was probably Leon Rom. Born in Mons in Belgium, a poorly educated Rom joined the Belgian army aged 16 and nine years later, aged 25 in 1886, he found himself in the Congo in search of adventure. He became district commissioner at Matadi and was put in charge of large numbers of African troops in the *Force Publique*. Rom's brutality became legendary and shocked even hardened Belgium Free State officials, and reports were sent to Brusells concerning agents who had 'the reputation of having killed masses of people for petty reasons'. Conrad probably heard of Rom, notorious for keeping a flower bed rigged with human heads, and keeping a gallows permanently erected in front of the station, when he had himself gone to Congo in 1890. *Heart of Darkness* is a reflection of actual events and members of this great imperial adventure. Again Conrad is scathing:

> This devoted band called itself the Eldorado Exploring Expedition and I believe they were sworn to secrecy. Their talk however was the talk of sordid buccaneers. It was reckless without hardihood, greedy without audacity, and cruel without courage. There was not an atom of foresight or of serious intention in the whole batch of them, and they did not seem aware these things are wanted for the work of the world. To tear treasure out of the bowels of the land was their desire, with no more moral purpose at the back of it than there is in burglars breaking into a safe. Who paid the expenses of the noble enterprise I don't know …

But this noble enterprise had victims, people beyond the representational language of war, civilising missions or crime. For the African labourers

> were dying slowly – it was very clear. They were not enemies, they were not criminals, they were nothing earthly now, nothing but black shadows of disease and starvation lying confusedly in the greenish gloom. Brought from all the recesses of the coast in all the legality of time contracts, lost in uncongenial surroundings, fed on unfamiliar food, they sickened, became inefficient, and were then allowed to crawl away and rest. [i.e. to die]

Chapter 6:
'A Living Lesson in the Museum of Order': The Case of the Royal Museum for Central Africa, Brussels

Long before he was regarded as an object of science, the criminal was imagined as a source of instruction ... now it was being suggested that children should come and learn how the benefits of the law are applied to crime – a living lesson in the museum of order. (Foucault 1977: 112)

[The modern prison] is not alone, but linked to a whole series of 'carceral' mechanisms which seem distinctive enough ... but which all tend ... to exercise a power of normalisation ... these mechanisms are applied not to transgressions against a 'central' law, but to the apparatus of production – 'commerce' and 'industry' ... ultimately what presides over all these mechanisms is not the unitary functioning of an apparatus or an institution, but the necessity of combat and the rules of strategy. ...

In this central and centralised humanity, the effect and instrument of complex power relations, bodies and forces subjected by multiple mechanisms of 'incarceration', objects for discourses that are in themselves elements for this strategy, we must hear the distant roar of battle. (Foucault 1977: 308)

Museums are one of society's principal agencies for defining culture, largely through their determination of what elements of the past are of value, memorable and worthy of preservation. This activity defines the present as much as it does the past. The significance of this task, not least for social stability, might itself suffice to explain why governments have played leading roles in establishing and maintaining museums. (MacDonald and Alsford 1995: 15)

The most serious blow suffered by the colonized is being removed from history and from the community. Colonization usurps any free role in either war or peace, every decision contributing to his destiny and that of the world, and all cultural and social responsibility. (Memmi 1991: 91)

Introduction: contemporary civilised space, exercising and expunging the power of normalisation

It takes under three hours to travel by Eurostar from London to Brussels, the home of the European Parliament and the administrative capital of the EU. The Channel Tunnel is a late modern testament to decreasing fears of European contamination and hopes for European integration. It can also appear as a conduit of crime:

A man from the Congo, living in Brussels, travelled regularly to London on Eurostar to collect housing benefit, an Old Bailey jury heard today.

Ngolompati Moka, 33, who is a Belgian national, used fake tenancy agreements to persuade the boroughs of Hounslow and Haringey to pay him a total of £4,653.36, said the prosecution. The court was told that Moka, who was born in the Congo, used a series of identities to claim the cash. After he was arrested in a Hounslow JobCentre last August, police found a number of documents that incriminated him. These included bogus tenancy agreements, a Belgian ID card and receipts from Eurostar trains. 'These show he was making trips from Brussels to claim benefit in this country', said counsel. (*Evening Standard*, 28 January 1999)

For the media this was an everyday crime, one that was moreover evidence of the need to strengthen immigration control and border policing. Doing justice meant punishing an individual. It did not invite analysis as to the complex intertwining of the Congo and Brussels, nor of past exploitation, justice and reparations. In this exercise of justice – concerning 'a man from the Congo, living in Brussels' – we are dealing with politics of the visible and the invisible.

Brussels offers a pace down from the postmodern world-city of London. The roar of battle certainly seems far from the idyllic scenes of modern Brussels' majestic urban *Parc du Cinquantenaire* with its imposing *Arc de Triomphe* and its Congo Monument although they are commemorated in the *Musee Royal de l'Armee et d'Histoire Militaire* whose sprawling building take up most of the north side. But the image of military campaigns celebrated therein, such as that against the Arab slave traders of central Africa in the 1890s, were not what Foucault meant by the roar of battle. Certainly, discipline, domination, surveillance and spectacle do not come to mind as one travels the quiet tram ride some ten kilometres out of central Brussels to the impressive neo-classical buildings and park spaces of the *Royal Museum for Central Africa* at Turveren. Nor do these urban spaces appear to bear any relationship to the history of the modern prison; certainly no imagery of prisons or other places of punishment intrudes, but complex plays of power link these seemingly discrete institutions and practices constituting the civilised space of contemporary Europe.

The normalcy of contemporary Brussels

The European Parliament and ever spreading mix of administrative buildings comprise an area now termed the EU quarter. One side of that quarter is the *Parc du Cinquantenaire.* Here we encounter that combination of civilised space and grandeur built by various enterprises under the direction of the Belgium King Léopold II as a belated celebration of the 50th anniversary of the Belgium state.

In *Heart of Darkness* Conrad had his narrator Marlow describe the city as 'a whited sepulchre', a reference to Matthew 23: 'Woe unto you, scribes and Pharisees, hypocrites! For ye are like whited sepulchres, which indeed appear beautiful outward, but are within full of dead men's bones ...' This is not the message on display. The *Arc de Triomphe* is larger than the corresponding Arc in Paris, the walks through the well-organised and tall trees are refreshing and the park is home to a number of monuments and pavilions.

One of these is the now rather crumbling monument to the Belgian pioneers in the Congo 'who brought civilisation to the Congo'. Near to it, an explanatory label states:

The monument to the Congo (1911–21) is typical of the colonial spirit of the age, which has since been called into question by History. In the lower section a young black man represents the River Congo. He is surrounded by two groups: on the right, a Belgian solider sacrifices himself for his fatally wounded captain; on the left, a Belgian soldier overcomes the slave-dealer. In the central strip, the African continent, now open to civilisation, advances towards the group of soldiers around Léopold II. Above, Belgium receiving the black race is depicted as a proud young lady.

Popular Belgium literature commemorated the fate of fallen Belgium officers (no private soldiers served in the Congo) and brought out the idea of sacrifice for a greater cause. One case was Charles-Eugene de Le Court, a young lieutenant who died bravely while covering the retreat of a *Force Publique* column (see Figure 6.1).

> The situation was desperate. All seemed lost. But brave De Le Court sprang into the breach. Together with two other Belgian officers and the remnants of their platoons, he immobilized the black demons who had rushed into the pursuit of the column. The rear-guard action raged with utter fury. Sinister black heads seemed to emerge from every corner, grinding their white teeth … It was a black nightmare, demonical, fantastic … One Belgian officer had already failed. And De Le Court understood that his turn too had come … But, calm, admirable, he continued to smile … with the hero's gentle and naïve smile … He fell … he understood that the supreme moment of death had come … Smiling, disdainful, sublime, thinking of his King, of his Flag … he looked for the last time upon the screaming horde of black demons … and collapsed. Thus Charles De Le Court died in the fullness of youth in the face of the enemy. (quoted Gann and Duignan 1979: 62–3)

As if to placate the contemporary feelings of anyone familiar with the 'reality' of the Congo to whom this would appear propaganda, the display text suggests it is typical of a the colonial spirit of the age that has since been called into question by History. It must be remembered, however, that work on this monument began some nine years after *Heart of Darkness* was published, seven years after Casement's report, and six years after the Belgian Parliament had forced Léopold to set up an independent commission of enquiry, which, despite the King's best efforts, had confirmed Casement's report. History was already known in 1911, at least to those who wanted to know it. Furthermore, the monument's completion in 1921, after the sufferings of Belgium from German occupation during World War I, may provide further testament to the normalising spirit that pushed such knowledge out from civilised space.

Further evidence as to the constitution of the civilised space of Brussels may be adduced by comparison of the monument with the fate of the closed neo-classical *Pavillon Horta* beside it. The proper title for the Pavilion is *Pavillon des passions humaines* (Pavilion of human passions) and the explanatory label explains its fate.

> Relief sculpture in Carra marble on the theme of the pleasures and misfortunes of unbridled humanity represented by the ghostly figure of Death, winged and draped in a shroud. Conceived in 1886 and purchased by the Belgian government in 1890, this was the first monument by the young architect Victor Horta, who created the pavilion in which the piece is exhibited. It was never finished. Officially inaugurated in 1899, the monument was permanently closed to the public three days later because of the scandal and controversy it aroused. The monument earned for its author the nickname 'Michelangelo of the gutter'.

Figure 6.1 Monument to the Congo (1911–21), Parc du Cinquantenaire (photo Wayne Morrison): a Belgian soldier sacrifices himself for his fatally wounded captain

A photograph of a small piece of the sculpture, showing hands on breast and buttocks is all that one is allowed still to see. The guidebooks suggest the contemporary reason may be out of respect for the new Mosque nearby. It may not matter whether it is closed today for reasons of economy or deference to those who come to pray in the Mosque. The fact that it has been closed since some three days after its opening as it was considered scandalous while the Congo monument was celebrated as a testament to national endeavour demonstrates the demarcations within European cultural sensitivities. Demarcations that place certain images and memories as material culture to be preserved and presented to the public, while others are repressed, rendered invisible and ineffective to contemporary social and political consciousness.

At the eastern end of the park colonnades swing round from the spectacular and imposing central *Arc de Triomphe* (officially entitled *Arcade de la Cinquantenaire*) to link the museums of the two wings of *Le Cinquantenaire*. These are the results of a plan to erect something that Léopold vaguely described as a *Walhalla*, to commemorate the heroic deeds of the dead of Belgium's past.[1] On the north side is the *Musee Royal de l'Armee et d'Histoire Military* (Royal Museum of the Army and Military History). Inside the history of the Belgian military is depicted through displays of armaments, uniforms, vehicles and planes. The revolution of 1830 that created an independent Belgium holds a central place but there are various somewhat unfocused collections. There are few attempts at providing any narrative and the displays are arranged in the now distinctly old fashioned trophy fashion; the effect, however, is to keep the visitor at a distance yet enticed. Belgium is placed at the centre of Europe's history and its future is that of the embodiment of the project of European integration, its past is presented as one of toil and sacrifice. Belgium the valiant, whose neutrality was all too easily overcome by German duplicity and might in two world wars and whose people suffered terribly at the hands of the German occupiers. Belgium, a somewhat hybrid nation state that contained a diversity of peoples divided between those speaking French and Flemish but united in their desire for normalcy – a state that wanted recognition, that desired peace, that was a victim. Leaving the site of these images for the peaceful surrounds, one may appreciate the message that contemporary Europe is a politic of peace and justice and Brussels is a fit location for the administration of that project, for Belgium was never an aggressor. But both the displays and the park outside are constituted spaces, requiring unpicking to appreciate the flows of power and complicity with subjective desire. Consider the presentation of the Arab Campaign 1892–97. In 2003 and again in 2005, I found these proudly arranged trophy style with a bust of Léopold taking centre place (Figure 6.2).[2]

The success of the Arab campaigns meant that an immense stretch of territory – the shores of Tanganyia, the Manyema, the Ituri and the Lomami basin – was brought effectively under the authority of the Congo Free State. After 1894 the men who had fought the most decisive engagements of the Arab campaign set about transforming this former 'Arab zone' into the *Province Orientale* of the Congo State. First Dhanis, and later Lothaire, were put in charge of the new province, the profits of which were to flow directly to Léopold. Certainly there is good reason for a bust of Léopold to take pride of place before the cabinets of mannequins of soldiers, portraits, collections of military weapons; but where are the explanations of how this campaign was by Belgium Officers (and other European officers and African solders of the *Force Publique*) not for the Belgium nation but of the personal state of the King of the Belgiums, Léopold II?

Figure 6.2 Representation of the Arab Campaign, 1892–7; Musee Royal de l'Armee et d' Histoire Military (photo Wayne Morrison)

No detailed narratives of explanation were provided; nor did inquiries for books on the Arab campaign at the museum shop bring any positive response. To examine the experiences of the young Belgian Officers in the *Campagne Arabe* we must turn to various journals and published diaries, now out of print and extracts from histories. One such officer was Emile Lémery, whose letters he wrote to his family from Nyangwe were not originally intended for public viewing (following discussion and quotes from Slade 1962: 114–16). After his military training Lémery entered the *Force Publique* in 1892, spent six months in the lower Congo before being sent to the east where men were desperately needed once the Arab campaigns had begun. He saw little of the main fighting, since Dhanis placed him at Nyangwe, together with another Belgian, to be in charge of native troops guarding the post and stop the scattered allies of Rumaliza from joining up with their leader. By August 1893 Lémery, had settled in at Nyangwe: 'The town must have been very big, but only ruins remain and there are skeletons in the streets.' He described Dhanis as charming and although 'a bit strange sometimes' he was an old Africa hand, very intelligent and able to speak all languages of the country as though they were his own. 'This is an immense advantage, and I think much of his success is due to it.' Lémery wrote that he himself was in possession of many pretty women (Arabs), a leopard, a monkey and twenty-four parrots. In early September he was hoping to leave Nyangwe to march against Rumaliza, which he thought would provide 'a famous massacre, for all the natives are for us and follow us'. Later in the month he was disappointed to find that he was expected to stay at Nyangwe but he made the best of the situation by studying Arab customs, exploring the neighbourhood and making maps. Although officially pacified he described Nyangwe as 'recently conquered country', its ground a 'cemetery of bones':

> We cannot take more than ten steps here without armed soldiers, and at night we sleep with loaded revolvers. Traitors abound in this recently conquered country. The ground is comparable to a cemetery of bones. At Nyangwe there was conspiracy to assassinate the Whites. It was discovered, and the same day began a massacre of St. Batholomew. Certainly a thousand people were killed in a few hours. Happily Gongo's men, cannibals *par excellence*, ate them up at the same rate. It's horrible but exceedingly useful and hygienic … It's impossible to stop it; you just have to shut your eyes and pretend not to see … I should have been horrified at the idea in Europe! But it seems quite natural to me here. Don't show this letter to anyone indiscreet, because I'm telling you things I ought to keep quiet about.

Lémery praised the Arabs for making pockets of civilisation out of the land, such as the plantations of rice, potatoes and sugar-cane at Kasongo, and for developing the flocks of sheep and goats, and the herds of cattle and donkeys which the European had inherited from the Arabs. He realised that the condemnation of Ngongo Lutete 'for treachery', which had provoked the confrontation that served as the excuse for waging war, was almost certainly wrong. However, this did not affect his desire to see action, as in October he expressed his disappointment at not having been able to join the expedition to Tanganyika:

> Adieu to decorations!!! For consolation I am telling myself that it shows great confidence in me to leave me at Nyangwe. … And on the other hand one buys a lot of ivory here, and if I stay it's likely that by the end of two years I shall have made quite a good commission. And that's not to be despised.

In December he relayed news of Ponthier's death and conveyed his regret that he was not in the front line of the fighting:

> a good death, for the cause is a noble one. I regret not having been in the fighting, although Dhanis says I have been in greater danger here. … Many a night I have spent on the watch; I could have been attacked at any moment and I only had a hundred men.

By January 1894 his letters revealed a changed perspective:

> *Vive le Congo*, there is nothing like it! We have liberty, independence, and life with wide horizons. Here you are free and not a mere slave of society.

Once transport in the Congo was better organised, he opined, full scale European colonisation would be possible, until then money was to be made from ivory, of which he said he was gathering in 2,000 pounds each month. By May the main fighting was over and Arabs who had been responsible for the murder of Europeans were being tried and condemned to death. Lémery related how he was looking after the children of those Arab leaders:

> I have adopted a son of Miserera, who is to be hung tomorrow; you know Miserera was the chief assassin of the Whites at Riba-Riba. The son in question is five years old,

completely white and very intelligent and good-looking. I intend to bring him to Europe and see to his education. I've gathered together at Nyangwe all the children of the upper class Arabs, the children of Sefu, Miserera, Bwana Zige, Mulenda, etc. … I have nine children of Miserera, all perfectly white, seven of them very pretty girls, as you'll see by their photographs.

This was a transforming administration: rebuilding the town, pacifying the surrounding country and organising regular river transport between Nyangwe and Riba-Riba – besides the profitable collection of ivory and some rubber. It was also time to congratulate himself on the 'complete success' of his 'political relations' with the 'natives'.

I hope that later on they will be grateful for all the efforts I have made here for the good of the State … Here one is everything! Warrior, diplomat, *trader*!! Why not, whatever they say, I am here for the good of the State … and all the means I use are permissible if they are honest.

But what were the standards for honesty? The agents of the Congo State performed all the roles, provided all the checks and balances. Soldiers were also administrators, for lieutenants or captains were at the same time *commissaries de district* – and State policy made them traders as well. Conrad had put it succinctly: 'out there, there were no external checks'. None of this is mentioned or hinted at: there is no insight to be gained from this museum into the historical complexity of the military involvement in the Congo. Or, of the military victory by the *Force Publique* in the events of World War I that led to Belgium taking over colonial responsibility for Rwanda. Did this change play a role in the later massacres post-independence and the 1994 genocide? There is no hint at complex legacies. One hundred years earlier Conrad structured *Heart of Darkness* so that the real message was located in Brussels; he ended his narrative with a scene that indicated that his audience preferred not to know his truths. Today, in rendering invisible the truths as to the cost of the building of these grand monuments, in the processes whereby the civilised space of central Brussels successfully excludes upsetting sights or knowledges of the Congo, we can understand that Conrad's message needs repeating. Again silence is probably the victor; and the greatest silence I encountered visiting this civilised Brussels in 2002 and 2003 was at the institutions dedicated to scientific study of Africa, The Royal Museum for Central Africa at Tervuren (RMCA).[3]

The Royal Museum for Central Africa at Tervuren

By 1897 profits were flowing back to Léopold from the rubber trade with the expectation of great wealth to be obtained. To counter growing rumours concerning the treatment of the native Africans, Léopold was concerned that the Belgium people appreciated his role as King – Sovereign of the Congo Free State and the benefits derived therefrom. In 1897 he was the driving force behind the temporary exhibition on the Congo constituting the Colonial Section of the Brussels World Fair. The fruits of which live on today as a wonderfully resourced National Museum, *The Royal Museum for Central Africa* situated in Tervuren, about ten kilometres from the city centre of Brussels. To appreciate the status of this institution, first listen to its 2003 self-description.

The colonial exhibition developed into a 'showcase' for 'his' Congo, and was intended to arouse more interest in that country among the Belgians. The exhibition's aims were as much propagandist and commercial as scientific. To house this great event, Léopold had the 'Palace of the Colonies' built on the royal estate in Tervuren. More than a million fascinated visitors became acquainted with the peoples, the fauna and flora, and the natural resources of Congo. To enable the visitors to get to the exhibition without delay, Léopold had a broad two-lane highway – the present-day Tervurenlaan – laid through the Zonien Forest. A year later, the temporary exhibition took on a permanent character and the *Musee du Congo* was created. Its purpose was not only museological; the new institution fulfilled a scientific task as well. However, it very soon became apparent that the 'Palace of the Colonies' was too small for its growing collections, and in 1902 the King decided to build a larger museum. French architect Charles Girault drew up the plans, and in 1904 the building of the present museum began. Originally, the museum was intended to be a part of a complex that would also include a World School, a restaurant, a concert hall and sports hall, as well as a Japanese and a Chinese museum. However, this ambitious project was brought to a halt when Léopold II died in 1909. In 1908, Léopold had sold his colony to the Belgian State. In 1910, King Albert I inaugurated Girault's building as the *MUSEE DU CONGO BELGE* – THE MUSEUM OF THE BELGIAN CONGO. In 1952 the 'Royal' appellation was added. When Congo gained Independence in 1960 – marking the end of Belgium's colonial era – the name changed once more, and the museum in Tervuren became THE ROYAL MUSEUM FOR CENTRAL AFRICA.[4]

The 2003 mission statement read:

The museum must be a world centre in research and knowledge dissemination on past and present societies and natural environments of Africa, and in particular central Africa, to foster – to the public at large and the scientific community – a better understanding and interest in this area and, through partnerships, to substantially contribute to its sustainable development. Thus the core tasks of this Africa-oriented institution consist of acquiring and managing collections, conducting scientific research, implementing the results of this research, disseminating knowledge, and presenting to the public a selection from its collections.

The museum complex consists of five buildings. A beautiful and imposing centrally situated main building in Louis XVI style contains the permanent exhibition. To the right of this edifice (as seen from the statue of the elephant) is the Administrative Pavilion and to the left, the Stanley Pavilion, where the complete Stanley Archive is housed. The Palace of the Colonies at the end of the Tervurenlaan and the CAPA building on the Leuvensesteenweg accommodate various scientific departments, laboratories and reserves.

This is part of contemporary cultural heritage; a heritage constructed blending classical appeals to the foundations of enlightenment thought and the profits of global positioning. During the nineteenth century and the beginning of the twentieth, impressive neo-classical museum buildings sprang up all over Europe. The golden age of museums had dawned giving us cultivated spaces – temple like – for displaying either the process of nation building (Anderson, 1981), natural history or the 'religion of art'. After the French Revolution the grand style or 'palace architecture' became pre-eminent architecture in which to emphasise the enduring nature of the Western cultural model.

The building French architect CHARLES GIRAULT created between 1904 and 1910 is a classic example of this kind of imposing museum architecture. Inspired by the Palace of

Versailles and the Petit Palais, the museum building enhanced the prestige of the still young Belgian State and contributed to the promotion of the then colony. The EXTENSIVE PARK WITH ITS LAKES AND FRENCH GARDENS added to the effect. The MAIN BUILDING is rectangular in plan and is structured around a large open court. It has undergone only one important alteration since it was built – the enclosing of the arcades around the inner court in order to create new exhibition space. On the park side of the building an imposing flight of steps leads the visitor to the prestigious ROTUNDA with its soaring 28 metre glass cupola. Like several other galleries in the museum, the walls of the rotunda are clad with marble in a rich geometric design. A star and crown motif – symbol of the Congo Free State – is incorporated in the pattern of the floor. To design the FRENCH GARDEN, Léopold II called on the Frenchman ELIE LAINE, who opted for an austere but harmonious pattern of parterres, lawns and pathways, embellished here and there with cast-iron statues on plinths. The stately garden facade of the main building is reflected in the water of the 'mirror pool'. Beyond, formal waterways lead to the large lakes of the park. The harmonious integration of the architecture in the natural environment is a *tour de force* of architectural and landscape design. (RMCA 2002: 14)

This celebratory tone does not concern the survival of the beautiful buildings of a discredited colonial tyrant in a revisionist history, far from it, for as late as 1997 a sculptural tribute in iron by the artist Tom Frantzen was installed in the gardens to celebrate Léopold and his work (Figure 6.3).

The visiting experience

The museum is a site for daily rituals of tourism or the weekend experience.[5] As the guide/map obtained from the tourist information office states: 'Tervuren, a haven of peace only a few miles from Brussels, invites you to explore its park, the Soignes forest, the Arboretum and its many country roads. In its museums you'll encounter Tervuren's glorious past – The Africa Museum … contains several remarkable collections, virtually all of them connected with Africa, including testimonies of the former presence of Belgium in the Congo. Its splendid façade faces the French Gardens and the park, which gradually leads to the Soignes Forest.' (Tervuren, Tourist Guide, January 2000)

The gardens are a favourite place for couples to have their wedding photos taken (Figure 6.4), while inside both adults and children gaze upon the various African artefacts, the thousands of stuffed animals, follow through the statues of women being protected from Arab slave traders (first cast for the 1897 exhibition), gaze upon the mementos of Livingston and Stanley, note the names of the more than 1,500 Belgium heroes killed in service there that are inscribed into the walls of a passage dedicated as a roll of honour, and marvel at the length of the grand canoe. There was in my visits of 2002 and 2003 little else to do, since the labelling of the pieces does not constitute any narrative of substance – no displays of social history, no confrontations of differing perspectives or narratives. Large amounts of ethnographic material presented, with simple labels, offering no comment on social location … it is as if ground, animals and natives were variations of one, then raised to civilisation (or nearly) by the mission of the white man. This was, almost certainly, the central organising narrative of this place, but without that being clearly expressed, the organising point disappears, the collection appears disjointed, inharmonious, a treat of imagery … but with no coherence to do combat with.

Figure 6.3 Léopold and three warrior chiefs (photo Wayne Morrison)

Figure 6.4 An example of civilised space: the foreground of the Royal Museum for Central Africa provides a great backdrop for wedding photos (from my visit in 2003, photo Wayne Morrison)

Revising ... locating ...

> Thirty years ago, but a small number of men had set foot in the Congo. There man was a wolf to man ... In the hundreds of millions of square kilometers that represented mysterious Africa, there was nothing that even resembled a work of civilization. It was only through Stanley, who followed the long ribbon of the Congo downriver, that one knew there were millions of human beings there, cannibals, slavers, victims of revolting diseases and horribly barbaric customs. Thirty years have passed! Central Africa is no longer mysterious it is criss-crossed with roads, railways, telegraph wires, scattered with towns, justice reigns, tribal warfare has vanished, the slave trade has been extirpated from the territory, numerous factories concentrate the riches of the forest and sustain thousands of our countrymen. (Baron A. de Haulleville, Director of the Royal Museum for Central Africa from 1910 to 1927)

That museums are formal embodiments of a *particular group's* 'public culture' – institutionally presenting sets of assumptions as if they were shared about the world and that group's place in it – is a central proposition of revisionist perspectives. Museums are institutionalised sites for seeing, for capturing the gaze, and then presenting it as if it were simple fact. We can tell the positivist history of this process: modern museums were produced in the transformation in collecting practices originating after the French revolution. Princely galleries were opened up to display the power of elites: 'The point of such show was to dazzle and overwhelm both foreign visitors and local dignitaries with the magnificence, luxury, and might of the sovereign, and, often – through special iconographies – the rightness or legitimacy of his rule' (Duncan 1995: 22). Hooper-Greenhill indicates how 'culture' became a particular sphere of a new governmental power.

> In the place of intensely personal, private collections housed in the palaces of princes and homes of the scholars, public collections in spaces open to the whole population were established ... Now the [governmental] gaze that surveyed an extended geographical space initially for military purposes surveyed that same space for cultural purposes. Material things, 'works of art' (*objects d'art*), were deployed in the same way as other strategic commodities. (Hooper-Greenhill 1992: 167)

Yet museums needed to be depicted as a sign of progress in knowledge and as part of a civilising process; at the same time as evidence of greater refinement and spread of elite practices. Influenced by Foucault's work on classification, on epistemes and his methodology of identifying the gaze of power, scholars engaged in revisionist museum studies, attempt to uncover the meaning of the emerging curatorial gaze that was constituted through a network of institutions and technologies of gathering together collections, filtering and (re)organising their objects. More than some abstract pursuit of the truth of the human condition was at stake when spaces and things that 'belonged' to the king, aristocracy and the church were utilised in establishing the new museums (the RMCA occupies land that was formerly the grounds of a Chateau). Partly celebration of new forms of 'public utility': partly reassurance. Governments (and quasi-governmental Boards of Trustees) presented alterity – 'things' of difference and things as 'different' – demonstrating that life conditions were improving for citizens of civilised space, the people who flocked to see the exhibits and 'world fairs'. The viewer – in some respects a self-selecting subject of modernity (in that he or she had chosen to come to the grand exhibition, was curious, was motivated) – participated in a display orientated around accepting that his/her life increased in security and richness as one consumed, that is as one gazed upon the variety of exhibits the patron(s) had brought, sometimes from the ends of the earth, and arranged expressly for viewing. This seduction into power flattered the power to organise exhibits, categories, displays, objects and their 'truths'; to locate. To accept these exhibitions as normal meant wondering at the increased power that new technologies expressed and enhanced, placed in greater variations of effects, rendered life seemingly transparent, almost democratic in our (Western) understanding of its effects.

Identification with the symbolic order through routinisation of the ritual

The modern grand museum's neo-classical architecture invites secular rituals (Carol Duncan). Referring to a pre-Classical world of highly evolved civic institutions, classical-looking buildings suggest secular Enlightenment principles and purposes. But monumental classical forms bring with them the space of rituals – corridors scaled for processionals and interior sanctuaries designed for awesome and potent effigies.

> Museums do not simply resemble temples architecturally; they work like temples, shrines, and other such monuments. Museumgoers today, like visitors to these other sites, bring with them the willingess and the ability to shift into a certain state of receptivity. And like traditional ritual sites, museum space is carefully marked off and culturally designated as special, reserved for a particular kind of contemplation and learning experience and demanding a special quality of attention. (Duncan 1991: 91)

Stage settings for visitors' performances, museums are structured around ritual scenarios, reflecting beliefs and values about social, sexual and political identity, enabling visual and direct experiences. Throughout the late nineteenth century many champions (e.g., Cole 1884) argued that museums could civilise the general populace by providing a new kind of civic ritual; educational and reflective, abstracted from the pressures of the workplace or the confines of cramped living space. Those needs may have now changed; but rituals remain, ever adapting. Drawn into this organised space one sees the sights in prescribed priority, ideally excluding our awareness of the outside. Rituals of cultural display and consumption discipline, even, perhaps, as one rebels; for rebelling would be to react against, and thus also to move within the webs of influence, of models and of training (and thus in this place the trap of, and for, neo-colonialism).

RMCA is a an active site of power, subtle and ideological, imposing a cultural experience that claims for its process of power the status of simple facts (as 'artefacts') and objective knowledge as it excludes confrontation with all that it does not present. 'To control a museum means precisely to control the representation of a community and its highest values and truths' (Duncan 1991: 8). RMCA civilises, its distancing of battle means we are in a place all-too-confident in its power to serve us. The relative standing of individuals within that community are invoked (in the museum café stand) colonial representations of caricatured blacks, having adopted the dress of their 'masters' (see Figure 6.5).

As I wandered around in 2002 and 2003 I wondered if to eat in the café was to accept this hierarchy? If I complained was that proof that I was strange, a trouble maker, a 'problem'? Perhaps those who are best prepared to perform its rituals – those who are most able to respond to it various cues – are also those whose identities (social, sexual, racial, etc.) the museum ritual most closely conforms. 'Seeing the sights in the prescribed priorities (and dismissing everything else) is one of the most disciplined of modern rituals. The ceremonial agenda can even direct us to view a scene from a special place' (Horne 1984: 11). Who was I? Was my dislocation a handicap to belonging; could I, as the past cast-away of Europe never be familiar here? Was this curse or blessing? Who or what process determines presence? Are the same forms that determine on what terms and by whose authority we do or do not see also working on questions about who constitutes the community of modern Europe and who defines its identity?[6] Did the man who took the Eurostar to London and was found guilty of benefit fraud ever come here? It is difficult, even for one who has read accounts of the history of Léopold's Congo to focus – what is the status of the following thoughts:

> In the walking of these spaces crime is filtered out, even though these spaces are only allowed by crime, they are the products of crime.

These thoughts can not enter into polite conversation; they are an uncultured intrusion – the attention paid to the ceremonial nature of this museum space and the need to differentiate it and the time one spends in it from the day-to-day time and space outside it was not wasted. To think thus intrudes upon the tranquillity, the civilised peace of the park, the fountains and statues fashioned so to prepare the visitors before they enter the main building leading them to appreciate the objects, encouraging them to bring a special kind of attention. An attention that focuses on the objects, that does not enter into the labyrinths of another time and place. What of the objects and their arrangement? Many of these objects were deposited by the missionaries that did so much to civilise the Congo. As Baron A. de Haulleville, Director of the Museum from 1910 to 1927 explained:

> One hundred and fifty thousand cannibals have been tamed by the cross, speak like us, think like us, and worship the same God as us! No other colonizing nation in Africa, not even those who have been established in the territories they control for more than a hundred years, can show such considerable results achieved among the natives. (quoted in Wastiau 2000: 20)

The museum benefited in that 'conversion meant the renouncing – voluntarily or otherwise – of "fetishes" (masks, amulets and suchlike heathen objects), prior to their destruction' (Wastiau 2000: 21). Many were destroyed (such as in the great fire of shields of 1909), but a considerable quantity were taken by the missionaries and in time found their way to the museum. But as to their presentation, the European practice of placing objects in settings designed for contemplation is historically speaking relatively recent. In the eighteenth century works of art began to have ascribed to them the power to transform

Figure 6.5 Photo of museum café, 2003 (photo Wayne Morrison)

their viewers spiritually, morally and emotionally. This newly discovered aspect of visual experience was extensively explored in a developing body of art criticism and philosophy. Although they may not be concerned with the experience of art as such but labelled questions of taste, the perception of beauty, the cognitive roles of the senses and imagination opened up a new terrain for art criticism. The rise of the art museum 'is a corollary to the philosophical invention of the aesthetic and moral powers of art objects' (Duncan 1991: 14). But is this an art museum? If they were once seen as fetishes, was there art in the (K)(C)ongo? Ambiguity still inheres in the presentation of the objects.

Visiting experience 2003: the visible of the museum

The temple form is apt (Cameron 1972: 201, 197). As a temple the museum 'plays a timeless and universal function, the use of a structured sample of reality, not just a reference but as an objective model against which to compare individuals' perceptions' (as contrasted to the idea of a forum, a place for 'confrontation, experimentation and debate').

So the neo-classical RMCA: the architecture of modern secular rationality. The main entrance faces the gardens and the park beyond, access up to it is via a grand flight of stairs; steps leading up to a 'ceremonial space' at the top, a magnificent rotunda with its soaring 28-metre glass cupola – the temple, a shrine. The rotunda was a popular style in the early twentieth century as memorials to donors whose private art collections were bequeathed to the nation, and their 'pristine forms of the mausoleum are derived from a variety of sources – circular temples (including the Pantheon)' (Duncan 1995: 88). Coming in from the garden one walks into the large rotunda, the marble walls of which form the main reception area in a rich geometric design with golden statues placed in elaborate niches. These thematically arranged statues celebrate the civilisation, salvation, mercy and justice that Belgium brought to the Congo. Placed with their backs against the half circle that faces the entrance, the statues representing Belgium are on the higher level and coated in gold; below, on the ground in front of their saviours, representational figures of the Congo sit on the ground, these are cast in black (see Figure 6.6). The wording on the plinths of the sets of statues – depicting Belgium and the Congolese are:

> La Belgique Apportant La Civilisation Au Congo – A Congo Artist
> La Belgique Apportant La Securite Au Congo – The Chief of the Tribe
> La Belgique Apportant Le Bien-Etre Au Congo – The Idol Maker
> L'Esclavage – Freedom from slavery.

So we find the material representation of European power with its saving grace, its enlightening actions, the bringer of equity, of justice, of education ... of reason.

Beyond the rotunda lie the passages, the research and display rooms, wherein are presented objects taken from the Congo. This is a mixture that represents an overlay of objects; as if all narratives are now uncoupled and there is little direction ... one could break the rules, one could take rooms out of order, for what is the order of enlightenment for the Kongo/Congo Free State/Belgium Congo/Congo/Zaire/DR Congo? Consider Figure 6.7; this represents a simple collection of artefacts of the natives of the Congo. They do not have their individual space, nor are there any extensive explanatory labels. Duncan's words fit:

> The art/artefact distinction marks the divide between the disciplines of anthropology on the one hand and art history and criticism on the other. At the same time, the dichotomy has provided a rationale for putting western and non western societies on a hierarchical scale, with the western ones (plus a few far eastern courtly cultures) on top as producers of art and non-western ones below as producers of artefacts. This scale is built on the

Figure 6.6 One of the set of four contrasting sets of sculptures. The top set were commissioned between 1910 and 1922 as a set of allegorical sculptures in gilded bronze for the niches in the rotunda; the theme was the relationship between the Belgian state and her colony – the brief was to be positive. The set is 'Belgium brings Civilisation to the Congo' (by Arsene Matton) in the rotunda, while below, and dwarfed by the white priest is the semi-naked 'native' (The Artist). The figure below was cast in plaster by the British sculptor, writer and collector Herbert Ward (1863–1919), who saw himself as a 'visual anthropologist'. Ward saw the native as occupying a lower rung on the evolutionary ladder, this image celebrates the primitive as untouched by civilization and thus able to produce primitive 'art'. In all four sets the figure above, representing the new order that Belgium brings, dwarfs the figure below who is clearly in a subordinate position (photo Wayne Morrison 2003)

Learning Resources

assumption that only works of art are philosophically and spiritually rich enough to merit isolated aesthetic contemplation, while 'artifacts' as products of presumably less evolved societies, lack such richness. (1995: 5)

Thus art belongs to the contemplative space of the art museum, while artefacts are placed in anthropological, ethnographical or natural history collections where they may be viewed as scientific specimens. We are in a version of a collecting complex that stretches from Darwin through Lombroso into the failed desires of the Nazi museum to the vanished European Jews. Darwin's acceptance of the unity of the evolution of mankind (as opposed to polygenesis) meant, as witnessed in the hands of Lombroso, that primitive or savage peoples could be seen (unfairly to what Darwin actually wrote in his major text) as examples of an earlier stage of species development through which Western societies had since progressed (although, Lambrosso assured us, in the case of criminals and gypsies, and so forth, we had examples of arrested development). Anthropology connected the histories of Western cultures and those of the regions it now subjected to imperial actions and gazes at the same time as it denied them a social–political history: 'Denied any history of their own, it was the fate of "primitive peoples" to be dropped out of the bottom of human history in order that they might serve, representationally, as its support – underlining the rhetoric of progress by serving as its

Figure 6.7 Layout of exhibition space for native artefacts, 2003 visit. On my 2005 visit to the 'Colonial Violence in the Congo' International Seminar I spent some time in the exhibitions with a participant from the Congo who argued that the Congo could never have peace while the spirits of the past Congo lay trapped, imprisoned, in these exhibition cases

counterpoints, representing the point at which human history emerges from nature but has not yet properly begun its course' (Bennett 1988: 94).

The disassociation of the histories is apparent in the distinctions of the galleries where animals and native artefacts are presented from those celebrating the human endeavours of 'discovery' exploration and the roll of honour to the Belgiun colonialists. Yet one has sometimes a shock of recognition and distaste at the non-narrative, at the absence. In a glass wall case amidst a small collection of 'Bronze pieces from Nigeria' there is a Queen Mother's Head from Benin (Figure 6.8).[7] But what is this doing there? How did this piece, almost certainly taken (stolen?) by the British 'Punitive' Expeditionary Force of 1897 (for background see Chapter 7) come to be in this museum on Central Africa? There are no explanations, no narrative confrontings, no questions raised in the viewer as to state power, victimisation or the ascription of civilised and barbaric or crime and actions to protect 'suffering natives'. Again I could not help but ask, 'where am I? What sort of place is this? Into what narratives am I being inscribed?'

Figure 6.8 Queen Mother's Head, Benin, bronze (RMCA, photo Wayne Morrison). Queen Mother Heads are in two styles, the first dates from the sixteenth century when Idia, the mother of Oba Esigie, was granted the right to establish her own palace and ancestral altars as a reward for using her mystic powers to bring victory in Benin's war against the Igala. Brass heads with the long beaded coral cap that covers the Queen Mother's hairstyle were cast for these altars. This piece with a long neck is a later eighteenth-century style

Placement by institutional history

The silences and incompatibilities of the exhibits are traceable to the origins as Léopold's desire to emulate the grand Imperial Exhibitions that were sweeping Europe after the Grand Exhibition of Crystal Palace of 1851. Hobson partially understood the complex in 1902:

> It is quite evident that the spectatorial lust is a most serious factor in imperialism. The dramatic falsification, both of war and of the whole policy of imperial expansion, required to feed this popular passion forms no small part of the art of the real organisers of imperialist exploits, the small groups of businessmen and politicians who know what they want and how to get it. (Hobson 1968: 215 [1st edition, 1902])

The ideology that underpinned those exhibits may no longer be defensible, but their organisational ethos lives on.

Consider the Native village that was built on the present site of the lake in front of the grand building (Figure 6.9). To gaze on the images of that time is to enter another realm, but it was real.

Today the only remnants are found by visiting the churchyard of Tervuren, where against one of the church's walls seven identical tombstones are lined up. A tourist office sign on the wall above serves as a simple memorial:

> Brussels Universal Exhibition 1897. On the occasion of the International Exhibition of Brussels in 1897 three African villages were erected along the lake of Tervuren. During daytime these villages were inhabited by 267 Congolese. Seven among them – EKIA,

Figure 6.9 Nineteenth-century postcard depicting the native village for the Universal Exhibition, 1897. Contrast with Figure 6.4, the same scene in 2003

GEMBA, KITUKWA, MPEIA, ZAO and MIBANGE – did not survive the chilly summer and lie buried here.

What were the rules and purposes of this display? Some natives subjected to the British Empire were present in the 1851 exhibition, but Native people were first 'part' of the exhibitory complex in the 1867 Paris Exposition Universelle. The 1878 Paris exhibition featured an Algerian bazaar and a Cairo street, and in the 1889 Paris Exposition colonial peoples were brought over not just to serve as waiters and so forth, but to be looked at in their 'natural settings' (Greenhalgh 1988: 85). One visitor was concerned whether they were the genuine article:

> A popular feature of the show is the street, not of an ancient civilised city, but of aboriginal savages. In the back settlements behind all the gorgeous finery of the pagodas and palaces of the further East the ingenious French have established colonies of savages whom they are attempting to civilise. They are the genuine article and make no mistake, living and working and amusing themselves as they and their kinfolk do in their country. Some day an enthusiast promises us we shall have a great anthropological exhibition of living samples of all nations and tribes and peoples that on earth do dwell. That may be the next Universal Exhibition. That it will not be without deep interest and instruction this street of colonies of natives suffices to prove. Each village is built in its own grounds, enclosed by a fence, and inhabited by its own natives … All these natives have been specially imported for the exhibition. They have brought with them the materials for their huts, their tools, and everything necessary for them to reproduce in the capital of the civilised world the everyday life of Africa, the Pacific and the Further East. To add to the attractiveness of this anthropological collection there is close to the streets of the Aborigines an Annamite restaurant. (Paris and its Exhibition, *Pall Mall Gazette Extra*, no. 49, Friday, 26 July 1889, quoted Greenhalgh 1988: 88)

Thus the image presented must be genuine, at least as far as it can be re-presented, but the image is devoid of context; the authentic lies in the object itself, not in the processes that surround it (Greenhalgh 1998: 82). Between 1889 and 1914, the exhibitions became human showcases, when people from all over the world were brought to sites in order to be seen by others for their gratification and education. 'The normal method of display was to create a backdrop in a more or less tableau-vivant fashion and situate the people in it, going about what was thought to be their daily business. An audience would pay to come and stare. Through this twenty-five year period it would be no exaggeration to say that as items of display, objects were seen to be less interesting than human beings, and through the medium of displays, human beings were transformed into objects.' These human showcases did not know the discourse of human rights and treatment of other living cultures as equals. Eskimos, Ceylonese, American Indians and others were displayed alongside animals The regard for the disabled, deformed, animals and other cultures as lowlier/inferior justified the control over them. Comparable to exhibits in human circuses of the freak-show, these exhibits/objects should, could and had to be disciplined and punished where appropriate (Greenhalgh 1988: 86).

In 2003 I saw a contemporary museum still following a system of exhibition wherein the exhibits were to speak to the Belgian people, to render visible the developing glory of the Belgian State. The collection of 'material culture' – not simple facts but objects and forms – was arranged in a living materialisation of the rhetorical power of persuasion. The Congo Free state, was not only anything but free, it was Léopold's personal (e)state, a personal domain in an increasingly rationalised realm of nation states. Yet, for the visitor, there was among the plays at work an inducement; one could take pride in the growing prowess of things done in the name of the Sovereign of Belgian. The citizens, Léopold's constitutional subjects, could see themselves as partakers of those developments that the citizens of the French or British state, with their imperial grandeur, were experiencing with their grand exhibitions. Thus the constituting power of Imperialism; for those who celebrated the exhibitions, therein was displayed the 'moral' workings of history; the nation could have evidence with which to examine its conscience and find itself pleased.

Policing and the creation of civilised space

> The people are to the Legislature what a child is to a parent. (Colquhoun 1797: 242–3)

> And it is no inconsiderable feature in the science of Police to encourage, protect, and control such as tend to innocent recreation, to preserve the good humour of the Public, and to give the minds of the people a right bias ... Since recreation is necessary to Civilised Society, all Public Exhibitions should be rendered subservient to improvement of morals, and to the means of infusing into the mind a love of the Constitution, and a reverence and respect for the Laws ... How superior this is to the odious practice of besotting themselves in Ale houses, hatching seditious and treasonable designs, or engaging in pursuits of vilest profligacy, destructive to health and morals. (Colquhoun 1806: 347–8)

In the development of scholarly disciplines old concepts are sometimes forgotten; so is it with policing. Contemporary narratives of policing, punishment and surveillance tend to forget the width that policing meant to classical eighteenth-century scholars such as Beccarria. The nineteenth century saw the disappearance of public punishment and the creation of various measures and institutions aiming at the creation of domestic civilised behaviour. In the discourses of criminology or the sociology of punishment, the work of Michel Foucault looms large in explaining the disappearance of the public spectacle of the pain of punishment. In large part Foucault's legacy is addressed in terms of the emergence of a disciplinary society with associated technologies of discipline and normalisation acting upon the human body in particular 'modern' ways. In taking *Discipline and Punish* as the exemplary text, Foucault's metanarrative becomes unduly reduced to a pessimistic account of the spread of the power to punish and control in ever increasingly subtle forms through a carceral society. The thesis is engaging but overdone and misses the seductive ability, or what we may call the rhetorical effect, of much of modern spectacle.

First, to restate the Foucaultean narrative – Foucault opens *Discipline and Punish* with the contrast between the public execution and the timetable of a juvenile reformatory stressing that each defines a certain penal style (1977: 7). Punishment was gradually ceasing to be a spectacle 'and whatever theatrical elements it still retained were now downgraded'. The power to punish was being 'redefined by knowledge'. In the reformist writings of the eighteenth century, Foucault discerns the utopia of the punitive city. One must 'imagine' it as exposing 'hundreds of tiny theatres of punishment. Each crime will have its law; each criminal his punishment. It will be a visible punishment, a punishment that tells all, that explains, justifies itself. …. The great terrifying ritual of the public execution gives way, day and day, street after street, to this serious theatre, with it multifarious and persuasive scenes' (p. 113). But punishment did not take this public path.

> The scaffold, where the body of the tortured criminal had been exposed to the ritually manifested force of the sovereign, the punitive theatre in which the representation of punishment was permanently available to the social body, was replaced by a great enclosed, complex and hierarchized structure that was integrated into the very body of the state apparatus. A quite different materiality, a quite different physics of power, a quite different way of investing men's bodies … emerged … The high wall … closed in upon the now mysterious work of punishment … [becoming] the monotonous figure, at once material and symbolic, of the power to punish. (p. 116)

Why did punishment take this hidden path with the development of the carceral system? A narrative, taken from Foucault, holds that removed from the public gaze in being enacted behind the closed walls of the penitentiary, punishment targeted not the production of signs for society but the correction of the offender. No longer an art of public effects, punishment aimed at a calculated transformation in the behaviour of the convicted. The body of the offender, no longer a medium for the relay of signs of power, was zoned as the target for disciplinary technologies, which sought to modify the behaviour through repetition.

> ultimately, what one is trying to restore in this technique of correction is not so much the juridical subject … but the obedient subject, the individual subjected to habits, rules, orders, an authority that is exercised continually around him and upon him, and which he must allow to function automatically in him. (p. 128)

We have two figures: our attention to the legal tradition with its emphasis upon restoring the juridical subject of the social pact should not blind us to the modern processes of shaping an obedient subject, according to general and detailed forms of developing powers (such as bio- or socio-power).

The account has been highly influential. But it has also been misapplied. Applied as a narrative of the penal development of modern Western societies the fear has been of 'the swarming of disciplinary mechanisms', or disciplinary technologies and forms of observation developed in the carceral system – and especially the principle of panopticism, rendering everything visible to the eye of power – that display a tendency 'to become "de-institutionalised", to emerge from the closed fortresses in which they once functioned and to circulate in a "free" state' (p. 211). We are thus subjected to systems of surveillance, mapping the social body so as to render it knowable and amenable to social regulation, which constitute 'a disciplinary society', a society that 'is one not of spectacle, but of surveillance'. While 'Antiquity had been a civilisation of spectacle', making accessible to a multitude of men the inspection of a small number of objects' in modernity individuality has replaced community and public life, 'relations can be regulated only in a form that is the exact reverse of the spectacle'. Instead the state must intervene 'in all the details and all the relations of social life' and develop 'buildings intended to observe a great multitude of men at the same time'.

We are neither in the amphitheatre, nor on the stage, but in the panoptic machine, invested by its effects of power, which we bring to ourselves since we are part of its mechanism. (pp. 216–17)

For all its power this imagery is partial. We may note that the mutilation of the body, in the case of Belgium, now took place in its colonial spaces. This displacement needs analysis, however even in the confines of European civilised space it is not simply that in a world of global communications the spectacle gains importance, but that spectacle was always there. The weakness of Foucault's account lies not so much in its negativity, but in the downplaying of notions of the desiring subject who can be seduced, albeit subtly, rather than coerced. A theory of the subject that focuses predominantly on society as the locus of repression and constraint necessarily denies the transformative nature of desire, while the contrary attempt to deny constraints can only produce a conception of freedom that is empty and abstract. The emergence of a secular subject reflects the process by which the transcendent authority of religious ideals came to be replaced by a series of increasingly normative social practices bound together by the newly formed subject of rational discourse. The disenchantment of the world is made sustainable and liveable through the secularisation of culture; this allows for the multiplicity of cultural forms, and this process constantly positions the subject in the symbolic order of society in ways that the subject seems to recognise his self as linked to the realisation of his hopes, establishing desire as a transformative force.

What then can control or constrain this desire? Partly it is a question of the limits of the imaginary world. Consider how writing in the shadow of post-revolutionary France, De Maistre (1971) could put forward the figure of the executioner as the central figure in a metaphysic of a bounded – through the true religion – yet universal humanity. The power of the executioner therein denoted a reality of submission and totality; De Maistre argued that some foundational imagery of totality was required by humans. In the twentieth century this found its realty in fascism and an impressive array of dictatorships. But liberal or civilised modernity was increasingly producing a located yet dislocated subjectivity. Increases in transport and communication, the great migration into urban life, the knowledge(s) brought from abroad (or overseas in the English parlance) gave an awareness of 'locality' itself not previously experienced. The power of the spectacle that public punishment had encoded, a terrifying power of subordination and placement was losing its meaning in these processes of increasing complexity and expansion of information. There was even more need for spectacles of displaying power, however, both the class relations within which power was to be exercised changed, as did the modalities of representation and communication.

The key to the functioning of the prison, as explained by in the late eighteenth and early nineteenth century by James Mill and John Austin was to place it at the limits of political economy. Prison set the limits of a modernising coercion, but the progressive subject had to be induced to labour, to perform, to act out the truths of political economy. The museum could offer a new pedagogic relation with the prison, another side to new powers: the prison and the grand exhibitions grew together (see Figure 6.10). In England, Greame Davison suggests that the Crystal Palace might serve as the emblem of an

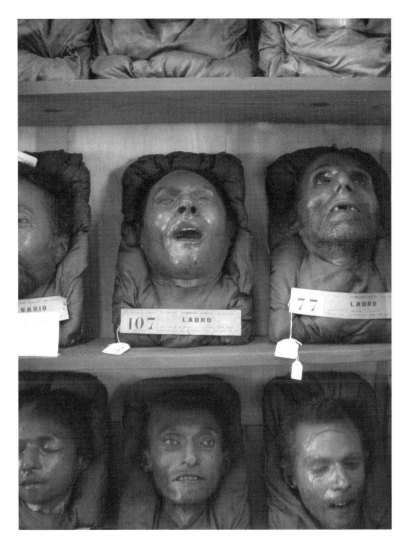

Figure 6.10 Part of the collection of wax death masks made for Lombroso and currently part of the collection at the Museo de Anthropologia 'Cesare Lombroso' in Turin, Italy (photo Wayne Morrison). These were made from the bodies of executed convicts, now executed behind prison walls and whose bodies were recorded as material 'facts' to be inscribed in a new regime of criminological knowledge (see further Morrison 2004b, also Leong 2004)

architectural series that could be ranged against that of the asylum, school, and prison in its continuing concern with the display of objects to a great multitude: 'The Crystal Palace reversed the panoptical principle by fixing the eyes of the multitude upon an assemblage of glamorous commodities. The Panopticon was designed so that everyone could be seen; the Crystal Palace was designed so that everyone could see' (Davison 1982/83: 7). In fact, as Tony Bennet suggests, the opposition is overstated since 'one of the architectural innovations of the Crystal

Palace consisted in the arrangement of relations between the public and exhibits so that, while everyone could see, there were also vantage points from which everyone could be seen, thus combining the functions of spectacle and surveillance' (Bennet 1995: 65). Bennet argues that even a cursory study of the literature of the nineteenth century demonstrates that it was 'quite unprecedented in the social effort it devoted to the organization of spectacles arranged for increasingly large and undifferentiated publics'. First, society itself – in its constituent parts and as a whole – was coming to be rendered as a spectacle. The city was to be rendered visible, and hence knowable, as a totality. 'Cities increasingly opened up their processes to public inspection, laying their secrets open not merely to the gaze of power but, in principle, to that of everyone; indeed, making the specular dominance of the eye of power available to all.' We see the development of city tours ranging from the Stock Exchange to the Sewers. Second, the state increasingly grew involved, albeit often indirectly, with the creation of massive public spectacles through the development of grand exhibitions, museums and art galleries – spectacles that took on an educative and civilising function. Third, these assumed a permanent quality, providing on-going displays of power/knowledge. Bennett calls this an *exhibitory complex* of which museums proved the best known example. The museum developed with rules of behaviour and rituals of visiting that distinguished 'the bourgeois public from the rough and raucous manners of the general public'. Through the visiting experience the rough and raucous 'might learn to civilise themselves by modelling their conduct on the middle class codes of behaviour' (1995: 28). If that was discipline through modelling, an invitation to join in the display of power was apparent. This new power-knowledge neither terrorised nor 'positioned the people on the other side of power as its potential recipients but sought rather to place the people – conceived as a nationalised citizenry – on this side of power, both its subject and its beneficiary'. Objects were transformed 'into material signifiers of progress – but of progress as a collective national achievement with capital as the great co-ordinator' (Bennett 1995: 67). Bennett captures this use of power in respect of the imperial webs that brought the 'other' close for the national subjects to observe in their human showcases.

This power thus subjugated by flattery, placing itself on the side of the people by affording them a place within its workings; a power which placed the people behind it, inveigled into complicity with it rather than cowed into submission before it. And this power marked out the distinction between the subjects and the objects of power not within the national body but, as organised by the many rhetorics of imperialism, between that body and other, 'non-civilised' peoples upon whose bodies the effects of power were unleashed with as much force and theatricality as had been manifest on the scaffold. This was, in other words, a power which aimed at a rhetorical effect through representation of otherness rather than at any disciplinary effects (Bennett 1995: 67).

The spectacle of seduction

The loyalising effect of such an exhibition is not the least of its moral recommendations. Every person who visited it would see in its treasures the result of social order and reverence for the majesty of the law (1849 opinion piece in the magazine *Art Union*, discussing the proposed Great Exhibition of 1851, quoted Greenhalgh 1988: 30).

To recap: the decline and stylisation of the spectacle of repressive coercion was accompanied by the flowering of the *spectacle of seduction*. As Norbert Elias ([1939] 1983), among others has argued, the civilising process involved the extension of 'high culture' from the court into wider society, a process where these cultural forms and practices helped form and shape the moral, mental and behavioural characteristics of the population. Rulers had already by 1600 seized upon the 'art of festival' as 'an instrument of rule' (Roy Strong 1984: 19). Court masques, the ballet, theatre and musical performances displayed aspects of royal power before courtly society and by the late seventeenth century the arena of this display began to incorporate a wider public, the populace of the emerging nation states whose relationship to the court needed newer forms of hegemony. Power needed to be displayed, but also to link in the populace not merely as objects of that power, but as participants.

> Imagine an area the size of a small city centre, bristling with dozens of vast buildings set in beautiful gardens; fill the buildings with every conceivable type of commodity and activity known, in the largest possible quantities; surround them with miraculous pieces of engineering technology, with tribes of primitive peoples, reconstructions of ancient and exotic streets, restaurants, theatres, sports stadiums and band-stands. Spare no expense. Invite all nations on earth to take part by sending objects for display and by erecting buildings of their own. After 6 months, raze this city to the ground and leave nothing behind, save one or two permanent land-marks.
>
> The international exhibitions held around the world between 1851 and 1939 were occurrences such as this, spectacular gestures which briefly held the attention of the world before disappearing into an abrupt oblivion, victims of their planned temporality. (Greenhalgh 1988: 1)

Temporal they may have been but millions of visitors came to them (six and a half million at the 1851 Exhibition alone) and were 'taught, indoctrinated and mesmerised'. Greenhalgh points out that they were the largest gatherings of people – war or peace time – of all time in Western societies, truly on both a high and a popular level they ranked amongst the most important events held in the nineteenth and twentieth centuries: 'remaining unsurpassed in their scale, opulence and confidence'. Beginning with displays of craft and industrial produce in France and then Britain, national displays of art and industry spread throughout Europe and across to New York in the first half of the nineteenth century. The Grand Exhibition held in London (christened Crystal Palace) became the symbol for a stunning, international festival dedicated to the new gods of capital and technology.

> The mix of exhibits was extraordinary, ranging from classical sculpture to giant lumps of coal, from a Nubian Court to wrought iron fire-places, from steam engines to Indian miniatures, from rubber plants to stained-glass windows. The artefacts in this lavishly orchestrated jamboree had only one thing in common, the awesome power of the technologies that had taken them there. (p. 13)

Paris took up the challenge and France remained in the ascendancy of an international game that between 1855 and 1914 saw an event involving more than twenty nations being held somewhere in the world on average every two years. The exhibitions of 1851 and 1862 in London and that of Paris in 1855 attracted millions mainly because of their novelty and the sheer scale of technological advance, but as exhibitions became more common technology alone could not be relied upon to fill a site and entertainment grew as a socio-economic factor. But so did education, particularly orientated to showing 'the progress civilization is making over the globe'. The first four French *Expositions Universelles* developed this idea until 'the last of these was seen by many as a museum of global explanation'. The organisers included influential Saint Simonians who sought to present a social and paternal image of world history, visions of 'total knowledge'. Thus individual location in family, work and history could be presented in a 'total display', such as in the *History of Human Habitation* in the 1889 Exposition. The dark side of this was the 'vulgar propaganda of government'. Education ... trade ... totality; ones place in the world largely revolved around the imperialist world vision buttressed by military technology. If trade had created Western power, the fact that trade being allowed by military advantage could not be directly celebrated in the exhibitions. The exhibition literature was often clear in explaining 'the hegemony of the Europeans and their descendents in terms of their ability to control and manipulate trading systems', yet this would also be clothed in a mystical eulogy where trade would unite peoples, solve the problems of the world and create happiness (p. 22).

The terminology of opening the globe for trade entailed conquest and controlling. Investment in the exhibitions could itself generate profits but they were also the principal means whereby government and private bodies presented their vision of the world to the masses, those who paid inevitably had motives not explained in the official literature. The Great Exhibition, for example, went international for a variety of reasons: to celebrate Britain's imperial and industrial lead; free trade demanded an international audience as did British manufacturers eager for foreign orders, but the home population had to play its part. The exhibition was designed to show the indigenous population the extent of British power and, by implication, their role within it. The year 1848 was marked by revolutionary activity throughout Europe, revealing the instability of regimes, thus the Great Exhibition was a giant counter-revolutionary measure instilling awe and some fear as well as pride in the British public.

To recap once again on Léopold's project: we have here in this museum the concrete manifestation of an exercise of power, a calculating King's ability to construct places of pleasure, of instruction, of cataloguing and education. But this ability of the King to sanction the happiness and instruction of his subjects is only a signature of the power of this manifestation of civilising process to inspire voluntary submission to its laws and processes of ordering. The order constructed must be accepted as internal (while it involves elements clearly imposed from above) and agreed by the desiring subjects themselves. An imaginary – wherein the desires of the subjects find a promise of satisfaction – is constructed that both acts to conceal the structuring of the 'wider' order(ing) from the subject who are both influenced (controlled) and contribute to it. Increased satisfactions internal to the pacified and wealthy space of the civilised are promised to those who build their techniques of self-constraint and social capital. Moreover, in acknowledging the sacrifices and privations experienced by those who lived and died in the civilising of the Congo, these subjects assume their share of the sovereign debt to the symbolic order. An heroic identification that can not just lie at the level of the noble individual but transfer to the order of the nation state and its authority.

A continuing process?

What lesson could be learnt from this calculation of presence and absence? What of justice? In contemporary historians' opinions (for example, Nelson 1994; Ascherson [1963] 1999; Anstey 1966; Edgerton 2002) Belgium inherited not only a colony but a system of exploitation that it changed the form of, but not the essence.

Léopold wanted profits from colonial possessions to buttress the financial security and ability to provide for military defence for a nation unsure of its identity and future survival; his wish was to be borne out in two disastrous European conflicts that became world wars. The 1916 offensive by Belgian colonial forces (*Force Publique*) successfully occupied an area of nearly 180,000 square kilometres, including Rwanda and Burundi, which passed to Belgian trusteeship after World War I. This was a substantial moral fillip for an occupied motherland. In a mostly occupied Belgium, the German occupation was harsh, with sometimes severe suffering, conscripted labour and confiscation of property and a number of 'punitive' actions taken to quell resistance. These are still a treasured part of Belgium collective memory. It is less remembered that although an occupied country, the Belgians could rely upon their colonial possessions as a territorial base as well as economic resource.

In World War II, during the Nazi occupation of Europe the Belgian state operated from London. It alone in Europe ended the war in credit. How was this possible? Robert Godding, the Belgian colonial affairs minister in 1945–6 proudly explained:

> During the war, the Congo was able to finance all the expenditures of the Belgian government in London, including the diplomatic service as well as the cost of our armed forces in Europe and Africa, a total of some 40 million pounds. In fact, thanks to the resources of the Congo, the Belgian government had not to borrow a shilling or a dollar, and the Belgian gold reserves could be left intact. (Quoted in Rodney 1974: 172)

To finance this, another system of neo-forced labour was instituted. Nzongola-Ntalaja (2003: 23) summarises: 'The Congo is a classic example of a colony that financed its own subjugation'. He asks,

> That a significant part of Belgium's economic growth and development was based on slave labour in the Congo raises the question of economic reparations for the economic plunder and political repression suffered by Africans for the benefits of Europeans. If it is morally right for Germany to pay reparations to Israel for the atrocities committed by the Nazis against Jews and to people who were coerced into slave labour during the Second World War, and if Iraq should be forced to pay reparations to some Persian Gulf countries because of the consequences of its invasion of Kuwait, why is it wrong for former colonial powers such as Belgium to pay reparations for the heinous crimes they committed in the African territories they administered?

But of course, this writing can (and will) be dismissed from consideration. For his use of the term 'crime' is only an emotive outburst; outwith the rational discourse of criminology, unrecognised by power. Yet today the Congo knows little peace, enjoys little security, its people denied justice, while pera in the 'west' either know or care of its war/pillage/rapes. ... It is effectively kept from the gaze of those in power, such as those who work – the wonderful EU Quarter of Brussels. Civilized space excludes.

The form the RMCA took and continued relatively comfortably until 2004–5 with its exclusions represented the (reality) power of civilised space. That it has now begun a process of rethinking its exhibitors and searchs for a new mission may make it a metaphor for change, for developing a global ethic. Yet the questions that imposed themselves so heavily during my previous visits remain: how could this museum realistically do any form of justice to the history of the (K)Congo and its colonial master and shaper of its present, Belgium? What would be its criminology if any? That the benefits of civilised 'peaceful' Western society are derived from a complex set of relations with its periphery – that in reality may be at its heart? But this would have then a state allowing one of its major cultural institutions to engage in a confrontation with its own constituting state power. Again would we not be living a fable?

But history keeps moving, eluding capture and yet always partly captured. If this museum was founded on the great exhibitory complexes we should remember that those lost their purposes. The World Trade Center in New York was a modern equivalent, connected to the trading populace through the technologies of communication, share trading, prices of the Dow Jones and Nasdaq. Its destruction (which in its scale hid the massacre of those within) was indeed a spectacle with a certain seductive power. No doubt it will have its own museum ... it would be a testament to enlightenment if it encouraged debate.

Appendix

Contrasting imagery: the battle over truth

Can a nation state inquire into the conditions of its own justice or must outside forces push open the veils of enlightenment? Daniel Goldhagen (1998b) suggests that in the case of post-World War II Germany an 'internationalisation of the "national" history', that is a process by which the country's past has been the subject of considerable outside scrutiny, has prevented the 'collective, narcissistic self-exaltation' often found (and expected) for national histories. The horrors of World War II have led to this enormous interest and prevented German history from being owned by Germans. German history has thus been an international enterprise with the result, Goldhagen argues, that Germans have a richer (and truer) history to access than otherwise.

It should be remembered though, that a major reason for the International Military tribunals (first Nuremberg and then Tokyo) after World War II was because Germany had not dealt with its 'war criminals' from World War I under the authority given it by Articles 228 and 229 of the Treaty of Versailles to prosecute and punish. Of the 901 individuals in respect of which the Allies gave evidence, 888 were acquitted by German courts and only token sentences imposed on the remaining 13, several of whom were shortly thereafter 'allowed to escape by prison officials who were publicly congratulated for assisting them' (Robertson 2000: 210–1; also reviewed Golt 1966).

Justice requires knowledge. In the case of the Congo Free State/Belgian Congo, first the propaganda machine of Léopold strove to prevent an accurate picture from being known, later the colonial state ethos provided an inbuilt assumption that the official story of the civilising mission and the preparation of the Congo to take its place in a European-led world order was correct. While there was some internal opposition, it was through the efforts of outside Missionaries and campaigners, Alice Harris and Morel, for example, that images were presented that broke the hegemony of the official story (see Hochschild 1998: 296–9 for the account of the one time Belgium diplomat Jules Marchal who grew curious and later, in the face of official silence, wrote the most comprehensive four-volume history of the Belgium Congo [in Dutch and French]). In Mark Twain's *King Léopold's Soliloquy*, an imaginary monologue conducted by Léopold and illustrated with photographs from the Harris collection, Léopold states that the Kodak camera was the only witness he has not been able to bribe. Yet this supposed realism for photography must be situated.

A popular magazine *Le Congo Illustre. Voyages et Traveaux des Belges dans l'Etat Independent du Congo* (Congo Illustrated. Travels and Works of Belgians in the Congo Free State), operated in 1892–5 and laid out many of the images that would establish the pictorial framework of representation of the Congo project (see Geary 2002, for a wide ranging discussion with many images of Central Africa). This was later strengthened by the set of volumes *Etat Independent du Congo* published by the Muse du Congo (forerunner of the RMCA) in 1903/4.

Published in 1904 as a series of Annex to the Annals of the Museum of the Congo under the title *L'Etat Independent du Congo – Document sur le pays et ses habitants*, the series used some 1,500 photographs. The preliminary notes set out the aim as bringing a reality to the people. Here the Kodak is used as the instrument of reassurance. These photos are fragments of complex processes with many intersecting determinants, but they are abstracted from this complex, whose 'actual' nature is not addressed but assumed as of no interest. Reassembled, they are gathered up to constitute a new entity, one stamped with the 'scientific' authenticity of the Museum. As a totality they are to constitute the evidence of the wholesome nature of the Independent State of the Congo's humanitarian colonial project. The text provides a narrative of a civilising process, turning the Africa native into a disciplined body, able to operate in the routinised and well-laid out new geo-social space which was to be the civilised state. The text functions as an institution of Western authority. Through the instrument of Western technology – the photograph – the 'reality' of life in the Congo is *pictured*; through writing those pictures are embedded into a narrative.

Through the museum and these texts Léopold sought recognition in Belgian eyes, through this mechanism the Belgium populace could be appropriated to the cause. The reader is seduced in the rhetoric of self-congratulation. If, and that was not actually likely – given the measures stifling publication – a member of the audience had heard of the rumours of the 'realty' of the Congo and the measures taken to produce rubber, here was an authentic rebuff. Consider two contrasting images of rubber collecting. Figure 6.11. Natives collecting rubber, Lusambo. And Figure 6.12, no label,

RUBBER.

NATIVES COLLECTING RUBBER, LUSAMBO.

Figure 6.11 The official image: sustainable agriculture (image: courtesy of Anti-Slavery International; oft reproduced in official post cards and in the *Annals*)

which shows a young boy with numerous sections of wild rubber vine that he has cut up and is waiting while the sap drains into the vessel that he has put below them. By themselves they escape understanding. However Figure 6.11 is one of the most reproduced official images of the Congo, it is of sustainable production. Figure 6.12 is from the Harris collection; it prefigures death.

In the official texts we have the appropriation of alterity; we see the 'evidence' that the 'law and order' of the European expansion functions so as to produce developed humanism. The *Annals* are testament to the civilising process. Proof of the operation of different categories is presented: Justice, education (in particular Christian), industry, construction, churches, progress

Figure 6.12 A different reality (image courtesy of Anti-Slavery International). Under extreme pressure to produce rubber this youth has cut the wild vine into sections; this will give maximum return this once, but will condemn him to diminishing return. Unable to reproduce this return, he has in reality signed his death warrant

in the sciences and arts, the production of music and fetes. Complexity has replaced the assumed simplicity of the African, progress is not only technical (in the construction of buildings we see a movement from rough wooden structures to the production of brick structures), but spiritual (in the centrality of places of Christian worship, in the changing recognition of state recognised 'legalised' marriage). The *Annals* were a series of six slim volumes containing short essays and over 1,200 photographs. These new volumes recycled many pictures. Each volume was presented in art nouveau design reflecting the idea that the colonial project was progressive. The first two volumes were concerned with the creation of the built environment depicting the creation of stone buildings and growing colonial towns which were built on the lines of Belgium architecture. The second section contrasted images of African villages with orderly new settlements established by the colonials for African workers. The volume on agriculture discusses the different crops and illustrates model farms with images of rubber production prominent. Volume four reflects the

Figure 6.13 The cover page of Léopold's response to the Congo Reform Association (image: courtesy of Anti-Slavery Society London). Here the prospect of an enlightened and civilised Congo is contrasted with its past

Figure 6.14 The supposed uncovering of intellectual fraud (image: courtesy of Anti-Slavery Society London)

establishment of communication and transportation networks and features, images replete with the realism of superiority, such as those illustrating early modes of European travel, namely being carried by natives in hammocks. The most labour intensive projects were the building of railways. In the volume, *The Protection and Moralisation of the Natives* the compilers give a story of the Belgium establishment of a new moral order in the Congo. The volume begins with a description of the legal system and prisons. Photographs of prisons trials and Africans in chains were common in the official publications and the privately produced sets of postcards and remain a popular theme long after Belgium took over the Congo Free Sate in 1908. Yet 1904 was the date of Caseman's report; in 1905 Mark Twain published his *Crime of the Congo*, for a time selling 25,000 copies a week. Léopold moved against Morel and Twain publishing a short booklet *An Answer to Mark Twain* (front cover reproduced as Figure 6.13). The booklet portrayed a new Congo of order, work and reason against the previous Congo of superstition, vice and indolence. It specifically questioned the reality of the images of Twain and Morel, attributing mutilation to act of wild animals. The back cover (Figure 6.14) featured two images: one was said to be of 'Potters at work in the Congo' – it was an image of three women at work with various pots; the second was said to be 'The same photo at Liverpool'. In the second image the pots had been replaced with human skulls. The implication was that the Reform Association had doctored the image to produce anti-Léopold propoganda; however, no trace of this supposed image has been found. It was rather an example of Léopold's agents doctoring an image and claiming they had uncovered intellectual fraud.

Chapter 7:
Contingencies of Encounter, Crime and Punishment: On the Purposeful Avoidance of 'Global Criminology'

There has never been any event which has had more impact on the human race in general and for Europeans in particular, as that of the discovery of the New World, and the passage to the Indies around the Cape of Good Hope. It was then that a commercial revolution began, a revolution in the balance of power, and in the customs, the industries and the government of every nation. It was through this event that men in the most distant lands were linked by new relationships and new needs. The produce of equatorial regions was consumed in Polar climes. The industrial products of the north were transported to the south, the textiles of the Orient became the luxuries of Westerners; and everywhere men mutually exchanged their opinions, their laws, their customs, their illnesses, and their medicines, their virtues and their vices. Everything changed, and will go on changing. But will the changes of the past and those that are to come, be useful to humanity? Will they give man one day more peace, more happiness, or more pleasure? Will his condition be better, or will it be simply one of constant change? (Abbe Guillaume Thomas Raynal, *Histoire philosophique et politique des etablissements et du commerce des europeens dans les deu Indes*, 1770, Book I: 1. [new edition as *L'Anti-colonialisme au xviiie siecle: Histoire philosophique et politique des etablissements et du commerce des europeens dans les deu Indes*, p. 43]).

I present to the Tribunal a certified photostatic copy of this notice as Exhibit USSR 262, and I read into the record an excerpt from this document. 'The Commander of the German State Security Police in Latvia hereby announces the following: ...
2. The inhabitants of the village of Audriny, in the Rezhetz District, concealed members of the Red Army for over one-quarter of a year, armed them, and assisted them in every way in their anti-government activities. As punishment I ordered the following: That the village of Audriny be wiped from the face of the earth.'

The Hitlerites practised punitive expeditions widely in the occupied districts of the Leningrad Region ...

Numerous punitive detachments, acting on the orders of the German Supreme Command, burnt down many hundreds of inhabited localities in the Yugoslav territory ... I refer, as evidence, to ... In these documents we find a number of facts concerning the burning and destruction of villages and hamlets by the special punitive expeditions of the Hitlerites. ... These districts of Yugoslavia were completely devastated after the Germans had been there. I also present to the Tribunal the original copy of a notice by the so-called Commander-in-Chief of Serbia ... I read into the record only one paragraph:

'The Commander-in-Chief of Serbia announces: the village of Skela has been burned and razed to the ground.'

German punitive detachments also destroyed inhabited localities in Poland ... I present reports [of 'punitive measures'] ... These reports, your Honours, are on Page 170 of your document book. Each of these reports consists of nine to ten lines. They are uniform in type and standardised. But these short official documents reveal in essence the monstrous system generally employed by the Hitlerites in the territories occupied by them. (The Trial of German Major War Criminals Sitting at Nuremberg, Germany 14 February to 26 February 1946, Sixty-Fifth Day: Friday, 22 February 1946. *Trials of German Major War Criminals*: Volume 7: 218–20)

Competing bars: competing judgements?

Institutionalised justice and history provide judgements frequently at odds, so it is with International tribunals. Perhaps it is always naive to hope that projects fixed with the passions and politics of the present may come to judgements that history finds acceptable. The structure of a criminal trial is orientated towards assigning responsibility primarily upon individuals as a prerequisite to punishing them, this means that 'their reductionist, bipolar logic and inherent barriers to the truth conceal and distort history' (Gustafson 1998: 75).

The first extract above is from a large text of 1770, written by an individual discoursing on the changes brought about by world exploration and seizure of colonies by the European powers; the second is part of an account setting the stage for judging what had officially been termed 'punitive' raids or actions conducted by the Nazis in occupied Europe in respect of which a number of apprehended German officers were being tried in 1946 by the International Military Tribunal (IMT) at Nuremberg. At first sight they appear united only in being reflections on the experience of encounter, the coming of people possessed of power on to the other and their dealing with the other and different power relations as to judging the justice of that interaction. That they are united in causal connections is a more contentious proposition; it would involve criminology moving beyond nation-state bearings.

Why did Nuremberg not move criminology beyond the nation-state?

As indicated in Chapter 2, criminology, the scholarly reflection on crime and its causes has historically a dependent relation with projects of criminal justice. One question arises, namely: given that we have had immediately post-World War II two major 'International' criminal tribunals, why did these not give rise to a criminology beyond the nation state; orientated, that is, to some foundational imaginary other than the defining power of nation-state sovereignty? A partial answer lies in the constitution of those tribunals, which simply put, reflected the interests of the political elites of a nation-state system; a system, moreover, committed to colonialism.

The trials of the IMTs at Nuremberg (in particular) and Tokyo formed the evidential basis for the immediate post-war historiography of mass murder and collective atrocity. They were processes of inclusion and exclusion. The charges were framed to avoid considering the actions of the victors during the war – as Telford Taylor (Chief Counsel for the prosecution and later an historian) explained with respect to the destruction of cities and their civilian populations: 'Since both sides had played the terrible game of urban destruction – the Allies more successfully – there was no basis for criminal charges against Germans or Japanese, and in fact no such charges were brought ... Aerial bombardment had been used so extensively and ruthlessly on the Allied side as well as the Axis side that neither at Nuremberg or Tokyo was the issue made a part of the trials.' The technology had moved the power of destruction on to the almost unimaginable: during the Sino-Japanese war in 1937 a single bomb dropped into the centre of Shanghai killed more than 1,000 civilians, a process almost able to be termed a war crime, but after 1945, that is, Hiroshima, the vision of what could be destroyed in a single bomb seemed limitless. And the Allies held the advantage (see Irving 1963; Hastings 1979; on the existential cost of the bombings on Germany see Sebald 2003; for the effect on the conscience of the Allies see Hopkins 1966, and Schaffer 1980; while Nazi Germany had developed the new campaigns of vast aerial bombardment [in August 1942, 1,200 German bombers attacked the refugee-swollen Stalingrad in one raid alone killing 40,000], in the 'conventional' attacks on Germany the British Royal Air Force dropped nearly 1 million tons of bombs, of the 131 towns and cities attacked many were almost entirely destroyed with 600,000 civilian deaths, 3.5 million homes destroyed and 7.5 million people left homeless). Not only must the conscience of the homeland citizens be kept secure (Hopkins 1966), but this advantage had to be preserved and so the charges gave a picture of changing customs of war; instead of saying that both sides engaged in war crimes, the criteria for determining what a war crime is was something liable to punishment by the victors and the circumstances determined that the victors would not be punished. Taylor tried to explain this as a principled stance: 'To punish the foe – especially the vanquished foe – for conduct in which the enforcer nation has engaged, would be so grossly inequitable as to discredit the laws themselves'. Reflexively the same discrediting applies to laws so created.[1]

The Tokyo trials have received less scholarly attention (the judgements were not even published in book form until Roling and Ruter 1977), albeit there was an effort to make the trials representative with some 11 main judges appointed. On individual charges it is easy to note obvious exclusions: the comfort women of Korea had no nation state to take up their claims and to raise the comfort women system more generally would have been to consider disturbing issues of colonial attitudes, institutional sexual violence, and the position of women in Asian societies; the US deal for the results covered up the actions of over 3,600 Japanese soldiers, doctors and scientists who had conducted biological testing on thousands of POWs and civilians; that chemical weapons had been widely used against the Chinese was only touched upon and the Japanese Emperor was not put on trial for fear of creating insurgency in occupied Japan.

There were other exclusions, notably chains of explanation that could have tied in the victors in other, more subtle ways; here, among others, the similarity in belief by the Nazis and some Japanese that they were engaged in a racial war for a new world order, more concretely links between Japanese territorial expansion, or the Nazi project to create Lebensraum (including the Holocaust of the Jews), and colonialism. At first sight the colonial issue seems clearer in the case of Japan: in that regard the question may be was Japan punished because it challenged Western imperialism (as many Japanese claimed) or because it tried to emulate it?[2] The Holocaust seems harder to link with colonialism yet slowly scholars are asserting a direct link between the colonial encounter and the holocaust (e.g. Zimmerer 2004). Such a linkage is not usually made, perhaps because the links are not immediately visible, or from a desire on the part of some commentators to own the Holocaust as a unique German–Jewish, or Christian–Jewish, problem, but it also flows more pragmatically from two central organising points of inclusion of material at the IMTs at Nuremberg and Tokyo.

The first was the interests of the victorious nation states to preserve their sovereignty (and their colonial possessions) by focussing upon outlawing waging aggressive war, defined, it is crucial to note, so as to include wars of national liberation; to preserve, in other words, the sovereign integrity of nation states and their colonial possessions as long as they do not interfere with other nation states. Note that the 25 defendants at Tokyo were found guilty of 'intricate preparation' for the 'waging of wars of aggression' against China, the US, the British Commonwealth, the Netherlands, France, the USSR and the Mongolian People's Republic: thus while all the activity took place in Asia, only two Asian countries were mentioned! While his officials were found guilty, the Emperor was not tried, a decision that caused the President of the Court, Justice Web, to dissent arguing that the authority of the Emperor was proved beyond question when he ended the war. The structure of the trials preserved a political framework of state sovereignty and colonial possession; they did not make the breakthrough to holding those in power to account for how they treated those subjected to the exercise of their sovereign power.

The second, was that a particular image of action and victim-hood was prioritised at the trials, again tied to seeing collective action as actually directed by a small group of responsible individuals linked in a criminal conspiracy against (essentially) the nationals of other nations and the IMTs were the consequence of a group of victorious (colonial) nations striving for a justice that was orientated around their structure of governance and appeasing the desires for 'justice' of their peoples. This is clear from Tokyo (The countries invaded and occupied by Japan were all Asian; yet, only three – Justice Mei Ju-ao from China, Justice Pal from India and Justice Delfin Jaranilla from the Philippines – of the eleven justices were Asians. The inclusion of Justices Pal and Jaranilla from colonised Asia was an afterthought. Pal dissented on all counts.) but also can be seen in the relatively weak attention paid to 'understanding' what happened to Jewish victims (as well as the gypsies and homosexuals). The full impact of a state-ordered biological reconstituting of Europe (and by extension, the world) was not entered into.

It is a popular assumption today that the trials of the major German War Criminals after World War II covered the activities we now call the Holocaust – the deliberate, systematic destruction of some 6 million Jews and their way of life – as a specific crime against humanity for which they were clearly charged. In fact the Holocaust was not dealt with as a separate punishable project at the trials and a self-sustaining concept of crimes against humanity did not provide a rationale for punishment; instead both were subsumed under the general concept of war crimes. The Holocaust 'never assumed a prominent place' (Marrus 1987: 4) in the Nuremberg trials, which were organised around the central task of punishing what was termed the supreme crime, namely waging aggressive war.[3]

The presentation of evidence and the linking in of individual defendants was structured by the central organising notion of conspiracy, a concept tactically used, with varying success, to tie together a range of persons whom otherwise may have been seen as functionaries rather than principal actors. Justice Jackson stated the conspiracy tactic aimed 'to bring within the scope of a single litigation the developments of a decade, covering a whole decade, and involving a score of nations, countless individuals, and innumerable events' (2 *Trial*, p. 100). But the Anglo-American legal concept of conspiracy, useful in tying together otherwise disparate members of a criminal gang, missed the whole edifice underpinning the social and political reality, that is, that the Nazis (and the Japanese government) were not some criminal gang that had illegally seized power; they were instead a legal government acting out many of the themes of modernity itself. That tactics of exclusion were in place is a reflexive awareness that is now part of the historical debate, but what exactly were the consequences is still an open issue.

The rule of law and the ambiguous use of the concept of conspiracy

The IMTs are seen, for all their faults, as advances in the rule of law. That trials were held, rather than simply rounding up top Nazis or Japanese and summarily executing them is portrayed as a victory for legalism over the scepticism of voices such as the British, who doubted whether many of the actions to be tried were indeed 'war crimes' as then envisaged.[4] At a conference in London in August 1945, a Charter was agreed, which became the basis for the international war crimes trials and gave jurisdiction to the Tribunals. This set out three interlinked definitions of crimes against peace, war crimes and crimes against humanity, while it removed sovereign immunity and the defences of 'head of state' or following superior orders. Crimes against humanity, while recognised 'whether or not in violation of the domestic law of the country where perpetrated', only came within the jurisdiction of the Tribunals because they were linked to the central charge of waging aggressive war. Against the argument that the Charter was making new law and applying it retrospectively to a defeated enemy, the reply of Jackson and others was in terms of shared common sense: these action were easily recognisable as crimes and the public back home would accept the legal process and punishment if the process was structured in such a way that it reflected key elements of the legal processes at work in the home nations. There were five questions that had to be asked before indicting a detainee:

1 Did the Nazi organisation have a common plan of criminal action?
2 Was a group's actions criminal?
3 Was a person's membership in such a group voluntary?
4 Was a person's membership a knowing one, that is, did the person have some knowledge of the criminal aims of the organisation?
5 Was there evidence that the person was such a member and that he or she acted to achieve the organisation's criminal goals? (UNWCC 1992: 45)

The conspiracy tactic rendered defendants liable in recognisable ways and assured the publics of the victorious states that it was their civilised, common sensibilities that provided the guiding principals of punishment; yet, it closed off broader conceptions of history.

To recap: while many hoped that the trial of the major German War Criminals at Nuremberg in 1946 would usher in a new era of international justice and the growth of accountability of state officials for crimes against humanity this was not to be. The power displayed was that of the representatives of nation states to organise legal proceedings and frame the legally relevant issues in such a way that the great issues of modernity were avoided and within criminology, broadly defined, the arguments of Sheldon Glueck [1943, 1944, 1946] for a permanent court to prosecute crimes of war and against humanity were ignored. It was more business as usual than a paradigm shift.

To example: the second extract at the beginning of this chapter covers a small sample of the evidence produced during the Nuremberg trial concerning punishing German punitive expeditions, but the concept of punitive expedition was itself an ambiguous concept to blame upon either the Germans or Japanese, and could only be controlled by constraining the range of evidence of what constituted valid customs of war. Simply put, the customs of war that were considered did not include those of colonial conquest or the past reality of exterminatory processes (intentional and unintentional) so central to the Europeanisation of the globe. In the Tokyo trial, when the Indian Judge Pal did consider such issues his judgement became a complete dissent, viewed as a travesty of justice by other judges and categorised as a personal mistake. Yet even in Nuremberg, given the centrality of the Holocaust to contemporary images of the Nazi programmes, it may appear surprising how small a profile the Nazi campaign to exterminate European Jewry occupied after the war's end. In an array of trials across Europe conducted in the shadow of Nuremberg, a sizeable number of German soldiers were tried and punished, many by death, for taking part in punitive expeditions or raids against civilian targets during their occupation of continental Europe. The punishment of German soldiers or other functionaries for their part in the Holocaust of the Jews was much more ambiguous; trials were directed by the agents of victorious nation states against 'criminal' Germans for their actions against the nationals of the nation states now directing matters.[5] The trial at Nuremberg itself was conducted largely through reading documents (with some film shown that achieved great, albeit temporary, effect; see Douglas 1995), and quickly became a boring spectacle (Bloxham 2001). The resultant 'Nuremberg view' or 'perpetrator history' focussed almost entirely on the intentions and ideologies of top leaders, as Browning (1992: 22, 26) explains: 'the evidentiary base was above all the German documents captured at the end of the war, which served … the prosecutors at post-war trials. The initial representation of the Holocaust perpetrators was that of criminal minds, infected with racism and anti-semiticism, carrying out criminal policies through criminal organisations.' This dislocation occurred from the centre outwards, for while waging aggressive war was recognised by the victorious Allied Powers as the most serious 'crime', genocide would have to wait for the UN to actually recognise its existence *as a separate crime* by the 1948 Convention (see discussion in Chapter 3) and the largest military power in the world, the US, did not ratify it until 1985, and then only in an attempt by the US administration to repair the public relations damage President Regan caused by his visit to Bitburg War Cemetery in West Germany, where 49 Waffen SS officers turned out to be buried. In reality, under the Charter used for the IMT, crimes against humanity could only be prosecuted if they had occurred in the course of waging an aggressive war and the party then lost: if the actions were taken by a sovereign power without waging aggressive war then the cloak of sovereignty protected him (as Steiner rightly opined, see Figure 7.1). It took several decades for the Holocaust to achieve recognition as a discrete and unique phenomenon. Western historians usually treated it as subsumed within the war's military history; Communist accounts subsumed it into a narrative of resistance to Nazism; Zionist historians located it as the culmination of a long tradition of anti-Semitic persecution. Later grew an awareness of the Holocaust as one of the defining instances of modern Western civilisation ('the' defining instance for some commentators); ambiguity and ambivalence accompany that new status as a symbol of the civilising process; but we should widen the frame for this symbolism should include its status as *a relatively unpunished action of a legitimate government*. Perhaps this is a shocking claim: but it is for historians and sociologists to put modernity, not a criminal gang, on trial.

Locating the Holocaust: uniqueness and symbol

Those who try to incorporate the Holocaust into more general theses on modernisation, 'modernity', rationalisation, comparative genocide studies, or continuing patterns of law and bio-power are sometimes criticised for (unintentionally) belittling it or not understanding the sheer scale of the horror. To deny that the Holocaust was a unique event of incredible evil is itself incredible. In the historiography of the Holocaust, the understandable focus on the uniqueness of the German exterminatory intent towards the European Jews, can, however, neglect the extent to which the Nazi programme depended upon a racial othering and cleansing of territory for the expansion of German living space. That the Nazi programme was a racial one of territorial expansion and cleansing of the population internal to that space meant that the Jews were not to be the only victims.[6] The particular and specific fate of the Jews was both an exception, in that a unique murderous intent and organisation was directed towards them, and part of general processes. In seeking to explain the Holocaust, specialised historians tend to divide into two camps that mirror criminological explanation generally: the intentionalists focus upon the specific role of Hitler and his inner circle, while the functionalists look for more general explanations. There are truths in both perspectives, for the Holocaust *would* not have taken place but for the intense hatred and personal focus of Hitler, and yet it *could* not have taken place were it not for certain general structural and cultural features (though these overlap as is obviously the case with anti-Semitism). While focussing on Hitler and his inner circle has revealed a twisted path to the 'final solution' and its implementation (on this see Browning 2004 for the most current synthesis of research), locating and making visible those more general structural and cultural features is difficult. It should not be forgotten here, that among those general features would lie the explanation for the indifference (some prefer ambivalence) of the other

Figure 7.1 Image of an attempt at a soap factory featuring Jewish corpses, source Taffet (ed.) 1945.

Writing in 1971 George Steiner opines:

> what would have happened if Hitler had played the game after Munich, if he had simply said, 'I will make no move outside the Reich so long as I am allowed a free hand inside my borders'. Dachau, Buchenwald, and Theresienstadt would have operated in the middle of twentieth-century European civilization until the last Jew in reach had been made soap. There would have been brave words on Trafalgar Square and in Carnegie Hall, to audiences diminishing and bored. Society might, on occasion, have boycotted German wines. But no foreign power would have taken action. Tourists would have crowded the Autobahn and spas of the Reich, passing near but not too near the death-camps as we now pass Portuguese jails or Greek prison-islands. There would have been numerous pundits and journalists to assure us that rumors were exaggerated, that Dachau had pleasant walks. And the Red Cross would have sent Christmas parcels.
>
> Below his breath, the Jew asks of his gentile neighbor: 'If you had known, would you have cried in the face of God and man that this hideousness must stop? Would you have made some attempt to get my children out? Or planned a skiing party to Garmisch?' The Jew 'is a living reproach' ... *Men are accomplices to that which leaves them indifferent.* It is this fact which must, I think, make the Jew wary inside Western society. (1971: 150)

Genocide has not been a feature in the experiences or the symbolic understandings of the normal for the vast majority of the inhabitants of Western, civilised space; thus the shock of the realisation of the true extent of the German ruthless concentration upon a task and Allied indifference (or lack of knowledge). In facing up to the Holocaust we should not forget ambivalence was and is central to attempts to integrate consciousness of the horror and claim ownership of victim hood. The victims are 'humanity' – true – but they were also Jews, gypsies and gays. Expressing victim hood in terms that allow greater emotional proximity and empathy thus goes counter to their perceived identity, that of being Jewish (and gays and gypsies). As Bloxham implies, the Jewish identity was downplayed precisely so that empathy (on the behalf of the imagined spectators for the trials) would not be lost. The other must be converted into the same; but it was as the other that they faced the ultimate exclusion.

countries, including the Allies, towards the fate of the Jews. The literary critic George Steiner once asked if this was an inevitable effect of the system of nation states under the deal of Westphalian sovereignty, but it also could be that this indifference was necessary to deal with the (non)knowledge of what had been, and, perhaps still was, required to master colonial possessions?

What global links are there to be observed for the overall perception of the causation of the holocaust? What of the process of territorial expansion and preparation for settlement? Burleigh states convincingly that the military campaigns in the Soviet Union 'were the means to realise a vision of territorial expansion which would bring both long-term economic security and perpetual racial renewal' (1997: 77). If so we are faced with the question of where the simple viewing of the country and its people as an object to be controlled, utilised, and its contents (including its inhabitants) to be disposed of as circumstances demanded (or allowed) came about? It was, of course, a fundamental imaginary for the colonial enterprise. (see Burleigh 1997: 77–80; Zimmerer 2004)

Certainly, there are many factors and contingencies at work pre-structuring the Holocaust; the realities of war and genocide have often moved in ways that eluded easy representation and that evoked emotions of resentment and resistance to social complexity. World War I was characterised by the high spirits of 1914 (and joyous volunteering for war) and latter despair at the constant destruction of human life. World War I experienced a growing porousness between soldier and civilian, battle front and home, thus reversing a process of controlling 'war' in play since Hobbes and Groitis wrote. Omer Bartov argues for a causal link between the emergence of industrial killing in World War I and the Nazi genocide; the link is 'the manner in which the European imagination grappled with (and redefined) the parameters of humanity in the nightmare of total war and destruction it had conjured up' (1996: 35). Against claims that Nazism was the lesser evil compared with the policies of the Soviet Union, he contends, rightly, 'that Nazi Germany was bent on murdering entire peoples, numbering many millions, in a highly organized, industrialized, and systematic manner; moreover, the regime had done its utmost to achieve this aim right to the last moment'.

> Not only were the Jews doomed to extermination, but at least twenty to thirty million Russians as well, along with countless other 'biological' and political enemies. Those who survived, particularly in the eastern *Lebensraum* of the Reich, were to be enslaved as complete and total *Untermenschen*, and to lead lives far worse than those of domestic animals. Wherever possible, this policy was carried out with what was called in the language of the time 'ruthless determination'. Had Nazi Germany won the war, Eastern Europe would have remained a vast death factory for centuries, ruled by a *Herrenvolk* who would refuse to consider its inhabitants as human beings. In no way can this be said about the Soviet Union. (1996: 87)

Bartov reminds us that we are dealing with practices of representation and evasions of connections. In locating the crucial turning point as the mass devastations and loss of life in World War I, however, he may have cast his net too narrowly in considering how the European imagination dealt with the destructive technologies of modern warfare.

The battle of Omdurman: control of the symbolic and killing at a distance

> The enthusiasm of the first months of [World War I] was rooted in an imagery of military glory that bore no relationship to the reality of the battlefield. The splendid bayonet charge over a field of flowers that so many soldiers had been taught to expect did not materialise. Instead, green fields were transformed into oceans of mud, frontal attacks ended up as massacres, great offensives rapidly ground to a bloody halt, and heroic gestures were soon replaced by grim determination and a desperate will to survive.
> (Bartov 2000: 11)

The battle of Omdurman pitted over 90,000 men against each other on 2 September, 1898. Kaplan (discussed in our introduction) gives us an institutional memory of it as the last of the era of honourable cavalry charges and hand-to-hand fighting. His reading of Churchill is partial for while Churchill did call the battle 'the last link in the long chain of those spectacular conflicts whose vivid and majestic splendour has done so much to invest war with glamour' his account also explained why that 'kind of war was full of fascinating thrills' and 'was not like the Great War'. The reason was simply that 'Nobody expected to be killed', or – put correctly – no white officer, possessing modern arms and commanding local native forces (which he was quick to put into the front of the battle), doubted that his technological superiority gave him a power to coerce, manipulate and ultimately determine the outcome to his advantage with relative immunity.[7]

The imagery of the battle is well known; glorious cavalry charges and close, hand-to-hand fighting in which the Anglo-Egyptian soldiers heroically capture the Black Standard. The reality was a massacre.

Omdurman was a victory for the astute leadership of Kitchener; but this occurred within a context of methodological planning, detailed preparations and technological superiority that overturned expectations connecting territoriality and security. Eighteen years before the battle, in 1881, the Sudanese preacher Muhammad Ahmad was declared as the Mahdi (the Guided One who will lead the victory over the Disbelievers). General Gordon, the British colonial governor, had alienated local support through a number of measures, some of which look progressive today (notably moves to abolish slavery), others as politically naïve (such as replacing Egyptian officials with Christian British ones). The Southern Anglo-Egyptian territories, what is now Sudan, were being used to finance the administration of Egypt. Few would dispute that 'there was no place more fitting nor ripe for revolution that the Sudan in 1881 – a corrupt and oppressive regime supported by a worthless army' ('Ismat Hasan Zulfo 1980: 6). Between 1881 and 1885, the Mahdists in Sudan defeated four British led armies and captured over 20,000 then modern weapons including early Maxim machine guns, artillery, rocket tubes, and many thousands of rounds of ammunition. The British ordered General Gordon to evacuate the Sudan; but he disobeyed orders and chose to stay in Khartoum.

The siege of the wall cities of Khartoum and Omdurman (defended by 7,000 British led troops) lasted from 21 October, 1884 to 21 January, 1885. The city fell and Gordon was killed three days before exhausted British relief forces arrived in steam-gunboats on the Nile. They immediately turned back. Despite great public outcry in England, it was nearly 14 years before the British returned.

This time (1898) they were as prepared as technologically possible. Transport and communication were to be key: a telegraph line was constructed and British forces took two years to build a 200-mile railway through one of Africa's most inhospitable semi-deserts to supply the campaign with adequate food and water. To enable fast passage on the Nile complete with its dangerous sections of rapids, steel-plated gunboats were designed that could be transported in sections, assembled and then armed with long distance artillery and 50 lb. exploding shells, along with new style high-powered Maxim machine guns. 15,000 troops packed into steamboats travelled down the Nile and, then undertook a rapid march of nearly 60 miles. The 'Anglo-Egyptian' forces comprised 8,200 British troops, 17,600 Egyptian and Sudanese soldiers, 44 field guns and 20 Maxims on the land, 36 big guns and 24 Maxims on water, 2,470 horses, 5,250 camels and 2,500 local Arabs. The ground troops possessed the new Lee-Metford MK II rifle, which had been introduced to the British Army in 1895. With modifications it survived for some 50 years and saw service in two World Wars. Its novelty lay in its introduction of a bolt and magazine mechanism for loading it with eight or nine bullets, in contrast to the old one-by-one muzzle or breach loading models. It had greater grooving, which made it accurate at long distances with new lighter ammunition.

The campaign was a media affair having some 16 correspondents who reported back to newspapers in the UK and elsewhere. It also included the young officer Winston Churchill, whose account became a best selling book.[8]

On the African side, Khalifa Abdullahi (the Mahdi had suddenly died in 1885) could call upon 70,000 fighters to his Standard at Omdurman. Defending the Sudan he had built 17 forts, mined the harbours and collected most of his artillery to two main points. The majority of his forces were, however, lightly armed and the heavier armaments captured from the British 18 years earlier now looked outdated. Moreover, he faced a tactical problem. Previous defensive measures appeared weak against the new British artillery that could bombard positions from three miles away. The only hope was to engage in close fighting where the courage and determination of the Sudanese would be effective. Khalifa decided he must attack the British forces on open ground.

This decision was forced on him by knowledge of the capabilities of the new weapons the British had brought with them and their effect in the defeat at Atbara. Atbara was a defensive battle that is estimated to have cost the Khalifa some 7,000 dead with the 4,000 who escaped relating the one-sidedness of the battle. The Anglo-Egyptian force lost 5 British officers and 21 men dead with 57 Egyptian dead and perhaps 350 wounded. The defenders, some armed with rifles, most with swords and spears, sheltered behind dirt and wooden fortifications and in trenches. They endured bombardment from modern batteries for over an hour and constant strafing by the new machine guns. Behind the covering fire the attacking forces advanced, taking some casualties but gaining the trenches for hand-to-hand fighting. The images presented in the press at home were of heroic hand-to-hand fighting, though several showed the imbalance in the dead. The Sudanese ('Ismat Hasan Zulfo 1980: 80) related that the trenches were filled with their dead and even considered that the British downplayed the numbers of dead defenders (officially reporting 3,000 dead), in case the advantage of the new armaments were too apparent and the public at home failed to see the vital distinction between what the Muslim Turkish forces were doing to the Greeks in Crete (unfair massacre) and towards their Armenian populations (systematic slaughter), which were the actions of uncivilised peoples, and what the Christian British were doing, namely bringing civilisation to a dark land.[9] Whatever the effect of the media images in the European metropolitan, as the survivors relayed the truth back to Omdurman and throughout the areas they had come from the Khaifia faced collapsing morale with many supporters, particularly in the north, changing sides to join with the British.

On 1 September Churchill (1899, reprint 1997: following extracts from pp. 82 to 160) first set eyes on Omdurman along with the advance cavalry.

> [T]urning the shoulder of the hill, I saw in the distance a yellow-brown pointed dome rising above the blurred horizon. It was the Mahdi's Tomb, standing in the very heart of Omdurman. From the high ground the field-glass disclosed rows and rows of mud houses, making a dark patch on the brown of the plain

The town was to be bombarded:

> At about eleven o'clock the gunboats had ascended the Nile, and now engaged the enemy's batteries on both banks. Throughout the day the loud reports of their guns could be heard, and, looking from our position on the ridge, we could see the white vessels steaming slowly forward against the current, under clouds of black smoke from their furnaces and amid other clouds of white smoke from the artillery. The forts, which mounted nearly fifty guns, replied vigorously; but the British aim was accurate and their fire crushing. The embrasures were smashed to bits and many of the Dervish guns dismounted. The rifle trenches which flanked the forts were swept by the Maxim guns. The heavier projectiles, striking the mud walls of the works and houses, dashed the red dust high into the air and scattered destruction around. Despite the tenacity and courage of the Dervish gunners, they were driven from their defences and took refuge among the streets of the city. The great wall of Omdurman was breached in many places, and a large number of unfortunate non-combatants were killed and wounded.

Perhaps a less one-sided battle would take place on the plains. The enemy was twice as strong in numbers to what Churchill called the 'army of scientific spirit'. If they had been attacked during the night, the British would probably have lost. But they were not; having advanced towards the British positions the Dervish forces stopped for the night and resumed at first light. As Churchill says: 'It seemed impossible to believe that they would attack by daylight across the open ground', but that is what they did opening themselves up to a technologically induced disaster. In the morning of 2 September they advanced slowly towards the waiting British forces.

> Great clouds of smoke appeared all along the front of the British and Sudanese brigades. One after another four batteries opened on the enemy at a range of about 3,000 yards. The sound of the cannonade rolled up to us on the ridge, and was re-echoed by the hills. Above the heads of the moving masses shells began to burst, dotting the air with smoke-balls and the ground with bodies. But they were nearly two miles away, and the distance rendered me unsympathetic ...

I looked back to the 'White Flags'; they were nearly over the crest. In another minute they would become visible to the batteries. Did they realize what would come to meet them? They were in a dense mass, 2,800 yards from the 32nd Field Battery and the gunboats. The ranges were known. It was a matter of machinery. The more distant slaughter passed unnoticed, as the mind was fascinated by the impending horror. I could see it coming. In a few seconds swift destruction would rush on these brave men. They topped the crest and drew out into full view of the whole army. Their white banners made them conspicuous above all … For a moment the White Flags advanced in regular order, and the whole division crossed the crest and were exposed. Forthwith the gunboats, the 32nd British Field Battery, and other guns from the zeriba opened on them. I was but 400 yards away, and with excellent glasses could almost see the faces of the Dervishes who met the fearful fire. About twenty shells struck them in the first minute. Some burst high in the air, others exactly in their faces.

Others, again, plunged into the sand and, exploding, dashed clouds of red dust, splinters, and bullets amid their ranks. The white banners toppled over in all directions. Yet they rose again immediately, as other men pressed forward to die for the Mahdi's sacred cause and in the defense of the successor of the True Prophet of the Only God. It was a terrible sight, for as yet they had not hurt us at all, and it seemed an unfair advantage to strike thus cruelly when they could not reply. Nevertheless, I watched the effect of the fire most carefully from a close and convenient position. About five men on the average fell to every shell: and there were many shells. Under their influence the mass of the 'White Flags' dissolved into thin lines of spearmen and skirmishers, and came on in altered formation and diminished numbers, but with unabated enthusiasm. And now, the whole attack being thoroughly exposed, it became the duty of the cavalry to clear the front as quickly as possible, and leave the further conduct of the debate to the infantry and the Maxim guns. All the patrols trotted or cantered back to their squadrons, and the regiment retired swiftly into the zeriba, while the shells from the gunboats screamed overhead and the whole length of the position began to burst into flame and smoke. Nor was it long before the tremendous banging of the artillery was swelled by the roar of musketry.

Eight hundred yards away a ragged line of men was coming on desperately, struggling forward in the face of the pitiless fire – white banners tossing and collapsing; white figures subsiding in dozens to the ground; little white puffs from their rifles, larger white puffs spreading in a row all along their front from the bursting shrapnel. The picture lasted only a moment, but the memory remains forever … Now it was the turn of the infantry. The long line of bayonets had been drawn up even before the sun had completely risen. The officers and men had watched the light grow in the plain, and had scanned the distant hills and nearer ridge with eager, anxious eyes. It made a great difference to them whether they were attacked in their impregnable position or had to clear the streets and houses of Omdurman – the difference probably between 200 killed and wounded and 2,000. They watched the squadrons push out towards the hills, and might see the tiny patrols vanish on the further side; and then suddenly horsemen began to come back. Orderlies, bearing important news, returned – spurring their weary horses to a full gallop. A rumour ran along the line. The enemy were advancing. The squadrons in the plain turned and retired towards the zeriba. Patrols drew in from all sides, leaving the dark outlines of Surgham Hill again deserted, catching up their squadrons, and disappearing in the ranks. Presently the whole expanse of ground was bare and deserted; but not for long.

One by one rows of flags appeared jerkily over a blur of dirty-white, which the field-glass developed into thousands of men. They approached, continually gaining ground to the left, and stretching out towards Kerreri … the Guards first at 2,700 yards, then the Seaforths at 2,000 yards, and the others following according to the taste and fancy of their commanding officers – the British division began to fire. As the range shortened Maxwell's Sudanese brigade, and a moment later MacDonald's, joined in the fusillade, until by 6.45 more than 12,000 infantry were engaged in that mechanical scattering of death which the polite nations of the earth have brought to such monstrous perfection.

They fired steadily and stolidly, without hurry or excitement, for the enemy were far away and the officers careful. Besides, the soldiers were interested in the work and took great pains. But presently the mere physical act became tedious. The tiny figures seen over the slide of the back-sight seemed a little larger, but also fewer at each successive volley. The rifles grew hot – so hot that they had to be changed for those of the reserve companies. The Maxim guns exhausted all the water in their jackets, and several had to be refreshed from the water-bottles of the Cameron Highlanders before they could go on with their deadly work. The empty cartridge-cases, tinkling to the ground, formed small but growing heaps beside each man. And all the time out on the plain on the other side bullets were shearing through flesh, smashing and splintering bone; blood spouted from terrible wounds; valiant men were struggling on through a hell of whistling metal, exploding shells, and spurting dust – suffering, despairing, dying. Such was the first phase of the battle of Omdurman.

Where was the glorious cavalry charge (so often presented and painted and which resulted in three Victoria Crosses [The highest British military honour] being awarded)? With the main Dervish army decimated the 21st Lancers (including Churchill) did charge so as to prevent some of the surviving forces from retreating back to the city; they encountered a large force hidden in a depression of the ground. A collision took place: 'the hand to hand fighting … lasted for perhaps one minute … within two minutes of the collision every living man was clear of the Dervish mass. All who had fallen were cut at with swords till they stopped quivering, but no artistic mutilations were attempted. The enemy's behaviour gave small ground for complaint'. The cavalry turned and regrouped: 'The general battle was forgotten, as it were unseen. This was a private quarrel. The other might have been a massacre; but here the fight was fair, for we too fought with sword and spear.' They sought to re-enter the fight …

But some realisation of the cost of our wild ride began to come to those who were responsible. Riderless horses galloped across the plain. Men clinging to their saddles, lurched helplessly about, covered with blood from perhaps a dozen wounds. Horses, streaming from tremendous gashes, limped and staggered with their riders. In 120 seconds five officers, 66 men, and 119 horses out of less than 400 had been killed or wounded.

It was best – 'on military considerations' – for the regiment to dismount and fire with their magazine carbines; thereby their superior range and massed fire forced the opposing forces to retreat to another hill, away from the city.

So much for the British cavalry charge; what of the Sudanese forces? The Dervishes had only 2,000 horsemen on the field but Churchill relates that at one stage around 400 of these, 'mostly the personal retainers of the various Emirs were formed into an irregular regiment'.

Now when these horsemen perceived that there was no hope of victory, they arranged themselves in a solid mass and charged … The distance was about 500 yards, and, wild as was the firing of the Sudanese, it was evident that they could not possibly succeed. Nevertheless, many carrying no weapon in their hands, and all urging their horses to their utmost speed, they rode unflinchingly to certain death. All were killed and fell as they entered the zone of fire – three, twenty, fifty, two hundred, sixty, thirty, five and one beyond them all – a brown smear across the sandy plain. A few riderless horses alone broke through the ranks of the infantry.

Was this heroism or fanaticism? Churchill thought – contrary to others – heroism. However, the next day many Anglo-Egyptian troops went through some of the lines of wounded Sudanese and killed them. The *Illustrated London News* explained why. It gave two illustrations, in one the wounded enemy are killed, and in another a wounded and apparently dead Dervish has partly risen and thrown his spear at an Anglo-Egyptian soldier. The accompanying message makes clear that the Dervish would not give up; hence it was necessary to kill the wounded soldiers to save allied forces from attack as they went across the body-strewn plain.[10] However, there are surviving photographs that also show looting by the Anglo-Egyptian forces on the corpses and the shooting of wounded from a sizeable distance. 'Ismat Hasan Zulfo (1980: 234) quotes Churchill's account:

> I [Churchill] personally record that there was a very general impression that the fewer the prisoners, the greater will be the satisfaction of the commander.' The meaning is clear. He [Churchill] went on to say that the slaughter was the consequence of the vast propaganda that preceded the campaign. 'It had inflamed their passions, and had led them to believe that it was quite correct to regard their enemies as VERMIN, unfit to live. The result was that there were many wounded who were killed.

'Ismat Hasan Zulfo deals dispassionately with these events, providing more of Churchill's account without commentary.

> Churchill divided the wounded into three categories. The first were those considered dangerous. This class was the largest and was wiped out. The second class was made up of those whose wounds were dangerous and painful. They were slaughtered out of compassion. The Sirdar [Ld. Kitchener] claimed that he was putting them out of their agony. In the third category were those who, in spite of their surrender and their disarmament, did not fall into either of the two categories, but were slaughtered none the less. 'About the third class there can be no dispute, how many were dispatched I cannot tell, although they threw down their arms and appealed for quarter.'

Stories of the slaughter provoked controversy in Britain; it did not seem the actions of troops on a civilising mission.[11] For his part, Churchill's account of the campaign gave the enemy a realist dignity; as he recounts while looking at the vast numbers of dead across the plain: 'There was nothing … of the dignity of unconquerable manhood, yet those were as brave men as ever walked the earth, destroyed not conquered by machinery'.

Omdurman was the template for reducing military outcome to a matter of calculation and technology. Churchill rather generously opines: 'The Khalifa's plan of attack appears to have been complex and ingenious. It was, however, based on an extraordinary miscalculation of the power of modern weapons; with the exception of this cardinal error, it is not necessary to criticize it.' Sudanese accounts state that it was actually meant to be a double pronged attack but because of bad communications it became a secession of single attacks, easily able to be destroyed. As for the immediate aftermath: in the Sudanese account there was widespread pillage of the city and the Mahdi's tomb destroyed. Their final image is of suffering:

> Some of the wounded remained on the field exposed to the sun each day for several days. Scores crawled a few years each day towards the Nile in quest of water. Many failed to reach the river, expiring with glazed eyes appealing for water.

Others lay in the same place under small bushes. Survivors were found a whole week after the battle. They were still alive thanks to the women of Omdurman who busied themselves each evening slipping out after dark to bury their dead, succour their wounded and to bring out food and water. The quiet hills each night listened to the wails of the bereaved digging graves or mumbling through tears that spilt into cups of drinking water. ('Ismat Hasan Zulfo 1980: 236)

This is not the account Kaplan presents for our contemporary consumption. Perhaps we should take lessons for today: namely that the success of this imperial war depended on the opponent *not* being in possession of a similar level of technology, one must control the spread of such weapons of mass destruction; it also depended on prowess in the art of representation. The war cannot be presented as for material gain alone; a higher ideal was needed to provide a convenient organising point. Today this battle is remembered only (and badly) by a few; it hardly registers as an historical occurrence to be analysed and fitted into our scholarly knowledge. It does not feature, for example, in the discourse of International Relations when matters of territoriality and security are mentioned. In that discipline a certain meta-narrative of security is espoused where the arrival of nuclear weapons completes the destruction of bounded security that modern aerial bombardment had started; John Herz (1973) is credited with the argument that the globalisation of security is traced to the introduction of nuclear weapons. Thus Harknett (1996: 145–6) concludes in drawing upon Herz: 'the pre-nuclear conceptualisation of territoriality as a hard shell of defence in which protection was achieved by planning to repulse an offensive attack had indeed been undermined by nuclear weapons'. But this conception of territorial security was never available to the colonised for their (lack of recognised) territoriality had continually been unbundled; European (later 'Western') possession of the power of modern weapons meant they determined the institutional forms through which territory was expressed and linked to security. A process in which the granting of nation-state status to ex-colonial spaces alongside an arms trade market in always not-quite-the-latest technology without any accounting of their leaders (or the arms sellers) to a global justice has all-too-usually condemned the newly constituted 'citizens' of those territories to existential insecurity and real death. To those who now argue that 'the relative security of the inhabitants of the North is purchased at the price of chronic insecurity for the vast majority of the world population' (Wyn Jones 1996: 203), one can reply that no matter how complex unpicking the current interactions of this may be, it is certainly not the product of late- or postmodernity; it constituted modernity.

Excursus: the destruction of territorial security: the case of China

The Great Wall of China is perhaps the best-known symbol of bounded territorial security. The destruction of Chinese governance by western forces in the nineteenth century was termed the Opium wars. Before 1840, China tightly controlled its contacts with the outside world. Trade relationships fell under the 'Canton Trade System', whereby only the port of Canton was

LE JOURNAL ILLUSTRÉ

Prise de la Porte de Chine par l'armée française
Dessin de Henri Meyer. — Gravure de Lenay. — Voir l'article, page 83.

Figure 7.2 An image, supposedly of French forces taking the China Gate in the Great Wall in the mid-nineteenth century (credit MEPL)

opened for foreign trade. From Canton Western merchants could only deal with a group of government authorized firms called (Gong Hang), which regulated the volume of the trade and prices as well as the personal activities of Western merchants. Western merchants were forbidden to have any contact with the Chinese except in trade and they had to live within a specific district in the city. These limitations were imposed from an ambivalent sense of Chinese status towards the external world. On the one hand a sense of superiority and self-sufficiency: (in the Chinese cosmic view Heaven was round, and the Earth was a square. The Heaven projected its circular shadow onto the centre of the Earth. The area under the shadow, Tian Xia or 'Zone Beneath the Heaven' was China itself. China was the 'Heavenly Middle Kingdom' and the corners of the square not under the celestial emanation were ruled by foreign 'yi' 'barbarians'). Economically, China had a large self-reliant economy and a self-sufficient domestic trade. But a second and crucial reason was its desire to protect itself. China viewed with alarm the Western conquest of the Philippines, the penetration of Malaysia, the rebellion of Christian converts in Japan and the British penetration and ultimately the conquest of China's neighbour, India. Chinese authorities understood that the overthrow of a dynasty was often successful when external threats were coupled with internal disturbances. The Manchu themselves used the civil unrest in China to conquer China and set up their Qing dynasty. At a time when the Manchu rule in China was becoming weaker, the rulers could not permit any forms of foreign power to enter China that may help to overthrow them. The 'closed-door' policy did not apply to Russia. From the seventeenth century, China's relations with Russia were based on equal participation. A well-balanced trade existed between the two countries. China welcomed peaceful merchants to the north while resisting the ones in the south.

Despite regulation, foreign trade in China expanded and China ran a considerable trade surplus. In 1820, the West found a product which China did not have, opium. Between 1829 and 1855, opium smuggling developed rapidly along China's South Coast. In 1820, 9,708 chests of opium were smuggled in per year; 15-years later 35,445 chests, a growth of 400 per cent. Opium became the vice of China with virtually all men under 40 smoking it. The entire army was addicted but it affected all classes of people, from rich merchants to Taoists with an estimated 12 million addicts in the 1830s. Opium turned the trade deficit Western countries had with China into a trade surplus. China could not export enough tea and silk to balance the trade. Instead the difference in trade was made up by the export of Chinese silver, which was highly valued for its fine qualities. In the 1835–6 fiscal year alone, China exported 4.5 million Spanish dollars worth of silver. In 1839, the Chinese opium smokers spent 100 million taels, while the government's entire annual revenue was only 40 million taels. The drain of silver greatly weakened the Chinese government resulting in a military badly affected by addiction and a central authority unable to pay their wages. In the debates among government officials an uncompromising stand prevailed. In 1839, the emperor issued 39 articles which imposed extremely severe punishments, including death, for smoking and trading opium. Special Commissioner Lin Ze-xu was sent to Canton to ensure the rules were carried out. Lin, while in Canton, made 1,600 arrests and confiscated 11,000 pounds of opium in 2 months. In June, Lin forced foreign merchants to hand over 20,000 chests of opium. He burned the opium in a public demonstration and scattered the ashes across the sea. When Lin gave the order that Canton should be completely closed to foreign trade, the British opened hostilities and started the First Opium War. The ill-equipped Chinese army was overwhelmed. Commissioner Lin was recalled in disgrace and sent to exile in the north-west. The First of the unequal treaties, the Treaty of Nanjing was signed. The First Opium War, which lasted from 1840 to 1842, ended with China losing in shame.

The Treaty of Nanjing and supplement treaties opened China to the world. China became a semi-feudal semi-colonial state. Its influences were far reaching and long lasting. However, because the Treaty of Nanjing was designed to obtain free trade, its economic effects were the most severe undermining the basis of its self-sufficient economy, the urban handicraft and rural homestead industries while greatly enhancing the development of China's urban market economy. There were dramatic ideological and social changes.

Losing to Western 'strong ships and sharp weapons', China was physically forced open and inadequacies in its social and political structures revealed. The treaties signed after the war opened Chinese ports, and along with it,

Chinese markets to Western capitalism. This almost entirely collapsed China's economy. However, it also forced China's economy to quickly adapt and evolve thus speeding up China's development of capitalism. The War greatly weakened the Manchu rule, and this, coupled with a collapsed economy, resulted in swelling poverty over the country along with social unrest and insurrections. But Chinese officials and intellectuals also rethought China's social and political system. In order for China to regain its past glories, it had to learn from the West as well as import Western technologies and industries. Some intellectuals also proposed a new, more democratic political system. But the Opium War had opened China against the will of the Chinese people, putting much of China effectively under the control of Western countries and made it a semi-feudal semi-colonial state. The Chinese perceived it as a shameful defeat and many vowed to strengthen China in order to prevent it from happening again.

Although there were dramatic increases in certain products France, UK and the US demanded revisions in the Treaty of Huangpu and Wangxia Treaty in an effort to expand their privileges in China. The Qing court rejected the revision demands and the resulting war may be viewed as a continuation of the First Opium War. On October 8, 1856, Chinese officials boarded the Arrow, a Chinese-owned ship registered in Hong Kong flying the British flag and suspected of piracy, smuggling and of being engaged in the opium trade. They captured 12 men and imprisoned them. The British responded by attacking Guangzhou from the Pearl River. American warships shelled Guangzhou on the pretext of 'protecting' its residents; however, resistance against the invaders forced them to retreat from Humen.

The British decided on a larger assault and requested France, the US and Russia to form an alliance. France eagerly joined the British action using as a pretext the execution by Chinese local authorities in Guangxi province of a French missionary. The US and Russia expected to be the third parties to benefit from the struggle. Although no army was dispatched, the US and Russia sent envoys to Hong Kong to offer help to the British–French Alliance in planning an assault on China.

The British and the French joined forces attacked and occupied Guangzhou in late 1857. Bo-gui, the governor of Guangdong surrendered. The British–French Alliance plundered the city. A joint committee of the Alliance was formed. Bo-gui remained at his original post to maintain order on behalf of the aggressors. This was China's earliest local puppet regime. The British–French Alliance maintained its colonial rule for nearly four years in Guangzhou.

After the Allied forces moved north the first part of the war ended with the Treaty of Tientsin, to which France, Russia, and the US were party. This treaty opened eleven more ports to Western trade.

The Chinese initially refused to ratify the treaties and in 1859, after China refused to allow the setting up of foreign legations in Beijing, a naval force attacked the forts guarding the mouth of the Peiho River. It was severely mauled and forced to withdraw under the cover of fire from an American naval squadron. In 1860, an Anglo-French force gathered at Hong Kong and then carried out a landing at Pei Tang on 1 August, and a successful assault on the

Figure 7.3 Illustration for the front cover of *Simplicissimus*, Number 15: 'The Europeans pour the blessings of their culture over the world' (collection of Author)

Taku Forts on 21 August. On 26 September, the force arrived at Beijing and had captured the city by 6 October. British–French troops in Beijing set the Summer Palace and the Old Summer Palace on fire. The Old Summer Palace was totally destroyed. Beijing was not occupied, however, the troops remained outside the city itself.

The motives for the destruction of the Summer Palace are unclear. The official reason stated by Elgin was to discourage the Chinese from using kidnappings as a bargaining tool, and to exact revenge on the emperor for his violation of the flag of truce. Other options were discussed but Elgin deemed this the 'least objectionable'. It is very likely, however, that it was largely to do with the treatment of the prisoners taken rather than the actual taking of prisoners. Another possible explanation is that Elgin was insulted by the decadence of the palace, and was especially offended by the European images in the Old Summer Palace. Chinese historians have claimed that is was to cover up the widespread looting which occurred, and there is some evidence for this, despite the fact that many people, such as Loch, and the French general Montauban, denied that widespread looting took place. The June 1858 Treaty of Tientsin was finally ratified by the emperor Xianfeng in the Convention of Peking on 18 October 1860. The opium trade was legalised. Christians were granted full legal and social and economic equal civil rights that were previously denied to them on the grounds of religious belief, including the right to own property. They were also allowed to proselytise and spread their faith unhindered. The Second Opium War came to an end with China now firmly under colonial influence. In the later action against the Boxers Japan joined in with the Allied forces. (For fuller discussion see Grasso, Corrin and Kort 2004.)

This destruction was not without critics, but it did not lead to any prosecutions

Western Imperialism: the avoided factor at the Tokyo trials?

Thus the Japanese invasion of China in the 1930s and use of a provocative 'incident' was continuing a tradition. With the notable exception of the wholly dissenting judgement of Pal, the complexity of the relations between the European powers, their subjection of China, and Japanese interests (both in ensuring their survival and in expansion) were ignored in the Tokyo trials; as was the right of resistance. For one should not forget that in the Sudanese accounts the 1885 fall of Khartoum and death of Gordon had meant that

> The Mahdi was now master of a million square miles. He was leader of the first African nation to be created by its own efforts. From this point ... the modern Sudanese nation was born. ('Ismat Hasan Zulfo 1980: 22)

Benin 1897: a celebrated punitive expedition

> Buried in the dirt of ages ... were several hundred unique bronze plaques, suggestive of almost Egyptian design, but of really superb casting. Castings of wonderful delicacy of detail, and some magnificently carved tusks were collected ... silver there was none, and gold there was none, and the coral was of little value. In fact, the only things of value were the tusks and bronze work ... of other ivory work, some bracelets suggestive of Chinese work and two magnificent leopards were the chief articles of note; bronze groups of idols and two large and beautifully worked stools were also found, and must have been of very old manufacture. (Bacon 1987: 91–2)

So Commander R. H. Bacon described the 'loot' that the British 'punitive expedition' captured and took from the city of Benin in 1897. At the time this expedition was portrayed in the media as an action of international penology and imperial global reach; the punitive expedition was presented as a remarkable achievement in assembling at short notice a task force from thousands of miles away, sending them to the coast of present-day Nigeria, capturing and sacking the city, before putting its King (the Oba) and the leading members of his court on trial. The Oba was sent into exile, several of his officers executed; thus the British punished for the murder of the peaceful party first sent to him. In addition they freed its inhabitants from the grip of 'disgusting customs' of human sacrifice and slavery. Today many are not quite so celebratory. Was the seizing of the Benin bronzes and the destruction of the city an act of international penology, or should we call it a crime? And what was the real motivation? Moreover, the actions of the Benin people can now be read as a desperate but doomed rebuttal of globalisation.

It is not overly cynical to suggest that a new source of profit was needed from the beginning of the nineteenth century to replace those from the abolished Slave Trade – on the West African coast British activity was turned towards legitimate trade supplying trade goods in return for raw materials or semi-processed commodities, in particular palm oil, a major lubricant for the industrial revolution and a major component of soap. Under the 1885 Berlin Conference's carve up of Africa, the British had an established 'legitimate' presence along the coast of present-day Nigeria, with some areas administered directly from Whitehall and others under trading company control (the British frequently used the device of the chartered company to annex blocks of land to their effective control). Spheres of influence were defined by European powers in relation to each other, and often had little meaning on the ground, being based on ambiguous treaties entered into with traditional rulers.

The Niger Coast Protectorate included the Niger Delta and the trading ports to the east. By 1895, the Protectorate government had established its authority, frequently by use of force, over all the major trading centres except the ancient kingdom of Benin, which insisted on retaining trading independence. Accounts favourable to British colonialism portray this autonomy as cause for Benin's fall in power (e.g. De Gramont 1975: 303; 'The Oba, in retaliation to English policies, closed his country to trade. Isolated in the delta, cut off from trade, in thrall to its king and priests, The Benin people fell into degradation, multiplying tortures and human sacrifices to please the gods and improve their fortunes'). A trade and protection treaty had been concluded with Benin in 1892 by Capt. Gallwey on the first official visit to the city in 30 years. Article VI of the document stated that trade should be open to all nations throughout the Oba's territory but trade was in practice conducted via the intermediary of the coastal Itsekiri people, and was less profitable than expected. The Protectorate administration was feeling the pressure from the rival British administrations of Lagos Colony and the Royal Niger Company, both desiring to open up the hinterland to trade. Ralph Moor, the Consul General of the Niger Coast Protectorate, felt hampered by the Foreign Office's reluctance to allow him to mount an armed expedition against the kingdom of Benin. Against this backdrop, the Illustrated London News depicted the Benin organisation as degenerate:

> Although little authentic knowledge of the Benin people is current, the main characteristics of the surrounding tribes are thought to be theirs also in an intensified degree finding expression in habits of disgusting brutality and scenes of hideous cruelty

and bloodshed, ordained by the superstitions of a degraded race of savages. (Illustrated London News, 23 January 1897: 123)

This image was at odds not only with the various historical accounts,[12] but even those of quite recent British visitors; for example, Auchterlonie in his talk to the Geographical Society in Liverpool, reported on the blacksmiths and other artisans who had evidently been productive at the time of his visit in 1890:

We saw blacksmiths at work. They make images, ornaments of various kinds for the hair, bracelets, anklets, knives out of hoop iron, etc., and, considering the appliances they have, they certainly turn out wonderfully good workmanship. And these were not the only craftsmen working in the City. There are also in the town good carvers in ivory and wood. (Auchterlonie 1897: 186–7)

In late 1986, Moor went on leave to England and a newly arrived Acting Consul General, James Phillips took up his post.

The events of 1897

Phillips had met Consul General Moor only once, in London, just before his departure. Moor had a history of violence against African rulers who did not submit to his authority and had already proposed a military operation against Benin but had been prevented by his more cautious superiors in Whitehall (military expeditions could become very expensive and produce disappointing returns if the outcome was not controllable or unintended consequences perceived). Phillips' intentions become clear in his despatches to the Foreign Office. Immediately on arrival he called a meeting of traders and officials and wrote a report to Whitehall:

The whole of the English merchants represented on the river have petitioned the government for aid to enable them to keep their factories (trading posts) open, and last but not least, the revenues of this Protectorate are suffering … I am certain that there is only one remedy. That is to depose the King of Benin … I am convinced that pacific measures are now quite useless, and that the time has now come to remove the obstruction … I do not anticipate any serious resistance from the people of the country – there is every reason to believe that they would be glad to get rid of their King – but in order to obviate any danger, I wish to take up sufficient armed force … I would add that I have reason to hope that sufficient ivory may be found in the King's house to pay the expenses incurred.

Phillips acted before he received a reply to this despatch sending out a message to the Oba informing him of his intention to visit Benin soon. The reply requested him to delay his visit for two months due to customary rituals – the festival of Igue – during which foreigners could not enter Benin City. Phillips replied it was necessary for him to come at once (ignoring the advice of a trusted Itsekiri chief) and led a small force of 10 British officers and a column of 200 African porters (and a drum-and-pipe band, which he later allowed to return to base in case their bright uniforms gave too militarist an appearance).

The religious significance of the Igue festival – a festival that European accounts recall being celebrated in 1651 – was such that it was only to be witnessed by the leading men of the city. The British insistence on coming was treated as an emergency. In the Benin account of why 'the Benin bronzes' when seized were heavily caked with blood, twelve men were taken with

12 cows, goats, sheep and chickens, the animals were killed near the altar and the blood from them was sprinkled on the ivories and the brass work while the 12 prisoners were led to 3 wells where they were beheaded.

Even if the British had known of this they may have still stated that this was part of vile practices of human sacrifice, one justification for the expedition. The Benin accounts stress that those sacrificed were criminals already sentenced to death. Unaware of these rituals, Lt Phillips pressed on; in Benin it was decided that Chief Ologbosheri, the Oba's son-in-law should be sent out with an armed group to check his advance. On 4 January 1897, the British force was ambushed by Ologbosheri. The African carriers were either captured or left dead. Lt Phillips and eight British officers were killed. It was an unexpected and unusual victory. Their only weapons, revolvers, were locked away in their luggage. Only two of the white men escaped and survived the attack.

Philips' decision to undertake this unsanctioned mission was either motivated by personal ambition – to achieve a result before Moor's return – or he was acting under Moor's orders and had, in fact been set up by him to provide an incontrovertible excuse for military intervention. Either way Moor's desire for the violent overthrow of the independent kingdom was satisfied. The British response was to raise a *Punitive Expedition* that looted and sacked the City.

Competing versions

The official version of these events was that a brave and humanitarian mission was massacred because of treachery and barbarity. A well-organised and successful military action then punished the perpetrators and freed the populace from the depredations of a 'Fetish-Priest-King' and his rule of terror. Much was made of the continuing practice of human sacrifice in Benin in the face of a treaty with a European power as a justification for interference:

> The King of Benin in the treaty he signed with captain Gallwey, had agreed to place himself and his county under H.M. Protectorate and it was becoming a perfect disgrace that in the Protectorate ... so terrible a state of affairs continued as that in what was not very improperly called the City of Blood.

The social space of Benin was then to be civilised. Captain Boisragon, Phillips' colleague on the journey, and one of the two Europeans to survive, wrote a sensationalist (and often contradictory in its opinion of Benin) account in which he stressed the humanitarian motive for the mission:

> The object to the expedition was to try and persuade the king to let the white men come up to his city whenever they wanted to. All their horrible customs could not be put down at once, except by a strong-armed expedition, but could be stamped out gradually by officials continually going up. (Boisragon 1897)

Another argument in Phillips' favour could be that this was to be a last chance visit, thus every pacific means towards approaching the King would not be complete until he as Acting Consul General paid a visit to the King. If unsuccessful, force would than be legitimate. However, having been advised that the timing would clash with the religious ceremonies, it was a last chance guaranteed to fail. From the Benin perspective: Phillip's visit was against the remonstrance's of the Itsekiri traders, the advice of the Chief Dogho (a trusted partner of the British), the Oba's stated refusal and constituted utter disregard for the traditions and susceptibilities of the Benin people. The few statements recorded from the Benin witnesses at the later trial of the Oba suggest a very different situation to the official version of planned attack on the British; they indicate that Oba Ovonramwen sought to avoid conflict. Benin had trading contacts with Europe since the fifteenth century with early Portuguese, Dutch and British visitors expressing admiration for the kingdom. Relations had become strained in the preceding decades as the British established permanent trading stations and consulates along the coast and sought to interfere – often by violent means – in the internal affairs of African kingdoms. The Gallwey Treaty had been concluded under veiled threats. The pro forma document was translated verbally from English via a dialect of Yoruba into Edo. It could have been understood as a statement of cooperation and trade, certainly not a relinquishing of tribal dominion. However, it was used to justify military action: it was an insult to the prestige of the Protectorate not to be able to assert its authority within these new territorial limits.

There were internal divisions within the Benin court, dating back to Ovonramwen's accession, and disagreements over an appropriate response to British pressure provided a focus for discontent. Ovonramwen's approach was to refuse visits for all official visits after Gallwey's and to withdraw into isolation from the British, although he still conducted trade via the Itsekiri middlemen. Despite the Oba's attempts to dissuade Phillips from coming, Phillips' insistence played into the hands of the radicals who sought to weaken the Oba in the name of defending Benin's autonomy. They argued that Phillips' incursion was a gross insult and that it was too dangerous to allow him into the city and the presence of the Oba.

As Ovonramwen foresaw, the attack on Phillips destroyed Benin's autonomy. The 'punitive expedition' organised under the command of Admiral Sir Harry Rawson, the commander-in-chief at Cape Town became a successful exercise of imperial power. Within a month, a force of 1,200 British soldiers, brought to the Benin River from 4,000 miles away (from London, Cape Town and Malta), had landed on the Nigerian coast, and teamed up with several hundred locally recruited black troops. Thousands of African porters were brought from the British military base at Sierra Leone.[13]

The actual assault on Benin City in February 1897 was not without difficulties; each of the advancing columns met resistance. The first one was harassed for several days – the second was attacked in its base camp and the commanding officer was killed. The naval surgeon, Felix Roth, recounts the story of the third in his diary providing matter-of-fact accounts of the methodological way in which machine guns 'cleared' Benin resistance.

> We shelled the village, and cleared it of the natives. As the launch and surf-boats grounded, we jumped into the water … at once placed our Maxims and guns in position, firing so as to clear the bush where the natives might be hiding.

Luckily, as Dr Roth recorded in his account entitled *Great Benin: its customs, art and horrors*: 'no white men were wounded; we all got off scot-free'. This providential protection was easily explained: 'Our black troops, with the scouts in front and a few Maxims, do all the fighting.' One notes that this was not the image produced in the *Illustrated London News*, which portrayed the action being conducted by White troops; the images circulating in England were of White power, White organisation and the white man's protection of native porters. Within six weeks of the ambush Benin City was captured as the Oba, the 36th of a dynasty stretching back to the thirteenth century, took flight when shelling began (in the Benin accounts they were shocked to find the sky raining destruction while no white men could be seen). The city was given the name *city of blood*. In Roth's account:

> It is a misnomer to call it a city: it is a charnel house. All about the houses and streets are dead natives, some crucified, some sacrificed on trees, others on stage erections ... In front of the king's compound stakes have been driven into the ground and cross-pieces of wood lashed to them. On this framework live human beings are tied, to die of thirst and heat, to be dried up by the sun and eaten by the carrion birds, till the bones get disarticulated and fall to the ground. At the base of them the whole ground was strewn with human bones and decomposing bodies, with their heads off. Three looked like white men, but it was impossible for me to decide, as they had been there for some time ... The bush too, was filled with dead bodies, the hands being tied to the ankles so as to keep them in a sitting posture. It was a gruesome sight to see these headless bodies about, the smell being awful.

The accumulated works of art from centuries that adorned the palaces were removed wholesale. Roth described the process: 'Every house had its alcove of various dimensions [containing "fetish" carvings and sculptures]. A large part of the loot was found embedded in the walls, and occasionally in so testing the walls the soldiers put their hands into human corpses built up in them'. Another officer took a remarkable photograph showing members of the expeditionary force posed in the middle of a large collection, piled up in one of the compounds. British marines put the palace and compounds to the torch. However, the fires got out of control, burning up what was left of the city as well as part of the equipment of the British force. Much of the carved woodwork in the Oba's palace was lost. On the Benin side, a strong sense of grievance of the events – comparatively recent in the oral history of a people whose dynastic legends are datable back through 40 generations to the thirteenth century – endures (see Akenzua 1960). In their perspective the British decided to burn the town as an appropriate finale to the punishment of the people who murdered their sons in cold blood. However, to have taken the works of art and still not returned them – in contrast to the process for the return of art stolen by the Nazi's in Europe – gives another message as to the civilising process.

For a further 6 months, a small British force harried the countryside in search of the Oba and his chiefs who had fled, cattle were seized and villages destroyed. In August the Oba was brought back to his ruined city where a large crowd was assembled to witness a ritual humiliation. The Oba was required to kneel down in front of the British military resident of the town and to literally trite the dust. Supported by two chiefs, the king made obeisance three times, rubbing his forehead on the ground three times. He was told that he had been deposed. Several weeks later Ralph Moor arrived reputedly to utter 'Now this is white man's country ... There is only one king in the country, and that is the white man'. The Oba and his chiefs were subjected to a show trial, charged with the murder of Lt Phillips: Moor was the judge. While the life of the Oba himself was spared, six of his chiefs were condemned to death. One of them, Ologhosheri, continued a guerrilla struggle against the British for another 2 years, but he too was eventually captured and hanged. The Oba was exiled to Calabar, and replaced by Chief Obaseki, a controller of many villages with rubber-producing forests. These were soon sold off to European firms.

Between 1897 and 1914 the Igue festival was not celebrated, but returned with the restoration of the monarchy in 1914 after the death of Oba Ovonramwen in exile when his eldest son was allowed to return to Benin and the dynasty was restored (see Igbafe 1979, for the story of Benin under British domination). The Oba of Benin is one of the most influential of modern Nigeria's traditional rulers.

The art treasures

Benin art was treated as little more than curios when first brought to Britain; as the wonderful quality of the ivory carving and bronze casting became appreciated it was reflected in increasing prices at art auctions. This in turn posed a paradox: how could a degenerate people make objects of such technical difficulty and artistic beauty? Coombes (1994) traces the early

Figure 7.4 Moore with the captured Oba

Figure 7.5 Benin bronze wall covering, currently at Horniman museum (photo Wayne Morrison)

assumptions that the artefacts were of ancient origin and in themselves evidence of the degenerate theory (see the views of Ling 1898a; 1898b). The bronzes could not be understood as made by the people and social order that had been subdued, as that would transgress the image of Benin as a degenerate culture. They must have had their birth in earlier times, and their existence could not be any material evidence against the project of imperial civilisation.

The Foreign Office sold considerable quantities of ivory to defray the costs of the expedition and many of the officers retained items. The British Museum acquired some but at the time there was considerable ill will at the sales to the US and Germany (the route whereby the Queen Mother's Head came to the RMCA is not apparent to the visitor). As Roth expressed it in 1903:

> Not only was the national institution thus deprived of its lawful acquisitions, but at the same time another government department sold for a few hundred pounds a large number of castings which had cost thousands to obtain, as well as much blood of our fellow countrymen ... it is especially annoying to Englishmen to think that such articles,

which for every reason should be retained in this country, have been allowed to go abroad.

Pieces were lost or destroyed during the World War II in Liverpool and Berlin (apparently quantities of Benin art have been rediscovered in the eastern part of Germany since renunciation). A diplomatic incident ensured when Nigeria was refused loan of an ivory mask, which was the visual symbol of the 2nd World Black and African Festival of Arts Culture (FESTAC) held in Nigeria in 1977. Since a major exhibition of Benin art at the Museum of Mankind in the early 1970s most of the British Museum's collection has lain in storage.[14]

The metaphysics of the images and the context for their creation were not fit subjects of analysis until relatively recently. It may now be accepted that the art of Benin was a way of capturing and fashioning historical recall; whoever controlled that production and display controlled the legitimacy of power. In the political and royal figure of the Oba, the controller of creation and production of royal art was also a key link into the powers of the cosmos. The Oba granted certain items of 'art' to Chiefs (which we may note reverted upon their death) and thus linked them with him and his influence with the cosmos (Ben-Amos 1999). The images and forms arose out of a struggle between competing claims for legitimacy; a rightful king has control over important symbolic resources and can argument them. Artistic creation or preservation of past events in oral tradition is not then innocent. Yet when the European analysis took place it was to position Benin art into a master-narrative of history that relegates the (sub)history of Benin's inhabitants essentially into some form of prehistory. Yet there is here a overcoming of visions of locality and transcendence: the Oba was considered a divine king, and as such could intercede with physical and spiritual forces to shape the outcome of events. The Oba should have ultimate say in the balance between the internal and the external, in protecting he internal from the intrusions of outside forces. Bosman had in 1705 recounted the Oba's terrible action against an Edo official who had murdered Dutch Company agents. Having been told his identity and the 'revenge' taken by the Dutch he ordered the person responsible to come before him and then 'caused him and his whole Race, to the third and fourth generation, to be cut into pieces' (Bosman [1705] 1967: 432). Gottlieb argued (1989: 254) that African kings revealed two sides to power: benevolent protectors of their land and people or agents of despotic acts of terror. Control over life and death had legal dimensions but also cosmic; denoting his ability to interact with powers beyond the normal structuring of the everyday locality. Thus the Oba had the right to make human sacrifice. Slaves and prisoners of war could be offered up as contributions to cosmic order. This is not the waging of war but an attempt at protection, which the phrase of Schechner (1993: 313) seems only to cover too accurately the events of 1897: the ritual sacrifice was a 'mortgaged actuality, awaiting while indefinitely postponing future catastrophe'. Only here the external could not be prevented from intruding.

In terms of the tactics of imperial domination the Benin expedition showed how the British could rule without committing vast numbers of their own troops. A combination of military discipline, technology and organised avenues of communication enabled a task force to move quickly to the locality and deliver a devastating message. Challenges to the imperial dynamic could not be met if they occurred simultaneously, but periodic offensive operations could be conducted utilising native forces under British Officers so that potential challengers would be aware of the response if they did not accommodate. As to its legitimacy, that was the task partly of controlling the media presentation. A subtle path must be tread: on the one side the message must be one of shock and awe, of the overwhelming force that can be assembled so that resistance should not be engaged in; on the other, hegemony requires that this force be used in the service of an idea, an idea that showed those who otherwise could be the subjects of the military option that there was benefit in avoidance. The contribution that that society could make to a global development – symbolised through its artistic expression and creation – must in turn be controlled, possessed by the imperial narrator.

Namibia: a successful German colonial genocide and prelude to the Holocaust?

> Driving women and children into the swamps was not as successful as it should have been, since the swamps were not deep enough for them to sink. Because of a depth of one metre, most cases reached solid ground (probably sand) so that drowning was not possible. (SS-Sturmbannfuhrer Franz Magill, commanding SS-cavalry Regiment involved in 'pacification' operations against 'Jewish plunderers', 'Bericht uber den Verlauf der Pripjet-Aktion', 12 August 1941, quoted Burleigh 1997: 109)

Burleigh uses this 'evasively matter-of-fact account' of operations that killed some 6,526 defenceless Jews by shooting and numerous others who actually drowned, as part of his thesis that the 'racial war in the Soviet Union' was a 'crucial catalyst, a final lowering of the threshold of what was thought humanly possible'. Burleigh's acute and nuanced account rescues the war on the Eastern front from military historians who have downplayed the racial aspects, but he nowhere draws any connections with an earlier German racial war in which the enemy were driven wholesale into an African desert in a successful genocide; that of the destruction of the Hereros. (For one text that does see Swan 1991) The accounts of Drechsler (first published in German 1963, in English 1980) and Bridgeman (1981) are of a somewhat romantic but futile resistance, thus we read that from 1904 to 1907 the tribes in South-West Africa, especially the Hereros, fought 'a heroic but futile war against their German masters. [which resulted in a genocide] that for all practical purposes has ... disappeared from history'.

The German destruction of the Hereros was the culmination of colonial activities and attitudes dealing with specific lands allocated in the 1884 Berlin Conference. The German chancellor Bismarck, not a keen supporter of colonial adventures, was virtually compelled by a well-organised public campaign to acquire a strip of land along the coast of South-West Africa (present-day Namibia) at Angra Pequeña (now Lüderitz Bay) in 1884. Further acquisitions followed in West Africa (Togo and Cameroon) and in German East Africa (now Tanzania). One driving force was Dr Friedrich Fabri, director of a German missionary society that had been active in Africa for decades, who became known as 'Father of the German Colonial Movement' through his forceful propaganda in promoting colonial development. As a result of his influence, several important elements of German society – bankers, intellectuals, businessmen and military leaders – joined in the establishment of a German Colonial Union (Kolonialverein) and similar societies. Fabri was convinced that possession of colonies would resolve many of the internal bitterness and divisions within German society and provide a grand cultural task for German renewal.

> We are convinced beyond doubt that the colonial question has become a matter of life-or-death for the development of Germany. Colonies will have a salutary effect on our economic situation as well as on our entire national progress. Here is a solution for many of the problems that face us. In this new Reich of ours there is so much bitterness, so much unfruitful, sour, and poisoned political wrangling, that the opening of a new, promising road of national effort will act as a kind of liberating influence. Our national spirit will be renewed, a gratifying thing, a great asset. A people that has been led to a high level of power can maintain its historical position only as long as it understands and proves itself to be the bearer of a culture mission. At the same time, this is the only way to stability and to the growth of national welfare, the necessary foundation for a lasting expansion of power. At one time Germany contributed only intellectual and literary activity to the tasks of our century. That era is now over. As a people we have become politically minded and powerful. But if political power becomes the primal goal of a nation, it will lead to harshness, even to barbarism. We must be ready to serve for the ideal, moral, and economic culture-tasks of our time … When the German Reich centuries ago stood at the pinnacle of the states of Europe, it was the Number One trade and sea power. If the New Germany wants to protect its newly won position of power for a long time, it must heed its Kultur-mission and, above all, delay no longer in the task of renewing the call for colonies. (Friedrich Fabri, *Does Germany Need Colonies*, 1879, extracted in Louis L. Snyder (ed.), 1962: 116–17)

Imperialism was said to be the destiny of the German people. This involved an appeal to the history of a glorious past and the need to follow its cultural mission. We should not neglect the flows of influence for this particular cultural mission furnished specific knowledges and models for the Nazis, among which was confirmation of the racial ordering of the world.[15]

Some of the 'knowledges' of mastery and racial superiority gained in this genocide were fed back to Hitler when while imprisoned and constructing Mein Kampf he read Eugen Fischer's work. Fischer went to the then South-West Africa in 1904 and made a study of the mixed ethnic children of German men and Herero women, the result of interbreeding from forced labour camps[16]. In *The Principles of Human Heredity of Race Hygiene*, Fisher supposedly demonstrated that these children were mentally and physically inferior to German children. When Hitler assumed the Chancellorship, Fischer was chancellor at the University of Berlin and taught select Nazi physicians in medical school; among his pupils was Josef Mengele, later tried for his medical 'experiments' at the Auschwitz concentration camp.

Destruction of the Hereros: an inevitable process or act of choice?

Herero culture and language is closely related to the Bantu people who had arrived in about 1750. Their language contains more than a thousand words for the colours and markings of the cattle they raised. Their diet consisted of sour milk mixed with blood drawn from the cattle and the wild fruits and berries that they gathered. German Marxist writers, such as Heinrich Lath, at the time of the early German occupation wrote that the Hereros were emerging politically from a purely tribal state into nomadic early feudalism. They noted that the land was held communally. The early German occupiers began the destruction of the traditional system which military action completed.

Bridgeman notes: 'After the uprising the Germans extinguished all the sacred fires and confiscated all the cattle, so that the whole traditional basis of Herero cooperative life, which was already beginning to decay by 1904, collapsed completely and the Hereros became hired herdsmen on white men's ranches'. In his classic text on colonialism, *The Wretched of the Earth* Frantz, Fanon (1963) expressed the relation between land and dignity: 'For a colonized people the most essential value … is first and foremost the land: the land which will bring them bread and above all, dignity.' In the eyes of the colonial there was no dignity in these inhabitants. 'All that the native has seen in his country is that they can freely arrest him, beat him, starve him: and no professor of ethics, no priest has ever come to be beaten in his place, nor to share their bread with him.' The few commentators who have investigated the actions of Hendrik Witbooi, the main Hottentot leader, and Samuel Makarero, the Herero leader, sympathetically recall their policies as one of futile resistance to an overwhelming external force. After struggles in the 1880s they signed a peace treaty in November 1892; but the Germans resumed the war; they attacked the followers of Witbooi first at their camp at Harukranz and killed 150, which included 78 women and children. The German commander's intentions were clear – to cleanse the Witbooi tribe from the land. However, events moved slowly due to overconfidence, exacerbated by increasing racism on the part of the Germans – Samuel Makarero planned actions of self-defence and in his instructions he forbade injuring women and children, Englishmen, Boers, and other neutral Africans. He also appealed for help to the other natives of Southern Africa, but without success.

On 12 January 1904, the Hereros launched attacks on German farms, villages, and forts in Hereroland and succeeded in destroying many of the farms. Magazines quickly gave images of heroic defence against the odds with White Settlers being overwhelmed by superior numbers of swarming natives; there was also, however, a theme of outside interference, particularly the implication that the English were arming native insurgents.

In February and March, German reinforcements arrived, giving 2,500 new troops. The Germans were armed with the Model 88 rifle, which in the hands of a good marksman could kill a man at ranges up to half a mile. They also had some light artillery and machine guns. The Hereros were armed only with rifles and handguns, and some had no guns at all. They surprised the Germans with their marksmanship and managed to maintain the initiative as well as determining where the small-scale battles, in which the Hereros proved effective and elusive, would be fought. This remained true even after there were far more armed Germans than armed Hereros. The German high command replaced their rather native-sympathetic commander with the more ruthless Gen. Lothar von Trotha. A rather weakly resourced Colonial Administration one that knew the necessity for cooperation, was replaced in a climate of few of losing control. The proclamation von Trotha issued on 2 October 1904 left little room for doubt that control was to be achieved

> The Hereros are no longer German subjects. They have murdered and stolen, have cut off the ears and noses and other body parts from wounded soldiers, and in cowardice no longer want to fight. I say to the people: Everyone, who brings one of the captains to one of my stations as prisoners, will receive 1,000 marks, whoever brings Samuel Maharero will receive 5,000 marks. However, the Herero people must leave the country. If the people does not do that, then I will force it to with the Groot Rohr [big cannon]. Within the German border every Herero, armed or not, with cattle or without, will be shot, I will not take up any more women or children, will drive them back to their people or let them be shot at.

The German forces slowly forced their opponents into a smaller area and at Waterbeg Makarero made a mistake. He gathered 25,000 of his people, including women and children (who always followed the men), in a sandy valley with steep bluffs on three sides. To the open side lay a 200-mile virtually waterless desert called the Omaheke sandveld. Von Trotha was able to force the people into the desert, where he had poisoned the few water wells. His troops locked the Hereros in the desert, where they died by the thousands and he had a series of German guardposts erected to prevent escape. Oral histories say men slit the throats of cattle to drink the blood; they suckled the breasts of new mothers; infants withered and died in days; some Hereros cut open the bellies of the dead to drink the liquid from their stomachs. Men who escaped the desert were lynched (a few photographs are in the public domain). Women and children survivors had chains placed around their necks and were worked to death, the few males remaining were rounded up, banned from owning land or cattle, and sent into labour camps to be the slaves of German settlers. Many more Herero died in the camps, of overwork, starvation and disease. By 1907, in the face of criticism both at home and abroad, von Trotha's orders had been cancelled and he himself recalled, but it was too late for the crushed Herero.

Bridgeman reports that the German losses in South-West Africa from January 1904 to March 1907 amounted to about 2,500 men killed, wounded, and missing; African losses cannot be determined with such precision. The Hereros were estimated to number 80,000 at the time the rebellion began; in 1911 only 15,130 were still alive. In 1904 there were believed to have been about 20,000 Hottentots in the colony; seven years later that number had been reduced to 9781.

The Colonial Office issued strict orders in 1907 that no native could own land or cattle (the Ovambos were an exception), all males over 17 had to carry passes, and all natives were subject to forced labour. In 1908 diamonds were discovered along the coast. As a result, by 1914 the white population had grown to 14,000. The few natives left were to serve their white masters. If the land had been cleared for white settlement, events elsewhere – World War I – intervened. But these changing patterns of land ownership and political alliances were also to impede knowledge of the events. South-West Africa was occupied by British forces in 1915 after which two officers were commissioned to investigate and draw up a report detailing the treatment of the South-West

Africans by German colonial authorities. The resulting 1918 report seemed relatively truthful to surviving accounts and detailing the German domination of the region and its consequences (extracts presented in Totten *et al.*, 1997: 26–40). This knowledge was not disinterested, for while it had the potential to bring the Herero genocide into mainstream consciousness the report's purpose was mainly to document the incompetence of the Germans as colonial administrators and thus rule out a possible return of South-West Africa to Germany after World War I. When the League of Nations mandated South-West Africa to the Union of South Africa the British-South African officials and German farmers were put on the same side and the aim of achieving a peaceful and prosperous (colonised) region was paramount. At a session of the South-West African Legislative Assembly on 19 July 1926, a resolution was adopted which first labelled the report an 'instrument of war', and said it was time for all such instruments to be set aside; second, asked for the removal of the report from the official files of the Government of the Union and the British Government; and third, requested the removal and destruction of all copies of the report found in public libraries and official bookstores (Drechsler 1980: 10).

This relegated the most damning record of the German genocide of the Hereros to virtual oblivion (as indeed it also rendered the cultural adaptation and future fight back by the surviving Hereros). In the light of this example, the vast clearing of population intended by the Nazis, and partly achieved, in their conquered east, as well as their intentions for enslaving the Slavonic peoples, was a continuation, not a radical break. This great policy of biological reordering was the exception – true – but it was the exception here in that it turned what had been conduct in the far flung areas of an imperial globe into state policy for incorporating into a transformed homeland a new European living space, cleansed of life not fit to live on equal terms or at all.

An alternative explanation for the impossibility of law and criminology?

I have charged that the Holocaust cannot be incorporated within criminology while the nation state continues as the definer of foundational concerns. There is another argument for the lack of a global criminology. That can be explained if we take the holocaust as the defining event of the twentieth century, namely that is it is beyond representation.

Hanna Arendt's comments on law and Nazism in correspondence with Jaspers (*Correspondence*, pp. 51–6) are often quoted, at least in part:

> The Nazi crimes ... explode the limits of the law; and that is precisely what constitutes their monstrousness. For these crimes no punishment is severe enough. It may be essential to hang Goering, but it is totally inadequate. That is, this guilt, in contrast to all criminal guilt, oversteps and shatters any and all legal systems ... And just as inhuman as their guilt is the innocence of the victims. Human beings simply can't be as innocent as they all were in the face of the gas chambers ... We are simply not equipped to deal, on a human, political level, with a guilt that is beyond crime and an innocence that is beyond goodness or virtue.

What is not usually included is her following description: 'That is the abyss that opened up … with the onset of imperialist politics'.

The argument that the Holocaust is beyond judgement, beyond representation, is sometimes made in recognition of its absolute horror and in respect of another form of knowledge. As Elie Wiesel (1978) put it: 'The dead are in possession of a secret that are, the living, are neither worthy of nor capable of recovering'. But while we acknowledge that relation to the past and the dead, we are also bound in relationships to the present and the future, to those alive and yet-to-be to seek comprehension, awareness and attempt judgements: those of the law and/or justice. But there we are caught in a politics of different spheres of representation and justice, varieties of 'whose justice, which rationality?' Or put in terms of our originating narrative, in which sphere of territory and epistemology can the judging occur? The search for a workable concept of a world justice under the processes of globalisation appears doomed not to find any secure place to stand from which to judge and thus is caught in perpetual movements with an absence of foundational security. While it was clear to Raynal in 1770 that there were great benefits from colonial trade, in the growth of industry, and the exploitation of the world's resources by the European powers, he could find no way of proving that they had any right to colonise. But colonising they were; today Niall Ferguson (2004: 165) calls for honesty in referring to actions in Afghanistan and Iraq: 'The main object had been to "root out" terrorists and their sponsors. The fundamental tendency, however, was imperialism in the name of internationalism'.

What then is the status of discourses of right, of justice, of crime and punishment, when they are spoken and written within a process that cannot be legitimated by its original right, but only by claims as to its advantages? To whose advantage? Raynal may again be a guide: ultimately his criterion for judgement was the self-interest of the European. Given that the contemporary US is the child of Europe, it would be rash to believe that his answer has been surpassed.

Chapter 8:
A Reflected Gaze of Humanity:
Reflections on Vision, Memory and Genocide

However the war may end, we have won the war against you; none of you will be left to bear witness, but even if someone were to survive, the world would not believe him. There will perhaps be suspicions, discussions, research by historians, but there will be no certainities, because we will destroy the evidence together with you. And even if some proof should remain and some of you survive, people will say that the events you describe are too monstrous to be believed ... We will be the ones to dictate the history of the Lagers [camps]. (Simon Wiesenthal recounting an SS officer's warning to the inhabitants of Auschwitz, Levi 1986: 11–12)

Cultural criminology uses the 'evidence' of everyday existence, wherever it is found and in whatever form it can be found; the debris of everyday life is its 'data'. (Presdee 2000: 15)

The first task in restoring the perpetrators to the center of our understanding of the Holocaust is to restore them to their identities, grammatically by using not the passive but the active voice in order to ensure that they, the actors are not absent from their own deeds. (Goldhagen 1996: 6)

My position is that those who, uncoerced chose to mock, degrade, torture, and kill other people and to boast about, celebrate, and memorialise their deeds [through taking photographs] did so because they hated their victims, held them to be guilty, and believed that they were right to treat them in this way. (Goldhagen 1998: 145)

Genocide and memories

The perfect genocide would leave no memories. Or, put more correctly, there would be neither words nor images that allowed the reality of genocide or the 'authentic' identity of the subject of that genocide to be acknowledged. There would, of course, be memories, words and images. But they would be those of the victors.[1] It was, after all, the intention of the Nazis to build a museum of the Jewish people, a testimony to an inferior race that the Nazis had, as the agents of progress, removed from our gaze.

In these politics of presence and absence, the perfect genocide becomes the iconally successful crime when no one can recognise it as such, and, unrecognised, it disappears. One looks, but cannot see – perhaps one is unguided, for one sees but does not look upon a scene that has relevance, one writes but does not mention; such, as has been stressed throughout this book, is the experience of the modernist discipline termed criminology. Conversely, the literature and art of survivors has contested the power of genocide and called upon the indifferent to bear witness to scenes that often defy representation. In the writings of survivors, laboured and sometimes even imaginary, many times felt by the articulator as fraudulent in their inability to render truth, scenes are revealed of a distressing humanity.[2] Humanity displays itself as both terrible and fragile; all too obviously straddling a ridge of destructive power with presence on one side and extinction on the other.

Yet what is it that one bears witness to? In *The Reawakening* Primo Levi – who survived Auschwitz because he managed to convince the camp authorities that he was useful for his knowledge of chemistry – acknowledged Hurbinek:

> Hurbinek was a nobody, a child of death, a child of Auschwitz. He looked maybe three years old, no one knew anything about him, he could not speak and he had no name; that curious name, Hurbinek, had been given to him by us, perhaps by one of the women who used these syllables to give shape to the inarticulate sounds the child sometimes made. He was paralyzed from the waist down, with atrophied legs, thin like sticks; but his eyes, lost in a triangular and wasted face, flashed, terribly alive, full of demand, assertion, of the will to break loose and shatter the tomb of his dumbness. The speech he lacked, which no one had bothered to teach him, this need for speech charged his stare with explosive urgency: it was a stare both savage and human, even mature, a judgement which none of us could support, so heavy was it with force and anguish. (1965: 11)

Like many of the inmates who somehow had survived until the Red Army liberated Auschwitz, Levi was put in an infirmary with Hurbinek. There Hurbinek succeeded in uttering a word, 'something like Massklo or Matisklo'. Was this his name or an attempt to name somebody or call for somebody? Although surrounded by representatives of every nation in Central Europe, Hurbinek's utterance did not reveal its secret.

Levi's survival disrupted more than the patterns of power of those who marked out his particular fate. For no trace of Hurbinek's place in time was intended to be preserved. The Nazi control over the ontology of European Jews had meant that Hurbinek was to be a child with no origin or language, who would die a death that the world was indifferent to note or record in words. Levi recorded – for he confronted and felt obliged to recount Hurbinek's stare.

> Hurbinek who was not yet three years old, who was perhaps born in Auschwitz and never saw a tree, Hurbinek who fought like a man till his very last breath to gain entry into the community of men from which a bestial power had excluded him, Hurbinek, the nameless one, whose tiny forearm bore the tattoo of Auschwitz, died in the first days of March 1945; free but not redeemed. Nothing remains of him: he only bears witness through my words.

Levi's ability to survive was also the contingent effect of a particular act of looking; an act that he believed contained the key to explaining how the Holocaust was made reality. In *Survival at Auschwitz* (1993: 105–6), Levi recounts how he escaped being sent to the gas chamber by passing a test of usefulness, a gaze of expertise, that distinguished those who could be used for *Kommando 98* (the Chemistry work unit). Levi, a chemist, had to pass a special test. His examiner was Doktor Engineer Pannwitz:

> Pannwitz is tall, thin and blond, with the kind of hair, eyes and nose that every German is supposed to have. He is seated menacingly behind an elaborate desk. And I, Haftling

174517, I stand in his office, which is a real office, neat and clean, with everything in order, feeling as if I would soil anything I touched.

When he finished writing, he raised his eyes and looked at me.

Since that day, I have thought about Doktor Pannwitz many times and in many different ways. I have often wondered about the inner workings of this man. What did he do with his time when he was not producing polymers in a chemistry lab, when he let his imagination wander beyond the reaches of Indo-Germanic consciousness? Above all, I wanted to meet him again, now that I was free, not out of revenge, but to satisfy my curiosity about the human soul.

Because the look he gave me was not the way one man looks at another. If I could fully explain the nature of that look – it was as if through the glass of an aquarium directed at some creature belonging to a different world – I would be able to explain the great madness of the Third Reich, down to its very core.

Everything we thought and said about the Germans took shape in that one moment. The brain commanding those blue eyes and manicured hands clearly said: 'This thing standing before me obviously belongs to a species that must be eliminated. But with this particular example, it is worth making sure that he has nothing we can use before we get rid of him.'

Levi is scanned for usefulness and distinguished from the mass. He would be sifted out and kept alive for a task, and – as history would have it – in time become a survivor. It was a fate he could never understand and ultimately could not live with.

Preventing vision: the closed world of the camp

It is a theme of this book that we *should* want to understand his experience. And that anyone who holds an academic position that involves the label criminologist at least some of the time, should be interested in analysing why that discipline has not been concerned to understand his fate or the context for the exercise of power over him. Yet, of course, there is the continual fact of the exception. The Holocaust is the exceptional state for western modernity – its excluded – which must be distanced else we come to understand the nature of the discourses and practices we work within.

The classical tropes of representation of the Holocaust may aid this distancing; for the iconic imagery of the Holocaust revolves around camps where slave labour and killing took on the appearance of an enclosed industrial practice. In that very modern process unity is disassembled; humanity and its effects – hair, shoes, bodily functions – are separated and glossed over, transformed into a language of statistics and euphemisms recorded in ways that recreate rational sets of linkages of things that take an effort to translate, to recognise as centreed on human subjects.[3] Social space is divided and common language torn.[4] It is as if this was a practice isolated out of shared pace at the time, and isolated in time from our space. This was perhaps part of the intentions of the creators of the system:

One of the purposes of the gas chambers was to isolate the killing. It sought to define limits: killing centered between walls and beneath a ceiling; the prey concentrated, cut off, isolated from the outside. So too the camp embodied outer limits, perimeters delimiting the outskirts of the city of death. (Horwitz 1991: 163)

Upon liberation, to enter the camps was to cross a line between the civilised and the uncivilised. When the Austrian priest, Franz Loidl, entered Mauthausen he did not encounter coherent speech. Instead:

> stories consist of solitary words, signs, and the showing of bodily wounds. In this babel of speech, in the reigning heat, the burdensome dust and the many-odored stench of perspiration clings to my brow. But the loathsome exhalations from the unwashed bodies and the shabbiest clothing of these poor people meant a true sacrifice for me. I do not know which of us was sickest. (following quotations from Horwitz 1991: chapter 8)

Leaving the barracks where the worst of the sick and infectious were put, he reflects:

> I am happy that I have again escaped the thick air inside there, which in the midday heat in the wooden barracks had become yet more unbearable. My hands have become sticky from the shaking of many hands. Hopefully I have not drawn an infection somehow. Danger is amply present. Even speaking with the people is not without danger, since with many the lungs have been attacked. There is much and painful coughing. A couple of times I was on the verge of throwing up. One indeed comes from civilization. And here, inside? … What a sad achievement of our arrogant century, this hideousness, this sinking into an unprecedented lack of civilization, and on top of that, in the heart of Europe!

The senses are opposed with sights, sounds and above all smells that civilisation was meant to design out.

> The nearer we approach the crematorium, the stronger the sweetish smell of corpses makes itself noticeable. Individuals have to take handkerchiefs to their noses, so unbearable it is. For days I could not get rid of it. Especially through the many burnings the air in the vicinity was poisoned, as the people complained. As long as I live I will never forget the view of the 140–50 corpses stacked upon one another in the storage room.

Do we hesitate over this recollection of the 'view of the 140–50 corpses'? Is there significance in the fact that he does not recount that he saw the bodies of people … but 'corpses'? This point may be returned to, but for now I note in his testimony that the smell was inescapable, whereas one could avert ones eyes. The eyes had difficulty coping: 'one does not tolerate the horrid all at once, and must first go away, and again look in, in order to catch a glimpse of the details'. Only with a certain time can one count the corpses, and notice the 'bluish-black skin' of bodies so dehydrated that they are almost mummified soon after death, but one cannot look into the open eyes of the corpses waiting burning. Loidl considered he had crossed into another world, where things had happened that he thought could only have been imagined in works of demented artists. How could one be faithful to the scenes that met American troops and an International Red Cross agent as they entered Mauthausen?

> By the thousands [the survivors] came streaming toward them, staggering toward them, crawling toward them to kiss and embrace them, to lift them upon weak, skeleton-thin shoulders, only to touch them like miracle-working holy men. Hollow, pallid ghosts from graves and tombs, terrifying, rot-colored figures of misery marked by disease, deeply ingrained filth, inner decay, incurable burn and frost damage to the soul, many of them become aged under the experience … lasting an eternity. All voices from out of the strange Ur-underground of human existence unite to a chorus, and a fugue upon the theme of horror and desperation. There are those who scream and rave in wild ecstasy, others are only able to whimper, to weep, suffocated, to stammer, to babble like

children ... One of them throws himself across the hood of the white Opel, kisses it and strokes it, worships it, clings tightly to it, cannot be removed from his fetish ... and the swelling heat of musty want develops in the open air to a flame, and rises, ignites rapidly forward and covers everything consumable.

Commandant's building, kitchen, and warehouse are stormed. Whatever is not edible or momentarily utilizable is destroyed. The recoil of an immense relaxation transforms itself into an explosive heat, and this into a blasting of the core of consciousness. Images from out of the portfolios of a Hogarth, a Brueghel; studies from a madhouse. There squat skeletons in rags and crazy grins drag themselves ... There people without strength, trembling from weakness, wrestle for sacks of flour and with shaking hands pour the Godly possession by the fistful down their throats. A quantity of precious, at first irreplaceable provisions becomes lost in the tumult, or else is sinfully and damagingly misused. Captured meat is devoured raw. Canned foods opened in feverish haste with beatings of stone fall victim to raging impatience. Heaps of wild creatures clustered from all nations of the sacred old world scuffle and strangle themselves on the ground for crumbs of bread, cigarette butts, potatoes, peas. Even the women furiously participate. The chaos howls toward heaven. (Fredrich von Gagern, quoted Horwitz 1991: 167)

So an observer recorded in a text published in 1948. But what did inmates see? Eug. Thome was perhaps more articulate than many in recalling the scene of an American tank entering Mauthausen's sister camp:

The joy, the rejoicing of the thousands who suddenly slid out of their numbers into civilian rank can be rendered neither by human speech, nor human song, nor human music. Here the unbridgeable gap between the abstract and the concrete manifested itself. That has to be experienced. Even the frontiers between the immense joy of self and community lack all separation, all polarization, all estimation. Dream and reality yield to an inextricable whole whose apotheosis is situated between silence and scream. (quoted Horwitz 1991: 166)

Some social scientific disciplines – criminology is said to be one – are labelled as belonging to the 'Humanities'. They have among their functions the task of recounting what it is to be human, additionally to provide scientific analyses of the human condition. Yet for whom are these accounts provided – for the inhabitants of a specific civilised space or set of such spaces, or some general 'humanity'? Moreover, how can scientific discourse do justice to that which is between silence and scream?

Crossing the boundaries of the ordinary and the genocidal: Browning, Goldhagen and Reserve Police Battalion 101

I have asserted as a matter of simple empiricism that there is not a coherent criminology that includes the great crimes of the twentieth century in its domain of facts; they are regarded as the exceptions to which criminology – as the science of the normal operations of state-sponsored control – need not be concerned. In the case of the Holocaust the imagery of the camps helps perpetuate this distance, for surely they were truly exceptional places that could never exist again.

Thus we have a strange irrelevancy. For the camps may be a symbol of the extreme evil of the modern era, but this is an exception beyond our concerns of the normal; they can be dismissed from those disciplines that deal with routine, everyday events and relegated to specialised historical studies.

But we need to face up to what it means to say that the camps are the true state of exception – namely that they were its absolute, methodologically pure, concretisation – they were that which modernity could legitimately produce as its ultimate; all the supporting mechanisms, all the other forms of killing, could or should be comprehended as an all-too-normal business for the state. Yet we also need to understand and interrogate the meaning of this support, of the fact that beyond the camps were the vast supporting processes of normal, routine, means-to-end, activities adapted to the eradication of European Jewry as an end; thus located the camps were only part of the totality. Browning (1998: xv–vi) reminded us that in mid-March 1942, some 75–80 per cent of all victims of the Holocaust were still alive, while 20–25 per cent had perished. A mere 11 months later, in mid-February 1943, the percentages were exactly the reverse. At the core of the Holocaust was a short, intense wave of mass murder centred on Poland: 'a veritable blitzkrieg, a massive offensive requiring the mobilisation of large number of shock troops'. This succeed because at the most basic level individual human beings killed other human beings in face-to-face conditions where there was no escape from the fact that one was looking at other human beings, unarmed, defenceless men, women and children, as one rounded them up, beat them, forced them to dig their own graves and shot them. Scenes that were often recorded producing diary transcripts, official reports and photographs, some official, some deliberately staged so as to present a misleading image,[5] but others, shockingly 'realistic', taken in acts of genocidal tourism.

A few historians have worked with the transference of 'ordinary' persons into the perpetrators of face to face killings. But it was the claim of *Hitler's Willing Executioners: Ordinary Germans and the Holocaust* (1996) – Daniel Goldhagen's international best selling text and recipient of several awards as well as severe academic criticism – that it was not ordinary men who were the perpetrators, instead and specifically, it was *ordinary Germans*. A lot is at stake for criminology, for if Goldhagen's thesis be accepted, and perhaps included as an extended essay in criminology, then contemporary criminology need not concern itself with the Holocaust; it was after all the unique historical product of 'Germans'. Is Goldhagen's work criminological? It applies, for example, some of methodological and explanatory precepts that we can see as central to the emerging strand of cultural criminology. Namely, the methodological injunctions of Jack Katz's *Seductions of Evil* to move to the foreground attractors of crime and the attention to the debris of everyday life as evidence, and culture as the explanatory medium for action. The popular acceptance of Goldhagen's text may reflect the ease with which he asserted particular cultural linkages and utilised cultural evidence; in particular his rendering of the testimony of the members of Reserve Police Battalion 101 and his interpretation of the photographs taken by the members of the battalion. But the reasons for this popular acceptance may be the very reasons for rejecting it as criminology, and conversely, *saving* the Holocaust as suitable material for criminology.

That Goldhagen's work was a publishing sensation may in itself need analysing as it followed closely the data and questions of a well-regarded genocide scholar, namely Christopher Browning's 1992 *Ordinary Men: Reserve Police Battalion 101 and the Final Solution in Poland* (revised edn 1998).

Goldhagen specifically targeted Browning's argument with the subtitle of this work: *Hitler's Willing Executioners: Ordinary Germans and the Holocaust*. Both men analysed the same data, predominantly records of police interviews with members of Reserve Police Battalion 101 conducted in the 1960s

> *when its members finally came under police investigation (several years after World War II) when only a few members were tried and then for reprisal killings – punitive actions – of Polish civilians.*

Ironically, a central member who had refused to join in the killing of Jews but who had participated in what he considered a legitimate action against Polish resistance was executed. Most members had returned to civilian life as ordinary policemen, a fact that may say something about the practices of everyday policing in modern western society *and make a point concerning the continuity of practices before and after the Holocaust*). Reserve Police Battalion 101 was composed mainly of reserve policemen from Hamburg (a noted Social Democratic city and not likely to be especially pro-Nazi) who became immersed in the very non-industrial killing of physically rounding up thousands of Jewish men, women and children and shooting them or herding them into transports to the death-camps. In the period July 1942 to November 1943, the men of this Battalion, totalling at the most 500, rounded up and shot at least 38,000 defenceless Jewish men, women and children and deported at least 45,200 to death-camps. Why did they do this?

Browning gives us a narrative of contingency and existential choice. In the early hours of 13 July 1942, the men were roused from their bunks and assembled before their commanding officer, Major Trapp, a 55-year-old career policeman who, 'pale and nervous, with choking voice and tears in his eyes', informed the battalion that it had been ordered 'to perform a frightfully unpleasant task'. Using the rhetorical myth of Jewish power, he told them that Jewish conspiracy had caused the war and even now 'bombs were falling on women and children' in German towns. The battalion had now been ordered to round up the Jews of the village of Jozefow. The male Jews of working age were to be separated and taken to a work camp. The remaining Jews – the women, children and elderly – were to be shot by the battalion. But he then offered that 'if any of the older men among them did not feel up to the task that lay before him, he could step out'. (1998: 2).

Significantly a few stepped out. There was adverse peer group pressure but it was possible to avoid the action; however, the majority did not choose to avoid. And among the majority who participated some clearly grew to enjoy the task, for this was only to be the first of many similar actions. Once engaged in genocide the individuals found themselves existentially immersed in the physical and gruesome task of killing. These were not men brutalised by war, even if they were to become brutalised by the process. Instead, Browning identifies explanatory factors in group conformity, deference to authority, the impact of alcohol, routinisation and various rationalisations used by the men; however, he concludes, some came to find their calling in killing, for he also tells us of the 'Jew hunt', the search and seeking out operations to locate small pockets of Jews or individual Jews who had somehow escaped from the sweeping operations. 'The Jew hunt was not a brief episode. It was a tenacious, ongoing campaign in which the "hunters" tracked down and killed their "prey" in direct and personal confrontation. It was not a passing phase but an existential condition of constant readiness and intention to kill every last Jew who could be found' (1998: 132). Browning's work was well received by fellow historians, but while reviewed in some 'serious' forms of the popular press, it was not a great commercial success and was only reprinted after the cultural phenomena of reaction to Goldhagen's work that brought greater attention to it. Goldhagen's text became a publishing sensation (over 500,000 copies were sold and it topped the non-fiction list in over 13 countries), and won the author several awards (including the Democracy prize in Germany) as well as being severely academically criticised.

Goldhagen claims two methodological aims. First, he denies the statistical approach ('The Jewish victims were not the "statistics" that they appear to us on paper. To the killers whom they faced, the Jews were people who were breathing one moment and lying lifeless, often before them, the next.'). Second, he seeks to be faithful to 'the horror of what the Germans were doing'. 'Any one in a killing detail who himself shot or who witnessed his comrades shoot Jews was immersed in scenes of unspeakable horror. To present mere clinical descriptions of the killing operations is to misrepresent the phenomenology of killing, to eviscerate the emotional components of the acts and to skew any understanding of them.'[6] Thus:

> I eschew the clinical approach and try to convey the horror, the gruesomeness, of the events for the perpetrators (which, of course, does not mean that they were always horrified). Blood, bone, and brains were flying about, often landing on the killers, smirching their faces and staining their clothes. Cries and wails of people awaiting their imminent slaughter or consumed in death throes reverberated in German ears. Such scenes – not the antiseptic descriptions that mere reportage of a killing operation presents – constituted the reality for many perpetrators. For us to comprehend the perpetrators' phenomenological world, we should describe for ourselves every gruesome image that they beheld, and every cry of anguish and pain that they heard. (1996: 22)

Goldhagen cannot of course present fully 'the horror, the gruesomeness, of the events for the perpetrators', instead he interweaves his interpretation of what it would have been like. The conduct of the Jews to be killed now affords 'each perpetrator an opportunity for reflection'. Thus we read that perpetrators walk 'side by side with [their] victim[s]', and are asked to think in what way did a perpetrator 'imbue the human form beside him with the projections of his mind'. What of the children? These men would likely back in Germany 'walked through woods with their own children by their sides, marching gaily and inquisitively along'. What emotions were now at play as they gazed

> sidelong at the form of, say, an eight- or twelve-year-old girl, who to the unideologized mind would have looked like any other girl? In these moments, each killer had a personalized, face-to-face relationship to his victim, to his little girl. Did he see a little girl, and ask himself why he was about to kill this little, delicate human being who, if seen as a little girl by him, would normally have received his compassion, protection, and nurturance? Or did he see a Jew, a young one, but a Jew nonetheless? Did he wonder incredulously what could possibly justify his blowing a vulnerable little girl's brains out? Or did he understand the reasonableness of the order, the necessity of nipping the believed-in Jewish blight in the bud? The 'Jew-child', after all, was mother to the Jew.

Goldhagen continues:

> The killing itself was a gruesome affair. After the walk through the woods, each of the Germans had to raise his gun to the back of the head, now face down on the ground, that had bobbed along beside him, pull the trigger, and watch the person, sometimes a little girl, twitch and then move no more. The Germans had to remain hardened to the crying of the victims, to the crying of women, to the whimpering of children. At such close range, the Germans often became splattered with human gore. In the words of one man, 'the supplementary shot struck the skull with such force that the entire back of the skull was torn off and blood, bone splinters, and brain matter soiled the marksmen' …. Although this is obviously viscerally unsettling, capable of disturbing even the most hardened of executioners, these German initiates returned to fetch new victims, new little girls, and to begin the journey back into the woods. They sought unstained locations in the woods for each new batch of Jews. (1996: 218)

LaCapra was one who found Goldhagen's methodology questionable.

> Goldhagen employs a rather uncontrolled narrative in which he mingles free indirect style (or Erlebte Rede), direct quotation, rhetorical questions, emotionally manipulative and stereotypical focusing on certain victims (little girls around the age of puberty play a prominent role), and interpolated speculations or projections about feelings seemingly ascribed to perpetrators but coming from a voice or perspective that is not simply their own – indeed, a voice or perspective that equivocates and involves an imputation from some other perspective of what perpetrators must have felt or at times should have felt but perhaps did not feel. Germans are monstrous and beyond the human pale in Goldhagen's account, and their monstrosity is related to the implicit exclamation or rhetorical question conveyed in Goldhagen's prose: How could humans possibly have done this to others, particularly to little girls? (LaCapra 2001: 118–19)

Other critics point out two obvious problems. The lack of previous attempts to bring forward the 'thick lives' of the perpetrators is as much due to lack of material as any reluctance of scholars, with so little material how can one be sure that one is really being faithful to their perspectives? Moreover, in using his material, Goldhagen mixes in his own imaginative effort to recreate the lived events, thus states Birn: 'it is his voice we hear!' (Finkelstein and Birn 1998: 147) Goldhagen (and his academic and popular supporters), however, was insistent that he had achieved a realism that no other scholar had, one which revealed a unique degree of cruelty; this provided the uniqueness of the Holocaust. An assertion, he claimed that was supported by comparative analysis: '… the quantity and quality of personalized brutality and cruelty that the Germans perpetrated upon Jews was … distinctive. This has been highlighted through comparisons with the Germans' treatment of other subject peoples. It could also be demonstrated through comparisons with other genocides and concentration camp systems.'

The art of looking: the role of photographs in Goldhagen's evidence

To repeat some material above to locate Goldhagen's use of the act of looking: he asserts that we need to be involved in the situational ethics and lived reality of the moments of action; we must look at what the perpetrator saw, we must share in the sensory experience of their doings. Perhaps this is the utopia of the historian's dream: to be able to understand fully by transferring oneself into the lived reality of the actors. But does his work result in scholarly naivety or progress?

In his favour Goldhagen helped adjust the (popular) collective imagery of the Holocaust by emphasising the face to face killings of the reserve police battalions and *Einsatzgruppen*, as well as the death marches, thus balancing the emphasis upon the camps and the ghettos.[7] We have a wider set of empirical activities to cover, however, instead of this leading onto claims for even more complex chains of causal factors – both macro and micro – and locating the camps alongside and within this array of activities, Goldhagen reduces, arguing that only a cultural explanation can explain the Holocaust. Goldhagen's text revolves around cultural readings at various levels. He firstly claims – similar to a 'seductions of evil' type of argument – to place the foreground factors as paramount in the lived reality of the events to be explained; he secondly utilises cultural fragments, in particular his own interpretation of perpetrators' experiences and photographs as evidence that links the reader into his arguments; but he thirdly seduces the reader by claiming that Germans exercised a unique degree of cruelty, which he combined with his other arguments to give a singular German causality for a singular phenomenon; thus ultimately offering a mono casual explanation dressed up in cultural terms.

For Goldhagen 'the quantity and quality of personalised brutality and cruelty that the Germans perpetrated upon Jews' was 'distinctive' and 'unprecedented' (p. 386); it 'stood out' in the 'long annals of human barbarism' (p. 414). For ordinary Germans, the killing was an opportunity for 'fun' (p. 231), the majority executed with 'gusto' (p. 241), they 'wanted to be genocidal executioners' (p. 279) and they 'killed for pleasure' (p. 451). Ultimately – he claims – only a deep-seated cultural explanation is believable:

> antisemitism moved many thousands of 'ordinary' Germans – and would have moved millions more, had they been appropriately positioned – to slaughter Jews. Not economic hardship, not the coercive means of a totalitarian state, not social psychological pressure, not invariable psycho-logical propensities, but ideas about Jews that were pervasive in Germany, and had been for decades, induced ordinary Germans to kill unarmed, defenceless Jewish men, women, and children by the thousands, systematically and without pity.

To the rhetorical question 'for what developments would a comprehensive explanation of the Holocaust have to account?' Goldhagen answers that four principal things were necessary: (1) The Nazis – that is, the leadership, specifically Hitler – had to decide to undertake the extermination; (2) They had to gain control over the Jews, namely over the territory in which they resided; (3) They had to organise the extermination and devote to it sufficient resources and (4) They had to induce a large number of people to carry out the killings. Goldhagen's appeal to the reader, as compared to the arguments stressing certain features of modernity (Bauman), the administrative thesis (Hindberg), the banality of evil (Ardent) or multilayered peer group dynamics (Christopher Browning), is his insistence that the Nazis did not have to do much to induce 'ordinary Germans' to participate in the processes.[8] And this conclusion, he asserts, is 'grounded in extensive research on the perpetrators, particularly on their own testimonies as given to the authorities of the Federal

Republic during postwar legal investigations and trials' and in reading the images they themselves created of their actions.

> It is the perpetrators who tell us of their own voluntarism in the slaughter, of their routine brutalities against the helpless Jewish victims, of their degrading and mocking of the Jews. It is they who tell us of their boasting, celebrations, and memorializations of their deeds, not the least of which are the many photographs that they took, passed around, put in their albums, and sent home to loved ones. This record of the perpetrators, their own words and photographs, much of which has never been used before, forms the empirical basis of my book and its conclusions. (1998: 130)

For Goldhagen, the words of the perpetators and the photographs that they took are evidence of his cultural determinants. Goldhagen's account, however, involves a strange disassociation of time. Germans *then*, as perpetrators of the Holocaust, were uniquely able to perform the Holocaust, but Germans *now* are not. He emphasised that the cultural conditions of contemporary Germany means that today's Germans are not the Germans of the Holocaust and neither could they have been us. West Germany, post World War II, rejoined the Western tradition, established liberal democracy – put in place, or had put in place by the occupying forces, political, cultural and structural impediments to anything remotely resembling the Holocaust.[9] Thus he can portray both an image of monstrous behaviours and normalcy, but the monstrous is not related to our normalcy. Their determinism is not ours, nor could it be. Thus, conversely to a situated cultural criminology in which it is humans who are members of a general social entity (humanity) but acting under specific cultural and social conditions who are the perpetrators, the Germans who did the Holocaust are both in culture and in history but outside of culture, outside of history.[10] They are also strangely divorced from the state: for conversely to the criminology that has, obliquely, tried to deal with mass killings, he ignores *authorisation*. He ignores the most basic fact that these men were *ordered*, as part of their state-sanctioned activities, *to participate* (irrespective of whether they could have refused, could have avoided).[11] This omission distorts his evidence.

Photography and looking

> These Germans' willingness to make an extensive photographic record of their deeds, including their killing operations, in which they appear with cheerful and proud demeanors as men entirely comfortable with their environment, their vocation, and with the images that are being preserved, is compelling evidence that they did not conceive of themselves as having been engaged in crime, let alone in one of the greatest crimes of the century.

For Goldhagen, photographs are a crucial evidence and provide a realism that transcends testimony in their immediacy. ('Photographic evidence, as the cliché tells us, often conveys more than do many words of testimony.') He asks us to consider a photograph of a group of German solider surrounding a bearded Jewish man. For Goldhagen:

> The photograph illustrates to us, as it celebrated for the Germans, their active disregard for the dignity of Jews, their denial that Jews possessed dignity. It is an example of the Germans' use of the socially dead Jews as playthings for their own satisfaction.

Goldhagen argues that the 'power of the visual evidence' is aided by words written on the back of the photograph 'giving his ironic commentary on it'. Together they

> represented the absolute mastery of the photographed German over the Jew ... The personal desecration was done, moreover, in front of the camera's recording eye, ensuring that the victim's shame would be displayed to people for years to come. This simple act conveyed unequivocally – to the German, to the Jew, and to all who watched, contemporaneously or later – the virtually limitless power of the shearer over his victim. The act, and its enjoyment by others, bespeaks a mind-set found among 'masters' dealing with the socially dead, particularly during those moments when they mark them physically in order to convey to them that they possess no honour. What better way for a man to display to his children and grandchildren his heroics during the war for the German Volk's survival than to have such a testament?

Goldhagen presents these photographs as if they were intended for the public domain, calling them 'keep-sakes of their work in Poland' and asserts they 'were generously shared among the entire battalion' (Figure 8.1).

> They were not private mementos, furtively taken, guarded, and husbanded by individuals. The affirmative atmosphere that reigned within the battalion regarding their work took on an almost celebratory, festive quality in the public displaying and sharing of the photographs. ... It is as if they were saying: 'Here is a great event. Anyone who wants to preserve for himself images of the heroic accomplishments can order copies.' It is reminiscent of travellers purchasing postcards or asking for duplicates of friends' snapshots that have captured favourite vistas and scenes from an enjoyable and memorable trip.

Elsewhere (Morrison 2004b), I have called these the products of 'genocidal tourism' (in similar fashion Vien Struk 2004 subheads a chapter on Cameras

Figure 8.1 Members of Reserve Police Battalion 101 look smiling at the camera as Jews are forced to undress down to their underwear prior to their being taken into the woods to be shot, source Taffet 1945

in the Ghettos as 'The Ghetto Tourist' to cover the various German soldiers who took cameras into particularly Lodz and Warsaw).

Goldhagen argues that the photos taken by German soldiers and reserve policemen of degrading humiliations and mass executions reveal that the men were not 'frightened, coerced, unwilling, disapproving, or horrified killers of people whom they considered to be innocent'. Instead, many photos 'capture men who look tranquil and happy, and others show them in poses of pride and joy as they undertake their dealings with their Jewish victims. It is difficult to see in the photographs men who viewed the killing to be a crime.' This interpretation may provide a route to fruitful analysis, but Goldhagen does not pursue further the paradoxical nature of this assertion of crime/non-crime.

Instead Goldhagen takes the photographs as refuting Browing's thesis of graduated choices and multilayered peer group pressure.

Figure 8.2 Members of Reserve Police Battalion 101 celebrating Christmas in their barracks. (Credit USHMM 47437, December 25, 1940, Lodz, Poland). To quote Goldhagen: 'In other photographs – taken at a time when the battalion was carrying out killings and deportations – we see officers and their wives sitting outdoors "drinking in what appears to be a convivial atmosphere" with many "evidently having a good time". Another photograph, from Czermierniki some time during the second half of 1942 was even more revealing since it captures more than fifteen men of Lieutenant Oscar Peters' Third Company platoon celebrating. The Germans are holding drinks, grinning broadly and appear to be singing to the accompaniment of violin playing. Hanging on the wall behind them is a hand-lettered ditty which they obviously composed themselves, a play upon the commanders names: "These Germans were celebrating, not cursing, the names of the men who repeatedly sent them to kill Jews. These men – whose lives were then dedicated to mass slaughter, who, in addition to the large company- and battalion-strength killings taking place during this period, were conducting numerous search-and-destroy missions in their own area – were feeling great" '

The perpetrators of the Holocaust took pride in their accomplishments, in their genocidal vocation, to which they were dedicated. They expressed this again and again in their actions, in the endless stream of choices that they made to tread the killing fields – and while they were there. They also expressed this in their words and actions while not on their killing forays. If they had indeed in principle disapproved of the genocide, then why would they have taken obviously approving photographs of their killing operations and their lives while executioners – and then circulate them and permit copies to be made for others?

Thus his central claim:

The German executioners, like other people, consistently made choices about how they would act, choices that consistently produced immense Jewish suffering and mortality. They individually made those choices as contented members of an assenting genocidal community, in which the killing of Jews was normative and often celebrated.

There are other interpretations as to the meaning inscribed in the act of photography: in her analysis of Holocaust photography Struk distinguishes a process of appropriation of the mythical Jew, a product of the 'the propagandists imagination'. In going into occupied Poland and Soviet Union, German troops and police battalions believed they were being confronted with real-life manifestations of the mythical Jew. Thus she suggests (2004: 58–62), against Goldhagen, some of the photographs would have been taken as a means of 'alleviating that [irrational] fear' of the dangers Jews posed. Moreover, Struk reveals how much the imagery of the criminal–normal continuum of 'types' became commonplace: images of Jewish types associated Jews 'with communism, criminal activity and the devil'. The photographs of the humiliations, of the beard cutting, prove that the perpetrators had indeed travelled there, had participated in the activity:

Photographing the enemy was equal to possessing or conquering it. Publicly to humiliate, degrade and possibly to kill the 'real' Jew was metaphorically to destroy the image of the mythical Jew. Taking photographs was an integral part of the humiliation process; in a sense it completed the violation. (Struk 2004: 64)

The photographs showed that real Jews could be dominated, rendered the playthings of Germans, eliminated, the ground cleansed for future German colonisation and occupation. There is some evidence that at least certain quarters wanted images to flow back to the home land. To quote Hans Frank (then Governor of Occupied Poland), speaking in late 1941 to German soldiers in Poland, urging them to write home:

In all these weeks, they [i.e. your families] will be thinking of you, saying to themselves: my God, there he sits in Poland where there are so many lice and Jews, perhaps he is hungry and cold, perhaps he is afraid to write. It would not be a bad idea to send our dear ones back home a picture, and tell them: well now, there are not so many lice and Jews anymore, and conditions here in the General Government have changed and improved somewhat already. Of course, I could not eliminate all lice and Jews in only one year's time. But in the course of time, and above all, if you help me, this end will be attained. After all, it is not necessary for us to accomplish everything within a year and right away, for what would otherwise be left for those who follow us to do? (US Government 1946, Vol II: 633–4)

In the quotations fronting the next chapter Susan Sontang (2002) refers to the large array of images of atrocities we now have, if we want to acknowledge them; Goldhagen, however, appears stunningly ignorant of the existence of this reservoir of data. He claims originality – of his work and for his subject matter – at the cost of withholding recognition of the widespread reality of genocidal activity. Even dealing with German actions he systematically downplays the many other accounts of real feelings, of real letters home as collected in the ironically entitled *The Good Old Days*. Consider the following:

Lemberg, 3 July 1941
On Monday, 30 June 1941 after a sleepless night I volunteered for a number of reasons to join an EK. By 9 o'clock I had heard that I had been accepted. It was not easy for me to leave. Suddenly everything had changed in me. I almost thought I would not be able to tear myself from a certain person. I felt acutely how attached one can become to another human being … .

At 4.00 pm on 2 July 1941 we arrived at Lemberg. First impression: Warsaw harmless in comparison. Shortly after our arrival the first Jews were shot by us. As usual a few of the new officers became megalomaniacs, they really enter into the role wholeheartedly. We took over another military school in the Bolshevik quarter. Here the Russians must have been caught in their sleep.

We quickly gathered together the bare essentials. At midnight after the Jews had cleaned the building, we went to bed.

3 July 1941. This morning I found out that we can write and it looks as though the post will actually be dispatched.

So while listening to wildly sensual music I wrote my first letter to my Trude. While I was writing the letter we were ordered to get ready. EK with steel helmets, carbines, thirty rounds of ammunition. We have just come back. Five hundred Jews were lined up ready to be shot. Beforehand we paid our respects to the murdered German airmen and Ukrainians. Eight hundred people were murdered here in Lemberg. The scum did not even draw the line at children. In the children's home they were nailed to the walls. Some of the occupants of a prison nailed to the wall …. I have little inclination to shoot defenceless people – even if they are only Jews. I would far rather good honest open combat. Now good night, my dear Hasi [Bunny].

It's 11.00 am. Wonderful music, 'Do You Hear My Secret Call' ('Hörst Du mein heimliches Rufen'). How weak can a heart become! My thoughts are so much with the person who caused me to come here. What I wouldn't give to see her for just ten minutes. I was up all of last night on guard duty, in other words kept watch.

A small incident demonstrated to me the fanaticism of these people. One of the Poles tried to put up some resistance. He tried to snatch the carbine out of the hands of one of the men but did not succeed. A few seconds later there was a crack of gunfire and it was all over. A few minutes later after a short interrogation a second one was finished off. I was just taking over the watch when a Kommando reported that just a few streets away from us a guard from the Wehrmacht had been discovered shot dead.

One hour later, at 5 in the morning, a further thirty-two Poles, members of the intelligentsia and Resistance, were shot about two hundred metres from our quarters after they had dug their own grave. One of them simply would not die. The first layer of sand had already been thrown on the first group when a hand emerged from out of the sand, waved and pointed to a place, presumably his heart. A couple more shots rang out, then someone shouted – in fact the Pole himself – 'Shoot faster!' What is a human being?

It looks like we will be getting our first warm meal today. We've all been given 10 RM so that we can buy ourselves a few small necessities. I bought myself a whip costing 2 RM. The stench of corpses is all-pervasive when you pass the burnt-out houses. We pass the time by sleeping.

During the afternoon, some three hundred Jews and Poles were finished off. In the evening we went into town just for an hour. There we saw things that are almost impossible to describe. We drove past a prison. You could already tell from a few streets away that a lot of killing had taken place here. We wanted to go in and visit it but did not have any gas masks with us so it was impossible to enter the rooms in the cellar of the cells. Then we set off back to our quarters. At a street corner we saw some Jews covered in sand from head to foot. We looked at one another. We were all thinking the same thing. These Jews must have crawled out of the grave where the executed are buried. We stopped a Jew who was unsteady on his feet. We were wrong. The Ukrainians had taken some Jews up to the former GPU citadel. These Jews had apparently helped the GPU persecute the Ukrainians and the Germans. They had rounded up 800 Jews there, who were also supposed to be shot by us tomorrow. They have now released them.

We continued going along the road. There were hundreds of Jews walking along the street with blood pouring down their faces, holes in their heads, their hands broken and their eyes hanging out of their sockets. They were covered in blood. Some of them were carrying others who had collapsed. We went to the citadel; there we saw things that few people had ever seen. At the entrance of the citadel there were soldiers standing guard. They were holding clubs as thick as a man's wrists and were lashing out and hitting anyone who crossed their path. The Jews were pouring out of the entrance. There were Jews lying on top of the other like pigs whimpering horribly. The Jews kept streaming out of the citadel completely covered in blood. We stopped and tried to see who was in charge of the Kommando. 'Nobody.' Someone had let the Jews go. They were just being hit out of rage and hatred.

Nothing against that – only they should not let the Jews walk about in such a state. Finally we learnt from the soldiers standing there that they had just visited some comrade of theirs, airmen in fact, in hospital here in Lemberg who had been brutally injured. They'd had their fingernails torn out, ears cut off and also eyes gouged out. This explained their actions: perfectly understandable.

Our work is over for today. Camaraderie is still good for the time being. Crazy, beautiful, sensuous music playing on the radio again and my longing for you, the person who has hurt me so much, is growing and growing. Our only hope is to get away from here – most would prefer to be back in Radom. I for one – like many of the other men – have been disillusioned with this Einsatz. Too little combat in my view, hence this lousy atmosphere.

This is literally horrifying as an account of the civilised killer, who plays music – perhaps therein searching for transcendence in the midst of this profanity, or perhaps the music is simply to forget, or even, most terrifying, a habit – who craves the love of another human, who desires and experiences common emotions. Given the subject matter of this account we are within an abyss; yet to what degree is this account *dissimilar* in its distancing between professional concern and moral gaze from the accounts Darwin gave of his great voyage? Put another way, how *similar* is it to the stories Stanley gave of his voyage through darkest Africa? Against Goldhagen, the editors of the collection this letter appears in (Klee, Dressen and Riess), argue

What kind of men were these who accepted murder as their daily work? They were perfectly ordinary people, with one difference: they could act as members of the 'master race'. They decided whether a person lived or died, they had power. Hitherto undreamt-of chances for promotion revealed themselves. There were pay bonuses, extra leave and privileges such as alcohol and cigarettes. And at all times a sense of power, for the state was happy to remove all sense of personal responsibility for them. (1991: xix)

Ordinary people, not ordinary Germans: ordinary people who were authorised and financed by the state and provided with a mass of legitimating discourses; we have a version of the control-opportunity nexus known to conventional criminology. And the transference of ordinary men (and sometimes women) into joyous killers is also shown in John Dower's (1986) study of the Pacific war, where he relates atrocities conducted by Allied troops, as well as Joanna Bourke's (1999) *Intimate History of Killing*. For Bourke, using accounts of British, Australian and US troops 'throughout this book, "ordinary" men and women have been heard rejoicing as they committed grotesque acts of cruelty': explained in part by 'obedience to the norms of the group' (p. 191), processes in training that induce racism, encouraged 'the actions of the morally detached' (p. 373); and beyond this the contextual fact of their being representatives of a 'society that promoted aggression'. (p. 368)

What of Goldhagen's other claim: that of the absolute unique nature of the cruelty imposed?

Nanjing and Japanese atrocities: the forgotten cruelty of a supposed comparative work

> It is estimated the more than 20 million Chinese died in the second Sino-Japanese war (1937–45), victims of various atrocities by the Japanese troops, including mass murder and random killings, chemical ad biological warfare, live experiments on human bodies, selling of opium and other drugs, and forced labour. Despite this fact, many Japanese today do not have a conscious memory of these historical facts of victimisation. (Tokushi 2002: 83)

There are a variety of reasons why Japanese atrocities during the campaigns in China, Asia and the Pacific do not enter into the historical memory in any way similar to German behaviour; one, simply put, is a variety of racism where Japanese cruelty is seen as less remarkable and less remarked upon as it was not the behaviour of such a civilised country as Germany, one of the centres of European civilisation.[12] There is however, little excuse for either Goldhagen – or the committee that awarded him his Phd in 'comparative political science', or his publishers, or many of the commentators who lavished praise upon his work – to accept – explicitly or implicitly – the argument that it was the level of cruelty of these 'ordinary Germans' that made the Holocaust unique. Goldhagen's comparative work is remarkable for its lack of comparative analysis or seeming knowledge of photographs and perpetrators' accounts from other cases of state-sanctioned mass killings, rapes and lootings.

> One way in which the Japanese fascists overshadowed their German counterparts in massacre was the abnormal enjoyment they derived from the killing. New tricks for killing the innocent gave them great satisfaction. (Young and Yin 1999: . further quotes in this section from same volume).

The words come from a large collection of photographs and text that makes a similar claim to Goldhagen. Again we have a cultural explanation and claims to show the intimate details of the cruelty of the Japanese soldiers in what Iris Chang called 'the Forgotten Holocaust of World War II'. We are given a narrative of man-made hell and presented with scenes aptly described as pornographic. Accounts of instances of great cruelty, of playing with civilians, young and old, before killing them; stories of burning alive, images of mass burials of live civilians before appreciative audiences of Japanese troops sit with chronicles of rapes and simple gratuitous cruelty.

> The Japanese military believed there were valuables hidden in a manure pit at Nanking's Eastern Kangtuo. They gathered more than thirty refugees and forced them into the pit, on a bitterly cold December day, to retrieve the valuables. Those who hesitated were shot on the spot. By the time the Japanese soldiers walked away, laughing and applauding, half of the refugees had been shot; the others had frozen to death in the pit.

And we have again the tactic of recounting events through the letters and photographs that were sent home by the Japanese soldiers. One example, taken from a diary found in 1984 at a peasant's home in Kitagou Village of Miyazaki County, Japan. The soldier, once a corporal, belonged to the 23rd Regiment of the 18th Division. (Asahi Shimbun, published part of his diary later that year).[13] The entry for 15, December 1937, reads:

> … we were very bored, we had some fun killing Chinese. We caught some innocent Chinese and either buried them alive, or pushed them into a fire, or beat them to death with clubs, or killed them by other cruel means …. [On 21 December] Today we did it again. We pushed innocent Chinese down and beat them up. When they were half dead, we pushed them into ditches and burned them, torturing them to death. Everyone gets his entertainment this way to get rid of the boredom. If this had happened in Japan, it would be an enormous incident. But here it's like killing dogs and cats.

Versions of the killings were published in the Japanese newspapers with glee. The outstanding example is the 'killing contest'. Photographs of two smiling Japanese officers were published by the Nichi Nichi Shimbun on 13 December 1937. The story was headlined: CONTEST TO KILL FIRST 100 CHINESE WITH SWORD EXTENDED WHEN BOTH FIGHTERS EXCEED MARK – MUKAI SCORES 106 AND NODA 105.

The newspaper did not clearly state that the Chinese killed were bound and defenceless prisoners or civilians. Indeed it made it appear as if military action was still proceeding.

> Sub-lieutenant Toshiaki MUKAI and Sub-lieutenant Takeshi NODA belonged to the Japanese army 16th Division. They started their contest from the west side of ju Rong, a town to the east of Nanking. On the same day December 12, MUKAI killed 89 people, while NODA felled 7 cavalry Next day when they arrived at the foot of the Zijin Mountain, MUKAI'S sword was partially damaged – he split a Chinese soldier in two, together with his helmet. Said MUKAI: 'That's a piece of cake.'[14]

The Young and Yin edited collection contains numerous photographs of beheadings by Japanese troops in front of appreciative audiences. The text 'explains' that Japanese soldiers dwelled with great relish upon the sword as a weapon and as a bushido spiritual symbol: 'This fanaticism was no doubt inculcated by the military culture from the day a man became a soldier.' Various perpetrators' accounts are included of the mass execution of captured soldiers and, in the confusion, many civilians.

Hiroki KAWANO, a former military photographer, related a more detailed account of the beheading of Chinese victims:

> I've seen all kinds of horrible scenes … headless corpses of children lying on the ground. They even made the prisoners dig a hole and kneel in front of it before being beheaded. Some soldiers were so skillful that they took care of the business in a way that severed the

head completely but left it hanging by a thin layer of skin on the victim's chest, so that the weight pulled the body down to the ditch. I captured that blink of a moment with my camera.

The text contains many photographs of another way of face to face killing – bayoneting. Thousands of Chinese were killed with 15-inch bayonets affixed to rifles. Live-bound captives were targets for bayonet drills. Sometimes the captive is blindfolded but often not. The Japanese historian Daikichi Shikikawa depicts one scene where Chinese prisoners were

> gathered at the city's open square and bound with wires into several columns. They were escorted to the walls on the river bank. One column was pulled out first and used as bayonet drill targets. The ones who were still alive after the bayoneting were finished off by being doused with gasoline and burned.

Kazuo Sone wrote in his *A Japanese Soldier's Confession*:

> To boost the morale and courage of new recruits during the war, we experimented with bayoneting the enemy. That meant using POWs or local civilians as live targets. New recruits without any battle experience would learn from this practice. It was unlucky for the people selected as targets, but it was also a painful experience for the new soldiers forced to participate in this experiment. …
>
> This kind of killing experience was every soldier's test and ordeal. After this they would be fearless in real battle, and would glory in the act of killing. War made people cruel, bestial, and insane. It was an abyss of inhuman crimes.

Shiro Asuma, a former soldier of the Japanese 16th Division, recounted:

> An old man who I think was a grandfather was holding onto his grandson. I killed the child while they were hugging. The boy was about 10 years old. And then the blood came out [after ASUMA'S thrust of his bayonet]. The grandfather started to suck the blood. When I saw this, I thought it was so cruel. In trying to resuscitate the dying child's life, the grandfather looked so pitiful. Still, I stabbed and killed the grandfather.

If Goldhagen had actually wanted to pursue the 'comparative' method that he stated he saw as proof of his claims to the uniqueness of the German cruelty he would also find material of the introduction of killing to untried Japanese soldiers. Here he can find accounts of learning to behead, learning to bayonet bound and defenceless prisoners. And if some found that 'the scene was so appalling that I felt I couldn't breathe', others were able to self-analyse. One, ordered to participate in killing practice related:

> I raised my bayoneted gun with trembling hands, and – directed by the lieutenant's almost hysterical cursing – I walked slowly towards the terror-stricken Chinese standing beside the pit – the grave he had helped to dig. In my heart, I begged his pardon, and – with my eyes shut and the lieutenant's curses in my ears – I plunged the bayonet into the petrified Chinese.
>
> When I opened my eyes again, he had slumped down into the pit. 'Murderer and Criminal!' I called myself.

For some, how many we do not know, enjoyment followed:

> I remember being driven in a truck along a path that had been cleared through piles of thousands and thousands of slaughtered bodies. Wild dogs were gnawing at the dead flesh as we stopped and pulled a group of Chinese prisoners out of the back. Then the Japanese officer proposed a test of my courage. He unsheathed his sword, spat on it, and with a sudden mighty swing he brought it down on the neck of a Chinese boy cowering before us. The head was cut dean off and tumbled away on the group as the body slumped

forward, blood spurting in two great gushing fountains from the neck. The officer suggested I take the head home as a souvenir. I remember smiling proudly as I took his sword and began killing people.

Then there are the many photographs of victims of rapes, the forced poses, the tied women and the dead with bamboo inserted into their vaginas. What does one make of the fact that these photographs were often confiscated from captured Japanese soldiers who had kept them as mementoes? Must we replay the argument between ordinary men and ordinary (Germans/Japanese ... [insert specific identity])? How can we be so sure that this is truly extraordinary, beyond our concerns?

The existential moment, turning the ordinary into the exceptional

Against Goldhagen's narrow concerns, Horwitz's study of Mauthausen, a second generation SS concentration camp that provided material for the Nazi construction projects gives material to show how 'everyone' could be turned into 'a potential executioner' (Horwitz 1991: 143). The main camp, Mauthausen, was built near Linz in Upper Austria, hard by a granite quarry. The base camp was operated by the SS who used concentration camp inmates as a ready supply of slave labour. In time Mauthausen expanded to comprise a network of some 49 satellite camps extending across the length and breadth of pre-war Austrian territory. Horwitz, similarly is concerned not to bypass the 'enormity' and 'horror' of 'crimes of unprecedented nature and magnitude' that occurred in the concentration camp network but he is also at pains to note that 'these crimes involved widespread complicity and were known in the major capitals of the world' (p. 4). Yet if that was to throw the web of complicity too far, he emphasises that every camp had civilian communities in the immediate vicinity. How then did Mauthausen operate so successfully in the civilised space of Austria?

This was a place of horror for its inmates, whose number rose to a peak of 84,500 in March 1945 with an inmate mortality rate of 58 per cent for 1941 (compared with 36 per cent at Dachau or 19 per cent at Buchenwald). From mid-1942 for at least a year, a gas van exterminated 30 victims at a time on a 3-mile route between Mauthausen to Guesen. Loaded on at one place, the corpses were unloaded for the crematorium at the other. In this way 1,900 to 2,800 were disposed of in addition to an estimated 4,000 in a 19-square yard, 8-foot high gas chamber developed at Mauthausen operating on Jews from May 1942 to April 1945 in groups of 65–70. The chamber had first been tested with rats in April 1942, then 200 Soviet prisoners of war.

Cruelty was ever present in the labour operations; SS men perched 'like gargoyles on the eaves of a cathedral' around the rim of the quarry, hurled prisoners off to raucous cries of 'Attention! Parachutists!' Others encouraged prisoners to go beyond the wire to pick fruits, shooting these 'raspberry picker details' for amusement.

Horwitz draws lines of connection between the camp system and everyday life in the surrounding towns, villages and farms. Land was leased to make room for the camp – people moved in and out providing labour, skills and supplies. Knowledge of the situation was widespread and he has many stories of interactions, including the SS beating prisoners at the railway station, casually shooting them in sight of nearby farmhouses, then recounting stories of their actions when drunk in pubs and bars as they attempt pick up lines with local girls which repeat those of the Japanese accounts such as: 'Today I killed two inmates ... I chased both of them into a pit of liquid manure, threw a crate over them, and stood on top of it until they drowned.'

There were some actions of assistance including dropping illicit food or even the simple act of looking with sympathy upon the Jewish captives; but the actions taken by the locals when 400 inmates escaped from the camp surpass even the normal comprehension of a jaded genocide reader. The local population far exceeded the SS in the savagery with which it tracked these fugitives down, shooting and clubbing them to death. Sanctions were for those (very few) who hid escapees, not for those who did nothing to help or hinder their escape. A local police chief recorded: 'How brutal were our people then. At close range they shot at the poor beings kneeling before them, and then observed with satisfaction their last shudders. Yes they boasted publicly of their deeds, heedless that their children listened to them in astonishment. In their stupidity many became murderers, and the just Judge of all things will know of it; but many fell victim to the intoxication of blood; the slumbering demon inside them broke forth and transformed them into beasts.'

> For the desperate 400 souls, bursting the cordon proved a life-affirming, if not ultimately a life-protecting, endeavor. Their drive beyond the wall was an expression of defiance in the face of certain death, and a reaching outward toward life. The inmates all escaped in the faint hope that the townsfolk would not simply stand aside but stand by them, nourish them, assist them in their flight. To the contrary, most of the citizenry rejected their pleas, drew up new cordons round their homesteads, and lowered their nets upon all save a very few. In their barns, farmers poked through the hay anxious to discover something live and trembling on the ends of their pitchforks. Captured, the inmates knew they had in fact never escaped the boundaries of Mauthausen. In giving chase to the fugitives, the citizenry made the camp coextensive with their own world.

> For a moment, the barriers had fallen. The inmates were no longer strictly confined but were dispersed. They penetrated the forests, the meadows, the market places, the barns, and the kitchens. The citizenry feared the inmates as a foreign and tainted presence in their midst. The official description of the prisoners as hardened criminals reinforced public fears that something safely confined had burst its bonds and now stalked the neighborhood. Yet, the popular designation of the fugitives as 'rabbits' offers a clue to a contrasting image that lodged in the mind of the citizenry. Rabbits are wily, elusive, yet ultimately meek and defenseless prey. Images of the hardened criminal escaped from a penitentiary overlapped with those of an amusing and harmless catch, offering the prospect of a sporting chase.

> And chase they did. Many responded to the challenge with zeal. They demonstrated initiative and resourcefulness in carrying out the order to root the fugitives from their hideouts. This was a release. Gladly they waded in, smearing themselves in blood. The SS offered the average citizen an opportunity to violate the most ancient of taboos: the killing of one's fellow man. In leaping the bounds of the camp, the inmates paradoxically afforded the onlookers an opportunity to transgress those same moral restraints they had for seven years witnessed the SS violate. Temptation gave way to intoxication. Such recklessness is embodied in the German word Rausch, 'something that just took hold', an unleashing of the senses, a drunken

madness, an unbridled surge of feeling in which 'one loses all hold on things and on reality'. (Horwitz 1991: 142–3)

Browning's account had put the German members of Battalion 101 in a position of choice and a path of increasing immersion in the existential dynamics of killing, what of the Jewish choices? As a narrative of ghetto complicity we have a story of original ambiguity but increasing knowledge of his role in the apparatus of killing provided by Calel Perechodnik, a 27-year-old French-educated engineer, from a well-to-do Jewish family. In early 1941 he joined the Jewish police in the Otwock ghetto near Warsaw in order to save the lives of his wife, small daughter and himself. Whatever his intentions, he was to be a pawn in the German strategies of enticing Jewish cooperation in their own destruction. In a context of acute angst and confusion in his reading and misreading German intentions, he was to help take his wife and child to the trains to the concentration camps and gain for himself only a pushing off of death.[15] Ultimately he died in the 1944 Warsaw Uprising already weaken by typhus. Towards the end, during a 105-day period spent hiding in 'Polish' Warsaw, Perechodnik wrote his *History of a Jewish Family during German Occupation*, which was published in Poland in 1993 under the title *Am I a Murderer?* This text disturbs categorisation in its ambivalence – it is confession, chronicle and diary. Here the easy story of Goldhagen is lost, for in this instance we have one of the few surviving testimonies of a widely despised group of people; but reading this account, moral judgment concerning such individuals becomes contingent, the circumstances are an existential hell and no one is to be trusted.

Perechodnik was a member of the Jewish Police, a crucial part of the array of support; others, as noted in the introduction, were members of the Kapos (*sonderkommandos*), the Jewish fellow-prisoners who performed the tasks for the SS in the camps for tragically 'the discipline which destroyed [the inmates] as sentient beings was largely in the hands of prisoners' (Clendinnen 1999: 36). Ultimately Goldhagen shows his reluctance to understand; for having defined a 'perpetrator' in broad fashion to include anyone who 'worked in an institution that was part of the system of brutal, lethal domination, a system that had as its apogee the institutions of direct mass slaughter ... for he knew that by his actions he was sustaining institutions of genocidal killing' (1996: 165), he excludes the very groups that did so much to destroy the self-esteem of the Jewish persons within their grasp (Levi 1987) and who by their very nature could not have been part of an eliminationist anti-Semitism culture, their being after all Jewish.[16]

There is much comparative material for the specifics of crossing the boundary from the normal to the exceptional. There are however, for all the inhuman weighing and comparing that it appears to entail, forms and practices to distinguish. There *is* much to be said for the Japanese explanation that the cruelty visited upon the victims by their troops was not by design, was not an essential part of a state-sponsored process, neither was it a means to an officially sanctioned end (the controversy occasioned by the death sentence being given and carried out on General Yamashita in respect of the massacres and other cruelties in the Philippines reflects this). There is an array of massacres, of cruelty, of tortures, of humiliations, of incredible degradations – there are the medical experiments, there is the germ and chemical warfare; but not the wholesale adoption of bio-power, not the state legitimating the internalisation of colonial methodology. (Can there be a paradox? Could the Tokyo tribunal's decision as to the atrocities be more logical as a reflection of the reality of war crimes than anything connected with the Holocaust as dealt with the IMT Nuremberg?)

Neither the cruelty that the perpetrators are described as carrying out nor the numbers of Germans implicated makes for the uniqueness of the Holocaust. Goldhagen cannot disprove that ordinary persons, normal humanity, could not be involved, he cannot prove the absolute ownership of the Holocaust by Germans as Hitler's willing executioners; he cannot put the Holocaust into a neat box, not logically, no matter how far he succeeded in doing that very localisation for the satisfaction of a mass readership who consumed his text as a story from another place, another time, and another set of Germans (read not ours). Conversely, it is much more shocking to assert that Germany, as the bearer of a legitimate government, one that was accepted internationally, pursued a radical policy of bio-power that included the systematic elimination of Jews, was the necessary component for the Holocaust. Germans mostly, but clearly not solely, carried it out; but this does not mark Germany, or Germans, off from the Enlightenment only returned to the correct path after World War II. For not only are the Holocaust and Japanese atrocities linked in ways indicated in chapter 7, but there was no such over-determining thing as the Enlightenment that set the structural norms for the development of the west or western societies. There have been many contingencies, the number of could-have-been immense; the number of might-still-be depressing.

Contingencies of seeing: between pornography and common humanity

Goldhagen's insistence on giving his interpretive recounting of the lived dynamics of the situation shocked many (and certainly contributed to his popular success). Dan Diner remarked on the aesthetic richness of the portrayal: 'He describes the cruelties of the perpetrators in all of their opulence'. For Ulrich Raulff, Goldhagen arranged the 'aesthetic of a horror film' that linked pornography with atrocity and his text was a 'step into the horror business' (*Frankfurter Allgemeine Zeitung*, 16 August 1996). Michael Bodeman agreed that 'this is pornography', since in trying to present the perpetrator's perspective, it brings out the 'pleasure derived from murder and torture' in a 'voyeuristic narration'.

'Pornography' here was not used as a descriptive sense alone but prescriptive, as a term of criticism. However, Steiner (1971: 54–5) comes closer to another understanding when he says of the camps that we found 'the technology of pain without meaning, of bestiality without end, of gratuitous terror … In the camps the millenary pornography of fear and vengeance cultivated in the Western mind by Christian doctrines of damnation was realised'. This Hell has a distorted and mythological link to justice; for even the Nazi ideology of scientific cleansing was infused with what Camus called a

Figure 8.3 Another image, said to be of the attempt to make soap from Jewish bodies: source Taffet, (1945). The camps processed out of sight, buttressed by an array of bureaucratic measures that did not speak the language of human dealing; thus the dehumanising, the essence of human life is closed off from man ... what sort of power is herein exercised, listen to Rudolf Hoss, Commandant of Auschwitz (1959: 171–3):

> I had to see everything. I had to watch hour after hour, by day and by night, the removal and burning of the bodies, the extraction of the teeth, the cutting of the hair, the whole grisly, interminable business. I had to stand for hours on end in the ghastly stench, while the mass graves were being opened and the bodies dragged out and burned.
>
> I had to look through the peephole of the gas chambers and watch the process of death itself, because the doctors wanted me to see it. I had to do all this because I was the one to whom everyone looked, because I had to show them all that I did not merely issue the orders and make the regulations but was also prepared myself to be present at whatever task I had assigned to my subordinates.
>
> The Reichsfuhrer SS sent various high-ranking Party leaders and SS officers to Auschwitz so that they might see for themselves the process of extermination of the Jews. They were all deeply impressed by what they saw. Some who had previously spoken most loudly about the necessity for this extermination fell silent once they had actually seen the "final solution of the Jewish question". I was repeatedly asked how I and my men could go on watching these operations, and how we were able to stand it.
>
> My invariable answer was that the iron determination with which we must carry out Hitler's orders could only be obtained by a stifling of all humans [sic] emotions. Each of these gentlemen declared that he was glad the job had not been given to him. .... This was one job which nobody envied me.
>
> I had many detailed discussions with Eichmann concerning all matters connected with the "final solution of the Jewish question", but without ever disclosing my inner anxieties. I tried in every way to discover Eichmann's innermost and real convictions about this "solution". Yes, every way. Yet even when we were quite alone together and the drink had been flowing freely so that he was in his most expansive mood, he showed that he was completely obsessed with the idea of destroying every single Jew that he could lay his hands on. Without pity and in cold blood we must complete this

'metaphysical revolt' against the conditions of human existence. The pornographic reigns through control, through the reestablishing of the terms of human interaction in which the other is dehumanised, rendered into the objects of the desire of power, of the rendering down of the humanity of the other. The Holocaust was the deepest pornography. The unclean are to be eliminated, the social body made pure; but the rendering down of Jewish bodies in an attempt to create soap escapes even the deepest pornography. The ultimate symbol in exchange value, in the co-modification of life, in the excess of the state's control over death, of globalisation: if the world would not accept live Jewish bodies as refugees, would they have accepted processed Jewish bodies as soap?

What of this production? Three images survive; we do not know under what conditions they were taken. Were they snapshots in the sense Erich Fromm once gave us[17], a substitute for seeing, or were they attempts to capture the indiscernible? The terrible reality of the state's immense power in the consumption of human life? This is a power that cannot speak its name. It is as if it was ashamed of its very existence. Let us contrast this image with those of the great exercise of sovereign power in the ancient regime as depicted in the very public torture and execution of Damiens.

With Damiens, sovereignty is not afraid to display itself; death is the occasion in which the sovereign's absolute power shone most clearly. The mechanism of death and the instruments of torture are very human in their calculated excess

extermination as rapidly as possible. Any compromise, even the slightest, would have to be paid for bitterly at a later date.

In the face of such grim determination I was forced to bury all my human considerations as deeply as possible. Indeed, I must freely confess that after these conversations with Eichmann I almost came to regard such emotions as a betrayal of the Fuhrer. There was no escape for me from this dilemma.

I had to go on with this process of extermination. I had to continue this mass murder and coldly to watch it, without regard for the doubts that were seething deep inside me. I had to observe every happening with a cold indifference. Even those petty incidents that others might not notice I found hard to forget. In Auschwitz I truly had no reason to complain that I was bored. If I was deeply affected by some incident, I found it impossible to go back to my home and my family. I would mount my horse and ride, until I had chased the terrible picture away. Often, at night, I would walk through the stables and seek relief among my beloved animals. It would often happen, when at home, that my thoughts suddenly turned to incidents that had occurred during the extermination. I then had to go out. I could no longer bear to be in my homely family circle.

When I saw my children happily playing, or observed my wife's delight over our youngest, the thought would often come to me: how long will our happiness last? My wife could never understand these gloomy moods of mine, and ascribed them to some annoyance connected with my work. When at night I stood out there beside the transports or by the gas chambers or the fires, I was often compelled to think of my wife and children, without, however, allowing myself to connect them closely with all that was happening. It was the same with the married men who worked in the crematoriums or at the fire pits. When they saw the women and children going into the gas chambers, their thoughts instinctively turned to their own families.

I was no longer happy in Auschwitz once the mass exterminations had begun. I had become dissatisfied with myself. To this must be added that I was worried because of anxiety about my principal task, the never-ending work, and the untrustworthiness of my colleagues.' contrast to Figure 8.4. (the execution of Damiens)

LE SUPPLICE DE DAMIENS

Figure 8.4 A state-sponsored etching of the public execution of Damiens in Paris, 1757 (image: MEPL)

The execution of Damiens was the ultimate point of public display of the power to punish, of combining guilt and horror, for the ancient regime.

Public executions took on a particular ritual: 'The day and hour set for the execution were cried throughout the streets, printed accounts of the trial were hawked by street-urchins. In this tumultuous and often passionately moved mass, women and children were not those less impatient. Each followed *avec ardeur* all the dramatic points of the execution which often lasted more than an hour.

The executioner, surrounded by his servants, bore the expression of a *seigneur* on display; he was barbered and powdered, clothed in white silk and looked about very proudly. His every movement was closely watched' (Bloch 1946: 68).

Damiens experienced a particular horror:

At half past four that dreadful spectacle began. In the middle of court was a low platform upon which the victim, who showed neither fear nor wonder, but asked only for a quick death, was bound fast with iron rings by the six executioners so that his body was completely bound. Thereupon his right hand was extended and was placed in a sulphurous fire; he let loose a dreadful outcry. According to Manselet, while his hair was burning, they stood on end. Thereupon his body was again attacked with glowing t[h]ongs and pieces of flesh were ripped from his bosom, thighs and other parts; molten lead and boiling oil were again spilled on the fresh wounds, the resulting stench (declared Richelieu in his *Memoirs*), infected the air of the entire court. Then four horses on the four sides of the platforms pulled hard on the heavy cables bound to his arms, shoulders, hands and feet. The horses were spurred that they might pull the victim apart. But they were unused to acting as the handmaids of executioners. For more than a[n] hour they were beaten to strain away so that they might tear off the legs or arms of the victim. Only the wailing cries of pain informed the "prodigious number of spectators" of the unbelievable sufferings that a human creature had to endure. The horses now increased to six, were whipped and forced to jerk away at the cables. The cries of Damiens increased to a maniacal roaring. And again the horses failed. Finally the executioner received permission from the judges to lighten the horrible task of the horses by cutting off the chains. First the hips were freed. The victim "turned his head to see what was happening", he did not cry but only turned close to the crucifix, which was held out to him and kissed it while the two father-confessors spoke to him. At last after one and one-half hours of this "unparalleled suffering" the left leg was torn off. *The people clapped their hands in applause while the* victim betrayed only "curiosity and indifference". But when the other leg was torn off he started anew his wailing. After the chains on his shoulders had been cut off his right arm was the first to go. His cries became weaker and his head began to totter. When the left arm was ripped off the head fell backwards. So there was only left a trembling rump that was still alive and head whose hair had suddenly become white. *He still lived!* As the head was cut off and his legs and hands collected and dropped into a basket the father-confessors stepped up to the *remainder* of Damiens. But Henry Sanson, the executioner, held them back and told them that Damiens had just drawn his last breath. "The fact is" wrote trustworthy Retif, "that many saw the body still move about and the lower jaw move up and down as if he wanted to speak". The rump still breathed! His eyes turned to spectators. It is not reported if the people clapped their hands a second time. At any rate during the length of the entire execution none moved from their places in the court or from the windows of adjoining buildings. The remainder of this martyr was burnt at a stake and the ashes strewn to the four winds. "Such was the end of that poor unfortunate who it may well be believed – suffered the greatest tortures that a human being has ever been called upon to endure".' (The account of The Duke de Croy, an eyewitness, quoted in Bloch 1946: 69) The audience had come from around France and even some, including Casanova (who commented, with some jealously, that two of his companions were 'busily engaged' achieving sexual satisfaction while watching the spectacle) from neighbouring countries.

Perhaps nobody has better expressed a holistic role for the executioner than the French philosophical writer Joseph de Maistre.[18] De Maistre held that the rationalist notion of the individual desiring subject was a recipe for existential disaster and political chaos. Man must belong, must surrender to a metaphysical totality. The Enlightenment ideals of reason, benevolence, belief in goodness, and the idea of progress, were illusionary images at odds with the dependant and created nature of man. The spectacle of punishment provided a bridge between the local and the universal/eternal. Violence (in all its guises such as disease, plague, war and famine) was inevitable in the universe, part of the problems included in the 'Divine Plan', or fate of the world. Men are inherently neither good nor perfectible, but subjects of original sin. Because of Adam and Eve's sinful actions in the Garden of Eden in Heaven and their eventual expulsion by God (as outlined in the Old Testament in the Bible), all men coming after them would be born bad and sinful.

De Maistre argued authority was imposed from above, extending all the way to the Christian Kingdom of Heaven and its ruler, God. Thus, the exercise of authority must justifiably be absolute, despotic and inevitably hierarchical. There could be no society without government, no government without sovereignty and no sovereignty without infallibility (incapability of political or social error). Therefore, social contracts and constitutions were unimportant, because both implied a creativity and independence in man that was not existent. The spectacle of the power to punish is the central element in affirming the social bond and the despised figure of the executioner was the figure on which society depended. The executioner was hated, but he was the very pinnacle of society for maintaining order and fear in the public mind, thereby enforcing discipline and respect towards authority. Executioners were 'instruments of God' who fulfilled the need for social dominance, and were therefore the source of all sovereignty. The writing is powerfully evocative:

> Wishing men to be governed by men at least in their external actions, God has given sovereigns the supreme prerogative of punishing crimes, in which above all they are his representatives …
>
> This formidable prerogative … results in the necessary existence of a man destined to inflict on criminals the punishments awarded by human justice …
>
> Who is this inexplicable being who has preferred to all the pleasant, lucrative, honest, and even honourable jobs that present themselves in hundreds to human power and dexterity that of torturing and putting to death his fellow creatures? Are this head and this heart made like ours? Do they not hold something peculiar and foreign to our nature? For my own part, I do not doubt this. He is made like us externally; he is born like us but he is an extraordinary being, and for him to exist in the human family a particular decree – a *fiat* of the creative power is necessary. He is a species to himself.
>
> Look at the place he holds in public opinion and see if you can understand how he can ignore or affront this opinion! Scarcely have the authorities fixed his dwelling-place, scarcely has he taken possession of it, than the other houses seem to shrink back until they no longer overlook his. In the midst of this solitude and this kind of vacuum that forms around him, he lives alone with his woman and his offspring who make the human voice known to him, for without them he would know only groans. A dismal signal is given; a minor judicial official comes to his house to warn him that he is needed; he leaves; he arrives at some public place packed with a dense and throbbing crowd. A poisoner, a parricide, or a blasphemer, is thrown to him; he seizes him, he stretches him on the ground, he ties him to a horizontal cross, he raises it up: then a dreadful silence falls, and nothing can be heard except the crack of bones breaking under the crossbar and the howls of the victim. He unfastens him; he carries him to a wheel: the shattered limbs interweave with the spokes; the head falls; the hair stands on end, and the mouth, open like a furnace, gives out spasmodically only a few blood-spattered words calling for death to come. He is finished: his heart mutters, but it is with joy; he congratulates himself, he says sincerely. No one can break men on the wheel better than I. He steps down; he stretches out his blood-stained hand, and Justice throws into it from a distance a few pieces of gold which he carries through a double row of men drawing back with horror. He sits down to a meal and eats; then to bed, where he sleeps. And next day, on

waking, he thinks of anything other than what he did the day before. Is this a man? Yes: God receives him in his temples and permits him to pray. He is not a criminal, yet it is impossible to say, for example, that he is virtuous, that he is an honest man, that he is estimable, and so on. No moral praise can be appropriate for him, since this assumes relationships with men, and he has none.

> And yet all grandeur, all power, all subordination rests on the executioner: he is the horror and the bond of human association. Remove this incomprehensible agent from the world, and at that very moment order gives way to chaos, thrones topple, and society disappears. God, who is the author of sovereignty, is the author also of chastisement …
> … The sword of justice has no scabbard; it must always threaten or strike. (De Maistre 1971: 191–3)

The visibility of the punishment is a conduit spanning the temporal and the divine. The spectacle is a necessary appeal to emotion and prejudice; it expresses the religious basis of institutions and the hierarchical order. In turn, the state requires these ceremonies of the order of things to remain healthy.

but they also reach out in an act of bridging a totality, partaking ritualistically in a created and interactive universe. Contrast to the attempted rendering of Jewish bodies into soap. Here death eludes display, is transformed into something to be hidden. What form of power is this that can dream of manufacturing soap from the bodies of Jews? Agamben (2002: 71–2) opinions: '… it is no longer possible truly to speak of death, that which took place in the camps was not death, but rather something infinitely more appalling. …. People did not die; rather, corpses were produced. Corpses without death, non-humans whose decease is debased into a matter of serial production'.

Yet this was law, it was in the name of the state: but it was a law that was afraid to assert, in the view of its practioners, its totality. Only by the action of the photographer can we experience the incandescence of a light showing the state's power, a light that captures and holds while the light of the fires of the ovens tries to extinguish knowledge. But is it the severity of the state revealed in this image that should make us tremble? Not that alone: for behind the state lay human desire, willing and willingness. It is causality for the severity of this will, of the totality, the calculation of the many acts of willing and willingness, that Goldhagen mistakenly tries to find it's secrete in the tired formula of anti-Semiticism. His monocausality is a weak reflection of the Nazis claims of legitimation in their narrative of social–historical totality, a narrative of totality that captures willing, and following Quetelet turns it into a matter of a social budget. Should we blame the claim of totality itself? Perhaps as Leyotard asserted, we are better off without it – but we cannot, some conception of totality is required. But this totality cannot be rigidly structured: certainly we cannot put ethics, or morality, within the same sphere as ontology. Against the heritage of Quetelet, Lombroso and positional ethics, morality should be considered as *outwith*.

Emmanuel Levinas tried to portray the ethical in the form of a narrative: that, similar to Plato, in encounter. By contrast to Plato's tale, however, Levinas finds not enlightenment by reference to the good but intrigue. 'Intrigue': morality without creating a moral system. Ethics, according to Levinas, is neither a sovereign good nor an immediate given that comes from knowing the difference between right or wrong; it displays itself in an event. Something must happen to me in order for me to stop being a 'force that continues on its way' and wake up instead to pangs of conscience. This dramatic event is not an encounter with reality made visible by the sun, but the other, or more precisely, the revelation of the other's face.

Yet there is more to this than a calling to recognise common humanity, for as Levi (1986: 202) said of those who manned the camps: 'They had our faces'. There are no logical rules for encounter; it is not an act of being taken to enlightenment, not an unmasking of reality. There is an existential instability of all accounts to impose determination: Javier Cercas tries to take us there in his *Soldiers of Salamis*. Therein he recounts his attempts to write the story of the survival of Rafael Sanchez Mazas – 'exquisite poet, fascist ideologue, Franco's future minister' – who has been captured by the anti-fascist forces and taken with others to be executed. Just before the executions he escapes and hides in a ditch but sees a soldier slowly advance towards the edge of the ditch 'rifle pointing at him unostentatiously'. He awaits the solider to announce his discovery and thus inevitable death, yet just as the soldier gets to the edge of the ditch when a commanding voice is heard to shout: 'Is anyone there?', the soldier simply looks straight at him; in return

> Sanchez Mazas is looking at the soldier, but his weak eyes don't understand what they see: beneath the sodden hair and wide forehead and eyebrows covered in raindrops the soldier's look doesn't express compassion or hatred, or even disdain, but a kind of secret or unfathomable joy, something verging on cruelty, something that resists reason, but nor is it instinct, something that remains there with the same blind stubbornness with which blood persists in its course and the earth in its immovable orbit and all beings in their obstinate condition of being, something that eludes words the way the water in the stream eludes stone, because words are only made for saying to each other, for saying the sayable, when the sayable is everything except what rules us or makes us live or matters or what we are or what this anonymous defeated soldier is, who now looks at this man whose body almost blends in with the earth and the brown water in the ditch, and who calls out loudly without taking his eyes off him:
>
> 'There's nobody over here!'
>
> Then he turns and walks away.

Chapter 9:
Teaching the Significance of Genocide and Our Indifference: The Liberation War Museum, Dhaka, Bangladesh

Part I: Representation and locality

When President Yahya Khan, the military Dictator of Pakistan, decided to massacre the Bengalis of East Pakistan for daring to demand regional autonomy, the world's tragic ignorance about the country was a factor of inestimable value to him. Since there were comparatively few people who knew or cared about the people of East Pakistan, fewer still would care how many he massacred. No journalists would be permitted to see what he was doing. The massacres would take place quietly, as though in some remote and unknown region. (Robert Payne, *Massacre*, Introduction, quoted in a display caption at the Liberation War Museum, Dhaka)

[S]omeone who is perennially surprised that depravity exists, who continues to experience disillusionment (even incredulity) when confronted with evidence of what humans are capable of inflicting in the way of gruesome, hands-on cruelties upon other human beings, has not reached moral or psychological adulthood.

No one after a certain age has the right to this kind of innocence, of superficiality, to this degree of ignorance, of amnesia.

We now have a vast repository of images that make it harder to maintain this kind of moral defectiveness. Let the atrocious images haunt us. Even if they are only tokens, and cannot possibly encompass most of the reality to which they refer, they still perform a vital function. The images say: keep these events in your memory. (Sontag 2002: 272)

Machination and murder have been the curse of Bangladesh – its legacy of blood. It will not end until public accountability and the sequence of crime and punishment is firmly established. (Mascarenhas 1986: 183)

In the imaginative apartheid of modernity, both the Congo under the administration of King Léopold II and East Pakistan in the 1960s and 1970s were remote and largely unknown regions; the 'crimes' that occurred there hardly register in any global historical consciousness. Today, both have sites, museums, which in their different ways demonstrate the play of power to institutionalise and present (or prevent) historical recall through displays of material culture. While the park spaces and buildings of the Royal Museum for Central Africa in Brussels recall the heritage of the site as previously part of the grounds of a Chateaux, they have largely hidden the crimes that gave the finances which so contributed to its redevelopment. By contrast, the Liberation War Museum, Dhaka, inhabits a different spatial and imaginative realm.[1] On a small side street in central Dhaka, the museum occupies a converted three-story rented house and its grounds (Figure 9.1). The house gives the visitor something of a feel for an older Dhaka (then called Dacca) but beside it is a cleared site for future building, a fate that may soon befall the museum.

Opposite is a house of similar age occupied and used by a well-known doctor as his clinic. Next to that is a small garage repairing cars in the shadow of an eight-storied apartment building, entitled Eastern Dream (with a sign on the entrance that declares that it is a no smoking zone). Much of the surrounding area has been converted into eight-storied blocks of mixed offices (The Consumer Society of Bangladesh; Dhaka Reporters Unity) and posters on adjoining street lamps point to Brand Marketing International Limited. Some large palm trees survive, somewhat discoloured by their light coating of dust while on the narrow streets rickshaws battle with a growing number of cars. Along with sounds of car horns and construction, come the cries of the ubiquitous black crows that fight across Dhaka with the street paupers over the rubbish of urban life. Inside the museum, a photographic display shows a time when the crows feasted on human flesh, it is entitled simply *Genocide*.

A different spatial terrain – a contrasting metaphysic to the RMCA Brussels, for this is a member of *The Museums of Conscience* group.[2] Its role is not to provide a place 'where people come and see [beautiful objects], but where people come and reflect' (Director, Akku Chowdhury). This is a location for the 'new museumology' of narrative and confrontation, where conservation means to handle the material culture of memories; memories of hope, struggle, blood, despair, loss and overcoming.

Figure 9.1 The Liberation War Museum, Dhaka (photo Wayne Morrison)

One enters below a sign, which in English reads 'let us remove hatred and prejudice from the world and let it begin with me'.[3] Rather incongruously a Mini Minor 1000 car (which was driven by a doctor in the 1971 struggle) sits opposite the two armed guards, who check your bag (this is after September 11 and the museum could be a target for terrorism). Behind the car is the entrance to the audioritoum, on its door a poster of the Asian Network for the International Criminal Court: 'With the International Criminal Court (ICC) Justice Wins. We all win. Ratify the ICC Statute Now.' In the mornings, the auditorium shows a video presentation to one of the many schools that visit on the outreach programme. When, on a visit in January 2003, I looked inside it was occupied by a member of staff watching a live telecast of India playing Pakistan at football. (Half an hour later he excitedly emerged to tell everyone that India had defeated Pakistan, which as Bangladesh had beaten India 2 – 1 two days earlier, was a source of some national satisfaction and ensured that Bangladesh progressed to the final of the competition, which they won.) Inside the administration office another sign gave a simple message: 'We want trial of Pakistani War Criminals for 1971 Genocide in Bangladesh'.

They are unlikely to get this. This is a museum devoted to establishing the significance of crime – specifically the museum claims, *genocide* – to the birth of a nation, Bangladesh.[4] The story it tells is how at the end of British colonial government the Indian sub-continent was divided into the 'two nations' of Hindu India and Islamic Pakistan (1947).[5] Pakistan was two culturally, socially and linguistically different entities separated by over one thousand miles, but united in the name of Islam in a political union that operationally left Bengali East Pakistan in effect a colony of West Pakistan. The political struggle of the people of East Pakistan, the Bengali speaking people of an area of land that was for centuries the place of diversity, was rejected, labelled as a rebellion, which was to be crushed. Consequently a horrifyingly bloody 9-months genocide was attempted by the military rulers from West Pakistan to subdue Bengali nationalism and cultural traditions in order to render a people docile and governable. In the narratives offered, that genocide was fought against and a new nation state created, while a culture reasserted its identity;[6] yet other voices tell of the open-ended nature of the struggle.

The museum and the materials sold through its shop offer narratives of national identity; struggle from below and of the resort to violence by the sovereign power against people that power was in theory to protect. It presents images of genocidal violence used in a desperate policy to preserve a political–religious entity that did not reflect the needs and desires of the people of East Pakistan. The narrative is seen to provide a universal message. As the dedication message printed in the flyer that visitors receive puts it, the museum is 'dedicated to all freedom loving people of the world and victims of mindless atrocities and destruction committed in the name of religion and sovereignty. This museum is proof that determination can overcome all odds to win freedom and liberty.'[7]

This narrative of successful resistance and struggle competes with another that is not articulated within the confines of the museum. That other message is of international neglect and ignorance, of a world order of cynical power ploys by states where global justice is not a concept with much attractive force.

Bangladesh was born amidst the plays of the Cold War and took its place in a global network of nation states in which the lack of power of Bangladesh contributes to an unresolved legacy. In his 1986 text Anthony Mascarenhas – the journalist who did so much to bring the situation in 1971 to world attention – calls this 'the legacy of blood'. He is not alone in contending that the drastic law and order situation and lack of stable political institutions that seem to have been common since independence is produced, in part at least, by unresolved tensions from the events of 1971.[8] The military actions of the Pakistan Army in East Pakistan during that time does receive mention in Western scholarly accounts of genocide in the twentieth-century;[9] they were however, never the subject of any truth and reconciliation proceedings, national justice commission, war trials or international justice symposiums (indeed the treatment of the issue at the United Nations occasioned observers to feel a sense of disgust with the organisation[10]). In this story the struggles, the hopes and bloodletting of the peoples of Bangladesh receive no authentic recognition; instead they were sacrificed to the expediency of those more powerful. Latterly, some commentators voice a further fear; namely, that in this ongoing struggle the genocide may have been rather more successful. In this later narrative the rich heritage of a tolerant Islamic Bengal has been stripped by the diverse demands of fundamental Islamic voices or forced client status of aid programmes that reads the nation state label 'Bangladesh' as equivalent to a corrupt 'basket case'(as Henry Kissinger once called it). Taking over a territory devastated by West Pakistan military actions, the governmental apparatus of the new Bangladesh dedicated in its rhetoric to political secularism, religious tolerance, progress and social justice, failed to deliver success against poverty and corruption, whereupon it turned to one-party government and was vanquished in a bloody coup; afterwards successive governments – often themselves the result of bloody military coups or in constant danger of them – turned to the (politically used) rhetoric of Islamic ideology in place of the secularism of the original 'liberation' constitution or in place of a sustained anti-corruption campaign. This content is deeply ambigious but crucial.

The trope of *surviving genocide* is the central theme of this museum (the first book published by the museum is entitled, *1971: Documents on Crimes against Humanity Committed by Pakistan Army and their Agents in Bangladesh during 1971*). In the literature concerning 1971, the first set of eyewitness accounts came from outsiders who drew attention to the events in many of the world's newspapers.[11] Their accounts moved many but were subject to discrediting tactics by the Pakistani government and calculated disinterest by others.[12] Some Bengali accounts were published in the immediate aftermath, but it was only in later years that the majority of Bengali accounts have been published.

The museum arose from a private initiative in the early 1990s; its exhibits are an attempt to preserve accounts and display a 'truth' that was in danger of being submerged. It also strives to educate through an 'outreach' programme (in which group visits by students come to the museum) and 'reach out' or mobile museum (in which a bus that has been specially fitted out with photographs and documents travels around the country visiting educational institutions). This aims at '(i) civic education, (ii) nation building and

(iii) conscience and moral development amongst the younger generation' (Guide brochure). There are many issues in educating about genocide. As Elie Wiesel, a survivor of Auschwitz said in respect of the holocaust:

> How do you teach events that defy knowledge, experiences that go beyond imagination? How do you tell children, big and small that society could lose its mind and start murdering its own soul and its own future? How do you unveil horrors without offering at the same time some measure of hope? Hope in what? In whom? In progress, in science and literature and God? (Wiesel 1978: 270)

To what extent must any educative exhibition provide social and political commentaries and global contexts for killing, rape and massacre? What kind of hope or trust in the world can be offered? Boundaries must, of necessity, be placed on perceptions of social–historical location. Such boundaries are in part a matter of intellectual awareness and of practical resources. In contrast to the facilities of the Holocaust Memorial Museum, Washington DC, or the RMCA Brussels, the Liberation War museum is financially fragile; its efforts to mount an international conference addressing genocide comparatively in January 2002 were frustrated by a combination of lack of resources and the reluctance of people to travel post-September 11. The exhibition and activities of the museum are a product of local endeavour and reflect a desire to preserve a memory of historical (national) struggle and sacrifice. The displays do not contain analysis of the duplicity and double standards of the international legal order in dealing with the events; this is instead an implicit theme in some of the books for sale in the small shop.

What sort of experience in the visitor does the museum aim for? We are in a different politics of looking and seeing than that discussed in Chapter 8. Certainly the gaze of the visitor can not be approximated to those theoretical accounts concerning public exhibitions of male appropriation or of possessing or consuming by proxy. In gazing upon the exhibition (as in Figure 9.2) a sense of wonder is perhaps invoked, but these are not golden images and if the notion of a precious legacy is invoked, wealth lies in other than material terms. It lies in memories – partly proud of achievements, partly appreciative of sacrifices – but also bewilderment at the level of cruelty and apparent sadism evidenced in the displays.

The potential public for this exhibition is large (the population of Bangladesh is now over 130 million, compared to 75 million in 1971). Due to the age spread the majority did not live through the events and owing to the subsequent political turmoil of the country people are widely perceived to be 'understandably confused about what really went on' (Akku Chawdry, Director). The task of designing the exhibition then entails enticing the viewer into an appreciation of the events; how they may structure present predicaments is left to the viewer. Given its resources the museum can only offer an attempt at this task. These are contentious memories; moreover, the context is now a highly charged political institutionalisation of memory and of continuing struggle (as is apparent from observing the changed emphasis in the Liberation War displays at the National Museum when governments change). Among the many issues that still have no settled or definite 'history' are the political leadership of Sheikh Mujibur Rahman and the role of the Awami league and other political organisations and leaders, the grassroots

Figure 9.2 A mother leads her daughter through Room 6 (photo Wayne Morrison)

support and drive of the students' movement, the resistance movement and the *mukti bahini,* the role of India and the identity of individuals involved, either directly or indirectly, in the coups and counter coups that prevailed after independence (many of the political leaders in the liberation struggle were killed in one or other coups or assassinations in the years that followed): on the other side, the schemes and intentions of the Pakistani military leadership, the atrocities of the Pakistani Army, the collaborators, the unsettled issue of justice, truth and atonement. Perhaps above all lies the complex intertwining of different strands of constructing a 'Bangladeshi' national identity, how the trope of genocide and the war of liberation fits with the interaction of Islam and the linguistic and cultural influences of Bengali heritage (Kabir 1995; Salahuddin Ahmed 1994; Osmany 1992).

Genocide: institutional memory and post-memory

Life is irreducibly played out in the confines of mortality; ageing places a natural constrain on human memory. Individual memory cannot last more than a life-time and the subjects of memory are often those who are no longer alive. Memories are not perfect recreations but fragments recalled out of the process of the past receding. Objects, such as family photo albums, provoke memories in acts of reading, in process of interpretation. Steiner (1989) reminds us that interpretation is active, it is 'understanding in action' by an actor who responds 'responsibly' to the material. To interpret is to give intelligible meaning to the material before one, in a process of transcending its materiality; interpretation invokes presence and awareness of 'vibrations of primal'. A responsible act of interpretation makes us answerable to the text and its meanings, in a sense at once moral, spiritual and psychological. Much interpretation involves an invitation to engage with the traditions of our communities, to enter into that shared presence with others who have gone before, joined by a commonality of meaning. Genocide changes the frame; for the act of remembering and interpretation for genocide disrupts the 'natural' flow of death's arrival and of human resistance and acceptance of death. Marianne Hirsch (1997) suggests that the material culture of holocaust memorials is 'postmemory', a set of objects – photographs and preserves accounts, such as letters – that are removed from the reader by generational distance and from abstract history by deep personal connection. Troubled by her own invocation of this term – post-memory – Hirsche seeks to understand how genocide breaks the 'umbilical' connection of the objects of normal memory to life, such as family photographs. For her those normal photographs affirm the past's existence and how the past gave life to the present, but genocide is calculated to destroy life's progression for death occurs on a scale and effect that takes it out of the frame of humanity's understanding. Even the most normal appearing photographs now are of a past, but a past that has been violently destroyed, and in the case of the holocaust, the notion of community torn impossibly. In the case of European Jewry, 'the destruction was such that not an image was left from the Jewish life before the war that was not in some way encumbered, tainted, marked by death' (Nadine Fresco, quoted Hirsch 1997: 243). In her holocaust-aware account, the level and specifics of causation involved in this mass death did more than take away the sensuality of specific human individuals through the time-bound flows of the finite world, it extinguished the light by which normal meaning was possible. Sustained acts of political violence and bestiality make inhabiting a communal space problematic, the holocaust extinguished hope of it. Yet there is further tragedy for the holocaust largely succeed; it removed Jews from areas of European sight where previously they were part of normal functioning. The violence of the holocaust is partly the irrecoverable destruction of a world, and a contribution to Europe that can not now be made and for which Steiner found Israel but little solace for the Jews hounded out of European history (Steiner 1971).

Thus photographs of pre-holocaust European life are post-memory, for even when viewed by the children of survivors, the community can not be entered into. The children live geographically and existentially removed from the social space that should have been the future of the past recalled. Instead the recall is of a void into which there is no light of continued presence.

By contrast the Liberation War Museum presents objects as memory for a shared but contested space. To view is to be called upon to interpret events that took place in the territorial and social space that is now Bangladesh, conducted by individuals many of whom remained and continued to engage in jobs and hold positions of political and economic influence. Presenting and encountering these objects – elements representing a period of collective violence – is to enter into a continuing relationship. In large part the exhibition and related work (such as the documentation centre, or work linked to the investigation of mass graves) is a bearing witness to a set of events and an attempt to capture images of some of the lives destroyed. In its theme of 'no just response' having been made to the genocide, it also hints of an unresolved trauma linked to subsequent occurrences.[13] Thus the narrative cannot ultimately have a satisfactory ending. On the one hand, we have a story of resistance to power with the exhibits offering a picture of an area of the world that was seen as subordinated and dominated, speaking back and asserting a successful counter-narrative of the right to expression and self-determination. This is a story told through the technology of lamination: the reproduction and preservation of photographs and newspaper cuttings. On the other, the narrative is unfinished, taking one onto the radically unsettled issues of justice, nationhood and unachieved human capabilities and potentialities.

The museum experience

The museum is arranged to guide visitors through an unfolding story. Before entering the exhibition rooms one passes in front of a flame of remembrance, a remembrance for dead who are not just the individuals covered by this museum for it burns 'for all those who laid down their lives for freedom and liberation throughout the world' (Gallery Guide).

Room 1 aims to give the viewer an outline of the heritage and culture of the Bengalis. The message comes through the labels, as with that headed 'Ancient Bengal'.

Bangladesh has a long and distinctive heritage:

- Language
- Poetry
- Autonomy of learning
- Industry
- Islam against a background of tolerance.

There are a number of plaster models, such as of Paharpu, the largest known Buddhist monastery south of the Himalayas, and the Shait Gumbad Masjid mosque built before 1459 by Ulugh Khan Jahn, the first Muslim ruler of a part of the sundarban forest on the sea coast in Khulan.

These themes of specificity of language, an expressive dynamic captured in poetry, a heritage of autonomous learning and the tolerance of Islam backed by pictures tell a story of transition from the time of 'Ancient Bengal'. In her work on *Bangladeshi Nationalism*, Shireen Osmany (1992) reflects the tone of the room. The period from the thirteenth century to 1757 of Muslim rule is described as 'a glorious period of communal peace and harmony, spread of Islam by the sheer merit of its superior spiritual and moral appeal, spread of education at a popular level and above all a historic process of restoring human dignity, respect and social justice among all classes'. In this 'golden period ... the success of Islam in integrating the society of Bengal through patronage of Bengali language and humanising process is a matter of historical fact'. Political rule was pragmatic, humanist and egalitarian, with 'a degree of convergence between the followers of all faiths in the socio-economic aspects of life' (Osmany 1992: 14).

However, with the collapse of the Moghul system of rule in the Indian sub-continent in the eighteenth century the Muslims of Bengal lost political power to the British and saw Hindu ascendancy in the economic spheres under the patronage of the British rulers. One of the icons of colonial rule, the Bengal Famine of 1943, is remembered by newspaper cuttings from the *Sunday Statesman* 22 August 1943, and *The Statesman* 23 September 1943. The headlines above the photographs are simple: *This Catastrophe is Man-Made.* There is however, no further explanation, nor any linkage to later events, such as the devastating cyclone in November 1970. The widespread perception that the damage caused by that cyclone was treated as a matter of little consequence by the West Pakistani 'rulers' contributed to the massive victory of the Awami league – a political party mostly based in East Pakistan – in the December elections. That 'event' is material for Room 3 and the opportunity is lost to draw out connecting themes. One theme, that is not addressed, perhaps connects the famine, the response to the cyclone and the genocide – namely the expendability of the weak to the powerful forces of rule; and the social and psychological factors which enable that distancing and exclusion.[14]

The role of poetry is prominent, with a small display on Kazi Nazrul Islam, a poet of the anti-British struggle. The Bengali Hindu poet Tagore, whose works were banned for some time under Pakistani rule, did much to raise the international profile of Bengali and expressed a longing for freedom;[15] the national anthem of contemporary Bangladesh comprise his ideas.

To go to Room 2 means crossing over a small passage which has inserted on the wall a brass plaque with the list of 29 Bengalis hung by the British. The inscription:

> The brave sons of the soil who were hung to death in the British prisons during the colonial period. These brave sons of Bengal wanted to achieve freedom of the country by acts of heroic sacrifice.

The list is simply arranged by name, age, place of birth, place of execution and date, for example, 'Charu Chandro Bosu, 19, Khulna, Alipur Jail, 19 March 1909'.

It is a simple plaque but resonance flows. If there is little visual stimulation, it invokes a pale shadow (at least) of the intense social experiences that lie behind the names. This simple list – name, age, place of birth, place where hung, age when killed – is the only clue to the identities and experiences of those who died and all those who participated with them in their struggles for the necessities of life and of the soul, of identities as desiring beings who once loved, wept, shouted political slogans, and ultimately were labelled as criminals and killed by the colonial state, enemies of Imperial sovereign power. The political importance of this in the context of the liberation struggle lies partly in the West Pakistani depiction of the Bengalis as non-martial, as easily able to be cowed, as politically docile. As a people about whom the military ruler Yahya asserted (according to popular belief) that if one killed a million or so the rest would be able to be ruled easily.

The objective behind Room 2 is to give a 'condensed historical tour of the Pakistan period ending with the 1970 election. This was the time when the

Bengalees struggled for their language, culture and economic, social and political parity. At last the election of 1970 through adult franchise was the opportune moment for the Bengalees to respond to the years of disparity suffered by them (Museum Guide). Here one confronts the impossibility of giving any thing more than a rendering to the history of movements and activities. The label on the wall reads:

> Independence in 1947 became domination by West Pakistan, disadvantaging Bengalis politically, economically and socially, and striking deep at their heritage:
> - Imposition of Urdu
> - Denial of intellectual rights: ban on Tagore
> - Economic disparity
> - Disparity in military and civil appointments
> - Martial law
> - The last straw: Pakistani's lack of interest in the 1970 cyclone.

Each line alludes to a complex history, a train of events, and a vehicle of struggle and change. On one side is a famous picture of a street urchin, fist high in defiance (Figure 9.3). This image was to give poets and fighters inspiration in the later dark time of 1971, as in the concluding stanza of Rahman's *From the Prison Camp* (July, 1971):

I never knew
I loved this word so much.
But with pointed guns
They have separated me
From such words as
Freedom and *Bangladesh.*
But little do they know
That in the leaves of the trees,
On the footpaths,
In the bird's feathers,
In the eyes of women,
In the dust of the roads,
In the clenched fist
Of the unruly child of our ghettos,
I always see Burning,
A word called *Freedom.*

Figure 9.3 Picture of a street urchin, fist high in defiance (image courtesy of Liberation Museum)

But how can one capture the multitude of human decisions, the opportunities not grasped, the interaction between myriad individual situations that comprise the collective and the statements of the elite (or those recorded as such) who make the 'historically significant' decisions? This room alludes to voices; voices that speak with the rhythm of Bengali, a dimly evoking a theme that runs throughout Bengali literature namely is the connection between the flows of the language and the earth, the rivers and the gentle landscape. It is as if the ground itself provided epistemological foundations for cultural life and expression.

The language was more than a medium. In 1948 language became a political issue when on 25 February, Pakistan's Prime Minister Liaquat Ali Khan declared,

> Pakistan is a Muslim state, and it must have its Lingua Franca, the language of a Muslim nation. It is necessary for a nation to have one language and that language can only be Urdu and no other language.

East Bengalis immediately resented the inference that their language, Bengali, was non-Islamic.[16] A national hartal (strike) was observed on 11 March, with over a thousand people jailed. Protests brought a decision by the ageing Governor-General of Pakistan, Mohammad Ali Jinnah, to visit Dhaka. However, at a public meeting he declared that Urdu alone would be the national language and those who opposed it were enemies of the state; large student protests ensued after his address at Dhaka University. Although the movement appeared to die down, the issue was picked up in 1951 by a coalition of interests with strong student involvement and a memorandum from the Dhaka University State Language Committee of Action was presented to members of the Constituent Assembly demanding a settlement of the state language issue. The then Prime Minister, Khwaja Nazimuddin, declared again that Urdu alone would be the state language. In meetings in 1952 the students decided to challenge Section 144, a martial law regulation forbidding public protest. In the following rallies police opened fire killing five, including three students. The deaths were the first of the 'language martyrs'. In the 1954 elections, a new political grouping, called the United Front campaigned on the language issue and promised to form a Bengali Academy. Their electoral success strengthened the cause of cultural nationalism. Although the Pakistan government had to compromise on the language issue tensions remained between the Urdu speaking people of East Pakistan, who had come from India at partition, and the Bengali speaking; tensions that were to flare violently in 1971.

Throughout the 1950s and 1960s, the language movement developed from a cultural movement into a broad-based social movement that expressed regional objectives and responded to economic distress and political frustration.[17] The emerging but small middle class had a particular relationship to the students. As the major universities became more Bengali Muslim, they served as the conduit to civil service posts – particularly at Dhaka University. Both the middle classes and the students found in the language movement a method of addressing the people as a coherent interest group and giving leadership in a way that the feudalist-village organisation could not

Figure 9.4(b) The tree in the background at Dhaka campus has iconic status (images courtesy N.A. Siddique)

Figure 9.4(a) From Dhaka campus to the village and town: speeches by N.A. Siddique, student leader

allow. Given that important circles in West Pakistan depreciated Bengalis as Muslims, Bengali tolerance and heritage was misrepresented.[18] In creating a discourse of national solidarity across two sections so separated in distance, newly educated urban Bengali's could not help but be trapped in a social ambivalence: 'The main stream of urban Muslim middle class never showed convincing evidence of being either totally secular in orientation or entirely sectarian (Muslim) in their political outlook' (Osmany 1992: 101).

Attempts by the sovereign centre (West Pakistan) to resolve this ambivalence by imposing a discourse of national unity was thus a project to impose a totalitarian guarantee. Bengali tolerance was in and of itself ambivalent. Dressing, wedding customs, rituals of address, mixed elements of Hindu and Muslim traditions; they offered evidence to some that a notion of a Bengali nation, combining Calcutta and Dacca, had not been fully given up.

Student activists who were arrested and imprisoned went on to find receptive audiences upon release and were able to spread the spirit of activism. Returning to villages, their speeches to gatherings were not some bowing to an oral tradition but the reality of communication in a land where less than 3 per cent of the population read newspapers and where the radio was primarily an urban communication form. (see Figures 9.4a and b)

The final straw

It is hard for a vehicle of material culture to capture the challenge to the governing elites of Pakistan posed by the expressions of power organised by the student leaders in the form of massive street rallies. In Dhaka, the University area comprises a substantial area within the city that even today has the largest open spaces and well laid-out avenues and buildings.

To re-present the existential meaning of the streets, the mass meetings called by the students and other political leaders is inherently difficult; contrast the following. One is a photograph (Figure 9.5) displayed on the walls of the museum with information about Maulana Bhashani, a people's activist and a communist. The photograph shows a meeting at the Puran Paltan – an open space or park – used for public meetings, called in early October 1971. But it could have easily referred to a number of large gatherings called at his insistence, such as one in November 1970 where he recounted his trip to the devastated coast. This meeting was put to poetry by Shamsur Rahman under the English title *The White Shirt*. It seeks to reveal the feel of that meeting.

The White Shirt

Artist, poet, journalist – local and foreign,
Shopper, worker, student, intellectual,
Female social worker, expert camera-man,
Professor, intelligence agent, office clerk, –
All of them rushed to Purana Paltan's open field,
All eager to hear what the aged Maulana Bhashani,
Just back from the scene of total devastation,
Had to relate.
He stood there in the sun's glare
Firm and unbending, straight as a rod,
Like Noah after the Great Deluge,

Figure 9.5 A mass meeting at Puran Paltan

His deeply carved face
Towering above his companions
Of the over-crowded Arc,
His catkin beard
Caught in the gusty north wind.
His heart is broken
Like the mourning, corpse-strewn
Coastline of southern Bengal.
His two staring eyes still see
The Scenes of mass slaughter
He flung at the seething multitude
The utter desolation of southern Bengal.
All of a sudden everyone saw
The familiar Purana Paltan
Turn slushy with thick mud,
Suddenly we are all carrying corpses
On our shoulders,
As if a farmer berserk with towering rage
Has turned into a vengeful demon
Tearing up his carefully nurtured
Field of ripening corn,
And now strewn all around
Lies his abandoned harvest.
Porter, beggar, worker, student
Female social worker, artist, poet,
Intellectual, journalist – Local and foreign,
Expert camera-man, the push-cart vendor,

> Intelligence agent, office worker,
> All the shops, theatres, traffic police,
> The racing rickshaws, taxis, over-sized double-deckers,
> The soft vanity bag and the historic canon,
> Pandal, television, lamp post,
> Restaurant, foot-path, office-building –
> All are swept into
> The storm-torn Bay of Bengal –
> Alas, what fell incantations
> Have been uttered by the Maulana!
> His eloquent hands flash out repeatedly
> Like quivering spears,
> The Maulana's flowing white shirt
> Swells quickly and billows out,
> As if with one spotless white shirt
> He anxiously seeks to cover the shame
> Of the scattered, unveiled, disrobed corpses.

Room 3 covers the events of March 1971. In 1969 the ruling military dictator attempted to stem political unrest by a return to democratic elections to be held in both parts of Pakistan leading to a unified national Assembly and a Prime Minister elected by the various MPs. While in West Pakistan the parties split on regional lines in East Pakistan the behaviour of the governing elites had resulted in a temporary consensus around a coherent set of demands best expressed by the Awami league, headed by the charismatic Sheikh Mujibur Rahman and dedicated to greater autonomy. The elections due in mid-1970 were postponed until December, which given the occurrence of the cyclone was a major disaster for the anti-Awami League forces. Yahya had reportedly asked for firm intelligence reports on the likely percentage of the seats that the Awami League would win. The biased nature of the intelligence services probably meant that significant underreporting was given.[19] In the event the Awami League obtained so many votes that they would be the legitimate party of government, not just for East Pakistan, but of the whole of Pakistan; this was too much for the West Pakistan military and political elites and the meeting of the national assembly that would have put Mujibur as Prime Minister was delayed. Out of the events of this month came delays, mass meetings and a highly successful campaign of non-cooperation in East Pakistan that showed the strength of social feelings. In response came a military crack down with what came to be the oft quoted utterance that if a million or so Bengalis could be got rid of then the country would be able to be governed. If the hope was that a set of arrests, massacres and intimidations of political and student leaders, or the removal of leading intellectuals, could remove the source of autonomy (and possible succession) the calculation was wrong. Massacres there were: members of the Awami League were central targets, as were the student leaders. Consider the operational orders for Operation Spotlight as the crack down was termed, copies of which are printed in several books. The basis for success was first that 'Awami League action and reactions to be treated as rebellion and those who support or defy Martial Law action be dealt with as hostile elements'. And second that 'as Awami League has widespread support even amongst the East Pakistani elements in the Army the operation has to be launched with great cunningness, surprise, deception and speed combined with shock action'. We find listed under 'the basic requirements for success' that the operation was to be launched all over the Province simultaneously; Maximum number of political and student leaders and extremists amongst teaching staffs, cultural organizations to be arrested. In the initial phase top political leaders and top student leaders must be arrested; the operation must achieve a hundred per cent success in Dacca. For that Dacca University will have to be occupied and searched; security of cantonments must be ensured. Greater and freer use of fire against those who dare attack the cantonment; all means of internal and international communications to be cut off. Telephone exchanges, Radio, TV, Teleprinter services, transmitters with foreign consulates to be closed down; EP troops were to be neutralised by controlling and guarding kotes and ammunition by West Pakistani troops.

Then there are the detailed instructions for top student and Awami League leaders to be 'arrested', Mujibur Rahman was to be treated without harm and taken to West Pakistan, but the intentions for the others are vague. In interpreting military orders the gap between the written and the intended needs bridging. Take the instructions for Comilla. This identifies the *Troops ...* and *Tasks*: (1) Disarm 4 East Bengal, Wing HQ East Pakistan Rifles, Reserve District Police; (2) Secure town and arrest Awami League leaders and students; (3) secure Exchange.

In actuality, 'in Comilla Cantonment 24 Bengali Officers and more than Bengali soldiers were arrested immediately after the crackdown and murdered in cold blood' (Imamuz Zaman 2001: 5). However, most of 4 East Bengal escaped. In each of the areas arrest and disarming translated into attempted massacre. The books later written by soldiers who served in the Liberation War all carry chapters detailing their escape from the massacres (e.g. Rafiqul Islam [1st ed. 1974] 1997: chapters 6, 7 and 8; Safiullah 1995: chapter 3; Akhtar Ahmed 2000 chapter 3). We then have various documentary records of journalists. Take John Pilger (1986: 325), one of the few who managed to travel into East Pakistan with resistance fighters in June 1971:

> Eric and I marched at night behind Moudud Ahmed and a guide bearing a green and red Bangladeshi flag and a ragged file of guerrillas armed with 25-year-old Lee Enfield rifles and Bren guns. One morning we came upon a mosque blown up, shops looted and a burned house without a wall, felled by a tank, from which its owner had not escaped.
>
> People emerged cautiously, asking if we had food. The Pakistani Army, which had come the previous night, had left them two piles of coarse nee: forty pounds to feed 5,000 people. An old man with a goatee and the lace cap of a maulana lifted his shirt, revealing a neat lattice-work of bayonet cuts on his stomach. An eight-year-old boy's ear was caked with blood, the lobe having been shot away at close range. A woman sat alone in a field nearby, grieving the burial alive of her husband. The Punjabi soldiers had put him and his two brothers, who had refused to go with them, in a trench beside the river and filled it with mud that came up to their noses and the crows had done the rest.
>
> And so the stories of systematic killing accumulated as we went from village to village, keeping well off the roads, waiting for a lone jet fighter to pass. Where there had been Hindu communities, whose ethnic place in Muslim East Bengal had been delicately but peacefully maintained since Partition, there were now deserted ruins. Whenever the Punjabis attacked, it was to the same pattern. Every young man in the village was ordered to display his penis. If he was circumcised and therefore a Muslim, he was taken away. If

he was uncircumcised and a Hindu, he was killed and, depending on the soldiers' whim, his penis was cut off. Anybody connected with Sheik Mujib's Awami League was shot. Food and animals, watches and family trinkets were taken; and those Bengalis who remained were threatened with the firing squad if they left their village.

The fact of massacres, state-sponsored and state directed, is unassailable as is a programme of ethnic cleansing, the deliberate attempts to force the minority Hindi population into India as refugees. Much of the repression was directed at destroying Bengali nationalism; it has not been possible to access details of meetings, policy discussions and orders which took place in West Pakistan, as the official Government reviews there has extended no further than an inquiry into the military loss of East Pakistan (one that did, implicitly, admit to widespread massacres). The explanatory factors include ideology: namely the idea that Bengali Muslims were recent converts – faith only skin deep, really heretics in disguise, lack of control – these are difficult subjects of representation in material form.

The centre of Room 3 has a clay sculpture of refugees (Figure 9.6). At the peak some 10 million people had made a desperate trek into India, many died on the way and many others died of cholera in the camps. Their reality is represented in one corner with a display organised around a cut off sewage pipe, which was the source of 'housing' in many of the camps. Newspaper reports above the pipe make reference to a young Senator Edward Kennedy, a key friend in America.[20]

Figure 9.6 A testament to the refugees, clay sculpture (photo Wayne Morrison)

One leaves this room and ascends stairs to the second floor. The walls are covered by photographs recording the early days of the armed struggle (The Recruit; Training). The accent is very much on becoming a 'freedom fighter'. Some of the posters prepared in Calcutta are displayed, but there is little hint of the divisions in the political structure of the government in exile or in the composition of the armed resistance.

The armed resistance that developed over the 9-month struggle had two sources of manpower. One was the military and police personnel who rebelled; the other was untrained students and other young men who were called freedom fighters (FFs). The FFs received a short basic training in various 'young camps' spread around the border areas, some of them located within Bangladesh territory. The camps were centrally administered by a department of the newly formed Bangladesh Government (in exile) and locally managed by Members of the National Assembly (MNAs), Members of Parliament (MPs) and senior political leaders. There were up to 100 camps with several hundred trainees in each camp. The military training was given mostly by Indian army instructors and the FFs moved to operational camps once they had gone through the training. Conditions in the camps were very basic with shortages of food and other supplies, and there were rumours of corruption and mismanagement. In the beginning there was discrimination in favour of National Awami Party (NAP) Awami League supporters but over time this lessened. There were also some camps run by the and the Communist Party of Bangladesh that were aided by leftist parties in India. All the camps suffered from lack of funds and supplies. The organisers complained that they were often harassed by the members of the Mujib Bahini who were much better trained and had superior arms. The seeds of the future use of armed groups by various political parties may be found here.

Room 5 provides a different social world to that of the military displays of the RMCA and the Military Museum in Brussels. There displays were arranged as trophy chests, which certainly did not feature the graveyards of the Congo. Rather than storehouses of the fruits or monuments to past triumphs this room of the Liberation War Museum presents further evidence of the killing and raping machinery of military power addressed to civilians.

Consider the caption for a photo of a girl looking at the camera …

> In our liberation war the women were the worst victims of Pakistani Army atrocities. While the male members of the household went off to fight the enemy the 'women' became the easy targets. Over 250,000 women were tortured and raped by the barbarian Pakistan soldiers. This 13-year-old girl was kept for months in a military camp to satisfy the Pakistani soldiers' lust. (Photo, Jill Durrance, National Geographic)

below were two photos of two young women, the caption reads

> Photographs of two women who were picked up and repeatedly raped by the occupying Pakistani Forces. During the liberation war they were under confinement by the Pakistani Army. After the war the society shunned them.

The issue of mass rape caught international attention and 1971 is often referred to as *The Rape of Bangladesh.* In a foundational text for the *1970s* western feminist movement, *Against Our Will: Men, Women and Rape,* Susan Brownmiller (1975) likened the 1971 events in Bangladesh to the Japanese rapes in Nanjing and German rapes in Russia during World War II.

> Hit-and-run rape of large numbers of Bengali women was brutally simple in terms of logistics as the Pakistani regulars swept through and occupied the tiny, populous land'. (p. 81)
>
> Rape in Bangladesh had hardly been restricted to beauty, Girls of eight and grandmothers of seventy-five had been sexually assaulted ... Pakistani soldiers had not only violated Bengali women on the spot; they abducted tens of hundreds and held them by force in their military barracks for nightly use. Some women may have been raped as many as eighty times in a night. (Brownmiller, 1975: 83)

Although a figure of between 200,000 and 300,000 is sometimes quoted, how many women were actually raped is difficult to accurately gauge. The numbers killed after rape or murdered as part of the generalised campaign of destruction and slaughter can only be guessed at. After liberation their futures were often uncertain.[21]

This is a room for the remembrance of suffering. On another wall is a photo of troops loading bodies of a mother and child into the back of a jeep-ambulance:

> Two victims of Pakistani genocide. The mother and child were not spared the brutality. The nameless victims of the senseless brutality being removed by Muktijuddhas in Balurghai on Nov. 30 after area was liberated.' (Amiya Taradar, photo)

Then there are the objects of the victims of Pakistani Army or collaborators killings. The first item donated to the museum was a T-shirt of a 4-month-old baby girl. It is displayed with a photograph of her father along with three small commentaries:

> Freedom Fighter Abdus Salam Khan. A valiant freedom fighter and feared by the Pakistan Army for his bravery. They wanted him dead or alive so badly they announced one lak rupees award on his head. On 30 April they surrounded his home looking for him. Not finding him they killed his 4-month daughter Rehana.
>
> Rehana: this T-shirt belonged to a 4-month old baby girl who was crushed to death by a Pakistani Jawan's boot in April 1971 in Senhati, Digholia, Khula. At the time of the killing she was wearing this shirt.
>
> Her crime: she was the daughter of valiant freedom fighter Abdus Salam Khan. He was commander of a group of freedom fighters in Digholia, Khulna. Salam had joined the liberation war from the beginning and was inducted as an instructor. The Pakistan Army and their collaborators put a price of TK 100,000 on his head. Unfortunately he had to pay a higher price as his first born girl Rehana was brutally murdered. Defenceless innocent Rehana fell prey to brutal Pakistan Army just like many other women and children whose husbands or fathers had to go off to fight for their motherland. (from the collection of Abdus Salam Khan)

In a near-by cabinet are the coat and electric shaver of Shaheed Altaf Mahmud.

> Born 1933, he was the lyricist of a song about the 1952 language movement 'Amar Bhaier Rokta Rangano' – My brother's blood soaked 21st February. Since the language movement he had been singing revolutionary songs to inspire the movement. During the liberation war his house was used as an arms and ammunition store house. On August 30 Pakistani Army surrounded the house obviously tipped off. Trunk full of weapons found underneath the floor. Taken away, presumed tortured and killed sometime in September.'

These items – bearers of personal stories but otherwise banal to a wider audience – are wounded artifacts. Torn from the context of their relationship with their wearer and user, they are evidence to the violence of human absence, of lives that did not live their potential. Once touched by their wearer and user in the rituals of everyday existence, the captions invoke unseen images of a more violent touch, the crushing weight of an army boot on a 4-year old baby girl's torso or the varied intrusions of the sophisticated torturer.

Room 6 is dominated by a display of death (of skulls and human bones). These were recovered from one of the many killing fields scattered around Bangladesh. This gallery is a place of witnessing 'the pain, sorrow and the gore of that time' (Museum guide). It recalls the role of the Indian Army 'and their sacrifice along with us', and, ultimately the surrender of the (West) Pakistan Army. Perhaps its most iconic display are the photographs concerning the killing of some 250 'intellectuals' by the collaborator groups, the Al-Babar, Al-Shams and the Razakers, on the eve of the surrender. A note on the door reads:

> There were some political organisation[s] like the Jaimati Islam and Muslim league that were not only against the Liberation War but actively collaborated with the Pakistan Army as informants about the whereabouts of the Freedom Fighters and providers of young women for the pleasure of the Pakistan troops. The members of these right wing fundamentalist parties were recruited and organised into paramilitary groups called Al-Babar, Al-Shams and Razakers. Ultimately when Pakistan Army realised their eminent [*sic*] defeat these groups ... helped the Pakistan Army to identify and pick up the intellectuals and elite of the Bengallee community who were massacred in the killing fields right before the Pakistani surrender. Obviously the ultimate motive was to create an intellectual and administrative vacuum in the newly liberated country.

The accompanying photos (e.g. Figure 9.7) are among the most reproduced images of the conflict. They are an eloquent testament to the imbalance in power and human universality of the victims. Can it be of any material concern that the persons – hands tied behind their backs, blindfolded, before execution (a legalist term of contestable appropriateness) were East Pakistani Muslim? It is of concern who they, as individuals were and

Figure 9.7 Image presented in Liberation Museum and often reproduced

who, in terrible, personal circumstances mourn their loss. But it is the implication of this museum's guidance that *we*, as Christians, Jews, Atheists, Buddhists, Taoists, urbanites, rural dwellers, are commonly affected.

The issue of the collaborators continues to divide. Many share an acute sense of wonder and this account is representative of an ongoing collective memory:

> It was almost unbelievable how fast these elements rallied around their military warlords. Fazlul Quader Chowdhury of Chittagong who was the speaker of the National Assembly during his heydays when Ayub Khan was the president of Pakistan went on the radio on April 24 and denounced Sheikh Mujib, the Awami League and all those millions who rose against the Pakistani rulers and their military oppression. He cried that December 1970 election was won by the Awami League based on their 'Six-Point' programme and the Awami League had no mandate from the people to fight for the independence of Bangladesh and thus dismember Pakistan. In fact this was the view of most of the Muslim Leaguers.
>
> The political stance taken by these parties and the raising of the Razakars etc. caused great concern among the pro-liberation forces. The Pakistanis in fact managed to divide the nation and thus created extra hardship for the pro-liberation forces. Much Bengali blood was spilt in frequent shooting between the FFs and the Razakars. No one knows exactly the extent of casualties suffered in such totally undesirable clashes and the number of innocent Bengalis who were killed by the Razakars, the Al-Badrs and the Al-Shams. These killer forces set up many slaughter houses throughout the country where large scale killings and executions were carried out during the entire period of the liberation war. The local Biharis gave all out support to the killer squads and many of them enlisted themselves in these squads. Mirpur, a suburb of Dhaka city, and a stronghold of the Biharis from the early days of Pakistan, and Rayerbazar near the city were famous slaughter grounds as were the Circuit House and the Foyes lake area outside the Chittagong city. Truck loads of unarmed and blindfolded Bengali young men were taken to the slaughter grounds and mercilessly killed in a bid to crush the liberation movement; it was a part of the Pakistani military strategy. (Exhibit label)

These later assertions amount to specific claims to genocide and the difficulty of judging. It was sometimes hard to distinguish FF and collaborator as many collaborators managed to gain FF certificates after the war.

So this Museum attempts to teach the facts of genocide and lack of recognition, it is a living counter to our states of denial. It is also an example of NGO activity; it contrasts strongly with the displays on the War housed in the National Museum.

The National Museum occupies a large grey concrete building of the 1970s in the administrative/cultural area of central Dhaka (near to the large complex of Dhaka University). Its display rooms are large, and rather drab. This exhibition lacks spirit. Perhaps its best exhibits on the war are artistic creations, such as 'In memory of '71' (MD. Hamiduzzaman Khan), made of mixed media, comprising the prostrate figure of a killed person half hidden by the water/dirt, bricks. (Nat Museum Acc. No. S – 88.1553). The Mezzanine floor with list and photographs of many of those (intellectuals) killed in 1971. Its entrance dominated by the portrait and photographs of Ziaur Rahman, including his wicker chair 'used during the time of liberation war 1971 in the battlefield' (Acc. No. E-92.1061). Many later photos include his wife and at times it is more a shrine to an individual. At my last visit, 2004, the stationery of Headquarters of Z force (Commanded by Major Ziaur Rahman) was on display.

The ethos and even the lay out of these articles varies with the party in power, under the Awami League Sheikh Mujibur Rahman is in turn given great prominence. History is clearly politicised, rather than the political (and the criminal) given a history. That the political has a disturbing history comes home with a visit to the house of Sheikh Mujibur Rahman, the scene of his assassination and of most of his family in 1975. It is preserved as it was, down to the blood stains on the stairs where he was shot; trademark pipe still in hand, he was assassinated while doing what he did best, trying to talk his attackers into alternative action.

Part II:

Identity and encountering reality,
past and future intervention

We cannot allow the annihilation of an entire people next door to us … it is not in our national interest that … the entire unarmed population of Bangladesh should be annihilated … I would certainly welcome the withdrawal of troops and *I think the troops that should be withdrawn straightaway are the Pakistani troops in Bangladesh … the very presence of Pakistani troops in Bangladesh is a threat to our security.* (Indira Gandhi, Indian Prime Minister, speaking at the Rajya Sabha (Upper House of Parliament) on 3 November 1971, quoted in *India and Bangladesh,* Delhi: Orient Longman, 1972, pp. 119–20)

The Indian Government asserts that it has launched the war in order to realize the national aspirations of the people in East Pakistan and bring about the return of the East Pakistani refugees to their homeland. This assertion is indeed absurd to the extreme. Many countries in the world have nationality problems, which need be solved properly and reasonably in conformity with the desire and the interests of the people, but these are the internal affairs of the respective countries, which can be solved only by their own government and people, and in which no foreign country has the right to interfere ….

What right has India to take over the affairs of others into its own hands, flagrantly interfere in Pakistan's internal affairs and even employ powerful armed forces to invade and occupy East Pakistan … the Indian government has single-handedly manufactured a so-called 'Bangladesh' and inserted it into East Pakistan by armed force … The Soviet government has played a shameful role in this war of aggression launched by India against Pakistan. The whole world has seen clearly that it is the backstage manager of the Indian expansionists.

The purpose of Soviet Union is to strengthen its control over India and theerby … contend with the other super power for hegemony in the whole of the South Asian subcontinent and the Indian ocean and at the same time foster India and turn it into a sub-superpower South Asian subcontinent as its assistant and partner in committing aggression against Asia. (Statement of the Government of the People's Republic of China, Hsinhua Dispatch No. 121607, 16 December 1971)

The new world order constructs itself partly in myth, one current example is the proposition that humanitarian intervention was invented in the 1990s with the NATO action in response to the Serbian Actions in Kosovo, there, we are told, military action was taken without Security Council authorization because of the clear and obvious breach of the human rights of the suffering Kosovians. Having not acted quickly enough for Bosnia the 'international community' intervened. It is illustrative that the precedents of Bangladesh and Cambodia are notable absences from the discussion.

Bangladesh was finally born with Indian military action and the surrender on 16 December 1971 of around 90,000 West Pakistan forces.[22] As indicated in the extracts above, India took the high moral ground claiming that it needed to intervene on grounds of humanitarian necessity that overwhelmed the state structured rules of international 'law'. China claimed this was a rhetorical flourish to obscure the great power plays involved, particularly as India was supported by the Soviet Union, Pakistan in large part by China and the US who had dispatched its Seventh Fleet to take up strategic position in an effort to halt the Indian advance. After full scale Indian military intervention pressure built at the UN Security Council headed by China and the US for an immediate ceasefire and withdrawal of troops, but the Soviet Union vetoed all proposals that did not provide for a political solution of the 'East Bengal' question as they and the Indian Government termed it. At a December 1971 meeting of the US National Security Council, Secretary of State, Henry Kissinger famously said Bangladesh would be 'an international basket case' but that 'it would not necessarily be our basket case' (Boyce and Hartmann 1990). Who would control its destiny? Whose justice would the events and the individuals involved in 1971 receive? Shelly (1979: 19) argues Bangladesh was 'the first state to be born in blood and iron in a polycentric world'. Post-World War II, the cold war between the Western Capitalist bloc and the Socialist Block of the Soviet Union and China had given way to a loose set of regional struggles albeit dominated by the competition between the nuclear superpowers of the US and the Soviet Union. For Myrdal (1968) in the 1960s the main protagonists understood the struggles of emerging states largely in terms of their significance for the superpowers' global interests; while the 'under-developed' countries understood only too well that the interests of the Western nations or Soviet Union, or other countries in their conditions and problems were largely due to 'the world tensions that gave significance to their internal affairs abroad'.

The absence

> My heart sang to be home again and among my people; but then I was brought face-to-face with the greatest man-made disaster in history. I could never imagine the magnitude of that catastrophe. They had killed more than three million of my people [the usual figure given in Bangladesh circles, the real figure is more likely to be 1.5–2.4 either killed or died as a result of disease WM]. They had raped our mothers and our sisters and have butchered our children. More than 30 per cent of our houses have been destroyed. Bangladesh has been flattened. There is danger of famine. We need help. ...
>
> What do we do about currency? Where do we get food? Industries are dead? [!] Commerce is dead? [!] How do we start again? What do you do about defence? I have no administration. Where do I get one? Tell me, how do you start a country? (Sheikh Mujibur Rahman, expressing his astonishment to Anthony Mascarenhas shortly after his release from prison and return to Dhaka, Mascarenhas 1986: 9–10)

> The great sacrifices made in the revolutionary war in 1971 have not gone in vain. The revolution created a nation of gallant men who wrested independence from the most brutal perpetrators of genocide. This traumatic birth of the nation is possibly the greatest force ensuring its continuinity. The revolution has created heroes, myths, and a vision of *Sonar Bangla* (Golden Bengal). Bangladeshi 'generations yet unborn' will continue to be proud of the nation born of a heroic revolution and this will sustain them in their attempt to complete the unfinished task of realising a Golden Bangladesh.' (Maniruzzaman 1980: 238)

The war and the trope of resisting genocide provide the constituting moment for Bangladesh; the images of Mujibur Rahman's return to Dhaka are widely reproduced (Figure 9.8.) Yet they are also a key to the problems that later occurred.

Contemporary Bangladesh is complex and confusing both to those who visit from abroad and to those who are raised there. Many visitors feel it cannot survive. As Paul Ryder Ryan expressed it in 1999 in a book recording his six months stay as a visiting fellow teaching journalism, in particular the ethos

Figure 9.8 Mujibur Rahman's arrival at Dhaka airport, after serving the nine months of the 'war' in prison in West Pakistan. An image of joy, it can also be read as revealing an over personification of the hopes and expectations for the future (image courtesy NA Siddique)

of reporting crime and law and order issues. His account

> was written as this tortured beggar nation … was wracked by widespread political violence, extreme poverty, economic and social disorder, an arsenic poisoned drinking water supply, excessive crime, endemic corruption, chronic power woes, and devastating seasonal flooding and cyclones. Added to these troubles was the spectre of nuclear war in the region between arch-rivals India and Pakistan over disputed Kashmir.
>
> [...]
>
> Discussions, travels, and observations in 1999 … led me to the conclusion that the country is headed inexorably for a bloody civil war in the not too distant future. (Ryder Ryan 2000: v–vi).

The highly experienced journalist and writer on social justice, Jeremy Seabrook's advocacy is strident. In his vision today,

> Bengali culture – pluralist, humanist, rooted, with its songs, dance, folklore, drama, and literature – confronts the austere discipline of Islam, often within the same people. The confusion this creates is immobilising, and helps to explain the stagnation of Bangladesh, the slow pace of development, the survival of feudal values, and the persistence of poverty. What some observers identity as fatalism and inertia are no such thing; they are symptoms of the uneasy stalemate that has produced a caricature of democracy and locked the country into its apparent beggar-role in the drama of globalisation. (2001: 3)

He raises the contemporary significance of the attempted genocide

> The ravages of nature, political violence, corruption – all conceal the fact that Bangladesh is still in the grip of a continuing and indeed undeclared civil war, the unfinished business of its creation in 1971. Bangladesh was lost to Pakistan then; a loss which Pakistan and a powerful minority in Bangladesh never accepted. What was lost to Pakistan may still be regained for Islam, but not the traditional fluid and tolerant Islam of Bengal. (Seabrook 2001: 3)

Other accounts, rightly, make reference to the 'quiet violence' of everyday village and urban life (Hartmann and Boyce 1983). The struggle for survival faces geographical, social, economic and global factors that seem overwhelming. These fears need to be placed against the life affirming resistance and ingenuity of the people; qualities that have not been well served by National or International governance.

The constitutional ethos of Bangladesh has proved problematic. The immediate problems facing the newly formed government were dramatic enough; issues of national identity seemed less pressing but perhaps of longer-term difficulty. Two strands of identity, which different factions either contrasted or saw as intertwined, namely those of Islamic religion and Bengali language and local customs, underly the events of independence. Indeed, even local commentators find 'the quick shifts in the prominence of religion and language in Bangladesh ... bewildering' (Kabir 1995: 213). In the early part of the twentieth century the questions of identity the people of Bangladesh did not exist; instead there were questions for the Muslims of Bengal, notably, whether they belong to 'India', whether their mother tongue was Bengali, what social justice meant in the context of village life, who and what were the obstacles to be overcome? Thus a turn to separatist politics, could link religious identification and the claims of oppression (by the British and more particularly a Hindu landowning class) and could, temporarily at least, paper over issues that would come to the fore as village life gave way to rapid urbanisation, when globalism left no corners self-sufficient.

In the context of my study there are two sides here: one is the question of genocide and justice, the other is the boundary between the internal and the external. To what extent would the Bengali use of the term genocide stand up to independent scrutiny? The requirements of the UN definition, legalist vision, leads one to issues of evidence and intention. Much of the original vision of Lemkin and the idea of the destruction of a cultural potential, much of did not survive into the convention. A theme of chapter IX was the 'preservation of the integrity of a people' (1944: 90). The target of genocide was 'national groups as distinguished from states and individuals'.

> The idea of a nation signifies constructive co-operation and original contributions, based upon genuine traditions, genuine culture, and a well-developed national psychology. The destruction of a nation, therefore, results in the loss of its future contributions to the world. Moreover such destruction offends our feelings of morality and justice in much the same way as does the criminal killing of a human being: the crime in the one case as in the other is murder, though on a vastly greater scale. Among the basic features which have marked progress in civilization are the respect for and appreciation of the national characteristics and qualities contributed to the world culture by the different nations – characteristics and qualities which, as illustrated in the contributions made by nations

weak in defence and poor in economic resources, are not to be measured in terms of national power and wealth. (Lemkin 1944: 91)

Lemkin saw genocide as a form of cultural destruction and prevention of potential being realised. It seems clear that the target of the West Pakistan military actions was the cultural integrity of a tolerant, largely Muslim East Bengal, one that still had a sizeable Hindu population and thus certainly would amount to attempted genocide under that original vision. The military actions were also to remove a political grouping.

The UN Convention is cast in more legal terminology and reflects political compromise by representatives of nation states: the 'exclusion of political groups from the Genocide Convention represents one such compromise. No legal principle can justify this blind spot' (Van Schaack 1997: 2261). Van Schaack argues however, that the exclusion of political groups 'is without legal force to the extent that it is inconsistent with the *jus cogens* prohibition of genocide': this 'the *jus cogens* prohibition of genocide, which predates the drafting of the Genocide Convention, provides broader protection than the Convention itself. Political compromises such as those that occurred during the drafting of the Genocide Convention, cannot limit *jus cogens* norms' (Van Schaack 1997: 2262, 2272).

The convention definition for genocide is also criticised for failing to embrace 'cultural genocide' the destruction of the language and culture of a group (Cassese 2003: 96; Morton and Singh 2003: 56). Schabas (2000: 187–8) puts the cultural element as a component of evidence of the intent to destroy a group.

Bangladesh experienced no war crimes trials, no truth and reconciliation commissions, no IMTs, but famously the Genocide convention was invoked in connection with the events in a way that shows the state-orientated nature of international legal order (*The Pakistani Prisoners Case*). In this instance Article IX of the Convention ('Disputes between the Contracting Parties relating to the interpretation, application or fulfillment of the present Convention, including those relating to the responsibility of a State for genocide or any of the other acts enumerated in Article III, shall be submitted to the International Court of Justice at the request of the parties to the dispute.') was invoked before the International Court of Justice in 1973. After the Pakistani army surrendered, India detained approximately 92,000 Pakistani troops and together with Bangladesh proposed to try some of these prisoners. Bangladesh passed 'An Act to provide for the detention, prosecution and punishment of persons for genocide, crimes against humanity, war crimes and other crimes under international law.' In response Pakistan instituted proceedings against India on 11 May 1973, alleging that India intended to hand 195 Pakistani prisoners over to Bangladesh for trial for genocide and crimes against humanity.

The argument of Pakistan was to the effect that measures adopted by Bangladesh indicated that it intended to try the Pakistani prisoners for genocide, including the adoption of the Bangladesh Collaborators (Special Tribunals) Order 1972, whose preamble made reference to those who 'have aided and abetted the Pakistani armed forces in occupation in committing genocide and crimes against humanity'. A number of exhibits showed Indian and Bangladeshi authorities using the term 'genocide' to describe the conduct of Pakistani troops. Pakistan argued that this would breach the Genocide Convention, in that Pakistan alone had an exclusive right to try the prisoners. Pakistan declared that by virtue of Article VI ('Persons charged with genocide or any of the other acts enumerated in Article III shall be tried by a competent tribunal of the State in the territory of which the act was committed, or by such international penal tribunal as may have jurisdiction with respect to those Contracting Parties which shall have accepted its jurisdiction.') persons charged with genocide shall be tried by the courts of the territory where the act was committed. 'This means that Pakistan has exclusive jurisdiction to the custody of persons accused of the crimes of genocide, since at the time the acts are alleged to have been committed, the territory of East Pakistan was universally recognized as part of Pakistan.' Pakistan cited Article IX of the Convention as the basis of jurisdiction. Pakistan also claimed that the courts of Bangladesh could not be deemed a 'competent tribunal': 'A "Competent Tribunal" within the meaning of Article VI of the Genocide Convention means a Tribunal of impartial judges, applying international law, and permitting the accused to be defended by counsel of their choice. ... In view of these and other requirements of a "Competent Tribunal", even if India could legally transfer Pakistani Prisoners of War to "Bangla Desh" for trial, which is not admitted, it would be divested of that freedom since in the atmosphere of hatred that prevails in "Bangla Desh", such a "Competent Tribunal" cannot be created in practice nor can it be expected to perform in accordance with accepted international standards of due process.' Pakistan's suit was accompanied by an application for provisional measures, requesting the repatriation of Pakistani prisoners of war and civilian internees to proceed without interruption, and that they not be sent to Bangladesh pending the proceedings. India replied in letters of late May and early June 1973 that the Court was without jurisdiction. India chose to argue that the Court did not have jurisdiction since at the time of ratification in 1959, India had formulated a reservation to Article IX: 'With reference to article IX of the Convention, the Government of India declares that, for the submission of any dispute in terms of this article to the jurisdiction of the International Court of Justice, the consent of all the parties to the dispute is required in each case.' Procedure, not any accounting of the substance of genocide would be the grounds for decision. Public hearings were held, but India did not attend; it knew that procedural discussions would not touch justice. In the event, Pakistan informed the Court that the issues before it would soon be discussed in negotiations with India, and asked that the request for provisional measures be postponed. On 13 July 1973, the Court held that the application by Pakistan for postponement meant that there was no longer any request for interim measures, which was, by definition, an urgent matter. Pakistan produced a memorial on the issue of jurisdiction on 2 November 1973 and on 14 December 1973, Pakistan informed the Court that in order to facilitate negotiations with India it would not be proceeding with the case. The following day, the President of the Court ordered that the case be removed from the docket.

In reading the accounts and counter-accounts, in interpreting the language of 'trouble-makers', and 'anti-state elements', it is clear that the West Pakistan military actions amounted to the destruction of legitimate politics and the attempted cleansing of minority elements. That this was successful in part can not be denied: the numbers of Hindus in Pakistan reduced post-1947 and again after 1971; the treatment of the non-Bengali hills people pose a continuing matter of concern.

Instead of a series of complex, difficult, and sometimes bewildering political processes (along with their setbacks) the 'attempted genocide' of East Pakistan must be labelled a 'criminal' substitution of state-elite power. Yet, who, and by what processes can that label be confirmed? We encounter, and live with the consequences of the great divide, which renders the suffering, the 'in justice', of this place of little consequence to the inhabitants of 'civilized space'. To what extent does the contemporary domestic Bangladeshi situation reflect the absence of trials, conducted openly and in accordance with due process? There are two images of trials and social solidarity: in one the trial reinforces a collective understanding, reflecting the common consciousness of the 'society'; in the other it represents a methodology of working through dissensus. The absence of trials must be counter-posed to actions such as taken by General Ziaur Rahman (then President) against those who participated in the failed mutiny of 1977.

> According to official records he hanged 1,142 men in the two months from 9 October 1977 ... by the stroke of the pen Zia created more than two dozen kangaroo courts which tried and executed the mutineers virtually by assembly-line methods. There was no question of justice. Men were convicted and executed on the flimsiest evidence, by a judicial licence to murder (Mascarenhas 1986: 148, 149).

Institution building requires adherence to a distinction between politics and crime; here many suspect we see the criminalization of politics and the political use of criminal methods.

The result is a clear tension between the hope and the reality. Chowdhury (2003: 63–4)

> 'For nearly two decades, Bangladesh experienced either pseudo-democratic or military regimes. A democratic constitution was enacted ... but democratic politics floundered largely because of the authoritarian style of democratically elected leaders, or military intervention into politics. Parliament was denied its befitting place in politics and governance. It served as an inert instrument of the strongman in power, used only to legitimise policies. The judiciary was not granted its independence from the executive. The party system has been and still is fluid, split into factions, personality-centred and undemocratic in its internal operations. Thus, except for the bureaucracy, all other political institutions have largely remained undeveloped ...

That is a challenge still to be met.

Chapter 10:
Enlightenment, Wedding Guests and Terror: The Exceptional and the Normal Revisited

You remember the scene: the Ancient Mariner accosts the wedding guests, who are thinking of the wedding and not paying attention to him, and he forces them to listen to his tale. Well, when I first returned from the concentration camp I did just that. I felt an unrestrainable need to tell my story to anyone and everyone! … Every situation was an occasion to tell my story to anyone and everyone: to tell it to the factory director as well as to the worker, even if they had other things to do. I was reduced to the state of the Ancient Mariner. Then I began to write on my typewriter at night … Every night I would write, and this was considered even crazier! (Levi 1997: 224–5)

As a symbol, then, Christopher Columbus vastly transcends himself. He stands before the bar of history and humanity, culpable not only for his deeds on Espanola, but, in spirit at least, for the carnage and cultural obliteration which attended the conquests of Mexico and Peru during the 1500s. He stands as exemplar of the massacre of Pequots at Mystic in 1637, and of Lord Jeffrey Amherst's calculated distribution of smallpox-laden blankets to the members of Pontiac's confederacy a century and a half later. His spirit informed the policies of John Evans and John Chivington as they set out to exterminate the Cheyennes in Colorado during 1864, and it road with the 7th U.S. cavalry to Wounded Knee in December of 1890. It guided lfredo Stroessner's machete-wielding butchers as they strove to eradicate the Ache people of Paraguay during the 1970s, and applauds the policies of Brazil toward the Jivaro, Yanomami, and other Amazon Basin peoples at the present moment.

And, the ghost of Columbus stood with the British in their wars against the Zulus and various Arab nations, with the United States against the 'Moros' of the Philippines, the French against the peoples of Algeria and Indochina, the Belgians in the Congo, the Dutch in Indonesia. He was there for the Opium Wars and the 'secret' bombing of Cambodia, for the systematic slaughter of the indigenous peoples of California during the nineteenth century and of the Mayans in Guatemala during the 1980s. And, yes, he was very much present in the corridors of Nazi power, present among the guards and commandants at Sobibor and Treblinka, and within the ranks of the Einsatzgruppen on the Eastern Front. The Third Reich was, after all, never so much a deviation from as it was a crystallization of the dominant themes – racial supremacism, conquest, and genocide – of the European culture Columbus so ably exemplifies. Nazism was never unique: it was instead only one of an endless succession of 'New World Orders' set in motion by 'the Discovery'. It was neither more nor less detestable than the order imposed by Christopher Columbus upon Espanola; 1493 or 1943, they are part of the same irreducible whole. (Ward Churchill 1997: 92)

Is it not time to end this terror, though we call it by another name? (Memo sent to the Air Ministry by British Prime Minister Winston Churchill, March 1945 after the Allied bombing of Dresden)

Enlightenment: modern style

On 6 August 1945, enlightenment came upon the citizens of the Japanese city of Hiroshima:

> The light was startling. Even if you had your back to it, you felt the shock go through, right to the centre of your brain. Such intense heat.

So recalled Shuntaro Hida, a military doctor at the time stationed in a village four miles from the hypocentre or original 'ground zero'; the atomic blast washed towards him over the intervening hills 'like an avalanche' and he was struck with enough force to throw him back into the building. Takakura-San, working in the concrete-walled Bank of Hiroshima, just 260 meters from the hypocentre, was knocked unconscious the instant she saw the light. Amazingly, she survived; outside bodies were virtually vaporized, their shadowy remains etched onto metal and stone surfaces. Around 40,000 people died instantly (240,000 died within 5 years; there were c.85,000 long-term survivors):

> People ask me how I survived. I find it strange too. People that had been walking the streets were doubled up dead over each other for as far as I could see. They had died immediately. Naked. Burnt. I just asked myself, why?[1]

We now know that there was no legitimate reason for Hiroshima (see e.g. Takaki 1995; Gar Alperovitz 1995); it was spectacle of power – designed to provide state terror prefiguring a new world order, one where the possessor of this weapon could write and enforce the rules of international order. Today Hiroshima and Tora Bora stand linked in an underlying set of similarities of attitude: that of reliance on technologies of killing at a distance, where those that kill are remote from experiencing the human consequence; the forced importation of terror takes the place of political negotiation, of awareness of cultural diversity, of compromise. Hiroshima, Tora Bora, September 11, the Holocaust – all partake in that fare served up in the combination of modernity and imperialism, with the nexus of racism and 'othering' that allows calculations concerning action safe in the knowledge that the holding to account will not involve the other as a possessor of power.

Bin Laden claims the right to engage in attacks and inspire insurgency and be called to account not by the Judge of Hobbes, satisfaction of human desire, but Allah's will. Yet his rejection only confirms that which he claims to reject. Hiroshima, a message to the Japanese (but really read a message for the Soviets); September 1996 Operation Desert Strike, from B-52 bombers and US Navy Warships 44 cruise missiles strike targets in Iraq: 'Our missiles sent following message to Saddam Hussein, when you abuse your own people or threaten your neighbors you must pay a price' (US President Bill Clinton, Statement by the President, 3 September 1996); On September 11, 2001 'three 300,000 pound cruise missiles' strike targets in the US (as US Secretary of Defense Donald Rumsfeld described the hijacked airliners, Press Briefing 13 September 2001) in an attack which bin Laden claimed sent a clear message to the US people (though few wanted to listen and the video tapes of his message were not allowed to be played after their initial screening for 'reasons of National Security').

Within the confines of civilised space Hobbes condemned the human subject to be the desiring being, to follow the never-ending games of felicity: to dream – as Robert Merton reinterpreted it – the American dream. In the introduction I presented Primo Levi's dream; Takakura-San also has a dream:

> I dream that the bomb has been dropped again, and I think this time I will get away from it. I decide that I shall escape, and then I wake up. It is impossible to escape from a nuclear bomb, but I suppose that is a desire making itself apparent in my dream.

One bomb, one manifestation:[2] Is it possible to escape? Who is to be listened to?

Wedding parties: ambivalent guests

> This is by far the most accurate bombing campaign ever. What the Air Force and Navy are doing today with smart bombs is the 'realisation of a dream', said military analyst Loren Thompson of the Lexington Institute. Since the Gulf War there have been significant advances in bomb technology to create so-called smart bombs. A key development is the Joint Direct Attack Munition, or J-dam – a satellite-guided kit that fits over the tail of a normal bomb to transform it into a smart bomb for precision attacks. ('Afghan bombing "most accurate ever" ', BBC online, 10 April 2002)

> US military officials in Afghanistan have refused to apologise following the mistaken bombing of an Afghan wedding party on Monday which killed at least 30 people [subsequently confirmed at 48 with 100 injured, WM], insisting that aircraft had come under sustained and hostile fire …

> Afghans claim the wedding guests, who were celebrating near Deh Rawud village, in the mountainous province of Oruzgan, north of Kandahar, had been firing into the air – a Pashtun wedding tradition – when American planes struck. But a US spokesman claimed yesterday that the shooting was 'not consistent' with a wedding, saying that the planes had come under attack. 'Normally when you think of celebratory fire … it's random, it's sprayed, it's not directed at a specific target', said Colonel Roger King at the US airbase at Bagram. 'In this instance, the people on board the aircraft felt that the weapons were tracking them and were [trying] to engage them.'

> The US planes – including a B-52 bomber and an AC-130 helicopter gunship – dropped seven 2,000 lb bombs, he added. ('No US apology over wedding bombing', *The Guardian*, 3 July 2002)

> The contrast couldn't be clearer between the intentions and the hearts of those who care deeply about human rights and human liberty, and those who kill; those who've got such evil in their hearts that they will take the lives of innocent folks. The war on terror goes on. (President George W. Bush, speaking after the suicide bombings on London public transport, BBC online Thursday, 10 July 2005)

We live the great divide, the double standards, the different weighing of being human: in London, as in New York, officials of the nation state counted the dead and wounded from the suicide attacks (terrorism); in the bombing campaign on Afghanistan it was left to concerned individuals to try and estimate the civilians killed by 'collateral damage', or (largely unacknowledged) 'mistakes'. It did not take long, specifically by mid-January 2002 – estimated Marc Herold (2002) of the University of New Hampshire – for the US military to kill the equivalent number of civilians that died on September 11, 2001. Few noticed: the head of CNN had early in the campaign stated it would be 'perverse' to grant extensive coverage to civilian causalities.[3]

Weddings should be an expression of joy. They involve a complex display of human interaction, of individual and family desire, no matter whether the partners were first 'arranged' by family or chosen by the individuals; they are not separated off from social, economic and political flows, they are more a pause for breath, for reorganising the team. A pause that is celebrated and recorded; we have noted the role played by the RMCA in Tureven as a setting for wedding photos. Weddings proved particularly unlucky occasions in Afghanistan once the response to September 11 began. On 29 December 2001, for example, a wedding in the Qalai Niazi village in eastern Afghanistan was bombed by US planes: the UN said 62 civilians were killed, while UK newspapers put the figure as high as 107. On 10 January 2002, the *Washington Post* told the story of another wedding attack at Qalai Niazi when about 3:30 AM, while the family and their guests slept in the largest house after an evening of celebration, the US planes attacked: 'After an initial series of blasts in which men, women and children died, people fled in panic out of Qalai Niazi, which is located north of Gardez in eastern Afghanistan's Paktia province. Then more bombs fell, killing a dozen other people as they moved across the barren landscape.' In early May 2002, Britain's Royal Marines launched Operation Condor after Australian troops had allegedly come under fire from al-Qaeda and Taliban forces, and called in American bombers to launch an attack. But according to an Afghan press agency based in Pakistan, the men 'engaged' by the Australian troops and later bombed by US forces in fact 'belonged to a wedding party, whose traditional AK-47 firing celebrations had been mistaken for offensive fire'.

These are places of singular tragedy: I have not come across images of their terror, perhaps they were meant to be unrecorded. Thus another set of innocents die, largely unreported, of little consequence to the collective symbols of the western civilised space they are called upon to protect. Beyond the particularity of these weddings we have differing tropes, not just the reliance on high technology or weak intelligence, but the avoidance of reflexivity, of recognising links. Yet September 11 should demonstrate to the most insular follower of the NASDEX or sports season that links should not be ignored … the 'dark corners' of the world are not simply places for actions which are then relayed, in the style of Henry Morton Stanley, by friendly media.

Certainly one should not obscure the Taliban's brutality against women on behalf of their version of a pure Islam, their insularity and intolerance, their cultural genocide towards the history and diversity of the space they had taken custody of. The Taliban needed to be engaged, intellectually and if they were 'judged' dangerous, fought and contained. Yet our late modernity had few resources intellectually and morally to deal with that which the west had in large part created to wrest out some more civilised space from the grip of its opponents in the cold war. Al-Qaeda is different, perhaps a global insurgency; in understanding which the first item would be to reposition it as a brand name, a state of mind, an insurgency yes: terrorist organization no.

The ally in understanding is history, globally conceived (the same standard of history that bin Laden uses); the enemy is double standards, which ultimately enslave only the internal inhabitants of now not-so-easily protected civilised space leaving the external viewers fee to see their cynical version of reality freed from any obligation to engage with your version. That message unheeded, the war waged on behalf of 'western civilization' post-September 11, soon became a moral and epistemological disaster. On a tactical level, truth would have required acknowledging that it was the US (along with key allies, such as China) that in the all-too-present past spawned the forces it is now engaged with to counter Soviet communism, then the essence of the enemy of freedom and values of Western democracy. To acknowledge that 'there are no innocents in the present war at the level of collectivities despite the powerful deployment of the figure of the "innocent" killed on both sides of the divide' (Veena Dass 2002) would have appeared to some a weakness but would have given play for a longer term game.

Bearers of the counter message are not welcome; they are as the wedding guest recounted in the Rime of the Ancient Marnier. This was a tale of global travel and consequences of rash decisions, of giving in to the temptation to label a little known entity (an albertros) as the reason for one's misfortune and to kill all-too-easily and then suffer the misfortune, to lose faith in your enterprise; ultimately in the narrative of the need for transcendence, of a truth that guides beyond the appeals of the immediate. Upon returning, the narrator cannot communicate his lesson to the inhabitants of civilised space who have the enjoyment of the wedding to engage them. I had already decided on an image of the Rime of the Ancient Marnier as the cover of this text before coming upon Levi's self-reference. The image I have used is from a set of late ninenteenth-century etchings by the Englishman William Strang. It hangs in my study, one example from a series, but the rest were stolen from the framer who was meant to be framing them for me some 20 years ago. A minor crime (and the framer had even given my name to the Police as a possible suspect!), but one that has more immediate register with my life course than the events that Levi or Ward Churchill recount.

Levi has by now attained the status of a wise sage – but we should also remember that he could not cope with his status as witness and had ultimately to kill himself. Ward Churchill is different – in the wake of his comments on September 11, 2001 (Ward Churchill 2001 Internet; book length 2003) he has been the target of the neo-right who branded him an intellectual danger to American values.[4] Immediately after September 11, 2001 there were admittedly scattered, and much more outside of the US than inside, voices that spoke of blowback time:

> [We] now have several thousand of our own disappeareds, and we are badly mistaken if we think that we in the United States are entirely blameless for what happened to them.
>
> The suicidal assassins of Sept. 11, 2001, did not 'attack America', as our political leaders and the news media like to maintain; they attacked American foreign policy.
>
> … On the day of the disaster President George W. Bush told the American people that we were attacked because we are 'a beacon for freedom', and because the attackers were 'evil'. In his address to Congress on Sept. 20, he said, 'This is civilization's fight.' This attempt to define difficult-to-grasp events as only a conflict over abstract values – as a 'clash of civilizations', in current post-cold war American jargon – is not only disingenuous, but also a way of evading responsibility for the 'blowback' that America's imperial projects have generated. (Chalmers Johnson, The Nation, 15 October 2001, using the language of disappeared from Chile)

Ward Churchill (Professor of Ethnic Studies at the University of Colorado, Boulder) went, however, further. He was different in two ways. First, his claims involved a wide vision of history, invoking the grand scheme of colonialism: branding the figure of Christopher Columbus – the semi-mythical foundational personage of American 'society' – as the prefigure implicated in the genocides of modernity.

In his essay, Churchill argued that September 11 was inevitable blowback in response to US global terrorism and imperialist policies against Islamic nations. Using a phrase of Malcolm X that the assassination of President Kennedy was an example of the 'chickens coming home to roost' (specifically, that leaders of a violent system may themselves become victims of violence), Churchill applied the same analogy to the US system as a whole. Thus, September 11 was the postponed but inevitable moment when the US paid a small fraction of the political costs it has incurred in its ruthless assault on nations and peoples around the globe. Unless the US drastically changed its imperialist policies, it would be struck again, likely in a bigger and more destructive way.

His target was the contradictions and hypocrisies in the thinking of the US government and citizenry, whereby the nation mourns the victims of the September 11 attacks, but sheds no tears for the half-million children killed in the US economic blockade of Iraq during the 1990s, the many thousands of innocent citizens killed in the US bombing and invasion of Iraq, or the many others who died as a result of US support for dictators or direct or covert action elsewhere. September 11 is condemned as a heinous act, mass occasions of remembrance of the victims engaged in, while the terrorist violence the US directs against many other people throughout the globe is … ignored.

In Chapter 1 it was noted that Chomsky gave vent to some similar opinions, but he clearly condemned September 11 as a terrorist action; by contrast Ward Churchill argued that the World Trade Center, like the Pentagon, was a military not a civilian target, and thus flying planes into the twin towers was not an act of terrorism. Recalling the holocaust, Ward Churchill declared that the 2,977 people killed in the 'sterile sanctuary of the twin towers' were not innocent victims, but rather 'little Eichmanns'. There was little nuance to his claim that those killed in the World Trade Center were as culpable for US violence as top Nazi bureaucrat Adolf Eichmann was for Hitler's 'final solution'.

> Those in the World Trade Center … were civilians of a sort. But innocent? Gimme a break. They formed a technocratic corps at the very heart of America's global financial empire – the 'mighty engine of profit' to which the military dimension of U.S. policy has always been enslaved – and they did so both willingly and knowingly. (Ward Churchill, 2001 Internet essay: enlarged as 2003)

This initial draft was an emotive and loose essay; it was not reflective and considered scholarship and was all to apt to cause offence. Ward Churchill rightly drew attention to the cost of US imperialism in terms of human victims and damage to the concept of justice as well as problematising the easy distinction between a righteous 'us' (read US) and an 'evil' them; but the dangers and real horrors of fundamentalist movements rooted in fanaticism, intolerance, and violence should not be dismissed. Nor should reflexivity ignore the very real benefits and principled strands of Western enlightenment. Opposition to aspects of US policy is not opposition to enlightenment or to globalisation in general, no matter how many specific consequences and claims may and must be countered. (And, it must be noted, the specific claim for current US policy in its global dimension – notably to champion democracy – must be supported – though one may dispute the means).

Politics and globalism, are the consequences of communication and non-communication,[5] of violence and (non)translation, of intellectual imagination and boundary drawing. The new righteous war required any inconvenient history to be deemed irrelevant and reflexivity not engaged in. Consequently, it is difficult to acknowledge culpability or even our various linkages in complex historical patterns. Real injustices that have led, or provided, excuses for actions in rage and despair are then ignored. But events have histories, political life has consequences, and acting as if they did not is not just to demean intellectual endeavour, but to bastardise social life.

Knowing and the return of the repressed: the seduction of imperialist imagery [1]

In my Introduction I drew attention to Kaplan's argument concerning the need for American imperialism and the lessons he claimed to draw from British endeavours in nineteenth-century Egypt and Sudan. There are two images from that time that reflect the ideas that seduce current US elites. The first, I place as Figure 10.1, and entitle 'The illusion of friendly forces'. As US forces took (or appeared to take) control of Iraq's capital western media sought the image of 'friendly forces'; they expected and looked for any evidence of Iraqi's embracing US forces as liberators. The hope, openly expressed by Niall Ferguson, was of a benign new 'liberal' colonialism; Ferguson looked to a past occupation for guidance.

The contrast with Abu-Ubayd al-Qurashi ('Why did Baghdad Fall?', Al-Ansar, 17 April 2003) was clear:

> After the fall of Baghdad, voices of wailing and mourning swelled in many Islamic countries, while total numbness and silence encompassed other circles. While some lamented the capital of al-Rashid, others recalled the fall of al-Andalus. They forgot that the entire Arab world is as good as fallen, as long as Islamic law is abrogated and the people of Islam fill the prisons and detention camps … Yes, direct colonialism has returned again. Another Arab capital has fallen into its hands, as Jerusalem, Beirut (before resistance flared), and Kabul fell.

In the face of the claim that 'the people of Islam fill the prisons and detention camps', what images could Western justice present?

First those of Guantánamo Bay, a piece of land occupied by forced colonial treaty dating from the 1898 war with Spain and part of the US deal for opening up Cuba, renewed in 1934, a legal black hole where persons given no legal status were detained. Morally, Guantánamo Bay is America's 'heart of darkness'. I will reserve full details to a footnote.[6] Then the Abu Ghraib prison photos.[7] At first a few images came to light that showed Iraqi detainees being forced into simulated sexual acts, looking like they had been beaten up; subsequently various other images came into the public domain:

- An unmuzzled dog appears to be used to frighten a detainee. (Two military dog handlers told investigators that intelligence personnel ordered them to use dogs to intimidate prisoners.)

Figure 10.1 'A Friendly Power in Egypt.' The Welsh Regiment marching through the Metwali Gate in the main street of the 'nature' part of Lairo, 1887. (From a painting by W. C. Horsley MEPL) Ferguson (2004, his discussion pp. 217–25) relates that the post 1883 British occupation of Egypt (along with Sudan after the battle of Orderman) for all the promises to leave lasted until 1956. Having, as with Iraq in 2003, had a quick military victory 'it swiftly became clear to the British administrators charged with the task that Egypt's finances could be stabilized only with sweeping reforms, but that these would be possible only if there were an ongoing British military presence'. In the supremely condescending words of Evelyn Baring, the all-powerful British agent and consul-general in Egypt from 1883 to 1907, "We need not always enquire too closely what these people … themselves think is in their own interests. … It is essential that each special issue should be decided mainly with reference to what, by the light of Western knowledge and experience we conscientiously think is best for the subject race." As Gladstone put it in his diary, the challenge was "how to plant solidly western & beneficent institutions in the soil of a Mohamedan community?" Ferguson sees

'[A] government reluctant to be labeled "imperialist", compelling economic reasons for intervention, a failure to arrive at a multilateral solution, indigenous resistance to occupation, popular support for it at home and technocratic reasons to maintain a military presence for an unspecified period. The net result offers an intriguing template for the United States in Iraq'.

Promising to leave Egypt, there soon appeared many 'protestations of the temporary nature of the British presence'. In 1922 they formally declared Egypt independent, and in 1936 they pronounced their military occupation at an end, yet as late as October 1954, 18 years after the occupation had supposedly ended, there were still 80,000 British troops in the canal zone, a huge military base covering an area the size of Massachusetts. Fergusson claims that the occupation brought financial and social stability to Egypt and strategic advantage to Britain. Perhaps, he finally suggests, the best thing we can hope for Iraq is 'an organized hypocrisy'

- An Iraqi detainee appears to be restrained after having suffered injuries to both legs with blob stained cloth in front of him. (It is unclear whether his injuries were from dog bites.)
- A US soldier gives the 'thumbs up' sign as she appears to be stitching up a prisoner's leg wound. It is unclear, though the wounds are suggestive, whether the injury was from a dog bite.

- A baton-wielding US soldier, appears to be ordering a naked detainee covered in a 'brown substance' (that appears similar to human excrement) to walk a straight line with his ankles handcuffed.
- A US soldier in a flak jacket appears to be using both hands to restrain a dog facing and very close to an Iraqi detainee.
- In what appears to be a hallway, a hooded detainee, seems to be handcuffed in an awkward position atop two boxes, while the frame seems to show the prisoner's ankle cuffed to the door handle behind him.
- An unidentified soldier appears to be kneeling on naked detainees.
- A US soldier with his right arm and fist cocked appears prepared to strike one detainee in a pile of detainees.
- Along a prison walkway, a hooded detainee seems to have collapsed with his wrists handcuffed to the railings.
- Two photos showing Spc. Charles Graner and Spc. Sabrina Harmon posing over the body of a detainee who was allegedly beaten to death by CIA or civilian interrogators in the prison's showers. [The detainee's identity and details of his death are now known.]
- A detainee with wires attached to his genitals.
- A dog attacking an Iraqi prisoner.
- An Iraqi prisoner and American military dog handlers. Other photographs show the Iraqi on the ground, bleeding, presumably from dog bites. (Variously published: *The New Yorker*, 9 May; *The Washington Post*, 20 May and 11 June; *ABC News* 19 May; CBS on *60 Minutes II*, June 2004)

These images of the 'liberation' of the Iraqi people are some of the photos that led to an investigation into conditions at the Abu Ghraib prison, once the detention and torture facility used by Saddam Hussain against his political opponents, and now run by the occupation authorities. Brig. Gen. Janice Karpinski, at that time in charge of the occupiers' detention facilities throughout Iraq (later dismissed from her post and reduced in rank to Cornol while 9 US soldiers were charged) had earlier stated: 'This is international standards. It's the best care available in a prison facility'. (CBS interview, 2003)

Thus the US administration internationalised the standards for its occupation.

So far the alleged grotesqueries are more analogous to the nightmares that occur occasionally at American prisons, when rogue and jaded guards freelance to intimidate and humiliate inmates. The crime, then, first appears not so much a product of endemic ethnic, racial, or religious hatred, as the unfortunate cargo of penal institutions, albeit exacerbated by the conditions of war, the world over. (Victor Davis Hanson, *Wall Street Journal* opinion piece of 3 May 2004)

This was intended to be reassuring; the images were after all only the product of the normal, though unfortunate, business of penal institutions. But the final words, 'the world over' are incorrect. This statement is rather an acceptance of the exceptional American penal system populated disproportionately by low-income blacks and Latinos. In this mainstream media presentation, guards 'occasionally' choose to 'freelance to intimidate and humiliate inmates'; in the world known to prisoners (and surely criminologists), guards frequently intimidate, humiliate – and brutalize.[8] This other world links here the external actions of the US military and the US incarceration industry. One of the main actors at Abu Ghraib, Staff Sgt. Ivan Frederick, had worked for 6 years as a guard for the Virginia Department of

Corrections. A special agent in the US Army's Criminal Investigation Division, Scott Bobeck, testified that Sgt. Frederick and a corporal apparently 'were put in charge because they were civilian prison guards and had knowledge of how things were supposed to be run' (Seymour Hersh, *The New Yorker*, 10 May).[9]

Trying to contain the outrage provoked by the prison images by speaking to viewers of Arabic-language television on 5 May, President George W. Bush said the people of Iraq 'must understand that what took place in that prison does not represent the America that I know'. We may take him at his word for in his term as Governor of Texas and then as President of the US, Bush rebuffed every plea to ameliorate the flagrant injustices and brutalities inside the courtrooms and prisons of Texas and the entire country. Bush's 'knowledge' is a politically constituted artifact.[10]

Converse positions

Bush's statement that he does not know criminological reality is met by bin Laden's claims to recognise criminological facts and identities:

> We regret to tell you that you are the worst civilization in the history of mankind. You ransack our lands, stealing our treasures and oil ... Your forces occupy our land .... You have starved the Muslims of Iraq ... So what is left on the list of the most heinous, evil and unjust acts that you have not done? (Bin Laden, 'Letter to Americans', *Waaqiah* [Internet site] posted 26 October 2002)

Earlier that month bin Laden stated that US leaders and people had not learnt 'the lessons of the New York and Washington raids' and had not changed the policies behind 'previous crimes'. However:

> Those who follow the movement of the criminal gang at the White House, the agents of the Jews, who are preparing to attack and partition the Islamic world, without disapproving of this, realize that you have not understood anything from the message of the two raids. Therefore, I am telling you, and God is my witness, whether America escalates or de-escalates the conflict, we will reply to it in kind, God willing. God is my witness, the youth of Islam are preparing things that will fill your hearts with fear. They will target key sectors of your economy until you stop your injustice and aggression or until the more short-lived of us die. ('Statement by Bin Laden', *AJSCT*, 6 October 2002)

Controlling language: situating war – national or global?: the seduction of imperialist imagery [2]

In the post-September 11 environment, the terms of 'war' and 'crime' ranged free of stable epistemological coordinates. War has become an overused term knowing not how to obey the internal – external divide. The 'war' on drugs that devastates social and political processes by legitimating neo-military 'policing' cannot be won because 'war' is an inappropriate concept to apply to a social problem. So to the 'war on terror' cannot be won, in part, as retired US Army general, William Odom, told C-SPAN viewers (October 2002): 'Terrorism is not an enemy. It cannot be defeated. It's a tactic. It's about as sensible to say we declare war on night attacks and expect we're going to win that war. We're not going to win the war on terrorism. All it does [this use of language] is whip up fear'. And this is fear with consequences, including Acts of Parliament or Senate that may close down liberal democracies by taking away due process and previously hard fought for rights. Defining the enemy as terrorism and terrorists maximises confusion, in part deliberately to maximise the range of possible targets, and provides a cloak of respectability to actions otherwise illegitimate.[11] Yet the language of war is not coherently applied to Osma bin Laden, who becomes a 'terrorist', and, those who were captured in Afghanistan become 'enemy non-combatants', neither enemy soldiers or criminals.

Internally incoherent, the actual tactics used in this war on terror reflects the failed calculations of Vietnam where US General Westmoreland laid out the phraseology used today with respect to Islamic (fundamentalist terrorists): 'The Oriental doesn't put the same high price on life as does a Westerner. Life is plentiful. Life is cheap in the Orient'. (As filmed in the 1974 documentary 'Hearts and Minds', quoted Derrick Jackson, 'The Westmoreland mind-set', *International Herald Tribunal,* July 2005.) Jackson surmised that assumption led to 'bombing without a conscience … admitting no mistakes along the way'.

The official media helped the cause repeating, without critically analysing, the body counts and reinforcing the notion that there were a fixed number of enemy combatants and that as you killed them you reduced the number left to fight – but this was wrong for it was not specific individuals that was the enemy, it was a cause. Similarly the two mistakes of this 'war'. First, to ignore the political and religious message behind bin Laden and conflate the issue into a matter of mindless terrorists (who would then by implication be limited in number and thus able to be killed or captured). Second, bin Laden can not be fought according to the rules of traditional warfare which call upon attacks on the enemy's 'center of gravity', or those vital areas that will ultimately defeat him. For as Anonymous summarises 'Bin Laden has no center of gravity in the traditional sense – no economy, no cities, no homeland, no power grids, no regular military … Bin Laden's center of gravity, rather, lies in the list of current US policies toward the Muslim world because that status quo enrages Muslims around the globe' (2004: 263). Consequently, the bombing – even when the (Western) media is kept away as with Iraqi towns being retaken provides messages that make bin Laden's case. Take the comments of the military historian and former war journalist Max Hastings upon a video that captured of the 'reality' of the freeing of Fallujah from insurgents:

> This is a scene straight out of Platoon or Full Metal Jacket. A soldier gazing down on a prostrate enemy sees him move and shouts: 'He's f***ing faking he's dead.' Another soldier fires a single contemptuous shot into the wounded man's head, and says laconically: 'Well, he's dead now.'
>
> On Saturday in Fallujah, that shocking melodrama was played out for real. US marines shot a wounded and helpless Iraqi – in a mosque, of all places – while an NBC television news camera recorded every detail. The images have flashed across the world, into the homes of thousands of millions of people, many of whom already hate what America is doing in Iraq.
>
> … Here are the crusaders for democracy, as George Bush and Tony Blair portray themselves and their soldiers, acting like animals. Even before this atrocity, the world recoiled from the spectacle of Fallujah shattered in the name of freedom.
>
> … Two months ago in Basra, a British officer said to me: 'We were appalled by those pictures from Abu Ghraib. They seemed to cut the legs off the whole moral basis for our presence here.' So they did. So, likewise, does the film footage from Fallujah.

Americans pursue a doctrine of firepower which causes NATO allies to think them unfit for any role in which 'hearts and minds' must be won. The fact is that the American way leaves few hearts and minds alive to parley with. American soldiers possess a contempt for people of alien races, which cost them defeat in Vietnam and could well cost them failure in Iraq.

... It is not enough for George Bush to declare from the distant citadels of Washington that the Coalition's forces are pursuing an honourable cause. On the battlefield, they must also be seen to be fighting in an honourable way.

... Not only have they abused Iraqis, they have been shown before the world to abuse Iraqis. The damning visual evidence is there.

... whatever happens afterwards to the Iraqi people, the way Bush has waged his war in Iraq has inflicted lasting injury on the cause of democracy. Who can again take seriously this President's claim to be fighting for freedom and virtue, when metaphorically he delivers such proclamations from the wreckage of Fallujah?

... I would suggest that what happened in Fallujah this weekend is arguably more the handiwork of Bush, Rumsfeld and Cheney than of the wretched marine who fired the shot.

... only a fool in the White House would suppose that he can win the War Against

Terror through so much blood recklessly shed, such mountains of rubble so carelessly created.

Every frame of film of Saturday's murder in Fallujah is worth another legion of recruits to al-Qaeda.

... Why shouldn't people hate George Bush? (Max Hastings, "Marine atrocities mock US cause", *The Daily Mail*, 17 November 2004)

Thus the incoherence of the second image of operative coercive power, notably Figure 10. 2, no matter how seductive the appeal of a power 'Imperially efficient, domestically clean'; the search for a technology of military power, or put simply, delivering destructive force, that is able to deliver firepower aboard, without threatening domestic political opinion runs up now against the millstone of the international media. And practically, for all the financial investment, security for an imperial military in a 'no body bags' environment is a mirage. As reports of suicide attacks in Iraq and Afghanistan demonstrate US grounds forces are susceptible to attack in ways they can not easily defend against (or only at the cost of killing civilians at road blocks and so forth); thus, the dream of the super weapon and the response of the suicide bomber.

The task: to build coherent criminological language in the shadow of empire?

If the language of war is inappropriate what of crime? In the face of September 11 should a strong president have stood tall, used the symbolism of sovereignty, yet acknowledged its global linkages, asked for the patience and resolve of the American public in tracking down the criminal perpetrators of the attacks, using the combined forces of intelligence and police services of various 'nations' in the process transcending bare national interest?

The answer here must be a qualified yes. The qualifications lie in the current weaknesses of a conception of global justice, jurisprudential, procedural and explanatory. Take the explanatory: the weakness of criminological language is that it has come from processes of production that destroy its ability to globalise, to cope with the crimes of imperialism, including the Holocaust. Thus inserting the terms 'terrorist' into a pseudo-criminological

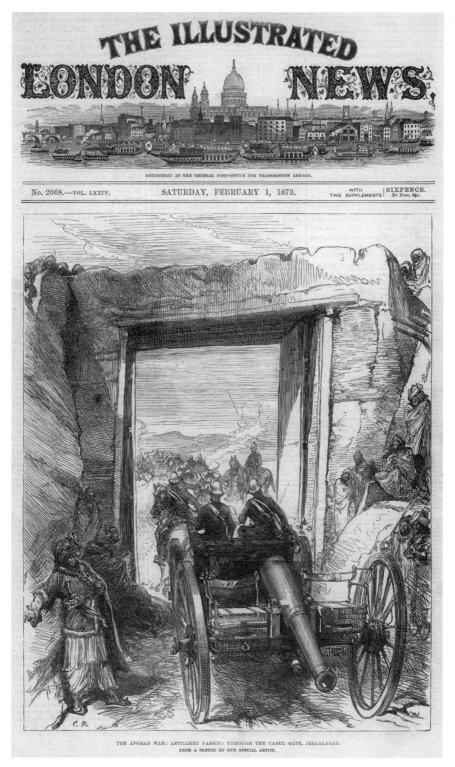

Figure 10.2 'In the current US temptation the canon has been replaced by the bomb and the cruise missile.' (Bacevich, 2002: 149)

sentence again fails: I thus agree with Anonymous (2004: 16–17) that Ralph Peters is wrong when he writes that bin Laden 'is an apocalyptic terrorist of the worst kind, and his superficial agenda ... is nothing compared to his compulsion to slaughter and destroy'. Bin Laden and those inspired by him 'are not trying to destroy the world in an Armageddon-like battle, and they are not psychologically deranged people prone to and delighting in the murder of innocents'. Claims that bin Laden and those inspired by him as psychopaths, sociopaths and inherently evil hark back to a criminological language long discredited that reduced a governmental project to claims about individuals and their criminality (and thus their suitability or lack of suitability to cope with social life). September 11 was a crime and it requires a global response; and that in turn requires a global justice. But this involves recognition of a legitimate global politics and the creation of avenues for real political opposition; real dissent.

This is not the current situation and it does not appear to be a realist prospect. I thus agree with Anonymous (2004: 17) that when those in the Islamic world 'ask Professor Lewis's question, "What went Wrong?" the answer comes back: the actions of the US as heir to the British Empire in the Muslim world, are what is wrong. As evidence for their claim, they point to specific real-world realities.' Anonymous is also cutting with his conclusion: either get used to a long war – and be prepared to accept far higher casualties and much greater use of violence than currently – or change US policies towards the Muslim world. But I disagree with (what I take at least) his realist position of national interest. He quotes Peters with favour, namely 'We Americans must avoid fantastic schemes to rescue those for whom we bear no responsibility. In dealing with nationalism and fundamentalism we must be willing to let the flames burn themselves out whenever we are not in danger of catching fire ourselves. If we want to avoid the needless, thankless deaths of our own countrymen, we must learn to watch others die with equanimity.' Anonymous continues:

> Can any U.S. official, academic, politician, or pundit credibly claim to know what is going on in Iraq's sectarian and tribal politics, Afghanistan's tribal and ethnic rivalries, or the tribal – religious – ethnic politics of the Balkans, Rwanda, Liberia, or Congo? Can anyone honestly believe the claim that Washington will broker a 'just peace' between Israel and Palestine is anything other than a thirty-year-old, mindlessly repeated mantra? Can anyone even describe the basic elements of the Islamic faith and their impact on world affairs? More to the point, can it be proven that it would make a substantive – vice emotional – difference to U.S. security if every Hutu killed every Tutsi, or vice versa; every Palestinian killed every Israeli, or vice versa; or if Serbs, Croats, and Bosnians exterminated each other to the last person? The brutal but correct answers are: we do not understand these conflicts, and none of them, regardless of who wins, endanger U.S. interests. All evoke empathy and stir emotion, but it is, as always, a cruel world, and each nation's one mandatory duty is to care for and defend itself.
>
> For our own welfare and survival, we must 'watch others die with equanimity' and help after 'the flames burn themselves out' by focusing our overseas intercourse on trade, sharing knowledge, and donating food and medicine. America must not commit abroad unless genuine national interests are at risk, and she must go to war only for survival and then act to annihilate the enemy. We must let our efforts to perfect self-government and ensure equality for all at home be the example that spurs democracy abroad. We must

unflinchingly let foreign dragons devour each other without expending American lives, treasure, and self-respect on an endless series of fool's errands.   (2004: 251–2)

Few have expressed so clearly the desire to return to the nation-state paradigm and oppose the case for the US policing the world. However, the forces of globalism have made the claim about 'those for whom we bear no responsibility' untenable: those 'others' are linked with the powerful and the less powerful in ways that mean that responsibility can not be shrugged off, no matter how effective the demarcations of civilised space are. The Holocaust haunts, even if we push it off to a specific time and place away from our new civilised space.

What then are the options?

Bush and Osama bin Laden dance as mirror images of each other (bin Laden is even credited by Bush's democratic opponent in the Presidential elections as making the crucial interjection that ensured Bush's re-election – 'It was the tape that did it': John Kerry), September 11, provides a global media event, the great exception, that underlies the deconstruction of the great divide. In the immediate aftermath of September 11, the US Congress authorized the President to 'use all necessary and appropriate force against those nations, organizations, or persons *he determines* planned, authorized, committed, or aided the terrorist attacks … or harbored such organizations or persons' (115 Stat. 224, September 18, 2001: Authorizations for Use of United States Armed Forces).

Thus under the measures adopted in 'the global war on terror', pace Guantánamo Bay, the US Military claims the authority to arrest and punish an accused terrorist without any federal court interference whatsoever. The play on discourse eludes categories: The 'war on terrorism' is claimed to be a real war, just like World War I and World War II. Terrorism is denied that status of a crime but instead made an act of war. Anyone whom the US Military accuses of terrorism becomes a prisoner of war, not a criminal defendant. But the prisoner is not entitled to the protections of the Geneva Convention, which governs prisoners of war, since these prisoners, the US terms, are 'illegal combatants' since terrorism is not a lawful way to wage war and because the combatants are not wearing military uniforms. The foundation stone of the procedure: the requirement that the US President sign a formal order designating the prisoner to be an unlawful combatant in the war on terrorism.

At this time the state of exception defines the sovereign: he who is given the power to make the definitions determines the preconditions for the new legal order; yet this state of exception is surprisingly familiar.

We return to that movement of the colonial declaration of martial law, or, when in Europe's turning of its colonial impulses upon itself, law bowed to a new sovereign with the seizure of the Furher principal. Thus law after Auschwitz reveals again its fractured weaknesses, its lack of learning from the past. In the face of this some may consider that the great divide must be overcome, that the illusions of civilized space be torn asunder, that the pursuit of a global justice be engaged in with a sense of crisis-stricken urgency … yet the response of power?

On the 17th February 2006, US Defense Secretary Donald Rumsfeld speaking to the Council of Foreign Relations could have paraphrased the

Figure 10.3 Image of a woman, East Pakistan (now Bangladesh) 1971, face lowered and with hair covering her face. Image courtesy of Liberation War Museum, Dhaka, where it is displayed with the message: 'one of the survivors of a West Pakistaini rape camp'. I had originally wished this image to form the front cover of this text. However, the graphic designer's reply was clear: the image was unsuitable, it was not dramatic enough, it was too ambiguous and it created uncertainty about the message (what is the woman doing? Is she ashamed or Ö). Other images of suffering were proposed as 'more in keeping with the desired impact'. We are now confronted almost daily with images of suffering from areas temporarily marketed as suitable for pity, concern and help. Attention is heldÖ then the image and issue forgotten. The proliferation of these images do not, as Stan Cohen rightly shows (States of Denial, 2001) lead to action and justice. When this text was first typeset the typesetters (located, in line with contemporary global realities) in India, no doubt anxious to fill in the gaps left by this author, ignored the words 'caption to follow' and substituted 'Hooded Iraqi detainee with wrists handcuffed to the railings'. Perhaps thereby they offered a lesson in the tropes of repetition and avoidance, in the instability in demarcating aggressor and victim. No image has a secure relation to 'reality' and this image originated in a conflict - a vast set of 'crimes' - located very much in the shadow of the 'cold war'. It was now misread in a 'new world order' where a main player is the dialectics between the intensification of a very postmodern American Empire and its opponents. Conscious of this repetition, the gamble that by force of arms, by a militarist global Pax America, agreement can be reached on the terms of remaking the world order in its own image, becomes a strange candidate for a comforting presence post September 11. Conversely, this image invokes, at least for me, the appeal of different striving, no doubt open to its own deconstruction, that of a global justice that reaches from the corridors of the White House to the villages of Bangladesh. In building jurisprudential and procedural resources scholarly disciplines such as criminology will need to overcome the false divides between civilised space and its other. Travelers on this voyage will also need to look to two paths, on one must engage the empire (bridges with power built, consciences pricked, differences translated) while constructing the conditions for the transformation

sentiments of Kaplan with which I structured my introduction when he said that some of the US' 'most crucial battles were now in the newsrooms ... Our enemies have skillfully adapted to fighting wars in today's media age, but ... our country has not'. The US must fight back by creating a more effective, 24-hour propaganda machine, or risk a 'dangerous deficiency' (BBC News-online, 'US losing media war to Al-Qaeda', 17th February 2006).

The inhabitants of civilized space must have their peace of mind.

Notes

Introduction

1 As Samuel Huntington put it in his famous 1993 essay entitled 'The Clash of Civilisations?' (1993: 39):

> The West is now at an extraordinary peak of power in relation to other civilisations. Its superpower opponent has disappeared from the map. … It dominates international political and security institutions and with Japan international economic institutions. Global political and security issues are effectively settled by a directorate of the United States, Britain and France, world economic issues by a directorate of the United States, Germany and Japan, all of which maintain extraordinarily close relations with each other to the exclusion of lesser and largely non-Western countries. Decisions made at the UN Security Council or in the International Monetary Fund that reflect the interests of the West are presented to the world as reflecting the desires of the world community. The very phrase 'the world community' has become the euphemistic collective noun (replacing 'the Free World') to give global legitimacy to actions reflecting the interests of the United States and other Western powers.

On celebratory accounts of a new globalism, see Ohmae (1990) and Bryan and Farrell (1996).

2 By criminology is meant sets of logos that pertain to the expression 'crime' and are loosely organised institutionally in university departments, publishing outlets, conferences and interpersonal networks. These organisational processes present a self-description where enlightened, mostly secular, rational, scientific discourses are orientated around the norm of objectivity and relevance. On tracing the first usage of the term criminology and criminologists to refer to those who took a modernist, scientific approach to the study of crime and its causes, see Beirne (1993: 233–8). My own use is not bounded by institutional histories or scientism but is consciously vague, allowing the field of criminology to include the normative and the emotive as well as the positivist.

3 A term later championed by the conservative economic historian Niall Ferguson (2003a, 2003b, 2004), who specifically agrees on the role of history: 'The dilemmas faced by America today have more in common with those faced by the later Caesars than with those faced by the Founding Fathers' (Ferguson 2004: viii).

Chapter 1

1 For example, 'How bin Laden Got Away', *The Christian Science Monitor*, 4 March, 2002; 'US Concludes bin Laden Escaped at Tora Bora Fight', *Washington Post*,

12 April 2002; 'Document Suggests bin Laden Escaped at Tora Bora', CNN 24 March 2005 (after the Bush administration had been at pains during the 2004 election campaign to suggest that bin Laden might already have been in Pakistan).

2   For a critical take on the campaign by an insider with 20 years experience in the US intelligence service, see Anonymous (2004); for the effect of the war on terror on civil liberties in the US, see Barber (2003); Cole and Dempsey (2002); for an example of the effect of September 11 on everyday relations between Euro-descent peoples and Arab immigrants and refugees see Poynting *et al.* (2004), *bin Laden in the Suburbs* (Australia).

3   For example, Van Creveld in a text aptly titled *The Transformation of War* (1991: 224) 'As war between states exits through one side of history's revolving door, low-intensity conflict among different organisations will enter through the other. Present-day low intensity conflict is overwhelmingly confined to the developing world ... So far the effects of these developments in the so-called "First World" had been marginal – but then this world comprises less than one-fifth of humanity. Who can point to a society so isolated, so homogeneous, so rich, and so wallowing in its contentment as to be in principle immune?' Howell (2001: 29) asserted: 'The weapons of choice have become back-pack bombs, computer and biological viruses, and chemicals. Military units are no longer divisions and battalions, but teams of two or ten. Terrorism is the next highest stage of war.'

4   The questions focused on narrow issues of 'intelligence', see for example, *Newsweek*, 27 May 2002, issue entitled, 'What Bush Knew'; *Newsweek*, 10 June 2002, issue entitled 'The 9/11 Terrorists the CIA Should Have Caught'; *Time*, 27 May 2002, 'Special Report: What Bush Knew Before 9/11'. In 2004, a Congressional Committee on the events of September 11 reported revealing systematic intelligence failures. The broader question lies in the attitude of complacency, both as to the moral fibre of the 'nation' that assumes the West is correct, and also, whether or not one shares that first assumption, safe.

5   The experience of British urban social theorist, David Harvey, who lives and teaches in New York, was typical for an internationalist: 'Desperate for news on the morning of September 11, I twiddled my radio dial and hit upon a station that was relaying accounts from the BBC. They reported events as an attack upon the main symbols of global U.S. financial and military power. This was such an obvious interpretation that I scarcely remarked upon it. But when I tuned in to the U.S. media, I noticed that no one took that line. In New York ... September 11 was represented as a local disaster of horrific magnitude with unfathomable causes and unthinkably tragic personal and local implications. Nationally, the media immediately followed President Bush in construing it as an attack upon "freedom", "American values", and the "American way of life". An amazing consensus was quickly forged throughout the nation on that point to the exclusion of almost anything else. But when I switched back to the international media, the BBC's phrasing was far from aberrant or unusual (2002: 57).

6   The precise combination Hobbes intended is a matter of speculation. In his own time his critics accused him of reducing God and religion to the status of human artefacts. See Mintz (1962). Others accused him of making secular power into a 'God'. However, Georges Lyon (1893: 210–11) displays a subtle grasp of the reciprocity and fragility involved: '(Power) is a god, yes, but a god crafted by

human hands and a god who disintegrates if human hands withdraw. If those who are equals by nature choose to elevate one among them to extraordinary heights, it is not out of idolatry, but to shelter themselves beneath him, and thereby to enjoy the benefits of peace.'

7 The legal origins of which are usually linked in the literature of political relations and International Law to the Treaty of Westphalia in 1648.

8 Hobbes's depiction left out two great advances in technology that were to change the course of history in favour of European 'nation states' (and their imperial projects) over the Islamic Empire and the Chinese, namely the ocean going ship and the musket/rifle. In the early 1600s the Ottoman rulers had been warned that while they were undoubtedly the strongest militarily on land, Europeans, particularly the Spanish and the Portuguese, now outside Islamic hegemony, had developed ships armed with cannon. Ships that were capable of taking an open ocean route from Europe to Asia (thus depriving the Ottomans of custom duties and providing new sources of income for Europe). Moreover, the European arms race, concentrating on developing ways of killing at a distance, was to render the sword obsolete in favour of the musket, then the rifle and the machine gun, a military advantage that the Islamic and Chinese Empires never overturned (cf. Lewis 2002; Keegan 2001).

9 Hobbes appeared to expect that the exiled English court outside Paris would see in the *Leviathan* a way of guaranteeing future *loyalty* of their subjects. The court did not however, read it this way. Instead of a quasi-patriarchal authority Hobbes presented reason. But what then guaranteed the privileges and powers of the Aristocracy? Could they not be replaced by other 'officers' who would be more efficient in new forms of power? Additionally, Hobbes did not make out a case for sovereignty as a right, it seemed more a responsibility.

10 Criminology discovered this respect of Hobbes – without realising it – when it picked up Merton's famous 1938 Article on the consequences of the American dream. For current account of urban life and consumerist culture see Hayward (2004).

11 Hobbes expressly described himself as a modern in his orientation to discourse, arguing that the authority of logos did not depend on the antiquity of the writing: 'Though I reverence those men of ancient time, that either have written truth perspicuously, or set us in a better way to find it out ourselves; yet to the antiquity itself I think nothing due. For if we will reverence the age, the present is the oldest' (*Leviathan* 1991: 487). The question was on what grounds to establish a new authority that did not depend on the old strategies of legitimisation, yet did not seem such a radical break that it would not find any acceptability, and this performability. Jeffrey Stout (1981: 2–3) tries to capture the ambiguity in the spirit of modernity in the phrase 'the flight from authority' (*The Flight from Authority: Religion, Morality and the Quest for Autonomy*). He also saw it as doomed: 'Modern thought was born in a crisis of authority, took shape in flight from authority, and aspired from the start to autonomy from all traditional influence whatsoever; that the quest for authority was also an attempt to deny the historical reality of having been influenced by tradition; and that this quest therefore could not but fail'.

12 Corrigan and Sayer (1985) recognise this as the central function of a modern State: 'States, if the pun be forgiven, state. They define in great detail, acceptable

forms and images of social activity and individual and collective identity; they regulate, in empirically specifiable ways much ... of social life'.

13 'And the grounds of these Rights [constituting Sovereignty], have the rather need to be diligently, and truly taught; because they cannot be maintained by any Civil Law, or terror of legal punishment. ... For the Punishment, they take it but for an act of Hostility; which when they think they have strength enough, they will endeavour by acts of Hostility, to avoid' (Hobbes 1991: 232).

14 'Time, and industry, produce every day new knowledge. And as the art of well building, is derived from Principles of Reason, observed by industrious men, that had long studied the nature of materials, and the divers effects of figure, and proportion, long after mankind began (though poorly) to build: So, long after men have begun to constitute Common-wealths, imperfect, and apt to relapse into disorder, there may, Principles of Reason be found out, by industrious meditation, to make their constitution (excepting by externall violence) everlasting. And such are those which I have in this discourse set forth' (Hobbes, 1991: 232).

15 Although it must be stated clearly that their actions were against central tenets of Islam (which, for example, prohibits suicide). In an article a week after September 11 under the title 'When the Innocent are Murdered, We All Go into the Dark With Them', Ziauddin Sardar (2001) argued that 'Islam cannot explain the actions of the suicide hijackers, just as Christianity cannot explain the gas chambers, Catholicism the bombing at Omagh. They are acts beyond belief, by people who long ago abandoned the path of Islam'. Yet this is to forget the history of the major religions: for Hobbes the 'wars' of the 1600s were enabled by sacred texts being misinterpreted for the personal power of the interpreter; the group around Osama bin Laden offered a reading of written texts in the name of enhancing their own power. But does this downplay their politics? What of the statement of the then Malaysian Prime Minister Mahathir Mohamad in a keynote speech 17 November 2001 (quoted Noor 2002: 162): 'any number of people can use it [Islam] for their own objectives. The main thing for them is to gain power. We are going to be faced with this problem for a long time. We know that we in Malaysia are vulnerable to such forms of extremism, like every other country in the world. Every one of us is vulnerable.' Although this acknowledges that power is at stake, it individualises the motive. But what if bin Laden was a genuinely religiously committed opponent of the American empire project? The point here is that bin Laden is a political actor, finding interpretations in Islam that can support his political programme; but few outside the Muslim world appear to accept him as a political actor, instead he is cast as a terrorist.

16 Samuel Huntington articulated a relatively common refrain, although one explicitly denied by George W. Bush and Tony Blair when he said that 'reactions to September 11 and the American response were strictly along civilisation lines', (*Newsweek*, Special Davos Edition, December 2001–February 2002: 13). Huntington's position was rejected by many, for example, Amitav Acharya, 'Clash of Civilisations? No, of National Interests and Principles', *International Herald Tribune*, 10 January 2002: 6. Huntington's thesis was first laid out in his 1993 article and expanded in his 1996 book, *The Clash of Civilisations and the Remaking of World Order*. The phrase derives from Bernard Lewis's attempts to uncover 'The

Roots of Muslim Rage' (1990): 'It should be clear that we are facing a mood and a movement far transcending the level of issues and policies and governments that pursue them. This is no less than a clash of civilisations – that perhaps irrational but surely historic reaction of an ancient rival against our Judeo-Christian heritage, our secular present, and the worldwide expansion of both.' Huntington (1996: 217) expanded: 'The underlying problem for the West is not Islamic fundamentalism. It is Islam, a different civilisation whose people are convinced of the superiority of their culture and are obsessed with the inferiority of their power.'

17 Booth and Dunne (2002: 11) implied that the events required an international court to establish guilt of the accused. 'On October 8 [2001], "Operation Enduring Freedom" began as B52s and F14s struck at suspected al-Qaeda bases. Was there an alternative to this strategy of using force against the Taliban? Could the crimes have been met with an international police operation?' They pointed out that a core principle of democratic states is that 'it is not for the victim of crime (or their political leaders) to establish the guilt of an accused, only an impartial court can do this'. While the logic of their position is correct, they seem to write without awareness of the historical link between the creation of central courts and the establishment of central state power: both in terms of policing and enforcement mechanisms. That their position seems so far from the reality of extra state processes may be intentional, perhaps pointing to the next stage of judicial processes? Historically, the choice of the terminology of a 'war' against terror is suspect: wars are not meant to drag on, as the impact of the 100 Years War and the 30 Years War showed. The 'war' against drugs is accepted by many commentators as increasing drug usage, or at least by those commentators who do not have a stake in perpetrating the conflicts and increasing the flow of resources to the 'fight'. By contrast, police actions are normal by definition, a fact of social life.

18 Others, in positions of power, would assert that the trap was not being walked into: 'The mad creatures who committed these terrible crimes ... may have hoped to provoke us into mindless revenge in order to create even more devastation, but they are wrong' (NATO Secretary-General George Robertson, quoted *Time*, 24 September 2001). An assertion that mixed together claims of irrationality (madness) and acute rationality and was, moreover, no response to the complexity or the time frame of the 'trap' that Fisk indicated.

19 And it should be clearly recognised that for many commentators, a movement towards ' "international justice" is, in fact, the abolition of international law' (Chandler 2002: 137). Since international law rested upon the notion of equal respect for 'territorial integrity', which in effect meant that 'I can not pursue you as a ruler for your crimes since I do not want you or others to pursue me for mine'. Or put in the more acceptable formulation of international law jurisprudence: 'If states have rights in international law, the bearers of the correlative duties are, in the standard formulation, other states. This reciprocal relationship is taken to provide the sanction in international law, as well as a description of the system ... In general, I observe your territorial integrity because in doing so I reinforce a system in which you are expected to observe mine' (Vincent 1992: 258).

20 A statement that may in hindsight be seen as the first step in destroying much of the sympathy felt for the victims of September 11 and the US; for if victim-hood was shared globally, it followed that the 'justice' to be sought must be global and not partial. If the achievement of 'justice' requires a struggle – as it must – it is necessarily a victory. But this victor's justice must be that of the victory of values, and not simply military might. Or to paraphrase Hobbes, it must be a victory whose virtues can be taught to subsequent generations and not debunked as soon as the threat of force is lifted.

21 About 40,000 usually worked in the twin towers, and around 150,000 visitors passed through the World Trade Center complex every day. At the time the first plane struck, a short time before normal working hours, between 16,000 and 18,600 people were in the towers and 87 per cent of them escaped.

22 As captured, for example, by the photographer Sebastiao Salgado in his book *Migrations* (2000).

23 In 1974, the twin towers were the site for 'the artistic crime of the century' (Petit 2003). In a demonstration of 'funabilism' a group around Philippe Petit smuggled themselves and their equipment up the towers and Petit spent an hour walking to and fro across a tightrope stretched between the two towers. The extensive planning and technological virtuosity involved in this act of claiming the symbol 'of late capitalism' for a 'joyous performance' were similar to those needed for an act of terrorism.

24 'Thirty-five years ago it was possible to build a development like the World Trade Center only by using the legal instrument of a public corporation. Private enterprise could not have pulled off what the Port Authority was able to do using its supragovernmental powers, which are beyond any public accountability; its public bond from financial risk, which no private developer could enjoy; and its capacity to exact tax abatements from the city and state' (Ross 2002: 127–8).

25 As a building, the World Trade Center was a spectacularly vulnerable adversary when symmetrically aligned with its attackers. Yamasaki's design for the World Trade Center was borne into a complex urbanism of weak building codes, real estate schemes, and urban master plans, a web-like, reciprocal organization, filled with productive lies, scams, and disguises. Contemporary journalism often focused on the building's 'smart' elevator network as just one of its intelligent building systems. But while the building appeared to be a giant, nondescript computing unit, filled with an efflorescent network, unlike the elevator technologies within or the global urbanity of the city outside its doors, the simple volumes contained in its spatial envelope had a much less intelligent organizational repertoire. To maximize rentable area, the floors were almost completely segregated, connected only by thin strands of exit stairways. Finally, the buildings rose from their urban context via a symmetrical, competitive urge: to offer the largest volume of commercial real estate in the world's tallest towers. (Easterling 2002: 192–3). The design of the WTC with its 'slow, sequential routes of circulation' gave it a vulnerability to this crime. Easterling also points out that the vulnerability was common to Yamasaki's other constructions: Yamasaki's own Pruitt-Igoe housing towers in St Louis, demolished in 1973, just a year before the completion of the World Trade Center, marked the beginning of a number of

intentional implosions of high-rise housing towers all across the country housing that had almost self-destructed in the face of adversaries like drugs and crime. Any user, dealer, criminal or maintenance problem affected the entire tower through the core, the unavoidable space of circulation. The towers were exactly the kinds of structures that an epidemiologist would regard as highly susceptible to contagions. Like these towers, the World Trade Center organization was so singular, so impossible to partition, that any negative influence could possibly unleash a deadly epidemic. The reductive and symmetrical organization, lacking resilience, with no means to dissipate disturbance, only enhanced the potential for catastrophe (pp. 193–4).

26 Publicly stated by the British Prime Minister Tony Blair, German Chancellor Gerhard Schroder and Peter Struck, German Social Democrat parliamentary leader, among others. There were many displays of international solidarity: the band played the US national anthem during the changing of the guard at Buckingham Palace, Dublin's shops closed for a day of mourning, Canadian stores sold out of American flags and Le Monde ran the headline: WE ARE ALL AMERICANS. The feeling was not to last. By late 2002/early 2003, Schroder had used anti-American feelings to gain re-election, the French President Chirac went on to use his veto powers in the UN Security Council to enhance his popularity, while Tony Blair waged a campaign of encouraging Bush to adopt a multilateral, rather than a unilateral approach in the 'war on terror' as America's closest ally; a campaign he was largely unsuccessful in and lost political credibility for apparently having already committed the UK to fully support the US in whatever actions it took. When stressing the need to abide by 'international law' the decision to join the US in war on Iraq required either a creative reading of such law or simple breach (a radical Hobbesian position, i.e. that in the absence of an international sovereign there was realistically no law was not a publicly espoused position), which in turn contributed to a further loss of political creditability. By March 2003 Richard Dawkins could write: 'Osama bin Ladin in his wildest dreams could hardly have hoped for this. A mere 18 months after he boosted the US to the peak of worldwide sympathy unprecedented since Pearl Harbour, that international goodwill has been squandered to near zero.' 'Bin Ladin's Victory', *The Guardian*, 22 March 2003. In the aftermath of the London bombings in July 2005, US signs read 'we are all British now'.

27 Homer-Dixon (2002: 55 and 60) typifies this changed awareness: 'modern societies are filled with supercharged devices packed with energy, combustibles and poisons, giving terrorists ample opportunities to destructive ends. To cause horrendous damage, all terrorists must do is figure out how to release this power and let it run wild or, as they did on September 11, take control of this power and retarget it.' Thus large gas pipelines running through urban areas, the radioactive waste pools of nuclear reactors, and chemical plants provide 'countless opportunities for turning supposedly benign technology to destructive ends'.

28 And when it was the turn of Afghanistan civilians to die in the bombing campaign of late 2001/2 it is hard to find accounts of their suffering in the mainstream Western media: this was other, them not us. Contrast Natasha Walter: 'don't think that just because they have suffered so much during the last generation that their grief is any the less now. Or because they don't get obituaries in *The New York Times*

that each of the civilian lives lost in Afghanistan isn't as precious to their loved ones as the people who died in the Twin Towers. Frankly, that's the way that terrorists think, that some civilian lives matter less than others, and that some – or even hundreds, or even thousands – of innocent people can be expended in the pursuit of the 'greater good'. ('These Refugees Are Our Responsibility', *The Independent*, 22 November 2001).

29 Four examples of immediate commentary in the UK press that consciously adopted an 'external' viewpoint (all from *The Guardian*, 12 September 2001): Faisal Bidi, 'Yesterday's attacks are the chickens of America's callous abuse of other's human rights coming home to roost'; Saskia Sassen, 'The attacks are a language of last resort for the oppressed'; Martin Woollacott, 'Western policy may have played a part in creating the anger which led to the attacks'; the left-wing MP George Gallaway's article was entitled 'Reaping the Whirlwind'.

30 For example, 'in the stunned weeks after Sept. 11, there was a powerful impulse to simply rebuild the towers, all 110 stories, to show that Americans could not be brought low by terrorists. Then people remembered that however much we love them in retrospect, the Twin Towers were a botch. At their completion in 1973, they were already anachronisms, products of an imperial Modernism that destroyed human-scale neighborhoods and in their place erected mammoth towers on desolate plazas. ... The towers were symbols of "the mid-century arrogance of architects ... What they did to lower Manhattan was an act of vandalism just as complete as Sept. 11." ' (David Childs, who had been commissioned by Larry Silverstein, the developer, to oversee the drawing up of proposals for the Trade Center site, reported in *Time*, 27 May 2002).

31 As Fidel Castro put it in a speech to the Non-Aligned Movement summit in Kuala Lumpur (Castro 2003 reported the *Guardian*) responding to the US President's dicta that American security will require a military that must be ready to strike at a moment's notice in any dark corner of the world.

> That is what we are, dark corners of the world. That is the perception some have of the third world nations. Never before had anyone offered a better definition; no one had shown such contempt. The former colonies of powers that divided the world among them and plundered it for centuries today make up the group of under-developed countries.
>
> There is nothing like full independence, fair treatment on an equal footing or national security for any of us; none is a permanent member of the UN security council with a veto right; none has any possibility of being involved in the decisions of the international financial institutions; none can keep its best talents; none can protect itself from capital flight or the destruction of nature and the environment caused by the squandering, selfish and insatiable consumerism of the economically developed countries.

32 'Americans were not accustomed to what so much of the world had already grown weary of the sudden, deafening explosion of a car bomb, a hail of glass and debris, the screams of innocent victims followed by the wailing sirens of ambulances. Terrorism seemed like something that happened somewhere else – *and somewhere else a safe distance over the horizon.* And then, last week, in an instant, the World Trade Centre in New York City became ground zero. At 12:18 on a snowy Friday afternoon, a massive explosion rocked the foundation of the Twin Towers of the Trade Centre in lower Manhattan ... [T]he landmark building near Wall Street seemed chosen with a fine sense of the symbols of the late

20th century. If the explosion, which killed five people and injured more than 1,000, turns out to be the work of terrorists, it will be a sharp reminder that the world is still a dangerous place. And that the dangers can come home.' *Time*, 8 March 1993 (emphasis added).

33 As well as 'secular' targets in the Muslim countries of Turkey, Egypt and Tunisia.

34 The quote is from the *Observer* header of 10 March 2002. It continues: 'The greatest change of all, however, has also been the most difficult to see. It is the way in which America, the world's only remaining superpower, has begun to think about itself. A state unrivalled in political, military and economic power has come to feel itself singularly vulnerable.'

35 Conversely, others could argue that they stemmed from America's reluctance to use its military might around the world. Compare Thomas Friedman: 'But the critics [of the American response to September 11] are missing the larger point, which is this: September 11 happened because America had lost its deterrent capability. We lost it because for 20 years we never retaliated against, or brought to justice, those who murdered Americans. ... The terrorists and the states that harbour them thought we were soft, and they were right. They thought they could always 'out-crazy' us, and they were right. They thought we would always listen to the Europeans and opt for 'constructive engagement' with rogues, not a fist in the face. America's enemies smelled weakness all over us, and we paid a huge price for that.

His solution? In part, to be willing 'to restore our deterrence and to be as crazy as some of our enemies'. (Comment, *The Guardian*, 16 February 2002 [First published *New York Times*.]). Friedman's comments may need to be read in the understanding that on 28 March 1999, the *New York Times Magazine* features as its cover story an earlier story by him in which the cover image was of a clenched fist, brightly painted with a Stars and Stripes. The image was to fit with Friedman's 'manifesto for the fast world', namely that 'the emerging global order needs an enforcer. That's America's new burden'. Walter Mead (2003) opines that the attacks were a consequence of the failure to force Saddam Hussein to disarm: 'The existence of al-Qaeda, and the attacks of September 11, 2001, are part of the price the United States has paid to contain Saddam Hussein. The link is clear and direct. Since 1991 the United States has had forces in Saudi Arabia. The forces are there for one purpose only: to defend the kingdom (and its neighbours) from attack. If Saddam Hussein had either fallen from power in 1991 or fulfilled the cease-fire agreement and disarmed, US forces would have left Saudi Arabia. But Iraqi defiance forced the US to stay, and one consequence was devastating. Osama bin Laden founded al-Qaeda because US forces stayed.'

36 As the Uruguayian writer Eduardo Galeano (2001) expressed it: 'Saddam Hussein was good, and so were the chemical weapons he used against the Iranians and the Kurds. Afterwards he became evil. They were calling him Satan Hussein when the US finished up their invasion of Panama to invade Iraq because Iraq invaded Kuwait ... [After the Gulf war of 1990] Satan Hussein stayed where he was, but this number one enemy of humanity had to step aside and accept becoming number two enemy of humanity in favour of Osama bin Laden. With Osama bin Laden proving difficult to catch or kill, by 2003, Saddam Hussein regained the number one spot'.

37 Officially, the process began when Bush authorised the CIA to assassinate suspected terrorists. *Time*, 18 November 2002, reported in an article entitled, 'They Didn't Know What Hit Them' that an American Predator drone operating by remote control fired a missile into a car in Yemen carrying suspected terrorists killing those inside. 'US officials think that one of the six killed was Kamal Derwish, a Yemeni American cited in federal court papers as the ringleader of an alleged sleeper cell in the US'. Another was a 'former bodyguard of bin Laden's'. In a letter to *Time*, 16 December 2002, a reader commented: 'Apparently, the US now kills without judicial trials and without questions. Are we nothing more than technically advanced snipers and terrorists?' On 21 March 2003, the opening action of the 2nd Gulf War, instituted by the US and aided by a small coalition with the UK and Australia actively contributing troops and officially aimed at destroying the 'regime' of the Iraqi President Saddam Hussein, and destroying the capacity of Iraq to make weapons of mass destruction, was a 'decapitation strike'. Acting on intelligence information that Saddam Hussein and key members of his party would be at one of three specific locations, 36 Tomahawk missiles and four 'smart' bombs dropped from two 'Stealth' fighter-bombers, attempted to assassinate him. A week later, in actions around the city of Basra, the British military command announced with some satisfaction that they had successfully targeted a building where some 200 plus members of the ruling Ba'ath party were meeting, ordering a bombing of the building that killed most of those inside. Here highly sophisticated and technically precise bombs were targeted at persons who were now a mixture of political–criminal–paramilitary status, 'legitimate' since the 'war' was against a 'criminal regime' and not a nation state. On 8 April, as Baghdad was surrounded by US forces, a restaurant was bombed in a western suburb where intelligence reports had indicated Saddam was in another attempt to kill him and his sons. However, it had previously been a policy of the CIA to plan and assist in the assassination of leaders deemed to be against the interests of the US: see William Blum (2003) for a list of CIA assassination plots between 1949 and 1991 (and, sobering as it may seem, it is an incomplete list).

38 It is still astonishing to appreciate Hobbes's clarity: 'But whatsoever is the object of man's Appetite or Desire; that is it, which he for his part calleth Good: And the object of his Hate, and Aversion, Evill; And of his contempt, Vile and Inconsiderable. For these words of Good, Evill, and Contemptible, are ever used with relation to the person that useth them: There being nothing simply and absolutely so; nor any common Rule of Good and Evil, to be taken from the nature of the objects themselves' (Hobbes: 1991: 39).

39 'In the midst of a large populated area which by and large is free of physical violence, a "good society" is formed. But even if the use of physical violence now receded from human intercourse, if even duelling is now forbidden, people now exert pressure and force on each other in a wide variety of different ways' (Elias 1982: 270–1). Elias stresses the widening out of the stratagems and behaviours of court society into the wider realm, 'high society' becomes spread as the realm of 'good society'; that realm is always however, geographical, an 'area'.

40 Israel's actions towards the 'terror' threat from the occupied territories may provide a sight of things to come: two Israeli lawyers drew up a detailed list of the

'liquidations' and 'attempted assassinations' carried out by Israel's security forces during the al-Aqsa Intifada, from November 2000 to April 2003. They found that Israel carried out no less than 175 liquidation attempts, averaging one attempt every five days which killed 235 persons, of whom 156 were suspected of crimes. They concluded: 'The consistent, wide-spread policy of targeted liquidations bounds on a crime against humanity' (reported Aryeh Dayan, *Ha'aretz*, 21 May 2003.

41 Writing soon after September 11 Said (2001) commented: 'There really is a feeling being manufactured by their media and government that a collective "we" exists and that "we" all act and feel together, as witnessed by such perhaps unimportant surface phenomena as flag-flying and the use of the collective "we" by journalists in describing events all over the world in which the US is involved. We bombed, we said, we decided, we acted, we feel, we believe, etc., etc. Of course, this has only marginally to do with reality, which is far more complicated and far less reassuring. Put more generally: all claims made in the name of a universalistic "we" face problems of universal aspiration and particularistic practice.'

42 *The Economist* (22–8 September 2001: 35) conveyed a flavour of the immediate post September 11 creation of what it called 'The home front': 'The whole country is aflutter with flags. They fly at half-mast from federal buildings. They fly from every other house and car you pass as you walk down the street. Huge flags decorate sports stadiums, tiny ones dangle from baby carriages … As well as patriotism, people are seeking solace in religion. Churches, synagogues and mosques are full to overflowing … In his sermon in Washington's National Cathedral, Mr Bush recalled Franklin Roosevelt's phrase about "the warm courage of national unity." … But this warm courage turns hot on the question of retribution. The opinion polls show nine out of ten Americans backing military action, and being willing to make whatever sacrifices are necessary so that this sort of thing does not happen again. The word "war" is heard everywhere.'

43 It is unlikely that either Bush or his advisors realised how closely the language mirrored the division the German catholic and later Nazi legal theorist Carl Schmitt drew between friend and foe (1923). For Schmitt, liberal democracy could only survive if in practice it excluded those who did not belong to the state. The cover of *The Economist*, 2–8 February 2002, portrayed a picture of Bush mid speech beneath the heading 'George Bush and the axis of evil'. The Leader called it 'a memorable phrase' noting that it was 'meant to galvanise support by turning a long and tricky foreign-policy challenge into a simple, moral issue'. The Leader called Bush's list of 'non-negotiable demands' about values to be defended 'impressive'. This list: 'the rule of law … respect for women … private property … free speech … equal justice … religious tolerance', was 'admirable' in aim; but *The Economist* warned that 'the application will be harder'. Not only do many countries that America would need on its side did not adhere to them, but 'alas, democracies that follow these values are also capable, on occasion, of being in the wrong and even of committing atrocities'. It warned that America would need to listen and engage in dialogue: 'To fight an axis of evil, even a superpower, needs an axis of its own'.

44 The attempts to make a coherent 'we' in the post-September 11 world seemed to echo the response to the verdict in O.J. Simpson's trial, 3 October 1995. As later

recounted, 'what Americans had in common that day was that we stopped using the phone for a few minutes: according to AT&T, phone traffic dropped 60 per cent from 10 AM to 10:05 AM P.T. In appliance stores and offices and diners, we dropped everything and watched as nine blacks, two whites and one Hispanic rendered their verdict: Orenthal James Simpson was not guilty of the murder of his ex-wife Nicole Brown Simpson and her friend Ronald Goldman. On the streets of African-American neighbourhoods and the campuses of black colleges, we high-fived total strangers in jubilation. In white communities, we sat in quiet shock or vocal disgust. On radio shows, we hailed the acquittal of the black former football hero as payback for years of police racism, and we condemned the decision as a simple case of money buying freedom. At New York City's Rokers Island prison, we broke into applause, guards and inmates alike. In the Harriet Tubman battered women's shelter in Minneapolis, Minnesota, we cried. Later that day, on the TV news, we watched each other watching, and soon that watching became the bigger news, for it taught us what else we had in common. We, each of us, could not believe that the other side could feel the way it did. We realised that we were not, in fact, 'we' (James Poniewozik, *Time*, 31 March 2003).

45 For example, in the opening decapitation strike Bush later told the NBC correspondent Brokaw: 'I was hesitant at first, to be frank with you, because I was worried that the first pictures coming out of Iraq would be a wounded grandchild of Saddam Hussein ... that the first images of the American attack would be death to young children'. Note that his concern appeared to be of the images of death to young children not concern as to their actual death ('Full Text of Brokaw's Interview with Bush', *The New York Times*, 25 April 2003).

46 Even presented to the outside world as the solution to American's security, as in the *International Herald Tribune* article of 2002, E. Eakin, ' "It Takes an Empire", say Several US Thinkers', 2 April 2002.

47 Conservative US commentators were rewriting the history of nineteenth-century imperialism. 'Afghanistan and other troubled lands today, cry out for the sort of enlightened foreign administration once provided by self-confident Englishmen in jodphurs and pith helmets ... the September 11 attack was a result of insufficient American involvement and ambition: the solution is to be more expansive in our goals and more assertive in their implementation' (Max Boot, 'The Case for American Empire', quoted *International Herald Tribune*, 2 April 2002). A decade ago Paul Kennedy was predicting American imperial overreach, now he notes that American military power far exceeds comparison with the reach of previous empires and asks that it be used. Robert Kaplan (2001) argued that only reference to the politics of past empires will give proper guidance to today's leaders. Bacevich, in a text entitled *The Imperial Tense: Prospects and Problems of American Empire* (2003) offers a selection of the best short articles published in 2002/3 on this. The British historian, now living in New York, Niall Ferguson, was clear: 'What is required is a liberal empire' (2004: 2).

48 Written self-consciously from the political left, Hardt and Negri's *Empire* (2000) postulates that only a concept of a new 'Imperial Sovereignty' is adequate to capture the new world order. There are three tiers of the imperial pyramid of power: the bomb, capital and ether (communication technologies). For these authors 'the spectacle of politics functions as if the media, the military, the government, the transnational corporations, the global financial institutions, and

so forth were all consciously and explicitly directed by a single power even though in reality they are not' (2000: 323). Thus while it has the appearance of domination, the US is a false target if seen as a sole imperial power. In their view 'the United States does not, and indeed no nation-state can today, form the centre of the imperialist project' (p. xiv).

49 As Polly Toynbee (*The Guardian*, 13 September 2002) wrote commentating upon Bush's UN speech: 'There he stood, this unlikely emperor of the world, telling the UN's 190 nations how it is going to be. The assembled nations may not be quite the toothless Roman senate of imperial times, but at the UN the hyperpower and its commander-in-chief are in control as never before: how could it be otherwise when the US army is the UN's only enforcer?' As the US seemed determined to push Saddam Hussein into total compliance or war, Toynbee rejected arguments that action in Iraq would be about oil ('if US companies want Saddam's oil, an oil-driven cynical administration could make peace not war and help themselves to fat contracts'), in favour of 'a new ideology', namely, 'Hyperpower is not enough unless it is exerted so forcefully that no state ever again challenges benign US authority'. The speech was a power to define: 'One thing was made crystal clear yesterday – there is no other source of authority but America, and that means there is no other law but US law'.

50 In Hobbes, the right to personal security, which the contract guarantees by means of the rule of law, is the result of a relation between the authorities and the citizen, the consequence of a political theory of sovereignty. It depends on a certain anti-imperial organisation of power. 'Not all states guarantee individual security, only those that refrain from exercising the right of life and death over their own citizens. Leviathan, the sovereign state, the state under the rule of law, is capable of terminating the wars within the body politic precisely because it does not make itself a conqueror or even military leader with respect to its own citizens; it takes the people's welfare as its objective.' (Kriegel 1995: 41)

51 To quote the Norwegian criminologist Nils Christie (1998: 126): 'In some states [of the US] the proportion of young males in the control of the penal system will be close to 20 per cent, which comes close to a civil war, a civil war where the privileged have created their protected territories, using the state machinery or private police as their soldiers and prisons as places for internment'.

52 As Bauman (2001: 209) puts it: 'In all order-building and order-maintenance endeavours legitimacy is, by necessity, the prime stake of the game and the most hotly contested concept. The fight is conducted around the borderline dividing proper (that is, unpunishable) from improper (that is, punishable) coercion and enforcement. The "war against violence" is waged in the name of the monopoly of coercion'.

53 Any figures were, however, a statistical construct. A WHO consultant epidemiologist relying on Iraqi figures in 1995 said that infant mortality rates had soared by 600 per cent and that estimate was argued by other agencies to translate to over half a million deaths. A 2000 UNICEF survey tried to obtain figures based on trends before the sanctions. Thus: 'If the substantial reduction in child mortality throughout Iraq during the 1980s had continued through the 1990s, there would have been half a million fewer deaths of children under five in the country as a whole in the eight year period 1991 to 1998.'

54 Note here the infamous comment of US Secretary of State Madeline Albright that 'we've decided that [the loss of life of Iraqi children] it's worth the cost' to 'set an example'; the example being of the consequences of defying the will of the US (interview broadcast on *60 Minutes* 1996). The ex-US Attorney General Ramsey Clark (1996) explored the issue in *The Impact of Sanctions on Iraq: The Children Are Dying.* UN Assistant Secretary General Denis Halliday resigned in protest at the effect of the sanctions and previous bombing of vital water plants, and so forth, calling it a 'policy of deliberate genocide': discussed in Ramsey Clark (1998) *Challenge to Genocide: Let Iraq Live.*

55 Or as Max Boot (editor of *The Wall Street Journal*) (2000) put it, since the West had conferred the status of nation states upon most of the territories in the current world order, if the powerful in these 'states' acted reprehensibly, the West should not feel bound by the discourses of sovereignty that it had itself created. Most of the world's nations do not have Westphalian legitimacy in the first place. They are highly artificial entities, most created by Western officials in the twentieth century ... There is no compelling reason, other than unthinking respect for the status quo, that the West should feel bound to the boundaries it created in the past. There is even less reason why the West should recognise the right of those who seize power within those borders to do whatever they want.'

56 For example Pfaff (2000/1: 58 and 64) who argues that the decline of the cold war 'left the United States with a huge military establishment of unprecedented policy influence' with the result that 'the prominence of military institutions ... and the availability of overwhelming force tend to influence the formulation of policy in ways that invite military remedies, even when these may be irrelevant.' The leading criminological example being the quasi-military response to the drug issue.

Chapter 2

1 Hence the *Sunday Telegraph* newspaper (29 February 2004: 24) opinion on the 'legality' of the war on Iraq goes too far in espousing (unwittingly no doubt) legal nihilism:

> The 'legality' or otherwise of the war is a non-subject, for the simple reason that there is no binding body of international law which compels obedience, either in morality or in fact, from the sovereign nations of the globe. ... The invasion of Iraq may or may not have been 'illegal' under international law. The point, however, is that the whole issue of 'international legality' is a gigantic irrelevance.

Against this statement: no, the moral bind is relevant even if there is indeed no binding force (presently) 'in fact'.

2 Usually referred to as *Vold*, after its original author; the above paragraph is paraphrased from Vold and Bernard, 1986, 'Theory, Research, and Policy', *Theoretical Criminology*, 3rd edn, chapter 18.

3 Though few would go as far as Wines (1910: 128) for whom Howard and Beccaria 'were chosen instruments in the hand of God for the elevation of the race by the better recognition of universal human rights'.

4 'Criminology was, in effect, an expression of the Enlightenment ambition to cure social ills by the application of Reason, and its emergence both expressed and

reinforced the developing administrative logic of nineteenth-century penal systems' (Garland 1990: 185).

5 By the time Winthrop Lane published a revised edition of Wines in 1919 he could close the text by noting the controversy whether universities should create whole departments of Criminology or fund individual Professorships of Criminology in various departments.

6 Leon Radzinowicz (1962: 168) provided a 'classic' formulation:

> Criminology, in its narrow sense, is concerned with the study of the phenomenon of crime and of the factors or circumstances … which may have an influence on or be associated with criminal behaviour and the state of crime in general. But this does not and should not exhaust the whole subject matter of criminology. There remains the vitally important problem of combating crime … To rob it of this practical function, is to divorce criminology from reality and render it sterile.

7 'The scholarly objective of criminology is the development of a body of knowledge regarding this process of law, crime, and reaction to crime … The practical objective of criminology, supplementing the scientific or theoretical objective, is to reduce the amount of pain and suffering in the world' (Sutherland and Cressey 1978: 3, 24).

8 This term is used in the sense ascribed it in chapter 9 'Mainstream criminology revisited' in *Criminology, theory and context*, 3rd edn (Lilly *et al.* 2002).

9 As the 'logical positivists' K. Popper, *The Logic of Scientific Discovery*; R. Carnap, *The Logical Structure of the World*; Hans Reichenbach, *Experience and Prediction*.

10 Or as Garland (2002: 17) comments on a related issue: 'As a discipline criminology is shaped only to a small extent by its own theoretical object and logic of inquiry. Its epistemological threshold is a low one, making it susceptible to pressures and interests generated elsewhere'.

11 Many of these features were known to more sophisticated writers. Thus Korn and McCorkle (1959: 367) argued that 'a considerable portion of penological literature has been devoted to constructing the universal evolution of principles and practices from ancient to modern times'. Analysing statements in the large earlier textbook of Barnes, for example, was founded on 'the assumption that an orderly evolution had taken place', with 'the implication that this progress came about as a result of a rational enlightenment among those who perceived the disadvantage of the older methods', an implication that the State had taken on a public role concerned with crime that previously was a matter of private vengeance and that this power (the State) was rationally controllable. They further argued that the evolutionary concept was compounded by a 'teleological implication', because the present was better, more progressive, more humane than the past, history was an accounting of how the past became the present under the influence of the progressive and the humane; thus the history was simply a confirmation of the present.

12 For an illustration of this see Garland's (2002) analysis of the rhetorical force of Radzinowicz's *Ideology and Crime*.

13 The discriminating feature of this criminology of the 'present' was apparent in Garland's (1999) review essay 'Crime in Late modernity', in which he favourably reviewed the everyday criminology of Marcus Felson. Garland was clear: 'Not all criminology is consonant with, or relevant to, the character of contemporary social

life. There is a huge inertia built into academic production which ensures that theoretical traditions continue long after they cease to connect to "the real world" ' (p. 362). He used this discriminating criterion – of connecting to the 'real world' – to warn against the dire predictions of Bennett *et al.* (1996), who had argued (with a rhetorical and selective use of 'civilisation') that 'previous civilisations have been overthrown from without: our present dissolution is from within'; namely, from 'a ticking crime bomb'. However, the same criterion could be used to argue that Garland gives a selective reading (and one strikingly resonant with that of Francis Fukuyama) of the nature of our contemporary social reality.

14 In an 'Author meets Critics' presentation at the British Society of Criminology Conference, Keele, UK, 2002, Garland stated that his history of the present was a history of those discourses that had been 'successful' as criminology. When he referred to criminology, he stated, he 'hoped he referred' to discourses that 'practitioners' would recognise, albeit partially, in their struggles and everyday routines.

15 As implicit in the accounts of several recognised 'criminologists' in *Thinking about Criminology* (Holdaway and Rock 1998). It is implicit in ethnomethodology, with its emphasis upon the contingent and moral basis of everyday life (Garfinkle 1967), and is explicit in most 'critical criminology', feminist writings and analyses of histories of punishment or 'crime and power'.

16 That provides a current emblem of public concern and connection with fighting crime, *Crimewatch*, through which the public are encouraged to identify otherwise anonymous assailants. This television programme, with its various manifestations in numerous countries, provides a means of connecting the public to a police performance in which incidents are reconstructed, closed circuit images of assailants screened, identikit pictures created. It responds to that image some commentators have identified, since in rural areas the majority of the victims know their assailants, while in cities, the killer and the mugger come out of the anonymous dark, their faces unrecognisable, their motives obscure. The viewers are encouraged to phone special incident lines and may themselves remain anonymous in throwing 'light on the incident'.

17 I have elsewhere (Morrison 2004a) acknowledged the few scattered voices that have been raised. See also Alvarez (2001) for a sustained attempt to integrate criminological approaches and examples of genocide. To this short list must now be added Hagen, Rymond-Richmond and Parker (2005).

18 An exception is de Haan's review of *The Oxford Handbook of Criminology* 2nd edn (de Haan 1999). While finding that 'it will allow criminology students to compete successfully with black letter law students by carrying around and showing off a truly disciplinary "Bible" ', he wonders at the localised answers to questions, such as what is criminology? that the text provides. 'As a reader from "abroad", I had expected an "Oxford Handbook" to be like the *Encyclopaedia Britannica*: a source of *general* knowledge. The editors decided, however, to provide a comprehensive map of criminological theory, research and debate in *Britain* ... such a narrow focus is ... wholly unacceptable where theoretical perspectives are concerned' (1999: 375). De Haan's remark concerning the *Encyclopaedia Britannica* may be more apt than he intended, as that text was originally conceived in the age of the nineteenth-century Empire.

19 As Ward Churchill, enrolled Keetoowah Cherokee, Professor of American Indian Studies in Boulder Colorado, lays out in his ironically entitled *A Little Matter of Genocide: Holocaust and Denial in the Americas, 1492 to the Present* (1997).

20 Indeed, Norbert Elias accepted the end of public executions as a key sign of the civilising process. However, others have seen them as linked to 'carnival culture' and their disappearance as more complex than Elias seems to suggest. See, for example, Bauman (1995: 149–152); Pratt (2002: chapter 2).

21 Such as Matza's (1969) distinction between 'correctional' and 'appreciative' criminology.

22 Source: Interpol International Criminal Statistics on the web. Accessed in 2003; as part of the anti-terrorist measures these figures are no longer available to the public!

23 'The prohibition placed on Magwitch's return is not only penal but imperial: subjects can be taken to places like Australia, but they cannot be allowed to "return" to metropolitan space, which, as all Dickens's fiction testifies, is meticulously charted, spoken for, inhabited by a hierarchy of metropolitan personages' (Said 1994: xvii).

24 The views of John Stuart Mill, who was both the leading English 'liberal' philosopher of the nineteenth century and a colonial administrator are revealing. In *Principles of Political Economy* he was clear:

> These [colonial territories] are hardly looked upon as countries ... but more properly as outlying agricultural or manufacturing estates belonging to a larger community. Our West Indian colonies, for example, cannot be regarded as countries with a productive capital of their own. ... [they are rather] the place where England finds it convenient to carry on the production of sugar, coffee and a few other tropical commodities. (J. Robson, ed., Vol. 3, 1965: 693)

25 Eric Hobsbawm (1975: 244) defined nineteenth-century European bourgeoisie as 'a body of persons of power and influence, independent of the power and influence of traditional birth and status. To belong to it a man had to be "someone"; a person who counted as an individual, because of his wealth, his capacity to command other men, or otherwise to influence them'. Magwitch achieved this in Australia but was subjected to an imperial spatial and culture apartheid with no possibility of cross over. Pip's use of Magwitch's money gives him great expectations, but his misuse results in debt. Some of this is paid off by a family member he had previously taken for granted but Pip clears his debts and achieves financial strength as partner of the firm in the Orient.

Chapter 3

1 The template is common today such as in the entire weekend magazine of *The Observer*, 27 April 2003, which had the title 'Crime Uncovered'. The cover posed the question: 'A Nation Under the Cosh? The truth about crime in Britain in 2003'. The centre spread was a map of crime in Britain 2003, with different areas shaded differently depending on figures taken from the latest British Crime Survey, 2001/2002. This was contrasted with the official criminal statistics and residents reported fear of crime. The theme of the report was the distinction between 'perception' and 'reality'.

2 As argued by Downes 1966: 71: 'the rate of delinquency in an area is the chief criterion for its 'social disorganisation' which, in turn is held to account for the delinquency rate'.

3 From the maps created by Guerry, for example, in his 1833 *Essai sur la statistique morale de la France* (reproduced, Beirne 1993: 120), it is apparent that the richest provinces in terms of total wealth were the location for the greatest number of reported offences against property. Guerry identifies that this may be because the greater total wealth may well be very unevenly distributed and may be accompanied by great poverty. Later theorists would look for 'relative deprivation', that is, even if the poorest were actually better off in terms of material living conditions, the fact that they were surrounded by images of greater wealth may stimulate feelings of frustration and encourage subjective desire to attain the wealth of the others.

4 Both Hart and Fraser may be sympathetic to Richard Rubinstein's (1996) belief that 'the Nazis did the dirty work for institutions that were destined to outlast them'; Hart, as with Kelsen, makes the positivist move to say that a lasting defence against this is to show that law is simply technique, but for Fraser law is, or should be, a shared social domain of ethical and social responsibility.

5 As apparent from the text above, Quetelet worked on the methodological assumption that human activity (or human nature) was to be studied as a phenomenon of the natural world, which he reinforced by arguing that it was possible to determine the average physical and intellectual features of a population. Through gathering the 'facts of life', the behaviour of individuals could be assessed against how an 'average man' would normally behave. He believed it possible to identify the underlying regularities for both normal and abnormal behaviour. The composition of the 'average man' could be known from graphically arraying the facts of life as bell-shaped curves. Society would have its normal state and its extremes or abnormal.

6 'Every race has its particular constitution, which differs from [the ideal type] more or less, and which is determined by the influence of climate, and the habits which characterise the average man of that peculiar country. Every individual again has his particular constitution ...' (Quetelet 1842: 99).

7 'The average man, indeed, is in a nation what is the center of gravity is in a body; it is by having that central point of view that we arrive at the apprehension of all the phenomena of equilibrium and motion ...' (1842: 96).

8 'In other words, there are no personal or social differences in *resistance* or *immunity* to contamination; all are equally vulnerable, and whether one escapes or succumbs depends on the degree of exposure (Korn and McCorkle, 1959: 298–9).

9 In common with many textbook accounts, the editor of this 2nd edition (as well as the 3rd), Bernard, appeared not to be concerned or, perhaps, simply not to notice, that mutually contradictory accounts of the data to be explained were presented in different chapters of the text as structuring the key questions for criminology. For – as has already been noted – in the chapter on social ecology theory the discussion was explained in terms of the data showing that delinquency was concentrated in the lower social class; this was later explicitly rebutted in later chapters but no reconciliation was attempted.

10 For a restatement of the need to keep on demanding for this conceptual separation, written by one of the authors, Bernard went on to include (see Stanley Cohen 1996), 'Crime and Politics, Spot the Difference'.

11 Burleigh and Wippermann (1991: 142) quote Hitler to a party rally of August 1929: 'If Germany were to get a million children a year and was to remove 700,000–800,000 of the weakest people, then the final result might even be an increase in strength'. Compare Quetelet (1842: 28): 'a country proceeds onwards to a more prosperous condition, when fewer citizens are produced, and when those existing are better preserved. The increase is then entirely to its advantage; for, if the fecundity be less, the useful men are more numerous, and generations are not renewed with such rapidity, to the great detriment of the nation'. Bonger himself was anti-Nazi and aged 63, took his own life on 15 May 1940 when the Nazis occupied his country. Whether his papers have been analysed and whether they provide a case study on academic sensibilities towards these issues I do not as yet know.

12 I will accept that Goldhagen (1996) demonstrates this in the case of ordinary 'Germans' participation in the holocaust (while not agreeing with his central thesis, see Chapter 8), and Gellately (1990) in the case of the Gestapo.

13 As Justice Jackson (US Chief Prosecution Counsel) declared: 'the crime against the Jews, insofar as it is a crime against humanity and not a war crime as well, is one that we indict because of its close association with the crime against peace' (Vol. XIX International Military Tribunal 1946: 470–71).

14 This can be doubted. Although there are similarities – especially at the level of motivations and perpetrators – the historical example of pogroms do not equate to the mass production killing of the Einsatzgruppen and the death camps. Some have suggested that it was the occurrence in history of pogroms against the Jews that allowed Jews to believe they would survive the Nazi programme. In Eastern Europe, for example in the Ukraine, Saul Friedman (1976: 3) states: 'During the nationalist uprising of Zaporoghian Cossacks in 1648–54, the … minions of Bogdan Chmielnicki slaughtered more than 200,000 Ukrainian and Polish Jews. Backs were broken, women raped, and children skewered in what Jewish historians refer to as "The Deluge" '. Yet Jews survived as part of social life. On past genocidal massacres, treated as an extreme form of ethnic population cleansing, see Andrew Bell-Fialkoff (1996).

15 Lemkin (1947: 150) stated: 'Germany's practices actually provided the basis for developing the concept of genocide'.

16 To quote Bauer (2001: 9–10): 'The historical context for Lemkin's work in early 1943 consisted of the information he possessed as to what was happening to Poles, Czechs, Serbs, Russians, and others. Horrifying information had been received concerning the fate of the Jews, but decent human beings evinced an understandable reluctance to believe that the accounts were literally and completely true. What was happening to some of these people, mainly perhaps the Poles, fitted Lemkin's description of denationalization accompanied by selective mass murder. It seems that he made his definition fit real historical developments as he saw them; the vagueness with which he contemplates the possibility of murdering all Jews reflects the state of consciousness in America of the Jewish fate.' Although I accept this summary it is also worth noting that several of the accounts

of those at the receiving end realised from an early stage the intent to eliminate. Note *The Warsaw Diary of Chaim A. Kaplan* (Katsh, ed. 1965: 65) '*1 November 1939. Today was a day of terror in unhappy Warsaw – that is in Jewish Warsaw. The conqueror is pouring out all his wrath upon the people he wishes to exterminate, and their distress is unbearable.*' For a full analysis of Lemkins' motives, role, beliefs (including the role of colonialism) see the recent volume of the *Journal of Genocide Research* (vol. 7, No 4, Dec 2005) devoted to Lemkin.

17 For the case of the Baha'I see Momen 2005.

Chapter 4

1 Anthropology – 'the science of man' – from its inception attempted to find a particular 'visuality' to bridge the realms of biology, the social and time. As Edwards (1998: 25) puts it for the British context: 'By the third quarter of the nineteenth century anthropology had begun to establish itself as a separate discipline in Britain. Its proponents saw themselves as scientists working in the tradition of the biological sciences on the science of mankind in both physical and cultural manifestations, and applying rigorous method to their data and analysis, classification being the primary aim for the ordering and thus understanding. Evolutionism, or at least progressivism, was the dominant model in analysis. Theories of evolution also encompassed such concepts as degeneration, diffusion and recapitulation. *What is important here is that evolutionism was a highly visualised theory.*' (emphasis added)

2 As Elsner and Cardinal (1994: 2) argue, changing taxonomies and systems of knowledge give the practice of classification; classification requires that objects be collected, but the process of collecting necessitates a reappraisal of the classification: '... the plenitude of taxonomy opens up the space for collectibles to be identified, but at the same time the plenitude of that which is to be collected hastens the need to classify. ... And if classification is the mirror of collective humanity's thoughts and perceptions, than collection is its material embodiment. Collection is classification lived, experienced in three dimensions.'

3 'Within a remarkably brief period, perhaps no more than twenty years after the appearance of Cesare Lombroso's *L'Uomo deliquente* in 1876, this knowledge developed from the idiosyncratic concerns of a few individuals into a programme of investigation and social action, which attracted support throughout the whole of Europe and North America' (Garland 1985: 77).

4 Manheim, for example, entitled his history *Pioneers of Criminology*.

5 See P. Beirne (1993), who links classical criminology and positivism together as different reading of the common project, that of a determinist enlightenment science of man(kind), and Morrison (1995), who claims that only a 'reforming' legality could constitute a legitimate space for criminological positivism to operate within.

6 A story lies behind my choice of this particular edition. In the mid-1980s I did some part-time work for the Workers Education Association holding classes in Bedford prison. On one occasion a prisoner asked to borrow my copy of Vold's *Theoretical Criminology*. I forgot that I lent it to him until about 6 months later when I received a letter from the prison saying they had confiscated a book from a prisoner they believed had been stolen from me. I wrote saying I had loaned it.

When it was returned to me the inmate had inscribed on the front page '....
Student, Roma University, July 1966' (to make it appear as if it was his, although
the book had not been published until 1979!); numerous drawings and tracings
of skulls and similar tropes of the Italian school that must have come from other
books were inserted. The chapter on 'The Positive School: Search for the Causes
of Crime' was heavily annotated with one sentence reading 'Darwin: change from
the idea of a fixed state to the evolutionary assent of man … Darwin speaks the
truth, where do I fit in?' There were also tables of various measurements, which
seemed to have been made of himself. [I should also note that my footnote here
is a continuation of a tradition, as much of the literature of the early Italian
Criminologists contained anecdotes of their experiences working either in
prisons or institutions for the insane.]

7 Parmelee's 1918 summary of Lombroso is characteristic of the institutionalised
and iconic role he plays within textbook histories. Lombroso is said to have
recognised 'a distinct biological and anthropological type', which he 'concluded
as a result of a study of the equivalents of crime among animals and among
primitive men and of the traits and conduct of children, that this congenital
criminal type is to a large extent an atavistic type … they revert to earlier human
types and to pre-human ancestors of man'.

8 Pick (1989) provides the most detailed study of Lombroso in the context of fears
over degeneration, 'social Darwinism' and the political developments in the
unification of Italy.

9 In *Crime: Its Causes and Remedies*, Cesare Lombroso (1911: 436–7) recounts when he
gave his assessment of which of the two stepsons was most likely to have killed a
woman. He had pointed out that one of them was 'in fact the most perfect type of
the born criminal; enormous jaws, frontal sinuses and zygomata, thin upper lip,
huge incisors, unusually large head (1620cc.) tactile obtuseness … with sensorial
manicinism. He was convicted.' In another case, Lombroso had argued for the
conviction of a 'certain Fazio', accused of robbing and murdering a rich farmer.
The evidence was purely circumstantial and seemingly rather flimsy. One witness
had testified that she had seen him sleeping near the murdered man; the next
morning he hid as the police approached. No other evidence of his guilt was
offered, however Lombroso was confident he could give the truth. 'Upon
examination I found that this man had outstanding ears, great maxillaries and
cheek bones, lemurine appendix, division of the frontal bone, premature wrinkles,
sinister look, nose twisted to the right – in short a physiognomy approaching the
criminal type; pupils very slightly mobile … a large picture of a woman tattooed
upon his breast, with the words, 'Remembrance of Celine Laura' (his wife), and on
his arm the picture of a girl. He had an epileptic aunt and an insane cousin, and
investigation showed that he was a gambler and an idler. In every way then biology
furnished in this case indications which joined with the other evidence, would have
been enough to convict him in a country less tender towards criminals.
Notwithstanding this he was acquitted.' See also comments in Gould (1981: 138–9).

10 Gina Lombroso-Ferrero (1911: 140) explained the differences between crime
and other social diseases as only a 'sensory illusion': 'The aetiology of crime,
therefore, mingles with that of all kinds of degeneration: rickets, deafness,
monstrosity, hairiness, and cretinism, of which crime is only a variation. It has,

however, always been regarded as a thing apart, owing to a general instinctive repugnance to admit that a phenomenon, whose extrinsications are so extensive and penetrate every fibre of social life, derives, in fact, from the same causes as socially insignificant forms like rickets, sterility, etc. But this repugnance is really only a sensory illusion, like many others of widely diverse nature.'

11 Quotes from Introduction 1911: xi–xx, New York: G.P. Putnam.

12 Note how closely this follows Quetelet. Cesare Lombroso stresses, however, that we may at first sight be confused. Young prostitutes may share 'a truly Darwinian trait', of 'delicacy of mien and a benevolent expression', but 'when youth vanishes, the jaws, the cheek-bones, hidden by adipose tissue, emerge, salient angles stand out, and the face grows virile, uglier than a man's; wrinkles deepen into the likeness of scars, and the countenance, once attractive, exhibits the full degenerate type which early grace had concealed' (Lombroso 1895: 102).

13 It has been claimed that Gall was 'the first criminologist', Savitz et al. (1997). Gall was clear that 'the object of his research was the brain and the cranium was 'a faithful cast of the brain'. De Guistina points out that phrenology offered a 'visually definite' field of investigation and dealt with 'precise measurable' data; see discussion of criminological claims in Savitz et al.

14 Galton recounts this in his journal published on his return in 1851 (3rd. edn 1891). The image of the 'Hottentot Venus' arose with Saartjie Baartman, a Khoi woman with extended buttocks, who travelled to Europe in the early nineteenth century to be exhibited by her keeper and later pathologised by the French scientist, Cuvier (see Gilman 1985: 204–42). She was the first of several women objectified in this fashion. Griqua communities in the northern Cape have asked for the return of her remains from the Musee de l'Homme in Paris for honourable reburial.

15 As an influence upon Cesare Lombroso, Vold and Bernard quote from Darwin's *Descent of Man and Selection in Relation to Sex* (1871: 137): 'With mankind some of the worst disposition which occasionally without any assignable cause make their appearance in families, may perhaps be reversions to a savage state, from which we are not removed by many generations'. The following year Darwin published his study on human expressions replete with photographs. In this he laid out a methodological and epistemological injunction: 'No doubt as long as man and all other animals are viewed as independent creations, an effectual stop is put to our natural desire to investigate as far as possible the causes of expression. By this doctrine, anything and everything can be equally well explained; and it has proved as pernicious with respect to expression, as to every other branch of natural history. With mankind some expressions, such as bristling of the hair under the influence of extreme terror, or the uncovering of the teeth under that of furious rage, can hardly be understood, except on the belief that man once existed in a much lower animal-like condition. The community of certain expressions in distinct though allied species, as in the movements of the same facial muscles during laughter by man and by various monkeys, is rendered more intelligible if we believe in their descent from a common progenitor. He who admits on general grounds that the structure and habits of all animals have been gradually evolved, will look at the whole subject of expression in a new and interesting light' (*The Expressions of Emotions in Man and Animals* [1872] 1999: 19).

16 The full title being *Journal of Researches into the Natural History and Geology of the Countries Visited During the Voyage of HMS Beagle Round The World.* The text used herein is the 7th edition, 1890, essentially a reprint of the 'corrected and enlarged edition of 1845', but which affords Darwin the chance of having made any corrections during his lifetime.

17 As the title, *European colonies in various parts of the world viewed in their social, moral and physical condition,* makes clear, he covered much of the territory Darwin was visiting: 'The continent of America has already been nearly depopulated of its aborigines by the introduction of the blessings of civilisation. The West Indian archipelago, from the same cause, no longer contains a single family of its primitive inhabitants. South Africa will soon be in a similar condition, and the islanders of the Pacific Ocean are rapidly diminishing in numbers from the ravages of European diseases and the despotism of self-interested and fanatical missionaries. It is surely time that the work of destruction should cease; and since long and melancholy experience has proved us to be invariably unsuccessful in rendering happier, wiser, or better, the barbarians whom we have visited or conquered, we may now conscientiously let them alone and turn a correcting hand towards ourselves and seek to repress … our avarice, our selfishness, and our vices.'

18 The following extract is from Chapter 5 (pp. 73 ff.) and described in the chapter heading as 'Indians' Wars and Massacres' (p. 58). This labelling is common, such events are almost never labelled as 'settler's wars'. The implication is that the Indians are at fault for resisting the invasion of the outsider.

19 Again one crucial motive was economics. In order to incorporate more suitable land for ranching into the *estanchieros* system General Roca moved on the Araucano Indians living south of Buenos Aires and in Patagonia. In Berger's (1991: 96–97) words: 'Roca's campaign, he said, was a civilizing mission, intended to bring scientists and engineers to the frontier. Indeed, Roca's army of 6,000 troops was to have the most modern technology available, including four pieces of heavy artillery. In addition, Roca ordered the construction of the first telegraph lines into the countryside, so that his orders could be carried immediately to the front … [Then he directed] lightning raids against unsuspecting villages, killing or imprisoning the inhabitants, seeking to sow terror through the tribes of the pampas. The battles were bloody. Often the Indians realized that their lances were no match for the soldiers' rifles and "they threw their lances to the ground and began to fight with us hand-to-hand, to grab the rifles out of our grasp". Many of the hand-to-hand battles ended with soldiers on horseback trampling fleeing Indians … Roca systematically exterminated the Indians. Vast estandas were established on what novelist V.S. Naipaul has called the "stolen, bloody land". Many of the estandas were allotted to the victorious generals. Roca himself was rewarded with the presidency.' (V.S. Naipaul 1980: 149) was scathing in stating that the pride that Argentines take concerning their 'martial prowess' in reality concerns 'a simple history of Indian genocide and European takeover'.)

20 Darwin recorded his impressions in 1834. In 1976 Wolf recorded his knowledge of the condition of the remaining Indians. 'One thing is certain: the Aché are not alone in their dying. Hunters and gatherers like them have been dying and

continue to die all along the internal margins of Latin America. Hundreds and thousands like them – in Peru, Brazil, Venezuela, Colombia – are driven daily from their former hunting territories to make room for incoming settlers and plantations, roads, airstrips, pipelines, oil wells. And this is hardly a new process, only the latest episode in the onward march of civilization. Wherever civilization advances, it spells the doom of the non-civilised. Out of the total range of human possibilities, civilization can tolerate only a few. In Latin America, this battle of the civilised against the non-civilised is fought by men who classify themselves as "men of reason" (*gente de razón*) against those who, bereft of that particular reason, can be classified with the animals. The Guarani-speaking Paraguayans who hunt the Aché, and the Aché, both speak varieties of the same language stock, Tupi-Guarani. But the Guarani-speaking settlers are men of reason, while the hunting and gathering Aché are in their terminology merely Guayaki, 'rabid rats'; and rabid rats must be exterminated. As the Aché die, others inherit their land. The progress of civilization across the face of the earth is also a process of primary accumulation, of robbery in the name of reason. Nor is this process confined to Latin America. What goes on there now is but what went on in North America when the land was 'discovered' and taken from its first occupants. It is only that in North America the process has been dignified by the passage of centuries: 'dead men tell no tales' (Wolf 1976: 52–3; see generally the other chapters also in Arens ed. 1976).

21 'We do not steadily bear in mind, how profoundly ignorant we are of the conditions of existence of every animal; nor do we always remember, that some check is constantly preventing the too rapid increase of every organised being left in a state of nature. The supply of food, on an average, remains constant; yet the tendency in every animal to increase by propagation is geometrical' (p. 126).

22 In reading the discourse of nineteenth-century degeneracy and biological evolution one is struck by the reappearance of common tropes. Lombroso was led in part to conclude that many offenders were 'veritable savages in the midst of this brilliant European civilization' as the shifty eyes of the thief reminded him of the beady, furtive eyes of the rat. He argued it was no coincidence that both these predators depended on 'stealth, quickness, and cunning.' In the *Descent of Man*, Darwin wrote: 'The New Zealander … compares his future fate with the native rat almost exterminated by the European rat'. Darwin was not to know the devastation to native bird species the introduction by the Maori of their rat had been. The sentiments can be dangerous: for example, the Paraguayans referred to the Ache Indians they nearly exterminated as 'Guayaki', meaning 'rabid rat' (Wolf 1976: 53).

23 Compare Lombroso's assumptions in the early chapters of *L'uomo delinquente* (1873) as picked out and quoted by Bonger (1936: 62): '... [among savages] crime is not considered an exception, but practically the general rule; in fact nobody looks upon it as such; on the contrary, its first appearances are, rather, ranked in the same class with the most irreproachable actions'.

24 Darwin saw nothing to upset his calculation that the inhabitants of Terra de Fuega were at the bottom of the list of savages. The missionary William Henry giving his impression of Aborigines in 1799 appeared to disagree: 'They are truely the most writched and deplorable beings my eyes have ever yet beheld. I think the Greenlanders and Labradorians or the inhabitants of Terra da Fuega, can not be more sunk to a level of brute creation than they. O Jesu, when will thy kingdom

come with power amongst them? When shall the rays of thine Eternal gospel penitrate the gross darkness of their minds (well represented by their faces) and illumine their benighted souls.' (quoted Elder 1998: 229)

25 The Aboriginal population of the Sydney basin was first affected by starvation in the winter of 1788 when the food supply was disrupted by the arrival of the white settlers, and then by smallpox in 1789. In less than a year half of the Aboriginal population perished. One settler recalled: 'The number that it swept off, by their own accounts, was incredible. At that time a native was living with us; and on our taking him down to the harbour to look for his former companions, those who witnessed his expression and agony can never forget either. He looked anxiously around him in the different coves we visited; not a vestige on the sand was to be found of human foot; the excavations in the rocks were filled with the putrid bones of those who had fallen victims to the disorder; not a living person was anywhere to be met with.

It seemed as if, flying the contagion, they had left the dead to bury the dead. He lifted up his hands and eyes in silent agony for some time; at last he exclaimed, "All dead! All dead!" and then hung his head in mournful silence.' (Quoted Elder 1998: 7–8)

26 In his study of whether 'genocide' occurred in Australia Reynolds (2001) relates how the then British secretary of state located in London, Earl Grey, in 1847 sought to point out to the colonists he duties they owed to the Aborigines: 'In assuming their Territory the settlers in Australia have incurred a moral obligation of the most sacred kind to make all necessary provision for the instruction and improvement of the Natives' (quoted p. 99). The settler view was somewhat different. In the Queensland parliament Lumley Hill stated: 'it must not be forgotten that the white man had undertaken to settle the country, to occupy it, and bring it as it were, into civilisation, and the blacks must always be a secondary consideration to him. The blacks must give way to the whites, and recede beyond the bounds of civilization' (quoted p. 111). The editor of a local newspaper could express his opposition in 1867 to the widespread violence used against the Aborigines as an unnecessary hastening of the natural process: 'whilst we regard the disappearance of the black race before the face of the white man as an inevitable fact to which we must of necessity submit as one of the conditions of successful colonisation, we must protest in the name of humanity and justice against seeking to attain this end by a ruthless and indiscriminate extermination of the doomed race. Their extinction is only a matter of time, and no unnecessary cruelty should be used to effect a result which the operation of natural causes will certainly accomplish.' (quoted p. 116)

27 During the first 20 years from 1788 to 1809, the average per annum was a modest 400. For 1810–19, it more than doubled to 1,100 a year. Between 1820 and 1829 it doubled again to 2,300. The peak was between 1830 and 1839 when the yearly average was 4,100. For 1840–52, the average declined to 2,700 (Radzinowicz and Hood 1990: 468).

28 This is a wonderful understatement. Some commentators argue that since the companies transporting the convicts had no financial interest in them other than the initial fee, conditions were worse than for the Atlantic slave trade. Pilger gives an account of the condition that his great-great-grandfather would have endured. 'Six of them shared a berth of less than six feet square where they lay "squeezed

up against one another, wallowing in each other's filth, sea-sickness and vermin, for the entire length of the voyage. If one wished to turn over in the cramped space, he had to wake the others so that all could roll over in their chains at the same time". They were fed like pigs, with potato peelings and crusts thrown at them, usually in darkness when the ship was rolling, and if they looked askance, let alone complained, the cruelties visited upon them included whipping with a knotted "cat" [cat-of-nine-tails, a form of whip], gang-rape for the women and the denial of sustenance until the point of death for children already half-starved. And the final cruelty, which was the twist in those lives resilient enough to survive such a purgatory, was that worse awaited them [in Australia].'

29 Eden Hooper (1935: 115–6) relates that the hundred convicts sent from a hulk in Chathan in 1829 to New South Wales included persons sentenced to life for stealing an apron, bacon or worsted material, and others sentenced to 14 years for stealing 2 pounds of potatoes, a pair of shoes or a bottle of spirits.

30 The fear of the effects of contamination was the most common worry of penal reformers. The hulks mixed together all manner of convicted persons and at night there were few wardens present. In his jointly authored 1862 text, Mayhew recounts that there 'are still officers in the Woolich hulks who remember a time when the *Justitia* [a particular hulk] … contained no less than 7000 convicts, and when at night these men were fastened in their dens – a single warden being left on board ship in charge of them! The state of morality under such circumstances may be easily conceived – crimes impossible to be mentioned being commonly perpetrated.'

31 'When, after the mutiny at Norfolk Island, in 1834 Dr (afterwards Bishop) Ullathorne, the Catholic priest, went to comfort the condemned and read out the names of those pronounced executed "they one after the other, as their names were pronounced, dropped to their knees and thanked God that they were to be delivered from that horrible place". Men in New South Wales and Van Diemen's Land chain gangs were locked up from sunset to sunrise in "caravans or boxes" so crowded that the occupants could neither all stand up together nor all sit down at the same time, except with their legs at right angles to their bodies. There were 22,000 summary convictions a year in New South Wales among 28,000 convicts, 3,000 of them were flogged with 108,000 lashes, "chiefly for insolence, insubordination and neglect of work". In Norfolk Island and Port Arthur the work was "of the most incessant and galling description", and any disobedience was "instantaneously punished by the lash".' (Radzinowicz and Hood 1990: 477)

32 Darwin himself was to give a liberal response to the dilemma posed by his own branch of science at least as far as the actions were to take place within civilised space. In *The Descent of Man* (1871) Darwin accepted Galton's argument concerning the eugenic effects of civilisation: 'With savages, the weak in body or mind are soon eliminated; and those that survive commonly exhibit a vigorous state of health. We civilised men, on the other hand, do our utmost to check the process of elimination; we build asylums for the imbecile, the maimed, and the sick; we institute poor-laws; and our medical exert their utmost skill to save the life of every one to the last moment … Thus the weak members of civilised societies propagate their kind. No one who has attended to the breeding of domestic animals will doubt that this must have been highly injurious to the race of man.'

Yet we most impose morality as our guide to action: 'The surgeon may harden himself whilst performing an operation, for he knows that he is acting for the good of his patient, but if we were intentionally to neglect the weak and helpless, it could only be for a contingent benefit, with a great and certain present evil. Hence we must bear without complaining the undoubtedly bad effects of the weak surviving and propagating their kind.' As we have seen Darwin was not so assertive for actions occurring outside the civilised realm. And others were soon prepared to be stronger of heart inside 'civilised societies'.

33 For a brief reading of the museum that Cesare Lombroso created and his ignorance of the role of Aboriginal art or tattooing see Morrison 2004b.

34 A similar inquiry and results can be addressed in many colonial situations. For the imposition of 'educational' programmes on Native (north) Americans see David Wallace Adams' (1995) aptly entitled *Education for Extinction: American Indians and the Boarding School Experience, 1875–1928* and J.R. Miller (1995) *Shingwauk's Vision: A History of Native Residential Schools.*

35 Darwin records his own attempt to plunder a grave, which, however, was empty. The return of aboriginal remains is now a political issue for many museums in the civilised world.

36 According to the English missionary L.E. Threlkeld in one of the massacres of Aboriginal people in the Bathurst region in the 1820s the police caught between 40 and 50 Aboriginal people in a swamp, surrounded them and killed them all. 'Forty-five heads were collected and boiled down for the sake of the skulls. My informant, a Magistrate, saw the skulls packed for exportation in a case at Bathurst ready for shipment to accompany the commanding officer on his voyage shortly afterwards taken to England' (quoted Elder 1998: 241).

37 On 1 May 1976 Trugannini's bones were cremated and her ashes cast to the winds in the D'Entrecasteaux Channel near her birthplace in Adventure Bay.

38 Many of these human remains are themselves 'collected'. Judy Ledgerwood (1997: 97) relates that the skulls in Tuol Sleng Museum of Genocidal Crimes in Phnom Penh, Cambodia, are presented as coming from every province and thus contribute to a meta-narrative of collective victimisation in the construction of a new national identity.

Chapter 5

1 The figure of 15,000,000 dead used by Mark Twain, see Chapter 3 of this text, is a rough halving of Stanley's later estimate of the population. The reality is probably *c.*8,000,000 dead through deliberate killing, malnourishment and disease due to weakened state that can be attributed to the conditions of labour employed by Léopold's Congo Free State (on the difficulty of making accurate estimates see the earlier comments in Chapter 3 of this text).

2 In his history of the Congo, Peter Forbath (The River Congo 1977) describes Léopold as 'a tall, imposing man … enjoying a reputation for hedonistic sensuality, cunning intelligence (his father once described him as subtle and sly as a fox), overweening ambition, and personal ruthlessness. He was, nevertheless, an extremely minor monarch in the realpolitik of the times, ruling a totally insignificant nation, a nation in fact that had come into existence barely four

decades before and lived under the constant threat of losing its precarious independence to the great European powers around it. He was a figure who, one might have had every reason to expect, would devote himself to maintaining his country's strict neutrality, avoiding giving offense to any of his powerful neighbours, and indulging his keenly developed tastes for the pleasures of the flesh, rather than one who would make a profound impact on history. Yet, in the most astonishing and improbable way imaginable, he managed virtually single-handedly to upset the balance of power in Africa and usher in the terrible age of European colonialism on the black continent.' Léopold was a constitutional monarch charged with the usual constitutional duties of opening parliaments, greeting diplomats and attending state funerals, but security was one of his pressing concerns and he saw in an Imperial enterprise all the pieces to ensure that for Belgium. He had no power to decide policy. But for over 20 years he had been agitating for Belgium to take its place among the great colonial powers of Europe. 'Our frontiers can never be extended into Europe, and since history teaches that colonies are useful, that they play a great part in that which makes up the power and prosperity of states, let us strive to get one in our turn.'

3 Hence Stanley could give the purpose of his 1879 activities in his later two volume account of the founding of the Congo Free State as 'to sow along its banks civilised settlements, to peacefully conquer and subdue it, to remould it in harmony with modern ideas into National States, within whose limits the European merchant shall go hand in hand with the dark African trader, and justice and law and order shall prevail, and murder and lawlessness and the cruel barter of slaves shall for ever cease' (1885, Vol. I: 59–60).

4 Struggle for advantage continued after the Conference and contributed to the advent of the Great War. By 1914, the conference participants had established control over Africa through their allocation of the 50 countries. The division was as follows: Great Britain desired a Cape-to-Cairo collection of colonies and almost succeeded though their control of Egypt, Sudan (Anglo-Egyptian Sudan), Uganda, Kenya (British East Africa), South Africa, and Zambia, Zimbabwe (Rhodesia) and Botswana; the British also controlled Nigeria and Ghana (Gold Coast); France had much of western Africa, from Mauritania to Chad (French West Africa) and Gabon and the Republic of Congo (French Equatorial Africa); Belgium (after King Léopold II had transferred it in 1908) controlled the Democratic Republic of Congo (Belgian Congo); Portugal had Mozambique in the east and Angola in the west; Italy had Somalia (Italian Somaliland) and a portion of Ethiopia; Germany had Namibia (German Southwest Africa) and Tanzania (German East Africa); while Spain had the smallest territory – Equatorial Guinea (Rio Muni).

5 The latter point was at issue when a certain piece of territory was in dispute between France and the Association; at one point in the negotiations it was important for the Association to prove that de Brazza had been mistaken in his estimate of the territorial influence of Makoko, a chief with whom he had concluded a treaty at Stanley Pool. Léopold had originally complained at the first version of the treaties Stanley was making asking that they be revised: 'they must be as brief as possible and in a couple of articles must grant us everything' (Maurice 1957: 161).

6 The records of which are kept by *Anti-Slavery International*, headquarters in London.

7 As revealed by a song which the Scheutist missionary Emeri Cambier heard in the lower Congo in 1888: O mother, how unfortunate we are! The white man has made us work; We were so happy before the white arrived; We would like to kill the white man who has made us work; But the whites have a more powerful fetish than ours; The white man is stronger than the black man; But the sun will kill the white man; But the moon will kill the white man; But the sorcerer will kill the white man; But the tiger will kill the white man; But the crocodile will kill the white man; But the elephant will kill the white man; But the river will kill the white man.

8 Joseph Clark, of the American Baptist Missionary Union, wrote on 25 March 1896: 'This rubber traffic is steeped in blood, and if the natives were to rise and sweep every white person on the Upper Congo into eternity there would, still be left a fearful balance to their credit. Is it not possible for some American of influence to see the King of the Belgians and let him know what is being done in his name? The Lake is reserved for the King – no traders allowed – and to collect rubber for him hundreds of men, women, and children have been shot' (Morel 1906: 54).

9 Bertram Russell (1934) summarises: 'From that day to the moment of his death, Morel was engaged in ceaseless battle – first against inhumanity in the Congo, then against secret diplomacy in Morocco, then against a one-sided view of the origin of the War, and last against the injustice of the Treaty of Versailles. His first fight, after incredible difficulties, was successful, and won him general respect; his second and greater fight, for justice to Germany, brought him obloquy, prison, ill health, and death, with no success except in the encouragement of those who loved him for his passionate disinterestedness. No other man known to me has had the same heroic simplicity in pursuing and proclaiming political truth'.

10 Hochschild reports that Casement's description of 'sliced hands and penises was far more graphic and forceful than the British government had expected'. When the Foreign Office finally published a sanitised version of his report, an angry Casement sent an 18-page letter of protest to his superiors in the Foreign Office, threatening to resign. He called his superiors 'a gang of stupidities' and 'a wretched set of incompetent noodles'.

11 And for his description, in the face of King Baudouin's praise for Léopold II's 'genius' and 'courage' and for having come to the Congo as 'civiliser rather than conqueror', of the conditions he had lived under: 'We have known harassing work, in return for wages that did not allow us to assuage our hunger or clothe or house ourselves decently ... We have been the victims of jokes, insults and blows morning, noon and night ... Our lands were expropriated with spurious legal documents ... The law was never the same for whites and blacks ... As exiles we have suffered for our political opinions and religious beliefs ... There were magnificent houses for the whites and crumbling grass huts for the blacks; the blacks were not admitted in cinemas, restaurants or so-called European shops; the blacks travelled in the holds of steamships, under the feet of the whites in the luxury cabins ... All this we have grievously suffered ... But all this is henceforth ended (quoted Stengers 1989: 266–9).

12 Recently, African critics like Chinua Achebe (Achebe 1988) have pointed out that the story can be read as a racist or colonialist parable in which Africans are depicted as innately irrational and violent, and in which Africa itself is reduced to a metaphor for that which white Europeans fear within themselves. The people of Africa and the land they live in remain inscrutably alien, 'other'. The title, they argue, implies that Africa is the 'heart of darkness', where whites who 'go native' risk releasing the 'savage' within themselves. Conrad may be using irony, however, to conceal the complexity of his true views.

13 Pigafetta records that when the Prince of the Congo first met the Portuguse they 'were looked upon and reverenced by him almost like gods come down to live on the earth', and they had to protest forcibly that they were men like himself (Pigafetta, *A Report of the Kingdom of Congo*, 1591, trans M. Hutchinson 1881: 71).

14 If one message of the story is to question authority, this applies to the tale itself. Marlow is the source of our story, but he is also a character within the story we read, and perhaps flawed. Marlow delivers macho comments about women and his insensitive reaction to the 'dead negro' with a 'bullet hole in his forehead' cause us to refocus our critical attention, to shift it from the story being retold, to the storyteller whose supposedly autobiographical yarn is being repeated. How much of this is intended by Conrad is debatable.

Chapter 6

1 Ascherson (1999: 275) provides the following story concerning the Arcade. It was to have been erected in time for the 50th anniversary of independence in 1880 but money ran out and successive governments would not allocate public funds to carry out the project. Léopold paid for the completion but so as not to offend the government of the day or arouse charges of extravagance with Congo money he had his equerry sign up a list of rich benefactors, who put their names to a letter stating that public spirit made them pay for the building of the Arcade, on the understanding that Léopold would reimburse them for the money spent. 'At the inauguration in 1905, these "benefactors" stood in the place of honour looking as foolish as they felt, while the King prowled about the monument grinning maliciously, affecting great surprise at the design (which he had helped to draw), and congratulating them on their generosity' (Ibid.: 275).

2 The now rather discredited trophy style has the advantage of being a clear statement that museums are inherently expressions of power. As in the creation and stocking of the Colonial palaces that became the Royal Museum for Central Africa Léopold's testament to the civilising mission was in the growing tradition where military conquest was accompanied by an associated seizure of possessions that were transferred to a national museum. But such conquest and forcible seizure was no longer being described as spoils of war but cast in terms of the liberation of peoples and objects from despotism and ignorance. The stocking of the Louvre, for example, was the prime beneficiary of that policy the Committee of Instruction's 1794 statement concerning what we may now refer to as 'organised art pillage' so confidently articulated. It was necessary to: 'dispatch secretly in the wake of our brothers in arms artists and men of letters with a solid

educational background. These honest citizens of proven patriotism will remove with all due care such masterpieces that exist in the territories into which republican arms have penetrated. The riches of our enemies are, as it were buried in their midst. Arts and letters are friends of liberty. The monuments erected by slaves will acquire, when set up among us, a splendour which a despotic government could never confer on them' (Hemmings 1987: 78).

3   I stress here my visits of 2002 and 2003; in 2001 the museum appointed a new director – who took his task as modernising the RMCA. In May 2005, I attended a path breaking colloquium on Colonial Violence and the Congo and visited the temporary exhibition. That exhibition broke ground in including some images of Abaes but still did not implicate a system, it was rather human failings and individual atrocities.

4   That description has a certain reflexive awareness. Contrast it to the proud openness of the propaganda purpose that one of the early Directors of the museum gave: 'The original idea of a Museum of the Belgian Congo dates from 1895. In those days, the State of Congo administration ordered that objects sent or donated by its African agents, and also some collections coming from the 1894 Antwerp Exhibition, be stored in the haylofts of the King's stables in the Place du Trone in Brussels. For the Brussels Exhibition of 1817, it was decided to make a great effort to substantially increase this store and to set before the public gaze the proofs of the progress made by the young State' (Baron A. de Haulleville, Director of the Museum from 1910 to 1927).

5   As Horne (1984: 11) puts it: 'sightseeing has established its own rituals. In what Erving Goffman calls the "ceremonial agenda of obligatory rites", there are established for us the monuments and exhibits we must see, and sometimes the order in which we must see them.' Horne describes this particular museum as having 'assembled leftovers showing something of the development of European consciousness of Africa – the maps which got the Europeans there, the crucifixes which gave them faith, animals and humans who gave curiosity to the "dark continent" '. It is also a memorial to 'the explorers' cult', with mementoes of Stanely and Livingstone, its Memorial room infused with 'astounding imperial arrogance' (Ibid.: 221–2).

6   These questions continue and in the process of constructing a new identity for this museum they come to the surface.

Chapter 7

1   The Dutch Judge Roling experienced it as an existential affront: 'in Japan we were all aware of the bombings and the burnings of Tokyo and Yokohama and other big cities. It was horrible that we went there for the purpose of vindicating the laws of war, and yet saw every day how the Allies had violated them dreadfully' (Roling and Cassese 1993: 87). Of the 153,000 tons of bombs dropped on Japan, 98,000 were firebombs. Hitler had first imagined the terrible consequences of incendiary attacks on London but was unable to carry them out (discussed, Sebald 2003: 104–5).

2   Expressed by Hawaiian rights activist Haunani-Kay Trask: 'Japan did not attack U.S. "home-territory" on 7 December 1941. It attacked the military forces of a

foreign power engaged in the illegal occupation of my homeland. Hawaiians are not "Native Americans", we are Polynesians. Our country, Hawai'I, is not American, it is Polynesian. Hawai'I is not part of the U.S., it is a colony of the U.S. (Lecture at University of Colorado, 1993, quoted Ward Churchill 2003: 31 n.92).

3 For Douglas (1996: 120) the IMT adopted 'an approach that placed the Holocaust at the margins of the legally relevant'.

4 The Soviets had initially been in favour of mass executions and there were voices in the US administration that favoured breaking Germany as a nation. Churchill refused to go along with those proposals. By the end of the war the US was more suspicious of the Soviet Union and came to push for trials. Churchill in turn had become more sceptical. An aide-memoire from the UK sent to Roosevelt on 23 April 1945, stated Churchill's later views: '[The British Government] is deeply impressed with the dangers and difficulties of this course [judicial proceedings], and they think that execution without trial is the preferable course. [A trial] would be exceedingly long and elaborate, [many of the Nazi's deeds] are not war crimes in the ordinary sense, nor is it clear that they can properly be described as crimes under international law.' (Quoted, Minear 1971: 9)

5 A telling example of this – the fate of the members of Reserve Police Battalion 101 – is discussed in Chapter 8.

6 The debate looked at in the following chapter (Chapter 8) concerning the participation in the Holocaust of ordinary men or ordinary Germans focuses around events of 1941 onwards, but we should note that executions of Polish intellectuals and others deemed important enough to stand in the way of the future use of Poland as German living space, in effect a colony, were carried out from the start. Rossino (2003) demonstrates how the Wehrmacht worked closely with the SS so that by the end of the Polish campaign in October 1939, 'Wehrmacht firing squads had executed no fewer than 16,000 Poles' (pp. 86–7) and when December closed the SS and Wehrmacht had murdered some 50,000 Polish citizens, 7,000 of whom were Jews (p. 234). From the beginning German armed forces worked with the SS towards the aim of a social space cleansed of Polish vitality, a social space that would be obedient to Nazi policies, a *Lebensraum* in which 'Germans are the masters and Poles the slaves' (as one army General put it in late September 1939, quoted p. 141).

7 As I wrote the first draft of this chapter, Easter Monday, 12 April 2004, in New Zealand, the lead story on TVNZ concerned the fighting in the Iraqi town of Falluja where some 600 Iraqis were said to have been killed in a week of US soldiers surrounding the town. The in-depth story concerned one US civilian who had been taken hostage with film, clearly made by a US team, showing the reactions of members of the small US town he came from who had no idea that one of them was going to be caught up in such drama. There was no such story on any of the 600 Iraqi dead. US military sources quoted on BBC online, stated that 95 per cent of them would be male insurgents, as the US weapons allowed for precision killing!

8 Winston Churchill's *The River War*, published in 1899, included two chapters devoted to the Battle of Omdurman. Churchill's account was written from his

firsthand experience of the battle as a supernumerary Lieutenant of the 21st Lancers and correspondent of the *Morning Post*. His application to take part in the Sudan campaign had originally been vetoed by Lord Kitchener and his presence had only been secured through his mother's entreaties to the Prime Minister, Lord Salisbury. Kitchener had objected on account of what Churchill might write as a newspaper correspondent. Churchill promised Lord Kitchener that he would not write for a newspaper but got around that by writing highly detailed and descriptive letters to his mother, which she made available to the *Morning Post*. In the early stages of the campaign the regiment's press coverage was not good and the relationship between the regular officers and Churchill became strained. The feeling was mutual and Churchill complained to his mother of being given 'a fearful lot of work of a petty and tedious kind' and 'the 21st Lancers are not on the whole a good business … I would much rather have been attached to the Egyptian cavalry staff'. However, as the regiment approached the northern outskirts of Omdurman and came in sight of the enemy greater camaraderie appears to have taken over. With the two armies poised waiting for battle to commence a naval officer on one of the gunboats threw a bottle of Champagne towards a group of Lancers; it fell short and Churchill was first in the water to recover it!

9 The campaign was closely followed by, for example, The *Illustrated London News*, which had first given images of English Officers drilling Egyptian troops in 1895, and Kitchener going down the Nile in steamboats. The main images of Atbara were those similar to the painting of Stanley Berkeley showing the Cameron Highlanders taking the stockade, namely close hand-to-hand fighting with equal portrayal of causalities. Other sketches, such as the Seaford Highlanders storming the Zareba again show fallen British soldiers. The *Graphic* contained an image of a lone British Officer picking his way over the massed corpses of the Sudanese dead in the trenches. Another image was of Anglo-Egyptian troops carefully moving about the dead and wounded in the stockade. There do not seem to be any images of wounded troops being killed by the Anglo-Egyptian forces and it was related elsewhere that the commander had given instruction that the troops were not to massacre the wounded.

10 The image is close to the Sudanese account: 'The battle of the standards and *rub's* was over. The battle of the individual began. The triumphant horsemen as they met the wounded were astonished to find they offered resistance. Each man waged his own individual battle before allowing the enemy to enter the city. Among a group of piled bodies one injured man would leap up and throw what was left of his strength into a final effort with a spear, sword or knife. Another would suddenly sit up after lying down for dead and hurl his spear at an enemy soldier. The scene was repeated a hundred times'. 'Ismat Hasan Zulfo (1980: 233). This contributed to the massacre of the wounded.

11 In the online The History Channel of the A&E Television Networks (http://boards.historychannel.com, accessed 7 May 2005, in the discussion board for Omdurman one post from ironmike of 2 September 2004 stands out. It reads: 'Aye, amigo, those wounded Dervish were still deadly. I experienced the very same thing, several times in Vietnam. Unpleasant duty, but you must care for yourself and your buddies. Gotta dash for a four day weekend …' The cares of the

everyday in civilised space prevent reflection on the fates of those defeated and wounded Dervish, as they are also present today for Iraq.

12 The Royal Palace is 'divided into many palaces, houses, and apartments of the courtiers', reads Olfert Dapper's enthusiastic 1668 account, 'and comprises beautiful and long square galleries ... resting on wooden pillars, from top to bottom covered with cast copper, on which are engraved the pictures of their war exploits and battles ... Every roof is decorated with a small turret ending in a point, on which birds are standing, birds cast in copper with outspread wings.' His description is accompanied by an engraving showing the soaring spires with their metal birds. These may have represented the Bird of Prophecy that Esigie, the seventeenth-century Oba of Benin is said to have killed after the bird squawked of disaster as he set out to war.

13 The news of the massacre of Phillips's party reached Rear-Admiral Rawson, the commander-in-chief on the Cape station, on the 4th of January 1897. The flagship was at Simons Town. The small crafts were dispersed. Two ships at Malta had been ordered to join the Cape command. A transport was chartered in the Thames for the purposes of the expedition. In 29 days a force of 1,200 men, coming from three places between 3,000 and 4,500 miles from Benin was landed, organised, equipped and provided with transport. Five days later the city of Benin was taken, and in 12 days more the men were re-embarked, and the ships coaled and ready for any further service.

14 In 1980 the Nigerian Government spent £800,000 on acquiring four Benin pieces and one Yoruba mask at auction in London. Increasingly within Nigeria, as well as within international organisations such as UNESCO, issues are raised over the legality of holding art collections expropriated by force (there are many precedents for the negotiated restitution of artworks, dating back to the Napoleonic wars). Parallels are drawn with the campaigns by Greece and Egypt for the return of their antiquities. The Benin artworks belong to a living culture and have a deep historical and social value, which goes far beyond the aesthetic and monetary value they hold in exile.

15 Contrast Hitler's explanation of Lebensraum: 'If the German people does not solve the problem of its lack of space, and if it does not open up the domestic market for its industry, then 2,000 years have been in vain. Germany will then make its exit from the world stage and peoples with more vigor will come into our heritage ... Space must be fought for and maintained. People who are lazy have no right to the soil. Soil is for him who tills it and protects it. If a people disclaims soil, it disclaims life. If a nation loses in the defense of its soil, then the individual loses. There is no high justice that decrees that a people must starve. There is only power, which creates justice. ... Parliaments do not create all of the rights on this earth; force also creates rights. The question is whether we wish to live or die. We have more right to soil than all the other nations because we are so thickly populated. I am of the opinion that in this respect too the principle can be applied: God helps him who helps himself.' (Hitler, *Voelkischer Beobachter*, May 7 1930, quoted Stavrianos 1991: 671).

16 During the destruction of the Herero many women were used as sex slaves. This was not the military commander von Trotha's intention. 'To receive women and children, most of them ill, is a serious danger to the German

troops. And to feed them is an impossibility. I find it appropriate that the nation perishes instead of infecting our soldiers.' In the Herero work camps, however, children were born to these abused women, and Fischer, who was interested in genetics, came to the camps to study them; he carried out medical experiments on them as well.

Chapter 8

1 'Survivors [of the Holocaust] who took upon themselves the task of bearing witness to the crimes of which they and their loved ones had been victim knew and valued the sanctity of memory. They feared the loss of memory as the necessary accompaniment of the disappearance of the suffering that underlay it, and instinctively knew that to erase its memory was tantamount to erasing the deeds. With the loss of memory, the world exonerated the killers, freed them of their burden of guilt, and simultaneously banished their victims to oblivion' (Horwitz 1991: 186).

2 I earlier placed authentic in scare quotes to denote the difficulty in rendering the identity of those who perished or survived and were inevitably, both individually and culturally, changed by that experience. Articulations to note include collections on the Holocaust of which I example *Art from the Ashes* (ed. Lawrence Langer 1995), or specific collections such as *Selected Poems* of Paul Celan (Michael Hamburger trans. 1972); for a collection of writings from survivors of 'other' massacres see Carolyn Firche (ed.) (1993) *Against Forgetting: Twentieth-Century Poetry of Witness*.

3 'For what was being done to the Jews there were different words, words that perpetuated the numbing ... by rendering murder non murderous' (Lifton 1986: 445). Nazi doctors used a language that made their actions seem 'responsible military-medical behaviour'; they 'lived increasingly within that language – and they used it with each other – Nazi doctors became imaginatively bound to a psychic realm of derealization, disavowal, and non-feeling' (*Ibid.*) 'Cargo, cargo', so Franz Strangl described the victims of Treblinka, the camp he commanded (Sereny 1983: 201). Arendt (1964: 86) said that the process institutionalised a new set of language rules that prevented the users from 'equating it with their old, "normal" knowledge of murder and lies'. However, while this is true and important to consider for its dehumanism that made the process easier for the perpetrators it is also the case that Hitler consistently warned what would be the fate of the Jews, as did his close associates. See Herf (2005: 55) who states: 'In fact, the public language of the Nazi regime was often a crude declaration of murderous intent always associated with projections of its own policies of mass murder onto "international Jewry".'

4 In a controversial statement (in that some though this too closely identified the Nazis with a Christian tradition) Steiner (1977: 99) said the German language gave 'hell a native tongue': 'That is what happened under the Reich. Not silence or evasion, but an immense out-pouring of precise, serviceable words. It was one of the peculiar horrors of the Nazi era that all that happened was recorded, catalogued, chronicled, set down; that words were committed to saying things no human mouth should ever have said and no paper made by man should ever have been inscribed with.'

5   To quote a scene from *The Warsaw Diary of Chaim A. Kaplan* (Katch, ed. 1965: 243) of *February 15, 1941* 'In the midst of the infected ghetto stands a varied group of people. It is apparent that no calamity has occurred; on the contrary, their faces reflect surprise and satisfaction at some exotic pleasure. What is the novelty today? The Jews of the ghetto have made a circle around two Nazi officers and the two faces are friendly. God in heaven! Have the laws of nature changed?

I guessed there was no danger, and so I approached. Nearby I noticed little Jewish children surrounding the Nazis and nearly embracing them. I was stunned. Was this a dream? Almost against my will I remained in the stream of traffic. I could not understand the explanation of the scene before me and I wanted to linger, although I'm not the kind to hang around street corners. One of the Nazis was lean, the other fat and paunchy. Suddenly I noticed that the fat one was holding a camera. As his companion fed a candy to a Jewish child, he would focus his camera for a picture. The riddle was answered. There is no Nazi without politics. Apparently they need pictures showing friendship to Jewish children for propaganda, to deceive mankind. Anything goes.'

6   Compare the criminology of Jack Katz (1988). Modern 'causal theories' had 'obliterated a natural fascination to follow in detail the lived contours of crime' (p. 317). Katza asks: 'What would follow if we stuck with the research tactic of defining the form of deviance to be explained from the inside and searching for explanations by examining how people construct the experiences at issue and then, only as a secondary matter, turned to trace connections from the phenomenal foreground to the generational and social ecological background?' (p. 317). Premise 'bodily comprehension', which may offer 'exceptional circumstances' where justifying rhetorics are 'undermined by an incongruent sensuality' (p. 7). Katz argues that few criminological accounts have focused on the varied emotional dynamics and experiential attractions that are an integral element of much crime. Consequently, the 'lived experience of criminality' rarely features in traditional criminological and sociological explanations of crime and deviance. Katz poses a question that many criminologists either take for granted, or completely ignore: namely 'why are people who were not determined to commit a crime one moment determined to do so the next?' (p. 4). The answer is to be found by going beyond background factors and delving deeper into the criminal act itself. The various mechanisms that move actors between 'background factors and subsequent acts' have been a kind of 'black box', assumed to have some motivational force but left essentially unexamined (p. 5).

7   Although both had been covered before – most notably, as indicated previously, by Christopher Browning in the case of Reserve Police Battalion 101 who used precisely the same research material as Goldghagen to come to a different array of causal factors. While the death marches had been material for Horwitz 1991, for example.

8   'The German perpetrators of the Holocaust were motivated to kill Jews principally by their belief that the extermination was necessary and just.' (Goldhagen 1998: 129–30)

9   No wonder the philosopher Jurgen Habermass was happy to present Goldhagen with the German Democracy prize. For Habermas (1983: 88) had earlier

accepted that American political culture had reintroduced West Germany into the path of the Enlightenment: 'The political culture of the Federal Republic would be worse today if it had not adopted impulses from American political culture during the first postwar decades. The Federal Republic opened itself for the first time to the West without reservations; we adopted the political theory of the Enlightenment, we grasped the pluralism which, first carried by religious sects, moulded the political mentality, and we became acquainted with the radical democratic spirit of the American pragmatism of Pierce, Mead, and Dewey'.

10 By contrast, Katz highlights the extreme and the normal of our everyday lives to build up a picture of the sensual, magical and creative appeals of crime. Evoking the notion of the Nietzschean superman, Katz asserts that deviance offers the perpetrator a means of 'self transcendence', a way of overcoming the conventionality and mundanity typically associated with the banal routines and practicalities of everyday 'regular life'. At the subjective level, crime is stimulating, exciting and liberating. To think of crime as either another form of rational activity or as the result of some innate or social pathology is to totally miss this point.

11 Goldhagen may have benefited from reading Mikhail Bakhtim (1985) and making use of his concept of 'authorised transgression'.

12 Another concerns the internal politics of China and its experiences of the twentieth century in which successive governments made disastrous choices and policies – not to mention purges and civil wars – which resulted in the deaths of many millions of their own people (See e.g. Rummel 1991).

13 Though I do acknowledge Justice Pal's comments on one particular diary reference (perhaps stimulated by the large number of diaries that were said to have been found and extracts translated and entered into prosecution testimony at the Tokyo IMT): '*We were not given the captured diary ... I hope it was written in Japanese*' (my emphasis): 'The head, detached from the trunk, rolls in front of it ... a superior seaman of the medical unit takes the Chief Medical Officer's sword and ... turns the headless body over on its back, and cuts the abdomen open with one clear stroke ... not a drop of blood comes out of the body ... If ever I get back alive it will make a good story to tell, so I have written it down' (Tokyo, IMT Proceedings, Vol. 14: 75–80).

14 There is doubt if the 'killing contest' actually took place. It may have been a media creation designed, in part, to enhance the marriage prospects of the two.' See Wakabayashi 2000 for a discussion of the trial and accounts of the 'Killing contest'.

15 Perhaps he was not as perceptive as Chaim A. Kaplan, who records in his *Warsaw Diary* (Katch ed. 1965: 243): 'February 18, 1941. The Jewish community is on a battlefield, but the battle is not conducted with weapons. It is conducted by means of various schemes, schemes of deception, schemes of smuggling, and so on. We don't want simply to disappear from the earth.' That diary contains great criticism of the Jewish ghetto police who carried out the instructions of the Nazi conquerors and also of those Jewish businessmen who, especially in the early days of the occupation, thought they could profit from the misfortune of other Jews.

16 In his 1998 essay replying to critics, Goldhagen appears to shift ground now constantly referring to the 'German perpetrators' of the Holocaust. If this tactic was meant to save his thesis from criticism on the grounds that it makes it specific

to Germans, it not only fails but also collapses his whole project. For it would then destroy any claims of uniqueness to 'ordinary Germans'; they would then just be a specific example of ordinary men.

17 'Taking pictures becomes a substitute for seeing. Of course, you have to look in order to direct your lens to the desired object … But looking is not seeing. Seeing is a human function, one of the greatest gifts with which man is endowed; it requires activity, inner openness, interests, patience, concentration. Today a snapshot (the aggressive expression is significant) means essentially to transform the act of seeing into an object' (Fromm 1974: 343). Clearly the majority of the photographs that Goldhagen relied upon fall into this category of snapshot; as the gun was fired so too the camera, the Jews were indeed just objects. The guns extinguished life, the camera captured an image whose meaning we now interpret; in this process one's ability to recognise common humanity is mortgaged to the good shot.

18 Joseph-Marie, Comte de Maistre, was born at Chambéry, in Savoy, in 1753, when Savoy did not belong to France; he died at Turin, 26 February 1821. For much of his active life he was a relatively poorly paid diplomatic agent for the King of Sardinia at St Petersburg. Afterwards he returned to Turin, where he filled the post of Minister of State and keeper of the great seal until his death. He was an avid anti-revolutionary and, some hold, forerunner of Fascism.

Chapter 9

1 Liberation War museum, 5 Segun Bagicha, Dhaka 1000, Bangladesh. Web page: www.liberationmuseum.org

2 International Coalition of Historic Site Museums of Conscience. (www.sitesofconscience.org)

3 When I checked my notes on a subsequent visit I realised I had first written this as 'let us remove hatred and prejudice from the world and let it belong to me'.

4 In *Imagined Communities* Benedict Anderson distinguishes the narratives of national identity from those of personal identity. Individuals may write their biographies as a set of natural 'begettings'. The narrative of nations are not fashioned by births, rather they are 'marked by deaths, which, in a curious inversion of conventional genealogy, start from an originary present. World War II begets World War I … the ancestor of the Warsaw uprising is the state of Israel'. These are not ordinary deaths since the narrative takes up the suicides, martyrdoms, assassinations, executions, wars, and mass killings to define the national story and they 'must be remembered/forgotten as "our own"' (1991: 205–6).

5 Modern Bangladesh constitutes part of the larger area of Bengal, which became independent of Delhi by 1341. After a succession of Muslim rulers, it was conquered by Akbar, the great Mughal emperor in 1576. By the beginning of the eighteenth-century, the governor of the province was virtually independent, but he lost control to the British East India Company, which after 1775 was the effective ruler of the vast area, which also included the Indian states of West Bengal, Orissa and Bihar. Bengal was divided by the British in 1905 into West Bengal and East Bengal, with East Bengal being more or less coterminous with

modern Bangladesh. Since the new province had a majority Muslim population, the partition was welcomed by Muslims, but it was fiercely resented by Indian nationalist leaders who saw it as an attempt to drive a wedge between Muslims and Hindus. The partition was withdrawn in 1911, but it had pointed the way to the events of 1947, when British India was partitioned into the states of India and Pakistan.

Pakistan consisted of two 'wings', one to the west of India, and the other to the east. The eastern section was constituted from the eastern portion of Bengal and the former Sylhet district of Assam and was known until 1955 as East Bengal and then as East Pakistan. Pakistan's two provinces, which differed considerably in natural setting, economy, and historical background, were separated from each other by more than one thousand miles (1,610 km) of India. The East Pakistanis, who comprised 56 per cent of the total population of Pakistan, were discontented by their treatment under a government centred in West Pakistan; the disparity in government investments and development funds given to each province also added to the resentment. Efforts over the years to secure increased economic benefits and political reforms proved unsuccessful, and serious riots broke out in 1968 and 1969. Bengali resistance was focused around recognition of the Bengali language, which the Pakistani Government had originally refused to have as one of the national languages.

6   This is a narrative central to the majority of works written on the history of Bangladesh by East Bengalis. For example (A. F. Salahuddin Ahmed 1994: 89): 'in the night of 25 March 1971 the Pakistan Army suddenly struck at the Bengali population in a treacherous and ruthless manner. It was the most gruesome genocide in history, which deeply shocked the conscience of the world community. But the people of Bangladesh were determined to resist unitedly this savage onslaught. The Bengalis were aroused by a new kind of nationalist and revolutionary consciousness. The war of national liberation had started which culminated in the creation of independent and sovereign Bangladesh.' The early books on the birth of Bangladesh contained genocide in their titles [for example, Chaudhuri, *Genocide in Bangladesh* (1972); Hasanat, *The Ugliest Genocide in History* (1974); Quaderi ed., *Bangladesh Genocide and World Press* (1972)] or devoted particular chapters to this [e.g. Chowdhury (1972) chapter 3, '*Crimes of a Soulless Regime*'].

7   As is the message of the three books so far published by the museum, for example, M.A. Rahman (2001: 15): 'The "war of liberation" mankind must ultimately win is for liberation of human values and not of geographical territories or of violated societies as such, and for this we all need to ask the ultimate question of our own failure to devise ways of settling our differences without needing a backing of brutal force. This is what, ultimately, "civilisation" means.'

8   As commentators on genocide note, political instability and violence with a succession of military upheavals did not end with Bangladeshi independence: 'the massive bloodletting by all parties in Bangladesh affected its politics for the following decades. The country has experienced military coup after military coup, some of them bloody.' (Rummel 1995: 334) What the actual linkages and tensions are however, is not analysed in any detail.

9   For example: Totten, Parsons and Charny, ed. 1994: chapter 10; Rummel 1997: chapter 13; Charny ed. Vol 2, 1991: 358–9.

10 See Kuper 1981: 173–4, who comments: 'I found it almost unbearable to read this discussion by a United Nations body of one of the major genocides of the twentieth century; it was so procedural and so devoid of human compassion.'

11 Many of which are collected in Mohan 1971, under the title *The Black Book of Genocide in Bangladesh*; and *Bangladesh Genocide and World Press*, ed. Fazlul Quaderi 1972.

12 As Pilger (1986: 325–6) instances his experience: 'My subsequent report and Eric Piper's pictures provided substantial evidence that the Islamabad government was practising genocide. A campaign was hurriedly mounted by the junta to discredit it. Three [British] Conservative Members of Parliament were invited to Pakistan by President Yahya Khan. They travelled by Army helicopter and used government interpreters, the Hindu hostel at Dacca University, where as many as 1,800 students [the actual figure is probably closer to 250 (WM)] were killed during the March 25 assault with rockets and mortar, was rebuilt for their visit. Their tour ended with a lavish party given by Yahya Khan. On her return to Britain, Jill Knight, the member for Edgbaston, reported to Parliament that stories of systematic killings in East Pakistan were grossly exaggerated and the situation was back to normal.'

13 In her comparative study of dealing with collective violence and reconciliation, Martha Minow points out that on a personal level 'coming to know that one's suffering is not solely a private experience, best forgiven, but instead an indictment of the social cataclysm, can permit individuals to move beyond trauma, hopelessness, numbness, and preoccupation with loss and injury' (1998: 67).

14 The famine of 1943 is regarded in some Bengali circles as a British 'war crime'. In Pilger's words (1986: 316), 'as many as a million and a half Bengalis starved to death after the British had stockpiled, transported or destroyed two crops in order to deny food to the advancing Japanese Army. Western war correspondents knew about this, but either they neglected to report it or their newspapers decided not to publish their dispatches.' By contrast: 'The disaster in East Pakistan in November 1970 was different in so far as it became an international "event" almost immediately the enormity of what had happened was revealed by Ian Brodie of *The Daily Express*, who had flown to Dacca from his Hong Kong base and was the first foreign journalist to send a detailed eye-witness account. After Brodie's reports, followed by mine in the *Mirror*, television squads arrived and "the story" gained momentum. It could easily have gone the other way: the international, mostly Western press is capricious by nature, especially in its troubled relationship with the third world, and had it been diverted by some other, more "newsworthy" event or had a reporter less experienced than Brodie led the way, television, the medium of impact, might well have stayed away and Bengal's agony would have gone unrecorded once again.' Thus the contingency of the spectacle; Pilger also relates how in spite of the headlines Western aid was weak and late in coming.

15 'Where the mind is without fear and the head is held high; Where knowledge is free; Where the world has not been broken up into fragments by narrow domestic walls; Where words come out from the depth of truth; Where tireless striving stretches its arms towards perfection; Where the clear stream of reason has not

lost its way into the dreary desert sand of dead habit; Where the mind is led forward by thee into ever-widening thought and action – Into that heaven of freedom, my Father, let my country awake.' (Rabindranath Tagore, from his Gitanjali)

16 Bengali was also not used on the coins, stamps, money and office forms issued by the Government of Pakistan. Given that the literacy rate was so low, this matter was not thought of as important in elite West Pakistani circles and one should note that Urdu was not even the majority language of West Pakistan. It was the language of the Governing elite, some of whom also claimed, that because Urdu was written in Arabic script, it was close to the language of the Prophet.

17 Economically, East Pakistan was treated as though it was a colony. Even though it had 54 per cent of the population, it got only 35 per cent of that spent on development. Its trade surplus was used to cover the deficits of West Pakistan, thus draining resources from East Pakistan. And income per capita in West Pakistan was 61 per cent higher. It was predominantly rural with many areas having very little contact with the world outside. Modern industries with their corresponding large urban centres were few.

18 Pakistan was not formed as constitutionally an Islamic Republic until a Constitution Bill was passed on 29 February 1956. The 'Objective Resolution' clause set forth the aims and objects of the constitution and gave governance as a trust from God. 'whereas sovereignty for the entire universe belonged to God Almighty alone and authority which He has delegated to the state of Pakistan through its people for being exercised within the limits prescribed by Him, is a sacred trust'. The resolution also declared that Muslims should be enabled to order their lives in accordance with the teachings of the Holy Quran and Sunnah. The name taken was Islamic Republic of Pakistan. The name of the east wing was changed from East Bengal to East Pakistan in the constitution.

19 Rafiqul Islam (1997: 59) suggests that as this request was made secretly to predominately non-Bengali officers, they were biased against believing that the Awami league would receive more than 40 per cent of the seats, while the few Bengali officers asked would have also given a low estimate 'in order to keep on official record their contempt for the Awami League, in the hope that they would thereby gain favour from their West Pakistani superiors'.

20 Senator Edward Kennedy toured some of these camps and on return to Washington reported at a press conference what he saw. 'You see infants with their skin hanging loosely in folds from their tiny bones – lacking the strength even to lift their hands. You see children with legs and feet swollen with oedema and malnutrition, limp in the arms of their mothers. You see babies going blind for lack of vitamins, or covered with sores that will not heal. You see in the eyes of their parents the despair of ever having their children well again. And, most difficult of all, you see the corpse of the child who died just the night before.'

21 'Prime Minister Mujibur Rahman's declaration that victims of rape were national heroines was the opening shot of an ill-starred campaign to reintegrate them into society – by smoothing the way for a return to their husbands or by finding bridegrooms for the unmarried [or widowed] ones from among his Mukti Bahini freedom fighters. Imaginative in concept for a country in which female chastity and purdah isolation are cardinal principles, the 'marry them off' campaign

never got off the ground. Few prospective bridegrooms stepped forward, and those who did made it plain that they expected the government, as father figure, to present them with handsome dowries.' (Brownmiller, 1975: 84)

22 Vietnam invaded Cambodia in December 1978, ending Pol Pot's atrocities. In return the US backed China to invade Vietnam, which Vietnam successfully repulsed, and subjected Vietnam to increased sanctions while giving the ousted Khmer Rouge regime direct support. 'A vast quanity of documents, mass graves and Pol Pot's torture chambers was discovered back in 1979. But where were the human rights lawyers, legal investigators and potential prosecutors? The world's first international genocide prosecution should have started long before it was eventually launched in 1998 at The Hague. The main reason for the 26 years of delay was that Washington and its allies persuaded the UN member states to accept the credentials of the Pol Pot regime, even after it had been driven out of Phnom Penh. ... Cambodia, already a victim of US B52 bombing and the Pol Pot regime, was made to suffer all over again because it had been liberated in 1979 by the wrong country, Vietnam' (Tom Fawthrop, 'The forgotten holocaust', *The Guardian*, 28 March 2005).

Chapter 10

1 Both quotations from 'The burning and the haunting: how for some the nightmare of Hiroshima will never end', *The Guardian*, 6 August 2005.

2 Of, among other things, the desire for the supreme technological fix, see H. Bruce Franklin, *Star Wars: The Superweapon and the American Imagination* 1988.

3 Thus, for example, continuing the pattern of Vietnam. On difficulties in ascertaining the numbers of civilians killed there see Franklin (2000), on trying to ascertain the way in which they were killed see John Duffett ed. 1968, and for US Vietnam Veterans trying to find the truth see *The Winter Soldier Investigation* 1972, for a citizens inquiry see *The Dellums Committee Hearings on War Crimes in Vietnam*, 1972.

4 The battle began with an objection to Ward Churchill's participation on an academic panel in upstate New York based on reactions to an essay he published on the Internet the day after September 11 entitled *Some People Push Back: On the Justice of Roosting Chickens*. Churchill was 'barbequed', to use a New Zealand expression and made into a minor media sensation; there were demands for termination of his tenured position, with the attacks shifting from the words of his essay to the body of his writings and even to scrutiny of his professed Indian heritage. To others, mindful of civil rights, provided an opportunity for the fundamentalist wing of the neo-conservative Right to further their culture campaign whereby they seek to demolish free speech rights, liberal and Left values, and the academic tenure system which in their view protects an army of crazed radicals corrupting the minds of youth. Churchill was labelled a 'madman' and 'cheerleader for terrorists' who spews vile 'hate speech'; his actions tantamount to treason. Churchill received 140 death threats within a four-day period after the story broke on national media. The Colorado governor excoriated Churchill and demanded termination of his tenure. The Colorado House of Representatives released a Joint Resolution in support of the September 11 victims' families and vilified

Churchill for striking 'an evil and inflammatory blow against America's healing process'. Within the Colorado university community, reaction was mixed. Some Board of Regent members demanded that Churchill be fired. The Board held a special meeting on February 3 to determine his fate, and decided to postpone the decision for a month while they scrutinised every word he had written and then decided on no action. The interim chancellor at Colorado University and Boulder Faculty Assembly declared Churchill's ideas to be 'repugnant', 'offensive' and 'odious' but nonetheless supported his right to express them, while his colleagues in the Ethnic Studies department provided 'full and unconditional support' for his free-speech rights. While College Republicans denounced Churchill and organised a petition drive for his dismissal, student supporters denounced the furor as a McCarthyesque witch-hunt engineered to silence a progressive member of their community. Some College Republicans chastised their Right-wing peers and formed the organisation Republicans for Churchill in support of his First Amendment rights. The American Union of University Professors and the American Civil Liberties Union came out strongly in favour of controversial speech and Churchill's First Amendment rights.

5   The idea of communicating by killing is also very familiar. In *War Is a Force That Gives Us Meaning*, former war correspondent Chris Hedges (2002) writes that he saw such transmissions up close: 'Corpses in wartime often deliver messages. The death squads in El Salvador dumped three bodies in the parking lot of the Camino Real Hotel in San Salvador, where the journalists were based, early one morning. Death threats against us were stuffed in the mouths of the bodies … And, on a larger scale, Washington uses murder and corpses to transmit its wrath. We delivered such incendiary messages in Vietnam, Iraq, Serbia, and Afghanistan. Osama bin Laden has learned to speak the language of modern industrial warfare.' Hedges notes: 'It was Robert McNamara, the American Secretary of Defense in the summer of 1965, who defined the bombing raids that would eventually leave hundreds of thousands of civilians north of Saigon dead as a means of communication to the Communist regime in Hanoi.'

6   In January 2002, the United States began transporting prisoners captured (predominantly by the Northern Alliance or other ad hoc groups) in the military conflict in Afghanistan to Camp X-Ray, at the United States Naval Base, at Guantánamo Bay, Cuba. Guantánamo Bay is a self-sufficient and essentially permanent town with approximately 7,000 military and civilian residents under the complete jurisdiction and control of the United States. Guantánamo Bay occupies nearly thirty-one square miles of land, an area larger than Manhattan, and nearly half the size of the District of Columbia. It has its own schools, generates its own power, provides its own internal transportation, and supplies its own water. Offenses committed by both civilians and foreign nationals living on Guantánamo are brought before federal courts on the mainland, where respondents enjoy the full range of Constitutional rights. The United States has occupied Guantánamo Bay since 1903, and has repeatedly declared its intention to remain there indefinitely. For several decades, the United States has resisted claims of national sovereignty made by Cuba over Guantánamo Bay.

The aim of these movements was expressly to hold the detainees in a physical and social space outwith any national legal jurisdiction and thus to hold them under military-administrative guidance safe from any legal supervision. A timeline of developments surrounding the legal status (with reference to the Geneva Conventions and the reach of the 'great writ' of habeas corpus) of US-held foreign prisoners at Guantánamo Bay Naval Base, Cuba is as follows:

Nov. 13. 2001: President Bush signs an Executive Order authorizing the Defense Secretary to hold non US citizens in indefinite detention.

Dec. 27, 2001: Defense Secretary Donald Rumsfeld confirms that the Pentagon will move 'war on terror' detainees from Afghanistan to the US Navy Base at Guantánamo Bay, Cuba, 'the least worst place' to hold them.

Jan. 11, 2002: The US military sends 20 prisoners from Afghanistan to Guantánamo, a figure that would swell to 750 men and teenaged boys in the course of three years. (By November 2002 the camp held more that 600 detainees, since then 260 have either been released or handed over to their national governments. In February 2006 the camp housed c. 490 detainees from c. 40 countries and was said to include terrorist suspects picked up in Eastern Europe and Africa. A full list of detainees has never been published.)

Jan. 19, 2002: Some clergy and law professors led by former Attorney General Ramsey Clark file a habeas corpus petition for Guantánamo detainees; it is dismissed because no petitioner is a captive's kin.

Defense Secretary Donald Rumsfeld declares them all to be unlawful combatants who 'do not have any rights' under the Geneva Conventions. The US, he said, would 'for the most part, treat them in a manner that is reasonably consistent with the Geneva Conventions, to the extent they are appropriate'.

At the end of January then White House counsel Alberto Gonzales (later Attorney-General) writes to President Bush that the Geneva Convention provisions on questioning enemy prisoners were 'obsolete' and argues, among other things, that rejecting the applicability of the Geneva Convention '[s]ubstantially reduces the threat of domestic criminal prosecution' of US officials for war crimes.

The day later, then Sectary of State Colin Powell attempted to rebuke. He wrote that declaring the Geneva Conventions inapplicable to the Afghan conflict would 'reverse over a century of US policy and practice in supporting the Geneva Conventions and undermine the protections of the law of war for our troops, both in this specific conflict and in general'; he warned that it would have 'a high cost in terms of negative international reaction, with immediate adverse consequences for our conduct of foreign policy'.

Feb. 7, 2002: President Bush issues a directive defining Taliban and al Qaeda captives as 'unlawful combatants' and not prisoners of war and therefore not entitled to the protections of the Geneva Convention. Rumsfeld tells journalists that same day: 'The reality is the set of facts that exist today with the Al Qaeda and the Taliban were not necessarily the set of facts that were considered when the Geneva Convention was fashioned.' The International Red Cross is granted full access to detainees (the only organization ever so allowed).

Feb. 19, 2002: Empowered by family members, The Center for Constitutional Rights files a habeas petition in federal court in Washington D.C. on behalf of Guantánamo detainees David Hicks of Australia and Shafiq Rasul and Asif Iqbal of Britain, Rasul v. Bush.

February 2002: more than 200 of the detainees begin the first of many hunger strikes; they are later force fed through nasal tubes.

March 18, 2002: US government asks the court to dismiss Rasul v. Bush, saying Guantánamo is not US jurisdiction.

April 5, 2002: US officials discover detainee Yaser Esam Hamdi, thought to be a Saudi, was born in Louisiana, and swiftly evacuate him from Guantánamo Bay to stave off federal court intrusion into the US Navy base in Cuba.

June 11, 2002: Hamdi, now held without access to an attorney at a Navy Brig in Norfolk, Va., files a writ of habeas corpus in the US District Court for the Eastern District of Virginia. The government replies that President Bush's war powers give him authority that extends beyond judicial review to detain him indefinitely and to deny him access to counsel and the courts.

Aug. 8, 2002: US District Court dismisses Rasul v. Bush, saying Guantánamo detainees cannot file habeas corpus petitions because they are non-US citizens detained outside US jurisdiction.

March 11, 2003: US Court of Appeals rejects appeal of Rasul v. Bush, setting the stage for a Supreme Court confrontation.

Nov. 10, 2003: The US Supreme Court agrees to hear Rasul v. Bush.

Feb. 13, 2004: Defense Secretary Rumsfeld tells the Greater Miami Chamber of Commerce that prisoners are not being tortured or otherwise mistreated at Guantánamo Bay.

March 9, 2004: Pentagon sends four Guantánamo prisoners to Britain, including Rasul and Iqbal, who are detained for a day and set free; the issue of whether Guantánamo detainees can sue for review is still bound for the Supreme Court.

April 20, 2004: Former Philadelphia federal judge John Gibbons, 79, a Nixon appointee, argues at the Supreme Court that Guantánamo is US jurisdiction and foreign detainees have right to file habeas petitions on behalf of the detainees. He has joined in written briefs by a former Japanese American internee, former judges and military lawyers, retired diplomats and civil liberties professors.

May 14, 2004: Freed Britons Rasul and Iqbal write an open letter to President Bush declaring that US soldiers abused and humiliated them at Guantánamo Bay. They said guards used strobe lights, dogs and loud rap music to extract information.

June 28, 2004: The Supreme Court rules 6-3 that Guantánamo detainees can challenge their captivity in federal courts. Chief Justice William Rehnquist, Antonin Scalia and Clarence Thomas dissent. In a related case, the court also says Hamdi can be held as an enemy combatant but he, too, may challenge his detention in US courts.

July 1, 2004: Civilian habeas corpus lawyers write Secretary Rumsfeld seeking to meet their clients at Guantánamo Bay.

July 30, 2004: In a bid to mollify the Supreme Court and create a substitution to challenge at the federal courts, the Pentagon creates military panels of officers to review each detainee's 'enemy combatant' status on a case-by-case basis. Lawyers are banned from the so-called Combatant Status Review Tribunals, CSRTs.

Aug. 24, 2004: The Pentagon convenes its first ever Military Commission at Guantánamo Bay. Five US military officers, only one an ex-lawyer, formally charge four of the 550 or so captives with war crimes, using rules written by the Defense Department rather than charge them in federal courts.

Aug. 30, 2004: The Pentagon permits the first civilian lawyer to meet a Guantánamo detainee filing a habeas suit. That lawyer sees British detainees Moazzam Begg and Feroz Abassi, who have since been sent home.

Oct. 20, 2004: US District Judge Colleen Kollar-Kotelly orders Pentagon to stop intelligence eavesdropping of lawyer-client conversations at Guantánamo, describing lawyer–client privacy as a 'bedrock' American principle.

Nov. 8, 2004: US District Judge James Robertson orders the Pentagon to halt the war crimes trial of alleged a Yemeni who worked as Osama bin Laden's driver, saying the Military Commissions are flawed and likewise calls the Pentagon's CSRTs an inadequate, non-judicial alternative to habeas proceedings in federal courts.

Dec. 17, 2004: Pentagon notifies Guantánamo detainees that they can sue for their freedom in a US court, distributing the court's Washington D.C. address to detainees for the first time.

Jan. 19, 2005: US District Judge Richard Leon dismisses seven Guantánamo prisoners habeas petitions, ruling that President Bush's war time powers permit the Pentagon to hold enemy combatants and review the detentions on their own.

Jan. 31, 2005: US District Judge Joyce Hens Green rules the opposite of Leon, saying Guantánamo Bay captives can sue for their freedom, and specifically citing torture allegations and criticizes the CSRTs as fundamentally flawed. The stage is set for a US Court of Appeals decision and likely later review by the Supreme Court.

May 3, 2005: The US District Court in Washington D.C. places on his docket the first 16 of what would become dozens of habeas corpus suits by captives who, through military contract linguists, wrote one-page letters to the court, from Camp Delta. Even though many of the captives are illiterate Afghanis, they are listed as pro se, or self-representation cases because they wrote the court directly, without attorneys.

May 2005: The Human Rights group Amnesty International calls the camp 'the gulag of our times' and calls for it to be shut down. (It also refers to Red Cross estimates that up to 70% of the inmates may be there by mistake or have little evidence against them.)

July 15, 2005: The US Court of Appeals for the District of Columbia Circuit unanimously upheld President Bush's war powers to create a Military Commission to try Salim Ahmed Hamdan, 35, of Yemen, overturning Judge Robertson's Nov. 8 order.

July 18, 2005: Defense Secretary Rumsfeld says at press appearance with Australian Prime Minster John Howard that the war crimes trials of Hamdan and Hicks will resume soon.

Nov. 7, 2005: The US Supreme Court announces that it will hear Hamdan v Rumsfeld, and decided it with the new Chief Justice John Roberts abstaining from the discussion.

Nov. 10, 2005: The US Senate votes 49-42 (along party lines) to adopt a proposal by Sen. Lindsey Graham, Rep-S.C., that strips Guantánamo detainees of the right to file habeas petitions, a proposal that will need to go next to the House of Representatives and then for President Bush's signature.

Nov. 14, 2005: Judge Kollar-Kotelly blocks the Pentagon from resuming Hicks' Military Commission until Supreme Court rules on its constitutionality in Hamdan v Rumsfeld.

In February 2006 a report by five inspectors for the UN human rights commissioner holds that the camp should be shut down without delay because activities amounting to torture were being conducted there. In particular it refers to shackling, hooding and forcing detainees to wear earphones and goggles (sensory deprivation), 'aggressive' interrogation techniques and excessive violence used to forcefeed detainees on hunger strikes.

Scott McClellan, the White House press secretary, dismisses the report as a 'rehash of old allegations', and 'a discredit to the organisation'. The detainees are being treated humanely, he states, 'remember these are terrorists'.

February 17 2006: At a hearing in London on the right of three UK detainees (two of which had been first apprehended in Africa) to require the British Foreign of State to petition the US on their behalf, the High Court judge remarks that the 'US idea of torture does not appear to coincide with that of most civilized countries'.

If Guantánamo Bay became a collecting place for all those who were apprehended globally in the 'war on terror', movement between domains was not simply outside of the US: on May 8, 2002, Jose Padilla, an American citizen, flew from Pakistan to Chicago's O'Hare International Airport, where he was taken into custody by federal agents as part of the 'war on terrorism'. Initially held as a 'material witness', Padilla was transferred to New York, where he was assigned an attorney. Soon thereafter, however, federal officials removed Padilla from the jurisdiction of the federal court and transferred him to the control of the Pentagon. Moved to a naval brig in South Carolina, the aim was to hold Padilla indefinitely as an 'enemy combatant' in the 'war on terrorism', denied the right to consult with his attorney, the right to due process of law, and the right to trial by jury. Thus the external could not be contained, the exceptional now threatened to take hold of internal space; later came the revelations of Bush's authorization of large scale telephone tapping on U.S. citizens. None of this, however, appeared to disturb public sentiment.

7 'Abu Ghraib' can be read as shorthand for the crimes committed in several dozen detention centers in Iraq, Afghanistan and at Guantánamo Bay. At last Pentagon count, no less than twenty-seven detainee deaths were criminal homicides. The CIA has admitted to using 'water boarding' (near drowning), unmistakably a form of torture. And documents released in 2005 under the Freedom of Information Act have confirmed some of the more outrageous accounts of detainee abuse. *The Washington Post*, Thursday, July 14, 2005, reported a military investigation had revealed that interrogators at the U.S. detention facility at Guantánamo Bay, Cuba, forced a stubborn detainee to wear women's underwear on his head, confronted him with snarling military working dogs and attached a leash to his chains: the tactics were employed there months before military police used them on detainees at the Abu Ghraib prison in Iraq. The techniques were an on-the-ground interpretation of the general approval Defense Secretary Donald H. Rumsfeld gave for the use of 'aggresive tactics' in interrogating Mohamed Qahtani — the alleged '20th hijacker' in the Sept. 11, 2001, terrorist attacks and were used at Guantánamo Bay in late 2002 as part of a special interrogation plan aimed at breaking down the silent detainee. Military investigators who briefed a Senate Armed Services Committee July 2005, called the tactics 'creative' and 'aggressive' but said they did not cross the line into torture. The report's findings indicate that the abusive practices seen in photographs at Abu Ghraib were not the acts of a small group of thrill-seeking military police officers but were used on Qahtani several months before the United States invaded Iraq. The investigation also supports the idea that soldiers believed that placing hoods on detainees, forcing them to appear nude in front of women and sexually humiliating them were approved interrogation techniques for use on detainees.

A central figure in the investigation, Maj. Gen. Geoffrey Miller, who commanded the detention facility at Guantánamo Bay and later helped set up U.S. operations at Abu Ghraib, was accused of failing to properly supervise Qahtani's interrogation plan and was recommended for reprimand by investigators. Miller would have been the highest-ranking officer to face discipline for detainee abuses so far, but Gen. Bantz Craddock, head of the U.S. Southern Command, declined to follow the recommendation.

Miller traveled to Iraq in September 2003 to assist in Abu Ghraib's startup, and he later sent in 'Tiger Teams' of Guantánamo Bay interrogators and analysts as advisers and trainers. Within weeks of his departure from Abu Ghraib, military working dogs were being used in interrogations, and naked detainees were humiliated and abused by military police soldiers working the night shift. Miller declined to respond to questions posed through a Defense Department liaison. Bryan Whitman, a Pentagon spokesman, said it is not appropriate to link the interrogation of Qahtani – an important al Qaeda operative captured shortly after the terrorist attacks – and events at Abu Ghraib. Whitman said interrogation tactics in the Army's field manual are the same worldwide but MPs at Abu Ghraib were not authorized to apply them, regardless of how they learned about them.

Some of the Abu Ghraib soldiers have said they were following the directions of military intelligence officials to soften up detainees for interrogation, in part by depriving them of sleep.

8 Ahdaf Soueif (*The Guardian*, 5 May 2004), almost repeats the lessons taken from reading accounts of genocide arguing that in the Arab world, the photographs 'have strengthened the feeling that there is a deep racism underlying the occupiers' attitudes to Arabs, Muslims and the Third World generally. The acts in the photos being flashed across the networks would not have taken place but for the profound racism that infects the American and British establishments. There have been reports of US troops outside Fallujah talking of the fun of being a sniper, of the different ways to kill people, of the 'rat's nest' that needs cleaning out. Some will say soldiers will be soldiers. But that language has been used by neocons at the heart of the US administration; both Kenneth Adelman and Paul Wolfowitz have spoken of 'snakes' and 'draining the swamps' in the 'uncivilised parts of the world'. It is implicit in the US administration's position that anyone who does not agree that all of history has been moving towards a glorious pinnacle expressed in the US political, ideological and economic system has 'rejected modernity'; that it is America's mission to 'civilise and to punish.'

9 That professional knowledge arose from experience in the US system of incarceration that now has 2,033,000 people behind bars – 63 per cent of them black or Latino. The over-representation of racial minorities in federal and state prisons and local jails reflect institutional biases that converge at the intersection of racism and unequal justice based on economic class. The Sentencing Project notes that 'black males have a 32 per cent chance of serving time in prison at some point in their lives; Hispanic males have a 17 per cent chance; white males have a 6 per cent chance'. The war on drugs equates to a semi-military action against inner-city problems. Penal conditions are often inherently abusive behind bars; many prisoners must cope with violence and duress. At the Stop Prisoner Rape organisation, executive director Lara Stemple points out: 'For women, whose abusers are often corrections officers, the rates of sexual assault are as high as one in four in some facilities.' (For more in-depth analysis of racial aspect of the war on terror, see Norman Solomon, *War Made Easy: How Presidents and Pundits Keep Spinning Us to Death.*)

10 Among the readings that Mr Bush could profitably look at, or not if his aim was to continue the system of neo-industrial profit from crime (see in that respect Dyer 2000, *The Perpetual Prisoner Machine: How America profits from Crime*), one could recommend Pratt *et al.* 2004; Mauer 1999; Monroe 1998.

11 As immediately recognized, post-September 11, by Michael Kinsley: 'if things go well it creates an opportunity to take care of other items on the agenda' ('Defining Terrorism', *Washington Post*, 5 October 2001). Nicholas Kristof had pointed out how open-ended the term terrorist was and how it enabled the administration to easily switch applicable enemies ('Our Friends the Terrorists', *New York Times*, 21 December 2001); yet others, sympathetic to Bush, pointed out that terror was a tactic and not an enemy (e.g. Daniel Pipes, 'What Bush Got Right – and Wrong', *Jerusalem Post*, 26 September 2001).

References

Achebe, Chinua (1988) 'An Image of Africa: Racism in Conrad's Heart of Darkness', in Conrad, Joseph, *Heart of Darkness*, 3rd edn, Robert Kimbrough, New York: W.W. Norton.

Adams, Simon (2004) *All the Troubles: Terrorism, War and the World After 9/11*. Freemantle, Western Australia: Freemantle Arts Centre Press.

Agamben, Giorgio (1998) *Homo Sacer: Sovereign Power and Bare Life*, trans. Daniel Heller-Roazen, Stanford, CA: Stanford University Press.

—— (1999) *Remnants of Auschwitz: The Witness and the Archive*, trans. Daniel Heller-Roazen, New York: Zone Books.

—— (2005) *State of Exception*, Chicago: University of Chicago Press.

Ahmed, A.F. Salahuddin (2000) *Bengali Nationalism and the Emergence of Bangladesh: An Introductory Outline*, Dhaka, Bangladesh: International Centre for Bengal Studies.

Ahmed, Akhtar (2000) *Advance to Contact: A Soldier's Account of Bangladesh Liberation War*, Dhaka, Bangladesh: The University Press Ltd.

Ahmed, Moudud (1979) *Bangladesh: Constitutional Quest for Autonomy 1950–1971*, Dhaka, Bangladesh: The University Press Ltd.

Ahmed, Nafeez Mosaddeq (2002) *September 11, 2001: The Great Deception: How and Why America was Attacked*, Selangor, Malaysia: Thinker's Library Sdn. Bhd.

Akenzua, Edun (1960) 'Benin – 1897: A Bini's View', *Nigeria Magazine*, No. 65 (June 1960).

Ali, S.M. (1994) *After the Dark Night: Problems of Sheikh Mujibur Rahman*, Dhaka, Bangladesh: The University Press Ltd.

Ali, Tariq (2003) *Bush in Babylon; The Recolonisation of Iraq*, London: Verso.

Alperovitz, Gar (1995) *The Decision to Drop the Bomb*, New York: Alfred A. Knopf.

Alvarez, A. (2001) *Governments, Citizens, and Genocide: A Comparative and Interdisciplinary Approach*, Bloomington, IN: Indiana University Press.

Aly, G., Chroust, P. and Pross, C. (1984) *Cleansing the Fatherland; Nazi Medicine and Racial Hygiene*, Baltimore, MD: John Hopkins University Press.

Amin, Samir (1997) *Capitalism in the Age of Globalization: The Management of Contemporary Society*, London: Zed Books.

Amnesty International (1996) *Brief Summary of Concerns about Human Rights Violations in the Chechen Republic*, London: Amnesty International.

Anghie, A (1999) 'Franciso de Vitoria and the colonial origins of international law', in P. Fitzpatrick and E. Darian-Smith (eds) *Laws of the Postcolonial*, Michigan: University of Michigan Press.

Aderson, Benedict ([1983], 1991) *Imagined Communities: Reflections on the Origin and Spread of Nationalism*, 2nd edn, London: Verso.

Annan, K. (1998) *Thirty–Fifty Annual Ditchley Foundation Lecture*, UN Press Release SG/SM 6613, 26 June 1988.

Anonymous (2002) *Through Our Enemies Eyes*, Dulles, VA: Brassey's Inc.

—— (2004) *Imperial Hubris: Why the West is Losing the War on Terror*, Virginia: Brassey's Inc.

Anstey, Roger (1966) *King Léopold's Legacy: The Congo under Belgium Rule 1908–1960*. Oxford, England: Oxford University Press.

Apter, David E. (ed.) (1997) *The Legitimization of Violence*, Washington Square, NY: New York University Press.

Arendt, Hannah (1958) *The Origins of Totalitarianism*, 2nd enlarged edn, Cleveland: World Publishing.

—— and Jaspers, Karl (1992) *Correspondence 1926–1969*, Lotte Kohler and Hans Saner (eds), Robert and Rita Kimber (Trans.), New York: Meridian.

—— (1994) *Eichmann in Jerusalem: A Report on the Banality of Evil*, London: Penguin Books.

Arens, Richard (ed.) (1976) *Genocide in Paraguay*, Philadelphia, PA: Temple University Press.

Arthur Berriedale Keith. *Belgian Congo and the Berlin Act*, London: Greenwood Press.

Ascherson, N. (1999) *The King Incorporated: Léopold the Second and the Congo*, London: George Allen & Unwin.

Aschheim, Steven E. (1996) *Culture and Catastrophe: German and Jewish Confrontations with National Socialism and Other Crises*, New York: New York University Press.

Atkinson, A. and Aveling, M. (eds) (1987) *Australians '38*, Broadway, NSW: Fairfax, Syme & Weldon.

Auchterlonie, T.B. and Pinnock, James (1898) 'The City of Benin: The Country Customs and Inhabitants', *Transactions of the Liverpool Geographical Society*, VI, 5–16.

Aziz, P. (1976) *Doctors of Death*, 4 vols, Geneva: Ferni Publishers.

Bacevich, Andrew J. (2002) *American Empire: The Realities and Consequences of U.S. Diplomacy*, Cambridge, MA: Harvard University Press.

—— (2003) *The Imperial Tense: Prospects and Problems of American Empire*, Chicago, IL: Ivan R. Dee.

Bacon, R.H. (1897) *Benin, City of Blood*, London: Arnold.

Bakhtin, Mikhail (1985) *Rabelais and His World*, trans. H. Iswlsky, Bloomington, IN: Indiana University Press.

Balakrishna, Gopal (ed.) (2003) *Debating Empire*, London: Verso.

Ball, Howard (1999) *Prosecuting War Crimes and Genocide: The Twentieth-Century Experience*, Lawrence, KS: The University Press of Kansas.

Barber, Benjamin R. (2003) *Fear's Empire: War, Terrorism, and Democracy*, New York: W.W. Norton & Co.

Barnett, Michael (2002) *Eyewitness to a Genocide: The United Nations and Rwanda*, New York: Cornell University Press.

Bartov, O. (1996) *Murder in Our Midst: The Holocaust, Industrial Killing, and Representation*, Oxford: Oxford University Press.

Bartov, O., Grossmann, A. and Nolan, M. (eds) (2002) *Crimes of War; Guilt and Denial in the Twentieth Century*, New York: The New Press.

Baudrillard, J. (1994) 'The System of Collecting', in J. Elsner and R. Cardinal, (eds), *The Cultures of Collecting*, pp. 7–24, London: Reaktion Books.

Bauer, Y. (2001) *Rethinking the Holocaust*, New Haven, CT: Yale University Press.

Bauman, Z. (1989) *Modernity and the Holocaust*, Cambridge: Polity.

—— (1991a) *Intimations of Postmodernity*, London: Routledge.

—— (1991b) *Modernity and Ambivalence*, Cambridge: Polity.

—— (1995) *Life in Fragments: Essays in Postmodern Morality*, Oxford: Blackwell.

—— (2001) *The Individualized Society*, Cambridge: Polity.

Bayart, J.-F., Ellis, S. and Hibou, B. (1999) *The Criminalization of the State in Africa*, Bloomington, IN: Indiana University Press.

Bayly, Christopher and Harper, Tim (2004) *Forgotten Armies: The Fall of British Asia 1941–1945*, London: Allen Lane, Penguin Books.

BBC News On Line, www.bbc.news.com

BBC News (2001) *The Day That Shook The World*, London: BBC Worldwide.

Beigbeder, Yves (1999) *Judging War Criminals: The Politics of International Justice*, New York: St. Martin's Press.

Beirne, Peirs (1993) *Inventing Criminology: Essays on the Rise of 'Homo Criminalis'*, Albany, NY: State University of New York Press.

Bell-Fialkoff, Andrew (1996) *Ethnic Cleansing*, New York: St. Martin's Press.

Ben-Amos, Paula Girshick (1999) *Art, Innovation, and Politics in Eighteenth-Century Benin*, Bloomington and Indianapolis, IN: Indiana University Press.

Benjamin, Walter (1969) 'On the Critique of Violence', in fragmentary translations in *Illuminations*, edited with Introduction by Hannah Arendt, New York: Schocken Books.

—— ([1973]) 'The Storyteller: Reflections on the Works of Nikolai Leskov', in Hannah Arendt (ed.), Harry Zohn (trans.), *Illuminations*, pp. 83–107, London: Fontana.

Bennett, T. (1988) 'The Exhibitionary Complex', *New Formations*, 4, 73–102.

—— (1995) *The Birth of the Museum: History, Theory, Politics*, London: Routledge.

Biaglioli, M. (1992) 'Science, Modernity and the "Final Solution"', in S. Friedlander (ed.), *Probing the Limits of Representation*, Cambridge: Harvard University Press.

Bikram, Imamuz Zaman Bir (2001) *Bangladesh War of Liberation*, Dhaka, Bangladesh: Columbia Prokashani.

Blaise Pascal (1950) *Pascal's Pensees*, trans. with an introduction by H.F. Stewart, New York: Pantheon.

Bloch, I. (1946) *Marquis de Sade: His Life and Works*, New York: Castle Books.

Blood, Archer K. (2002) *The Cruel Birth of Bangladesh: Memoirs of an American Diplomat*, Dhaka, Bangladesh: The University Press Ltd.

Bloxham, D. (2001) *Genocide on Trial*, Oxford: Oxford University Press.

Blum, William (2003) *Killing Hope*, London: Zed Books (rev. edn originally published as *The CIA: A Forgotten History*, 1986).

Boggs, Carl (ed.) (2003) *Masters of War; Militarism and Blowback in the Era of American Empire*, New York: Routledge.

Boll, Bernol (1999) *The German Army and Genocide*, edited by Hamburg Institute for Social Research trans. Scott Abbott, New York: New Press.

Boisragon, Captain Alan (1897) *The Benin Massacre*, London: Methuen.

Bonger, W.A. (1936) *An Introduction to Criminology*, London: Methuen.

Booth, Ken and Dunne, Tim (2002) 'Worlds in Collision', in Ken Booth and Tim Dunne (eds), *Worlds in Collision: Terror and the Future of Global Order*, Hampshire, England: Palgrave Macmillan.

Bosman, Willam (1967 [1705]) A New and Accurate Description of the Coast of Guinea Divided into the Gold, the Slave, and the Ivory Coasts, London Reprint, with notes by J.D. Fage and R.E. Bradbury.

Bosworth, R.J.B. (1993) *Explaining Auschwitz and Hiroshima: History Writing and the Second World War 1945–1990*, London: Routledge.

Bourke, Joanna (1999) *An Intimate History of Killing: Face-to-Face Killing in Twentieth-Century Warfare*, London: Granta Books.

Boutros-Ghali, B. (1992) *An Agenda for Peace: Preventive Diplomacy, Peace-making, and Peace-keeping*, New York: United Nations.

Boyce, James and Hartmann, Betsy (1990) *A Quiet Violence*, Dhaka: University Press Limited.

Bransch, Georges (1987) *Belgian Administration in the Congo*, London: Greenwood Press.

Bridgeman, Jon M. (1981) *The Revolt of the Hereros*, Berkeley, CA: University of California Press.

Broeckmann, A. (1995) *A Visual Economy of Individuals*. Web publication accessed 20 June 2003, http://www.v2.nl/~andreas/phd/

Browning Christopher, R. (1992) 'German Memory, Judicial Interrogation, and Historical Reconstruction: Writing Perpetrator History from Postwar Testimony', in S. Friedlander (ed.), *Probing the Limits of Representation: Nazism and the 'Final Solution'*, Cambridge, MA: Harvard University Press.

—— (1995) *The Path to Genocide: Essays on Launching the Final Solution*, Cambridge: Canto, Cambridge University Press.

—— (1998 [1992]) *Ordinary Men: Reserve Police Battalion and the Final Solution in Poland*, New York: Harper Perennial.

—— (2004) *The Origins of the Final Solution: The Evolution of Nazi Jewish Policy 1939–1942*, Yad Vashem, Jerusalem, Israel (Arrow Books edition 2005, London).

Brownmiller, Susan (1975) *Against Our Will: Men Women and Rape*, New York: Simon & Schuster.

Bryan, Lowell and Farrell, Diana (eds) (1996) *Market Unbound: Unleashing Global Capitalism*, New York: John Wiley.

Brzezinski, Z. ([1993] 1995) *Out of Control: Global Turmoil on the Eve of the 21st Century*, New York: Touchstone.

Burbach, Roger and Clarke, Ben (eds) (2002) *September 11 and the U.S. War: Beyond the Curtain of Smoke*, San Francisco, CA: City Lights Books.

Burke, James Lee (2003) *Last Car to Elysian Fields*, New York: Pocket Star Books.

Burleigh, Michael and Wippermann, Wolfgang (eds) (1991) *The Racial State: Germany 1933–1945*, Cambridge: Cambridge University Press.

Burleigh, Michael (1997) *Ethics and Extermination: Reflections on Nazi Genocide*, Cambridge: Cambridge University Press.

Caporaso, J. (1997) 'Across the Great Divide: Integrating Comparative and International Politics', *International Studies Quarterly*, 41(4), 563–92.

Casement, R. (1904) 'The Congo Report', *British Parliamentary Papers*, LXII, Cmd 1933.

Cassese, Antonio (2003) *International Criminal Law*, Oxford: Oxford University Press.

Cercas, Javier (2003) *Soldiers of Salamis*, London: Bloomsbury.

Césaire, Aimé (1972) *Discourse on Colonialism*, New York: Monthly Review Press.

Chalk, Frank and Jonassohn, Kurt (1990) *The History and Sociology of Genocide: Analysis and Case Studies*, New Haven, CT: Yale University Press.

Chamberlin, Russell (1983) *Loot! The Heritage of Plunder*, New York: Facts on File Inc.

Chandler, D. (2002) *From Kosovo to Kabul*, London: Pluto.

Chang, Iris (1997) *The Rape of Nanking: The Forgotten Holocaust of World War II*, New York: Basic Books.

Charny, Israel (1991) *Genocide: A Critical Bibliographic Review*, London: Mansell.

Chevallier, P. (1989) *Les Regicides: Clement, Ravaillac, Damiens*, Paris: Fayard.

Chomsky, Noam (1989a) *Necessary Illusions: Thought Control in Democratic Societies*, London: Pluto Press.

—— (1989b) *The Culture of Terrorism*, London: Pluto Press.

—— (1999a) *Acts of Aggression: Policing 'Rogue' States*, New York: Seven Stories Press.

—— (1999b) *The Umbrella of U.S. Power: The Universal Declaration of Human Rights and the Contradictions of U.S. Policy*, New York: Seven Stories Press.

—— (2001) *An Evening with Noam Chomsky*, Recording from the Technology and Cultural Forum, MIT, 18 October, 2001.

—— (2003) *Hegemony or Survival: America's Quest for Global Dominance*, New York: Metropolitan Books.

Chowdhury, Sabir Ahmed (1999) *The Mystic Bard: Songs of Sabir Ahmed Chowdhury*, trans. M. Mizanur Rahman, Dhaka, Bangladesh: Tanjeela Ferdous Ayshee.

Christie, Nils (1993, 2nd edn 1994, 3rd edn 2000) *Crime Control as Industry: Towards Gulags, Western Style*, London: Routledge.

Christie, Nils (1998) 'Roots of a Perspective', in Holdaway, Simon and Rock, Paul (eds), *Thinking about Criminology*, London: UCL Press.

Churchill, Ward (1997) *A Little Matter of Genocide: Holocaust and Denial in the Americas, 1492 to the Present*, San Francisco, CA: City Lights Books.

Churchill, Ward (2003) *On the Justice of Roosting Chickens: Reflections on the Consequences of U.S. Imperial Arrogance and Criminality*, Edinburgh: AK Press UK.

Churchill, Winston (1997 [1899]) *The River War: An Historical Account of the Re-conquest of the Soudan*, 2 vols, London: Longmans Green, reprint London: Prion.

Citizens Commission of Inquiry (1972) *The Dellums Committee Hearings on War Crimes in Vietnam*, New York: Vintage.

Clark, G.N. (1958) *War and Society in the Seventeenth Century*, Cambridge: Cambridge University Press.

Clark, Ramsey (1996) *The Impact of Sanctions on Iraqi: The Children are Dying*, Washington, DC: Maisonneuve Press.

—— (1998) *Challenge to Genocide: Let Iraq Live*, Washington, DC: International Action Center.

Clarke, Ronald V. and Marcus Felson (eds) (1993) *Advances in Criminological Theory, Vol. 5: Routine Activity and Rational Choice*, New Brunswick, NJ: Transaction.

Clendinnen, Inga (1999) *Reading the Holocaust*, New York: Cambridge University Press.

Cohen, Stanley (1996) 'Crime and Politics: Spot the Difference', *British Journal of Sociology*, 47(1), 1–21.

—— (2001) *States of Denial: Knowing about Atrocities and Suffering*, Cambridge: Polity Press.

Cole, David (2003) *Enemy Aliens: Double Standards and Constitutional Freedoms in the War on Terrorism*, New York: The New Press.

Cole, David and Dempsey, James X. (2002) *Terrorism and the Constitution: Sacrificing Civil Liberties in the Name of National Security*, New York: The New Press.

Colquhoun, P. (1797) *Treatise on the Police of the Metropolis*, 4th edn, London: J. Mawman.

—— (1806) *Treatise on Indigence*, London: J. Mawman.

Conan Doyle, Sir Arthur (1909) *The Crime of the Congo*, New York: Doubleday, Page & Co.

Conrad, Joseph ([1899] 1988) *Heart of Darkness*, Robert Kimbrough (3rd ed.) New York: W.W. Norton & Company.

Cookey, S.J.S. (1968) *Britain and the Congo Question 1885–1913*, London: Longmans, Green & Co. Ltd.

Coombes, Annie E. (1994) *Reinventing Africa: Museums, Material Culture and Popular Imagination*, New Haven, CT: Yale University Press.

Cooper, Robert (2003) *The Breaking of Nations: Order and Chaos in the Twenty-First Century*, Atlantic Books.

Cornelis, S., Creemers-Palmers, M., Goris, J.M., Hambrouck, G., Jespers, P.H., Luwel, M. and Marechal, Ph. (1991) *H. M. Stanley: Explorateur au Service du Roi*, Brussels, Belgium: Royal Museum for Central Africa, Tervuren.

Corrigan, Phillip and Sayer, Derek (1985) *The Great Arch: English State Formation as Cultural Revolution*, Oxford: Blackwell.

Cotterrell, Roger (2003) *The Politics of Jurisprudence*, 2nd edn, London: Lexis Nexis.

Cowling, Mary (1989) *The Artist as Anthropologist: The Representation of Type and Character in Victorian Art*, Cambridge: Cambridge University Press.

Cunneen, Chris (2001) *Conflict, Politics and Crime: Aboriginal Communities and the Police*, Sydney: Allen & Unwin.

Damrel, D. (1995) 'The Religious Roots of Conflict: Russia and Chechnya', *Religious Studies News*, September, 10(3), 10.

Danner, Mark (1998) 'The Killing Fields of Bosnia', *New York Review of Books*, 24 September, 63–77.

Darton, Eric (1999) *Divided We Stand: A Biography of New York's World Trade Center*, New York: Basic Books.

—— (2002) 'The Janus Face of Architectural Terrorism: Minoru Yamasaki, Mohammed Atta, and Our World Trade Centre', in Michael Sorkin and Sharon Zukin (eds). *After the World Trade Center: Rethinking*, New York City, London: Routledge.

Darwin, Charles (1871) *Descent of Man and Selection in Relation to Sex*, London: John Murray.

—— (1890) *Darwin's Journal, or Darwin's Voyage on the Beagle, or Journal of Researches into the Natural History and Ecology of the Countries Visited During the Voyage of H.M.S. 'Beagle' Around the World*, 7th edn, London: Ward, Lock and Co.

Dass, Veena (2002) 'Violence and Translation', *Anthropology Quarterly*, 75(1).

Davidson, Basil (1992) *The Black Man's Burden: Africa and the Curse of the Nation State*, New York: Three Rivers Press.

Davidson, Eugene (1973/1998) *The Nuremberg Fallacy*, New York: Macmillan.

De Lichtervelds, Comte Louis (1928) *Léopold of the Belgians*, trans. Thomas H. Reed, London: Stanley Paul.

De Maistre, J. (1971) *The Works of Joseph de Maistre*, trans. Jack Lively, New York: Schocken.

De Quiros, Bernaldo (1911) *Modern Theories of Criminality*, Alfanso de Salvio (trans.) Boston: Little Brown and Company.

De Witte, Ludo (2002) *The Assassination of Lumumba*, trans. Ann Wright and Rene Fenby, London: Verso.

Dembour, M.-B. (1992) 'La chicotte comme symbole du colonialisme belge?', *Canadian Journal of African Studies*, 26(2).

Depelchin, Jacques (1992) *From the Congo Free State to Zaire (1885–1974): Towards a Demystification of Economic and Political History*, Senegal, Africa: Codesria.

Deutsch, Eberhard P. (1972) 'Biafra, Bengal, and Beyond: International Responsibility and Genocidal Conflict', *American Journal of International Law*, 66, 89–107.

Dickens, Charles (2002 [1860]) *Great Expectations*, London: Penguin.

Dixit, J.N. (1999) *Liberation and Beyond: Indo-Bangladesh Relations*, Dhaka, Bangladesh: The University Press Ltd.

Douglas, Lawrence (1966) 'The Memory of Judgement', *History and Memory*, 7.

Douglas, Lawrence (1995) Film as Witness: Screening 'Nazi Concentration Camps' Before the Nuremberg Tribunal', *Yale Law Journal*, 105, 449–81.

Douzinas, C. (2000) *The End of Human Rights*, Oxford: Hart Publishing.

Dower, John W. (1986) *War Without Mercy: Race and Power in the Pacific War*, New York: Pantheon Books.

Downes, David (1966) *The Delinquent Solution*, London: Routledge & Kegan Paul.

Duffett, John (ed.) (1968) *Against the Crime of Silence: Proceedings of the International Crimes Tribunal*, Stockholm-Copenhagen, New York: Simon & Schuster.

Drechsler, Horst (1980) *'Let Us Die Fighting': The Struggle of the Herero and Nama against German Imperialism* (1884–1915), Bernd Zollner (trans.) London: Zed Books.

Duncan, Cameron (1972) 'The Museum: A Temple or the Forum', *Journal of World History*, 14(1), 197–201.

Duncan, Carol (1991) 'Museums and Citizenship', in Ivan Karp and Steven Lavine (eds), *Exhibiting Cultures: The Poetics and Politics of Museum Display*, Washington and London: Smithsonian Institution Press.

—— (1995) *Civilising Rituals: Inside Public Art Museums*, London: Routledge.

Durkheim, Emile (1965) *The Elementary Forms of Religious Life*, New York: Free Press.

—— (1982) *The Rules of Sociological Method*, edited with an introduction by Steven Lukes, trans. W.D. Halls, New York: Free Press.

Dyer, Joel (2000) *The Perpetual Prisoner Machine: How America Profits from Crime*, Boulder, CO: Westview Press.

Easterling, Kelloer (2002) 'Enduring Innocence', in Sorkin, Michael and Zukin, Sharon (eds) (2002) *After the World Trade Center: Rethinking New York City*, London: Routledge.

Edgerton, Robert B. (2002) *The Troubled Heart of Africa: A History of the Congo*, New York: St. Martin's Press.

Elder, Bruce (1998) *Blood on the Wattle: Massacres and Maltreatment of Aboriginal Australians since 1788*, (expanded edn) Sydney: New Holland.

Elias, Norbert (1982) *Power and Civility*, New York: Pantheon Books.

Elias, N. (1984) *The Civilising Process*, trans. Jephcott, Oxford: Blackwell.

—— (1991) *The Symbol Theory*, ed. Richard Kilminister, London: Sage.

—— (1996) *The Germans*, ed. Michael Schroter, Cambridge: Polity.

Elliot, G. (1972) *Twentieth Century Book of the Dead*, London: Allen Lane.

Elsner, J. and Cardinal, R. (1994a) *The Cultures of Collecting*, London: Reaktion Books Ltd.

—— (1994b) 'Introduction', in J. Elsner and R. Cardinal (eds), *The Cultures of Collecting*, London: Reaktion Books.

Evans, Julie (2005) 'Colonialism and the rule of law: the case of South Australia', in Barry Godfrey and Graeme Dunstall (eds) *Crime and Empire 184-1940: Criminal Justice in Local and Global Context*, Devon: Willan Publishing

Ewans, Martin (2002) *European Atrocity, African Catastrophe: Léopold II, the Congo Free State and its Aftermath*, London: Routledge Curzon.

Fanon, Frantz (1963) *The Wretched of the Earth*, New York: Grove Press.

Fein, H. (1979) *Accounting for Genocide*, New York: The Free Press.

Fein, H. (1993) *Genocide: A Sociological Perspective*, London: Sage.

Felson, Marcus (1998) *Crime and Everyday Life*, Thousand Oaks, CA: Pine Forge Press.

Ferguson, Niall (2003a) 'Hegemony or Empire?' *Foreign Affairs*, September–October 82(5).

—— (2003b) *Empire: The Rise and Demise of the British World Order and the Lessons for Global Power*, New York: Basic Books.

—— (2004) *Colossus: The Rise and Fall of the American Empire*, London: Penguin.

Ferrell, J., Hayward, K., Morrison, W. and Presdee, M. (2004) *Cultural Criminology Unleashed*, London: Glasshouse.

Finkelstein, Norman G. and Birn, Ruth Bettina (1998) *A Nation on Trial: The Goldhagen Thesis and Historical Truth*, New York: Henry Holt & Co.

Finkielkraut, Alain (2000) *In the Name of Humanity: Reflections on the Twentieth Century*, trans. Judith Friedlander, New York: Columbia University Press.

Firche, Carolyn (ed.) (1993) *Against Forgetting: Twentieth-Century Poetry of Witness*, New York: W.W. Norton.

Fletcher, R. (1971 [1882]) 'Tattooing Among Civilised People', an address illustrated by photographs and drawings at the 61st regular meeting of the Anthropology Society of Washington 1882, *Transactions of the Anthropology Society of Washington*, New York: Kraus Reprint Co.

Fo'a, Piero P. (2003) 'Science, Pseudoscience and Public Policy in Fascist Italy, Physical Anthropology, Phrenology, Constitutional Medicine and Eugenics: The Slippery Slope of Racism', Web publication accessed 4 April 2004, at www.reed.edu/~sheaa/primary%20documents/eugenics_paper.pdf

Fogel, Joshua A. (ed.) (2000) *The Nanjing Massacre in History and Historiography*, Los Angeles, CA: University of California Press.

Foucault, M. (1969) *The Archaeology of Knowledge*, London: Tavistock Publications.

—— (1977a) *Discipline and Punish*, Harmondsworth: Penguin.

—— (1977b) *Discipline and Punishment: The Birth of the Prison*, London: Penguin Books.

Franklin, H. Bruce (1988) *Star Wars: The Superweapon and the American Imagination*, New York: Oxford University Press.

—— (2000) *Vietnam and Other American Fantasies*, Amherst, MA: University of Massachusetts Press.

Fraser, David (2005) *Law After Auschwitz: Towards a Jurisprudence of the Holocaust*, Durham, NC: Carolina Academic Press.

Friedlander, H. (1995) *When Medicine Went Mad; Bioethics and the Holocaust*, Totowa, NJ: Humana Press.

Friedlander, Saul (1976) *Pogromchik: The Assassination of Simon Petlura*, New York: Hart.

—— (1997) *Nazi Germany and the Jews*, New York: Harper Collins.

Friedman, Thomas L. (2002) *Longitudes and Attitudes: Exploring the World Before and After September 11*, London: Penguin Books.

Friedrich, Otto (1994) *The Kingdom of Auschwitz*, Harmondsworth: Penguin Books.

—— (1996) *The Kingdom of Auschwitz*, London: Penguin Books.

Frigessi, D. (2003) *Cesare Lombroso*, Turin: Giulio Einaudi Editore.

Frigessi, D., Giacanelli, F. and Mangoni, L. (2000) *Delitto, genio, follia: Scritti scelti*, Turin: Bollati Boringhieri.

Fromm, Erich (1974) *The Anatomy of Human Destructiveness*, London: Jonathan Cape.

Fukuyama, Francis (1989) 'The End of History?', *The National Interest*, 16 (Summer), 18.

—— (1992) *The End of History and the Last Man*, New York: Free Press.

G Blanchart and Cie (eds) (1993) *Le Rail au Congo Belge 1890–1920 – Tome I*. Brussels, Belgium: GBB.

Galeano, Eduardo (2002) 'The Theatre of Good and Evil', in Roger Burbach and Ben Clarke (eds), *September 11 and the US War: Beyond the Curtain of Smoke*, San Francisco, CA: City Lights Books.

Galton, Francis (1878) 'Composite Portraits', in *Journal of the Anthropological Institute*, Vol. VIII.

Gann, Lewis H. and Duignan, Peter (1979) *The Rulers of Belgian Africa, 1884–1914*, Princeton, NJ: Princeton University Press.

Garland, D. (1985a) *Punishment and Welfare*, Aldershot: Gower.

—— (1985b) 'The Criminal and his Science', *British Journal of Criminology*, 25(2), 109–37.

—— (1988) 'British Criminology before 1935', in Paul Rock (ed.), *A History of British Criminology*, pp. 1–17, Oxford: Oxford University Press.

——(1992) 'Criminological Knowledge and Its Relation to power: Foucault's Genealogy and Criminology Today', *British Journal of Criminology*, Vol. 32. No. 4. 1992.

—— (1994) 'Of Crimes and Criminals: The Development of Criminology in Britain', in Mike Maguire, Rod Morgan and Robert Reiner (eds.), *The Oxford Handbook of Criminology*, Oxford: Clarendon Press.

——(1997) 'Of Crimes and Criminals: The Development of Criminology in Britain', in *The Oxford Handbook of Criminology*, 2nd revised (edn.) Maguire, Morgan and Reiner (eds). Oxford: Oxford University Press.

—— and Sparks, R. (2000) 'Criminology, Social Theory and the Challenge of Our Times', in D. Garland and R. Sparks (eds), *Criminology and Social Theory*, Oxford: Oxford University Press.

—— (2001) *The Culture of Control: Crime and Social Order in Contemporary Society*, Oxford: Oxford University Press.

——(2002) 'Of Crimes and Criminals: The Development of Criminology in Britain', in *The Oxford Handbook of Criminology*, 3rd revised edn, Maguire, Morgan and Reiner (eds)Oxford: Oxford University Press.

Gatrell, V. and Hadden, T. (1972) 'Criminal Statistics and Their interpretation', in E. Wrigley (ed.), *Nineteenth Century Society. Essays in the Use of Quantitative Methods for the Study of Social Data*, Cambridge: Cambridge University Press.

Geary, Christraud (2002) *In and Out of Focus: Images from Central Africa, 1885–1960*, London: Philip Wilson Publishers.

Gellateley, Robert (1990) *The Gestapo and German Society: Enforcing Racial Policy 1933–1945*, Oxford: Clarendon.

Gibbons, D. (1994) *Talking about Crime and Criminals: Problems and Issues in Theory Development in Criminology*, Englewood Cliffs, NJ: Prentice Hall.

Giddens, Anthony (2000) *Runaway World: How Globalization is Reshaping Our Lives*, pp. 20–21, New York: Routledge.

Gilman, S. (1985) *Difference and Pathology: Stereotypes of Sexuality, Race and Madness*, Ithaca and London: Cornell University Press.

Giorgio, C. (1975) *La scienza infelice: Il Museo di antropologia criminale di Cesare Lombroso*, Turin: Bollati Boringhieri.

Glass, James M. (1997) *Life Unworthy of Life*, New York: Basic Books.

Glover, J. (2001) *Humanity: A Moral History of the Twentieth Century*, London: Pimlico.

Goldberg, Arthur J. and Gardner, Richard N. (1972) 'Time to Act on the Genocide Convention', *American Bar Association Journal*, 58, 141–5.

Goldhagen, D. (1996) *Hitler's Willing Executioners: Ordinary Germans and the Holocaust*, London: Little, Brown.

—— (1998a) 'The Failure of the Critics', in Robert Shandley (ed.), *Unwilling Germans?*

—— (1998b) 'Modell Bundescrepublik: National History, Democracy, and Internationalization in Germany', in Robert Shandley (ed.), *The Goldhagen Debate*, pp. 129–50, Minneapolis, MN: University of Minnesota Press.

Golt, Maynard (1966) 'The Necessity of an International Court of Justice', *Washburn Law Review*, 6.

Goring, C. (1913) *The English Convict: A Statistical Study*, London: HMSO.

Gottfredson, M. and Hirschi, T. (1990) *A General Theory of Crime*, Stanford, CA: Stanford University Press.

Gottlieb, Alma (1989) 'Witches, Kings, and the Sacrifice of Identity or the Power of Paradox and the Paradox of Power among the Beng of Ivory Coast', in W. Arens and I. Karps (eds.), *Creativity of Power: Cosmology and Action in African Societies*, pp. 245–72, Washington, DC: Smithsonian Institution Press.

Gould, S. (1981) *The Mismeasure of Man*, New York: W. W. Norton.

Grasso, June, Corrin, Jay and Kort, Michael (2004) *Modernization and Revolution in China: From the Opium Wars to World Power*, 3rd edn, Armonk, New York and London: M.E. Sharpe Inc.

Greenfield, J. (1996) *The Return of Cultural Treasures*, 2nd edn, Cambridge: Cambridge University Press.

Greenhalgh, Paul (1988) *Ephemeral Vistas: The Expositions Universelles, Great Exhibitions and World's Fairs, 1851–1939*, Manchester, NH: Manchester University Press.

Gross, Hyman (1979) *A Theory of Criminal Justice*, New York: Oxford University Press.

Grossman, Dave (1996) *On Killing: The Psychological Cost of Learning to Kill in War and Society*, Toronto: Little Brown.

Grosvenor, I., McLean, R. and Roberts, S. (eds) (2002) *Making Connections: Birmingham's Black International History*, Birmingham, AL: Black Pasts, Birmingham Futures Group.

Gudenkauf, Abbe (1986) *Belgian Congo Study Circle*, Cockrill Buoklet 44.

Gustafson, Carrie (1998) 'International Criminal Courts: Some Dissident Views on the Continuation of War by Penal Means', *Houston Journal of International Law*, 21 (Fall), 51.

Habermas, Jurgen (1983) 'Neoconservative Cultural Criticism in the United States and West Germany: An Intellectual Movement in Two Political Cultural', trans. Russell A. Berman, *Telos*, 56 (reprinted in Richard J. Berstein [1985] *Habermas and Modernity*, Cambridge, MA).

Habib, Haroon (ed.) (2000) *Bangladesh Blood and Brutality*, Dhaka, Bangladesh: Magnum Opus.

Hagen John. Rymond-Richmond, Wenona and Parker, Patricia (2005) 'The Criminology of Genocide: The Death and Rape of Darfur', *Criminology*, 43 (3).

Hall, C. (ed.) (2000a) Introduction: Thinking the Postcolonial, Thinking the Empire, *Cultures of Empire: Colonizers in Britain and the Empire in the Nineteenth and Twentieth Centuries*, Manchester, NH: Manchester University Press.

—— (2000b) *Cultures of Empire: Colonizers in Britain and the Empire in the Nineteenth and Twentieth Centuries*, Manchester, NH: Manchester University Press.

Hamilton, Peter and Hargreaves, Roger (2001) *The Beautiful and the Damned: The Creation of Identity in Nineteenth Century Photography*, London: Lund Humphries.

Hannan, Mohammed (2001) *Political History of Bangladesh*, Dhaka, Bangladesh: Anannya.

Harff, Barabara and Gurr, Ted Robert (1988) 'Toward an Empirical Theory of Genocides and Politicides', *International Studies Quarterly*, 32, 359.

Harknett, R.J. (1996) 'Territoriality in the Nuclear Era', in E. Kofman and G. Youngs (eds), *Globalisation: Theory and Practice*, London: Pinter.

Harris, Sheldon H. (2002) *Factories of Death: Japanese Biological Warfare, 1932–1945, and the American Cover-up*, rev. edn, New York: Routledge.

Hartmann, Betsy and Boyce, James K. (1983) *A Quiet Violence: View from a Bangladesh Village*, London: Zed Books.

Harvey, David (2002) 'Cracks in the Edifice of the Empire State', in Michael Sorkin and Sharon Zukin (eds), *After the World Trade Center: Rethinking New York City*, pp. 57–67, New York: Routledge.

Hasanuzzaman, Al Masud (1998) *Role of Opposition in Bangladesh Politics*, Dhaka, Bangladesh: The University Press Ltd.

Haskel, Francis (1971) 'The Manufacture of the Past in Nineteenth-Century Painting' *Past and Present*, 53.

Hass, Amira (2002) 'Human Rights Watch Blasts Palestinians for War Crimes. New Report Calls Suicide Strikes against Civilians a Violation of International Law', *Haaretz*, 1 November 2002, www.haaretzdaily.com

Hastings, Max (1979) *Bomber Command*, London: Dial.

Hastings, C. (27 August 2001). UK Museums to Return Aboriginal Artefacts in Policy Switch, *The Age*, Retrieved 28 February 2003, http://www.theage.com.au/news/world/2001/08/27/FFXNFETPTQC.html

Hawkins (1981–2) 'Joseph Conrad, Roger Casement, and the Congo Reform Movement', *Journal of Modern Literature*, 9(1), 65–80.

Hayner, Priscilla (2001) *Unspeakable Truths: How Truth Commissions Around the World are Challenging the Past and Shaping the Future*, London: Routledge.

Hayward, K. (2004) *City Limits: Crime, Consumer Culture and the Urban Experience*, London: Glasshouse.

Hedges, Chris (2002) *War Is a Force That Gives US Meaning*, New York: Anchor Books.

Heers, Jacques (2003) *The Barbary Corsairs; Warfare in the Mediterranean, 1480–1580*, trans. Jonathan North, London: Greenhill Books.

Heidegger, Martin (1977) *The Question Concerning Technology and Other Essays*, New York: Harper & Row.

Herold, Marc W. (2002) 'Who Will Count the Dead?', in *September 11 and the US War: Behind the Curtain of Smoke*, Roger Burbach and Ben Clarke (eds), San Franciso: City Lights Books, 2002 (originally posted as a web article, entitled 'A Dossier of Civilian Victims of United States Aerial Bombing of Afghanistan: A Comprehensive Accounting' @ http://www.media-alliance.org/mediafile/20-5/).

Herz, John (1976) *The Nation-state and the Crisis of World Politics*, New York: David Mckay.

Heschel, Abraham Joshua (1955) *God in Search of Man: A Philosophy of Judaism*, New York: Farrar, Straus & Cudahy.

Heyer, Paul (1966) *Architects on Architecture: New Directions in America*, New York: Walker and Company.

Hilberg, Raul (1965) 'German Motivations for the Destruction of the Jews', *Midstream*, June 1956.

Hilberg, Raul (1979) *The Destruction of European Jews*, New York: Harper & Row.

Hillyard, Paddy, Pantazis, Christina, Tombs, Steve and Gordon, Dave (eds) (2004) *Beyond Criminology: Taking Harm Seriously*, London: Pluto Press.

Hinton, Alexander Laban (ed.) (2002) *Annihilating Difference: The Anthropology of Genocide*, Los Angeles, CA: University of California Press.

Hiro, Dilip (2002) *War without End: The Rise of Islamist Terrorism and Global Response*, London: Routledge.

Hirsh, Marianne (1997) *Family Frames: Photography, Narrative and Postmemory*, Cambridge, MA: Harvard University Press.

Hobbes, T. ([1651] 1998) De Cive [The Citizen], printed by J.C. for R. Royston, at the Angel in Ivie-Lane, Cambridge Edition, Cambridge: Cambridge University Press.

Hobbes, T. (1991 [1651]) *Leviathan*, ed. Richard Tuck, Cambridge: Cambridge University Press.

Hobson, J.A. (1902) *Imperialism, A Study*, London: George Allen and Unwin Ltd (1938 reprint).

Hobsbawm, Eric (1975) *The Age of Capital: 1845–1878*, New York: Scribner.

Hochschild, A. (1998) *King Léopold's Ghost: A Story of Greed, Terror and Heroism in Colonial Africa*, Boston and New York: Mariner Books/Houghton Mifflin Company.

Hochschild, A. (1998) *King Léopold's Ghost*, London: Houghton Mifflin.

—— (1999) *King Léopold's Ghost*, New York: Mariner.

Hoes, Rudolf (1959) *Commandant of Auschwitz: The Autobiography of Rudolf Hoess*, New York: George, Weidenfeld and Nicholson.

Hofstede, Geert (1984) *Culture's Consequences*, 2. Get. Aufl., Beverly Hills: Sage.

Homer-Dixon, Thomas (2002) 'The Rise of Complex Terrorism', *Foreign Policy*, January/February 2002.

Hooper-Greenhill, E. (1992) *Museums and the Shaping of Knowledge*, London: Routledge.

Hopkins, F. (1966) 'Bombing and the American Conscience During World War II', *The Historian*, Vol. 28. No. 3, May 1966.

Horne, D. (1984) *The Great Museum: The Re-presentation of History*, London: Pluto.

—— (2003) *The Criminal Body: Lombroso and the Anatomy of Deviance*, London: Routledge.

Horowitz, Solis (1950) 'The Tokyo Trial', *International Conciliation*, 465, 473–584.

Horwitz, Gordon J. (1991) *In the Shadow of Death: Living Outside the Gates of Mauthausen*, London: L B Taurus.

Hossain, T. (2001) *Involvement in Bangladesh's Struggle for Freedom*, Dhaka, Bangladesh: Manabatabadi Karmakendra Centre for Humanist Activities.

Howard, Michael (1976) *War in European History*, Oxford: Oxford University Press.

Howell, Llewellyn D. (2001) 'Terrorism: The 21st-Century War', *US Today*, March.

Huntington, Samuel P. (1993) 'The Clash of Civilizations and the Remaking of World Order', *Foreign Affairs*, 72 (summer), 22–49.

—— (1996) *The Clash of Civilizations and the Remaking of World Order*, London: The Free Press.

Huque, Kazi Anwarul (1991) *In Quest of Freedom*, Dhaka, Bangladesh: The University Press Ltd.

Igbafe, P.A. (1979) *Benin under British Administration: The Impact of Colonial Rule on an African Kingdom 1897-1938*, London: Longman.

Imam, Jahanara (1998) *Of Blood and Fire: The Untold Story of Bangladesh's War of Independence*, trans. Mustafizur Rahman, Dhaka, Bangladesh: The University Press Ltd.

Ingold, Tim (1986) *Evolution and Social Life*, Cambridge: Cambridge University Press.

International Commission of Jurists (1973) 'Bangladesh', *The Review*, 11, 30–3.

Islam B.U., Rafiqul (1997) *A Tale of Millions: Bangladesh Liberation War 1971*, Dhaka, Bangladesh: Anannya.

'Ismat Hasan Zulfo (1980) *Karari: The Sudanese Account of the Battle of Omdurman*, London: Frederick Warne.

Jacobson, Norman (1986) *Pride & Solace: The Functions and Limits of Political Theory*, New York: Methuen.

Jochmann, Werner (ed.) (1980) *Monologe im Fuhrerhauptquartier 1941–1944: Die Aufzeichungen Heinrich Heims*, Hamburg: Albrecht Knaus Verlag.

Johnston, H.H. (1895) *The River Congo: From Its Mouth to Bolobo*, London: Sampson, Low, Marston & Company.

Juergensmeyer, Mark (1993) *The New Cold War? Religious Nationalism Confronts the Secular State*, Berkeley, CA: University of California Press.

Kabir, Amanullah (2002) *The Struggling Democracy of Bangladesh*, Dhaka, Bangladesh: Adorn Publication.

Kabir, Muhammad Ghulam (1995) *Changing Face of Nationalism: The Case of Bangladesh*, Dhaka, Bangladesh: The University Press Ltd.

Kagan, Robert (2003) *Paradise & Power: America and Europe in the New World Order*, London: Atlantic Books, Grove Atlantic Ltd.

Kaplan, Robert (2001) *Warrior Politics: Why Leadership Demands a Pagan Ethos*, New York: Random House.

—— (2003) 'Supremacy by Stealth: Ten Rules for Managing the World', *The Atlantic Monthly*, July/August, 65–83.

Katch, J. (1965) *Scroll of Agony: The Warsaw Diary of Chaim A. Kaplan*, J. Katch (ed. and trans.), New York: Macmillan .

Katsuichi, Honda (1999) *The Nanjing Massacre: A Japanese Journalist Confronts Japan's National Shame*, trans. Karen Sandness, New York: M. E. Sharpe Inc.

Katz, J. (1988) *Seductions of Crime: Moral and Sensual Attractions in Doing Evil*, New York: Basic Books.

Keegan, John (1998) *War and Our World*, New York: Vintage Books.

Keeley, Lawrence H. (1996) *War before Civilization: The Myth of the Peaceful Savage*, New York: Oxford University Press Inc.

Kelman, H. and Hamilton, V. (1989) *Crimes of Obedience*, New Haven, CT: Yale University Press.

Khan, Faruq Aziz (1993) *Spring 1971: A Centre Stage Account of Bangladesh War of Liberation*, Dhaka, Bangladesh: The University Press Ltd.

Khan, Zillur R. (1996) *The Third World Charismatic: Sheikh Mujib and the Struggle for Freedom*, Dhaka, Bangladesh: The University Press Ltd.

Kimbrough, Robert (ed.) (1988) *Heart of Darkness: Joseph Conrad*, London: W. W. Norton & Company.

King, Michael (1996) *Maori: A Photographic and Social History*, rev. edn, Auckland: Reed Publishing.

Kolko, Gabriel (2002) *Another Century of War?* New York: The New Press.

Korn, Richard R. and McCorkle, Lloyd W. (1959) *Criminology and Penology*, New York: Henry Holt & Company, Inc.

Kriegel, Blandine (1995) *The State and the Rule of Law*, Princeton, NJ: Princeton University Press.

Kuper, L. (1982) *Genocide: Its Political Use in the Twentieth Century*, London: Penguin books [1981] New Haven, CT: Yale University Press.

—— (1985) *The Prevention of Genocide*, New Haven, CT: Yale University Press.

LaCapra, Dominick (2001) *Writing History, Writing Trauma*, London: The John Hopkins University Press.

Landas, Mark (2004) *The Fallen: A True Story of American POWS and Japanese Wartime Atrocities*, Hoboken, NJ: John Wiley & Sons Inc.

Langbein, John E. (1977) *Torture and the Law of Proof; Europe and England in the Ancient Regime*, Chicago, IL: University of Chicago Press.

Langer, Lawrence L. (ed.) (1995) *Art from the Ashes: A Holocaust Anthology*, Oxford: Oxford University Press.

Lee Burk, James (2003) *Last Car to Elysian Fields*, New York: Pocket Star Books.

Lemert, Charles C. and Gillan, Garth (1982) *Michel Foucault: Social Theory and Transgression*, New York: Columbia University Press.

Lemkin, R. (1944) *Axis Rule in Occupied Europe*, Washington, DC: Carnegie Endowment for International Peace.

—— (1947) 'Genocide as a Crime under International Law', *American Journal of International Law*, 41(1), 145–51.

Leong, M (2004) *Il Museo di Anthropologia Criminale 'Cesare Lombroso'*, unpublished Masters Thesis for MA in Museum Studies, London: UCL.

Levene, Mark and Roberts, Penny (eds) (1999) *Massacre in History*, New York: Berghahn Books.

Levi, Primo (1986) *The Drowned and the Saved*, trans. Raymond Rosenthal, New York: Summit Books.

—— (1987) *If this is a Mann*, trans. Stuart Woolf, London: Abacus.

—— (1993) *Survival at Auschwitz*, trans. Stuart Woolf, New York: Collier.

—— (1995) *The Reawakening*, Stuart Woolf (trans.), New York: Collier.

Lévinas, Emmanuel (1985) *Ethics and Infinity: Conversations with Philippe Nemo*, trans. Richard A. Cohen, Pittsburgh, PA: Duquesne University Press.

—— (1990) *Difficult Freedom: Essays on Judaism*, trans. Sean Hand, Baltimore, MD: The John Hopkins University Press.

Lewis, Bernard (2002) *What Went Wrong? Western Impact and Middle Eastern Response*, London: Phoenix, Orion Books Ltd.

Li, F.F., Sabella, R. and Liu, D. (eds) (2002) *Nanking 1937: Memory and Healing*, New York: M. E. Sharpe Inc.

Libaridian, G. (2000) 'The Ultimate Repression: The Genocide of the Armenians, 1915–1917', in I. Wallimann and M. Dobkowski (eds), *Genocide and the Modern Age*, pp. 203–36, Syracuse, NY: Syracuse University Press.

Liberation War Museum (n.d.) *1971: Documents on Crimes against Humanity Committed by Pakistan Army and their Agents in Bangladesh during 1971*, Dhaka, Bangladesh: Liberation War Museum.

Liebrechts, C. (1909) *Souvenirs d'Afrique*, Brussels: Lebegue.

Lifton, Robert Jay (1986) *The Nazi Doctors: Medical Killing and the Psychology of Genocide*, New York: Basic Books.

Lindqvist, Sven (1997) *Exterminate All the Brutes*, London: Granta Books.

Ling, Roth, H. (1898a) 'Notes on Benin Art', *Reliquary*, Vol. 4.

—— (1898b) 'Primitive Art from Benin', Studio, Vol. 15, no. 69.

—— (1903) *Great Benin: Its Customs, Arts and Horrors*, Halifax: F. King.

Linenthal, Edward T. (1995) *Preserving Memory: The Struggle to Create America's Holocaust Museum*, New York: Columbia University Press.

Liss, Andrea (1998) *Trespassing through Shadows: Memory, Photography & The Holocaust*, Minneapolis, MN: University of Minnesota Press.

Loader, I. and Sparks, R. (2002) 'Contemporary Landscapes of Crime, Order, and Control: Governance, Risk, and Globalisation', in M. Maguire, R. Morgan and R. Reiner (2002) *The Oxford Handbook of Criminology*, 3rd edn., Oxford: Oxford University Press.

Lombroso, C. (1896) 'The Savage Origin of Tattooing', *Popular Science Monthly*, April, 793–803.

—— (1972 [1876, 1877]) [*L'Uomo Delinquente*] 'Criminal Man', in Sawyer F. Sylvester, Jr. (ed.), *The Heritage of Modern Criminology*, Cambridge, MA: Schenkman Publishing.

Lombroso-Ferrero, G. (1911) *Criminal Man, According to the Classification of Cesare Lombroso, with an Introduction by Cesare Lombroso*, New York: G.P. Putman.

—— (1915) *Cesare Lombroso: Storia della vita e delle opere narrate dalla figlia*, Turin: Bocca.

Louis L. Snyder (ed.) (1962) *The Imperialism Reader*, Princeton, NJ: Van Nostrand.

Luttwak, E. (2000) 'No-score War', *Times Literary Supplement*, 14 July, 11.

Lyon, Georges (1893) *La Philosophie de Hobbes*, Paris: F. Alcan.

MacDonnell, John DeCourcy (1905) *King Léopold II, His Rule in Belgian and the Congo*, London: Cassell.

Mack, John (n.d.) *Emil Torday and the Art of the Congo, 1900–1909*, Seattle, WA: University of Washington Press.

Maga, T. (2001) *Judgment at Tokyo: The Japanese War Crimes Trial*, Lexington, KY: University Press of Kentucky.

Magnusson, W. (1990) 'The Reification of Political Community', in R.B.J. Walker and S.H. Mendlovitz (eds), *Contending Sovereignties: Redefining Political Community*, Boulder, CO: Lynne Rienner Publishers.

Maniruzzaman, Talukder (1980) *The Bangladesh Revolution and Its Aftermath*, Dhaka, Bangladesh: The University Press Ltd.

Mannheim, H. (1972) *Pioneers in Criminology*, 2nd edn, Montclair, NJ: Patterson Smith.

Mansergh, Nicholas (1965) *The Irish Question 1840–1921*, London: Unwin University Books.

Marchak, P. (2003) *Reigns of Terror*, Montreal & Kingston: McGill-Queen's University Press.

Margolis, E. (31 August 1999a) 'Following in Stalin's Footsteps', *Toronto Sun*.

—— (1999b) 'US Aids Russia's Crimes in the Caucasus', *Toronto Sun*, 12 October.

—— (2000) 'Forgotten Chechens Face Extermination', *Toronto Sun*, 23 January.

Marrus, Michael (1989) *The Holocaust in History*, New York: Oxford University Press.

Marx, K. (1967 [1867]) *Capital Vol. 1*, London: Lawrence and Wishart (reprint).

Marx, K. (1971 [1865]) *Capital Vol. 3*, Moscow: Progress (reprint).

Mascarenhas, A. (1986) *Bangladesh: A Legacy of Blood*, London: Hodder and Stoughton.

Matza, David (1964) *Delinquency and Drift*, New York: Wiley.

Matza, D. (1969) *Becoming Deviant*, Englewood Cliffs, NJ: Prentice Hall.

Mauer, Marc (1999) *The Race to Incarcerate*, New York: Free Press.

Maurice, A. (1957) *Stanley, Unpublished Letters*, London.

Mazower, Mark (1997) *The Policing of Politics in the Twentieth Century*.

McGoldrick, Dominic (2004) *From '9:11' to the 'Iraq War 2003': International Law in an Age of Complexity*, Oxford: Hart Publishing.

McGreal, C. (February 21 2002). Coming Home: Remains of 'Hottentot Venus'. *Guardian Unlimited* web site. Retrieved 28 February 2003, http://www.education.guardian.co.uk/museums/comment/0,11727,660396,00.html

Mecklenburg, A.F. Duke (1913) *From the Congo to the Niger and the Nile: An Account of the German Central African Expedition 1910–1911*. London: Duckworth.

Memmi, Albert (1991/[1967] 1991) *The Colonizer and the Colonized*, rev. edn, Boston, MA: Beacon Press.

Mendlovitz, S.H. (1990) in R.B.J. Walker and S.H. Mendlovitz (eds), *Contending Sovereignties: Redefining Political Community*, Bolder, CO: Lynne Rienner Publishers.

Merriam, A.P. (1961) *Congo, Background of Conflict*, Londres: Northwestern University Press.

Merival, H ([1861] 1967) *Lectures on Colonization and Colonies*, delivered before the University of Ozford in 1839, 1840 and 1841 and printed in 1861, reprinted London: Frank Cass 1967.

Mills, C (1997) *The Racial Contract*, Ithaca, NY: Cornell University Press.

Milne, Seumas (14 February 2002) 'Can the US Be Defeated', *The Guardian*, Thursday.

Minear, Richard H. (1971) *Victors' Justice: The Tokyo War Crime Trial*, Princeton, NJ: Princeton University Press.

Minow, Martha (1998) *Between Vengeance and Forgiveness: Facing History after Mass Genocide and Mass Violence*, Boston, MA: Beacon Press.

Mintz, Samuel I. (1962) *The Hunting of Leviathan: Seventeenth-century Reactions to the Materialism and Moral Philosophy of Thomas Hobbes*, Cambridge: Cambridge University Press.

Mohamad, Mahathir (2003) *Terrorism and the Real Issues*, Malaysia: Pelanduk Publications (M) Sdn Bhd.

Mohan, Jag (1971) *The Black Book of Genocide in Bangla Desh: A Documentary Book Compiled and Edited by Jag Mohan*, New Delhi: Geeta Book Centre.

Momen, Moojan (2005) 'The Babi and Baha'I Community of Iran: A Case of "Suspended Genocide"?', *Journal of Genocide Research*, 7(2), 221–41.

Money, J.W.B. (1861) *Java, or How to Manage a Colony: Showing a Practical Solution of the Questions Now Affecting British India.* London: Hurst and Blackett.

Morel, E.D. (1904) *King Léopold's Rule in Africa*, London: William Heinemann.

—— (1909) *Great Britain and the Congo: The pillage of the Congo Basin*, London: Smith, Elder & Co.,

—— (1919) *Red Rubber: The Story of the Rubber Slave Trade Which Flourished on the Congo for Twenty Years, 1890–1910*. Revised edn, Manchester: National Labour Press.

Morrison, Wayne (1995) *Theoretical Criminology: From Modernity to Post-Modernism.* London: Cavendish.

—— (1997) *Jurisprudence: From the Greeks to Postmodernism*, London: Cavendish.

—— (2004a) 'Criminology, Genocide, and Modernity: Remarks on the Companion that Criminology Ignored', in C. Sumner (ed.), *The Blackwell Companion to Criminology*, Malden, MA: Blackwell.

—— (2004b) 'Lombroso and the Birth of Criminological Positivism: Scientific Mastery or Cultural Artifice?', in Jeff Ferrell, Keith Hayward, Wayne Morrison and Mike Presdee (eds), *Cultural Criminology Unleashed*, London: Glasshouse.

Morrison, William M. (1903) 'Personal Observations of Congo Misgovernment', *American Monthly Review of Reviews*, July, 28.

Morton, Jeffrey S. and Singh, Neil V. (2003) 'The International Legal Regime of Genocide', *Journal of Genocide Research*, 5(1).

Moses, A. Dirk (ed.) (2004) *Genocide and Settler Society: Frontier Violence and Stolen Indigenous Children in Australian History*, New York: Berghahn Books.

Muhith, AMA. (1978) *Bangladesh: Emergence of a Nation*, Dhaka, Bangladesh: The University Press Ltd.

—— (1996) *American Response to Bangladesh Liberation War*, Dhaka, Bangladesh: The University Press Ltd.

Muller-Hill, B. (1988) *Murderous Science; Elimination by Scientific Selection of Jews, Gypsies and Others, Germany, 1933–1945*, Oxford: Oxford University Press.

Mumford, Lewis (1955) *Sticks and Stones: A Study of American Architecture and Civilization*, 2nd rev. edn, New York: Dover Publishing.

Murray, C. (1984) *Losing Ground*, New York: Basic Books.

—— (1999) *The Underclass Revisited*, American Enterprise Institute for Public Policy Research: Papers and Studies, http://www.aei.org/ps/psmurray.htm

Musee royal de L'Afrique central (2005) *La memoire du Congo le temps colonial*, Gand: Editions Snoeck.

Nelson, Samuel H. (1994) *Colonialism in the Congo Basin, 1880–1940*. Ohio: Ohio University Center for International Studies. Monographs in International Studies, Africa Series no: 64.

Newsweek (28 June 1971) Tony Clifton, *The Terrible Blood Bath of Tikka Khan*.

Noor, Farish A. (2002) 'Globalization, Resistance and the Discursive Politics of Terror, Post-September 11', in Andrew Tan and Kumar Ramakrishna (eds) *The New Terrorism: Anatomy, Trends and Counter-strategies*, Singapore: Eastern University Press.

Nzongola-Ntalaja, Georges (2002) *The Congo: From Léopold to Kabila*, London: Zed Books.

Ó Síocháin, Séamas and O' Sullivan, Michael (eds) (2003) *The Eyes of Another Race: Roger Casement's Congo Report and 1903 Diary*, Dublin: University College Dublin Press.

Ohmae, Kenichi (1990) *The Borderless World: Power and Strategy in the Interlinked in the Economy*, New York: Harpers.

Orend, Brian (2000) *War and International Justice: A Kantian Perspective*, Canada: Wilfrid Laurier University Press.

Osiel, Mark (1997) *Mass Atrocity, Collective Memory, and the Law*, New Brunswick, NJ: Transaction Publishers.

Osmany, Shireen Hasan (1992) *Bangladesh Nationalism: History of Dialectics and Dimensions*, Dhaka, Bangladesh: The University Press Ltd.

Paffen, Paul (2001) 'A Grand Illusion: Benjamin Duterrau and The Conciliation', *Melbourne Art Journal*, 5.

Pakenham, Thomas (1991) *The Scramble for Africa: White Man's Conquest of the Dark Continent from 1876–1912*, New York: Avon Books.

Parenti, Michael (1995) *Against Empire: A Brilliant Expose of the Brutal Realities of U.S. Global Domination*, San Francisco, CA: City Lights Books.

Paul T.V. and Hall John, A. (eds) (1999) *International Order and the Future of World Politics*, Cambridge: Cambridge University Press.

Perechodnik, Calel (1996) *Am I a Murderer? Testament of a Jewish Ghetto Policeman*, trans. Frank Fox, Colorado: Westview Press, Harper Collins Publisher.

Perez de Cuellar, J. (24 April 1991) 'Secretary-General's Address at the University of Bordeaux', Bordeaux, France: United Nations Press Release SG/SM 4560.

Perkin, H. (1969) *The Origins of Modern English Society*, London: Routledge and Kegan Paul.

Peterson, N. (1989) 'A Colonial Image: Penetrating the Reality of the Image', *Australian Aboriginal Studies* 2, 59–62.

Pfaff, William (2000/1) 'The Praetorian Guard', *The National Interest* (Winter).

Pick, D. (1989) *Faces of Degeneration: A European Disorder, c. 1848–1919*, Cambridge, Cambridge University Press.

Pigafetta, F. ([1591] 1881) *A Report of the Kingdom of Congo ... Drawn Out of the Writings and Discourses of the Portuguese*, Duarte Lopez (Rome, 1591), (trans.) M. Hutchinson, London: John Murray.

Pieper, Josep (1957) *The Silence of Saint Thomas*, New York: Pantheon Books.

Pilger, John (1987) *Heroes*, London: Pan Books Ltd.

—— (2004) *Tell Me No Lies: Investigative Journalism and Its Triumphs*, London: Jonathan Cape.

Poynting, S., Noble, G., Tabar, P. and Collins, J. (2004) *Bin Laden in the Suburbs: Criminalising the Arab Other*, Sydney: Sydney Institute of Criminology Series.

Popper, Karl (1956 [1945]) *The Open Society and Its Enemies*, London: Routledge and Kegan Paul.

—— (1957) *The Poverty of Historicism*, London: Routledge and Kegan Paul.

Pratt, John (2002) *Punishment and Civilization*, London: Sage.

Pratt, John, Brown, David, Brown, Mark, Hallsworth, Simon and Morrison, Wayne (2005) *The New Punitiveness: Trends, Theories, Perspectives*, Devon, UK: Willan.

Presdee, M. (2000) *Cultural Criminology and the Carnival of Crime*, London: Routledge.

Procter, R. (1988) *Racial Hygiene; Medicine under the Nazis*, Cambridge: Harvard University Press.

Quaderi, Fazlul Quader (ed.) (1972) *Bangladesh Genocide and World Press*, Dhaka, Bangladesh: Amatul Quader.

Quetelet, M.A. (1842) *A Treatise on Man and the Development of His Faculties*, trans. R. Knox and T. Smibert, Edinburgh: Willam and Robert Chambers.

—— (1869) *Physique sociale, ou Essai sur le developpement des facultes*, Brussels: C. Murquardt.

—— (1871) *Anthropometrie, ou mesure des differentes facultes de l'homme*, Brussels: C. Muquardt.

Radzinowicz, Leon (1962) *In Search of Criminology*, Cambridge MA: Harvard University Press.

—— and Hood, Roger (1990) *The Emergence of Penal Policy in Victorian and Edwardian England*, Oxford: Clarendon Press.

Rae-Ellis, Vivienne (1992) 'The Representation of Trucanini', in *Anthropology and Photography 1860–1920*, Elizabeth Edwards (ed.), New Haven: Yale University Press.

Rahim, Enayetur and Rahim, Joyce L. (2000) *Bangladesh Liberation War and the Nixon White House 1971*, Dhaka, Bangladesh: Pustaka.

Rahman, Muhammad Anisur (1993) *The Lost Moment: Papers on Political Economy of Bangladesh*, Dhaka, Bangladesh: The University Press Ltd.

—— (2001) *My Story of 1971: Through the Holocaust that Created Bangladesh*, Dhaka, Bangladesh: Liberation War Museum.

Rahman, Shamsur (2000) *The Devotee, The Combatant: Selected Poems of Shamsur Rahman*, trans. Syed Najmuddin Hashim, Dhaka, Bangladesh: Pathak Shamabesh Books.

Rauschning, Hermann (1940) *The Voice of Destruction*, New York: Putnam.

Reynolds, Henry (1971) *An Indelible Stain? The Question of Genocide in Australia's History*, Victoria, Australia: Penguin Viking.

—— (1987) *The Law of the Land*, Australia: Penguin Books Australia Ltd.

—— (1999) *Why Weren't We Told? A Personal Search for Truth about Our History*, London: Penguin Books.

Reyntjens, F. (1999) Talking or Fighting? Political Evaluation in Rwanda and Burundi, 1998–99, *Current African Issues*, 21. Nordiska Afrikainstitutet.

Rhodes, Richard (2002) Masters of Death: The SS-Einsatzgruppen and the Invention of the Holocaust, New York: Vintage Books.

Riles, Annelise (1993) 'Aspiration and Control: International Legal Rhetoric and the Essentialisation of Culture', *Harvard Law Review*, 106(3): 723–40.

Robert F. (ed.) (1997) *Theory in Criminology: Contemporary Views*, Beverley Hills, CA: Sage Publications with the American Society of Criminology.

Robertson, Geoffrey (2000) *The Struggle for Global Justice*, New York: Free Press.

Robley, H. (1998 [1896]) *Moko: The Art and History of Maori Tattooing*, Twickenham: Senate.

Rodney, Walter (1974) *How Europe Underdeveloped Africa*, Washington, DC: Howard University Press.

Roling, B.V.A. and Cassese, Antonio (1993) *The Tokyo Trial and Beyond*, Cambridge: Polity.

Roling, B.V.A. and Ruter, C.F. (eds.) (1977) *The Tokyo Judgment: The International Military Tribunal for the Far East (IMTFE), 29 April 1946–12 November 1948*, Amsterdam: APA-University Press Amsterdam.

Roosevelt, Theodore (1889–1896) *The Winning of the West*, 4 Vols (ed.) [1906], New York: G.P. Putman.

Rorty, Richard (1999) *Philosophy and Social Hope*, London: Penguin Books.

Roshier, B. (1989) *Controlling Crime: The Classical Perspective in Criminology*, Milton Keynes: Open University Press.

Ross, Andrew (2002) 'The Odor of Publicity', in Sorkin, Michael and Zukin, Sharon (eds) (2002) *After the World Trade Center: Rethinking New York City*, London: Routledge.

Rossino, Alexander B. (2003) *Hitler Strikes Poland: Blitzkrieg, Ideology, and Atrocity*, Lawrence, KS: University Press of Kansas.

Roth, H. Ling (1903) *Great Benin: Its Customs, Art and Horrors*, Halifax: F. King & Sons.

Roy, Arundhati (29 September 2001) 'The Algebra of Infinite Justice', *The Guardian*, Saturday.

Rubenstein, R. (2000) 'Afterword: Genocide and Civilisation', in I. Wallimann and M. Dobkowski (eds), *Genocide and the Modern Age*, Syracuse, NY: Syracuse University Press.

Rubinstein, Richard (1996) 'Religion and the Uniqueness of the Holocaust', in Rosenbaum, Alan S. (ed.) *Is the Holocaust Unique? Perspectives on Comparative Genocide*, Bolder, CO.: Westview Press.

Rubinstein, William D. (2004) *Genocide: A History*, London: Pearson, Longman.

Rummel, Rudolph, J. (1990) *Lethal Politics: Soviet Genocide and Mass Murder since 1917*, New Brunswick, NJ: Transaction Publishers.

—— (1991) *China's Bloody Century: Genocide and Mass Murder since 1900*, New Brunswick, NJ: Transaction Publishers.

—— (1992) *Democide*, New Brunswick, NJ: Transaction Publishers.

—— (1994) *Death by Government*, New Brunswick, NJ: Transaction Publishers.

Russell, B. (1934) *Freedom and Organization 1814–1914*, London: George Allen & Unwin.

Ryan, James R. (1997) *Picturing Empire: Photography and the Visualisation of the British Empire*, London: Reaktion Books.

Ryan, Paul Ryder (2000) *Bangladesh 2000 on the Brink of Civil War: Fragments from Inside a Coming Explosion*, Cummington, MA: Munewata Press.

Said, Edward W. (1994) *Culture and Imperialism*, London: Vintage.

—— (2001) Internet postings.

Sands, Philippe (2005) *Lawless World: America and the Making and Breaking of Global Rules*, London: Allen Lane.

Sardar, Ziauddin and Davies, Merryl Wyn (eds) (2002) *Why Do People hate America?* Cambridge: Icon Books.

Savitz, Leonard, Turner, Stanley H. and Dickman, Toby (eds) *(The Origin) of Scientific Criminology: Franz Joseph Gall as the First Criminologist*, in Meier,

Scarry, Elaine (1985) *The Body in Pain: The Making and Unmaking of the World*, New York: Oxford University Press.

Schabas, William A. (2000) *Genocide in International Law: The Crimes of Crimes*, Cambridge: Cambridge University Press.

Schaffer, Ronald (1965) *Wings of Judgement: American Bombing in World War II*, New York: Oxford University Press.

—— (1980) 'American Military Ethics in World War II: The Bombing of German Civilians', *Journal of American History*, Vol. 67, no. 2, September 1980.

Scharf, R. (1993) *In the Warsaw Ghetto: Summer 1941, with Passages from Warsaw Ghetto Diaries, Photographs by Willy Georg*, London: Aperture.

Schechner, Richard (1993) 'Ritual, Violence, and Creativity', in Smadar Lavie, Kirin Narayan and Renato Rosaldo (eds), *Creativity/Anthropology*, Ithaca: Cornell University Press.

Scheper-Hughes, Nancy and Bourgois, Philippe (2004) *Violence in War and Peace: An Anthology*, Massachusetts: Blackwell Publishing.

Schmitt, Carl ([1922] 1985) *Political Theology*, George Schwab (trans.), Cambridge, MA: MIT Press.

Schwarz, Daniel R. (1999) *Imagining the Holocaust*, New York: St. Martin's Press.

Scraton, Phil (2002) *Beyond September 11: An Anthology of Dissent*, London: Pluto Press.

Seabrook, Jeremy (2001) *Freedom Unfinished: Fundamentalism and Popular Resistance in Bangladesh Today*, London: Zed Books with Proshika Books, Dhaka.

Sebald, W.G. (2003) *On the Natural History of Destruction*, London: Penguin.

Sellars, K. (2002) *The Rise and Rise of Human Rights*, Phoenix Mill: Sutton.

Sellin, J. Thorsten (1976) *Slavery and the Penal System*, New York: Elsevier.

Sereny, Gitta (1983) *Into That Darkness*, New York: Vintage Books.

Serres Guiraldes, Alfredo M. (1979) *La Estrategia de General Roca*, Buenos Aires, Pleamar.

Shaloff, S. (1970) *Reforms of Léopold's Congo*, Richmond, VA: John Knox Press.

Shandley, Robert R. (ed.) (1998) *Unwilling Germans? The Goldhagen Debate*, Minneapolis, MN: University of Minnesota Press.

Shaw, Clifford R. and McKay, Henry D. (1969) *Juvenile Delinquency and Urban Areas*, Chicago, IL: University of Chicago Press.

Sheikh Hasina (1997) *People and Democracy*, Dhaka, Bangladesh: Agamee Prakashoni.

Shelly, M.R. (1979) *Emergence of a Nation in a Multi-polar World: Bangladesh*, Dhaka: Academic Press and Publishers Limited.

Sherry, Micheal (1987) *The Rise of American Air Power: The Creation of Armageddon*, New Haven, CT: Yale University Press.

Siddiqui, Zillur Rahman (2001) *Quest for a Civil Society*, Dhaka, Bangladesh: Sucheepatra Publication.

Sinclair, Andrew (2003) *An Anatomy of Terror: A History of Terrorism*, London: Macmillan, Pan MacMillan Ltd.

Singer, Peter (2004) *The President of Good and Evil: Questioning the Ethics of George W. Bush*, London: Plume.

Sisson, Richard and Rose, Leo E. (1990) *War and Secession: Pakistan, India, and the Creation of Bangladesh*, Berkeley, CA: University of California Press.

Slade, Ruth (1962) *King Léopold's Congo: Aspects of the Development of Race Relations in the Congo Independent State*. Oxford: Oxford University Press.

Smith, Neil (2002) *Scales of Terror: The Manufacturing of Nationalism and the War for U.S. Globalism*, in Michael Sorkin and Sharon Zukin (eds), *After the World Trade Center: Rethinking New York City*, pp. 97–108, New York: Routledge.

Smith, R. (2000) 'Human Destructiveness and Politics: The Twentieth Century as an Age of Genocide', p. 21, in I. Wallimann and M. Dobkowski (eds), *Genocide and the Modern Age*, Syracuse, NY: Syracuse University Press.

Snyder, Louis L. (ed.) (1962) *The Imperialism Reader*, Princeton, NJ: Van Nostrand.

Sontag, Susan (1997) *On Photography*, London: Penguin Books.

Sorkin, Michael (2002) 'The Center Cannot Hold', in Michael Sorkin and Sharon Zukin (eds), *After the World Trade Center: Rethinking New York City*, pp. 197–207, New York: Routledge.

Sorkin, Michael and Zukin, Sharon (2002a) 'Introduction', in Michael Sorkin and Sharon Zukin (eds), *After the World Trade Center: Rethinking New York City*, New York: Routledge.

Sorkin, Michael and Zukin, Sharon (eds) (2002b) *After the World Trade Center: Rethinking New York City*, London: Routledge.

Soyinka, Wole (2004) *Climate of Fear*, London: Profile Books.

Spencer, H. (1967) *The Evolution of Society*, Chicago, IL: University of Chicago Press.

Stanley, Henry Morton (1872) *How I Found Livingstone: Travels, Adventures and Discoveries in Central Africa, Including Four Months' Residence with Dr. Livingstone*, London: Sampson, Low, Marston, Low and Searle.

—— (1878) *Through the Dark Continent; or the Sources of the Nile around the Great Lakes of Equatorial Africa and Down the Livingstone River to the Atlantic Ocean*, 2 Vols. 1899 edn, Reprinted by Dover Publications, New York, 1988.

—— (1885) *The Congo and the Founding of Its Free State: A Story of Work and Exploration*, 2 Vols. New York: Harper & Brothers.

—— (1890) *In Darkest Africa; or the Quest, Rescue and Retreat of Emin, Governor of Equatoria*, 2 Vols. New York: Charles Scribners's Sons.

—— (1909) *The Autobiography of Sir Henry Morton Stanley* (ed.), Dorothy Stanley, Boston: Houghton Mifflin Company.

Stannard, David E. (1992) *American Holocaust: The Conquest of the New World*, Oxford, England: Oxford University Press.

Staub, E. (1989) *The Roots of Evil: The Origins of Genocide and Other Group Violence*, Cambridge: Cambridge University Press.

Stavrianos, L.S. (1991) *The World since 1500: A Global History*, Englewood Cliffs, NJ: Prentice Hall.

Stein, Stuart (2005) 'Conception and Terms: Templates for the Analysis of Holocausts and Genocides', *Journal of Genocide Research*, 7(2).

Steiner, G. (1977) *Language and Silence: Essays in Language, Literature and the Inhuman*, New York: Atheneum.

Stengers, J. (1989) *Congo: Mythes et Realities. 100 ans d'histoire*, Paris: Louvain-la-Neuve, Duculot.

Steiner, George (1971) *In Bluebeard's Castle: Some Notes Towards the Redefinition of Culture*, New Haven, CT: Yale University Press.

Stout, Jeffrey (1981) *The Flight from Authority: Religion, Morality and the Quest for Autonomy*, Notre Dame Indiana: University of Notre Dame Press.

Struk, J. (2004) *Photographing the Holocaust: Interpretations of the Evidence*, London: I.B. Tauris.

Sumner, C.S. (ed.) (1982) *Crime, Justice and Underdevelopment*, London: Heinemann.

—— (1997) *Violence, Culture and Censure*, London: Taylor & Francis.

Sutherland, E.H. (1939) *Principles of Criminology*, 3rd edn, Philadelphia, PA: Lippincott.

—— (1947) *Principles of Criminology*, 4th edn, Philadelphia: Lippincott.

Sutherland, E.H. and Cressey, D.R. (1978) *Criminology*, 10th edn, Philadelphia: Lippincott.

Swan, Jon (1991) 'The Final Solution in South West Africa', *MHQ: The Quarterly Journal of Military History* Vol. 3, no. 4.

Sykes, G.M. and Matza, David (1961) 'Delinquency and Subterranean Values', *American Sociological Review*, 26.

Tappen, Paul (1947) 'Who is the Criminal?', *American Sociological Review*, no. 12: 96–102.

Taffet, G. (ed.) (1945) *Extermination of Polish Jews: Album of Pictures (ZagLada Zydostwa Poliskiego: Album Zdjec,)* Centralna Zydowska Komisja Historyczna Polsce, Lodz (Central Jewish Historical Committee in Poland).

Takaki, Ronald (1995) *Why America Dropped the Atomic Bomb*, Boston, MA: Little Brown.

Tanaka, Yuki (1996) *Hidden Horrors: Japanese War Crimes in World War II*, Westview Press.

Taylor, Ian, Walton, Paul, and Young, Jock (1973) *The New Criminology: For a Social Theory of Deviance*, London: Routledge and Kegan Paul.

Tervuren Tourist Information Booklet (2000), Brussels, Belgium: Tervuren Tourist Office.

Thomas, Nicholas (1994) *Colonialism's Culture: Anthropology, Travel and Government*, Princeton, NJ: Princeton University Press.

Tokushi, Kasahara (2002) 'Remembering the Nanking Massacre', in F.F. Li, R. Sabella and D. Liu (eds), *Nanking 1937: Memory and Healing*, pp. 75–94, New York: M.E. Sharpe.

Totten, S., Parsons, W.S. and Charny, I.W. (eds) (1997) *Century of Genocide: Eyewitness Accounts and Critical Views*, New York: Garland Publishing, Inc.

Traverso, Enzo (1999) *Understanding the Nazi Genocide: Marxism after Auschwitz*, London: Pluto Press.

Twain, Mark (1907) *King Léopold's Soliloquy: A Defence of His Congo Rule*, E.D. Morel (ed.), London: T. Fisher Unwin.

United Nations (March 1966) *Convention on the Prevention and Punishment of the Crime of Genocide*, London: Her Majesty's Stationery Office. Originally Paris, 9 December 1948 (see Part I).

United Nations War Crimes Commission (1992) *Law Reports of War Criminals: Four Genocide Trials*, New York: Fertig.

U.S. Government (1946) *Nazi Conspiracy and Aggression*, U.S. Government Printing Office, vol. II, p. 634.

Vahakn, D. (1995) *The History of the Armenian Genocide: Ethnic Conflict from the Balkans to Anatolia to the Caucasus*, Providence, RI: Berghahn Books.

Van Creveld, Martin (1991) *The Transformation of War*, New York: Free Press.

Van Dyke, Vernon (1960) *Political Science*, Stanford: Stanford University Press.

Van Schaack, Beth (1997) 'The Crime of Political Genocide: Repairing the Genocide Convention's Blind Spot', *Yale law Journal*, 5(1).

Vattimo, Gianni (1992) *The Transparent Society*, Cambridge: Polity Press.

Vermeersch, Father A. (1906) *La Question Congolaise*, Brussels: Impr. Sci.

Vidal-Naquet, P. (1992) *Assassins of Memory: Essays on the Denial of the Holocaust*, New York: Columbia University Press.

Vietnam Veterans Against the War (1972) *The Winter Soldier Investigation: An Inquiry into U.S. War Crimes in Vietnam*, Boston, MA: Beacon Press.

Vincent, R.J. (1992) 'The Idea of Rights in International Ethics', in T. Nardin and D.R. Mapel (eds), *Traditions of International Ethics*, Cambridge: Cambridge University Press.

Vines, Frederick Howard (1919) *Punishment and Reformation: A Study of the Penitentiary System*, rev. edn, New York: Thomas Y. Crowell Co.

Vold, G.B. (1958) *Theoretical Criminology*, New York & Oxford: Oxford University Press.

—— (1979) *Theoretical Criminology*, 2nd edn, Prepared by Thomas J. Bernard. New York and Oxford: Oxford University Press.

—— and Bernard, Thomas J. (1986) *Theoretical Criminology*, 3rd edn, New York: Oxford University Press.

Wakabayashi, Bob Tadashi (2000) 'The Nanking 100-Man Killing Contest Debate: War Guilt and Fabricated Illusions, 1971-75', *Journal of Japanese Studies* 26 (2)

Walker, R.B.J. (1990) 'Sovereignty, Identity, Community: Reflections on the Horizons of Contemporary Political Practice', in R.B.J. Walker and S.H. Mendlovitz (eds), *Contending Sovereignties: Redefining Political Community*, Boulder, CO: Lynne Rienner Publishers.

—— (1993) *Inside/Outside: International Relations as Political Theory*, Cambridge: Cambridge University Press.

Wallimann, Isidor and Dobkowski, Michael N. (2000) *Genocide and the Modern Age: Etiology and Case Studies of Mass Death*, Syracuse, NY: Syracuse University Press.

Ward, Churchill (2001) 'Some People Push Back: Reflections on the Justice of Roosting Chickens', *Pockets of Resistance*, no. 27, Sept. 2001 [First appearing posted on the Internet].

—— (2003) *On the Justice of Roosting Chickens*, Oakland, CA: AK Press.

Wastiau, Boris (2000) *Exit Congo Museum: A Century of Art With/Without Papers*, Brussels, Belgium: Royal Museum for Central Africa, Tervuren.

Watson, G.J. (1989) *Irish Identity and the Literary Revival*, London: Croom Heln.

Wedgewood, C.V. (1938) *The Thirty Years' War*, reprint, London: Jonathan Cape, 1971.

West, Rebecca (1955) *A Train of Powder: Six Reports on the Problem of Guilt and Punishment in Our Time*, Chicago, IL: Ivan R. Dee.

Wetzell, R. (2000) *Inventing the Criminal: A History of German Criminology, 1880–1914*. Chapel Hill, NC: The University of North Carolina Press.

Wiesel, Elie (1978) 'Trivialising the Holocaust: Semi-Fact and Semi-Fiction', *New York Times*, April 16, 1978, section 2.

Wigley, Mark (2002) 'Insecurity by Design', in Michael Sorkin and Sharon Zukin (eds), *After the World Trade Center: Rethinking New York City*, pp. 69–85, New York: Routledge.

Williams, Hywel (22 December 2001) 'A Haunting Beauty', *The Guardian*, Saturday.

Wilson, J.Q. and Herrnstein, R. (1985) *Crime and Human Nature*. New York: Simon & Schuster.

Wines, Fredrick (1910) *Punishment and Reformation*, (revised edn) New York: Thomas Y. Crowell, Co.

Wistrich, Robert (2001) *Hitler and the Holocaust*, New York: The Modern Library.

Wolf, Eric R. (1976) 'Killing the Achés', in Arens (ed.), *Genocide in Paraguay*, 57.

Wolf, Eric R. (1990) *Europe and the People without History*, Berkeley, CA: University of California Press.

Wrong, Michela (2001) *In the Footsteps of Mr Kurtz: Living on the Brink of Disaster in Mobutu's Congo*, New York: Harper Collins Publishers Inc.

Wyn Jones, R. (1996) 'Travel without Maps', in E. Kofman and G. Youngs (eds),

Yamamoto, M. (2000) *Nanking: Anatomy of an Atrocity*, London: Praeger.

Young, S. and Yin, J. (1999) *The Rape of Nanking: An Undeniable History in Photographs*, Login Publishers Consortium.

Zaheer, Hasan (1998) *The Separation of East Pakistan: The Rise and Realization of Bengali Muslim Nationalism*, Dhaka, Bangladesh: The University Press Ltd.

Zelizer, Barbie and Allan, Stuart (eds) (2002) *Journalism after September 11*, London: Routledge.

Zimmerer, Jurgen (2004) 'Colonialism and the Holocaust: Towards an Archaeology of Genocide', in A. Dirk Moses (ed.), *Genocide and Settler Society: Frontier Violence and Stolen Aboriginal Children in Australian History*, New York: Berghahn Books.

Ziring, Lawrence (1992) *Bangladesh, from Mujib to Ershad: An Interpretative Study*, Dhaka, Bangladesh: The University Press Ltd with Oxford University Press, Karachi.

Zukin, Sharon (2002) 'Our World Trade Center', in Sorkin, Michael and Zukin, Sharon (eds.) (2002) *After the World Trade Center: Rethinking New York City*, London: Routledge.

Zygmunt Bauman (2001) *The Individualised Society*, Oxford: Polity.

Index